Millicent Garrett Fawcett

'Millicent Fawcett's influence in the suffrage movement is often overlooked in favour of the more radical suffragette Emmeline Pankhurst. Millicent was hugely important, concentrating on non-violent rational persuasion. This book explains the work of this dogged suffragist.'
Dame Jenni Murray, former President, Fawcett Society

'*Millicent Garrett Fawcett: Selected writings* invites the reader to delve into the life and passions of this great suffragist leader. Millicent Fawcett paved the way for women to take their place in public life, that's why I'm so proud that in 2018, her sculpture was unveiled in London, becoming Parliament Square's first-ever statue of a woman. The statue depicts Millicent holding a banner bearing the powerful quote, "Courage Calls to Courage Everywhere". This book explores important aspects of the rich and too-often untold history of women's rights, including the origins of that inspirational quote.'
Sadiq Khan, Mayor of London

'This is a vital collection of the vital speeches of a vital person. You need to read this to understand the history of Millicent Fawcett and if you don't understand the history of Millicent Fawcett you don't understand one of the most important developments in modern civilisation.'
Lord Daniel Finkelstein

'Millicent Fawcett is one of the pivotal voices in UK political history. Her work paved the way for every woman who has ever taken her place in a parliament anywhere on these islands. When any of us talk about standing on the shoulders of giants, Millicent Fawcett was that giant of female empowerment.'
Baroness Ruth Davidson

'Millicent Fawcett was one of the most influential figures of her age, yet history has tended to overlook her. Extraordinarily astute and forward-thinking, she inspired women to change their world by giving them a political voice, and the confidence to use it. Thanks to this collection, which is both scholarly and accessible, we can now hear her own voice as never before. She continues to inspire us to speak out on behalf of women's progress everywhere.'
Jane Robinson, Senior Associate, Somerville College, Oxford; author of Ladies Can't Climb Ladders: The pioneering adventures of the first professional women

Millicent Garrett Fawcett

Selected Writings

Edited by Melissa Terras and Elizabeth Crawford

First published in 2022 by
UCL Press
University College London
Gower Street
London WC1E 6BT

Available to download free: www.uclpress.co.uk

Introductory material and notes © Editors, 2022
Images © Contributors and copyright holders named in captions, 2022

The authors have asserted their rights under the Copyright, Designs and Patents Act 1988 to be identified as the authors of this work.

A CIP catalogue record for this book is available from the British Library.

This book is published under a Creative Commons Attribution Non-commercial Non-derivative 4.0 International licence (CC BY-NC-ND 4.0). This licence allows you to share, copy, distribute and transmit the work for personal and non-commercial use provided author and publisher attribution is clearly stated. Attribution should include the following information:

This book is published under a Creative Commons Attribution Non-commercial Non-derivative 4.0 International licence (CC BY-NC-ND 4.0), https://creativecommons.org/licenses/by-nc-nd/4.0/. This licence allows you to share, copy, distribute and transmit the work for personal and non-commercial use providing author and publisher attribution is clearly stated. If you wish to use the work commercially, use extracts or undertake translation you must seek permission from the author. Attribution should include the following information:

Terras, M. and Crawford, E. (eds) 2022. *Millicent Garret Fawcett: Selected Writings*. London: UCL Press. https://doi.org/10.14324/111.9781787358638

Further details about Creative Commons licences are available at
http://creativecommons.org/licenses/

ISBN: 978-1-78735-865-2 (Hbk.)
ISBN: 978-1-78735-864-5 (Pbk.)
ISBN: 978-1-78735-863-8 (PDF)
ISBN: 978-1-78735-866-9 (epub)
ISBN: 978-1-78735-867-6 (mobi)
DOI: https://doi.org/10.14324/111.9781787358638

Contents

List of figures	viii
Foreword	
Fiona Mactaggart (Former Chair, Fawcett Society)	xi
Introduction	1

1	Picturing Fawcett: Millicent Garrett Fawcett with Henry Fawcett, 1868	22
2	The education of women of middle and upper classes, 1868	24
3	Electoral disabilities of women, 1871	37
4	Picturing Fawcett: A meeting at the Hanover Square Rooms, 1872	56
5	Picturing Fawcett: Professor and Mrs Fawcett by Ford Madox Brown, 1872	58
6	Mrs Fawcett on women's suffrage, 1872	61
7	Mr Fitzjames Stephen on the position of women, 1873	69
8	Picturing Fawcett: Millicent Fawcett's lecture at the Unitarian Church, Glasgow, 1875	78
9	Reporting Fawcett: The women of modern fiction lectures, 1874	80
10	*Janet Doncaster*, an excerpt, 1875	85
11	Women and representative government, 1883	92
12	The protection of girls: speech or silence, 1885	101
13	Employment for girls: the civil service (the Post Office), 1887	109
14	The employment of children in theatres, 1889	118
15	Picturing Fawcett: Mrs Fawcett, 1890	128
16	Introduction to Wollstonecraft's *A Vindication of the Rights of Woman*, 1891	130
17	Home and politics, 1892	148
18	The story of the opening of university education to women, 1894	156
19	Reporting Fawcett: Women's suffrage, London 1897	178

20	Picturing Fawcett: Millicent Fawcett by Theodore Blake Wirgman, 1898	194
21	Women's suffrage, Manchester, 1899	197
22	The white slave trade: its causes, and the best means of preventing it, 1899	212
23	The concentration camps in South Africa, 1901	224
24	Why we women want votes, 1906	232
25	The prisoners of hope in Holloway Gaol, 1906	238
26	Picturing Fawcett: NUWSS procession, 1908	250
27	Picturing Fawcett: Millicent Fawcett, 1908	254
28	National Union manifesto, 1908	256
29	Picturing Fawcett: A woman speaking at the Oxford Union for the first time, 1908	264
30	Men are men and women are women, 1909	266
31	Picturing Fawcett: International Woman Suffrage Alliance Congress, 1909	284
32	Picturing Fawcett: Mrs Henry Fawcett, LLD, president of the National Union, 1909	286
33	Reporting Fawcett: Wanted: a statesman, 1909	288
34	Picturing Fawcett: Dame Millicent Fawcett, CBE, LLD, by Annie Louisa Swynnerton, c. 1910	302
35	Broken windows – and after, 1912	306
36	Picturing Fawcett: Millicent Garrett Fawcett, 1912	312
37	Who's for us? For him are we, 1912	314
38	Picturing Fawcett: Millicent Fawcett's Hyde Park address, 1913	322
39	To the members of the National Union, 1914	324
40	Picturing Fawcett: Millicent Garrett Fawcett, 1914	328
41	Life's cost, 1915	331
42	Lift up your hearts, 1916	336
43	An immense and significant advance, 1917	347
44	Sing, rejoice and give thanks, 1918	354
45	Still in thy right hand carry gentle peace, 1918	359
46	Courage calls to courage everywhere, 1920	365
47	Picturing Fawcett: Dame Millicent Fawcett, 1925	372
48	Picturing Fawcett: Dame Millicent Fawcett at NUSEC garden party, 1925	374
49	What the vote has done, 1926 and 1927	376
50	How University College, London led the way in the education of women, 1927	391
51	The end crowns all, and that old common arbitrator, Time, will one day end it, 1928	396

52	Picturing Fawcett: Royal Assent to the Equal Franchise Act, 1928	402
53	Picturing Fawcett: Dame Millicent Fawcett at the Victory Breakfast, 1928	406
54	Picturing Fawcett: Dame Millicent Fawcett, by Lionel Ellis, 1928	408
55	Can women influence international policy? 1929	411

Bibliography 417
Appendix: Additions to Fawcett's bibliography 454

Index 457

List of figures

1	Millicent Garrett Fawcett with Henry Fawcett, 1868, by Henry Joseph Whitlock. From the Women's Library at LSE. No known copyright restrictions.	22
2	'Women's rights – A meeting at the Hanover Square Rooms' in the *Graphic* (1872). No known copyright restrictions. Digitised from editor's own copy.	56
3	Portrait of Professor and Mrs Fawcett by Ford Madox Brown. Oil on canvas, 1872. © National Portrait Gallery, London. Licensed for use.	58
	Mrs Fawcett's lecture on the female characters of Dickens, Thackeray, and George Eliot, at the Unitarian Church, Glasgow'. Pen-and-ink illustration by Jim Karnie (1875) in the *Pictorial World*. No known copyright restrictions. Digitised from editor's own copy.	78
5	Mrs Fawcett, 1890, carbon print by W. & D. Downey, London. No known copyright restrictions. Digitised from editor's own copy.	128
6	Millicent Fawcett, oil on canvas, by Theodore Blake Wirgman, 1898. Royal Holloway, University of London. Licensed for use.	194
7	NUWSS procession, 13 June 1908. The Sport and General Illustration Co. From the Women's Library at LSE. No known copyright restrictions.	250
8	Millicent Fawcett, 1908, matte bromide print by O. and K. Edis. © National Portrait Gallery, London.	254
9	'A woman speaking at the Oxford Union for the first time'. Illustration by Samuel Begg. *Illustrated London News* (November 1908), 745. © Illustrated London News Ltd/Mary Evans Picture Library.	264

10	International Woman Suffrage Alliance Congress, London, April 1909, with Millicent Fawcett, first vice-president, seated centre. From the Nasjonalbiblioteket/National Library of Norway. No known copyright restrictions.	284
11	Mrs Henry Fawcett, LLD, president of the National Union, 1909. Elliott & Fry, London. No known copyright restrictions.	286
12	Dame Millicent Fawcett, CBE, LLD, by Annie Louisa Swynnerton. Preparatory oil painting, likely painted c. 1910. Sold at Christie's London in 1959 (when the photograph was taken), Sotheby's in 1970 and Christie's again in 1973. Current whereabouts unknown. Picture from negative held at the National Portrait Gallery. Permission given for use by the National Portrait Gallery.	302
13	Dame Millicent Fawcett, CBE, LLD, by Annie Louisa Swynnerton. Exhibited 1930, likely painted c. 1910. Oil on canvas. © Tate, London 2020. Licensed for use.	303
14	Millicent Garrett Fawcett, bromide print by Lizzie Caswall Smith, 1912. From the Women's Library at LSE. No known copyright restrictions.	312
15	Millicent Fawcett's Hyde Park address on 26 July 1913. Postcard. Photograph taken by Central News Agency, originally featured in the *Daily Telegraph* on 28 July (1913, 5), reprinted in the *Common Cause* on 1 August (1913i) and the *Illustrated London News* (1913, 177) on 2 August. From the Women's Library at LSE. No known copyright restrictions.	322
16	Millicent Garrett Fawcett by Lena Connell, 1914, with Fawcett's signature. From the Women's Library at LSE. No known copyright restrictions.	328
17	Fawcett photographed outside her home at 2 Gower Street, London, on the day of her investiture as Dame Grand Cross of the Order of the British Empire (GBE) on Thursday, 12 February 1925. The Topical Press Photographic Agency, 1925. In Lang (1929, 91). No known copyright restrictions.	372

18	Dame Millicent Garrett Fawcett speaking in the garden of Aubrey House at a party organised in her honour by the National Union of Societies for Equal Citizenship, on Thursday, 23 July 1925. From the Women's Library at LSE. No known copyright restrictions.	374
19	'Officers and members of the National Union of Societies for Equal Citizenship, after the Royal Assent to the Equal Franchise Act', 2 July 1928. Postcard. From the Women's Library at LSE. No known copyright restrictions.	402
20	'Dame Millicent Fawcett, Miss Fawcett, Miss Garrett and Mrs Strachey after the Royal Assent to the Equal Franchise Act', 2 July 1928. Postcard. From the Women's Library at LSE. No known copyright restrictions.	403
21	Dame Millicent Fawcett at the Victory Breakfast, Hotel Cecil, Thursday, 5 July 1928. From the Women's Library at LSE. No known copyright restrictions.	406
22	Millicent Garrett Fawcett, oil on canvas, by Lionel Ellis, 1928. Now in Newnham College, University of Cambridge. Orphan work, due diligence undertaken, permission granted by Newnham College for inclusion.	408

Foreword

As the former chair of the Fawcett Society, I am pleased to welcome this volume, which brings together many of the writings and speeches of our eponymous predecessor Millicent Fawcett. We aim to continue in the tradition she built of campaigning for equality between women and men, focusing particularly on political power, education and work. Like her, we depend on robust research, clear argument and building alliances with women and men to advance our cause. It is a joy to present this collection, which will increase understanding of the role Millicent Fawcett played, not only in the struggle for the women's franchise but in the series of other causes which she promoted.

The quality I have always most admired in Millicent Fawcett is persistence. She gathered signatures on the petition for women's suffrage at the age of 18 in 1866, and she persisted with the cause, becoming its leader for many years, until the women of Britain had achieved her aim of the right to vote on the same terms as men, 62 years later in 1928. The Fawcett Society is the successor to the National Union of Women's Suffrage Societies (NUWSS), which Millicent Fawcett led for many years. We inherited the brooch that appears in pictures reproduced in this volume, which was given to her by members of the society to recognise her leadership. It is engraved on the reverse with the words 'Steadfastness and Courage' and is now in the Museum of London.

This scholarly work, peppered with pictures of Millicent, shows her persistence in making the argument for the vote to audiences, many of whom were deeply hostile, and her determination to advance the cause of women through education. When women did gain a limited franchise, she was careful to record how this change had led to many new laws which benefitted women, from protection from forced marriage to the right to join the police.

Fawcett's words on her statue, a comment made relating to the death of Emily Wilding Davison, who was fatally injured by the King's horse while carrying a banner that demanded votes for women (see Section 46), were a declaration of fact rather than a rallying call. While Fawcett recognised that the militant suffragettes had put the issue on the public agenda ('They've rose the country', in the words of an audience member at one of her speeches – see Section 25), she was critical of their tactics. And in some ways, the record of her doggedly persistent campaign to advance the cause of women without resorting to the violent tactics of the suffragettes is a lesson for feminists in the twenty-first century.

When I find myself disagreeing with other people who are concerned about issues facing women today, I take inspiration from Millicent. She was often generous in her appreciation of what the militant suffragists had done, while always rejecting their tactics. For universities and public platforms to exclude people because they take one side of a debate is unacceptable in a democratic society. I hope that the middle way which the Fawcett Society adopts can win wider acceptance, so that we can all stop being angry and upset with each other and carry on the dogged work which is still needed to build a society where women and men are truly equal.

The approach to the campaign for votes for women which Millicent Fawcett led has lessons for us today: be clear in your arguments, do not abuse those who disagree with you, build alliances and, above all, be persistent in working towards the changes we need.

Fiona Mactaggart
Chair, Fawcett Society, 2018–21
August 2021

Introduction

Nothing is duller reading than speeches on issues which are dead and gone (Millicent Garrett Fawcett 1924, 91).

We think our readers will be glad to have the actual words of Mrs Fawcett (*Common Cause* 1919b).

On 24 April 2018, a statue of Dame Millicent Garrett Fawcett, the leading UK suffragist and campaigner of the late nineteenth and early twentieth centuries, was unveiled in Parliament Square, London. Marking 100 years since some of the women in the UK were given the right to vote and following a campaign by the activist Caroline Criado Perez to increase the visibility of political women, this artwork by Gillian Wearing is the first statue of a woman, and the first by a woman, in a public space that had previously featured only statues of male politicians. Wearing portrays Fawcett at the age of 50 in 1897, when she became a leading figure within the democratic National Union of Women's Suffrage Societies (NUWSS),[1] carrying a banner emblazoned with her own words: 'Courage calls to courage everywhere' (Buck 2018). The statue itself has since become a place of pilgrimage (Thorpe 2018), remembrance and vigil (Rose 2021), and a meeting point for organised protest regarding women's rights (Oppenheim 2019; Gayle and Mohdin 2021). Its featured phrase has been appropriated as a battle cry by modern feminists (Reilly 2019), adorning necklaces, t-shirts, tote bags and fridge magnets and becoming part of common parlance (Begum 2018).

But what is the source of Fawcett's quote? And where can one read Fawcett's own words, in context? Those simple questions were the spark for this volume, which provides access to Dame Millicent Garrett Fawcett's essential speeches, pamphlets and newspaper columns. In doing so, it tells the story of her many-faceted contribution to public life, using primary source material she created herself. However, these are complex sources, often situated in particular political and social contexts which can make it hard for the modern reader to fully comprehend their meaning or purpose. In this volume we introduce 35 texts and 22 images, providing detailed notes for each, plumbing the original material into the rich nexus of historical and literary references used by Fawcett, as well as into contemporary news coverage, and linking them further to 75 other sources written by Fawcett. These speeches, articles, artworks and photographs cover both advances and defeats in the campaign for women's votes, but also other topics and causes that Fawcett pursued, such as: the provision of education for women; lives of great women and feminist history; literature, and her unsuccessful attempt at establishing a career as a novelist; purity and temperance; the campaign against the employment of children; her investigation into the conduct of the concentration camps instituted by the British Army during the South African War; the Unionist cause against Home Rule for Ireland; and the role of suffrage organisations in supporting the nation during the Great War. Making these links reveals a rich, intertextual network of outputs, preferred reading material, organisations, contacts, friends and sometimes enemies, providing an insight into Fawcett as an individual throughout her 61 years of campaigning in the public eye.

Unlike her male near-contemporaries, such as John Stuart Mill (1806–73)[2] and Winston Churchill (1874–1965)[3], Fawcett (1847–1929) does not have an online library that details and documents her oeuvre in order to provide access to interested readers. In fact, very few women publicly active in the political sphere have been paid this type of attention.[4] The last large-scale scholarly work on Fawcett was published 30 years ago,[5] David Rubinstein's *A Different World for Women: The life of Millicent Garrett Fawcett* (1991). A phenomenal piece of detailed scholarship with pointers to source material (now freely available online[6]), it also provides, as an appendix, a list of publications by Fawcett, including columns, speeches and pamphlets, as well as noting her books (Rubinstein 1991, 291–9): we collated these in an archival version of Pokémon's *Gotta catch 'em all*. From this, a selection of texts were chosen, combined with related images and artworks, that would explain and contextualise Fawcett's social campaigning, opinions and character, over her professional life. These texts were carefully transcribed from the originals and explained in both brief introductions to contextualise each chosen piece and footnotes which outline Fawcett's references to individuals, institutions, news events and literary sources. This volume will therefore be useful to a reader wishing to understand the contribution Fawcett made to political and cultural society but will also add to the information available about her life and her achievements, providing a trusted, open-access source for a wide readership.

Millicent Garrett Fawcett: a brief biography

Millicent Garrett was born on 11 June 1847 at The Uplands, Aldeburgh, Suffolk. Her father, Newson Garrett (1812–93), was a politically active merchant, shipowner and maltster with interests including coal, corn and the maltings at Snape (where 'Millie' spent her childhood). Her mother, the evangelical Louisa Dunnell (1813–1903), was born in London. Millicent was the seventh of the surviving ten children in a large family of six daughters and five sons;[7] the family was a close and happy one, and the children were encouraged to read widely, discuss politics and intellectual matters and be physically active. Taught by 'a governess at home over whom we tyrannised' (*Women's Penny Paper* 1888, 4), Millie then attended a boarding school at Blackheath in south London between the ages of 11 and 15 (run by Louisa Browning [1807–87], half-aunt of the poet Robert Browning [1812–89]), further furnishing her with an interest in education and the arts.

Millicent's elder sisters were instrumental in introducing her to the embryonic women's movement, and their encouragement supported her determined conviction that women's emancipation and access to education for women were crucial issues to address. An apocryphal story has it that an early conversation with her older sister Elizabeth's friend, the suffragist Emily Davies (1830–1921), saw Emily commit to securing higher education and Elizabeth (1836–1917) tasked with opening up the medical profession, leaving Millie to 'see about getting the vote' (Strachey 1928, 101). Louisa Garrett (then Smith, 1835–67) provided a London base in Manchester Square, Elizabeth became Britain's first legally qualified woman doctor in 1865 and Agnes Garrett (1845–1935) became London's first female interior designer with their cousin Rhoda Garrett (1841–82). In London, the young Millicent heard the progressive sermons of the Christian socialist Rev. Frederick Denison Maurice (1805–72), and in 1865 she first saw the philosopher and economist John Stuart Mill speak. It was also in 1865 that she first met her husband-to-be, the Liberal member of Parliament for Brighton, Henry Fawcett (1833–84). In 1866, Elizabeth Garrett was part of the informal committee which organised a petition requesting 'that women who met the requisite property qualifications, as set out in the Reform bill then under discussion, should be able to cast a parliamentary vote alongside men' (Crawford 2014b). 'They consulted Mr Mill about the petition, and he promised to present it if they could collect as many as a hundred names' (Fawcett 1912a, 20). Millicent was then too young to sign, but was probably, with her sister Agnes, responsible for gathering signatures for it from the women of Aldeburgh. 'After a fortnight's work they secured 1499 [signatures], including many of the most distinguished women of the day . . . Mr Mill . . . was greatly delighted by the large number of names which had been obtained and exclaimed, "Ah, this I can brandish with great effect"' (Fawcett 1912a, 20). These connections, shared attitudes and opportunities set the young Millicent towards a lifetime of campaigning.

Millicent married Henry Fawcett in 1867 (see Figure 1), and 'as a young married woman was invited in May 1867' to join a women's suffrage committee 'which had already been formed the previous year' (Fawcett 1927f). This coincided with the first time women's suffrage was 'raised in parliament as a practical issue in 1867, when John Stuart Mill . . . moved an amendment to the Reform Bill of that year. It was, of course, defeated: but 73 members voted for it, including ten leading Conservatives. Mill's speech made a very deep impression' (Fawcett 1927d, 697). It was important to Fawcett that she had been there to witness the 1867 events in Parliament: in later recollections she defines herself as 'I, who was in the struggle ever since Mill's speech in the House of Commons in 1867' (Fawcett 1928c; see also Fawcett 1928a).

The approach of this book is to place focus on Millicent's publications, which began shortly after her marriage to Henry. His support, encouragement, career and connections were key in giving her the opportunity to engage with many social issues in Victorian Britain, and resulted in pathways towards publication to express her views. As a public figure, Millicent was styled as Mrs Henry Fawcett, but from the outset she maintained and published under her own name: Millicent Garrett Fawcett. Introductions to the featured texts cover major life events, but a brief trajectory here will be useful to the reader.

After marrying, Millicent and Henry spent their time between Cambridge and London, and their daughter Philippa was born in April 1868. Millicent, as well as acting as her husband's guide and secretary, established a speaking and writing career of her own throughout the 1870s. As a result, press coverage painted her as a neglectful mother, but it was said later that to 'her friends she is known as a devoted mother to her only child, and one of her favourite pastimes is knitting stockings by her own fireside while her daughter reads aloud to her' (*Matron* 1915).

Millicent supported the education of women, and became a co-founder in 1875 of Cambridge's second college for women, Newnham Hall (later College). The early and sudden death of Henry in 1884 saw Millicent widowed at the age of 37, moving with Philippa to the Gower Street home of her sister Agnes Garrett. Fawcett's return to public life in 1885 saw her renewed interest in and public campaigning around a range of topics related to the emancipation of women, including education, purity, the evils of prostitution and constructive employment opportunities. From 1893, Fawcett chaired a committee on behalf of London suffrage societies, leading directly to the foundation in 1897 of the NUWSS, a democratic and non-militant organisation that coordinated the activities of hundreds of different groups and tens of thousands of members nationwide, aiming to achieve the vote for women via peaceful and constitutional approaches. By the close of the nineteenth century, Fawcett was an establishment, if conservative, figure: she was awarded an honorary LLD by the University of St Andrews in 1899 for her services to education, and in 1901 she was trusted by the British government to lead the commission of women sent to South Africa to investigate unsanitary conditions and disease in British Army concentration camps (Fawcett being largely unsympathetic to the Boer situation).

After the NUWSS reorganised along democratic lines in 1907, Fawcett officially became president, tactically and strategically negotiating steps towards women's suffrage, always pragmatically looking for the approach most likely to move the cause forward and emphatically distancing the suffragists from the increasingly militant activities of the suffragettes. The outbreak of the Great War in 1914 saw all suffrage activism halted, although Fawcett led the NUWSS's war work, organising activities to support the country via their established networks. However, Fawcett's vocal, fiercely patriotic support for the war and its violence saw her lose many pacifist colleagues and friends. The changes war had wrought to society meant it was accepted that the franchise should be extended to all servicemen, and in these 1918 reforms there was also a recommendation that women over 30 who met the property qualification be granted the right to vote: Fawcett urged the NUWSS to compromise, and lobbied to support this development. Resigning from the leadership of the NUWSS in 1919 after achieving votes for some women, Fawcett continued to write, edit, campaign, lobby and protest, as well as travelling widely in her retirement. She was made a Dame Grand Cross of the Order of the British Empire (GBE) in the 1925 New Year Honours list. Although little involved in organising the later campaign to gain the vote for all women (Law 1997), Fawcett remained supportive of the younger generation[8] and gladly joined in activities celebrating the gaining of women's suffrage in 1928, being by then a renowned public figure. She died after a short illness, aged 82, at home in Gower Street on 5 August 1929, and was cremated at Golders Green. The resting place of her ashes was never made public (Fawcett 1924; Strachey 1931; Rubinstein 1989; Rubinstein 1991; Howarth 2007).

Millicent Garrett Fawcett: memorialisation

By the end of her long and successful life, Fawcett was a household name, synonymous with women's rights and emancipation, associated in the public consciousness with the continuous and eventually successful campaign for women gaining the vote on the same terms as men. Her achievements were rightly celebrated at the time: a 1932 memorial in Westminster Abbey, sympathetically added to Henry's (see Section 55); a meeting room at the heart of Women's Service House – the new building for the Westminster premises of the main women's rights organisation in London, then called the London and National Society for Women's Service[9] – being named after her in 1931 as 'Millicent Fawcett Hall' (Fawcett had laid the foundation stone in 1929); the renaming of the London and National Society for Women's Service[10] to the Fawcett Society in 1953 (Grant 2016; Fawcett Society 2020) and, with that, the renaming of the library of materials originating from the society – known as the 'Women's Service Library' – to the 'Fawcett Library'. A blue plaque was erected at what had been Millicent's Gower Street home in 1954 (OpenPlaques.org 2009). Various programmes explaining Fawcett's achievements appeared on British Broadcasting Corporation (BBC) Radio.[11] Millicent Fawcett Court, a compact, modern council housing estate in Haringey, North London, was completed in 1971 (Cherry and Pevsner 2002, 587). In 2008, Fawcett was one of six 'Women of Distinction' honoured on a set of UK postal stamps[12] (*British Philatelic Bulletin* 2008).

However, over the course of the later twentieth and early twenty-first centuries, it became harder to remember what she had accomplished and what causes she embodied, and her name slipped from public memorialisation. After World War II, lack of finance forced the Fawcett Society to move premises and eventually to part company with its library, which in 1977 was given a home in Whitechapel by the City Polytechnic. Then, in 2002, by this time renamed the Women's Library, it moved into new, purpose-built premises (BBC 2002) before relocating to the London School of Economics (LSE) in 2013 (Murphy 2016). By now the link to Millicent Fawcett was no longer visible. In 2013 the memorial to Henry and Millicent in Westminster Abbey was moved to a less prominent position (Westminster Abbey 2021), where it is harder to see or read. At least Millicent Fawcett Hall (which was purchased from the Fawcett Society in 1957 under a compulsory order by Westminster Council) was saved from demolition in 1992 (Ghazi 1992; Abdela 1992). However, although it retains Fawcett's name, it is now privately owned as part of the independent Westminster School (Historic England n.d.), and there is a certain irony that the only remaining part of London's first custom-built premises to support women's rights, named after a known promoter of women's education, is now inaccessible to most and being used to educate society's most privileged sons.

Institutionally, it is easier to change the name, situation or purpose of libraries, plaques or meeting halls than statues. Recently, we have seen the stressing of the political, nationalistic, jingoistic as well as emotional, memorial and educational power of statuary of historical figures, which has long been understood: statues are 'ideological powerhouses: physical objects that compress whole systems of authority into bodies of bronze or marble. Elevated on bases and columns, accompanied by inscriptions and framed by grand, civic architecture, they enshrine the deeds of the men (and it is usually men) that they represent'[13] (Platt 2020). It had long been noted that there was no statue of Fawcett – anywhere, even if it might or might not be appropriate (Abdela 1992; Blackburn 1996; Bakewell 2004; Stevenson 2013) – and there were recent calls for one in Parliament Square itself (Finkelstein 2015; Crawford 2016a). Criado Perez' 2016 petition and Wearing's 2018 statue have seen public interest in Fawcett reignited,[14] although modern scholarship has not yet reassessed her contribution. The recent reframing of Fawcett as a feminist icon means it is time to consider what – and how – Fawcett argued, in her own words.

Selecting Fawcett's texts

Fawcett was an industrious, productive and successful author, producing 12 books and hundreds of individual pieces that appeared in a wide variety of outlets, including pamphlets, articles, chapters, introductions, newspaper columns and reviews (categorised and listed in Rubinstein 1991, 291–9), as well as volumes of open letters, and statements and letters representing the NUWSS. Many of these were syndicated and republished in various versions. Taking Rubinstein's list as a starting point and adding material to it via online searches from WorldCat,[15] marketplaces such as eBay and AbeBooks and contemporaneous adverts in digitised historical newspapers reveals a voluminous print legacy, giving a surfeit of material to select from. Materials were accessed in reading rooms, within digital editions and online resources, via digitisation on demand or (where affordable or available) through purchase. A process of resolving thematic and temporal spread saw the selection of 35 speeches, columns and excerpts and 22 images, covering the entire period of Fawcett's public life between 1868 and 1929. These give a sense of the range of her interests, while also demonstrating the changing political and social landscape, focusing on Fawcett in the round, rather than only the story of votes for women.

The featured texts foreground the many professional interests Fawcett maintained. Some themes are constant, such as the campaign for votes for women. Fawcett's writings on the developing constitutional women's suffrage movement, its achievements and sometimes its disappointments necessarily dominate the table of contents, from her early speeches on the subject in 1871 (Section 3) to the celebrations upon achieving votes on the same basis as men in 1928 (Section 51). These writings on the campaign for women's enfranchisement navigate some of the major issues of the day, including how the suffragists – and Fawcett – responded to the increasing militancy of the suffragettes between 1906 and 1914 (Sections 24 to 39); the intersection with the Unionist cause against Home Rule for Ireland in 1912 and 1913 (Sections 35 and 37); World War I (1914–18), how women were affected by it and how pacifist suffragists responded to the war effort (Sections 39 to 42); and how the changed nature of the country after the war afforded some women the vote (Sections 44 and 45).

However, amid this theme of votes for women are many explorations of Fawcett's other concerns. One of her lifelong interests was the provision of education to women and how it could be encouraged (see Sections 2, 18 and 50), as well as employment opportunities and issues for women and children (Sections 13 and 14). Less well known is her love and knowledge of literature (Section 9) and her failure to establish herself as a career novelist (Section 10); if her fiction had succeeded, we may not have had Fawcett the statesperson, who effected so much societal change. Fawcett's role in the purity movement in the 1880s and 1890s is covered (Sections 12 and 22), and her views on women, and their place in society, sit very differently from modern feminist approaches to women's emancipation (Section 17). Most contentious are Fawcett's role in supporting the British Army's approach to the South African War in 1901 (Section 23) and her judgements regarding the deserving and undeserving foreign poor, as well as on sexuality and purity (Section 22).

We have deliberately chosen not to include content from Fawcett's books, except where apposite (showing her attempt as a novelist in *Janet Doncaster* [1875], and the exact source of 'Courage calls to courage everywhere' from *The Women's Victory – and After* [1920], which is much mis-cited).[16] Fawcett's books are wide-ranging, including her best-selling introductory text *Political Economy for Beginners* (1870a), the collection with Henry Fawcett, *Essays and Lectures on Social and Political Subjects* (1872), and *Tales in Political Economy* (1874). As Fawcett increasingly wrote on women's emancipation matters for reviews, journals and newspapers, her books covered more historical matters; examples include: *Some Eminent Women of our Times: Short biographical sketches* (1889c); *Life of Her Majesty Queen Victoria* (1895); *Life of the Right Hon. Sir William Molesworth, Bart., M.P., F.R.S.* (1901a); and *Five Famous French Women* (1905). Her autobiographical reflections are important source material in order to explain the significance of many of the excerpts featured in this text, including: *Women's Suffrage: A short history of a great movement* (1912a); *The Women's Victory – and After: Personal reminiscences, 1911–1918* (1920a); and *What I Remember* (1924). Her last books were *Easter in Palestine, 1921–1922* (1926b) – a compilation of travel writings – and, with Ethel M. Turner, *Josephine Butler: Her work and principles and their meaning for the twentieth century* (1927). Nearly all of Fawcett's books are digitised and freely available online:[17] we leave interested readers to consult these full texts, although we refer to them where relevant, while foregrounding less easily accessible material.

It would be possible to edit together other selections of Fawcett's writings; for example, thinking of what we can learn about Fawcett herself, we have not included any of her travel writings,[18] which provide rich source material on her colonialist view of England in the international context. More politically, although we feature one section (37) on Ireland, further research into the relationship Fawcett had with it is needed, including the interlinking of the votes for women campaign with the campaign for Irish Home Rule (which Fawcett was opposed to), the many visits to Ireland she made, and whether any of her many speeches there survive (extended archival research was not possible due to the Covid-19 outbreak). Further analysis and foregrounding of the letters Fawcett wrote and the statements she made on behalf of the NUWSS would be useful in understanding the contribution the constitutional approach made to gaining the vote for women. Indeed, one of the reasons that a collection such as this has not been attempted before is probably because there is just so much content to locate, synthesise and draw from: while the relatively brief period of militant suffragette action has attracted much recent scholarly and public attention, the decades of constitutional suffragist work remain ripe for further study.[19] The sections here show the complexity, too, in drawing clear distinctions between the suffragists and suffragettes: all groups were respectful of each other's activities before violent militancy (Section 25) and, after World War I and the granting of votes to some women, celebrated various achievements and memorials together, in a once-again supportive relationship (see Figure 21): this, too, merits further analysis.

Editorial approach

Much in Fawcett's speeches and columns seems strange to modern comprehension: the political parties and establishments, the legal framework, the popular culture of the day and even the humour. As a result, in order to be fully appreciated by the interested modern reader, these texts require adequate commentary, situating them within the wider historical, political and social climate and describing Fawcett's engagement with it. The commentary-writing stage took place between February 2020 and June 2021 in a tag-team approach, led by Terras and supported by Crawford. Luckily, the vast majority of archival and library material was accessed, gathered, digitised and transcribed throughout 2018 and 2019, before the UK Covid-19 lockdowns. There are a few places in the book where further access to archives would have improved or clarified information: these are signposted so that future researchers can enjoy their time in the reading room.

Beyond collating Fawcett's written material from libraries and archives, the analysis presented here is utterly dependent on online access to library sources that are available while home-working, demonstrating the wealth of digitised historical material that now exists (particularly from the Victorian, Edwardian and World War I periods). Fawcett was writing in what turns out to be an ideal phase for research, as 'Chronologically, the nineteenth century is particularly well represented in digital archives, owing perhaps to its "goldilocks" (or just right) conservation-copyright status. Most pre-1900 material can be safely considered to be in the global public domain' (Hauswedell et al. 2020, 150). Indeed, the out-of-copyright status of Fawcett's own materials[20] has made this collection possible, while cross-referencing them at scale is possible because of the preferential choices made about digitising material that has no known copyright restrictions.

After texts were selected and transcribed, only light editing was undertaken to resolve typographical and other obvious print errors, and the pieces here are presented, for the most part, in their entirety. This, however, means that terms and phrases, particularly relating to race, are of their time, although we have discussed this where apposite in our endnotes. Introductory material to each piece draws primarily on Rubinstein 1991, but also on Fawcett's own memoirs (*Women's Suffrage: A short history of a great movement* [1912a]; *The Women's Victory – and After: Personal reminiscences, 1911–1918* [1920a]; and *What I Remember* [1924]) and Strachey's fawning biography, *Millicent Garrett Fawcett* (1931). It also uses the wider wealth of Fawcett's writings not included here and the periodicals Fawcett was involved with, such as the *Common Cause*, *Englishwoman* and *Woman's Leader*, before turning to the wider historical and scholarly literature available.

The people, places, events, phrases, cultural references, parliamentary processes and legal frameworks that Fawcett mentions were identified. These are presented in generous endnotes which should be read alongside the original sources. For efficiency, unless another source is stated, the *Oxford Dictionary of National Biography* was used to give dates of birth and death, titles and brief descriptions of individuals· individual biographies are only cited when further information is useful to understand context. Quotations derived from Shakespeare's work were noted using the *New Oxford Shakespeare*.[21] Biblical references were identified using *Bible Gateway*.[22]

Determining the sources of more complex references and allusions within the texts required searching the full gamut of online digitised content available to modern researchers. Indeed, this activity has only become possible very recently, given the large repositories of digitised content now available which offer a full text search: our approach is absolutely dependent on this complex network of prior digitisation of cultural heritage. Resources used included those on the open web, such as Wikipedia and Wikidata, Flickr Commons, Internet Archive Books (including the National Emergency Library), Google Books, the HathiTrust Digital Library and Project Gutenberg. Institutional and scholarly digital resources were essential, including those from the LSE Digital Library, British Library,[23] National Library of Australia (Trove) and Online Library of Liberty. This research benefitted from subscription-based access to digital resources via the University of Edinburgh,[24] UCL and the National Library of Scotland (NLS – and on-site access in the NLS to Electronic Legal Deposit[25] materials including the UK Web Archive).[26] Essential licensed online resources included Gale Historical Newspapers[27] (in particular the *Times* Digital Archive),[28] ProQuest Historical Newspapers[29] and LexisNexis for modern news coverage. In addition, a personal subscription to the British Newspaper Archive was invaluable.[30] Finding previously published research was facilitated by JSTOR and Google Scholar. Where absolutely necessary, given the physical Covid-19 restrictions in place throughout the writing of the text, Library Genesis was also used.[31] Substantial quotations from these varied sources are provided in footnotes to avoid readers having to navigate paywalled and restricted-access content.

The Fawcett in Fawcett's texts

What we know about Fawcett, including her relationships, network and approach, has to come from written material, photography and artworks: there are no known recordings of her voice, and so we do not know her intonation, timing or response to the particular audience around her (although there may be brief captures of her on silent newsreel).[32] Newspaper coverage of speeches suggests she read from the page and did not deviate from prepared speeches: see, for example, Fawcett's speech at Owens College, Manchester, in 1899 (Section 21) and its coverage in the *Manchester Courier and Lancashire General Advertiser* (1899). Such reports often record audience responses at specific points, such as laughter and applause (see Sections 19 and 33). Fawcett herself said in 1888 that she always prepared her speeches – 'that is, I always know what I want to say' – although she was frequently nervous: 'I don't like it at all, I never like speaking . . . what I should like to do would be to sit down all day with my books' (*Women's Penny Paper* 1888, 5).

Others have looked at these speeches and columns to see what is revealed about Fawcett herself. Contemporaneous reports and obituaries note that, although 'widely read and of keen intellect' and 'a writer of considerable importance on her own account' (*New York Times* 1929), '[s]he was never eloquent; her speeches were generally a record of recent events relevant to her subject and always optimistically interpreted, together with shrewd digs at her opponents' (*Manchester Guardian* 1929). This is a harsh but fair assessment, and, paradoxically, it is what makes an edited collection of her speeches so rich a sketch of the time, filled as they are with news events, people, places, asides and allusions to Victorian popular culture (however obscure these may be now: see, for example, the misquoted lines from the then popular Irish ballad 'By the Lake Whose Gloomy Shore' in Section 30). Her discursive approach was always careful and measured: 'Her weapons were those of reason and argument . . . though vigilant and making the most of every public opportunity, she never let herself be provoked into saying or writing anything which would have lowered the dignity of the controversy' (*Times* 1929). It has been noted that in the careful textual legacy we see the development of a leader of women who strategically understood that she would best accomplish what she wanted by being accepted and supported by leading men. Fawcett was an efficient, law-abiding, well-read and well-connected Christian English mother, who merely asked for one core thing for 60 years: for women to have equality with men. As Rubinstein said, she 'long pursued unacceptable goals by acceptable means' (1991, 251). It was these well-known, modest characteristics, as well as her achievements in leading the NUWSS (and her unblemished criminal record),[33] that made her an appropriate candidate to the authorities for a 2018 statue in Parliament Square commemorating 100 years of votes for (some) women. However, it has also been noted more recently that although she was a leading Victorian feminist in 'scholarship and practice', her feminism was limited by being 'white and middle class' (Dalley 2021, 13) and from an entirely English viewpoint (Fawcett regularly used the term England to encompass Scotland, Ireland and Wales). For example, she was angered that Māori women in Aotearoa, New Zealand, or Black men in South Africa had more rights than British women in England (Sanghani 2015; see Section 33). Fawcett also ignored the plight of Black African prisoners in the South African War and believed British approaches to be superior, blaming Boer women for the high mortality rate in the South African concentration camps (Section 23). Her views on prostitution, purity (Section 12) and the deserving and undeserving poor (Section 22) are aspects of Fawcett's arguments that many modern feminists find difficult to reconcile with her recent standing as a feminist icon.

Beyond these noted characteristics, what is added to our knowledge of Fawcett through undertaking this close reading of her publications? Fawcett quotes other sources often, although – perhaps as a result of her childhood education, since 'it was the fashion then to learn . . . things by heart' (*Women's Penny Paper* 1888, 4) – she often slightly tweaks, or rephrases. Given she had a reputation for being a good Christian, it is not surprising that biblical references appear throughout her works, and she quotes equally from the Hebrew Bible (Genesis, Deuteronomy, Nehemiah, Job, Psalms, Isaiah) and the New Testament (Matthew, Luke, John, Corinthians, Ephesians, Hebrews) – although what is unexpected is that she does not actually quote the scriptures very fully, or often. From her phrasing, it is most likely that her Bible was the King James Version. Fawcett knew her Shakespeare, from the sonnets to *Hamlet*, *King Lear* and *Romeo and Juliet*, but also *Troilus and Cressida*, *Twelfth Night* and the histories. She was up to speed with modern literature, quoting a minor work from Wordsworth[34] and a major one from Ibsen, although not respecting Dickens (and also criticising Thackeray and Fielding). She often quoted Tennyson, hugely admired George Eliot, alluded to the popular work of Maria Edgeworth, and regularly mentioned Mark Twain's travel memoirs, given his comments on women's suffrage.

Her penchant for almost remembering quotes is seen in her description of news items (although there were times when Fawcett also deliberately reframed stories and bent quotations to suit her argument: these are clearly noted, as, at times, she could be quite selective in her evidence). She was an avid reader of the press, particularly the *Times*, London (which should always be the first port of call when trying to find a news item she refers to, however obliquely), but also other London newspapers and perhaps those from further afield (such as the *Western Times*). Her comments on Ireland suggest she kept up with the Irish newspapers, too. As is to be expected, Fawcett paid close attention to suffrage publications, being a regular contributor to the NUWSS publication the *Common Cause* and having editorial duties for the *Woman's Leader*, and contributing often to *Jus Suffragi* (the journal of the International Woman Suffrage Alliance [IWSA]) and the suffrage magazine the *Englishwoman*. She evidently also read publications from the militant factions closely, including the *Vote* and *Votes for Women*, and closely scrutinised the *Anti-Suffrage Review* published by her major nemesis, the Women's National Anti-Suffrage League (WNASL), as well as reading widely around women's issues, including publications such as the *Woman Worker*.

It becomes clear throughout these pieces how wide Fawcett's networks were. There are mentions of various individuals working with her in the suffrage movement, some well known, some not. There are frequent, if passing, mentions of those she knew and respected in academia, including, in particular, colleagues from the University of Cambridge and the London institutions. She also knew, and respected, various liberal-minded (in the modern sense) politicians. Evidently, she was quite the networker, and while this is to be expected, the mentions of these individuals in the texts, which are fully explained throughout, give concrete instances of her incredibly wide social and professional circles. More surprising, given her pledged allegiance to the widening international suffrage movement, is that there is little evidence of international friendships, beyond correspondence with Carrie Chapman Catt (1859–1947), the president of the National American Woman Suffrage Association (NAWSA; see Section 30).[35] We also see evidence of Fawcett bearing obstinate grudges – for example, in her relationship with the leader of the WNASL, Mary Augusta Ward (Mrs Humphry Ward, 1851–1920; see Section 30), or towards the welfare campaigner Emily Hobhouse (1860–1926), who first drew widespread attention to the unsanitary conditions in the British government's concentration camps in South Africa (see Section 23). Her stubborn allegiance to Britain's Great War effort saw her lose the support and friendship of many pacifist suffragists (see Section 41), but it was also her stubbornness which made her 'go-on – go on – go on!' (see Figure 21).

An aspect that is most touching in her writings is her dependence on, and pride in, family networks (Crawford 2002), which she evidently learnt a lot from. Fawcett often gives examples that are linked to her extended family, even if they are not directly named or mentioned. For example, Fawcett talks knowledgeably about South Africa and having 'recently received cuttings from a Cape paper' (Section 22): these would have been from her cousin Edmund Garrett (1865–1907), who had lived at Gower Street with Agnes and probably Millicent before going on to become a Member of the Parliament of the Cape of Good Hope in 1898 (Cook 1909, 6). Their correspondence helped them both navigate constitutional matters in the UK and South Africa. In Section 45 Fawcett talks proudly of the war effort and the work of UK women doctors, who had been snubbed by the British Red Cross but successfully established hospitals abroad: this is a reference to Fawcett's niece Louisa Garrett Anderson (1873–1943), daughter of Elizabeth Garrett Anderson, who had established a hospital in Paris with Flora Murray (1869–1923), working with the French Red Cross. Fawcett, despite her reputation, high energy levels and organisational and networking abilities, strategically presented herself as a 'womanly woman . . . devoted to her home and to homely pursuits' (*Star* 1929, 322), although that home, and her family network, were exceptional (Crawford 2002). The attachment to and support of her family shines through these pieces and (where not obvious) is signposted to the reader.

This book's contribution

The aim of this book is not only to present material in an accessible format, but also to research into Fawcett's published works and life. As a result, it has made particular contributions of its own. Highlights include:

- Expanding Fawcett's known bibliography, identifying 24 published works beyond Rubinstein's excellent list (5 of which are included in full in this volume).[36]

- Establishing the seriousness of her injuries from a fall from a horse in 1874, which led her to write her only surviving novel (Sections 9 and 10).
- Discovering the contribution that Fawcett made to the World's Columbian Exposition (the Chicago World's Fair) of 1893, which had previously been undocumented (Section 18).
- Establishing the iconography and heraldic meaning of the brooch Fawcett was given by the NUWSS in 1913 and noting its importance on her Westminster Abbey memorial and Wearing's statue (Figures 16 and 22 and Section 55).
- Identifying Fawcett's speeches on the early BBC Radio service (Sections 50 and 52) and the transcript of the radio speech that Fawcett made after the Royal Assent to the Equal Franchise Act, 2 July 1928 (Section 52).
- Establishing concrete evidence of Fawcett's relationship to University College, London (near her home on Gower Street: see Section 50).
- The potential identification of footage of Fawcett in a British Pathé newsreel (1928).
- Clarifying discussions regarding her cremation and memorialisation (Section 55).

This book has also:

- Gathered in one place, for the first time, the four known oil portraits made of Fawcett in her lifetime, providing full information about them, while also publishing Swynnerton's preparatory study for the first time (Figure 12).
- Properly attributed the Lionel Ellis portrait (Figure 22), as previous to this research it was wrongly thought to have been painted by the English portrait artist William D. Dring (1904–90).
- Accurately dated various photographs in common circulation, while also attributing their photographers and their place of first publication (for example, the provenance of both Figure 17 [Fawcett photographed on her doorstep on the day of her investiture as Dame in 1925] and Figure 21 [Fawcett at the Victory Breakfast in 1928] had been lost).
- Shown how current Fawcett's arguments still are, particularly on: inequalities between men and women; societal and institutional approaches to violence against women; the need to fight for equality in education, employment and equal pay; navigating prejudices; and confronting the double standards by which women are judged.

- And, finally, ensured that consistency, accuracy and reference to primary sources were maintained throughout, pointing other readers to essential source material and correcting common misconceptions and misattributions circulating online.

Acknowledgements

This reader has been an ambitious endeavour, and is dependent on the input of many other people: we thank them all for their supportive efforts. Julianne Nyhan has provided support and commentary on all aspects of the book, from idea to proposal to draft and finalisation, and we acknowledge the contribution this has made to the final product. Kinda Dahlan, David Beavan and Bethany Johnstone assisted in photographing original sources in various libraries and archives. Source materials were carefully and efficiently transcribed from the originals by Alys McDonough, who is available for all your scholarly transcription needs.[37] Lara Speicher and Pat Gordon-Smith at UCL Press have provided encouragement and helpful input since the germination of this project. We also thank Sam Smethers and the Fawcett Society for their encouragement, and Fiona Mactaggart for her generous foreword. Melissa would also like to thank: Anthony, Edward and Fergusson for their bemusement; Os for his unwavering assistance and reassurance that this was a project worth pursuing; Robert and Margaret Terras for their interest; and Claire Easingwood for her support. Elizabeth, as ever, thanks her family, especially Grant, for their support and kindness.

 The research presented here benefitted from the generous support and assistance of various librarians, curators, archivists and information professionals, and in particular we would like to thank: Ksenya Blokhina, ArtUK; Elizabeth Bruton, Science Museum; Sian Collins, Cambridge University Library; Beverley Cook, Museum of London; Paul Cox, National Portrait Gallery; Laura Dennis, Newnham College, University of Cambridge; Rachel Hosker, Centre for Research Collections, University of Edinburgh; Tim Jerrome, Museum of English Rural Life and Special Collections, University of Reading; Kirsty Lingstadt, Library and University Collections, University of Edinburgh; Laura MacCulloch, Royal Holloway Art Collections and Picture Gallery; Gillian Murphy, LSE Library; Heather Pascall and Stewart Gillies, British Library; Matthew Payne, Westminster Abbey; John Petrie, College of Arms; Susan Pettigrew and Norman Rodger, Digital Imaging Unit, University of Edinburgh; Sian Phillips, Bridgeman Images;

Rachel Pierce and Mats Dahlström, University of Borås; Lesley Pitman, Former Librarian, UCL School of Slavonic and East European Studies at UCL; Rachel Roberts, Cheltenham Ladies' College; and Mari Takayanagi and Richard Ward, Parliamentary Archives.

We thank all the galleries, libraries, archives and museums mentioned throughout this volume for their stewardship: although Fawcett's writings are out of copyright, we appreciate the efforts made to retain and provide access to the originals, to allow us to bring these materials to a wider readership. This publication would not have been possible without using resources from the British Library and the Women's Library at LSE, but also Wikipedia and the Internet Archive. A donation has been made to each of these organisations in order to contribute to their activities and infrastructure.

Finally, any income from the sale of this book will support the future work of UCL Press. We chose to publish with UCL Press due to their open-access policy, but also because of Fawcett's relationship to University College London (as it is now known) as an engaged neighbour of the Bloomsbury campus (Section 50). Print copies of this volume have been donated to the Fawcett Society to support them in their work. The commentary and other contents of this book (unless otherwise clearly stated, as for Figures 3, 6, 8, 9, 12, 13 and 22) are available via a Creative Commons Attribution-NonCommercial 4.0 International license (CC BY-NC 4.0), which allows any non-commercial reuse without further permission needed, as long as the source is credited. Fawcett's own words have no known copyright restrictions. Millicent Garrett Fawcett's words belong to everyone.

September 2021

Notes

1. It 'was not until 1907 that the NUWSS was reconstituted as a body with a president and an elected executive', when Fawcett officially became president (Rubinstein 1991, 137).
2. John Stuart Mill (1806–73), philosopher, economist and member of Parliament, was a strong influence on Millicent. His works are available at https://oll.libertyfund.org/title/robson-collected-works-of-john-stuart-mill-in-33-vols. An early essay by Fawcett, assessing Mill's contribution as a politician, published a few weeks after his death in 1873, stresses the contribution he made to the women's movement: 'What he has done for women is final: he gave to their service the best powers of his mind and the best years of his life' (Fawcett 1873c, 85–6). Mill did not hold the same high opinion of Fawcett, however: 'Mrs Fawcett is an excellent woman, with plenty of sense and energy but no experience, and a great deal of self-confidence; a person, therefore admirably calculated to fall headlong into mistakes. She never originated this movement, and is not likely to originate any' (Mill 1872, Letter 1760, in Mineka and Lindley [1972, p. 1921]).
3. Winston Churchill, British statesman. See https://winstonchurchill.org for speeches and other publications.

4 Margaret Thatcher is the exception: https://www.margaretthatcher.org/archive was funded by private philanthropy.
5 Steinbach's *Millicent Garrett Fawcett* (2008) usefully provides a collection of newspaper clippings and other sources that mention Fawcett, showing how she was viewed by her contemporaries, rather than providing an analysis of her works.
6 https://kb.osu.edu/handle/1811/29265.
7 A son, born nine years before Millicent, had died (Fawcett 1924, 9).
8 In 1928, Fawcett commented on modern women: 'there has been a good deal of nonsense about this so-called "flapper vote" . . . A girl of 21 is no longer a flapper. She is a highly developed individual . . . Beneath their shingled hair is an alert brain and a ready wit, able to give clear, quick decisions, and to laugh at obstacles . . . She has been splendid . . . in a hundred and one other ways, and I have nothing but praise for her' (*Derby Daily Telegraph* 1928).
9 The Central Society for Women's Suffrage was formed in 1900, amalgamating other societies (Crawford 2001a, 104). In 1907 it became the London Society for Women's Suffrage. The society had established a Women's Service Bureau at the start of World War I, providing practical support, training and employment. The society officially changed its name to the London Society for Women's Service in 1919 (*Common Cause* 1919a), and then to the London and National Society for Women's Service in 1926 (*Woman's Leader* 1926b): these name changes reflect the society's broadening activities.
10 Fawcett was chair of the Central Society for Women's Suffrage, renamed the London and National Society for Women's Suffrage, until 1909, remaining on its executive until 1913 (Rubinstein 1991, 168), then succeeding her daughter Philippa as president of the London Society for Women's Service in 1923 (p. 268).
11 See, for example, 'Great Lives: Millicent Garrett Fawcett' (BBC 2006), which is still available to listen to online. Earlier programmes include: the plays 'Louisa Wants a Bicycle' (BBC 1936) and 'Queen Victoria was Furious' (BBC 1946); an interview 'I Knew Her' with the writer Mary Stocks (1891–1975) (BBC 1954); retrospectives asking why she is now forgotten (BBC 1989, BBC 2000), and a programme on the campaign to stop children working in Victorian theatres (BBC 2004; see Section 14).
12 The picture chosen was an Elliott & Fry portrait taken in late 1916. A portrait from the same sitting appears in *War Illustrated* (Fawcett 1917d). (See Figure 11 for an earlier Elliott & Fry portrait of Fawcett.)
13 Fawcett herself knew the power of statuary and the importance of maintaining statues to women, raising and contributing funds for the conservation of a contemporary statue to Queen Elizabeth I in Fleet Street in 1928 (*Belfast News Letter* 1928), and leaving a sizeable legacy of £700 in her will for its upkeep (*Times* 2001).
14 See, for example, the naming of a new closing race at the annual Müller Anniversary Games (now the London Grand Prix) athletics event. The race, first organised in 2018, was named 'The Millicent Fawcett Mile . . . commemorating 100 years since British women secured the right to vote' (British Athletics 2018). Fawcett was also celebrated by a Google Doodle on her 171st birthday on 11 June 2018 (Google 2018).
15 https://www.worldcat.org.
16 Much of the news coverage states an incorrect source: see Section 46.
17 Most are available on the Internet Archive, with the exception of: *Some Eminent Women of Our Times*, available via Project Gutenberg; a section of *Easter in Palestine*, available via Bahá'í Library Online; and *Josephine Butler*, with search-only access currently available via the HathiTrust Digital Library.
18 Fawcett travelled widely, both for work and pleasure; she wrote about the UK, including the New Forest (1884a, 1884b) and Burnham Beeches (1885a), and various international experiences, including entries for the *Orient Line Guide* on: Italy and European cities (1885b); Naples, Cities of Italy and Germany (1888e); Gibraltar to Naples (1894b); and London to Marseilles and Naples, and Cairo (1901b). Fawcett's sister Elizabeth was married to James George Skelton Anderson (1838–1907), who was joint-founder of the Orient Steamship Company with his uncle. Fawcett also wrote reflections on experiences in South Africa (1903, 1904) and trips to Palestine in 1921, 1922 and 1927 (Fawcett 1921, 1922 [reprinted as 1926b], 1927b), among others.
19 'Young women students today are becoming very interested in their feminist history . . . But it is usually the fighting Pankhursts these girls call to mind, not the boring old constitutionals, who started long before the Pankhursts and steadfastly continued long after the militant

meteorites had flashed into virtual oblivion' (Stott 1978, 11). Research on the constitutional approach within the women's suffrage movement includes Holton 1986 and Harrison 1987. There has also been research on the constitutional approach of the suffragist, writer and social reformer Isabella Ormston Ford (1855–1924) (Hannam 1989), as well as prior work on Millicent Fawcett (Oakley 1983; Crawford 2001b).

20 The UK copyright for published works authored by Fawcett expired in 1999, 70 years after her death. A risk-management approach was taken to material included in this volume (Korn 2016).
21 https://www.oxfordscholarlyeditions.com/nos.
22 https://www.biblegateway.com.
23 https://www.bl.uk/catalogues-and-collections/digital-collections.
24 https://www.ed.ac.uk/information-services/library-museum-gallery.
25 https://www.nls.uk/about-us/legal-deposit/.
26 https://www.webarchive.org.uk.
27 https://www.gale.com/intl/primary-sources/historical-newspapers.
28 https://www.gale.com/intl/c/the-times-digital-archive.
29 https://about.proquest.com/en/products-services/pq-hist-news/.
30 https://www.britishnewspaperarchive.co.uk.
31 http://libgen.li.
32 A head and shoulders – potentially Fawcett's – can be seen in the window near the statue in the British Pathé 1928 newsreel 'A Queen Cleaned – Dame Millicent Fawcett unveils only contemporary statue of Queen Elizabeth . . . repaired, repainted and restored as it was in the 16th century' (see note 13). Silent newsreel footage of the suffrage pageants and Hyde Park 1913 meeting (see Figure 15) also exists: these items are worthy of further analysis to identify individuals.
33 Militant suffragettes in the UK have not been pardoned for their civil disobedience (see Hinsliff 2004; Fisher 2018).
34 Fawcett included a chapter on Dorothy Mae Ann Wordsworth (1771–1855), the sister of William Wordsworth (1770–1850), in *Some Eminent Women of Our Times* (1889c, 176–85).
35 The papers of Millicent Garrett Fawcett held in Manchester Central Library contain much of her correspondence, further evidencing her wide networks. These are available in microfilm (Adam Matthew Digital 2021). Contained within these is correspondence with many leading figures from the international feminist movement: perhaps they are just not mentioned in this volume's selection.
36 Listed in the Appendix.
37 https://epodcentral.com/transcribingandvideocaptions.

1
Picturing Fawcett: Millicent Garrett Fawcett with Henry Fawcett, 1868

Figure 1: Millicent Garrett Fawcett with Henry Fawcett, 1868, by Henry Joseph Whitlock. From the Women's Library at LSE. No known copyright restrictions.

Henry Fawcett (1833–84), an economist and Liberal politician who had been blinded in a shooting accident in 1858, encountered 17-year-old Millicent Garrett in April 1865 at a party in Aubrey House, London. His attention was drawn to her when she decried the assassination of Abraham Lincoln, the news of which had just reached London (Fawcett 1924, 54; Strachey 1931, 21–2). A year later, he proposed marriage to Millicent's elder sister, Elizabeth, whom he had also met via mutual friends. Elizabeth rejected him, citing her intention of devoting herself to medicine. It is thought that Millicent was unaware of this proposal and in October 1866 she became engaged to Fawcett, who had by then been the member of Parliament for Brighton for just over a year (Rubinstein 1991, 13–21). They were married in Aldeburgh on 23 April 1867, and from the outset Millicent continued to use her family name.

The marriage 'made an enormous difference' to Millicent's life, 'an even greater difference than is usual... From the quietest of quiet country life I was transplanted into a society of surpassing interest and novelty both in London and Cambridge.' Millicent suddenly found herself at the centre of political and academic society while maintaining two homes, being a 'dragon over every unnecessary expenditure' (Fawcett 1924, 55). She noted that her 'political education was just beginning: naturally I had to read and write for my husband. I grappled with newspapers and blue books, and learned more or less to convey their import to him' (Fawcett 1924, 64), contributing 'directly to his essays, lectures and speeches' (Strachey 1931, 37). 'He took care that I should hear important debates in the House of Commons... the whole scene was new to me and very interesting' (Fawcett 1924, 64).

This double portrait was taken in the year after they were married, when Millicent was 21 years old. Their only child, Philippa Fawcett (1868–1948), was born earlier in the year this photograph was taken, which also saw the publication of Fawcett's first essay (see Section 2). An albumen *carte-de-visite* from the same sitting is credited to Henry Joseph Whitlock (1835–1918), a photographer based in Birmingham and Wolverhampton (National Portrait Gallery 2021a).

2
The education of women of middle and upper classes, 1868

Macmillan's Magazine. Vol. 17 (November 1867–April 1868), 511–17.

When Millicent Fawcett published her first article, women in Victorian Britain had extremely limited rights: they could not vote, and if they married, their husbands owned both their property and their earnings and were the sole legal guardians of their children. Indeed, the social expectation was that women would marry and be content with motherly and domestic duties, rather than seek formal education or political advancement (Gordon and Nair 2003; Steinbach 2016; Roderick 2016). Nevertheless, women had been actively involved in relatively recent campaigns, such as the anti-slavery movement, the Anti-Corn Law League and Chartism, and knew that change could be effected. Drawn particularly from Quaker and Unitarian families, they were in touch with counterparts in the USA who, in 1848 at Seneca Falls, had held their first convention to discuss women's rights.

Ideas travelled across the Atlantic: in 1851 a Female Political Association was formed in Sheffield and presented a petition to the House of Lords, calling for the vote for women (Gleadle 1995). Like-minded women kept in touch over the years, inculcating their beliefs into their daughters and, with them, signing the suffrage petition in 1866. But it was now a younger generation, and women such as Elizabeth Garrett and Emily Davies, who led the multi-faceted campaign for women's rights. Living in Aldeburgh and still so young, Millicent had not been a member of the Kensington Society, formed in 1865 to discuss the social and political position of women, of which Emily Davies was secretary and Elizabeth Garrett a member. However, a mere three years later, Fawcett's first article appeared shortly after her marriage to Henry Fawcett, in whom she found a supportive equal who encouraged her to engage in social and political activities (see Introduction), which was a circumstance somewhat unusual for the period:

> From the early years of our marriage, my husband was constantly urging me to write. Without his perpetual encouragement I certainly should not have embarked on authorship at the age of twenty-one. I was also helped and encouraged by his old friend Mr Alexander Macmillan, the head of the publishing firm which bears his name. My first article appeared in 1868, in *Macmillan's Magazine*. Its subject was 'The Lectures for Women in Cambridge' which had lately been started by Henry Sidgwick.[1] These lectures proved to be the seed of which, in a few years, Newnham College was the fruit.[2] I mention this little article partly because I received £7 for it. It was the first money I had ever earned.[3] So I made a sort of Feast of the First Fruits, and gave my £7 to the fund then being formed for paying Mr Mill's[4] expenses at the general Election of that year. It was about this time that I began to have business talks with Mr Macmillan[5] ... He was a real friend to both of us ... Mr Macmillan's business experience convinced him that there was a demand for an elementary book upon Political Economy ... He was convinced I could write this book, and my husband was of the same opinion (Fawcett 1924, 85–6).

Fawcett's *Political Economy for Beginners* was published in 1870, and was so successful that it ran for 10 editions over 41 years, establishing her profile (and an income).

*

At a time, like the present, when the education of the people is engaging so much attention, and when it becomes daily more evident from speeches delivered both in and out of the House of Commons, by men of all political creeds,[6] that the reform and extension of national education will assume, in the future, supreme importance, it seems not inappropriate that something should be said regarding the education of women.

When such phrases as 'national education', and 'the education of the people', are made use of, it is usually implied that they mean the extension of education to the working classes; and it is also implied when the reform of national education is spoken of, that the only part of the nation whose education is neglected, and which therefore needs reform, is that part which receives the designation of 'the lower orders'. We think that the education of women in the middle and upper classes is at least as important, almost as much neglected, and that it needs even more strenuous efforts to effect reform in it. For scarcely any one now openly opposes, in theory, the education of the poor; but with regard to women, before substantial and national reform is effected in their education, an immense amount of opposition, prejudice and undisguised hostility must be overcome.

Let it therefore be considered what is the present state of education among women of the upper and middle classes: what are the results of such education: what reforms it is desirable to introduce: and what results may be expected from them. We will first endeavour to give a fair representation of the education girls usually receive, and then proceed to enumerate some of the consequences to which such an education inevitably leads. A girl, between the ages of twelve and seventeen, generally gives from five to seven hours a day to study. This time is devoted chiefly to music, French, German and sometimes Latin, and to committing to memory and repeating the ordinary school lessons; a very small portion of her time is given to arithmetic, or rather to cyphering.[7] If this list of studies is analysed and examined, it is found that a girl usually spends her time not in learning music, but in acquiring dexterity in playing upon the piano; not in studying language, but in obtaining conversational fluency in French and perhaps German; and, with regard to the ordinary school lessons, the object of these seems to be to cultivate not the understanding but the memory. The cyphering is still worse: it is seldom that a girl has the advantage of being taught arithmetic well, and it is almost an unknown thing for her ever to enter upon the far higher intellectual study of mathematics. To the loss of the discipline which this great science affords the mind may be attributed the defects so common in a woman's intellect, as to be by many considered inherent in it, viz. a certain looseness of thought and incapacity of close logical reasoning.

It must not be supposed that we at all despise the above-mentioned accomplishments, of facility in playing upon a musical instrument, the power of conversing in a foreign language and strength of memory; on the contrary, we consider all of these most charming and useful appendages to a cultivated mind. But they do not form a substitute for education, and no one can pursue them to the exclusion of real mental training without bringing on themselves great, nay, irreparable loss.

At many schools, girls are now taught either a little botany or a little geology. But what does this really amount to? It is contrary to the first principles of women's education to teach them anything scientifically: so the young lady botanist is generally a mere collector of plants, and geology is reduced to the power of repeating by heart the names of the various rocks to be found in the earth's crust, together with a knowledge of some geologist's opinion as to whether they are igneous or aqueous, and to a vague impression that the first chapter of Genesis does not contain all that it is desirable to know about the creation of the world. When we hear from men whose education and mental faculties have enabled them really to pursue astronomy, botany, chemistry or geology scientifically, that these studies afford to them an unparalleled amount of the highest intellectual happiness, we cannot but regret that access to these branches of knowledge is practically denied to women through the superficiality of their education.

The effect of this lack of mental training in women has been to produce such a deterioration in their intellects as, in some measure, to justify the widely spread opinion that they are innately possessed of less powerful minds than men, that they are incapable of the highest mental culture, that they are born illogical, created more impetuous and rash than men. This it is at present, owing to the want of education amongst women, impossible absolutely to disprove. If this inferiority really exists, society must abide the consequences; but in this case, surely, everything which education could do should be done to produce in women the highest mental development of which they are capable; whereas, the present system of education heightens and aggravates the difference between the intellectual acquirements of men and women.

The belief, however, in the innate inferiority of women's minds, though it is impossible from want of sufficient data to prove its absurdity, we do not for one instant hold. All reasoning from analogy points to the fallacy of such a belief. There is no marked difference in the minds and characters of male and female children. When they are all in the nursery together the stereotyped characteristics, in the boys of caution and sound judgement, in the girls of impetuosity and excitability, are not observable. On the contrary, I have frequently noticed more difference in character and disposition between two boys of the same family than exists between either of them and one of their sisters; and when in the members of a family there is a marked and invariable difference between the two sexes, it is sometimes amusing to find the little girls manly, and the little boys what is usually called girlish. All this, however, changes as soon as the divergence of a girl's from a boy's education begins to exert its influence. Let any man, however gifted and whatever intellectual distinction he may have attained, consider what the state of his mind would have been, had he been subjected to the treatment which ninety-nine out of a hundred women of his acquaintance have undergone. He probably, from the time he was ten years old or younger, had the advantage of possessing a real stimulus to mental exertion; he has spent years probably at some great school where there were many rewards in the shape of exhibitions and scholarships given to those boys who distinguished themselves by special proficiency, and where he has perhaps been taught by such men as Arnold,[8] Temple[9] or Kennedy.[10] At eighteen or nineteen, he probably went to one of the universities where not only great and almost unparalleled distinction is the reward of the most highly gifted, but where intellects of not extraordinary powers are capable, by perseverance, of carrying off valuable pecuniary prizes. But a far higher advantage than any pecuniary prize can afford is possessed by the university student; at Oxford and Cambridge, and at the Scotch universities, the highest branches of knowledge may be studied under the guidance of men whose scientific fame is European, and all the enthusiasm with which genius in the teacher can inspire the pupil is thus awakened. But these pecuniary and educational advantages are not the only benefits which a young man derives from a university training. Many men who have not sufficient intellectual power to obtain the former or appreciate the latter, nevertheless would not be justified in thinking that the years they have spent at Oxford or Cambridge have been thrown away. The social and moral advantages conferred by free intercourse among young men of all shades of character, talent and position cannot be easily exaggerated. Friendships, which last through life, are thus frequently formed; and many lessons are thus learned which are never forgotten, and which no other teaching could have imparted. Nor, in enumerating the benefits to be derived from a university life, must the inspiring and ennobling associations be forgotten which are always connected with an ancient seat of learning.

We have now mentioned some of the principal educational and social advantages which form part of the mental training of a large proportion of the young men of the middle and upper classes. What a contrast does the education of girls in the same social position present! They can by no possibility obtain any pecuniary stimulus to mental exertion, neither do they share with boys the immense advantage of being the pupils of the foremost minds of the age. At about eighteen, when a boy is just beginning his university career, a girl is supposed to have 'completed her education'. She is too often practically debarred from further intellectual progress by entering into a society where pleasure, in the shape of balls, fetes, &c., engrosses all her time; or, hers being a country life, and it being her supposed duty to be what is called domesticated, she devotes her life to fancy needlework, or to doing badly the work of a curate, a nurse or a cook. If she does attempt to carry on her education by means of reading, many almost insuperable difficulties beset her. For example, she probably finds it nearly impossible to secure her time against those who consider any sort of idleness better for a woman than mental culture; she also has to endure the reproach which a woman incurs when she exhibits a wish to quit the ignorance to which society has consigned her. It may be denied that a woman does incur reproach by desiring to improve herself; but there is implied contempt in the term 'blue-stocking',[11] though this originally meant simply an intellectual or learned woman; and the epithet 'strong-minded', though anything in itself but uncomplimentary, is considered highly condemnatory when applied to a woman.

The principal reform, therefore, which it is desirable to carry out in women's education is their admittance to all the sources of mental and moral development from which they have hitherto been excluded. Let all, both men and women, have equal chances of maturing such intellect as God has given them. Let those institutions which were originally intended to provide an education for girls as well as boys be restored to what their founders intended. Christ's Hospital[12] is a glaring instance of the very secondary importance which is attached to the instruction of girls. It was originally an educational establishment for the purpose of maintaining and teaching a certain number of boys and girls. It is now a great and flourishing boys' school. It gives to about 1,200 boys, free of all expense, a regular public school education – it has produced some of our most distinguished scholars and men of letters. Scarcely any one knows that there is an endowed girls' school connected with this establishment; it has been for some years moved out of London, and maintains about forty girls, and trains them as domestic servants. Gross as are the facts of this case, it does not stand alone in its culpable neglect of women's education. Many charitable institutions, for the purpose of providing an asylum for a certain specified number of old men and women, were endowed with land which was not at the time considered more than sufficient to provide for their support. Owing to the immense increase in the value of land, the property of these charities has been found much more than adequate to fulfil the intentions of their founders. The surplus property has frequently been appropriated to found not schools for boys and girls, but schools for boys only. It is indisputably unjust, the property having been left for the benefit of both sexes, that one sex only should reap the advantage of its increased value.

We should therefore wish to see equal educational advantages given to both sexes; to open all the professions to women; and, if they prove worthy of them, to allow them to share with men all those distinctions, intellectual, literary and political, which are such valuable incentives to mental and moral progress. The University of Cambridge was the first learned body that took an important step in the reform of women's education, by admitting girls to its local examinations.[13] The importance of this as a first step can hardly be exaggerated; it has been attended by none of those evil consequences which its original opponents so greatly feared; on the contrary, it has worked with such success that those who at first were most opposed to it are now some of its most ardent upholders. We trust, however, that Cambridge will not be content to rest here, but that, in the future, some scheme will be carried into operation by means of which women could, with perfect propriety, become graduates of the University. I believe few, even university men, are aware how easily this could be accomplished at Cambridge. The only conditions which the University of Cambridge imposes on students prior to their passing their examinations are that they keep a certain term of residence and that they should attend professors' lectures. Now, residence may be kept in two ways; either by entering at some college, in which case residence is kept either within its walls or in lodgings; or by residing in the house of some Master of Arts who has licensed his house as a 'hostel'. In this latter manner, residence may be kept by students without their ever setting foot within the walls of a college. There would, therefore, be no difficulty or impropriety in ladies fulfilling the conditions of residence imposed by the University; any married Master of Arts who is living at Cambridge could, by obtaining from the Vice-Chancellor the necessary licence, convert his house into a hostel, and his sons or daughters, by residence in it, and by attending professors' lectures, would do all that the University requires of students previous to their passing, or trying to pass, their examinations. Of course, it would be exceptionally easy for those ladies to keep residence whose fathers are Masters of Arts living at Cambridge; but there would be no conceivable danger or impropriety in allowing a respectable married MA to license his house as a hostel for girls not so favourably situated. The difficulty of residence, therefore, which many people regard as insuperable, being thus disposed of, what remains? Simply attendance at professors' lectures, and the admittance of girls to the examinations which the University imposes on those who are desirous of obtaining degrees. As for attendance at professors' lectures, so many ladies in Cambridge already do attend them, that it is unnecessary to say that there is no difficulty whatsoever in their doing so. It is no uncommon thing in Cambridge for a professor to have a course for lectures largely and regularly attended by ladies.

The opening of all the university examinations to girls[14] is therefore the only remaining hindrance to the possibility of their obtaining a degree which has not been here discussed. One examination has been opened to them, and with great success. The Cambridge local examinations have been held at Cambridge, and boys and girls have both been examined there, in different rooms, but at the same time, without the least difficulty or inconvenience resulting;[15] and if it is safe and practicable thus to examine boys and girls of sixteen or seventeen years of age, what are the insuperable difficulties which attend their examination at nineteen and twenty-one?

In these days religious disabilities are fast becoming obsolete; we trust that university reformers will not rest satisfied with their downfall, but will continue the attack with even increased vigour against sexual disabilities, which inflict even greater injuries upon society by entirely excluding from the university those to whom her training would be so highly beneficial.

The results of such reform as is above suggested would be in time so vast and manifold that it is impossible to give here any but a general survey of them.

To describe the consequences of this increased diffusion of sound mental training in a few words, we conceive that it would add as much as any other proposed reform to the general happiness and welfare of mankind. In the first place, every woman who had had the advantage of sound mental training could make the best possible use of her special faculties or talent, simply because education would have discovered what those faculties or talents were, and with this assistance she would have a much greater chance than at present of finding and occupying her proper sphere. For woman's – the same as man's – sphere is precisely that situation in which she is doing the highest and best work of which she is capable. This is a high standard, and one which, with every advantage society can afford, is too frequently found unattainable; nevertheless, it is one to which all educational schemes should aspire, and their approach to, or neglect of, it should be deemed the only valid test of worth.

We also confidently believe that with the possession of mental culture and development women would gain much of that public spirit and sense of the importance of public duties, the lack of which now so frequently pains us. It could no longer then be said with impunity in a public place – and it was said last year in the House of Commons – that a woman, if she had a vote, would sell it to the man who could offer her the highest bribe;[16] and we should then no longer hear, what was far worse, this accusation smilingly acknowledged to be just, at least of themselves individually, by women on whom the important social duty had devolved of training the tender minds of children and implanting in them the first and frequently indelible impressions of their duty to God and man.

Of those who say that education will unfit women to fulfil the duties of wives and mothers, we ask if ignorance – call it simplicity if you will – and an utter incapacity of comprehending the chief interests of her husband's life are qualities which so eminently conduce to domestic happiness. Or, is a want of education the thing of all others which it is desirable to foster in those who have the charge of children. A mother, to be a good mother, ought to have it in her power not only to attend to the physical wants of her children, but to train and direct their minds during their childhood, and, when they have reached man or womanhood, either to have a community of interests with them, or if that be from difference of disposition impossible, to be capable of affording them that sympathy which an uncultivated mind can never feel for one from which it differs. We do not say that a good education invariably produces these good results, but the want of it, we believe, is in almost all cases the cause of that want of communion and sympathy which is too common between a mother and her children.

It would also be a considerable pecuniary advantage if married women were able to assist their husbands in their business or profession. Of course, there are cases where this would be impracticable; but there are hundreds of cases where, if the woman had been properly trained, she could with great ease render the most valuable assistance to her husband. Take the case of an architect in a large practice; he probably is either greatly overworked, or is forced to employ a considerable number of paid assistants; while his wife, unless she happened to have a very large family, or was otherwise incapacitated, would be, in most cases, a wiser, healthier and happier woman if she were in the habit of working some hours a day in his office. If women were accustomed to enter into this sort of partnership with their husbands, they could carry on his business or profession in case of his sickness or death: in the latter case, the burden of a heavy life insurance, which a thoughtful husband feels bound to lay upon himself in order to form some provision for his family, would be rendered to a great extent unnecessary, and much destitution and misery would be avoided. Widows and unmarried women with property frequently suffer most severe pecuniary loss through their entire ignorance of business, which often renders it necessary for their trustees to invest their money otherwise than to the greatest advantage, and which, if they have the control of their own property, frequently makes them the dupes of unprincipled speculators.

Important, however, as is the claim of married women to an improved education, the burden of an ill-cultivated mind falls much heavier on unmarried women, for they are as devoid as married women of general interests, without having an occupation found for them in the direction of a household, or the care of children. We hardly know on which portion of this large class the injustice of their position weighs most heavily – on those who earn their own living, or on those who do not. The former frequently find themselves, without any previous warning, without a home or means of subsistence; they are forced to do something to earn a livelihood, and there is usually no hesitation in the minds of themselves or their friends as to what they had better do. There is but one occupation open to them; true, it is already frightfully over-stocked, and they are not improbably eminently unfitted to become teachers, but whether by following this occupation they have a reasonable chance of providing for old age or sickness or not, whether they are fitted for the position or not, they must be governesses. All the professions are hermetically sealed against women, and therefore a woman who supported herself by teaching would not gain much if she did contrive to save 200l. or 300l.,[17] for she would be unable to use this money to apprentice herself, with a view to entering any of the professions. It is true that one woman has obtained the degree of LSA and that she is now in practice in London,[18] but the door through which she entered the profession has since been closed, for fear other women should follow her example; as indeed they were showing little hesitation in doing. As the case stands at present, therefore, a lady, unless she has special talents as an artist, an actress or a singer, cannot earn enough to support herself except by teaching, which of all businesses requires in those who undertake it special moral and mental qualifications, wanting which it is eminently disagreeable to the teacher and unprofitable to those who are taught.

There is another consideration also which makes the case of women who are forced to take up this occupation particularly hard. As it is the only employment which is open to ladies of commonplace education and acquirements, it is very much over-crowded, and the remuneration in it is therefore excessively low. I have no hesitation in saying that nine governesses out of ten, even if they are in regular employment, find it impossible to save enough out of their earnings to provide for sickness and old age. The consequence is that unless they marry, they are forced in old age to be to a great extent dependent on private or public charity.

The other unmarried women in the middle and upper classes – those who possess full control of their time, and who are independent of their own exertions for a living – suffer equally with the above from the want of education. Though it entails on them no serious pecuniary loss, or what is usually called hardship, yet their very exemption from toil makes them more dependent on their own mental resources. As it is, they bring to a life so idle as in itself to be highly dangerous to mental activity, a mind so ill-trained and ill-stored that they either succumb at once to the terrible dullness of their lives, or they perhaps seek fictitious relief in those pursuits and amusements which are characteristic of the 'fast' young lady. The better sort, those who if they had been well educated would have achieved something in life, resolutely set apart some portion of each day for solid reading; but this reading is nearly always of the most desultory character, and though it is much better than nothing, it goes further towards storing the memory with facts than strengthening and developing the mind. It is not too much to say that one of the great curses of society is the enforced idleness of such a large proportion of its members as is formed by the women who have nothing to do. We say enforced idleness, for we believe it to be enforced by bad education. When it is considered how many people are overworked, how many are underfed and how precious a boon leisure is when it is rest from labour, we do say that society cannot afford to maintain a large and increasing class in absolute idleness. The leisure which is so pernicious to these women, properly distributed, would take much of the hardship from toil, and would greatly increase the happiness of mankind; whereas, when it is concentrated on the lives of individuals, it loses all its value, and becomes as great a curse to its possessor as the want of it is to the over-worked labourer. But if society stands in need of the labour of women, it stands much more in need of their purity and unselfishness, their heroism and public spirit, which are at present too rare. If this is not the case, what is the meaning of the taunts which the keenest observers of mankind – such as Fielding, Thackeray and Dickens[19] – cast upon women? They constantly portray them either as unprincipled schemers, or as affectionate fools. There is too much justice in these sarcasms for us to put them aside as meaningless. George Eliot has, it is true, given us many a type of noble womanhood; but we cannot afford to neglect the lessons of our censors, and if we are forced to the conclusion that the present training of women tends to produce creatures like Becky Sharp[20] or Amelia Osborne,[21] it is the duty of all who care for the welfare of mankind to strive earnestly after every reform that may effect an improvement in that training. The first thing to be sought is education, and we are glad that in this direction by far the greatest advance has been made in the position of women, by the opening to girls of the Cambridge local examinations; for following close upon improved education must come the extension to women of those legal, social and political rights, the withholding of which is felt, by a daily increasing number of men and women, to be unworthy of the civilization of the nineteenth century.

Transcribed from a copy in the University of Michigan,[22] digitised by Google. Public domain.

Notes

1. Henry Sidgwick (1838–1900), philosopher and economist.
2. Fawcett co-founded Newnham College, Cambridge, in 1871, with a group organising 'Lectures for Ladies' that included the philosopher Henry Sidgwick. It was the second women's college to be founded at Cambridge as a 'house in which young women could reside while attending lectures in Cambridge, long before they were allowed to become full members of the university with the granting of degrees to women in 1948' (Newnham College 2020).
3. Strachey notes, 'though, as the law then stood, it belonged to her husband!' (1931, 53).
4. John Stuart Mill; see Introduction, note 2.
5. Alexander Macmillan (1818–96), co-founder of Macmillan Publishers.
6. See, for example, the Factory Acts (Education Clauses) debate in the House of Commons (House of Commons Debates [hereafter HC Deb] 1867a, cols 1066–88), a speech delivered by Henry Fawcett, followed by a debate.
7. Handwritten books on arithmetic produced by children when they were at school, which set out rules and model examples on a sequence of mathematical topics, especially commercial arithmetic. See Ellerton and Clements 2014.
8. Thomas Arnold (1795–1842), headmaster of Rugby, a major English independent school in Warwickshire.
9. Frederick Temple (1821–1902), headmaster of Rugby.
10. Benjamin Hall Kennedy (1804–89), headmaster of Shrewsbury School, an English independent school in Shropshire. Kennedy was a supporter of the establishment of Newnham College, Cambridge, with his daughter Marion becoming the 'indefatigable Secretary of the Council' in 1876 (Sutherland 2006, 103).
11. Originally a member of an eighteenth-century literary society founded by women, the term came to refer to 'learned and literary ladies, who display their acquirements in a vain and pedantic manner, to the neglect of womanly duties and virtues' (*Chambers's Encyclopaedia* 1876, 172).
12. An English independent school founded in 1552; one of the oldest boarding schools in England, originally in Newgate, London, then Hertford, but now in Horsham, West Sussex (Christ's Hospital 2020). 'With the girls also, who form part of the establishment at Hertford . . . they are taught reading, writing, the rudiments of arithmetic, and needlework. Part of their occupation consists in making the linen of both the boys and themselves; and every attention is paid to formation of those habits of industry, which are calculated to render them useful members of society in the humbler walks of life, wherein they may be expected to move' (Trollope 1834, 189).
13. In 1863. See Tullberg 1998, 15–18 and Section 18.
14. See Section 18.
15. See Tullberg 1998, 15–18.
16. The threat of bribery was often used in the House of Commons to argue against household, and then female, enfranchisement: 'the suffrage having been extended to the lower orders, who, though they might be honest, were more open to be influenced than those who occupied a more independent position – that at the next general election a state of things would prevail which all lovers of their country must greatly regret; intimidation would become stronger than ever, and bribery would be found in every corner of the country' – Mr Berkeley MP reporting on the words of Sir James Graham (HC Deb 1867c). Fawcett here is likely referring to the 1867 debates on Parliamentary Reform: the Representation of the People Bill, Bill 79, such as '[i]t was absurd to

suppose that a woman when she obtained the franchise would, as the hon. Gentleman suggested, be better able to protect herself against the brutality of man. Man must be "unbrutalized", if he might use the expression, by some other means . . . He was, however, surprised to hear the hon. Gentlemen the other day tell the Gentlemen who sat upon his [Mr Karslake's] side of the House that their weapon was their pocket' – Mr Karslake (HC Deb 1867b).

17 The 'l.' was used to represent 'pounds sterling' until late in the nineteenth century. Two hundred pounds in 1870 was worth approximately £12,522 in 2017, according to the UK National Archives' Currency Converter (National Archives 2017).
18 Elizabeth Garrett Anderson, Fawcett's older sister, received a licence (LSA) from the Society of Apothecaries in 1865, the first woman qualified in Britain to do so openly. Although initially barred from taking up a medical post in a hospital due to her sex, she established her own successful practice, and in 1870 became the first woman in Britain to be appointed to a medical post (Manton 1958), although others could not easily follow (see Section 18).
19 See Fawcett's lectures on the women of modern fiction, Section 9.
20 Becky Sharp, later Rebecca, Lady Crawley, the social-climbing protagonist of *Vanity Fair* (Thackeray 1848).
21 Weak, naive Amelia (Osborne née Sedley), the antithesis of Becky Sharp (Thackeray 1848).
22 https://babel.hathitrust.org/cgi/pt?id=mdp.39015004987296&view=1up&seq=517.

3
Electoral disabilities of women, 1871

A Lecture Delivered at the New Hall, Tavistock, 11 March 1871. *Chi dura vince*.[1] Printed for the Bristol & West of England Society for Women's Suffrage. Tavistock: Tavistock Printing Company, 1–23.

Fawcett joined the campaign for women's suffrage directly after her marriage, and spoke at the first pro-suffrage public meeting in London on 17 July 1869. Her first substantial lecture on women's suffrage was in Brighton in March 1870, followed by speeches in London, Greenwich and Dublin. She 'had quickly become one of the very few women to make regular appearances on the platform. In March 1871, less than two years after her initial speech, she undertook a tour of the West Country, speaking at Frome, Bath, Bristol, Taunton, Tavistock,[2] Plymouth and Exeter to large and enthusiastic audiences' (Rubinstein 1991, 37–9). The speech presented here was delivered in various forms in Brighton, Dublin, the West Country and London, and featured as an article in the *Fortnightly Review* (Fawcett 1870b). Published coverage and responses indicate that the format remained constant: a 'classic expression of her early views, a list of up to sixteen objections to women's suffrage, each of which was then demolished' (Rubinstein 1991, 40).[3] In it she sets out an argument that she was to return to over the next 60 years: that the franchise could not be denied because of the inferior physical strength of women, as that would mean granting more power to those who were physically and mentally superior and removing the franchise from the elderly and weak, regardless of gender. Although a serious message, newspaper reports show that the lecture was punctuated by laughter from the audience (*Tavistock Gazette* 1871; *Western Times* 1871).

A similar version of this speech given in London in July 1871 appears in *Essays and Lectures on Social and Political Subjects*, the book co-authored with Henry Fawcett (Fawcett and Fawcett 1872, 230–61). Fawcett maintained that 'Writing came more easily to me than public speaking ever did, although for many years work for Women's Suffrage compelled me to do it' (Fawcett 1924, 87). Strachey recalls, 'She would speak perhaps half a dozen times, and go on one or two short tours in the year, from which she would bring home the most entertaining tales' (Strachey 1931, 48).

*

The subject of this lecture is one which few are prepared to discuss quite dispassionately. Most people are either enthusiastically in favour of the extension of the suffrage to women, or are violently opposed to it. The former are inclined to think that those who disagree with them must be blinded by prejudice or wilfully opposed to the principles of justice and freedom: the latter look upon a 'women's rights' woman as the incarnation of all that is repulsive; and a woman's rights man, they think, must be bereft of his senses. I desire to approach the subject of the claims of women to the suffrage in a different spirit to either of these concerning parties. I will attempt to state fairly and impartially the main arguments on both sides. If I fail in doing justice to the views of those with whom I differ, I shall not do so wilfully, but through ignorance. I will only add before entering upon the general subject that in my opinion this is not exclusively a woman's question, above all, it is not one in which the interests of men and women are opposed. If the exclusion of women from political power be right and just, women as well as men are interested in maintaining it: if it be unjust and antagonistic to the principles of freedom, then men as well as women are interested in destroying it. 'If one member suffer, all the members suffer with it'[4] is as true as regards national as individual life. Praying your indulgence for many shortcomings, I will at once proceed to give a categorical list of the principal arguments urged against the removal of electoral disabilities of women. You will probably observe that all these arguments could not be used by the same person, as some of them neutralize others. It is, however, better to mention them all, as I am anxious not to omit anything which has been urged in objection to women's suffrage. The objections are:

1. Women are sufficiently represented already by men, and their interests have always been jealously protected by the legislature.
2. A woman who is so easily influenced that if she had a vote it would practically have the same effect as giving two votes to her nearest male relation, or to her favorite clergyman.

3. Women are so obstinate that if they had votes endless family discord would ensue.
4. The ideal of domestic life is a miniature despotism. One supreme head, to whom all the other members of the family are subject. This ideal would be destroyed if the equality of women with men were recognised by extending the suffrage to women.
5. Women are intellectually inferior to men.
6. The family is woman's proper sphere, and if she entered into politics, she would be withdrawn from domestic duties.
7. The line must be drawn somewhere, and if women had votes, they would soon be wanting to enter the House of Commons.
8. Women do not want the franchise.
9. Most women are Conservatives, and, therefore their enfranchisement would have a reactionary influence on politics.
10. The indulgence and courtesy with which women are now treated by men would cease, if women exercised all the rights and privileges of citizenship. Women would, therefore, on the whole, be losers if they obtained the franchise.
11. The keen and intense excitement kindled by political strife would, if shared by women, deteriorate their physical powers, and would probably lead to the insanity of considerable numbers of them.
12. The exercise of political power by women is repugnant to the feelings and quite at variance with a due sense of propriety.
13. The notion that women have any claim to representation is so monstrous and absurd, that no reasonable being would ever give the subject a moment's serious consideration.

The first of these arguments, viz. that women are sufficiently represented under the present system, is an old friend. Its face must be very familiar to all who took part in or remember the great agitation which preceded the Reform Bill of 1867.[5] Those who were opposed to an extension of the suffrage were never weary of repeating that working men were quite well represented; there was no need to give them votes, for their interests were watched over with the most anxious solicitude by noblemen and gentlemen, who knew far better than the artizans themselves, what was good for the working classes. We all know that this opinion was not shared by working men; they pointed to the inequality of the law relating to masters and servants, and the unjust efforts which legislation had made to suppress trade societies. They said, 'These laws are unequal and unfair, they will not be amended until we have some hand in choosing the law makers.' Besides this, they said, 'We bear a large portion of the taxation of the country; for every pound of tea and sugar we consume we contribute so much to the national revenue, and in common justice we ought to be allowed to exercise a corresponding control over the national expenditure.' For years and years these arguments were repeated in every town in Great Britain; orators like Mr Bright,[6] Mr Ernest Jones[7] and Mr Cobden[8] devoted immense energy and splendid eloquence in forcing the claims of the working men to representation on the reluctant middle classes. We all know how that struggle terminated; the obstacles were at length surmounted, and the rights of working men to citizenship were fully recognised. Now I appeal to working men and to all who took their side in the great reform agitation, not to cast aside and repudiate the very arguments which they found so useful during that struggle. I would say to them, 'You have reached the top of the wall, don't push down the ladder by which you have ascended.' Apply your arguments to the case of women. Are women sufficiently represented? Are there no laws which press unjustly on them? Is that state of the law equitable which relates to the property of a married woman? Is the law equitable which gives a married woman no legal right to the guardianship of her own children? Perhaps you do not know that 'the married women of this country, when their children are seven years old, have no kind of power to prevent their children from being removed if their husbands choose to remove them'! Would this be the case if women were virtually represented? Finally, using the very same argument which has been so often applied to the working classes – is it right or just that anyone should be forced to contribute to the revenue of the country, and at the same time be debarred from controlling the national expenditure? Either this argument is good for nothing, or it applies to women as forcibly as it does to men. I think it does apply both to men and women, and that, therefore, it is not accurate to say that women are already sufficiently represented, and that their interests are, under the present system, fully protected.

Now let us turn to the second argument urged against the extension of the suffrage to women, namely, a woman is so easily influenced that if she had a vote it would practically have the same effect as giving two votes to her nearest male relation, or to her favourite clergyman. This is a curious argument; if it were applied indiscriminately to both men and women, very few people indeed would have votes. For instance, it might be said that the *Times* newspaper exercises an extraordinary influence over the political opinions of thousands of people. This is perfectly true; nearly everyone must have noticed how, in ordinary society, the conversation of nine people out of ten echoes the general tone of the leading articles in the day's *Times*. Now it may be said, following out the argument just quoted, the effect of giving all these people votes is only to multiply a million-fold the voting power of the editor of the *Times*, or the writers of the articles in that journal; therefore all people who take their political views from the *Times* ought to be precluded from exercising the franchise. By carrying out the principle, nearly everyone would be disfranchised, except the great leaders of political thought, such as Mr Gladstone,[9] Mr Disraeli,[10] Mr Bright, Mr Mill, Lord Salisbury[11] and the editors of some of the principal papers. For there are very few indeed whose political opinions are not biased by the views of some of these distinguished and able men. But perhaps this argument, that women's suffrage would only double the voting power of some men, can best be answered by making way for the next argument, namely, that women are so obstinate, that if they had votes, endless family discord would ensue. Now the people who urge this as a reason why women should not be allowed to exercise the franchise, seem to have an erroneous notion of what a vote is. The mere possession of a vote does not confirm or intensify any opinion. If any man here, at present without electoral power, became a voter to-morrow, would the mere possession of a vote affect any change in his political convictions? A vote is not an opinion, but an expression of opinion. Now let us suppose the case of a family in which the husband and wife hold similar political views; their talk is probably often of politics, and I cannot see that it would make any difference to their domestic happiness if the wife could vote as well as her husband. But you say it is all very well for me to illustrate my argument by the case of a husband and wife whose political views are similar; how would it answer for a wife to have a vote if she disagreed with her husband's political opinions? I reply by asking in return – how does the present system answer? In those cases in which the husband and wife hold different political opinions, one of three things happens: either politics are suppressed as a subject of conversation – the husband goes his own way, and the wife never interferes or obtrudes her own views; or the husband and wife are sensible enough to discuss political subjects and defend their respective opinions with energy, and yet without temper; or else, finally, they take no pains to smooth over or hide their differences. The wife, for instance, fasts every 30th of January in honor of the sacred memory of King Charles the martyr,[12] whilst the husband hangs up the death warrant of that monarch, and treasures it as a glorious memento of British freedom. Now in each of these cases the perfect concord and sympathy which form the ideal of marriage are more or less destroyed. What is it which destroys this concord and sympathy? The answer must be – essential difference of opinion on a subject constantly affecting every-day life. It is the divergence of opinion which destroys the harmony, not the expression of that divergence. Under the present system, women cannot be prevented from having political opinions, or from expressing them, and I venture to think that if they had votes, there would be more domestic harmony on political subjects than there now is; for then marriages would not so frequently take place between those who held diametrically opposite political views. Suppose, for instance, that in order to insure conjugal harmony on religious matters, a law were passed to prevent all women going to church. The advocates of such a law might say, 'Suppose an Evangelical married a Roman Catholic, what disagreement it would lead to, if the husband went off to one place of worship and the wife to another.' As a fact such marriages seldom take place; for it is recognised that women have a right to think for themselves on religious subjects, and there is therefore a strong and reasonable feeling against marriages between people of opposite religious opinions. Would not the same feeling come into existence against marriages between people of opposite political parties, if the political independence of women were recognised. If this feeling were prevalent, I believe a higher harmony than any yet generally known would gradually pervade domestic life.

Let us now consider the validity of the fourth objection raised against the enfranchisement of women, namely, 'The ideal of domestic life is a miniature despotism, in which there is one supreme head, to whom all other members of the family are subject. This ideal would be destroyed if the equality of women with men were recognised, by extending the suffrage to women.' I am ready at once to concede that if the truth of the premise be granted, the truth of the conclusion must be granted also. Family despotism would receive a deadly blow from the extension of political power to women. But let us enquire how and why men – Englishmen at least – have come to consider despotic national government immoral and then let us see whether despotic family government differs essentially in principle from other despotisms. First let us enquire why despotic national government has been so successfully opposed in this country, and why representative government has been set up in its place. It may be briefly said that despotic government has been got rid of in this country because it has been felt to interfere unwarrantably with individual liberty. The leaders of popular rights from the time of Magna Charta to this day, have always insisted on the importance of preserving individual liberty. Why has the name 'Liberty' always had such a magic spell over men? Why has liberty been valued more than life itself by all those whose names make our history glorious? Why have our greatest poets sung the praises of liberty in words that will never be forgotten as long as our language lasts? Is it not because it has been felt more or less strongly at all times that man's liberty is essential to the observance of man's duty? A contemporary philosopher[13] has thus analysed the right to mankind to liberty. He says,

> It may be admitted that human happiness is the Divine Will. We become conscious of happiness through the sensations. How do we receive sensations? Through what are called faculties. It is certain that a man cannot hear without ears. Equally certain that he can experience no impression of any kind unless he is endowed with some power fitted to take in that impression; that is, a faculty. All the mental states, which he calls feelings and ideas, are affections of his consciousness, received through his faculties. There next comes the question – under what circumstances do the faculties yield those sensations of which happiness consists? The reply is – when they are exercised. It is from the activity of most of them that gratification arises. Every faculty in turn affords its special emotion; and the sum of these constitutes happiness; therefore happiness consists in the due exercise of all faculties. Now if God wills man's happiness, and man's happiness can be obtained only by the exercise of his faculties; that is, it is man's duty to exercise his faculties, for duty means the fulfilment of the Divine Will.
>
> As God wills man's happiness, that line of conduct which produces unhappiness is contrary to His Will. Therefore the non-exercise of the faculties is contrary to His Will. Either way, then, we find the exercise of the faculties to be God's Will and man's duty. But the fulfilment of this duty necessarily supposes freedom of action. Man cannot exercise his faculties without certain scope. He must have liberty to go and come, to see, to feel, to speak, to work, to get food, raiment, shelter and to provide for all the needs of his nature. He must be free to do everything which is directly or indirectly requisite for the due satisfaction of every mental and bodily want. Without this he cannot fulfil his duty or God's Will. He has Divine authority therefore for claiming this freedom of action. God intended him to have it; that is, he has a right to it. From this conclusion there seems no possibility of escape. Let us repeat the steps by which we arrive at it. God wills man's happiness. Man's happiness can only be produced by the exercise of his faculties. Then God wills that he should exercise his faculties. To exercise his faculties he must have liberty to do all that his faculties naturally impel him to do. Then God wills that he should have that liberty. Therefore he has a *right* to that liberty.[14]

The only limitation to perfect liberty of action is the equal liberty of all.

> Liberty is not the right of one, but of all! All are endowed with faculties. All are bound to fulfil the Divine will by exercising them. All, therefore, must be free to do those things in which the exercise of them consists. That is, all must have rights to liberty of action. Wherefore we arrive at the general proposition that everyone (man or woman) may claim the fullest liberty to exercise his faculties compatible with the possession of like liberty by every other person.[15]

Never has the basis of individual liberty been more clearly explained than in this passage. It proves conclusively that despotism, being antagonistic to the principle of 'the perfect freedom of each, limited only by the like freedom of all,' is at variance with the Divine will. How, then, can the ideal of family life be despotism, when despotism is proved to be antagonistic to the Divine will? If I have dwelt at some length on the importance of recognising the real basis of the rights of man, it is not to prove to you that these rights exist – all in this room are probably willing to concede that – but to 'show that the rights of women must stand or fall with those of men; derived as they are from the same authority; involved in the same axiom; demonstrated by the same argument'.[16] Much more could be said in defence of the assertion that despotic family government is very far removed from the ideal state. If time permitted, I think it could be shown that command is blighting to the affections, and that where anything approaching the ideal of domestic happiness at present exists, the subjugation of all members of the family to the husband and father is not enforced. But it is necessary to pass to the consideration of the next objection to the extension of political power to women, namely, that women are intellectually inferior to men. I am not going to enter upon the vexed question whether the mental powers of men and women are equal. It is almost impossible from want of evidence to prove whether they are or not. It may be very interesting as a philosophical discussion, but I maintain that it is quite irrelevant to the present subject – that is, whether women ought to have political power. Suppose it could be proved beyond the slightest doubt that on the average the intellectual powers of women were inferior to those of men. If this were fully and satisfactorily established, as a fact, it would not furnish the slightest justification for depriving women of electoral power. Suppose it were also proved that the intellectual powers of the inhabitants of the north of England are superior to those of the inhabitants of the south of England. I can assure you I have often heard very accomplished people assert seriously that is the case.

Would you recognise that as a reason why the inhabitants of the south of England should be deprived of electoral power? Would the people of Tavistock be willing to relinquish their right to the franchise if it were proved to demonstration that on an average and taking them altogether they were intellectually inferior to the inhabitants of Edinburgh? It is ridiculous to suggest such a thing, and yet this absurdity is exactly similar to what is really urged against allowing women to exercise the franchise. But the question may be looked at from another point of view. It is said that women on the whole are not the intellectual equals of men. Whether this is true I neither affirm nor deny; but even the most ardent asserters of the inferiority of women have never said that all women are inferior to all men. In the sphere of Government I need only mention Zenobia,[17] Maria Theresa[18] and Elizabeth[19] to remind you that these women's names stand preeminent. Let us hear what the authority previously quoted has to say on this subject. Granting, for the sake of argument, that the intellect of woman is less profound than that of man, he adds:

> Let all this be granted, and let us now see what basis such an admission affords to the doctrine that the rights of women are not co-extensive with those of men:
> 1. If rights are to be meted out to the two sexes in the ratio of their respective amounts of intelligence, then must the same system be acted upon in the appointment of rights between man and man.
> 2. In like manner, it will follow, that as there are here and there women of unquestionably greater ability than the average of men, some women ought to have greater rights than some men.
> 3. Wherefore, instead of a certain fixed allotment of rights to all males and another to all females, the hypothesis involves an infinite graduation of rights, irrespective of sex entirely, and sends us once more in search of those unattainable desiderata – a standard by which to measure capacity, and another by which to measure rights. Not only, however, does the theory thus fall to pieces under the mere process of inspection; it is absurd on the very face of it, when freed from the disguise of hackneyed phraseology. For what is it that we mean by rights? Nothing else than freedom to exercise the faculties. And what is the meaning of the assertion that woman is mentally inferior to man? Simply that her faculties are less powerful. What then does the dogma that because woman is mentally inferior to man she has less extensive rights, amount to? Just this – that

because woman has weaker faculties than man, she ought not to have like liberty with him to exercise the faculties she has![20]

We will now pass to the sixth objection to women's suffrage – that the family is woman's proper sphere, and if she entered into politics she would be withdrawn from her domestic duties. I may mention in passing – it is a fact to which I do not attach any special importance or regret – that there are some million or so of women in this country without families and without domestic affairs to superintend. The number of women is constantly in excess of the number of men, and so there must always be a certain percentage of women unmarried, and who therefore have no families to be withdrawn from. It is all very well to tell a woman that her sphere is to be a wife and a mother, when there must always be a large number of women unmarried, owing to the simple fact that there are more women in the world than men. But let us look at the case of women who are married, and see whether the objection that politics would withdraw them from domestic duties is valid. I should like to find out exactly how many hours in the year an elector in such a town as this devotes to his political duties. Do you think that on an average, taking one with another, they spend an hour a week, every week in the year, in discharging their electoral duties? I don't know whether they do, but I doubt it. I don't think an elector, unless he is engaged in some particular work, such as superintending the registration, or as secretary of some political society, need devote as much as an hour a week, no, nor half-an-hour a week, to duties which the franchise imposes on him. Then what does this objection, that the right to vote at Parliamentary elections would withdraw women from domestic duties, really come to? Why soon it will be objected that women should not go to church or out for a walk, because so doing withdraws them from their domestic duties. But it may be urged that it is not merely the exercise of the franchise, but all that an interest in political questions involves – the reading of newspapers, the attending of meetings, and the like – that would have a mischievous influence in withdrawing women from their domestic duties. But surely the wife and mother of a family ought to be something more than a housekeeper or a nurse – how will she be able to minister to the mental wants of her husband and her children if she makes the care of their physical comforts the only object of her life? I do not say that physical comfort is to be despised, but if there is no moral and intellectual sympathy between a husband and a wife, or between a mother and her children, a permanent and life-long injury is inflicted on them all, which no amount of physical comfort can in the slightest degree compensate. It is, however, quite erroneous to suppose that an attention to domestic duties and to intellectual pursuits cannot be combined. There is no reason whatever, why wives and mothers should not cultivate their minds and at the same time give proper attention to their domestic affairs. As far as my experience goes, the notion that a woman, in order to manage her house and family well, must devote her whole time and mind to it and do nothing else, is quite incorrect. If I were asked to name the most orderly, neat, bright and best managed houses that I am acquainted with, I should name those which are respectively presided over by women whose names are justly celebrated for their achievements in literature and science, or for their activity in promoting educational and social reform. Perhaps my experience is exceptionally favourable, but I do not think I know one distinguished woman whose home does not do credit to her taste, refinement and love of order. I do not, therefore, think the plea that the franchise would withdraw women from their domestic duties is a valid objection to their enfranchisement.

We now come to the seventh objection. That the line must be drawn somewhere, and if women had votes they would soon be wanting to enter the House of Commons. This objection was some years back considered a conclusive argument against removing the electoral disabilities of working men. At any rate, said the Tories, let us have gentlemen in the House of Commons – fancy sitting next a man who didn't sound his h's. They were also quite certain that working men would be great failures in the House. We all know the reply of the Reformers to such objections as these. They said, 'These are questions for constituencies to decide; they are not likely to select a man to serve them in the House of Commons unless he is capable of devoting sufficient time, trouble, and ability to the discharge of his duties.' The selection of a fit person to serve them in Parliament may safely be left to constituencies. At the present time there is no necessity to pass a law that a man wholly immersed in the conduct of a large business should not offer himself as a candidate for a seat in Parliament. All these things are settled by candidates and constituencies without any legislative interference. As Mr Mill very justly says – I quote from memory – there is no necessity to pass laws to forbid people doing what they cannot do. There is no Act of Parliament needed to enact that none but strong-armed men should be blacksmiths.[21] And so it would prove if all the electoral disabilities were swept away. The would-be-witty caricatures of sickly women fainting in the House of Commons under the weight of their legislative responsibilities would lose their brilliancy and point in the cold light of stern reality. No constituency would deliberately choose a representative who would be quite incapable of serving it faithfully and well. All questions about who should or who should not have seats in Parliament may safely be left to constituencies.

I now turn to the consideration of the eighth objection to the extension of political power to women – that women do not want votes. Notwithstanding the obvious reply that a considerable number of women do want votes, and are continually petitioning Parliament to remove their electoral disabilities, I must confess that this objection to the enfranchisement of women appears to me more formidable than any other which has ever reached me. Of course it makes no difference at all so far as abstract justice is concerned; but still in practical politics abstract justice does not usually weigh much with statesmen, unless it is accompanied by an urgent and pressing demand for the amelioration of the law. There must always be a certain adaption between the characters of the people, and the rule under which they live. The existence of the Irish Church Establishment was as much opposed to abstract justice in 1769 as it was in 1869, but disestablishment did not take place until the demand for it was so urgent that it could no longer be disregarded.[22] The demand for the extension of the suffrage to women is daily growing more earnest and more general. The bill now before Parliament has been supported by petitions from every part of the kingdom, signed by many tens of thousands of men and women. In the presence of such facts it cannot be said that there is no demand on the part of women for the suffrage. There is also this very strong argument, which is sometimes overlooked by those who consider that the suffrage should not be extended to women, because the majority of women do not desire to exercise their electoral rights. None of us who desire the extension of the franchise to women wish women to be compelled to vote. Only those who desire political power need exercise their newly acquired rights. Any woman who thinks that voting would be unfeminine or injurious to her health, would be quite at liberty to refrain from taking part in elections. But it seems to me very unfair that those who don't wish for political power should be enabled to deprive those who do wish for it, of the right to exercise the franchise. Let us now turn to the next objection, namely, that most women are Conservatives, and that their enfranchisement would consequently have a reactionary influence on politics. I have often heard this argument from the lips of men for whom I have the greatest respect, but I never hear it without astonishment and regret. What is representative government if not government by a national assembly chosen by the people to represent their views, and to produce a corresponding influence on the state of the laws? Do those who object to the enfranchisement of women, on the ground that they are usually Conservatives, think that all Conservatives ought to be disfranchised? Surely the representative institutions require that all differences of opinion should have their due and proportionate weight in the legislature. No class of persons should be excluded on account of their political opinions. What would be thought of a Conservative who gravely asserted that he thought all Dissenters should be disfranchised because they are generally Liberals? I am almost afraid even to suggest the hard names which such a misguided person would be called by the very people who oppose women's suffrage, because most women are Conservatives. And yet the two cases are exactly parallel, and equally antagonistic to the fundamental principle of representative government. A representative system which excludes half the community from representation surely is a farce. In my opinion the question ought not even to be asked. 'How would women vote if they had the franchise?' The only question ought to be, 'Is representative government the best form of government that can be devised?' If the answer is in the affirmative, the exclusion of women from electoral rights can in no way be justified.

The next objection which I have set down is that the indulgence and courtesy with which women are now treated by men would cease if women exercised all the rights and privileges of citizenship. As I hear this objection the old Bible story forcibly recurs to my mind, of Esau, and how he sold his birthright for a mess of pottage.[23] Let it be granted that women would no longer be treated with exceptional courtesy and indulgence if they exercised the rights and privileges of citizenship. What do this exceptional courtesy and this indulgence really amount to? I am not going to say that they are valueless, but let us analyse them and see of what sort of things they consist. Women are usually assisted in and out of carriages; they also take precedence of men in entering and leaving a room; the door also is frequently opened for them; they are helped first at dinner; and they are always permitted to walk on the inside side of the pavement. Besides these there are more substantial privileges, such as being allowed to monopolise the seats in a room, or in a railway carriage, in those cases where, owing to overcrowding, some of those present are compelled to stand. I hope I do not unduly underrate these little amenities of social life; they are very harmless and perhaps even pleasant in their way; but I think it must be confessed that their practical value is small indeed, especially if the price paid for them consists of all the rights and privileges of citizenship. If the courtesy of men to women is bought at this price, it must not be forgotten that the *sale* is compulsory, and can in no case be regarded as a free contract. But now let us consider whether women would really lose all the politeness now shown to them if their right to the franchise were recognised. At elections it is not usually the case that those who have votes are treated with the least consideration; but apart from this, how would the courtesy of every day life be affected by an extension of the suffrage to women? I incline to the belief that some of the mere forms of politeness which have no practical value, such as always giving precedence to a woman in entering and leaving a room, would slowly but gradually fall into disuse if the electoral disabilities of women were removed; but I am quite convinced that true politeness, which is inseparately associated with kindness of heart, would not suffer any decrease from the extension of the suffrage to women. As far as my experience goes, those who are invested with political power of any kind are always treated with more deference and respect than those that are destitute of that valuable commodity. The highest political power in the kingdom is vested in a woman, and what man is inclined on that account to be less courteous to her, or less considerate of her feelings? Have the women who have taken part in late municipal and school board elections[24] been treated more rudely since they acquired that instalment of political power? In answer to this objection to women's suffrage – that women would lose in the politeness with which they are now treated more than they would gain in political power – I reply in the first place that women are compelled to pay a great deal too dearly for this politeness, if they are forced to sacrifice for it all the rights and privileges of citizens. And secondly, there is no reason to suppose that the acquisition of political power would cause women to be treated with less courtesy and respect, though some of the mere forms of politeness might disappear, if the equality of the rights of men and women were recognized.

The next objection to the enfranchisement of women is one which has probably never occurred to anyone in this room. I certainly should never have thought of it had I not noticed it in a daily paper, the writers of which have shown the greatest inventiveness and originality in their persistent attacks on women's suffrage. Argument after argument they have advanced against it, and as no one took much notice of these attacks, I suppose the editor thought that something quite new must be tried. The following was the result. 'The keen and intense excitement kindled by political strife would, if shared by women, deteriorate their physical powers, and would probably lead to the insanity of considerable numbers of them.' I think if medical men were called upon to reply to such an objection as this, they could easily prove that a great many more people – especially women – suffer in regard to their health through having nothing to do, and no absorbing interest in life, than through overwork and excitement. If the Editor of the journal just quoted would condescend to practical experience, perhaps he will enquire if those women who have lately taken part in the municipal contests and the school board elections have since exhibited any alarming symptoms. Such an argument as that just mentioned would be more comprehensible if women were entirely debarred from mixing with the outside world; but as it is, there is nothing to prevent women from sharing the general excitement caused by elections. It is notorious to everyone that they do share it, and I have no hesitation in saying that many of them are a great deal better for it. But suppose it were satisfactorily proved that the health of some women would be injured by the excitement caused by taking part in elections; is that a reason for excluding all women from political power? The health of many men is frequently injured by excessive political work and excitement. Instances of such cases must occur to everyone present. The illness from which Mr Bright is now suffering,[25] and the extreme exhaustion of the Prime Minister, at the end of the session of 1869,[26] were both doubtless produced by the mental strain attendant on too much political work. But such facts furnish no argument against the exercise of political power by these eminent persons. We all hope the only practical result of their maladies may be to make them more solicitous of their own health than they have hitherto been. It may safely be left to the inhabitants of a free country to take the necessary precautions for preserving their own health; and if any woman found that the excitement of elections endangered either her mind or her body, no Act of Parliament would be necessary to induce her to withdraw from political strife. It has almost become a proverb that you cannot make people moral by Act of Parliament.[27] I am sure it is equally true that you cannot make them healthy by Act of Parliament.

The next objection urged against the enfranchisement of women, is one which I am not perhaps wrong in saying is the one which has had the most powerful influence in producing the opposition to women's suffrage. Consciously, or unconsciously, most of us are greatly under the dominion of our feelings, even when they are directly opposed to the dictates of our reason. But let it not be forgotten that reason must be listened to sooner or later, and the feelings must ultimately submit to be modified by the understanding. This objection which I believe to be so potent with most people who oppose women's suffrage is 'that the exercise of political power by women is repugnant to the feelings, and quite at variance with a due sense of propriety'. In Turkey, a woman who walked out with her face uncovered would be considered to have lost all sense of propriety – her conduct would be highly repugnant to the feelings of the community. In China, a woman who refused to pinch her feet to about a quarter of their natural size, would be looked upon as entirely destitute of female refinement. We censure these customs as ignorant, and the feelings on which they are based as quite devoid of the sanction of reason. It is therefore clear that it is not enough, in order to prove the undesirability of the enfranchisement of women, to say that it is repugnant to the feelings. It must be further enquired to what feelings women's suffrage is repugnant, and whether these feelings are 'necessary and eternal', or 'being the results of custom, they are changeable and evanescent'.[28] I think these feelings may be shown to belong to the latter class. In the first place, a feeling that is necessary and eternal must be consistent, and the feeling of repugnance towards the exercise of political power by the women is not consistent; for no one feels this repugnance towards the exercise of political power by Queen Victoria. In the second place it has been previously shown that the equal freedom of all is a necessary prerequisite of the fulfilment of the Divine Will, and that the equal freedom of a part of the community is destroyed if it is deprived of political power. Now it seems to me in the highest degree blasphemous to assert that the Supreme Being has implanted in man necessary and eternal feelings in opposition to his own will. Again, the state of popular opinion as to what women may, or may not, do is constantly changing in the same country and even in the minds of the same individuals, and the feelings on this subject differ in different classes of the community; it is, therefore, quite impossible to say that these feelings are necessary and eternal. If they are not necessary and eternal, they are the result of custom, changeable and evanescent, and are destined to be modified by advancing civilization. It may be that a great deal of the repugnance which undoubtedly exists against women taking parts in politics arises from the disturbance and disorder which are too often the disgraceful characteristics of elections in this country. I should like to say a few words on this point. In the first place the adoption of the ballot[29] and the abolition of nominations, which are almost certain to take place before the next dissolution, will, in all probability, cause elections to be conducted with perfect order and tranquillity. A distinguished statesman, whose name I could mention, lately told a friend of mine that his last objection to woman's suffrage would be removed by the adoption of the ballot. In the second place I think the danger of women proceeding to polling places under the present system is greatly exaggerated. As the result of my own experience I can testify that during the last election at Brighton, I was walking about from one polling place to another, the whole of the day; the town was in a state of great excitement; the contest was very severe, and party feeling ran high.[30] I walked through an excited crowd just previous to the close of the poll, after having been assured that it was not safe for me to venture, and I never heard one word or saw one gesture which would have caused reasonable annoyance to the most sensitive and refined lady. But I can give another and perhaps more striking example from my own experience. During the general election of 1865, I went round to many of the polling places in Westminster, accompanied only by a young girl. We met with no incident whatever which could have alarmed or annoyed anyone. My experience on this point has always been the same, and it is corroborated by the experience of all ladies with whom I am acquainted, who, like myself, have tested by personal experience whether it is either unpleasant or unsafe for a woman to go to a polling place. Their unanimous testimony has been that there is nothing to deter a woman from recording her vote. I, for one, have too good an opinion of my countrymen to believe that they would insult or annoy a well-conducted woman in the discharge of what she believed to be a public duty.

I now pass to the last objection, for by this time I am sure you must be getting weary of me. This objection, that the notion of women's suffrage is monstrous and absurd and deserves only to be treated as a joke, is one which is slowly dying a natural death. You still hear of it in remote country districts, but it has received its death blow from the names of the many very eminent persons who are the warm advocates of women's suffrage. Perhaps I need only mention such names as Mr Mill, Canon Kingsley,[31] Mr Darwin,[32] Professor Huxley[33] and Professor Maurice[34] to remind you that women's suffrage is advocated by men occupying the highest ranks in philosophy, science and literature. Mr Mill and others have shown in their writings the grounds on which they base their support of the claims of women to representation. It is easy to laugh; but when the leading philosophical thinkers of the day use all their weight and influence, and employ their great genius in striving to produce a recognition of the rights of women, their arguments must be met with arguments; they will never be answered by a sneer. I think I have now made a reply to all the objections previously enumerated against women's suffrage. In doing so I have perhaps sufficiently indicated the grounds on which I advocate it. I have endeavoured to show that men's rights and women's rights must stand or fall together; their maintenance is necessary to the fulfilment of the Divine will – man's happiness. For if God wills man's happiness, and man's happiness depends on his freedom, then God wills man's freedom. 'Equity knows no difference of sex. The law of equal freedom necessarily applies to the whole race – female as well as male. The same reasoning which establishes that law for men may be used with equal cogency on behalf of women.'[35] These are not my words, they are the words of a great philosopher, whose writings will probably mould the opinions of unborn generations. I refer to Mr Spencer, and as I have, perhaps, passed rather too briefly over the objections of those who urge that women's suffrage would destroy the harmony of home, I cannot do better than quote in conclusion what he has said on the effect of the complete enfranchisement of women on domestic happiness.

> Married life under this ultimate state of things will not be characterised by perpetual squabbles but by mutual concessions. Instead of a desire on the part of the husband to assert his claims to the uttermost, regardless of those of his wife, or on the part of the wife to do the like, there will be a watchful desire on both sides not to transgress. Neither will have to stand on the defensive, because each will be solicitous for the rights of the other. Not encroachment but self-sacrifice will be the ruling principle. The struggle will be, not which shall gain the mastery, but which shall give way. Committing a trespass will be the thing feared, and not the being trespassed against. And thus instead of domestic discord will come a higher harmony than any we yet know.[36]

Transcribed from an original in Special Collections, the University of Iowa Libraries. No known copyright restrictions.

Notes

1. Who endures wins.
2. This article does not appear in the bibliography compiled by Rubinstein (1991, 291–302).
3. See the Grosvenor Papers 1870, *Irish Times* 1870 and LeGeyt 1871 for contemporaneous coverage and responses to the earliest speeches, indicating that their contents were similar to, and perhaps the same as, the speech featured here. The detailed ripostes, equating her even at this early stage with John Stuart Mill, indicate how seriously her arguments were being taken.
4. 1 Corinthians 12:26.
5. In 1867, the Conservative government had introduced the second Parliamentary Reform Act, granting the vote to men who were occupiers (rather than owners) of property in urban areas, which increased the electorate to almost 2.5 million, after much political upheaval (Parliament. uk n.d.c).
6. John Bright (1811–89), radical and Liberal member of Parliament for Birmingham at this time.
7. Ernest Charles Jones (1819–69), poet, novelist and Chartist.
8. Richard Cobden (1804–65), radical, Liberal member of Parliament and calico manufacturer.
9. William Ewart Gladstone (1809–98), British statesman and Liberal politician, who was prime minister of the United Kingdom at the time of this speech.
10. Benjamin Disraeli (1804–81), 1st Earl of Beaconsfield, Conservative Party politician who served as leader of the opposition at the time of this speech.
11. Robert Gascoyne-Cecil (1830–1903), 3rd Marquess of Salisbury, a politician who later became prime minister but at the time of this article was not in office, following his resignation from the Cabinet over the Reform Act 1867.
12. Charles I (1600–49), King of England, Scotland and Ireland. 30 January, the anniversary of his execution, is his feast day in the Anglican calendar of saints.

13 Herbert Spencer (1820–1903), English philosopher, sociologist and biologist, in *Social Statistics* (Spencer 1850, 75–6). Fawcett slightly alters the quote. Fawcett and Spencer both contributed an essay to *John Stuart Mill, His Life and Work: Twelve sketches* (Fawcett 1873c).
14 Spencer (1850, 76–7).
15 Spencer (1850, 77).
16 Spencer (1850, 171).
17 Septimia Zenobia (c. 240–74 CE), queen of the Roman colony of Palmyra, in modern-day Syria.
18 Maria Theresa (1717–80), archduchess of Austria and queen of Hungary and Bohemia.
19 Elizabeth I (1533–1603), Queen of England and Ireland.
20 Spencer (1850, 158).
21 'Nobody thinks it necessary to make a law that only a strong-armed man shall be a blacksmith. Freedom and competition suffice to make blacksmiths strong-armed men, because the weak-armed can earn more by engaging in occupations for which they are more fit. In consonance with this doctrine, it is felt to be an overstepping of the proper bounds of authority to fix beforehand, on some general presumption, that certain persons are not fit to do certain things' (Mill 1869, 32).
22 Reference to the Irish Church Act 1869, which separated the Church of Ireland from the Church of England. See Parliament.uk n.d.a.
23 Genesis 25:29–25:34.
24 See Section 21, note 20.
25 'He is not likely, it is said, to be able to take his place in Parliament again . . . He is suffering from excess of mental labour' (*Sheffield Daily Telegraph* 1870).
26 'Mr Gladstone's illness, according to the *Lancet*, was to a large extent caused by the fatigue and anxiety he has of late undergone. The honours of statesmanship are not acquired without cost, and the extent to which Mr Gladstone has risked his health to secure the passing of the Irish Church Bill will give the nation still greater confidence in him' (*Bradford Daily Telegraph* 1869).
27 A common phrase used in parliamentary debates in the nineteenth and early twentieth centuries, dating back to at least the 1830s (*Sun* 1834).
28 Spencer (1850, 184).
29 The Ballot Act, passed in 1872, introduced the secret ballot to parliamentary and local government elections (Parliament.uk 2021).
30 Henry Fawcett was standing for re-election as Brighton's MP in 1868. 'Throughout the day [the polling booths] were surrounded by crowds more or less dense in character and larkish in conduct . . . in the afternoon the crowds there grew dense and excited' (*Brighton Guardian* 1868).
31 Charles Kingsley (1819–75), priest, professor, social reformer and novelist, famous for his 1863 novel, *The Water-Babies: A fairy tale for a land baby*.
32 Charles Robert Darwin (1809–82), naturalist, geologist and biologist, known for his work on evolution.
33 Thomas Henry Huxley (1825–95), biologist and anthropologist and staunch advocate for Darwin's theories of evolution, known for his work on comparative anatomy.
34 John Frederick Denison Maurice (1805–72), Anglican theologian, author, and co-founder of Christian socialism.
35 Spencer (1850, 155).
36 Spencer (1850, 168).

4
Picturing Fawcett: A meeting at the Hanover Square Rooms, 1872

Figure 2: 'Women's rights – A meeting at the Hanover Square Rooms' in the *Graphic* (1872). No known copyright restrictions. Digitised from editor's own copy.

The Hanover Square Rooms, on the east side of Hanover Square, London, were used from 1868 to 1874 for public meetings of the women's suffrage movement (Crawford 2001a, 263). This engraving illustrates a meeting held on Friday, 10 May 1872, 'of ladies and gentlemen who desire that women should vote for members of Parliament to thank the supporters of Mr Jacob Bright's bill,[1] and to reply to the arguments urged in the House of Commons against that measure' (*Illustrated London News* 1872). It is the first image of Fawcett engaged in suffrage-related work. From left to right, it depicts suffragists Mrs Millicent Garrett Fawcett, Mrs Mark Pattison (later known as Lady Emilia Dilke [1840–1904]; see text under Figure 3), the American Mrs Ernestine Rose (1810–92), Miss Lydia Becker (1827–90, who was an early leader of the cause until her death) and Rhoda Garrett (Fawcett's cousin).

They are speaking in a discussion chaired by the Liberal politician Mr Lyon Playfair (1818–98), 'whose presence speaks to the women's desire to work within modes of patriarchal hegemony. They wished to work alongside the men rather than be seen as separatists' (Denney 2017). 'Miss Becker moved the first resolution, expressing thanks to the members of Parliament who supported the Woman Suffrage Bill by speeches and votes . . . Miss Garrett said that the House of Commons seemed to find it impossible to hear the word woman mentioned without roars of laughter' (*Shields Daily Gazette* 1872). In her speech, 'Mrs Fawcett skeched [sic] the history of the movement, and showed from an analysis of the division list that there was a gain of one this year. Referring to the four members of Parliament who had seceded from the movement, Mrs Fawcett was consoled by reflecting on the Shakespearian song: "Men were deceivers ever / One foot on sea and one on shore / To one thing constant never"'[2] (*Leicester Journal* 1872). Her 'humorous speech, supported the motion, which was carried by a large majority' (*Shields Daily Gazette* 1872).

Notes

1 HC Deb, 1872, Second Reading. Women's Disabilities Removal Bill. 1 May 1872, vol. 211 cc1–72. https://api.parliament.uk/historic-hansard/commons/1872/may/01/second-reading.
2 Balthasar's song in *Much Ado about Nothing* 2.3.882–5.

5
Picturing Fawcett: Professor and Mrs Fawcett by Ford Madox Brown, 1872

Figure 3: Portrait of Professor and Mrs Fawcett by Ford Madox Brown. Oil on canvas, 1872. © National Portrait Gallery, London. Licensed for use.

Ford Madox Brown (1821–93) was a Pre-Raphaelite painter known for his Hogarthian depictions of social and moral subjects (Ford 1896). In this intimate portrait, Henry Fawcett, in academical dress, is seen dictating to his wife, who 'acted as her husband's guide and for some years as his secretary' (Howarth 2004). This portrait has a more equal pose than the photograph taken four years earlier: the 24-year-old Millicent, sitting on the arm of Henry's chair, is raised above her husband, with one protective hand on his shoulder while holding her pen, the other hand entwined in his, clutching a letter, which Henry is animatedly discussing. The letter in the painting is signed by them both as 'Your Obt. Servants', indicating it is intended for an official correspondent. The jointly signed letter in the portrait underlines that Millicent was not acting as a mere amanuensis, but that their work in the public sphere was a shared endeavour.

A relatively early painting of protagonists of the women's movement, this painting was commissioned in the same year that Professor and Mrs Fawcett published their jointly authored book, *Essays and Lectures on Social and Political Subjects* (Fawcett and Fawcett 1872). This is one of only two works painted by Brown in 1872, as he was ill for much of the year. Brown mentioned the double portrait in a letter to his friend Frederic Shields in July 1872: 'I am painting Fawcett, the blind member, and his wife in one picture for Sir Charles Dilke – quite a pathetic-looking group' (quoted in Ford 1896, 273). A preparatory sketch in crayon and chalk, with similar poses, resides in Wightwick Manor (National Trust n.d.). The suggestion that a portrait of Henry should include Millicent seems to have come from Brown: '"My idea of painting Fawcett & his wife seems to me the most interesting" he wrote, "a group might be made of them full of character & pathos." . . . He suggested the proper treatment would be a group down to the knees of a proper size to suit' for 'a final figure of £210' (Bennett 2010, 398). The picture was completed in July 1872, but added to in September: '"one reason" Madox Brown wrote "is that Mr Fawcett has not yet sent me *his* signature to put on the paper along with *her's* [sic] as I intended in the picture"' (Bennett 2010, 399).

Dilke, a Liberal politician, was a close friend and colleague of Henry Fawcett, having been his student at Trinity Hall in Cambridge in the 1860s, with both supporting women's suffrage in the House of Commons from the 1870s (see Goldman 2003, 16, 82). However, Dilke's political career was punctuated by various scandals caused by his unorthodox extramarital history. Dilke wrote 'to John Stuart Mill in 1871 to recommend Millicent Fawcett's election as the first woman member of the Political Economy club, a prestigious group of Liberal economists and men of affairs' (Rubinstein 1989, 77). In 1885 Dilke married Mrs Mark Pattison, née

Emily Francis Strong, known as Lady Emilia Dilke, who is pictured in Figure 2. Dilke 'delighted in having near him the pictures of his friends' (Gwynn 1917, 235), and the painting remained in his home until his death in 1911, when it was bequeathed to the National Portrait Gallery (*Times* 1911a) and 'added to the exhibition' in November of that year (*Common Cause* 1911b). The *Common Cause* reported soon afterwards:

> We believe that Mrs Fawcett is the only living person whose portrait has been added to the national collection. It is a great happiness to members of the National Union that it is there, and the knowledge that the long years since it was painted have been filled with toil for the cause of women, will be an inspiration for their own struggles (*Common Cause* 1912a).

In March 1987 the portrait went on display with other nineteenth-century National Portrait Gallery works in Bodelwyddan Castle, Wales, returning to gallery display in London in 2017 (*Sunday Times* 1988; BBC 2017a; Cox 2021). This 'rarely seen and intimate painting' was 'part of the Gallery's year-long Rebel Women season' to mark the centenary of some women gaining the vote in Britain (National Portrait Gallery 2018).

6
Mrs Fawcett on women's suffrage, 1872

A Speech Delivered in the Town Hall, Birmingham, 6 December 1872. George Dixon, Esq., MP, in the chair.[1] Reprinted from the *Birmingham Morning News*. Birmingham: C. N. Wright, 1–8.

> A public meeting was held . . . in Birmingham in connection with the Conference sitting there on the subject of women suffrage. Resolutions in favour of the extension of the suffrage to women were spoken to by Mrs Fawcett, Miss Sturge,[2] Miss Garrett, Professor Fawcett, and others (*Sheffield Daily Telegraph* 1872).

Birmingham was one of the cities where women's suffrage meetings were regularly held. As Fawcett later reminisced,

> With our five centres in London, Bristol, Birmingham, Manchester and Edinburgh, and the work which each was doing in forming societies and influencing opinion in its own neighbourhood, we had, as it were, the framework ready made of what afterwards became the 'National Union of Women's Suffrage Societies'; but this did not come into actual existence until later . . . My speaking was done from the 'seventies onward, chiefly in connection with these large societies; a group of meetings would be arranged in a given geographical area . . . Of course, one gets (at least, I got) frightfully weary of constant speaking on the same subject, and I had to refuse to speak more than

once a day or more than four times a week. I tried to get home for weekends, not always successfully' (Fawcett 1924, 123–4).

By 1872, Fawcett was a 'respected, even a formidable figure' and was 'undeterred by public rebuke, and by private remonstrance that "No Christian Woman"[3] should take part in politics or speak on the platform' (Rubinstein 1991, 41) and by unkind rumours that she was neglecting her daughter, Philippa (Strachey 1931, 61–2). 'I worked hard when I was at work, speaking and lecturing up and down the country, writing for the magazine and for the Press, hitting the Anti-Suffragists, metaphorically, on the head, whenever opportunity offered' (Fawcett 1924, 103).

*

It gives me great pleasure to have the opportunity of speaking once more on the subject of Women's Suffrage to a Birmingham audience; for I have a very pleasant recollection of a former meeting here, in a smaller hall, about a year ago.[4] Perhaps my pleasant associations with that meeting may have something to do with the fact that after it was ended, I received from two women among the audience the greatest compliment it has ever been my good luck to obtain. They came round to the door of the hall and said, 'Good night, ma'am, and thank you; you have made us feel two inches taller.' Now, it is exactly what we want to do, translated into a homely metaphor: to make women feel two inches taller. You may smile at this, because you are used to hear the same idea put into longer words, and called the elevation of women, or some phrase of this kind; and I am sure you will agree with me that if this meeting serves to promote the cause of the elevation of women, it will fully justify the action of those who have brought us together tonight. We have just heard the words of the Resolution which I have been asked to second. It asserts the principle that as long as the Parliamentary Suffrage is based on certain property qualifications, none who fulfil those qualifications ought to be excluded from the list of voters. This principle is maintained by our law with the most undeviating rigidity in all cases except in that of women. You all remember the elaborate pains that were taken to secure the political rights of the illiterate voter. The male householder who can neither read nor write must not be disfranchised; and no end of time and trouble is spent in enabling him to record his vote. I do not say this is wrong; but I do say that it reduces to an absurdity, to an insult, the exclusion of women who fulfil the necessary qualifications, and who are, besides, very frequently persons of high intelligence and general culture. The principle of associating property with representation is maintained by our law even with regard to the votes of persons of unsound mind. I am told on good authority that the vote of a lunatic is good and valid if it can be shown that at the time he recorded it he was enjoying a lucid interval. Ignorance, therefore, however dense, is no disqualification for the franchise; lunacy is not invariably a disqualification. The only absolute disqualification, beside those of crime and pauperism, is that of sex; and in this way cultivated and intelligent women are placed politically in a position inferior to that enjoyed by the illiterate lunatic who may happen to record his vote in a lucid interval. The constitutional arguments in favour of extending the suffrage to those women who fulfil all the qualifications required of the male elector have been already most ably treated by those who have preceded me; and I can scarcely imagine that the Birmingham politicians, who took so prominent a part in the reform agitation for the extension of the suffrage to working men, can be blind to the patent fact that all the most convincing arguments used during that agitation in favour of admitting the working classes to representation apply with equal cogency to the case of women. Page after page of John Bright's speeches[5] might be read from this platform to-night, and they would furnish much more effective arguments than any I could use in favour of the object of the present meeting. The reason why we have not so many of our Liberal[6] Friends with us as we could wish is not, I suspect, that our arguments are new, strange or distasteful to them; they admit the justice of our claim, but refuse to take up our cause on the ground that women are Conservatives. I doubt very much if this is true; but even granting, for the sake of argument, that the majority of women are Conservatives, I think this is, to a great extent, the fault of the Liberals themselves. What benefits have the Liberal party, as a party, bestowed upon women? They have moved heaven and earth to get rid of abuses oppressive to themselves; they have very seldom lifted a finger to redress any of the wrongs special to women. Two Reform Bills have passed in this century[7] – they did nothing for women. The abolition of University tests still left untouched the test of sex.[8] The Divorce Act is framed with the most flagrant injustice to women. A Bill to permit marriage with a deceased wife's sister has several times passed through the House of Commons;[9] no provision is contained in that Bill to sanction a woman marrying her deceased husband's brother, and I am told that the author of the Bill has threatened to abandon it should such a clause be inserted. Can it be wondered at if these, and many other similar instances, have alienated the sympathy of women from the Liberal party? I do not think that the complaint that women are Conservatives would long be heard if justice to women were a plank in the platform of the Liberal party. I do not wish to forget that women owe a Liberal minister the possession of the Municipal and the Educational vote.[10] I am not very well versed in municipal politics, but with regard to the educational franchise, there is a good deal of evidence to show that the virtue of the Liberal party has been rewarded. With one or two exceptions, all the women on the School Boards are Liberals, not to say Radicals.[11] They nearly all owed their election to the support of women voters; they nearly all are known to be supporters of Women's Suffrage, and of the general elevation of the condition of women. I do not, therefore, think there need be any fear that when women see that they are no longer to be excluded from sharing in the benefits which the Liberal party hopes to obtain, they will withhold their sympathy from Liberal principles. There is another circumstance which stands in the way of the admission of women's claim to political independence in the minds of some people, and it is this: that it is an almost universal belief that women are unfit to exercise political power. This opinion, it is said, has been held by so many wise people that there must be something in it; or, to quote from Charles Dickens, 'everybody said so, and what everybody says must be true'.[12] It may be pointed out in reply to this objection, that if you multiply folly and prejudice a thousand million times, the result is an exceedingly large quantity of folly and prejudice; and because there is a great deal of it, it does not become one whit more like wisdom and reasonableness. If the universality of an opinion is evidence of its truth, this would have been in the Middle Ages a conclusive proof of the truth of the belief in witchcraft. Nay, it would even now be very strong evidence in its favour, for it is reckoned by Mr Tylor, in his work on Primitive Culture, that four-fifths of the inhabitants of the world believe in it.[13] I think it may be fairly concluded that almost as many inroads have been made into the notion that women ought to not possess political power as into the belief in witchcraft. In Italy, women are permitted to exercise the suffrage,[14] and nearly all the greatest European powers have at different periods of their history been presided over by female sovereigns. The names of Catherine of Russia, Isabella of Spain, Maria Theresa of Austria and Elizabeth of England[15] will serve to remind you that these female names stand out conspicuously among the long list of incapables who have usually occupied thrones. It is true that in our own history, although there have been distinguished female sovereigns, there never yet has been a general diffusion of political power among women, and this fact is not unfrequently used as an argument against us. It is urged that our present exclusion from the franchise is justified by history. 'Women', it is said, 'have always, save a few extraordinary instances, been in a condition of political subordination. Look back into the past and you will find the lot of women to be a perpetual record of submission and dependence. What always has been always will be; you cannot fight against nature.' If the lot of women always had been what it is now, I confess this argument would carry some weight with me. But it is not true that the condition of women is the same now as it was in the past. It is immensely better now than it was in the past. The history of civilization is the history also of a steady progressive improvement in the condition of women. And this improvement is a thing which is still going on; it is not a thing that belongs to the past only. Women are better off in England to-day; they have more freedom, more independence, they are more trusted with responsible work than they were 30 years ago. They will be still better off 30 years hence.[16] The admission of women to the municipal and educational franchise, the efforts now being made to secure to women the advantages of higher education are among the proofs that the elevation of women is still going on. Among savage races women have little better lives than beasts of burden. In India a widow is sometimes compelled to sacrifice her own life at the death of her husband. In the semi-civilizations of the East, we know that women are principally valued as inmates of the Seraglio.[17] From this deep degradation they have gradually, slowly, but steadily been elevated, until they have reached such a measure of freedom and independence as they possess at the present day. And are we to be told that this gradual elevation has now reached its utmost limit? That the history of womankind is one of progressive improvement up to 1872 but that, after that fatal date, women must stay where they are, and ask for no further additions to their privileges and responsibilities? We are often told of the debt which women owe to Christianity, and a contrast is drawn between the condition of women in Christian countries and in countries where other religions prevail. There are few women who are not willing to acknowledge what they owe to Christianity. But the debt was not all incurred in one day. It has been accumulating all through the 1800 years that Christianity has influenced mankind. And are we to be told that the benefits that Christianity is capable of bestowing on women are now exhausted, that it can do nothing further for us, that the sum of our indebtedness can never be increased? Do not believe it for a single moment. No nation, no race can cut itself off from its past history. We have inherited a tradition of progress and advancement, and it is as idle to say that this progress must now come to an end as it is to say to the waves of the sea, 'Thus far shalt thou come, and no farther.'[18] There seems to be a sort of idea that the present age is the headstone of the corner in the great building of history, that growth and development were very good things once, but that we have had enough of them now. We hear the civilization of the 19th century spoken of as if it were so perfect that there could be nothing beyond it. But what is this civilization that we are so proud of? It is the spread of knowledge, the throwing off of superstition, the gradual relinquishment of beliefs that are not based on reason and experience; it is the assertion of the sovereignty of law, and the repression of the tyranny of brute force. Who will say there is not much to be desired in each of these directions, and that, therefore, the civilization that we possess at the present time is a very imperfect one; and that there is much to be done in the way of improving and increasing it, both for this and for many succeeding generations? If you were asked to describe one of the special characteristics of an uncivilized age, would you not say that it was a time when the laws and the administration of justice failed either to prevent or to punish the most brutal assaults on the persons and property of the less physically strong members of the community? A time, for instance, when it is not robbery for a man to appropriate his wife's property to his own use, without her consent and contrary to her wish. A time when it is not murder for a man to hold his wife on the fire till she is burned to death. The case I refer to is no imaginary one. I allude to the case of W. Bradley of Preston, who on the 5th of April last, when quarrelling with his wife, seized her and held her on the fire. She was so severely burned that she died, and the coroner's jury brought in a verdict of manslaughter against her husband. He was tried for manslaughter, and the jury found him guilty, but recommended him to mercy. Mr Justice Willes sentenced the prisoner to ten years' penal servitude, adding that but for the recommendation of the jury he would have passed a heavier sentence.[19] The *Times*, in commenting on this and several similar cases – for, unfortunately, they might be quoted by the dozen – said: 'Recent trials have revealed a prevalent indifference to the maltreatment of women, which is a heinous disgrace to English nature.'[20] The laws relating to the property of married women, and the administration of the law relating to cases of assault on women, are some of the remnants of barbarism which have been handed down by the past to the present generation. We have received many blessings from the past, but we have also received an inheritance of ignorance, brutality and superstition. It is pleasanter to look at the bright side, and to talk about the blessings, but we should never forget that the chief of them all is the example of improvement and progress – the fact that each generation has done something to make the one that succeeds it happier and wiser than itself. The aim of each generation should be to follow this example, to add its contribution to the store of human well-being, and to do something to diminish the strength of the forces which tend to make us superstitious and brutal. And is not the extension of the suffrage to women a step in the direction of increasing civilization? Will it not bring about a retreat of the forces of savagery and barbarism? It would place women in a position of equality before the law; it would recognise their status as citizens of a free country; it would insure the speedy abolition of those laws by which their rights are disregarded and their liberties trampled under foot. If women had votes, do you suppose the punishments for murderous assaults on women would much longer be as trifling as they are now? If women had votes, do you think that the laws relating to the property of married women would long remain what they are? If women had votes, do you not think they would put in a claim for the guardianship of their own children? Do you not think they would make an effective demand for a fair share of the educational endowments of the country? But I think I hear some women say, 'Are all these good things certain to follow our political enfranchisement; if we could make quite sure of them, we would make any sacrifice in order to obtain the recognition of our claim to citizenship.' They hesitate and falter; they are like Thomas when he was told of the resurrection of the Lord – 'Except I put my finger into the prints of the nails, and thrust my hand into his side, I will not believe.'[21] To such I would reply:

> Nay, never falter. No great deed is done
> By falterers, who ask for certainty.
> No good is certain but the steadfast mind,
> The undivided will to seek the good.
> 'Tis that, compels the elements, and wrings
> A human music from indifferent air.[22]

To promote the improvement of the condition of women is a great and noble cause to devote one's life to. Success in such a cause is a goal worthy of the noblest ambition; and failure in such a cause is a better thing than success in any meaner or pettier object.

Transcribed from a copy in the Women's Library at LSE.
No known copyright restrictions.

Notes

1 George Dixon (1820–98), Liberal MP for Birmingham (1867–76) and supporter of education for all children.
2 Eliza Mary Sturge (1842–1905), women's activist, secretary and later vice-president of the Birmingham Society of Women's Suffrage. Sturge's speech was reprinted in the *Birmingham Morning News* and followed as a pamphlet entitled *On Women's Suffrage* (Sturge 1872).

3   'A follower of Christ and of Paul his Apostle', to MGF, 11 May 1872 (M50/2/1/6), quoted in Rubinstein (1991, 42).
4   The meeting in support of the granting of suffrage to women was held in the Masonic Hall on Tuesday, 5 December 1871. Fawcett's speech (and those of the other speakers, including Sturge) is detailed in the *Birmingham Daily Post* 1871.
5   See Section 3, note 6.
6   In the nineteenth and twentieth centuries, the Liberal Party was one of the two major political parties in the United Kingdom, the other being the Conservative Party. Its members believed in personal liberty, free trade, social reform and reducing the powers of the Crown and the Church of England (see Bentley 1987).
7   The Reform Acts of 1832 and 1867. There was a third in the nineteenth century: the 1884 Reform Act. See Parliament.uk n.d.g for an overview.
8   The Universities Tests Act 1871, which abolished religious tests, allowing non-Christians, Roman Catholics and non-conformists to enter or be employed by the universities of Oxford, Cambridge and Durham (Batorowicz 2012).
9   The Marriage Act 1835 had made it illegal for a man to marry his dead wife's sister. In 1842, the Marriage to a Deceased Wife's Sister Bill was introduced but strongly defeated, with the bill becoming a '"hardy annual" repeatedly debated and then defeated in most of the parliamentary sessions in the last half of the nineteenth century' (Anderson 1982, 68).
10 The Municipal Franchise Act 1869 had given single female ratepayers the right to vote under a Liberal government led by William Gladstone (Rix 2019).
11 'Radicals' here refers to a parliamentary grouping that supported parliamentary reform from the late eighteenth to the mid-nineteenth century, drawing on previous progressive ideologies that had emerged with the French Revolution (see Harris 1885).
12 The actual quote is 'Everybody said so. Far be it from me to assert that what everybody says must be true. Everybody is, often, as likely to be wrong as right' (Dickens 1848, 1).
13 Sir Edward Burnett Tylor (1832–1917), an English anthropologist and founder of cultural anthropology, who states that 'four-fifths of the human race' believe in the 'Magical arts' (Tylor 1873, 117–19).
14 This was only true in some areas of Italy, for some women: in 1848 in the pre-unitary Italian states of Lombardy, the Venetian Region and the Grand Duchy of Tuscany, 'a tiny number of propertied women had been able to vote (via proxies) and some early suffrage campaigners tried to build on this precedent' (Willson 2009, 38). Women throughout Italy were only allowed to vote in local elections in 1925, eventually gaining full suffrage in 1945.
15 As in the previous speech, Fawcett is keen to point out female monarchs, although they are exceptional.
16 Given that this speech was made in 1872, 30 years later women still did not have the vote. It was 46 years later, in 1918, that women over the age of 30 were enfranchised, and 56 years later that the Representation of the People Act 1928 gave women the vote on the same terms as men.
17 The living quarters used by wives and concubines in an Ottoman household.
18 Job 38:11.
19 This distressing case had much media coverage, given the leniency of the sentencing. See *Preston Chronicle* 1872 for details.
20 *Times* 1872a, which does not actually quote this case, but does mention plenty of other horrific, violent murders.
21 John 20:25.
22 Lines from *The Spanish Gypsy* by George Eliot (1868, 162), spoken by Zarca, the heroine's long-lost father. This poem, mostly forgotten today, had been profitably published and was successful in its time (Marks 1983).

7
Mr Fitzjames Stephen on the position of women, 1873

Examiner. Saturday, 24 May 1873, 539–41.

Fawcett spent time raising issues surrounding gender equality. '[S]he had a great many other things to do as well. One of these was the writing of pamphlets and letters to the Press, at which she was exceedingly efficient' (Strachey 1931, 48). Sir James Fitzjames Stephen (1829–94) was a lawyer educated at Eton, King's College London and Cambridge, as well as a High Court judge and author. His book *Liberty, Equality, Fraternity* (1873) was written in a series of articles during the voyage home from British India, where he had been working as a legal member of the Imperial Legislative Council. In an attack on John Stuart Mill's neo-liberalism and a riposte to *On Liberty* (1859), he argues for restraint and legal compulsion and the upholding of conservative moral and religious mores. Stephen had previously voiced disdain for Henry Fawcett:[1] here Mrs Fawcett sharpens her pen to present her argument against his views on gender equality. The retort proved so popular that it was reprinted and sold as a stand-alone pamphlet (Fawcett 1873b).

*

In a book entitled *Liberty, Equality, Fraternity*, consisting of reprints from the *Pall Mall Gazette*,[2] the English-speaking nations of the world have just received the latest revelation of the Gospel according to St Stephen. Upon nearly all the most important subjects of contemporary politics, upon the gravest questions of religion and metaphysics, we are fully instructed what we ought to do, and how we ought to think. 'This is the way, walk ye in it'[3] ought to be printed in letters an inch high on the top of every page. The manner in which the law is laid down on such questions, for instance, as the connection of Church and State, the social position of women, the Parliamentary suffrage and the right of the State to persecute, strikes one as not only clear, but loud. The reader feels as he studies these passages that the author is shouting in his ear. If, as is probable, he resents being bawled at, he may console himself with the reflection that Mr Stephen would despise him as one of the bad results of modern civilisation, a creature full of nervous sensibility, afraid of pain for himself and others. We therefore advise him not to complain of the shock to his nerves, but to provide himself with a little cotton-wool.

It is impossible to consider here one quarter of the subjects dealt with in *Liberty, Equality, Fraternity*. Even if the time and space at our disposal permitted it, our limited faculties render it impossible for us to follow Mr Stephen into the heights and depths to which he would conduct his readers. We therefore propose to criticise only one portion of Mr Stephen's book – that which refers to the position of women.

Mr Stephen's case is this: men are stronger than women in every shape. They have greater muscular and nervous force, greater intellectual force, greater vigour of character. The physical differences between men and women affect every part of the human body, from the hair of the head to the sole of the foot. This inequality ought to be recognised by the law and by society. Therefore the law and public opinion ought to make the man master; in married life, if differences of opinion arise between husband and wife – on such questions, for instance, as their place of residence or the education of their children – the will of the husband ought to be supreme: the duty of the wife is submission, even although she may disapprove the decision of her husband, and may be better able than he to come to a trustworthy judgement on the matter in hand. Mr Stephen writes:

> I say the wife ought to give way. She ought to obey her husband, and carry out the view at which he deliberately arrives, just as, when the captain gives the word to cut away the masts, the lieutenant carries out his orders at once, though he may be a better seaman and may disapprove them.[4]

Mr Stephen's theory is the theory of the common law. It will be remembered that this theory was maintained in a very remarkable manner at the trial of Mrs Torpey for robbery and for smothering a jeweller's assistant with chloroform.[5] The facts were proved against Mrs Torpey, but she was acquitted, because in stupefying a young man and afterwards robbing him, she had done her duty as a wife. She had obeyed her husband and carried out the view at which he had deliberately arrived. Mrs Torpey might have been a person with the most delicate sense of honour, but the captain had given the word and the lieutenant had but to obey. Those who maintain the absolute authority of the husband must be prepared to meet cases of this kind. Is the wife to obey the husband when, in obeying him, she does something she believes to be wrong? If the answer is 'yes', the possession of a husband may become the screen of all kinds of iniquity, from murder to robbery downwards. If the answer is 'no', everything is conceded that the advocates of equality in marriage demand, for many wives may and do think it is wrong to encourage a spirit of despotism in their husbands by invariably allowing the husband's authority to be supreme. We are very far, indeed, from wishing to imply that all men or all husbands have the spirit of despotism; but some men have it and some women too, and we think it the duty of their friends and relations to check it by resistance before it becomes overpoweringly strong. Every one must know domestic tyrants of both sexes who might have been immensely changed for the better if their disposition to insist invariably on their own way had been nipped in the bud. Mr Stephen's simile is a great favourite with those who maintain the absolute authority of the husband in married life. The government of a family resembles, they say, the management of a vessel, in which every one admits that it is necessary to maintain military discipline, and where the captain is entrusted with supreme and unquestioned authority, not only over the conduct of the vessel, but also over the liberty, and sometimes even over the lives of every other person on the ship. There seems, however, to us to be a very remote analogy between the relations subsisting between a captain and lieutenant of a ship, and those between a husband and wife. Except under circumstances of very great emergency, a lieutenant could scarcely venture to offer advice to his captain unsolicited. The security which the officers, passengers and crew have against abuse of authority on the part of the captain is that they are able to report any cases of misconduct to the owners of the ship at the end of the voyage or, as a less extreme measure, to refuse to serve or sail under the same captain on another voyage. We never heard anyone propose to give the same remedy against oppression to the wives and children of tyrannical husbands.

No true analogy exists between the government of a ship and the government of a family. There is, however, a real resemblance between the government of a family and Parliamentary government as it exists in this country. In Constitutional government no one person, no one chamber, has absolute authority; no change can be effected in the law without the consent of the three estates of the realm. We are constantly being told that the State is founded on the family; and we are certainly of the opinion that in the family as in the State it should be necessary to obtain the consent of the husband and the wife, who in this case stand for the two chambers, for any change affecting the interests of the whole family. As the children grow up, they too should be admitted to the family parliament, and their advice and consent should be sought before the parents decide any matter of importance. Every one must know plenty of instances of this kind of family government; and nearly every one will admit that in practice it contrasts favourably with the ship-captain kind of family government. The law sanctions the ship-captain theory, but the moral sentiment of many persons is superior to the law, and therefore there are many happy marriages. If the existing state of things were as bad as the laws relating to marriage would permit it to be, society would be, as Mr Mill has said, 'a hell upon earth'.[6] From this proposition Mr Stephen strongly dissents. 'I say,' . . . he writes, 'the law is good and the people in question (those who have married happily) obey it.'[7] And yet he admits in a previous page that in many particulars men have made laws for their own supposed advantage, as husbands, which are in fact greatly to the injury of both men and women; and he goes on to speak of the 'stupid coarseness of the laws about the effects of marriage on property'.[8] Mr Stephen has, in fact, made a decided improvement on the spelling-book story beginning, 'I once knew a very nice little girl; she was cross, and told fibs.' 'The laws regulating the relations between men and women are very good; they are in many important respects injurious to both parties, partial, coarse, and stupid.'[9]

To illustrate the necessity of the legal supremacy of the husband, and also, we suppose, the position of a wife in her husband's house, Mr Stephen describes the position of guests in a well-appointed house, and of clerks in a Government office. An 'exact parallel to the case of married life is to be found in the common case of hospitality'.

> Everyone is anxious to promote the enjoyment of others; the host considers everyone before himself, but he has an undoubted legal right to order all his guests out of the house in the middle of the night – to forbid them to touch an article of furniture, or to eat a crumb of bread.
>
> This appears harsh; yet if he were deprived of that right, if the presence of his guests rendered its existence doubtful for a moment in any particular, not one of them would cross his doors; matters go well, not because the master of the house has no powers, but

because no one questions them, and he wishes to use them for the general comfort of the society.[10]

Mr Stephen's other parallel is that of the contract a man makes to serve the Government on certain terms. In this case the employer has complete control over the employed; there is a contract, as in the contract of marriage, a weaker and a stronger person, and the weaker is subject to the authority of the stronger.

The obvious reply to the argument, based on these illustrations, is that the guests and that the Government clerk are free to go the moment that the powers possessed by the host or by the employer are unfairly exercised. If the owner of a country-house, unprovoked by any ill conduct on the part of his guests, availed himself of the powers so graphically described by Mr Stephen, his guests would instantly take their departure; no one who knew the circumstance would ever stay with him, he would be looked upon as a madman, he would be cut by all his neighbours, and after his death, his will would probably be disputed on the ground of his insanity. Even a slight ostentation of his authority as master of the house would probably be sufficient to hasten the departure of his guests, and would prevent their making him another visit. The clerk in a Government office is likewise free to go if there is any abuse of authority on the part of his superiors. Such an abuse of authority would also give the office a bad name, and would tend to prevent men who had any self-respect from becoming clerks in it.

If these parallels are 'exact', Mr Stephen ought to wish a wife to have the same means of escape from an abuse of authority as guests and clerks have. This means they have not. The indissolubility of marriage renders all those so-called parallels entirely fallacious, and makes it necessary for the protection of the wife that she should not be either actually or legally subjugated to her husband. Every one of Mr Stephen's parallels, including that of the ship captain, leads to the conclusion from which he would shrink: that the marriage contract should cease to be permanent.

Mr Stephen is desirous to make his readers believe that the laws regulating the relations of men and women are very advantageous to the latter. Women, it is true, are subjugated to men, but then in return they get the protection of men. 'Submission and protection are correlative. Withdraw the one and the other is lost, and force will assert itself a hundred times more harshly through the law of contract than ever it did through the law of status.'[11] That is to say, in return for submission married women get the protection of losing all control over their own property; they also have the inestimable advantage of possessing no legal right to the guardianship of their own children even after the death of their husbands. In return for the submissiveness of women, little girls of twelve years old are, for purposes of seduction, legally regarded as women – a most noteworthy instance, this, of the kind of protection the present state of the law affords. With regard to the protection women enjoy through the administration of the law, it is notorious that brutal assaults upon women are often treated with the most extraordinary leniency. In case any of our readers should imagine that we are prejudiced on this subject, we will quote from an article which appeared in the *Times* in April 1872:

> Every day the reports of our police-courts and of our criminal tribunals still repeat the tale of savage and cowardly outrages upon women; and every day we have reason to marvel, not without a mixture of indignation at the leniency with which some of our judges treat offences of this kind. Let it be remembered that the decisions of our tribunals have much to do in forming the opinion of those who possess but little mental or moral training in regard to the comparative heinousness of crimes . . . The only moral teaching which at present effectually enters into the conduct of a 'London rough' is that which he learns before the magistrate and the judge. What, then, is likely to be the effect upon his mind of a series of sentences which prove to him that for one in his position it is safer to disfigure or maim, or even trample the life out of a wretched woman who, in her folly, not unmixed with tenderness, may have linked her life to his, than to snatch a watch-chain from an old gentleman in a crowd, or to filch a few pounds of old metal from a workshop? Yet this is the lesson which is taught almost daily in our Criminal Courts . . . Cases that were tried last week in our Criminal Courts might make us doubt whether some of our judges do not still hold to the principle that an Englishman may do what he likes with his own; and, within certain limits, may beat his wife as much as he pleases. Nay, it seems as though, if by accident apparently, he should a little overstep the limits of his manly privilege, and by such a chance relieve himself of an uncongenial companion, the Courts will not too harshly scrutinise his conduct.[12]

The article then describes in detail cases of the most brutal outrage upon women, in several of which the victim, fortunately for herself, was killed, and for which the culprits received sentences of three or four months' hard labour. The *Times* concludes by demanding why a quasi-legality unrecognised by the law should be given to outrages upon women. In another article in the same journal, in August 1872, the complaint is reiterated that 'recent trials have revealed a prevalent indifference to the maltreatment of women, which is a heinous disgrace to English nature'.[13]

The subjects to which reference has just been made indicate the nature of the protection which women receive in return for their submission to men. But Mr Stephen would probably admit that in these cases women are treated with something less than justice. He would, however, urge upon our consideration the courtesy with which well-bred men always treat well-bred women; he makes special mention of 'the cheerful concessions to acknowledged weakness, the obligation to do for women a thousand things which it would be insulting to offer to do for a man'.[14] We wish Mr Stephen had not in this part of his essay employed such general language; he can at times be explicit enough. What are these cheerful concessions to acknowledged weakness, and the thousand things that men do for women which it would be insulting to offer to do for a man? We are convinced that Mr Stephen must refer to very important and substantial privileges, for he speaks as though their proper price was the subjection of women to men; but for the life of us we cannot think of anything but such matters as being 'seen home' from evening parties, being helped first at dinner, having chairs offered, doors opened, umbrellas carried and the like. For such privileges as these, women of the middle class make what we always thought an ample return by sewing on buttons, working slippers and making puddings for the man-kind of their domestic circles. Probably all women give back in small services of some kind the full value of the little attentions they receive as women from men. But even if this is not the case, it is a small consolation for Nancy Jones, in Whitechapel, who is kicked and beaten at discretion by her husband, to know that Lady Jones, in Belgravia, is always assisted in and out of her carriage as if she were a cripple. It is a small consolation to a widow whose children are taken from her and handed over to the guardianship of a stranger, to know that a gentleman will never pass out of the room before her and that she may always take the inner side of the pavement. If Sir John Lubbock carries his Bill called 'The Shop Hours Regulation Bill',[15] it will be a small consolation to the hundreds of women who will be thrown out of employment thereby, to hear that Anonyma's diamonds[16] are as splendid as a princess's, and that gentlemen of the very highest rank would vie with each other for the honour of picking up her fan. If women are to understand that the courtesies they now enjoy are simply yielded to them on condition of their legal and actual subjection to men, there are few women who would not at once declare that they were being grossly overcharged for the article, and also that these small privileges become utterly valueless unless they are completely voluntary in their character. We believe they are entirely voluntary, and that those who assert that they are simply given in exchange for submission make a very unjustifiable charge on the characters of their fellow-men. Old men and men who are disabled by any physical infirmity are in the habit of receiving from women the little considerate attentions which men usually show to women. In these cases is there any kind of stipulation expressed or implied that these services are to be paid for by submission on the one side and dominion on the other? The very idea would render it almost impossible that the services should ever be given or received. In the same way, we believe it to be entirely erroneous to say that when men are polite to women, and anxious to help them in all things in which the superior physical strength of a man is serviceable, they demand in return the submission of women.

In the passage in which Mr Stephen speaks of 'the cheerful concessions' and the 'thousand things' that women now obtain on condition of their subjection, he must either mean the politeness and kindliness of men to women in social intercourse, or else he must refer to some weighty and substantial advantages of the existence of which we are entirely ignorant. It is quite an appalling thought to a woman in whom the English virtue of resistance to arbitrary authority is strongly developed that, although she is ignorant of the fact, she is daily receiving concessions, and having a thousand things done for her on condition of a submission which she never intends to give. When the settling day comes, she will have nothing to meet the demands of her creditors.

It is in many respects satisfactory that the opponents of the social and legal equality of women should have found so able a spokesman as Mr Stephen. He advances in support of his view intelligible and honest arguments, to which it is possible to reply; whereas there is an absolute impossibility in arguing with a man who says, for instance, that women ought not to have votes because no women came over as soldiers with the Norman army which invaded England in 1066, or because if they had votes they would go to Parliament, would become attorneys-general and would be fallen in love with by solicitors-general. This is the usual style of argument employed in the House of Commons by the Home Secretary and other opponents of woman suffrage. In contrast with it we welcome the attack of Mr Stephen's heavy artillery; it is one among the many proofs of the growing importance of the movement for the emancipation of women.

Transcribed from a copy in the British Library.
No known copyright restrictions.

Notes

1. Rubinstein reports (1991, 53), 'After meeting Fitzjames Stephen at a dinner party in India in 1872 Alice Cowell wrote to her father: "He told me of Harry having skated from Cambridge to Ely soon after his blindness with his brother Leslie Stephen and seemed to think the fearless way in which he went ahead regardless of holes and other people's toes typical of his whole career." Alice Cowell to Newson Garrett, 10 April 1872, Anderson Papers.'
2. Stephen 1873. The essays on utilitarianism were published in the *Pall Mall Gazette* in June 1869 (Stephen 1873, 355).
3. Isaiah 30:21.
4. Stephen (1873, 217).
5. An account of this robbery of a diamond necklace and other articles valued at £2,500, which took place on Thursday, 12 January 1871, in the shop of Messrs London and Ryder, jewellers and goldsmiths, Bond Street, London, can be found in the *Express and Echo* 1871. The robbery, the trial and the subsequent sentencing were much featured in the press. In March 1871, Martha Torpey was tried for theft and applying chloroform to the shop assistant, and appeared 'in the dock carrying a baby in her arms . . . The jury, after deliberating a few moments, said their opinion was that the whole matter had been pre-arranged by the husband, and that the wife acted under his coercion, and that she was therefore not guilty. The verdict was received with loud applause' (*Dundee Advertiser* 1871). Michael Torpey was found guilty of the robbery in May 1871 (*Clerkenwell News* 1871).
6. Mill (1869, 60).
7. Stephen (1873, 229).
8. Stephen (1873, 219).
9. Presumably Fawcett has constructed these quotes for effect: they are not found in the text.
10. Stephen (1873, 231).
11. Stephen (1873, 237).
12. *Times* 1872b.
13. *Times* 1872a, which Fawcett also quotes in her speech in Birmingham in 1872 (see Section 6).
14. Stephen (1873, 237).
15. Sir John Lubbock (1834–1913) was a banker, Liberal politician, philanthropist and scientific researcher. In 1873, he 'proposed that the Factory Acts be extended to shops. His Shop Hours Regulation Bill . . . proposed that the working hours of women, apprentices and children be cut to ten and a half per day. Lubbock was already a household name: it was thanks to him that bank holidays had been introduced two years previously' (Cox and Hobley 2015, 43). This new legislation was eventually passed as the Shop Hours Act in 1886.
16. Presumably a reference to Anonyma, a 'pseudonym for the author of a set of licentious books in the 1860s' (At the Circulating Library 2020); Fawcett sets up scandalous behaviour against royalty here.

8
Picturing Fawcett: Millicent Fawcett's lecture at the Unitarian Church, Glasgow, 1875

Figure 4: 'Mrs Fawcett's lecture on the female characters of Dickens, Thackeray, and George Eliot, at the Unitarian Church, Glasgow'. Pen and ink illustration by Jim Karnie (1875) in the *Pictorial World*. No known copyright restrictions. Digitised from editor's own copy.

This is a frequently used image which depicts the popularity of the young Fawcett's lectures: the pair of speeches she delivered on this tour were detailed widely in the press (see Section 9 for transcripts and tour details). Little is known about the artist, Jim Karnie, who contributed one other pen-and-ink sketch of Glaswegian life to the *Pictorial World*, in 1874 (Karnie 1874).

9
Reporting Fawcett: The women of modern fiction lectures, 1874

Coverage of Lecture on Women of Modern Fiction, Glasgow (*Pictorial World*, Saturday, 2 January 1875) and Kirkcaldy (*Fife Free Press*, Saturday, 5 December 1874).

By the mid-1870s Fawcett had become a household name. Between '1867 and 1874 she had married, become a mother, written two economics books, much of a third and many articles, been heavily involved in opening higher education at Cambridge to women, and carved out for herself a novel and controversial role as a public speaker on women's suffrage' (Rubinstein 1991, 45). In February 1874 she was due to undertake a lecture tour throughout the United Kingdom speaking 'On Women of Modern Fiction'. Unfortunately, when out riding with Henry Fawcett 'her horse fell with her, and she was thrown with great force and rendered unconscious. Harry could not see for himself what had happened, and thought that she had been killed' (Strachey 1931, 67). 1874 was a quiet year as a result, as she recuperated from serious injury.[1] While considering the way women were represented in modern fiction, Fawcett used the pause to plan and write her first novel, *Janet Doncaster* (see Section 10). The lecture series was postponed,[2] although later rescheduled.[3]

Dates included in the reorganised listings at the end of the year show the pace and geographical spread of Fawcett's tours:[4]

Middlesbrough (Oddfellow's Hall): Monday, 30 November 1874.
Edinburgh (Philosophical Institution): Tuesday, 1 December 1874.
Leven (Greig Institute): Wednesday, 2 December 1874.
Kirkcaldy (Corn Exchange): Thursday, 3 December 1874.

Edinburgh (Philosophical Institution): Friday, 4 December 1874.
Paisley (Public Library): Monday, 7 December 1874.
Glasgow (Crosshill Unitarian Church): Thursday, 10 December 1874.
Bothwell (Free Church): Monday, 14 December 1874.

Featured here are reports of two different lectures on the topic, one given in Glasgow and one in Kirkcaldy. Together, and alongside the engraving from the *Pictorial World* (Figure 4), their content, coverage and reception can be ascertained. The Glasgow lecture, in particular, was widely reported (via telegram) in local newspapers throughout the United Kingdom.

*

Mrs Fawcett's lecture at Glasgow

The 'Women of Modern Fiction' was the subject of Mrs Fawcett's lecture in Glasgow a week or two ago. It was delivered at Cross Hill[5] and contained many good points. She dwelt on the women characters of Dickens, Thackeray and George Eliot. Of the first-named writer's heroines she holds a similar opinion to that expressed by the great French critic, M. Taine.[6] She observed that Dickens's heroines were, as a rule, imbecile and idiotic, fascinating and undersized. He drew some splendid caricatures of female failings, and some wonderfully amusing characters, but they were unlike any person that ever lived. Dickens lacked true insight into woman's heart. The women of Thackeray and George Eliot, on the other hand, breathed and lived before us. With that, however, the likeness of the women of Thackeray and George Eliot ceased. In the case of Thackeray one saw the face of the clock, but did not see the works; while in the case of George Eliot you saw the very balance of the machine, and were taken behind the scenes in a manner which made you know the people themselves, and not their words and actions only. If, she said, all Thackeray's women were suddenly to be endowed with real existence, you would not feel any great eagerness to make them your friends; but, on the other hand, it would be a widening of one's whole existence to know Dorothea, Videlmah and Romola.[7] You could not know them without being influenced for good by them. If you knew them, they would be people to whom you would look for sympathy in joy and help in trouble. George Eliot had done incalculable service to women in raising before her in the central figures of her books types of character worthy of the deepest admiration. No one could read her books without being in some degree elevated above the petty and selfish objects that are too apt to engross us.

Lecture on the women of modern fiction

The third of the interesting course of lectures under the Kirkcaldy Literary Association was delivered in the Corn Exchange on Thursday evening by Mrs Fawcett, wife of Henry Fawcett, Esq., Professor of Political Economy at Cambridge, formerly member of Parliament for Brighton and now colleague of Mr Holms as member for Hackney – her subject being 'Some of the Women's Characters of Dickens, Thackeray, and George Eliot'. There was a large attendance, the whole body of the Exchange being filled, while the front seats were also well occupied; and Robert Douglas, Esq., engineer, president of the association, in a few well chosen remarks, introduced the lady lecturer to her hearers.

Mrs Fawcett, who was received with applause, dwelt, in the opening of her lecture, on the delights of novel reading, which were unknown to our ancestors two centuries ago, and the disadvantages which we have to labour under while studying life and character when depicted on the stage as compared with the knowledge of these subjects to be obtained by a perusal of good novels. Referring to the enormous number of bad novels which are now annually published, the lecturer brought under the notice of her audience the sarcastic allusions to be found in Dickens' and Thackeray's works on the unnatural style of writing which prevails among a large class of authors. One question which was largely discussed was: Should an author have a moral lesson to enforce, or should he simply give a picture of life as it presents itself to his imagination? Should he preach us a sermon or should he paint us a picture? The latter was the course almost invariably adopted by the greatest of writers. Not that our best writers had no strong convictions on the principal matters of interest of our day, but their artistic sense was so keen, their sympathy with human nature was so broad, that it was impossible for them to group together characters and events with the sole purpose of portraying some single phase of human experience, or enforcing one doctrine, however important. She did not wish to imply from this that the greatest novelists could not teach us any lessons, but they taught us these lessons from a skilful interpretation of nature, not from a direct dogmatic assertion. There was no more important function exercised by the novelist than that by which they extended, almost indefinitely, their readers' knowledge of society, and their acquaintance with the characters and motives of men and women situated in positions of life, surrounded by temptations and actuated by motives very different from our own. The most valuable novels to the historian were not those which were called historical, but those which represented the society of which the writer formed a part. Such novels were social historical photographs, important in our day, and which would doubtless go far towards forming a part of the history of the future. A great effect on the public mind had been produced with regard to the subject of the character, sphere and duties of women, and described by authors. Take, for instance, the women of Dickens' novels. What ideas did they convey of woman's duties, and her power of fulfilling them? Feminine fortitude in Dickens' novels was below the medium height, always babyish and infantile; while his proud, wicked women were tall and masculine. His heroines were maimed and helpless phantoms, who were constantly swooning into the arms of any one, and every one who would catch them. (Laughter.) The chief part of their lives must have been spent in drying their eyes and recovering from fainting fits. (Great laughter.) After illustrating her remarks by a reference to the characters of Kate Nickleby, Dora, and Ruth Pinch,[8] Mrs Fawcett said that one idea that Dickens entertained regarding women was very misleading and had done and was doing a great deal of harm. They had met with the opinion that if women interested themselves in any public question, if in any way they cared for anything, either in literature, politics or religion, outside the limits of their own home, then that very fact would render them neglectful of their domestic duties, untidy in their dress, careless of their husbands and children and a nuisance to every one who came in contact with them. That opinion she believed to be entirely false, and without common sense. (Applause.) What reason could there be for saying that if a woman had been taught mathematics, she would not love her children; and that if she took an interest in politics she would have no interest in pudding. To judge from Mrs Jellyby and Mrs Pardiggle in 'Bleak House',[9] evidently considered, that women who cared for anything in the world save their husbands and children, were unbearable in all their social relations. The moral of Mrs Jellyby was: 'This is what you will come to, young woman, if you give your mind to public questions; and this is what you will come to, young man, if you marry a strong minded woman' (Laughter.) Never was caricature more uncalled for and untrue. Dickens' characters were not real living creatures – and that criticism applied to some of his male and nearly all of his female characters. He could make Old Weller[10] or the Boots at the Holly-Tree Inn[11] live because he knew the characters and had studied their peculiarities; but women he did not know in the same way. He could not draw them from the life, therefore he evolved them from his inner consciousness, and he never acquired the skill of making his wax figures look as if they were living. If they compared his gallery of women's portraits with his gallery of men's portraits, the former would be seen to be immeasurably inferior.

At the close a cordial vote of thanks was given, on the motion of the chairman, awarded to the lady lecturer.

Transcribed from copies in the British Library.
No known copyright restrictions.

Notes

1. Although Strachey maintains 'She was not seriously hurt, and was soon herself again' (1931, 67), Fawcett later replied to a 'Hallucinations Census' carried out by the Society for Psychical Research in 1891/2 recalling the incident, indicating that she had experienced significant injury: 'faces I saw were visible at intervals for about 2 months after my fall' and the 'appearances were frequent – generally by day' but 'I did not speak of them to anyone at the time because I thought my friends would imagine that my brain was affected if I told them I was seeing visions' (Fawcett c. 1892a, CUL SPR 24/13).
2. '. . . owing to the recent accident which had been sustained by Mrs Henry Fawcett, the two lectures . . . would not take place. Mrs Fawcett said that she would be happy to place herself at the service of the directors next session' (*Scotsman* 1874a).
3. These articles do not appear in the bibliography compiled by Rubinstein (1991, 291–302).
4. Dates from the *Scotsman* 1874b, *Paisley Herald and Renfrewshire Advertiser* 1874, *Fifeshire Journal* 1874, *Fife Free Press* 1874, *Western Morning News* 1874, *Hamilton Advertiser* 1874, *Northern Echo* 1874.
5. The illustration in the *Pictorial World* 1875 shows this to be at the Unitarian Church, Crosshill. Newspaper coverage dates it to Thursday, 10 December 1874.
6. Monsieur Hippolyte Taine (1828–93), a French critic and historian who attempted to provide a scientific account of literature.
7. Characters from George Eliot's writings: Dorothea Brooke from *Middlemarch* (1871), presumably Fedalma, the Spanish Gypsy from the title of Eliot's tragic play in blank verse (1868), and Romola de' Bardi from *Romola* (1863).
8. Kate Nickleby from *The Life and Adventures of Nicholas Nickleby* (Dickens 1839), Dora Spenlow from *David Copperfield* (1850) and Ruth Pinch from *The Life and Adventures of Martin Chuzzlewit* (1844).
9. *Bleak House* (Dickens 1853). Friends and both philanthropists, Mrs Jellyby squanders her fortune abroad while ignoring her family and the nearby needy, and Mrs Pardiggle disregards her own family's needs and condescends and irritates the local poor.
10. Mr Weller Senior, personable widower in *The Pickwick Papers* (first printed as *The Posthumous Papers of the Pickwick Club* [Dickens 1837]).
11. The Boots was a kindly, low-ranking servant who looked after the boots and shoes. He was introduced in the extra Christmas number of *Household Words* (Dickens 1855), which was later published as a stand-alone edition (Dickens 1856). The character appears in later editions of sentimental stories about the *Holly-Tree Inn* (Dickens 1858).

10
Janet Doncaster, an excerpt, 1875

'The Old Home and a New One', Chapter XIV, *Janet Doncaster*. May 1875. London: Smith, Elder and Co., 218–32.

Having had success as a writer of textbooks, including *Political Economy for Beginners* (1870a), *Essays and Lectures on Social and Political Subjects* (Fawcett and Fawcett 1872) and *Tales in Political Economy* (1874), Fawcett experimented by turning her hand to fiction. While recovering from her fall in 1874 (see Section 9), Fawcett wrote her only surviving novel.[1] Set in Fawcett's birthplace of Aldeburgh, Suffolk, *Janet Doncaster* chronicles an impoverished young woman's struggle for independence as she is lured into an unwanted, then disastrous, marriage. Fawcett criticises the legal system that would force a woman to live with an unsuitable spouse, and 'like the author, Janet possesses an alarmingly rigid moral code, which causes her to leave her husband at once and permanently at the first manifestation of his hereditary drunkenness' in a book that is 'characterised not only by pronounced feminism but also by wit, puritan morality and a marked dislike both of upper-class pretensions and adherence to outward forms of Christianity' (Rubinstein 1989, 75). The book received much attention in the press,[2] but critics were politely lukewarm to unkind. Even the ever-positive Strachey admits 'the book as a whole was not written with the skill of a great novelist' (1931, 55).

Included here is an excerpt, Chapter XIV, 'The Old Home and a New One', which is the zenith of the novel: Janet Doncaster resolves to leave the marital home. The chapter stresses Fawcett's interest in education, and access to knowledge, for women, as well as her understanding of the limited occupations available to educated women at the time.

*

> Love is not love which alters when it alteration finds.[3]

It was a relief to Janet to sob out her story to the good old servant. Mrs Barker[4] listened to everything and shared to the full Janet's grief and anger, but she decidedly and strongly opposed Janet's determination to leave her husband. '"*For* better and *for* worse" you took him,' she said with particular emphasis on the prepositions. Janet only replied by repeating her determination never to see him again. The poor child had never known the strength of over-mastering love for her husband. She had liked him, thought him kind and affectionate and had been grateful for his affection. She imagined even that she loved him, but her love had not been of the kind 'that looks on tempests and is never shaken';[5] and the storm that had overtaken her had carried away in its fury such affection as she had once felt for her husband. She could not think of him now except as she last saw him in a drunken sleep, with discoloured face and half-closed eyes and with Marston watching at his side. When Mrs Barker talked to her of instances of wifely devotion, and told her of women who had gone through fire and water to serve men whom Mrs Barker described as 'drunkards and worse', Janet's self-reproach was greater than her anger. 'I cannot bear what those poor women bore', she thought; 'their love gave them strength. I never loved him as wives should love their husbands. I was very wicked to marry him, and now I am punished. O God! I am punished.'

Her thoughts turned in this direction as good Mrs Barker proceeded with her simple sermon. 'What I say is,' she concluded, 'hev he a wife or hev he not? If he hev, he don't ought to be left alone, whatever he is, or whatever he's done!'

But Janet was immovable. Though the whole world should tell her that she ought to go back to her husband, she would not go back to him. She now told herself that she had done wrong in marrying him, and evil had come of that wrongdoing. The evil was quite inevitable, and she must endure the consequences of it to the end of her life, but it would be making bad worse to go back to her husband. She thought with a shudder of the luxuries and all the wealthy surroundings of her life as Mrs Leighton; if she accepted them now, it would be accepting the price of her own degradation. She would reject them all. She refused to fulfil all wifely duties, and she would also refuse every privilege she would have claimed as a wife. As far as in her lay, she would wash her hands of the marriage altogether; she would not be beholden to the Leightons for a penny; she would work for her own living, as she would have had to do, in case of her mother's death, if she had remained unmarried.

Work for her own living! But what work? That was a question that Janet had great difficulty in answering. If she offered herself as governess in a private family or school, would her services be accepted? In the first place, she knew very little except French; and she had seen enough of the world to be aware that a woman living apart from her husband, whatever were the circumstances of her separation, would not be likely to find many people willing to engage her as a governess. Could she wait in a shop, or be a telegraph clerk, or learn to cut ladies' hair and get engaged at Douglas's, or any of the other London hairdressers that employ women.[6] The fact that the women in these employments are not ladies did not weigh with her. 'I daresay they are as good as I am,' she said to herself, 'and I must live.'

She did not, of course, forget that she had 50*l*.[7] a year on her own. The possession of that little fortune was the one ray of light that shone upon Janet's life at that time. It enabled her to wait, to keep Mrs Barker with her, and, above all, it gave her the power to be her own mistress. Very soon after her arrival in Norborough, she wrote and told her story to her friend Margaret, and begged her advice as to what she could do for a living. The reply was a letter from both Mr and Mrs Williams pressing Janet most warmly to come to them at Oakhurst at once. Margaret said she was sure if they talked it over together, they could think of something better for Janet to do than anything that had yet been suggested. So it was arranged that Janet should go to Oakhurst. Mrs Barker remained at Norborough for a week or two, till the house and the furniture were sold; then she followed her mistress to the New Forest, and they felt that they had said a last good-bye to Norborough.

Mr Williams was a very good friend to Janet, notwithstanding that he strongly disapproved of her determination to live apart from her husband, and that he found that she was quite immovable on the point.

'Since you have written to ask our advice, Mrs Leighton,' he said, 'I do not hesitate to say that I am most strongly of opinion that you ought to go back to your husband.' He forgot, till his wife reminded him, that it was not about returning to her husband that Janet had asked their advice, but about what work she could do to support herself, as she would accept none of her husband's money. But Mr Williams, thoroughly kindhearted and helpful as he was, had a mind that rather despised details. Janet had certainly written to ask advice, and Mr Williams was quite ready to give it on all subjects; it was a mere detail on what subject it was that Janet had wished to be advised. People who knew Mr Williams well used to say that the way to ingratiate oneself with him was to ask him for his advice; he gave it in floods and torrents, but he was your friend for life. One of his best points was that he did not resent it if his advice was not taken. He had so happy a disposition that if the advisee succeeded in any undertaking, Mr Williams was confident that it was because his advice had been followed. Whereas all failures were accounted for in a manner equally satisfactory to himself; the person who failed had not taken Mr Williams's advice. Now that Janet was staying in his house, and had written before she came to ask advice, he found her a charming companion. He advised her on every conceivable subject: Where to get Stilton cheese; how to supply herself with Welsh mutton; what walks to take; to go back to her husband; to travel third-class and not to mind what people said; to not get into debt; not to part with Mrs Barker; what boot-laces wore the best; who was the best tutor and the best coach at Cambridge; what college to send her sons to; where to spend the long vacation; and finally, how to turn her knowledge of French to good account. On this last subject his advice was triumphant. Janet and Mrs Williams had thought that it might be a good plan if Janet entered a training-college, and qualified herself to become the certificated mistress of a national school. If she did this, she could get 70*l.* or 80*l.* a year and a house, and might perhaps get appointed to the Oakhurst school which was then being built by Mr Williams. She could live at Oakhurst very comfortably with Mrs Barker on her salary plus her 50*l.* a year. But Mr Williams could not see that this scheme had a single recommendation. 'Mrs Leighton's knowledge of French would be completely thrown away in such an occupation.' Finally, he wrote to his own publishers, pointing out the urgent necessity, in the interests of theological research, that English translations should be published at once of several volumes of French theology written by eminent Protestant *pasteurs*; and added that there was a lady now staying in his house, a first-rate translator, who would undertake to do the work on moderate terms. He enclosed a specimen of Janet's translation of a few pages of a work by M. de Pressensé,[8] which he said he was sure would astonish Messrs Parsons and Hitchcock by its vigour and fidelity. Janet was most grateful; the training college scheme was put on one side, pending the receipt of Messrs Parsons and Hitchcock's reply. It came at last, and was favourable; and in a few days Janet had agreed to translate for 150*l.* three ponderous tomes of French Protestant theology.

'How delightful!!' exclaimed Janet, hugging her volumes. 'How good you have been to me, Mr Williams; I can never thank you enough!'

'Not at all. I can give you an order to read in the library of the British Museum if you would like to do your work in London, or if you would like to do it here, I could get you books of reference from the University library. It wouldn't be the least trouble. I should simply write a note, and say, "Oakhurst Rectory, March 12. – My dear Elliot, – I shall be much obliged if you will take out of the University Library, in my name, so-and-so and so-and-so, and send them to the above address. Believe me, my dear Elliot, sincerely yours, Robert Williams."'

Did we say Mr Williams despised details? He did in most things, but when he once committed himself to a description in detail he left nothing to the imagination.

When Mrs Williams and Janet were alone, the former suggested that the work would be a little dull. 'It's a dreary subject, Janet,' she said.

'O Margaret, that is nothing. I am so delighted to have the work; it won't be nearly so dull as cutting hair and fastening together sham chignons.'

'That was a most absurd notion of yours, certainly.'

'But I believe I should have been obliged to do it if it hadn't been for you and Mr Williams,' said Janet, kissing her friend.

Before Janet had left Norborough, she had endured visits from her old friends there. Of course, her story, or some version of it, was in everybody's mouth before she had been four-and-twenty hours in the village. Mrs Sedgely heard so many different accounts of the matter that she was fairly baffled. With the best intentions firmly to believe one version and regard all the others as 'Norborough tales,' she could not make the selection; so at last she persuaded herself that as an old friend she ought to call upon Janet. 'After all,' she reflected, 'there's nothing like going to the fountain head.' But she did not find Janet very communicative. 'I am very unhappy, but I would rather not talk about it,' was all that Mrs Sedgely could obtain. So Mrs Sedgely repaired next to Mrs Barker, whom she might have compared, if she had wished to develop her simile of the fountain head, to the fountain's tap. When Mrs Grey heard that Mrs Sedgely had called, and had ascertained that Janet refused to live with her husband, she too went to see Janet. She felt that the motherless girl had some claim upon her for affection, and for reproof, for Mrs Grey strongly condemned Janet's conduct. Janet responded gratefully to Mrs Grey's affection, and accepted the reproof with meekness.

'My dear Janet,' said Mrs Grey, 'you ought to take the advice of your friends in this; you are putting yourself quite in the wrong by staying here. Everyone says so. If you will go back to your husband, everyone's sympathy will be with you. But you shut yourself off from the pity we all feel for you in this misfortune by your present conduct.'

'I cannot help it, Mrs Grey; it is very hard, but I cannot help it. I would rather have everyone against me than be against myself. I don't mean that I don't blame myself now. I do. But if I went back to him I should be selling myself, body and soul. I should be no better than those poor creatures on the streets. I should be much worse.'

Mrs Grey left Janet, but the door had hardly closed upon her before the clergyman, Mr Doubleday, was announced. His counsel was identical with Mrs Grey's. Then Mrs Sedgely called again to back up what 'dear Mrs Grey' had said. Then Captain Macduff wrote a long letter in the same strain; and finally Mr Broadley came down from London on purpose to give the same advice. From Mrs Barker upwards, everyone said, 'Go back to your husband, whatever he is, however you may have been deceived.' But she swore to herself, and declared to her counsellors, that she would never go back to him.

It was after receiving all these visits that Janet had written to Mrs Williams; she could not endure her life in Norborough any longer. At Oakhurst it would be more tolerable to be alive than at Norborough, where no day passed without the irritating necessity of justifying or excusing herself to people who believed that no justification or excuse for her conduct could under any circumstances be found. Janet hardly knew how much this contest with the Norborians had exhausted her till she found that, for the first time since her troubles came upon her, she had a keen sense of pleasure and relief, arising from the fact that Margaret thought her conduct right.

'It is such a rest, Margaret,' she said, 'that you understand it, and think I should be wrong to go back.'

'Of course you have no legal right to separate yourself from him; but it seems to me that your moral right is plain. He married you under false pretences, as false as they would have been if he had had another wife living at the time. If this horrible propensity for drinking had come upon him after you were married, I should have thought that you ought to have borne everything rather than have left him. It would have been an unforeseen misfortune which you should have borne together. But the case is quite different now. He has wilfully deceived you; if you had known the truth about him, you never would have married him.'

'You don't know how glad I am to hear you say this. I feel now that I am not alone; that I have a friend on whose arm I can lean. Dear Margaret, I shall think of you when I hear "I was sick and ye visited me; I was in prison and ye came unto me."'[9]

Janet did not establish herself in London with Mrs Barker and her French theology, without having an encounter with Lady Ann's lawyer. She first received a letter enclosing a cheque due to her 'as per settlement', and requiring her to join Mr Leighton at Leighton Court. This she replied to by returning the cheque, and by saying that she entirely refused to live with Mr Leighton, or to accept anything from him. 'If any attempt is made to force me to live with him,' she wrote, 'I will advertise in every way that is open to me the circumstances of my marriage. Everyone shall know that I am living with him against my will; that he is a drunkard, and that he married me under false pretences.' When she sent off this letter, she also wrote to Lady Ann Leighton, repeating the threat of giving the greatest possible publicity to the circumstances of her marriage if any attempt was made to force her to live with Mr Leighton. And she concluded by saying that she was earning her own living, and would continue to do so, without any pecuniary assistance from her husband's family. Lady Ann replied by imploring her not to disgrace the name she bore by performing menial work, or mixing with uncultivated people. She promised that no effort should be made to force her to return to her husband, although she expressed confidence that in time Janet's better feelings would prevail, and that she would return to him. In conclusion, she begged Janet as a personal favour to accept an allowance of 500*l*. a year, to maintain her in that station of life to which it had pleased Mr Leighton to call her. This offer was once more refused, and at last Janet was undisturbed in her new life in London.

> *Transcribed from a copy in the Internet Archive, from the Bodleian Library, University of Oxford. Not in copyright.*

Notes

1. Tantalisingly, Strachey recounts that Fawcett 'suspected that her name and her friends were the chief element in the flutter her book made, and she determined to test the matter properly. She wrote a second novel, without letting anyone into the secret, and published it under another name. It fell perfectly flat – as she had feared it might – and she was satisfied – if naturally disappointed – that the career of a novelist was not for her. Unfortunately, all traces of this novel . . . are lost' (1931, 55–6).
2. For example, anonymous, but mildly favourable, reviews appeared in the *Examiner* (Anonymous 1875a) and the *Times* (Anonymous 1875b), with a more critical appraisal appearing in the *British Quarterly Review*: '*Janet Doncaster* as a whole, fresh, original and powerful as it is, tires us, and utterly fails to touch our best sympathies. It is put together by a hard, intellectual process, the result of keen and somewhat sarcastic observation, and consists of cold, utilitarian inter-relations. It may represent actual types of human nature, but it does not even suggest an ideal of what men and women should be. We prefer Mrs Fawcett as a writer of political economy; although we note the same qualifications of her power even in this department of social exposition' (Anonymous 1875c, 557).
3. Shakespeare, Sonnet 116.
4. Mrs Barker resembles Mrs Barham, the Garretts' own faithful servant in Aldeburgh, including in her speech patterns (Fawcett 1924, 18–24).
5. Shakespeare, Sonnet 116.
6. In a speech of 1869 at the Hanover Square Rooms, the English women's rights activist Emily Faithfull (1835–95) revealed that 'women were now employed instead of men at a hairdresser's shop at the West-end. This opens up another sphere of female employment in London. Female barbers have hitherto been confined to Wales' (*Suffolk and Essex Free Press* 1869). In 1869, 'a Mr Douglas of Bond Street has a strike among his employees and took the opportunity of employing twelve women in their place' (Jordan 2001, 176; see also Clark 2020, 83–6).
7. According to the National Archives Currency Converter (National Archives 2017), 50*l*. in 1880 was equivalent to £3,309.24 in 2017, although in 1880 this represented a working-class income which would allow a person to rent a room and live humbly.
8. Edmond de Pressensé (1824–91), French Protestant theologian.
9. Matthew 25:36.

11
Women and representative government, 1883

Nineteenth Century. August 1883, 285–91.

The period between 1874 and 1883 represented 'quiet years' for Fawcett (Rubinstein 1991, 45–55), in a time where 'the lack of parliamentary progress and the divisions within the movement must have been dispiriting' (p. 49). Fawcett 'continued her work for Newnham and served on the college council from 1881' and worked on the improvement of university facilities for women in London (p. 50), becoming 'a prominent and respected figure, no longer a shocking novelty as she had been a decade earlier' (p. 55).

In July 1883, a resolution to enfranchise qualified women in the UK was narrowly defeated (HC Deb 1883), suggesting that future success was possible. Shortly afterwards, Fawcett demonstrated her knowledge of parliamentary legislation, modern history, contemporary political events and cultural theory in this tightly argued, confident appeal for women's representation, showing her maturing skill as a writer.

*

Those who have been labouring in behalf of the removal of the electoral disabilities of women feel that a very critical time in the history of the agitation is now approaching. The question of parliamentary reform, and a further extension of the principle of household suffrage, will probably occupy the attention of the House of Commons during a great part of next session.[1] The old familiar arguments that taxation without representation is tyranny,[2] that those who are subject to the law and fulfil the obligations of citizenship cannot be justly excluded from all share of making the laws, will be heard again and again; and it will moreover be urged that it is alike unjust and inexpedient to place the stigma of political subjection upon whole classes of loyal, peaccable[3] and industrious citizens by making the qualifications for the franchise such as they cannot fulfil. On one side of the House it will be urged that property ought to be represented; on the other side of the House the words of Mr Chamberlain at the Cobden Club dinner will be repeated, that 'full confidence in the people is the only sure foundation on which the government of this country can rest'.[4] And what the advocates of a real representation of the people want to make sure of, is to remind the orators who make use of these telling phrases, that the human race consists of women as well as of men. They wish to remind the Radicals and Liberals, who have done so much to get rid of political disabilities, that the disability of sex is as repugnant to true Liberalism as are the disabilities of race and religion. They want to remind the Tory party that if a fair representation of property is what they are aiming at, they will be acting very inconsistently if they support a system which gives no kind of representation to property, however vast, which happens to be owned by a woman.

It is sometimes said by those who do not deny the justice of women's claim to representation that it is necessary to show what practical good will be done to women and to the community at large by giving women votes. The answer is not far to seek. Exactly the same good that is done to other people by self-government and representative government, as opposed to government by an autocracy or an oligarchy. One overwhelming advantage which results from representative government is that it teaches people to take care of themselves; it teaches them that faults in their system of government are due not to the tyranny of those who are set over them, but to their own lassitude and want of zeal in correcting these faults. What better remedy than this can exist against revolution? And what a miserable waste of noble qualities results from the opposite system – the system of repression and autocracy. It is not necessary to look further than to the contemporary history of Russia for examples.[5] We see their courage, compassion, fidelity, devotion, ingenuity and patience turned aside from channels in which they might have made the whole world a better place to live in, into channels which lead to conspiracy, murder and insatiable longings for revenge. These are the fruits of tyranny when tyranny is carried to extremes. It is the aim of representative government to avoid these social cankers; and it is the aim of those who favour the representation of women to make representative government in our own country as complete as possible by including all citizens, men and women, who fulfil the legal qualifications and who have not forfeited their political liberty by crime or pauperism.

It is not necessary here to dwell at any length on the painful subject of laws that are unjust to women. No one who has ever given even a few minutes' attention to the subject will deny that there are many laws which, to use Mr Gladstone's expression, give to women 'something less than justice'.[6] If it is necessary to quote examples, the inequality which the law has created between men and women in divorce suits furnishes one. The cruel law which gives a mother no legal guardianship over her children is another. I think there can be little doubt that if similar hardships had affected any represented class, they would long ago have been swept away. As it is, however, though the injustice of these and other laws affecting women is fully and almost universally recognised, year after year rolls by and nothing is done to remedy them. Here are matters almost universally admitted to involve injustice and wrong, and no one tries to remedy them. Why is this? It is because the motive power is wanting. Representation is the motive power for the redress of legislative grievances. If not, what is the use of representation? Before the working classes were represented,[7] trades-unions were illegal associations, and consequently an absconding treasurer of one of these societies was liable to no legal punishment. Not one man in a thousand attempted to justify such an iniquity, even when it was an established institution. It was a recognised injustice; but it was not till the working classes were on the eve of obtaining a just share of representation that the motive power for the redress of that injustice was forthcoming.[8] The same thing can be said with regard to those laws which press unjustly on women. Hardly anyone defends them; it is not so much the sense of justice in parliament or in the country that is wanting as the motive power which representation alone in a self-governed country can give, to get a recognised wrong righted. Another illustration of the value of representation may be found in looking back at recent discussions on alterations in the land laws of England and Ireland. This legislation has been discussed, month in and month out, in the House of Commons and on every platform in the United Kingdom, as if the interests of two classes and two classes only had to be considered: those of the farmers and the landowners. The labourers have been apparently as much forgotten as if the land were ploughed and weeded and sown by fairies, and not by men and women, who stand at least as much in need of any good that law-making can do them as the other classes who are directly interested in the soil.

A curious illustration of the absolute neglect, so far as politics are concerned, of all who are not represented, or whom, it is expected, will be shortly represented, may be found in the accounts of the recent celebration of the Bright festival at Birmingham.[9] The Liberals who assembled to do the honour to Mr Bright which he so richly deserves, enumerated, in honest pride, the main achievements of Mr Bright's career; but they did not point to any chapter in the statute book and say, 'Here he succeeded in changing a condition of the law that was oppressive to women.' And this was so, although Mr Bright has, on more than one occasion – as, for example, on behalf of a bill enabling women to receive medical degrees[10] – lifted his powerful voice in favour of justice being done to women. Matters which affect injuriously, or the reverse, unrepresented classes, lie outside what are called practical politics. The politicians' field of vision is entirely filled by those who are represented; the unrepresented are forgotten. So, again, when the Birmingham Liberals let their imagination range over what was to be expected and worked for in the future, no mention was made of anything being done for women. Their ideal seemed rather to be manhood as opposed to universal suffrage; that is, all men not being either paupers or felons to be admitted to political power, no matter how ignorant, how poor, how degraded, in virtue of their manhood; while all women are to be excluded in virtue of their womanhood. The Birmingham imagination sees also with the eye of faith the payment of members. Members can only be paid by the taxpayers, that is the men and women of England; but the anomaly in a self-governed country of taking money from women to pay representatives without giving women any representation does not seem to have occurred to the political seer.

When, on July 6, the question of the removal of women's electoral disabilities was discussed in the House of Commons,[11] the chief point relied upon by the opponents of the resolution moved by Mr Mason[12] was that it was not clear whether the resolution, if carried, would have the effect of enfranchising married women, who, in virtue of the Married Women's Property Act,[13] are no longer precluded from possessing the necessary qualifications. It is no secret that some of those – for instance, Mr Mason himself – who are in favour of removing the disability of sex are not in favour of removing the disability of marriage, whilst others desire the removal of both disabilities. If Parliament should see fit to admit women to the benefits of representation, opportunity would no doubt be afforded, during the passage of a Reform Bill that extended the suffrage to women, for the House of Commons to declare distinctly whether it wishes to give the right of voting to married women who possess the qualification or not. In this, as in other matters, it appears to me very unpractical to reject a substantial measure of reform because it does not grant all that may be thought desirable. Personally I entirely sympathise with those who wish to see the disability of coverture removed.[14] If, however, the House of Commons is willing to remove the disability of sex but unwilling to remove the disability of coverture, I think those who represent the women's suffrage movement outside the House of Commons would be acting most unwisely to reject what is offered to them. Many of the supporters of the Reform Bills of '32[15] and '68[16] were in favour of universal suffrage, but had to be content with a smaller instalment of enfranchisement. Mr Chamberlain said the other day, at Birmingham, that Radicals nearly always had 'to accept a composition',[17] and the women's suffrage party may have to do the same.

I have said that the sense of justice is not so much wanting as the motive power which will convert a passive recognition of the existence of wrong into an active determination to get that wrong righted. It must not, however, be forgotten that, without being consciously unjust or cruel, there is such a thing as a torpid sense of justice. As the ear gets deafened and the vision gets blurred by frequent misuse, so the sense of justice becomes feeble and dim by constant association with laws and customs which are unjust. To live in a society whose laws give women 'something less than justice' is apt to pervert the conscience, and make those whose imagination is not very active acquiesce in injustice as if it were part of the inevitable nature of things. Magistrates, for example, who sometimes punish men less severely for half-killing their wives than for stealing half-a-crown, are partly responsible for this faulty sense of justice, and may be partly regarded as the victims of it. We want – to use an expression of Mr Matthew Arnold's – to call forth 'a fresh flow of consciousness'[18] on all these questions where the interests of women are concerned. We want to ask ourselves, and to set others to ask themselves, 'Ought these things to be supported because they exist?' 'Could we not come nearer to righteousness if we aimed at a higher ideal of justice?'

It will no doubt be argued by some, that while much yet remains to be done before the balance is adjusted, so as to give perfect justice to women, yet that much has already been done to improve their legal status, and that it is not too much to hope that in time all grievances will be redressed without giving women votes.[19] The Married Women's Property Act, it is said, has redressed a great and crying evil; why may not other evils be redressed in the same way? To such as use this argument it may be replied that, in the first place, the Married Women's Property Act would probably never have been introduced or heard of, if it had not been for the wider movement for the parliamentary representation of women. The women's suffrage societies, by constant and untiring efforts actively carried on for sixteen years, have done something to awaken that keener sense of justice to women to which reference has just been made. However, let it be supposed that this view of the history of the passing of the Married Women's Property Act is entirely erroneous, and let it be supposed that the Legislature have, of their own free will, quite unmoved by any representations made to them by women, been graciously pleased to say that married women may have what is their own. What right has any set of human beings to say to another, 'I concede to you that piece of justice, and I withhold this, not because you ask for either or can make me give you either, but because I choose to act so'? What is the policy, what is the sense, of compelling half the English people to hold their liberty on such terms as these? All this circumlocution is unnecessary and inexpedient. Give women the rights of free citizenship, the power to protect themselves, and they will let their representatives know what they want and why they want it. They will find, no doubt – as other classes have found – that though the price of liberty is vigilance, the House of Commons will never turn a deaf ear to well-considered measures of reform which are demanded by the constituencies.

This movement for the representation of women is nothing more nor less than a simple outgrowth of the democracy which has been the gradual product of this century. The old ideal of government, even in England, which has had representative institutions so long, was that the few should govern the many. The democratic ideal – which has been steadily growing here, on the Continent and in America – is that the many should govern themselves. When the representatives of the present electorate undertake a further extension of the suffrage, we ask them to be true to their own principles, to be just – even to women – without fear. If women are not excluded from the next Reform Bill, may we not anticipate the growth of new bonds of sympathy and union between men and women? Their lives will be less separated than they have hitherto been. It is one of the most disastrous things that can happen to a nation to have a great wall of separation, as regards opinion and feeling, grow up between men and women. This state of things is to be seen very conspicuously in some Catholic countries – such, for instance, as Belgium – where the women influenced by Catholicism, and the men influenced by a revolt against Catholicism, belong, as it were, to two entirely different strata of civilisation; and hence each sex loses a great part of what it might otherwise gain from sympathy and companionship with the other.[20] Every circumstance which widens the education of women – their political as well as their literary education – renders impossible the building up of that wall of separation. It may be said there is no danger of such a state of things in England; but if there is no danger of it, is it not because we have already gone so far along the road of giving equal justice to women? We have gone so far and with such good results there could hardly be a better reason for going further.

It is possible there may be some who have rather a dread of this demand for giving women votes, because it is so essentially modern. Few of the leading statesmen of the present day ever say anything in its favour, and fewer still of the political leaders of the past have supported it. It must, however, be remembered that when a politician becomes a political leader, his time is so much engrossed in carrying on the work of practical politics – that is, in one form or another, in obeying the behests of those who have political power – that he very seldom has time to give to other people's wants. We must not expect the initiative in this matter to come from Governments. We must ask those who have votes to help us, and let Governments know that they wish for justice for women as well as for themselves. All good things must have a beginning, and if this demand on the part of women for representation is good in itself, it is none the worse for being, as compared, say, with tyranny and selfishness, new. Christianity was a new thing once; even now – as we were reminded the other day – it is held to be true only by a minority of mankind; the belief in witchcraft was once universal and was shared even by the wisest and most cultivated of men. If there is a soul of goodness in things evil, may we not observingly distil out of the mistakes of the past something that will strengthen our hopes for the future? No one is wise enough or great enough to be able to set a limit upon the progress of mankind towards knowledge and well-doing. In the chapter of Grote's *History of Greece* on the attitude of the Greek mind towards the Greek myths,[21] the author shows how in the early dawn of Greek history, the belief was universal and unquestioned that all natural phenomena were the direct result of the personal intervention of gods and semi-divine beings. Then came, slowly and hesitantly, the beginning of what we have now learned to call 'natural science'; and little by little, the most cultivated classes began to seek to explain things according to some rational theory of the universe. They ceased to regard the personal intervention of Zeus or Demeter or Athene as a satisfactory explanation of the cause of storms, the fertility of the earth and other similar things. It is, however, remarkable that Socrates, although he lived well within the time when this dawn of natural science had begun, only partially discerned its future sway. He taught that there were two classes of phenomena, one produced by natural causes and one resulting from divine interposition; and he held that 'physics and astronomy belonged to the divine class of phenomena, in which human research was insane, fruitless and impious'.[22] Now is it not possible to take both courage and warning from this: courage not to limit our hopes for the future, not to say this aim is too high ever to be realised, and warning to have no *popes* in our protestant minds? The best and wisest of human beings is liable to err. Let us think for ourselves – weigh diligently the reasons of the faith that is in us, and strive earnestly for all things that we believe to be just and reasonable.

Transcribed from editor's own copy. No known copyright restrictions.

Notes

1. The Third Reform Act, 1884, which 'established a uniform franchise throughout the country' and 'brought the franchise in the counties into line with the 1867 householder and lodger franchise for boroughs', while still excluding women from the vote (Parliament.uk n.d.h).
2. In 1635, the English landowner and politician John Hampden (1595–1643) opposed arbitrary 'ship money' taxes imposed by Charles I, establishing the principle of 'no taxation without representation', which contributed to the constitutional crises leading to the English Civil War. (This phrase also went on to become one of the avowed principles of the American Revolution in 1776.) Hampden was a major inspiration to the women's suffrage cause, appearing, for example, on the Women's Tax Resistance League banner (Joannou and Purvis 1998, 65).
3. An older form of 'peaceable', or of a peaceful character.
4. The Cobden Club was a Victorian gentlemen's club, only without its own premises. It was founded in 1866 for believers in free trade, and named after Richard Cobden (1804–65). Joseph Chamberlain (1836–1914), then president of the Board of Trade, presided over the Cobden Club annual dinner on 30 June 1883 at the Ship Hotel, Greenwich, which was reported widely in the press, saying words to this effect. See, for example, *St James's Gazette* (1883, 11).
5. Presumably referring to the assassination of Alexander II (1818–81), who had emancipated Russia's serfs in 1861, and the reign of Alexander III (1845–94), who reversed many of his father's liberal reforms (Lieven 2015).
6. Fawcett's footnote: 'Mr Gladstone's speech in the House of Commons on the Women's Suffrage Bill 1871.' See HC Deb 1871a. William Ewart Gladstone, then the prime minister, used this phrase upon various occasions in his speeches.
7. Under the Second Reform Act, 1867; see note 8.
8. The Trade Union Act of 1871 established the legal status of trade unions (HC Deb 1871b).
9. On 14 June 1883, 'Mr Bright was entertained by the Liberals of Birmingham at a banquet in the Town Hall. The gathering was one of the most brilliant of the kind that had taken place in the town for many years . . . in honour of the twenty-fifth anniversary of Mr Bright's representation of Birmingham' (*Birmingham Daily Post* 1883). The menu included clear turtle soup, pigeon pies, *suedoise* of apricots and vol-au-vent of gooseberries.
10. See, for example, his speeches on the Enabling Act, which meant that women doctors who had trained abroad could potentially register to practise in Britain (HC Deb 1876).
11. Parliamentary Franchise (Extension to Women); see HC Deb (1883, 664–724).
12. Hugh Mason (1817–86), English mill owner, social reformer and Liberal politician. His daughter Bertha (1855–1939) was an English suffragist and temperance campaigner.
13. Presumably a reference to the 1882 Act which had significantly changed the property rights of married women in England, Wales and Ireland, allowing them to own and control property themselves. There had been a previous act in 1870, amended in 1874. See Erickson 2002.
14. Coverture was the legal doctrine 'which subsumed a married woman's legal and financial identity under that of her husband', placing 'strict limits on the formal economic activities of English women' (Finn 1996, 704). Fawcett herself was acutely aware of 'this monstrous state of the law': attending a London court at the trial of a youth who had snatched her handbag at Waterloo station, 'I saw the charge sheet, and noted that the thief was charged with "stealing from the person of Millicent Fawcett a purse . . . the property of Henry Fawcett". I felt as if I had been charged with theft myself' (Fawcett 1924, 62).
15. The Representation of the People Act 1832, which created new constituencies, 'broadened the franchise's property qualification in the counties to include small landowners . . . and created a uniform franchise in the boroughs, giving the vote to all householders who paid a yearly rental of £10 or more and some lodgers' (Parliament.uk n.d.f).

16. The 1867 Reform Act 'granted the vote to all householders in the boroughs as well as lodgers who paid rent of £10 a year or more' and 'reduced the property threshold in the counties and gave the vote to agricultural landowners and tenants with very small amounts of land' (Parliament.uk n.d.c).
17. Mr Chamberlain, speaking after Mr John Bright at a meeting of the Birmingham Liberal Association in Bingley Hall, 13 June 1883. 'What was now wanted, he said, was an extension of the suffrage, equal electoral districts, and payment of members, and although they might have once more to accept a composition in the matter of bankruptcy, yet under his bill they would not give a debtor his discharge' (*Morning Post* 1883).
18. Matthew Arnold (1822–88) was an English poet and cultural critic. This is presumably a reference to Arnold's *Culture and Anarchy* (1869), where he regularly refers to consciousness; for example: 'In the meanwhile, since our Liberal friends keep loudly and resolutely assuring us that their actual operations at present are fruitful and solid, let us in each case keep testing these operations in the simple way we have indicated, by letting the natural stream of our consciousness flow over them freely' (Arnold 1869, 254).
19. Fawcett's footnote: 'The Birmingham programme does not lend much probability to this hopeful view of women's prospects of getting the benefits of representation without votes.'
20. This is a very simplified account of the waves of secularisation, and resulting societal tensions with the Catholic Church, throughout Belgium in the nineteenth century. See Lesthaeghe and Lopez Gay (2013, 85) for a more evidenced overview.
21. 'Grecian Mythes, as understood, felt and interpreted by the Greeks themselves' (Grote 1854, Chapter XVI, 460–615). The historian and politician George Grote (1794–1871) and his wife Harriet Grote (1792–1878) were friends of the Fawcetts, and Harriet was herself a suffragist and author (Fawcett 1924, 60–1).
22. Grote (1854, 500).

12
The protection of girls: speech or silence, 1885

Contemporary Review. September 1885, 326–31.

Following a period of mourning after the sudden death of her husband in late 1884, Fawcett returned 'both to feminist and wider political activity with undiminished enthusiasm and effectiveness' (Rubinstein 1991, 65). 'For several years good men in both Houses of Parliament had been trying to pass a Criminal Law Amendment Bill, giving additional protection to young children', with little success (Fawcett 1924, 128). To force the issue, in July 1885, the *Pall Mall Gazette* published a series of controversial articles on child prostitution titled 'The Maiden Tribute of Modern Babylon' (referring to the Minotaur's virgin sacrifice). The editor, William Thomas Stead (1849–1912), undertook risky (and unlawful) investigative journalism to show that the abduction, procurement and sale of young English girls aged twelve or thirteen was possible in London, by himself purchasing and drugging a girl named Eliza Armstrong (although she remained otherwise unharmed, he claimed). Salacious and licentious, the articles contained headings such as 'Virgins Willing and Unwilling' and 'Strapping Girls Down'. 'The effect was instantaneous and worldwide. The articles set all London and the whole country in a blaze of indignation' and 'The Bill, which a few weeks previously the Government had said they could not touch, and was consequently regarded as hopeless, was now revised and strengthened and passed into law with utmost despatch: one man, single handed, had coerced an unwilling legislature' (Fawcett 1924, 130).[1]

However, the scandal grew throughout the summer, and in September 1885, Stead was convicted of assault and abduction while undertaking his investigation: 'It mattered nothing that the child had been protected and sheltered at every turn from any possible evil befalling her. Stead was believed to have broken the law, and could, and should, bear the penalty' (Fawcett 1924, 130). This public controversy had a lasting effect on journalism (Soderlund 2013). Fawcett also believed that this directly impacted public opinion on the suffrage of women, and wrote the following about the incident in a letter to her friend, the trade union organiser Emma Miller (1839–1917): 'I think all the deep feeling that has been aroused by a knowledge of the facts will make a great many people understand for the first time one of the reasons why women ought to have votes' (Fawcett, quoted in Strachey 1931, 109).

Fawcett had strong views on the topic of purity and morality and, originally influenced by John Stuart Mill, had previously believed that suffrage work should not be 'associated in the public mind with issues arising from prostitution' (Rubinstein 1991, 46). In 1875 she had objected to the pregnancy of the unmarried suffrage campaigner Elizabeth Wolstenholme (1833–1918), being one of those who forced her to marry the father of her unborn child, the silk mill owner and feminist Benjamin Elmy (1838–1906), under threat of being barred from any further involvement in the women's movement (Rubinstein 1991, 55).[2] By the 1880s, however, attitudes had changed, and the topic of social purity was one to which Fawcett now devoted herself. 'The Protection of Girls: Speech or Silence' argues for better legislative frameworks to protect young women and children. The Criminal Law Amendment Act was passed in August 1885 (close to the time of publication of this column): the Act raised the age of consent for women from 13 to 16, suppressed brothels and strengthened existing legislation against prostitution, criminalising the procuring of girls by fraud, intimidation or the administration of drugs. Fawcett's approach to how outspoken and frank she should be on these topics did change over time: in 1917 she produced a measured, factual account of 'The Problem of Venereal Diseases', which had seen increased outbreaks since the start of the Great War. Fawcett characteristically proposed 'more efficient organisation for dealing with it' (1917c, 156).

*

The whole of England has during the last six weeks been deeply stirred, as it only is when some great question is being discussed which involves a principle of faith or morals. In such questions every one is, as it were, compelled to form an opinion and take a side. No one is neutral. In our time such questions have generally been mixed up with foreign affairs, and therefore with party politics. The long struggle for Italian independence,[3] the American Civil War,[4] involving the principles of human freedom, the treatment of Bulgaria by Turkey,[5] evoking sentiments somewhat similar to those raised by the present agitation, directly concerned the political action of England; became immediately, therefore, party questions, and were fully discussed by leading newspapers and by leading public men on both sides. The present agitation resembles those to which reference has just been made, as regards to the deep and passionate emotion of which it is the outcome; it differs from them in the fact that it is not mixed up with party politics, and that in the endeavour to form a just and fair opinion on the questions raised, the people have been deprived of the guidance of their usual leaders. Nearly the whole of the London press has been silent, or has spoken only to advocate silence and condemn speech. Political leaders have been silent; and for the first time probably in their experience they have been dumb spectators of a movement which has deeply stirred the heart and conscience of the nation. The result has been for the moment to turn the mind of part at least of the public from the question 'How can the evils exposed by the *Pall Mall Gazette* best be combated?' to another question: 'Is more harm than good done by speech of any kind about these evils?'

A hideously perverted state of morals have been exposed, running through, so far as one sex is concerned, the whole of Society, from the highest to the lowest; whilst, so far as the other sex is concerned, it condemns the poorest, most ignorant and most helpless to a living death of unspeakable degradation, and drags down certain others, through appeals to their cupidity, to a much lower depth of infamy and shame, that of living in luxury on the trade of decoying and selling children and their fellow-women. There are those who, following the lead of the *Pall Mall*, say the first step towards finding a remedy for this terrible social evil is to let in the light upon these deeds of darkness, to bring the force of public opinion to bear on those who commit them and on those who profit by them; and there are others, of whom the ablest and most respected are well represented by Mr Llewelyn Davies, who strongly condemn open speech on these subjects, who deeply deplore 'the tearing aside of the veils',[6] and who believe that this agitation is setting at naught the traditions of civilization and morality; they quote St Paul in the verse where he says, 'It is a shame even to speak of those things that are done of them in secret.'[7]

It seems not inopportune to offer a few considerations in support of those who believe that the balance of evidence inclines in favour of plain speech and against silence. In the first place, the silent system has had a long trial, and the most optimistic can hardly claim that it has succeeded. Crimes against children, according to the testimony of those who have sifted the facts, have been, of recent years, alarmingly on the increase. Those who, with Mr Hopwood, condemn the agitation, and condemn the effect it has had in hastening a change in the law, rely principally upon the statement that the law, as it stood before the recent passing of the Criminal Law Amendment Act, was strong enough, and that what was defective was the administration of the law. Can anything be plainer proof of the want of a good wholesome severity of public opinion on these matters? Children were entrapped and sold and ruined; and though the law condemned the crime, the criminals remained unpunished because the administration of the law was defective: the police would not move, the Home Office would not move and the law remained a dead letter. Was it not time for speech when silence had led to such a state of things as this?

Those who have the best opportunity of knowing the truth have of late spoken with the deepest grief of the state of the public schools as regards morals. May not this also be a result of the silent system? If fathers and mothers and schoolmasters would realize the duty of speech on this most vital and solemn of questions, might not some good result be looked for? If lying or stealing, or if any merely ungentlemanly habit were rife in schools, would it be best dealt with by absolute silence on the subject, and by a careful veiling from the general public of all knowledge of the mischief? The secrecy which has hitherto surrounded these sins can hardly have acted otherwise than as an encouragement to them. Crimes that are nearly certain to be followed by exposure and disgrace are very rare except in what are known as the criminal classes. It takes away one of the safeguards against immorality to cloak it in an impenetrable mystery.

A great part of the evil, everyone agrees, comes from the want of a good tone of morals running through society. A man who, a few years ago, was turned out of the English army for a criminal assault upon a girl was last year re-elected to one of the most select and fashionable of London clubs, and a petition was signed by large numbers of great people, praying that he might be reinstated in the English army.[8] Rumour said that the petition would have been successful but for the fact that the ultimate decision lay with the Queen. The case is significant as an illustration of the want of a healthy tone of public opinion. No one tries to reinstate in his clubs or in the army a man who has cheated at cards, or who has been condemned for cowardice by a court-martial. Public opinion is strong and outspoken with regard to deeds like these, and they are correspondingly rare. By encouraging expressions condemnatory of the kind of vice exposed by the *Pall Mall,* even on the part of those who do not approve of the agitation, a more healthy tone of public opinion is being formed. The *Times*, following the counsel of Mr Llewelyn Davies, advocates the formation of 'Vigilance Committees' throughout the country[9] to see that the new law does not remain a dead letter: the *Spectator* writes in favour of the use of the lash for the worst kind of offenders. These, and many similar expressions of opinion, might be quoted, partly as evidence of the improvement in moral tone that has already taken place, and partly as the means by which a still further improvement may be looked for. It is difficult to avoid the conclusion that one of the first results of the recent outspokenness is that people have been in some cases awakened from a lethargy, and in others stimulated to a greater activity of mind in regard to the efforts to be made to suppress the lowest forms of vice. Almost every one has the same experience to record. Those who were already, with noble self-devotion, giving up their lives to promote the cause of purity[10] are greatly strengthened and encouraged by what has recently taken place; their only anxiety seems to be lest there should be a reaction of indifference after this great outburst of grief and shame. Those who have never worked before in any of these questions are saying to themselves with anxious heart-searching, 'What can I do to help on the right side?'

A comparison has frequently been made between the present agitation and that concerning the Bulgarian atrocities.[11] There is a resemblance, but there is also a great difference. There has been little or no Pharisaism in the present agitation. The pervading tone of the meetings have been one of deep humiliation and self-reproach. Men and women have been made to feel that simply to live encased in the hard shell of their own righteousness, without making any effort to save those poor children from their destroyers, is to be guilty of the worst of cowardice. Those who loved purity before do not love it less now; but they can no longer believe it to be consistent with their duty to hug the robe of their holiness around them and stretch out no helping hand to those who are wallowing in the mire. Better even that their own snowy whiteness should be smirched than that they should leave their brothers and sisters to perish.

There is some fear of falling into a sort of insincerity in speaking of these subjects, as if they had never been known or heard of till the *Pall Mall* proclaimed them. There are probably no men and very few women to whom the statements were really revelations. The *Pall Mall* has not so much told us what we did not know before, as whipped and lashed us up to a sense of our dastardly cowardice in knowing these things and making no effort to stop them. We have all seen and known people whose characters might otherwise have been beautiful and noble, who have shipwrecked their own lives, and the lives of many others, on the rock of coarse and brutal sensualism; and hardly an effort has been made either to save them or to warn others. If we had seen similar shipwreck made by drunkenness or gambling, we should not have been so cowardly; but on one of the most dangerous shores we have raised no lighthouse and manned no lifeboat. There are many men and women of saint-like lives, who have been showing us our duty by patient example for years; but this did not suffice to rouse us: we needed a coarser instrument – the lash – and we have had it from the editor of the *Pall Mall*.

It has been not a little surprising that during the recent controversy as to the duty of speech or silence, certain passages from the Epistles of St Paul have been quoted in support of silence. It would be difficult to find an epistle to any of the churches that does not specifically and in detail denounce the moral evils of the world Paul lived in. When he says, 'It's a shame *even to speak* of those things that are done of them in secret', or, 'Let it not be once named amongst you',[12] surely the whole context shows that this was an emphatic way of warning the Christian Churches against certain evil deeds, and that these passages cannot fairly be interpreted to mean that the deeds themselves, when rife, should be unreproved. Indeed, when St Paul makes use of the expression, 'Let it not be once named amongst you,' he refers not only to uncleanness, but also to coveteousness [sic], foolish talking and jesting; thereby making it clear (even if, by his own example, it were not clear already) what his meaning was. The Bible has before now been used to support slavery and polygamy; and even efforts to lift up the poor from the depths of their misery have been reproved by the text, 'The poor you have always with you.'[13] Isolated texts do not count for much in such matters. The spirit of the New Testament is the spirit of equality, and it is this spirit which, as it gradually gains strength, condemns institutions, such as slavery and polygamy, which are based on inequality. This spirit also condemns the making of one law for the rich, another for the poor; one law for the man, another for the woman. In regard to the present agitation, this spirit of equality is making itself felt and heard. The evil state of the law, the evil state of the general tone of public opinion in regard to morals, is an outcome of the subjection of women, of the notion that women are possessions or chattels, with whom men are fully justified in dealing as they please. If women had been able to protect themselves by legitimate use of the parliamentary franchise, the Criminal Law Amendment Bill would have been passed in the ordinary course of things without the necessity of shaking the whole of England by the recent agitation. Parliament cannot, as a rule, spare time for a serious effort to remedy the grievances of non-electors. If an illustration is wanted, it may be found in the fate of the Infants Bill, giving married mothers some minimum of legal right to the guardianship of their own children. The subject has not been dealt with seriously in Parliament. In the session of 1884, it was passed in the House of Commons and rejected by the House of Lords; in the session of 1885, it was passed by the House of Lords and allowed to lapse in the House of Commons.[14] How differently the Medical Relief Bill[15] fared, that had the supposed interests of the newly enfranchised agricultural labourers behind it; in the House of Commons the rival parties were eagerly outbidding each other in regard to it, and in the House of Peers noble lords quarrelled over the honour of having charge of it.

Deep down at the bottom of the questions that have been raised by the recent agitation is the economical and political subjection of women; their miserably low wages in the poorest classes, wages on which life can hardly be supported unless recourse is had to the better-paid trade of sin. If a real remedy is to be found, it must be sought in two ways, both full of difficulties and needing patience, enthusiasm, courage and faith. The demand for victims must be diminished by a growth of unselfishness and of purity of heart among men; the supply of victims must be diminished by giving the poorest women more opportunities of fairly remunerative employment, by insisting on an extension to women of the trades-union doctrine of a fair day's pay for a fair day's work, by improvement in the dwellings of the poorest classes, and by endeavouring to form in every girl's mind a worthy ideal of womanhood. Every one of these agencies of reform will need prolonged and incessant effort; the widest experience and wisdom will be needed; the best men and women in England ought to be called upon to occupy themselves with any fragment of this work for which they feel any aptitude. How is this great machinery of moral reform to be set going? Some maintain that it will best be set going by saying nothing about the need for it, or by referring to the need for it in veiled language which few can understand. Others say, by proclaiming the need for it far and wide, so that the whole nation shall not choose but hear.

Transcribed from a copy in the British Library.
No known copyright restrictions.

Notes

1 The Criminal Law Amendment Act 1885.
2 Sylvia Pankhurst provides the background to this incident and describes the reaction as 'much fluttering in the suffrage dovecotes' (1931, 31).
3 Rebellions in Italy contesting the Congress of Vienna and the restoration of old boundaries began in the 1820s, followed by the revolutions of 1848 and the Italian wars of independence, which finally saw Italy declared a united nation-state in 1861 (see Collier 2003).

4 1861 to 1865 (see Weigley 2004).
5 The conflict to free the Balkan nations from the Ottoman Empire (see Glenny 2012).
6 The Reverend John Llewelyn Davies (1826–1916) in a letter to the *Times* (Davies 1885, 6): 'It must be perplexing to many persons to find that so grave a difference of opinion exists among those to whose authority they would naturally defer on such a subject, with regard to the revelations of brutal wickedness with which the air has lately been poisoned . . . Let me add that almost every clergyman with whom I have conversed on the subject has deplored and condemned in the strongest manner the free unveiling of things over which it has been hitherto usual to draw a cover of decency. A master of a great public school has spoken to me with emotion of the irreparable mischief being done by this tearing aside of veils.' John was brother to Emily Davies (see Introduction), who was a friend of Elizabeth Garrett Anderson.
7 Ephesians 5:12.
8 Colonel Valentine Baker (or 'Baker Pasha', 1827–87), a distinguished officer, aged 50, who on 17 June 1875 assaulted and attempted to rape Miss Kate Rebecca Dickinson in a train carriage near Woking. He was sentenced to a year in prison and dismissed from service: the trial is detailed in the *Gloucester Journal* 1875. He then served in the Ottoman Army, demonstrating much bravery. He commanded the Egyptian police from 1882 until his death in 1887. A campaign to have him reinstated to the British Army (because of this gallantry) began in the early 1880s, and by 1884 a petition had 'been signed by 12,000 persons, including several Peers and members of the House of Commons' (*Edinburgh Evening News* 1884).
9 In his letter to the *Times* (Davies 1885).
10 The 'Cause of Purity' was the campaign against prostitution, which had a relationship with the campaign for votes for women and with the Christian morality of the age; see Roberts 1912 for a pamphlet on the subject.
11 The April Uprising was an insurrection organised by the Bulgarians in the Ottoman Empire in 1876 which was brutally suppressed. Henry Fawcett led protests: 'He shared the indignation aroused in England by the Bulgarian atrocities: he presided at a great meeting held at Exeter Hall on 19 September 1876 and called upon his hearers to pronounce themselves emphatically in support of Mr Gladstone, who now came from his partial retirement to head the popular movement' (Stephen 2011, 406).
12 Ephesians 5:3.
13 Matthew 26:11; also, John 12:8.
14 See HC Deb 1885. The Guardianship of Infants Act was passed in 1886, which granted judges 'the authority to consider the welfare of the infant as a point of concern equal to that of the interests of both parents'; see Holmes (1997, 52).
15 The Medical Relief Bill of 1885, which removed the disqualification from voting for those whose only income was parish medical aid. The disparity between the treatment of these two bills is covered in Stanton, Anthony and Gage 1887: 'This delay stands in sharp and painful contrast . . . parliament therefore found time amidst all the press of business and party divisions to pass the Medical Relief bill removing this disfranchisement from men, though we are repeatedly assured that nothing but the want of time prevents their fair consideration of the enfranchisement of women. It is another proof that there is always time for a representative government to attend to the wants of its constituents' (p. 890).

13
Employment for girls: the civil service (the Post Office), 1887

Atalanta. Vol. 1, No. 3, 174–6.

In this article Millicent Fawcett details the practical ways in which her husband Henry Fawcett, who had been an innovative Postmaster General from 1880 until his death in 1884, had improved working conditions for women and opportunities for their employment. 'The new Postal Order Branch was placed entirely in women's hands. I remember being taken over this branch and seeing the women clerks there . . . This to me was miraculous' (Fawcett 1924, 109). Here, she presents it as an attractive employment option for the readers of *Atalanta*, a popular monthly girls' magazine published between 1887 and 1898 which sought to widen girls' aspirations via articles and stories.[1] Interestingly, Rubinstein mentions that W. T. Stead, the editor of the *Pall Mall Gazette*, wrote to Millicent Fawcett in 1883, asking her 'to contribute an article on the work of women in the Post Office' (1991, 60). This was the start of their 30-year working relationship, although at that time she replied to say she would rather write about the suffrage question.[2]

*

There is a very familiar problem which is submitted to some of us almost daily for solution: 'What can a fairly educated girl, not of the working class, do to earn her own living if she is not fitted for teaching?' Eighty or a hundred years ago the answer would have been: 'By needlework.' Many women whose names afterwards gained an honourable place in our literature maintained themselves for a time, or assisted to support their families, by their needle. The sprigged muslins and tambour work of our grandmothers were often the product of the industry of gentlewomen.

Among those who earned money in this way before they learnt that the pen was more profitable than the needle, were Mary Wollstonecraft,[3] Mary Lamb[4] and Harriet Martineau.[5] 'I do dearly love worked muslin,' wrote Mary Lamb,[6] and the taste in her day was very general. Machinery and printing have almost superseded this industry as a means of livelihood; and so far as there is still a demand for hand-worked embroidery, it is supplied from Ireland, Switzerland and other localities at prices which leave a very bare remuneration for the labour entailed in production. Readers of Harriet Martineau's autobiography will remember her touching account, how, in her girlhood, she pored over fine needlework all day and sat up till two or three o'clock in the morning, night after night, to study and work with her pen, and how when she first began to feel that she had something to say and the power to say it, nearly all her relatives strongly opposed her giving up the substance, i.e. the pittance she earned by needlework, for the shadow, literary success.[7]

Artistic needlework requires a considerable degree of artistic faculty; and what are girls to do, if they are not artists and are not qualified to teach?

Employment in the several departments of the Post Office where women are engaged offers many advantages for the class of girls to whom I am referring. There are some rather general misconceptions on this subject which it would be well to remove. Very often when a girl, brought up as a lady, is asked if she would like to go into the Post Office, she answers in the negative, because she thinks she is being asked if she would like the work which she sees being done by young women behind the counter in the baker's or stationer's shop round the corner. These shops in which postal business is carried on are called in familiar parlance 'post offices'; but they are more strictly termed in official language 'receiving offices'. The young women employed in them are not in the service of the General Post Office at all. They are employed by the owner of the shop and are responsible to him; he only is responsible to the Department. They are not 'in the service' even in the sense that the letter-carrier is, and it is almost as great a mistake to confound them with the female clerks in the General Post Office as it would be to confuse in one's mind a shopman in an Italian warehouse with a Foreign Office clerk.

A large part of the clerical work in the Savings Bank Department of the General Post Office has always been done by ladies. At first the appointments were reserved exclusively for 'the daughters of gentlemen'. Nominations were given by the Postmaster-General of the day to these ladies, and private interest or political patronage was generally needed to obtain a nomination. When nominated, a limited form of competition took place, three of the nominees competing for each appointment. In 1881, Mr Fawcett, who was then Postmaster-General, felt that it would be better for the public service, and for the female clerks themselves, to remove this limitation of the service to daughters of gentlemen. He would have found it an unendurable burden to have to decide upon each application that was made to him, whether the social position of the father of the candidate was on this side or that of the shadowy boundary line which separates gentle from simple. He endeavoured for a time to select for nomination those applicants who stood most in need of remunerative employment. But the choice was often extremely difficult, and where there were so many needy applicants, it can easily be imagined that the duty of discriminating among them was very distressing. For a short time previous to his abolition of the nomination system, he nominated every applicant who was within the regulation limits of age and could give satisfactory assurances with regard to health and character. The girls thus nominated, as well as those whose names were on the nomination list of his predecessor in the office of Postmaster-General, competed against one another for the female clerkships vacant between the middle of 1880 and the middle of 1881. In the latter year the appointments were thrown open to unrestricted competition, and the nomination system was entirely abolished. The only restrictions upon the candidates from 1881 and onwards are:

1. That their age on the first day of the competitive examination is not less than 18 nor more than 20.
2. That they are unmarried, or widows.
3. That they are duly qualified in respect of health and character.

Candidates have also, before entering upon the competitive examination, to submit to a preliminary test examination in handwriting, spelling and arithmetic, the object of which is to prevent disappointment and waste of time by sifting out any who are obviously unfit, through defective education, for the work expected of them.

The subjects of the Competitive Examination are Arithmetic, English Composition, Geography and English History. Of these subjects, I believe it is no secret that arithmetic is the most important; the work in the Savings Bank Department consists almost entirely of book-keeping, and a good head for figures is one of the most necessary qualifications which a candidate can have. It is hardly necessary, perhaps, to add that orthography[8] and handwriting are also very important. A considerable proportion of the failures are due to bad spelling and untidy writing.

A savings bank clerk must not only have a good head for figures, but must be capable of keeping up the high standard of marvellously neat bookkeeping, which tradition has handed down in the department. The salary attaching to these clerkships for women commence in London at £65 a year, and increases by £3 a year to £80. In Dublin and Edinburgh the salary begins at £55 and rises to £70. Higher salaries in all the offices are obtained by those who are promoted to the higher classes of the service: such promotion depends on merit and capacity. The highest salary earned by women in the General Post Office is £300.

When Mr Fawcett first became Postmaster-General, the initial salary of the 2nd class female clerks in the Savings Bank was only £40. He became convinced, as a result of careful personal inquiry, that this rate of salary, rather less than 15*s*. 6*d*. a week, was less than what was paid for equally skilled labour in the open market: it was less, for instance, than what could be earned by a tolerably skilful needlewoman or charwoman. He also found that the health of the female clerks decidedly improved as soon as they had been long enough in the service to have secured a higher rate of remuneration. It must be remembered that the Postmaster-General is himself a servant of the Treasury, and he cannot do anything which involves expenditure of the funds of the department without the consent of the Treasury. Mr Fawcett was not therefore able himself to raise the salaries of the female clerks, but he wrote a minute to the Lords of the Treasury strongly urging the claim of these women to a more liberal scale of remuneration. He had the altogether unprecedented pleasure and satisfaction of getting from the Treasury more than he had asked for. I shall not easily forget his jubilation over this good fortune. Lavish generosity is, very properly, not a quality which distinguishes the guardians of the public purse. They had been known, very frequently, to refuse altogether to entertain applications for an increase of salary: they had been known, less frequently, to grant a quarter of the increase asked for: they had been known in a very few instances to grant all that had been asked; but they never before had been known to grant more than they had been asked for. Mr Fawcett asked that the initial salary should be raised from £40 to £50, and the sum actually granted was £65. The late Lord Frederick Cavendish[9] was Secretary to the Treasury at the time; and to him was probably due the substantial increase just referred to.

It will be easily understood that the opening of the appointments to competition, unrestricted by the nomination system, coupled with the subsequent increase in the scale of salary, caused a great increase in the number of applicants for vacant posts. This rendered it necessary to increase considerably the difficulty of the examination, and to further restrict the limit of age according to the rule which has been already quoted. Only those can now become candidates who are between eighteen and twenty. This rule not only limits the number competing for appointments, but tends to the efficiency of the service. Generally speaking, those girls make the best clerks who take to the work while they are young: at eighteen or thereabouts, they are fairly fresh from school and are used to regular hours and steady work, and are sufficiently teachable to learn their new duties without difficulty and without friction.

The popularity of the service and the need there is for similar employment among women may be measured by the enormous number of candidates who present themselves for the competitive examinations. On one occasion, when 145 additional women clerks were needed, there were 2,500 candidates for the vacant posts. Facts like these always weighed on Mr Fawcett's mind: he vividly pictured to himself the urgent need for employment among women and the keen disappointment felt by the unsuccessful candidates. He placed himself, in imagination, in the position of these girls, and he often said that the eagerness with which the appointments were sought by well-educated women lifted a veil from an amount of want and privation, patiently borne and carefully hidden, which he had not previously guessed at. From this time he did all he could to open to women additional branches of Post Office work. The clerical work connected with the Postal-Order branch, established in 1881, was entrusted entirely to women. A large number of women had long been employed in the Receiver and Accountant General's office. The number of women employed here, in the Savings Bank and in the Postal Order branch gradually increased. More employment for women in the lower branches of the service was also offered. The number of female telegraphists and counterwomen grew with the natural growth of the business of the department, and a new class of employment was offered for girls of the upper artisan class, that of 'sorter' in the Savings Bank. The number of women employed in the General Post-Office increased very considerably between the years 1880 and 1884. In the Postmaster General's Report of 1881, the number of women employed in the service is quoted as over 2,000. In 1884 the number given is 2,731, of whom 586 were clerks in the central establishments of London, Edinburgh and Dublin. The number of female clerks in these establishments is now (1887) 750, and there are also 36 women thus employed in the provinces. The number of women now employed throughout the country as telegraphists, counterwomen, sorters, &c. is 2,981. (See pp. 24 and 25 of the Postmaster-General's Report of 1887.)

It may be surprising to some readers to know how eagerly these positions in the Post Office, at very moderate salaries, are competed for.

The money earned is not so much as that gained by a high school teacher; but it must be remembered that a high school teacher requires to be able to give proof of an exceptionally good education. She will probably be spending money, or her parents will be spending it for her, in procuring her the necessary training, long after the girl clerk in the Post Office has begun to earn her £65 or £70 a year. It is one of the things most important for women to remember that good work and good wages can only be performed and secured by those who submit to a due amount of professional training and preparation. Miss Nightingale has spoken with great force on this subject. In a letter of advice to young women about their work, she says: 'I would say also to all young ladies who are called to any particular vocation, qualify yourselves for it as a man does for his work. Don't think you can undertake it otherwise.'[10] The time and expense required in the preparation for teaching are greater than for success in becoming a Post Office clerk. This is one reason of the greater competition for these posts. But other reasons are to be found in the inherent attractiveness of Government employment. One great charm about it is certainty. Unless a girl marries, or voluntarily retires for some reason, her appointment in the Civil Service is for life, barring, of course, crass incapacity or misconduct. Another charm is that an annuity is secured after long years of service; and the salary is not stopped or withdrawn during temporary sickness. The hours are not heavy, from ten to four, for five days in the week, with a shorter day on Saturday; extra work means extra pay. Medical attendance is provided at the expense of the Department. In London, Liverpool and Manchester, the post of medical officer falling vacant in these places during the time Mr Fawcett was Postmaster-General, he appointed female medical officers to take charge of the health of the women employed in those Post Offices.

It will naturally be inquired how the women clerks do their work. It is not very long since it was considered an almost self-evident proposition that women were incapable of arithmetic. Dora's figures that would not add up[11] were supposed to be typical of all female attempts at book-keeping. As a matter of fact, the women clerks in the Savings Bank have done, and are doing, their work excellently. I have seen girls rapidly turning over a large pile of statements of the Savings Bank transactions that are sent in daily from every provincial post office to the London centre, and adding the totals together by mental arithmetic so quickly that the process, to one unaccustomed to such feats, seemed nothing less than miraculous.

The conduct of the female clerks is excellent; their health is not all that could be wished, but they generally become stronger after a few years' experience of the best way of taking care of themselves. They require, or at least they have, less superintendence than the men clerks in the same division; in the female branch there are ten superintending officers to two hundred and sixty clerks, or one superintendent to every twenty-six clerks, while in the men's branch there are fifty-five superior appointments to six hundred ordinary clerks, or one superintendent over every eleven clerks. The women clerks do the same amount of work at the same average per hour as the men. They have shown themselves particularly capable of figure-work and book-keeping. I remember being shown some of the books of the Savings Bank Division by the late Mr Ramsay, who was head of that branch of the department. He was a Scotchman, who measured every word he said, and he was very proud of the exquisite order and neatness with which the huge tomes were filled with closely packed ranks of figures. Laying his hand upon one of the open ledgers, he said, 'There was a time when I did not believe that females were capable of keeping books like this.' On more than one occasion the work done by women in the Post Office has been referred to in the Annual Reports of the Postmaster-General as particularly good, and to the advantage of the public service. It is obvious that the public gain by the employment of women; the quality of their work is as good as that of the men in the same branches, and their salary is a good deal lower, hence a considerable departmental economy is secured by extending the employment of women wherever work suitable for them is to be found.

It is one of the objects of this paper to supply as much practical information as possible to those who may be thinking of Post Office employment for themselves or their friends. It is therefore desirable to add that all applications from those who wish to become candidates should be sent to the Civil Service Commissioners, Cannon Row, Westminster, from whom also can be obtained information about the time of the examinations, and the qualifications and conditions imposed on candidates. Full information on these points, besides more detailed accounts of what is expected of candidates, can be obtained from a very useful shilling manual published by Messrs Cassell, called a 'Guide to Female Employment in Government Offices'.[12] In this little book are given specimens of the examination papers, and a number of useful hints to intending candidates. I have purposely refrained from entering in detail upon the employment of women as telegraphists and counterwomen in the General Post Office, as I intend this paper more especially for the use of girls of a higher class. Much of what has been said, however, as to the advantages of Government employment, is as applicable to the telegraphists and counterwomen as to the clerks. Female telegraph learners begin on 10s. a week; when they are capable of taking charge of an instrument they have 14s., and their wages are gradually raised in the 2nd class to 27s. a week. When they reach the 1st class, their wages begin at 28s. a week, to 34s. There are also a few superior appointments, which form the prizes of this branch of the Service, with salaries ranging from £110 to £250 a year. Messrs Cassell's guide will supply all information about the conditions of employment and the nature of the requisite examination and training.

It may fairly be quoted as one of the grievances of women that although their employment as civil servants has been so highly successful, no attempt has been made to open to them work in any other Government office besides the Post Office. Royal Commissions sit from time to time to consider how economy may best be secured in the Civil Service, but it does not seem to occur to the Commissioners to recommend that the example set by the Post Office should be copied, and that women should be employed as clerks in the fashionable Government offices about Whitehall. Men clerks have votes and women clerks have none; and probably no Government could materially extend the employment of women in the Civil Service without losing votes in every constituency. The women's salaries, even at the higher scale adopted in 1881, are about one-third of what is paid to men for doing exactly the same work, and, as previously pointed out, the proportion of superior appointments is much higher on the men's side than on the women's. I do not urge, as some may think I ought, that men and women should be paid exactly the same for the same work. As long as there are twenty channels of remunerative employment for men, for one which exists for women, it must needs be that women will command a lower scale of wages. But women ought to get the advantages of their lower rate of salary as surely as they bear its disadvantages, and they do not do so as long as every branch of employment in the Civil Service except one is still closed to them.

Transcribed from a copy in the British Library.
No known copyright restrictions.

Notes

1 This article does not appear in the bibliography compiled by Rubinstein (1991, 291–302).
2 Stead to MGF, 31 December 1883; MGF to Stead, 2 January 1884 (quoted in Rubinstein [1991, 60], cited as M50/2/1/14 and 15).
3 Mary Wollstonecraft (1759–97), English author and advocate of women's rights; see Section 16.
4 Mary Anne Lamb (1764–1847), English children's author.
5 Harriet Martineau (1802–76), English writer and sociologist.
6 Quoted in Hazlitt (1874, 65).

7 'Thus was I saved from being a literary lady who could not sew; and when, in after years, I have been insulted by admiration at not being helpless in regard to household employments, I have been wont to explain, for my mother's sake, that I could make shirts and puddings, and iron and mend, and get my bread by my needle, if necessary, (as it once was necessary, for a few months), before I won a better place and occupation with my pen' (Martineau 1885, 20–1).
8 Spelling, particularly when related to accepted usage or convention.
9 Lord Frederick Charles Cavendish (1836–82), an English Liberal politician who was financial secretary to the Treasury from April 1880 to May 1882.
10 From a letter to Charles Plowden, September 1868, Wellcome Ms 5480/15, quoted in McDonald (2005, 70).
11 Dora Spenlow, from Dickens's *David Copperfield*, who does not have the emotional capacity to deal with household expenses: '"If you will . . . look about now and then at your papa's housekeeping, and endeavour to acquire a little habit – of accounts, for instance –" Poor little Dora received this suggestion with something that was half a sob and half a scream' (Dickens 1850, 383).
12 Kidd and Maywood 1884.

14
The employment of children in theatres, 1889

Contemporary Review. December 1889, 822–9.

Between 1887 and 1889 Fawcett was a leading figure in the movement calling for the prevention of the employment of young children in the theatre. This was linked to her work with the Preventive and Rescue Sub-Committee of the National Vigilance Association (NVA).[1] In 1880, the Factory Act had been passed to regulate the employment of children between the ages of 5 and 10, but did not include those working in the theatre, causing campaigners to carry out investigations, compile papers, write letters and articles and contribute to the Royal Commission on Education reports, lobbying for change in the legislation (Varty 2008). In 1889, Fawcett published a series of articles in the *Echo* to highlight the working conditions and lives of theatre children:[2]

> I have come to the conclusion, after a long investigation, that theatrical work is highly prejudicial to children, physically, educationally and morally, I do not look upon it as the sole or even the chief case of the juvenile immorality which is such an appalling fact in our social life, but I do regard it as one of the causes (Fawcett 1888a).

In response, Mrs Mary Jeune (1845–1931), the well-connected 'London hostess, prolific essayist, and worker on behalf of women and poor children' (Coustillas 2008, 18; see also Young 2009), wrote a public response to Fawcett about the social and economic *benefits* of young children working in theatres, suggesting that 'Mrs Fawcett can never have been behind the scenes' (Jeune 1889, 10) and accusing her of exaggerating the stated risks to children. Fawcett replies, here, demonstrating her characteristic spirit, but also her views on purity and temperance.

*

An article in the October number of the *English Illustrated Magazine*, by Mrs Jeune, in defence of the employment of little children in theatres,[3] appears to call for reply on the part of those who have supported the recent legislation on the subject.

In the first place, Mrs Jeune's arguments, if they hold good at all, hold good against the whole principle of the Factory Acts,[4] so far as they limit the employment of young children. She dwells on the undoubted capacity of children, through their earnings, to provide necessaries for their families, and thus help to keep up the home; and she holds that it is 'little short of a crime to pass any law which would diminish the power of the children' of contributing to the income on which the home depends. This crime our country has been guilty of these forty years past, ever since the Factory Acts have been in operation. At first the principle of forbidding the employment of children under a certain age was applied tentatively to certain trades; the experiment was found to work well, and the principle was extended to other trades and industries, till at last, by the Education Act,[5] it was laid down as a principle, applying to all children, that their employment for wages under the age of ten years was illegal, and that the hours of their employment between the ages of ten and fourteen should be regulated. In any handbook referring to the subject of legislation as regards the limitation of the hours of labour in various countries under the head 'England', some such entry as this will be found: 'Children under ten years of age are not to be employed at all; children under fourteen are not to be employed more than half-time.' It is to be noted as a characteristic of the gradual spread of this principle of our legislation from trade to trade, first to children in mines, then to children in factories, then to children in workshops and last to children in agricultural and miscellaneous employments, that the representatives of each trade in turn thought it 'little less than a crime' to apply the restrictions upon juvenile labour to their own business. When the master chimney-sweeps were forbidden to use little naked bleeding children to clean chimneys, they said the risk of London being destroyed by fire was indefinitely increased by the prohibition. When the little children under ten were excluded from the cotton factories, manufacturers said the cotton trade of England would perish in consequence; but there was one voice heard,[6] even among the manufacturers themselves, which replied: 'Very well, then perish the cotton trade!'[7] The exception, however, only proves the rule, which has been that each trade in turn has resisted limitation and restriction as applied to itself.

In this respect the theatrical profession has not been in any way exceptional; its leaders have considerable power of influencing the press; and providing, as the stage does, so largely for the amusement of the public, a thousand pens are ready to leap from their inkstands in its defence, if there is any idea of an attack being made upon it. We who wish the labour of children on the stage be limited and regulated, do not necessarily attack the theatrical profession in itself, but we urge that no case has been made out for its exceptional treatment. Children under ten are debarred, with admittedly good results, from all other employments: why should they not also be debarred from theatrical employment?

To allow parents to depend on the earnings of their infants is one of those cruel kindnesses akin to indiscriminate almsgiving and other pauperizing influences. While apparently beneficial to the home, by allowing the little children to contribute their mite to its support, it is really prejudicial to it, because it weakens the sense of parental responsibility and obscures the fact, which Mrs Jeune admits as readily as we do, that it is the duty of parents to support their children, and not that of children during the tender years of infancy to support their parents.

The good results attendant on the prohibition of the labour of little children and the provision for them of the rudiments of education are year by year becoming more apparent. Those who can contrast the condition of the population affected by it tell us that the improvement is little short of miraculous. There is a lower death-rate, a decreased expenditure per head on alcohol, larger deposits in the savings-banks, building societies and provident clubs, and a very large diminution in juvenile crime. It may no doubt be urged that other influences besides the Factory Acts and Education Acts have been at work to produce the improvement referred to, and this no doubt is true; but that security against premature employment and the provision of the means, through education, of other than animal pleasures have had their share in causing this improvement is so obvious that it cannot be called in question. Why not do for the theatre child what has been done already for the children in factories and other employments?

While referring to Mrs Jeune's remarks on the preciousness of home-life, and on the cases in which the children's earnings at the theatre are used to keep the home together, we would point out that the home life of the child is in many cases quite destroyed and put an end to by its employment on the stage. What will be said by those who defend, in the interest of the home, the employment of babies on the stage, of the case of children of five and six years of age, who are sent from their homes in London for the whole winter to fulfil theatrical engagements in Glasgow or Newcastle? Careful inquiry has been made by a School Board officer who knows the home life of large numbers of theatre children, into the sort of home which the wages of the children are used to support. With the exception of the children belonging to regular theatrical families, he asserts positively that in ninety-nine cases out of a hundred where children are sent on the stage, either the father or the mother drinks.[8] Even Mrs Jeune, in spite of her enthusiastic words about 'that most sacred and holy place – the Home',[9] states that it would be useless to send large classes of theatre children to bed at hours when most children of their age are tucked up for the night, because they would 'often get no rest owing to dirt and vermin'; and she adds that she knew one little girl who cried with vexation after she was in bed because she could get no sleep on account of fleas 'and other insects'.[10] A plentiful use of carbolic soap would do more to preserve the purity of the sentiment of 'Home, sweet Home' in these cases than sending the children to dance and pirouette night after night in the theatres and music-halls of London. Mrs Jeune's assertions about the low standard of cleanliness in the homes from which many of the children are drawn, go far to confirm what we have been told from other sources as to the drinking habits of the parents. My own knowledge of this subject is confined in the main to London and London children, but inquiries made in Liverpool, Glasgow and elsewhere show that what is true in London is true there – viz. that the children employed in pantomimes and music-halls come in a large proportion from homes that are hardly worth the name. A lady, writing from Liverpool, who has had much experience there with School Board work, says: 'In ninety per cent of these cases the books show that the parents, one or both, are classed as bad, drinking, neglectful, or of doubtful character.' Mrs Jeune does not deny that the earnings of theatrical children are often spent by idle and drunken parents in a public-house; but she says that a similar remark is applicable to the earnings of children who beg in the streets at night, or who make a pretence of selling things, while in reality they are begging. Exactly so, and in the same Act which deals with the employment of children in theatres, their employment by their parents to beg, or to offer things for sale in the streets at night, is also prohibited. The object of legislation in these matters is to make it difficult for the lazy, selfish, drunken parent to muddle on in his lazy, selfish, drunken way on the pence brought in by his wretched children. 'But', says Mrs Jeune, 'a man who is lazy and drunken will not work one bit the more because his children are starving.'[11] Perhaps not; but he will work the more if he is starving himself, and if the possibility of subsisting in idleness on the wages of his little children is denied to him. If his children are still neglected and starved, the resources of civilization on their behalf are not yet exhausted. There are in many towns, though not at present in London, day industrial schools to which children belonging to this lowest class of home can be sent.

It appears to me that throughout her article Mrs Jeune assumes more than she is justified in doing, that she and those who think with her have their knowledge at first-hand, while those who wish the principle of the Factory Acts to be applied to theatre children have nothing but second-hand information and have 'no practical knowledge of their subject'.[12] I have always said frankly that my knowledge on the subject is second-hand. I have never been a theatre child, or employed in a theatre in any capacity whatever, and what I know is gained from the children themselves, from their parents, from what theatrical people themselves say about their profession, from the careful and systematic investigation of the subject by Miss A. Bear[13] and others, and from the school teachers who know the children and their home-life and the effect of their employment in theatres thoroughly well. I have always considered that the evidence of the parents and the employers should be received with some caution, because they are profiting pecuniarily from the employment of the children; and we do not make any charge against them as being worse than the rest of the world, in saying that self-interest often perverts the judgment. I have therefore always attached special importance to the evidence of the teachers of the children; they have opportunities of knowing the children before and after and during their engagement in theatres such as is thrown in the way of very few except those who profit by their employment. I have been astonished at the unanimity with which the teachers, whether under the School Board or belonging to voluntary schools, have condemned the employment of these children. Their education, the teachers say, practically comes to an end; there is not a doubt their health suffers; they come to school so tired that the teacher, out of kindness, exacts no work from them; and finally, with terrible iteration, the teachers say that the moral evil arising from theatre work is indescribable. Mrs Jeune says that all this is second-hand information. True, but her information is second-hand also, only she relies solely on the parents and the employers, while we rely mainly on those who make no profit out of the children's work. But even out of her own mouth, I think her article contains facts and statements quite sufficient to condemn that which she seeks to uphold. In the first place, although she says, referring to the theatre children, that there is 'no drawback or disadvantage in their professional life' (p. 9), in another place (p. 11) she says there are two points with regard to these children that are unsatisfactory: 'they are the questions of *education and food*'. It will be admitted that these are rather important items in the life-history of a little child. She says also that she is filled with sorrow and indignation at the thought of little children of eight or nine having to work. So are we; but our indignation and sorrow lead us to try to stop them from working, while Mrs Jeune's lead her to encourage their employment. But there is more than this in Mrs Jeune's article condemnatory of the employment of little children on the stage. There is abundant proof that the parents, although they deny categorically that their children are exposed to any special risk or disadvantage, are in reality fully aware of it. Mrs Jeune tells us of a poor woman whose daughter was in a theatre, and who said, 'with tears in her eyes', that she 'never would have let her go on the stage'[14] if she could have got other regular work for her, but that she did all she could for her in the way of special watchfulness and protection. Again, in another case, cited by Mrs Jeune, of a gifted child who acted in the 'Silver King', we are told that this child's mother, Mrs H., *'never let her out of her sight . . . never let her act with any one whom she did not know well, and felt her child was safe with; above all, she never let the child go to the theatre without her, and when Florrie went with Miss Mary Anderson to America her mother left her husband and their children and went with her child'* (p. 8). These rigid and incessant precautions are necessary, then, in the opinion of those who have the best means of judging, for the safeguarding of a little child in a theatre, even in a company presided over by a lady so thoroughly *sans reproche* as Miss Mary Anderson.[15] These precautions can be insisted on by the parents of highly gifted children whose talents give them a natural monopoly and enable their guardians to make what terms they please for the safety of their own precious little ones. But what chance would the mothers of the hundreds of little children who come from 'homes' swarming 'with fleas and other insects' have of taking care of their children in a similar way? Of course it would be absolutely impossible. There are many mothers as careful as Mrs H. in a lower position of life, but they would never dream of allowing their children to be on stage at all. Mrs Jeune apparently thinks that she has a monopoly of personal acquaintance with theatre children and their parents; she may therefore be surprised to hear that I have known a family for many years, a member of which, a little child of eleven, is on the stage. Her mother's account of her experience is an almost exact parallel to that which Mrs Jeune gives of Mrs H. and 'Florrie'. The little girl I am speaking of is an extremely gifted child: she has real innate dramatic power. She was discovered by the managers of a theatre, and her mother consented to let her take an engagement. The Zs are an extremely respectable, middle-class family, but the money offered no doubt was a temptation to them, as was also the chance of letting their child's great gifts be known beyond her own small circle. Mrs Z. went with the child once or twice to the theatre for rehearsals. After a very short experience of this, she said she would withdraw her child altogether and cancel the engagements unless the rehearsals could be at her own house. She absolutely refused to let the child go to the theatre for rehearsals on the ground of harm to the child from what she saw and heard there. She also bargained that another and older daughter, with no particular talent for acting, should be engaged in the piece, in order that she might be on the stage with the child. She laid great stress on this, and that either she or her elder daughter *always* had their eyes on the little thing, *they never let her out of their sight for a minute*. Mrs Z. also bargained that, when the company travelled, she and her child should have the use of a separate dressing-room, and that she should *never* be required to associate with the other members of the company. Mrs Z. is a sensible, practical, clever woman; she would not have exacted such terms as these for a mere whim. If those who are in a position to enforce them make such terms as these, we can without much difficulty picture to ourselves what are the dangers of stage employment for those children whose parents make no terms for them, except for the receipt of so many shillings a week.

Mrs Jeune emphatically denies that there is any special moral danger in theatrical life, and she thinks that this is proved because out of a large number of cases that have passed through a 'home' for fallen women, of which she is the manager, only two have formerly been on the stage. It would certainly be a rather startling development of religious revival that would bring a Miss Jocelyn Montague and a Miss Nina Montmorency,[16] who make five toilettes a day, whose persons are adorned with diamonds, laces and furs, who drive a smart Victoria by day and a neat Brougham by night, on the modest salary of £2 a week, if they trooped in crowds as applicants for admission to Mrs Jeune's home. One who has a first-hand, not a second-hand, knowledge of the theatre life during rehearsal, has written of the dazzling image of these houris that are constantly in evidence before the eyes and mind of the pantomime child: 'Poor as the attire and humble as the rank of the pantomime child may be, she is not without social advantages. That fashionably attired young person yonder in the crimson-braided mantle trimmed with sable fur, is her aunt by her mother's side'; but her ears are boxed if she addresses Miss Jocelyn Montague as 'Aunt Polly'.[17] While the pantomime child, if of the poorer sort, has a meal of bread and dripping brought from home; or, if of wealthier class, repairs to a neighbouring cook-shop to have 'a sossidge', Aunt Polly drives away in her Brougham to a luxurious dinner, comes back resplendent in another toilette, and the rehearsal begins again. Wonderful contrast between Aunt Polly on £1 a week and the pantomime child! The child has been up at six, has attended school before rehearsal, has had hardly anything to eat, and has fallen asleep in some cobwebby corner, protecting as well as she can with a frowsy, beaded mantle her two little sisters of five and six who are being trained with her. The long hours go on, midnight passes, the small hours begin to grow into tolerably big hours, Aunt Polly has rolled home in her Brougham again, and the pantomime child is to be seen in the cold, wet, slippery streets, dragging two smaller and still more weary children homewards over Waterloo Bridge or towards Vauxhall Road.

We claim that it is not making an excessive demand to ask for these children the same protection from premature employment that prevails in other trades. The House of Commons twice, by a substantial majority, affirmed the principle that children should not be employed in theatres under ten years old, and the clause embodying this was supported in a powerful speech by the Right Hon. L. Courtney, MP,[18] whom we may regard as a typical specimen of the 'gushing sentimentalists' against whom Mrs Jeune is appealing. In the House of Lords this clause was altered; the limit of age was reduced to seven, but the proviso was added that no child may be employed between the ages of seven and ten without a license; and when licensed children are employed, an inspector, corresponding to a factory inspector, is to be appointed, who shall have power to enter and inspect the premises and see that the conditions of the license are strictly observed. We have not done all that we aimed at doing, or all that we hope to see accomplished at some future date; but it is worth something to have prevented the employment of children under seven and to have got a beginning, although it may be only a small beginning, of the inspection of theatres by a public officer corresponding to a factory inspector. Since I have taken an interest in this subject, I have received letters from all parts of the country making strong complaints of the inadequacy of the arrangements for the safety, comfort and decency of the employés of many theatres. It is satisfactory to see that Mrs Jeune is with us in the matter of wishing for the appointment of inspectors.

One word more in reference to the statements of which we have heard so much with regard to the school for theatre children that has been started in Drury Lane. Mrs Jeune says that Mr Augustus Harris[19] employs from 150 to 200 children.[20] The school accommodation at Drury

Lane was thus commented on by a Board inspector in February 1888 – fifteen children were present:

> The premises are wretched and even dangerous. Persons are constantly at work just outside the canvas walls of the schoolroom, and often the noise is so great as to drown the voice of the teacher. Most of the children appeared to suffer from cold on the day of my visit. There are no proper registers, and only one set of reading-books.

This year the housing of the school was greatly improved, and the children met in a warm comfortable room; there were, on January 15, 1889, twenty-three children on the roll (out of the 150 to 200 employed); only fourteen, however, were present. There were *no registers* kept of the attendances, but this was remedied later, and duplicate registers were furnished to the School Board for the twelve weeks from January 12 to March 30. These registers showed that the children under ten made many fewer attendances than would have been required of them had they been attending a Board school. I believe that a school has also been started for the children at the Crystal Palace; but out of an estimated number of something like a thousand children employed in theatres and music-halls in London alone, school accommodation has been provided at the theatres for considerably less than forty. The actual average attendances would probably not amount to thirty. If we take the theatre children attending ordinary schools, we find that one child attended twenty-five times out of a possible ninety-one; another attended thirty-four times out of a possible ninety-one, and was late twenty-nine times. But this is a matter not requiring the support of an army of figures. Every one must know that a little child of less than ten years old cannot be actively at work day after day and night after night in a theatre, and be at school regularly too. And even Mrs Jeune admits that in the little matters of education and food the position of the theatre child leaves something to be desired. She complains that the compromise arrived at by the Act of last Session was illogical. In this we are also at one with her, and feel that the only logical position is to give to theatre children exactly the same protection from premature employment and work at unsuitable hours which has been afforded to children in all other occupations.

Transcribed from a copy in the British Library.
No known copyright restrictions.

Notes

1. See Section 22.
2. Fawcett 1888a, 1888b, 1888c, 1888d.
3. Jeune 1889.
4. The Factory Acts are a series of laws passed in the UK to set out conditions of industrial employment, initially covering the working conditions and welfare of children working in cotton mills and gradually extending to other industries. While the prevention of Cruelty to, and Protection of, Children Act (1889) had given further protection to working children, the 1891 Factory Act raised the minimum age for employment in factories to 11 (Parliament.uk n.d.b).
5. The Education Act of 1870 established a commitment to the education of children: the 1880 Act made school compulsory between the ages of 5 and 10 (Parliament.uk n.d.d).
6. Fawcett's footnote: 'Robert Owen's. He was then the head of a large cotton manufactory at New Lanark.'
7. 'For deeply as I am interested in the cotton manufacture ... yet knowing as I do, from long experience ... the miseries which this trade ... inflicts on those to whom it gives employment, I do not hesitate to say, Perish the cotton trade! Perish even the political superiority of our country! If it depends on the cotton trade – rather than they shall be upheld by the sacrifice of everything valuable in life.' Robert Owen (1771–1858), textile manufacturer and social reformer, in a speech of 1815 in Glasgow, which was copied and much circulated (quoted in Jones 1919, 143).
8. Fawcett abhorred intemperance throughout her life. 'The habitual drunkard is usually incapable, even when he is sober, of performing any severe labour, and habits of intemperance nearly always produce decay and death' (1876, 19). See also *Janet Doncaster* (Fawcett 1875), Section 10 in this volume.
9. Jeune (1889, 12).
10. Jeune (1889, 10).
11. Jeune (1889, 12).
12. Jeune (1889, 13).
13. Annette Bear (1853–99, later Bear-Crawford), 'one of Fawcett's most active assistants in collective evidence ... she began by looking at the obvious flashpoints of risk: the kind of company kept by the children in the dressing rooms, in the green room, at the stage door and on the journey home after the show. She discovered that although access backstage was supposed to be restricted, door keepers could be bribed to permit entrance, or to reveal a child's name and address to anyone interested enough to pay for it' (Varty 2008, 210).
14. Jeune (1889, 8).
15. Mary Anderson (1859–1940), an American actress performing on the London stage in the 1880s.
16. Fictional names, used for effect.
17. *St James's Gazette* (1888, 6).
18. Leonard Henry Courtney (1832–1918), professor of political economy at University College, London and radical British politician, in a speech in the House of Commons supporting the Cruelty to Children Prevention Bill on 10 July 1889: 'I take my stand upon this – that the advocates of such employment have not discharged the onus probandi that lay upon them, and have shown no good ground why children under 10 years of age, who are debarred from other employment, should be permitted to be employed at Drury Lane and other theatres. Why should this special exemption be made? We have been told of the grievous necessities of poor parents, and of the hardships which will be inflicted on them if they are deprived of the scanty earnings of their children. But we have heard those arguments on previous occasions, and yet we relentlessly interfered with the employment of children under 10 in factories.' (HC Deb 1889).
19. Sir Augustus Henry Glossop Harris (1852–96), actor and theatre manager.
20. Jeune (1889, 7).

15
Picturing Fawcett: Mrs Fawcett, 1890

Figure 5: Mrs Fawcett, 1890, carbon print by W. & D. Downey, London. No known copyright restrictions. Digitised from editor's own copy.

William and Daniel Downey's London portrait studio, active from the 1860s to the 1920s, enjoyed the patronage of many leading Victorians, including Queen Victoria and the Prince of Wales (Lyden 2014, 142). In 1890, Fawcett remarked in a letter to her friend William Thomas Stead (see Section 12) that she regarded being photographed as a 'penance' (quoted in Rubinstein 1991, 38). However, she recognised the benefit to the cause of these promotional materials and 'it was a penance to which she repeatedly subjected herself' (Rubinstein 1991, 38).

This portrait of Fawcett, then aged 43, was featured in the first book of Downey and Downey's 'The Cabinet Portrait Gallery' series (1890–4), which contained portraits of notable personalities from the Late Victorian period alongside biographical details. Fawcett is therefore firmly depicted as an establishment figure, alongside Prince George of Wales (later King George V, 1865–1936), Professor Thomas Henry Huxley (1825–95) and the actress Miss Maude Millett (1867–1920). Fawcett's entry notes the following:

> At a time when it was regarded as an unpardonable breach of conventionality for a woman to speak in public, Mrs Fawcett appeared as a lecturer on Women's Suffrage, and by her unassuming womanliness and charm of voice and manner, won many of her opponents to her side. While others have merely talked of 'the cause', Mrs Fawcett has been quietly working for it. Her ability makes her one of the strongest arguments in favour of women representatives; and if ever the day comes when women may be returned to Parliament, one of our first lady members will probably be Mrs Fawcett (Downey and Downey 1890, 68).

It also noted Fawcett's books, including *Janet Doncaster* (1875), and that as well as 'magazine articles on Women's Suffrage', Fawcett 'wrote the article on Communism for the ninth edition of the *Encylopædia Britannica*'.[1]

> To those who know her only as a writer, personal acquaintance with Mrs Fawcett is a revelation, especially if they are imbued with the old-fashioned prejudice that high intellectual power cannot be combined with sympathetic womanliness: while they may discover a fund of humour which makes a story told by Mrs Fawcett something to be pleasantly remembered (Downey and Downey 1890, 69).

Notes

1 Fawcett 1877.

16
Introduction to Wollstonecraft's *A Vindication of the Rights of Woman*, 1891

New edition, London: T. Fisher Unwin Ltd, 2–30.

Throughout her writing career, Fawcett wrote many introductory texts and biographical overviews of leading feminist, political or historical figures, including *Some Eminent Women of Our Times: Short biographical sketches* (1889c), *Life of Her Majesty Queen Victoria* (1895) and *Five Famous French Women* (1905). Originally published in 1792, *A Vindication of the Rights of Woman*, by the philosopher and writer Mary Wollstonecraft (1759–97), is one of the earliest works of feminist philosophy, and argued for fundamental rights for women. This new edition, commissioned by Fisher Unwin to mark the centenary of the work's publication, was the first since 1844; knowledge of Mary Wollstonecraft's personal history[1] had ensured the rejection of her writings during the latter half of the nineteenth century. In her lengthy introduction, Fawcett demonstrates her knowledge of both Wollstonecraft's sources and influence, and draws contemporary parallels, while also expressing disapproval of the 'errors of Mary Wollstonecraft's own life' and her 'irregular relations' (this obvious distaste showing Fawcett's own traditionally purist moral views; see Oakley [1983, 193] and Harrison [1987, 21]). Fawcett was instrumental in restoring the unfashionable Wollstonecraft to the feminist canon through her own respectability. Rubinstein, however, suggests that 'her intention was to make Wollstonecraft acceptable to the later Victorian reading public and, indeed, to herself', introducing Wollstonecraft 'to a new audience as a pioneer feminist who urged the case for political representation and economic independence of women', showing that 'the women's movement could claim links with a tradition dating from the enlightenment . . . and a powerful and original feminist mind' (1991, 89–90).

*

The near approach of the completion of a hundred years since Mary Wollstonecraft wrote her *Vindication of the Rights of Woman* and its republication in the present year, suggest considerations concerning the progress which has already been made in Europe and America in establishing the personal and proprietary independence of women, and also concerning Mary Wollstonecraft's relation to the great movement of which her book was in England almost the first conscious expression.

There is no truer or more consolatory observation concerning the great movements of thought which change the social history of the world than that no individual is indispensable to their growth. The Reformation in England and Germany would have come and would have changed men's thoughts concerning the relations of man to God, and of the Church to society, if Wiclif[2] and Erasmus[3] and Luther[4] had never lived, and if Henry VIII had never wished to put away his first wife. The democratic movement, changing men's thoughts concerning the relations of the State to society, would have come even if the roll of famous and infamous names associated with the revolution in England and France had been a blank. And the change which nearly the whole of civilized society throughout the world is conscious of in its estimation of the duties, rights, occupations and sphere of women in a like manner is not due to any individual or set of individuals. The vastness of the change, its appearance, almost simultaneously, in various ways in different parts of the world, indicate that it proceeds from causes too powerful and too universal to be attributed to any particular individual. Individuals, indeed, have expressed in the most remote periods of history what we should now consider modern ideas concerning the duties and rights of women. Plato's *Republic*, Solomon's description of the virtuous woman, Sir Thomas More's *Utopia*,[5] contain arguments and theories that satisfy the most modern advocate of women's rights. But these and other indications that many master minds did not placidly accept as satisfactory the relation of man and woman as master and slave were for long ages powerless to affect the realities of life. The hour had come as well as the man: and till the hour was favourable, the most conclusive arguments, the most patent facts, fell on deaf ears and on blind eyes, and had no practical result in modifying the conduct of men and women, or in ameliorating the laws and customs concerning their relation to one another.

It was Mary Wollstonecraft's good fortune that when she spoke, the ears of men had been prepared to hear and their minds to assimilate what she had to say. In one sense she was as much the product of the women's rights movement as its earliest confessor. The fermentation in men's minds which had already produced new thoughts about the rights of man, which was destined presently to overthrow the authority of unrestrained despotism wherever it existed in Western Europe, did not pass by without producing its effect on the greatest despotism of all, that of men over women. The idea that women are created simply to be ministers to the amusement, enjoyment and gratification of men was closely allied to the idea that peasants and workmen exist solely for the satisfaction of the wants and pleasures of the aristocratic classes. Ideas of this kind die hard, and it is Mary Wollstonecraft's chief claim to the regard of posterity that while she proved to demonstration the falsity of the notion that makes the place of women in creation entirely dependent on their usefulness and agreeableness to men, she had a keen appreciation of the sanctity of women's domestic duties, and she never undervalued for a moment the high importance of these duties, either to the individual, the family or the State. On the contrary, one of her chief arguments against the subjection of women was that it prevented them from performing these duties as efficiently and as conscientiously as would otherwise be the case. She wanted, as she says in her preface, to see women placed in a station where they would advance instead of retard the progress of the human race. Her argument, she adds, is built upon the simple principle that if women be not prepared by education to become the companions of men, they will stop the progress of knowledge, and that so far from knowledge and freedom inducing women to neglect their duties to their families, 'the more understanding women acquire, the more they will be attached to their duty – comprehending it – for unless they comprehend it . . . no authority can make them discharge it in a virtuous manner.'[6] She argues with force and justice against the habit of regarding women and their duties simply from the sexual point of view, and draws a vivid picture of the domestic miseries and the moral degradation to both men and women arising from women being trained in the idea that the one object in an unmarried woman's life is to catch a husband. In the scathing and cruel light of common sense she places in close juxtaposition two leading facts which ate like acids into the moral fibre of the whole of society in her time. The one aim and object of women was to get married; an unmarried woman was a social failure. Women who had passed the marrying and child-bearing age were treated with scant courtesy. A writer quoted by Mary Wollstonecraft had expressed this sentiment in plain language by exclaiming, 'What business have women turned of forty to do in the world?'[7] Yet while in a variety of ways it was dinned into the minds and consciences of women that husband-catching was the end of their existence, they were at the same time enjoined that this object must never be avowed. The aim must be pursued with unceasing vigilance, the whole of women's education, dress, manners and thoughts must be subordinated to this one object, but they must never openly avow it. In Mary Wollstonecraft's time those who undertook to lead the female mind in the principles of virtue advised women never to avow their love for the man they were about to marry; it was argued that it was 'indelicate in a female'[8] to let it appear that she married from inclination; she must always strive to make it appear that her physical and mental weakness had caused her to yield to force. On the first of these two nonsensical theories, that marriage is the one aim and object of women's existence, Mary Wollstonecraft, with her habitual reference to the religious sanction, pertinently asks how women are to exist in that state where there is neither marrying nor giving in marriage. 'Man', she adds, 'is always being told to prepare for a future state, but women are enjoined to prepare only for this.'[9] She also shows how wretchedly the sacredness of marriage and the charities of domestic life are violated by making marriage the only honourable career for women. As long as this is the case, and so far as it is the case, women are apt to marry 'to better themselves', as the housemaids say, or 'for a support, as men accept of places under government',[10] and not because they are heartily and honestly in love, or because they have any real vocation for married life. Mary Wollstonecraft had had abundant experience, in her own circle, of domestic wretchedness, brought about partly by this cause and partly by the bestial vices of domestic tyrants invested with the irresponsible power associated with 'the divine right of husbands'.[11]

On the second of these false theories, i.e. that women must never openly acknowledge that they wish to marry while secretly making marriage the one object of their existence, she has no difficulty in showing how antagonism between the real and avowed objects of life breeds dissimulation and cuts at the root of all openness and spontaneity of character. The authors she quotes as maintaining this absurd view of female delicacy seem to leave the moral atmosphere laden with impurities and utterly destitute of the ozone necessary to healthy lungs. Dr Gregory, for instance, whose book, *A Legacy to his Daughters*, seems to have been regarded as a standard work on female propriety at the end of the eighteenth century, recommends constant dissimulation to girls to whom nature has given a robust physical constitution.[12] A sickly delicacy was supposed to be an essential part of feminine charm. This will perhaps be believed with difficulty at the present time; one more quotation may therefore be given in support of the assertion. The Rev. Dr James Fordyce, in his sermons addressed to women, says:

> Let it be observed that in your sex manly exercises are never graceful; that in them a tone and figure, as well as an air and deportment, of the masculine kind, are always forbidding; that men of sensibility desire in every woman soft features and a flowing voice, a form not robust, and demeanour delicate and gentle.[13]

The lordly protector, man, was supposed to have his vanity tickled by a constant exhibition of female feebleness. A healthy girl was therefore counselled by sage Dr Gregory 'not to dance with spirit when gaiety of heart would make her feet eloquent',[14] lest the men who beheld her might either suppose that she was not entirely dependent on their protection for her safety, or else might entertain dark suspicions as to her modesty. Well might Mary Wollstonecraft protest against such 'indecent cautions',[15] and in respect of nine-tenths of the advice proffered to girls by Dr Gregory and other writers of the same stamp, one is inclined to cry, 'Give me an ounce of civet, good apothecary, to sweeten my imagination.'[16]

The essence of the absurdity now under consideration was dissimulation, and dissimulation was, we find, exalted by these writers as the pole-star to the wandering bark of women's lives. As indicated by these sages, womanly prudence and virtue consist in one long series of pretences. Behaviour, appearance, decorum, the applause of Mrs Grundy, 'constant attention to keep the varnish fresh',[17] are set before women as ends to be sedulously sought for on account of their bearing on the grand aim of women's existence, the admiration of the other sex. To this end everything else was subordinated. Even piety is recommended in one of Dr Fordyce's sermons, not because it bends the whole power of the nature more intently on its duty to God and man, but because piety is becoming to the face and figure. He recommends holiness as a cosmetic. 'Never,' exclaims the preacher, 'perhaps, does a fine woman *strike more deeply* than when composed into pious recollection; . . . she assumes, without knowing it, *superior dignity and new graces*; so that the beauties of holiness seem to radiate about her.'[18] On this passage Mary Wollstonecraft exclaims that the intrusion of the idea of conquest and admiration as influencing a woman at her devotions gives her a 'sickly qualm'.[19] Profanation could hardly go lower than this; but there was much more modelled on the same pattern. Cowardice, as well as physical weakness, was regarded as part of what every woman ought to aim at. Ignorance was likewise extolled. Female modesty was held to be outraged by the confession of strong and enduring love from a woman to a man, even when that man was her husband. Dr Gregory advises a wife 'never to let her husband know the extent of her sensibility or affection'. He likewise cautions all women carefully to hide their good sense and knowledge if they happen to possess any. 'Be cautious', he says, 'even in displaying your good sense. It will be thought you assume a superiority over the rest of the company. But if you happen to have any learning, keep it a profound secret, especially from the men, who generally look with a jealous and malignant eye on a woman of great parts, and a cultivated understanding.'[20] Pretence, seeming, outward show were the standards by which a woman's character was measured. A man is taught to dread the eye of God; but women were taught to dread nothing but the eye of man. Rousseau embodies the then current doctrine, that reputation in the case of women takes the place of virtue, in a passage which Mary Wollstonecraft quotes. 'To women,' he says, 'reputation is no less indispensable than chastity: ... what is thought of her is as important to her as what she really is. It follows hence that the system of a woman's education should in this respect be directly contrary to that of ours. Opinion is the grave of virtue among the men; but its throne among women.'[21] Right through this tangle of pretences and affectations Mary Wollstonecraft cuts with the double-edged knife of a sound heart and clear head. It is against the system of dissimulation that she protests; instead of telling women how they are most likely to avoid censure and win praise, to gain a reputation for decorum and propriety of behaviour, she tells them to leave appearances out of consideration: 'Make the heart clean, give the head employment',[22] and behaviour will take care of itself. Dr Gregory's remarks relative to reputation and the applause of the world, she complains, begin at the wrong end, because he treats them as ends in themselves, and not in their proper relative position as advantages usually, but by no means universally, attendant on nobility of character and purpose. How much sounder than Dr Gregory's petty maxims, she reminds her readers, is the scriptural injunction, 'Get wisdom, get understanding; forget it not; ... forsake her not, and she shall preserve thee; love her, and she shall keep thee. Wisdom is the principal thing; therefore get wisdom, and with all thy getting get understanding.'[23] With a touch of humour, more common in her private letters than in her more studied works, Mary Wollstonecraft expresses her conviction that there is really no cause to counsel women to pretend to be sillier and more ignorant than they are. 'When a woman has sufficient sense not to pretend to anything which she does not understand in some degree, there is no need of determining to hide her talents under a bushel. Let things take their natural course, and all will be well.'[24]

In combating false views concerning what women ought to be, and to what ends their lives should be directed, Mary Wollstonecraft did not concentrate herself only on the orthodox immoralities propounded by Dr Gregory and Dr Fordyce. She challenges the whole field, and deals with Pope, Lord Chesterfield[25] and Rousseau as fearlessly as with teachers more in harmony with the ordinarily received opinions of her day. In contrast with Dr Fordyce's recommendation of the consolations of religion to women on the ground that 'a fine woman never strikes more deeply' than when she is communing in the spirit with her Creator, she reminds us of the opposite pole of male and female depravity expressed by Pope in the lines where, speaking on behalf of the whole male sex, he says:

> Yet ne'er so sure our passion to create
> As when she touch'd the brink of all we hate.[26]

The appearance of wantonness, just short of its reality, if indeed it was desirable to stop short of it, is recommended to women by Pope exactly in the same spirit as that in which Dr Fordyce recommended piety. The centre of both systems is the assumption that women have nothing better to do or think of in this world than 'to make conquests', as the old phrase was. The falsity, the immorality of this assumption, and the miserable consequences of acting upon it, it was the aim of *The Vindication of the Rights of Woman* to demonstrate. In combating Rousseau's views on education, especially his antagonism to teaching boys and girls together or according to the same methods, she refers to his argument that if women are educated like men, the more they will resemble men, and the less power will they have over the other sex. 'This is the very point', Mary Wollstonecraft says, 'I aim at. I do not wish them to have power over men, but over themselves.'[27]

Rousseau in many respects gave a compendium of all Mary Wollstonecraft most objected to in his views relating to the position of women. Profoundly influenced by his writings as she had at one time been, she was intensely antagonistic to his professions and his practice in regard to all that touched upon the position of women and upon domestic life. There is nothing in her book to show that she was aware of the indelible stain on Rousseau as a man which has been left by his disposing of his five children immediately after their birth by placing them in the turnstile of the Foundling Hospital.[28] The knowledge of this fact has perhaps relieved posterity from the necessity of paying any very strenuous attention to his arguments on the cultivation of the domestic virtues. Mary Wollstonecraft speaks contemptuously of Rousseau's wife as 'the fool Theresa',[29] and she probably knew what we know also, that Theresa was a kitchen wench whose state of mind closely approached absolute imbecility. 'She could never', says Mr John Morley, 'be taught to read with any approach to success. She could never follow the order of the twelve months of the year, nor master a single arithmetical figure, nor count a sum of money, nor reckon the price of a thing. A month's instruction was not enough to give knowledge of the hours of the day upon a dial-plate. The words she used were often the direct opposites of the words she meant to use.'[30]

But nearly imbecile as she was, she loved her children, and deeply resented the cruel wrong her husband did her in snatching them from her. 'The fool Theresa', with almost nothing to commend her but the primitive maternal instinct, may seem to many of us a more touching and instructive spectacle than a score of philosophers maundering over the thesis that woman has been formed for the sole purpose of being pleasing to man and subject to his rule. Mary Wollstonecraft seems to have known of Theresa's mental limitations and nothing more, and this was enough to show her that what Rousseau looked for in a wife was not a companion who could share his aims and stimulate his thoughts and imagination by her sympathy, but just a creature who had the physical capacity of bearing children, and who was present without necessarily being spoken to – he sometimes passed weeks without addressing her a single word – when complete solitude would have been distasteful to him.

There is a peculiar satisfaction on the part of those who are trying to produce a change in general feeling in regard to any subject, when one of their opponents will state boldly, in so many words, what is the real foundation of the sentiment which inspires them. The majority of their spokesmen feel that the real reason of their opposition is too little respectable for open avowal; they count upon its secret influence, but never refer to it in public. It is therefore with a cry of delight that those on the other side seize upon an indiscreet avowal of the real principles on which their enemies rely. It was a service of this kind which Rousseau rendered to those who wished to promote the independence of women, when in a passage in 'Emilius' he avowed his reason for belittling women from the cradle to the grave to be that otherwise they would be less subservient to men. The battle in which Mary Wollstonecraft took a leading part is still being waged, and it may be useful to those who are now carrying on this contest to be able to quote Rousseau's reason for keeping women in a perpetual state of tutelage and childhood. These are his words:

> For this reason, the education of women should always be relative to that of men. To please, to be useful to US, to make US love and esteem them, to educate US when young, and take care of US when grown up, to advise, to console US, to render OUR lives easy and agreeable: these are the duties of women at all times, and what they should be taught in their infancy.[31]

Take this and contrast it, as containing a worthy and dignified theory of human life, with the well-known first question and answer of the Scottish Shorter Catechism, of which Carlyle said,

> The older I grow – and I now stand on the brink of eternity – the more comes back to me the first sentence in the catechism which I learned when a child, and the fuller and deeper its meaning becomes: 'What is the chief end of man? To glorify God, and to enjoy Him for ever.'[32]

Rousseau and his disciples would disinherit women from this birthright, and to the question, 'What is the chief end of woman?' would reply, 'To glorify man, and to help him to enjoy himself for a little time.' But Rousseau and those who follow in his footsteps do not even succeed in this poor aim. Happiness is one of those things of which it may with truth be said, 'I was found of them that sought me not; I was made manifest unto them that asked not after me.'[33] Poor Theresa nursing in her dull brain undying resentment against the man who had robbed her of her children, the squalor and degradation of the pair and the miserable end of Rousseau's life are all a terrible commentary on the rottenness of the principles on which he founded their joint existence. All the beauty of personal devotion and self-abnegation, which count for so much in the happiness of family life, disappear and wither when they are selfishly claimed by one member of the family as due to him from the others, and are entirely unreciprocated on his part. The affectionate mutual consideration and the happy companionship of human beings with equal rights, but different capacities and different occupations, are exchanged by those who adopt Rousseau's doctrines for a state of things which develops the vices of tyranny on the one side and the vices of slavery on the other; the husband becomes a harsh, exacting master, the wife and other members of the household too often become obsequious and deceitful serfs. Mary Wollstonecraft's husband wrote of her shortly after her death, 'She was a worshipper of domestic life',[34] and the truth of the expression is felt in every line of the numerous passages in *The Vindication* where she contends that the subjection of women is inimical to domestic happiness, and appeals to men to 'be content with rational fellowship instead of slavish obedience'. If this were more so, 'they would find us', she adds, 'more observant daughters, more affectionate sisters, more faithful wives, more reasonable mothers – in a word, better citizens'.[35] The relation of Milton to his daughters may be mentioned as an object lesson in the truth of Mary Wollstonecraft's contention. He tyrannized over them, they deceived and cheated him and the domestic life of one of the greatest Englishmen, instead of being full of beauty and a source of strength to those who come after him, is a thing that we try not to think of, and can never remember without a sense of pain and loss.[36]

Mary Wollstonecraft, as Mr Kegan Paul says in his sketch of her life and work prefixed to her *Letters to Imlay*,[37] makes, in her *Vindication of the Rights of Women* [sic], a reiterated claim that women should be treated as the friends and equals of men, and not as their toys and slaves;[38] but she does not claim for women intellectual or physical or moral equality with men. Her argument is that being weaker than men, physically and mentally, and not superior morally, the way in which women are brought up, and their subordination throughout life, first to their fathers, then to their husbands, prevents the due natural development of their physical, mental and moral capacities. How can the powers of the body be developed without physical exercise? And in her day the ordinary rule for women in the upper ranks of society seems to have been to take none whatever. Their clothes and shoes rendered outdoor exercise entirely out of the question. A white muslin gown damped to cling more closely to the figure and satin slippers are not an equipment even for a walk on the London pavements; they would make a country ramble still more completely out of the question. Miss Edgeworth makes great fun of one of her sentimental heroines, who insists on admiring the beauties of nature otherwise than from the windows of a coach. She takes a country walk, the lanes are muddy, and she leaves the satin slipper of her right foot in one of them.[39] Mary Wollstonecraft pleaded that the lower degree of physical strength of women, and the strain upon that strength caused by maternity, ought to secure for them such conditions as regards exercise, clothing and food as would make the most of that strength, and not reduce it to a vanishing point.

In the same spirit she argues about the mental capacity of women. Perpetual obedience, she contends, weakens the understanding; responsibility, and the necessity of thinking and deciding, strengthen it. She draws a picture of the obvious practical disadvantage of women being guided in everything by their husbands, and supposes a case in which the husband is a perfectly benevolent and perfectly intelligent despot. He manages everything, decides from the depths of his wisdom all difficulties; his wife, to quote Mrs Poyser, does not know which end she stands uppermost till her husband tells her.[40] But even intelligent and benevolent despots do not live forever. Her husband dies, and leaves his wife with a large family of young children. Her previous life has not prepared her by experience to fulfil the arduous task of being both father and mother to them. She is ignorant of the management of their property and of their education. She is utterly unfit for the weight that suddenly falls on her shoulders. What is left for her to do except transfer to some other husband the direction of her family, or in some other way shift to other shoulders the responsibility that she ought to discharge?

In Mary Wollstonecraft's remarks respecting what she considers the moral inferiority of women to men, I think we see more than anywhere else evidence of the salutary change that has already been brought about in the very social position and education of women. Very few modern writers or observers consider women less sensible to the claims of duty than men. The late Rev. F. D. Maurice, writing in support of women's suffrage and speaking of English women as he knew them, said, 'In any sphere wherein women feel their responsibility they are, as a rule, far more conscientious than men';[41] and I think there is a general consensus of opinion that where large and important duties have been confided to women, they have been on the whole faithful in the discharge of them. The moral trustworthiness of the run of women is accepted by most of us, in our every-day life, as part of the natural order of things on which we can rely as implicitly as on the continuity of the forces of nature. Mary Wollstonecraft, however, finds great fault with women in her time, and roundly accuses them of cunning, superstition, want of generosity, low sense of justice, gross mismanagement of their children and of their households, and of a domestic selfishness which, in some respects, is worse than neglect. This last subject is worth referring to, because some of those who wish to maintain the subjection of women are to be found even now who argue that if a woman is happy in her own children she has no occasion to occupy herself at all with the circumstances that make or mar the lives of other children. On this point Mary Wollstonecraft says:

> In short, speaking of the majority of mothers, they leave their children entirely to the care of servants; or, because they are their children, treat them as if they were little demi-gods, though I have always observed that the women who thus idolize their children seldom show common humanity to servants, or feel the least tenderness for any children but their own.[42]

If this were true a hundred years ago, the majority of candid observers certainly would not maintain that it is true now. From the time of Mrs Fry[43] downwards there has been a constantly growing army of women who both idolize their own children and spend themselves with unstinting devotion to render the lives of other children happy and healthy. Women have used the greater freedom and the better education they have received since Mary Wollstonecraft's time just as she predicted they would. They care for their own children as much, and they care for other children more. They are not content with securing favourable conditions in life for their own children but in almost innumerable ways are making efforts to check the waste in children's lives that went on unheeded in Mary Wollstonecraft's time.

The faults of *The Vindication* as a literary work are patent upon the face of it. There is a want of order and system in it which may, perhaps, be attributed to the desultory education of the writer. As she herself points out, the want of order in women's education is answerable to a large extent for the want of order in their after-work. A more important blemish to modern ears consists in the formal and frequently stilted language in which the writer conveys her meaning. The reaction against the formalities of the Johnsonian period had begun, but had not as yet conquered; the triumph of the naturalistic school in literature led by Cowper, Burns, Wordsworth and Joanna Baillie[44] was yet to come. There are other faults in the book deeper than those of order and style, which are probably to be traced to a reaction against the school of ethics, which proclaimed that appearances and decorum were ends in themselves to be diligently sought for. To this reaction may also, I believe, be attributed the errors of Mary Wollstonecraft's own life, and those of so many members of the circle in which she moved. In unravelling the curious tangle of relationships, intrigues, suicides and attempted suicides of the remarkable group of personalities to whom Mary Wollstonecraft belonged, one is sickened for ever, as Mr Matthew Arnold has said, of the subject of irregular relations.[45] Mary Wollstonecraft's great merit, however, lies in this: that with a detachment of mind from the prejudices and errors of her time, in regard to the position of women, that was quite extraordinary, she did not sanction any depreciation of the immense importance of the domestic duties of women. She constantly exalted what was truly feminine as the aim of woman's education and training; she recognized love and attraction between the sexes as a cardinal fact in human nature, and 'marriage as the foundation of almost every social virtue'.[46] Hence very largely from her initiative the women's rights movement in England has kept free from the excesses and follies that in some other countries have marred its course. Mary Wollstonecraft, in her writings as well as her life, with its sorrows and errors, is the essentially womanly woman, with the motherly and wifely instincts strong within her, and caring for all she claims and pleads for on behalf of her sex, because she is convinced that a concession of a large measure of women's rights is essential to the highest possible conception and fulfilment of women's duties. In words that recall Mazzini's memorable saying, 'the sole origin of every right is in a duty fulfilled',[47] she says, 'a right always includes a duty',[48] and again, 'rights and duties are inseparable'.[49]

The remarkable degree in which she was ahead of her time is shown on almost every page of *The Vindication*. She claims for women the right to share in the advantages of representation in Parliament, nearly seventy years before women's suffrage was heard of in the House of Commons. She knows that few, if any, at that time would be found to sympathize with her, but that does not prevent her from claiming for women what she felt was simple justice. She also perceives the enormous importance of the economic independence of women, and its bearing on social health and disease. The possibility of women earning a comfortable livelihood by honest labour tends in some degree to prevent them from marrying merely for a living, and on the other hand cuts at one fruitful source of prostitution. She pointed out fifty years before any English woman had become a qualified medical practitioner that the profession of medicine was particularly well suited to women, and entirely congenial to the womanly character; and she argued that there were a number of other businesses and professions in which women might suitably and honourably engage. These opinions have now become the commonplaces of ordinary conversation; but it must not be forgotten, in estimating the originality of her mind, that she was writing only a very few years after the time when the great lion of the literary and social world of London had condemned even the harmless wielding of the paint-brush and mahlstick by a woman. Boswell records that Dr Johnson 'thought portrait painting an improper employment for a woman. Public practice of any art, he observed, and staring in men's faces, is very indelicate in a female'; and in another place Boswell tells how the great doctor thought literature as little suited to a 'delicate female' as painting. Of a literary lady of his time who was reported to have become attentive to her dress and appearance, Johnson remarked that 'she was better employed at her toilet than using her pen'.[50]

It need hardly be said that Mary Wollstonecraft anticipated the change that has come about in the public mind as to what is needful in the education of women. How great that change has been is forcibly illustrated by a passage quoted in *The Vindication* from a writer who propounds the view that the study of botany is inconsistent with the preservation of 'female delicacy'.[51] This might well provoke another 'sickly qualm' in its essential coarseness of feeling and degrading conception of the works of Nature. Mary Wollstonecraft brings this indelicate delicacy to the right touchstone when she says,

> On reading similar passages, I have reverentially lifted up my eyes and heart to Him who liveth for ever and ever, and said, 'O my Father, hast Thou by the very constitution of her nature forbid Thy child to seek Thee in the fair forms of truth? And can her soul be sullied by the knowledge that awfully calls her to Thee?'[52]

In another all-important respect, Mary Wollstonecraft was ahead of her time, and may be regarded, though opinion has moved in the direction in which she pointed, as ahead of ours. In numerous passages she points out the inseparable connection between male and female chastity. One would have thought the fact so self-evident as to need no asseveration; but as a matter of experience we know that even now the mass of people mete out to the two partners in the same action an entirely different degree of blame, and judge them by entirely different standards; the one who is condemned the most severely is not the one who has had the advantage, generally speaking, in wealth, education, experience and knowledge of the world, and on whom therefore, if any difference be made, a greater responsibility ought to rest; 'the strong lance of justice hurtless breaks' on him, and reserves all its terrors for her who stands at a disadvantage in all these respects. An action that is one and the same is regarded as in the last degree heinous in one of the actors and as quite excusable in the other. Against the essential immorality and injustice of this doctrine and practice, Mary Wollstonecraft protested with her whole strength. She exposes the insincerity of those who profess zeal for virtue by pointing the finger of scorn at the woman who has transgressed, while her partner, who may have tempted her by money, ease and flattery to her doom, is received with every mark of consideration and respect. 'To little respect has that woman a claim . . . who smiles on the libertine while she spurns the victims of his lawless appetites and their own folly.'[53] The injustice of this attitude of mind is as conspicuous as its hypocrisy; and in the different measure meted out by the world to the partners in each other's degradation Mary Wollstonecraft perceives a fruitful source of immorality. The two sexes must in this, as nearly every other respect, rise or sink together. Unchastity in men means unchastity in women; and the cure for the ills which unchastity brings with it is not to be found in penitentiaries and in Magdalen institutions, but in a truer measure of justice as regards the responsibilities of both sexes, in opening to women a variety of honourable means of earning a living, and in developing in men and women self-government and a sense of their responsibility to each other, themselves, their children and the nation.

In many respects, Mary Wollstonecraft's book gives us a pleasing assurance that with all the faults of our time we have made way upon the whole, and are several steps higher up on the ladder of decency and self-control than our forerunners were a hundred years ago. She speaks of the almost universal habit in her time among the wealthier classes of drinking to excess, and of what is even less familiar to her readers of the present day, 'of a degree of gluttony which is so beastly'[54] as to destroy all sense of seemliness. She also states that so far from chastity being held in honour among men, it was positively despised by them.[55]

In all these matters the end of the nineteenth century compares favourably with the end of the eighteenth; and one great factor in the progress made is the far greater concession of women's rights at this time compared with that. The development of the womanliness of women that comes with their greater freedom makes itself felt in helping to form a sounder public opinion upon all forms of physical excess, and with this a truer and nobler ideal of manly virtue.

In one other important respect Mary Wollstonecraft was ahead of her own time in regard to women, and in line with the foremost thinkers on this subject in ours. Henrik Ibsen has taken the lead among the moderns in teaching that women have a duty to themselves as well as to their parents, husbands and children, and that truth and freedom are needed for the growth of true womanliness as well as of true manliness. But Mary Wollstonecraft anticipated him in teaching that self-government, self-knowledge and self-respect, a worship of truth and not of mere outward observances, are what women's lives mainly need to make them noble. I have already quoted her saying: 'I do not want them to have power over men, but over themselves', and other quotations of a similar drift may be given: 'It is not empire, but equality and friendship which women want';[56] and again: 'Speaking of women at large, *their first duty is to themselves as rational creatures*, and the next, in point of importance, as citizens, is that, which includes so many, of a mother.'[57] The words italicised foreshadow almost verbatim Nora's expression in the well-known scene in *A Doll's House*, where she tells her astounded husband that she has discovered that she has duties to herself as well as to him and to their children.[58]

The facts of Mary Wollstonecraft's life are now so well known through the biographies of Mr Kegan Paul and Mrs Pennell,[59] and her memory has been so thoroughly vindicated from the contumely that was one time[60] heaped upon it, that I do not propose to dwell upon her personal history. I have here endeavoured to consider the character of the initiative which she gave to the women's rights movement in England, and I find that she stamped upon it from the outset the word Duty, and has impressed it with a character that it has never since lost. Women need education, need economic independence, need political enfranchisement, need social equality and friendship, mainly because without them they are less able to do their duty to themselves and to their neighbours. What was false and unreal in the old system of treating women she showed up in its ugliness, the native ugliness of all shams. That woman must choose between being a slave and a queen; 'quickly scorn'd when not ador'd'[61] is a theory of pinchbeck and tinsel; it is difficult to discover its relation to the realities of life. Upon this theory, and all that hangs upon it, Mary Wollstonecraft made the first systematic and concentrated attack; and the women's rights movement in England and America owes as much to her as modern Political Economy owes to her famous contemporary, Adam Smith.[62]

Transcribed from a copy in the Internet Archive, from the University of Toronto Library. Not in copyright.

Notes

1 The posthumous publication in 1798 of *Memoirs of the Author of a Vindication of the Rights of Woman* by Wollstonecraft's husband, William Godwin (1756–1836), had the unintentional outcome of destroying her reputation by discussing her lovers, illegitimate child and suicide attempts.
2 John Wycliffe (1320s–1384), English theologian and reformer. Variations in the spelling of his name are common.
3 Desiderius Erasmus Roterodamus (1466–1536), Dutch philosopher and Catholic theologian.
4 Martin Luther (1483–1546), German professor of theology and a central figure in the Protestant Reformation.
5 Sir Thomas More (1478–1535), English lawyer, judge and humanist, who published *Utopia* in 1516. 'And the better part of the people, both men and women throughout all their whole life do bestow in learning those spare hours, which we said they have vacant from bodily labours' (1909, 206).
6 Wollstonecraft (1891, x). Note: quotations will be cited from the edition that Fawcett introduced.
7 Wollstonecraft cannot recall the source: 'A lively writer, I cannot recollect his name, asks . . .' (1891, 36). No original text has been found.
8 Fawcett refers to a famous quote from Samuel Johnson about portrait painting: 'He thought portrait-painting an improper employment for a woman. "Public practice of any art (he observed) and staring in men's faces, is very indelicate in a female"' (Boswell 1791, 251).
9 Fawcett paraphrases: 'For though moralists have agreed that the tenor of life seems to prove that *man* is prepared by various circumstances for a future state, they constantly concur in advising *woman* only to provide for the present' (Wollstonecraft 1891, 68).

10 Wollstonecraft (1891, 222).
11 Wollstonecraft (1891, 78).
12 The posthumously published bestseller *A Father's Legacy to His Daughters* (1774) by Scottish physician Dr John Gregory (1724–73) takes the form of a sequence of letters of advice to his daughters, given his declining health, covering religion, conduct and behaviour, amusements and relationships with men including friendship, love and marriage. Wollstonecraft comments, 'I respect his heart; but entirely disapprove of his celebrated *Legacy to His Daughters*' (1891, 61).
13 James Fordyce (1720–96), Scottish Presbyterian minister and poet, best known for his *Sermons to Young Women* (1775, 236).
14 'Many a girl dancing in the gaiety and innocence of her heart, is thought to discover a spirit she little dreams of' (Gregory 1774, 34).
15 Wollstonecraft (1891, 62).
16 *King Lear* 4.6.
17 Wollstonecraft (1891, 206).
18 Fordyce (1775, 217).
19 Wollstonecraft (1891, 150).
20 Gregory (1774, 19).
21 Jean-Jacques Rousseau (1712–78), philosopher and writer. His book *Emile, or Education* is a treatise on the nature of education, with its Book V providing an overview of his views on the education of women and the requirement that they be weak and subservient (1762, 354). Quoted in Wollstonecraft (1891, 201).
22 Wollstonecraft (1891, 155).
23 Proverbs 4:5–7. Wollstonecraft actually only quotes from 'Wisdom is the principal thing . . .' (1891, 158).
24 Wollstonecraft (1891, 156).
25 Philip Dormer Stanhope (1694–1773), 4th Earl of Chesterfield, known for his *Letters to His Son* (1774), which Wollstonecraft criticises (1891, 99).
26 From a poem by Alexander Pope (1688–1744), *Of the Characters of Women: An epistle to a lady* (1735, 8), which sets out the qualities of an ideal woman and compares these to undesirable characteristics.
27 Wollstonecraft (1891, 107).
28 See Damrosh (2005, 191–5) for an account.
29 Wollstonecraft (1891, 259).
30 Fawcett's note: 'Life of Rousseau, p. 72.' See Morley (1878, 72).
31 Rousseau (1762, 328).
32 Thomas Carlyle (1795–1881), historian, author, philosopher and teacher. Quoted in Wylie (1881, 328).
33 Romans 10:20.
34 Godwin (1798, 108).
35 Wollstonecraft (1891, 224).
36 Edward Phillips (1630–96), Milton's nephew, in his famous account has Milton's daughters 'condemned to the performance of reading' in a 'trial of patience, almost beyond endurance; yet it was endured . . . for a long time' (1694, 40).
37 Wollstonecraft 1879.
38 '. . . it should be ever remembered, if not read, as the herald of the demand that woman should be the equal and the friend, not the slave and toy of man' (Kegan Paul 1879, xxix).
39 Maria Edgeworth (1768–1849) was a prolific writer, known for her novels of Irish society and *Tales of Fashionable Life* (1809). Fawcett probably refers to Edgeworth's novel *Angelina, Or, L'Amie Inconnue* (1801): 'One of her slippers fell off as she scrambled up the hill – there was no recovering it; her other slipper, which was of the thinnest kid leather, was cut through by the stones; her silk stockings were soon stained with the blood of her tender feet; and it was with real gratitude that she accepted the farmer's offer, to let her pass the night at his farm-house' (1801, 277).
40 Mrs Poyser, the outspoken farmwife in Eliot's *Adam Bede*: '"Yes", said Mrs Poyser, "I know what the men like – a poor soft, as 'ud simper at 'em like the picture o' the sun, whether they did right or wrong, an' say thank you for a kick, an' pretend she didna know which end she stood uppermost, till her husband told her. That's what a man wants in a wife, mostly: he wants to make sure o' one fool as 'll tell him he's wise"' (Eliot 1859, 306).
41 Rev. John Frederick Denison Maurice (1805–72), author and theologian, quoted in the *Calcutta Review* (1870, 243).

42 Wollstonecraft (1891, 282).
43 Elizabeth Fry (1780–1845), a British Quaker, philanthropist and prison reformer (de Haan 2017).
44 The poets William Cowper (1731–1800), Robert Burns (1759–96), William Wordsworth (1770–1850) and Joanna Baillie (1762–1851).
45 Here Arnold refers to Shelley's behaviour and relationship history. See Arnold (1990, 322).
46 Wollstonecraft (1891, 119).
47 Mazzini (1862, xiii).
48 Wollstonecraft (1891, 233).
49 Wollstonecraft (1891, 297).
50 See note 8 and Boswell (1791, 301).
51 Wollstonecraft (1891, 187).
52 Wollstonecraft (1891, 187).
53 Wollstonecraft (1891, 210).
54 Wollstonecraft (1891, 207).
55 '. . . as this regard for the reputation of chastity is prized by women, it is despised by men: and the two extremes are equally destructive to morality' (1891, 207).
56 Wollstonecraft (1891, 162).
57 Wollstonecraft (1891, 218).
58 Ibsen (1889, act 3).
59 Pennell 1884.
60 Fawcett's footnote: 'Horace Walpole called her "a hyena in petticoats."' This quotation comes from a letter to Hannah More on 26 January 1795 (Oxford Reference 2020a).
61 A quotation from Anna Letitia Barbauld (1743–1825), English poet and editor. Greatly admired by Wollstonecraft, she is referred to twice in *Vindication*, but Fawcett here chooses her own quotation to add to the comparison, from 'Song III', lines 16–18 (Barbauld and Aikin 1826, 90–1).
62 Adam Smith (1723–90), philosopher and economist.

17
Home and politics, 1892

An address delivered at Toynbee Hall and elsewhere, 4th edition. London: Women's Printing Society, 1–8.

Many of the political assumptions that underwrote the Victorian women's movement are fundamentally different to views commonly held today. Liberal approaches 'promoted women's emancipation with an eye both to extending women's opportunities for self-development and to encouraging socially responsible attitudes', although the home, and the upkeep of one, still had 'a crucial role in socializing individuals' (Pederson 1999, 44–8). This challenged 'classical liberalism's opposition between public and private spheres by illuminating interconnections between the domains of home and politics . . . Liberal feminism sought to add a feminine dimension to the public world . . . to feminize democracy' (Nym Mayhall 2001, 189–90). In this speech, Fawcett argues 'that women's natures made their full participation as citizens necessary, increasingly urging that women be enfranchised on the grounds of the contributions they would make to the polity' (Nym Mayhall 2003, 20), both gaining from and engaging with society. Rubinstein also points out that her distinctive approach aimed to maximise support for women's suffrage, and that

> anti-suffragists based much of their case on the alleged fact that the two sexes had different qualities and that for women to take part in politics would 'unsex' them . . . Mrs Fawcett therefore took her stand on the ground that men and women differed in nature, occupation and training, but that both would benefit from the passage of women's suffrage (1991, 139).

Essentially, to ensure the support of her cause, Fawcett stresses that suffrage will not be a threat to domesticity, motherhood, or wifely duties (a view that echoes that of Wollstonecraft's: see Section 16), reiterating a point she regularly had to emphasise. In another speech given to NUWSS members around this time, Fawcett describes the 'present situation' of the suffrage movement as being stuck in a cycle of these same debates: 'We have no new enemies and they have no new arguments' (National Society for Women's Suffrage 1892, 72).

This speech is described in the Women's Printing Society 1894 edition as having been given in the East End of London in Toynbee Hall, a charitable institution established in 1884 as part of the 'settlement movement' that aimed for better integration of the rich and poor in society, working to address the causes and impacts of poverty; it was named after the social reformer Arnold Toynbee (1852–83). Fawcett regularly spoke at Toynbee Hall throughout the later 1880s, on topics ranging from 'The Influence on Character of Political Conditions' (*Pall Mall Gazette* 1886), 'John Wycliffe and the Dawn of the Reformation in England' (*Times* 1886b), 'The Social Progress of Women During the Last Century' (*Times* 1888a) and 'Men and Women' (*Times* 1888b). The speech here was given earlier than this publication in 1894: Fawcett gave a lecture tour of the same name in Eastbourne, Brighton, Hastings, Portsmouth and Gloucester in late January and early February 1888,[1] and possibly printed it in pamphlet form thereafter. It was published in the *Albemarle* in 1892 as 'Politics in the Home' (Fawcett 1892c, 195–200), reprinted in the *Humanitarian*[2] journal (Fawcett 1893a), and condensed from that version for a US audience in the *Literary Digest* (Fawcett 1893b). It is best known in its 1894 pamphlet form, published by the Women's Printing Society, a cooperative venture founded in 1876 by Mrs Emma Paterson (1848–86) to give women opportunities for working in the printing trade (Crawford 2020). This may be the pamphlet mentioned in the Central Committee of the National Society for Women's Suffrage Annual General Meeting report as being sold for fundraising at the price of 1*d*. (National Society for Women's Suffrage 1894). The text here is taken from that edition, although it is little changed from the *Albemarle* text of 1892.

*

It is now more than twenty years ago since I delivered the first lecture I had ever given in public, on a Brighton platform, in support of women's suffrage.[3] Twenty years is a long time in the life of an individual; it is a very short time in the life of a great movement, and I think, as we look back over these twenty years, those who have devoted themselves to the cause of the enfranchisement of women have good reason to congratulate themselves on the substantial progress which has been made.

We have a direct increase of our strength in Parliament, and we have further cause for congratulation on side issues bearing upon the general position of women; their admission to the Municipal and School Board Suffrages; their activity in many invaluable efforts of social and moral regeneration; their work as poor law guardians;[4] and their success in the higher fields of education.[5] There is also the increased activity of women in political life. Each party now seems to vie with the other in its eagerness in calling upon the women within its ranks to come forward and work for what they believe to be the right side in politics. But, perhaps, more encouraging than any of these direct evidences of the progress the women's movement is making is the general feeling that is beginning to prevail that women's suffrage is a thing that is bound to come. The tendency of public opinion is felt to be set in that direction, and even those who oppose us seem to know that they are fighting a lost battle. Mr Lowell used to say, 'There is a sort of glacial drift in English public opinion; you cannot see it move, but when you look again you see that it has moved.'[6] I think there is no doubt that the glacial drift of English public opinion has moved and is moving in the direction of the active participation of women in politics. We have evidences of this in all parties.

With regard to the differences between men and women, those who advocate the enfranchisement of women have no wish to disregard them or make little of them. On the contrary, we base our claim to representation to a large extent on them. If men and women were exactly alike, the representation of men would represent us; but not being alike, that wherein we differ is unrepresented under the present system.

The motherhood of women, either actual or potential, is one of those great facts of everyday life which we must never lose sight of. To women, as mothers, is given the charge of the home and the care of children. Women are, therefore, by nature as well as by occupation and training, more accustomed than men to concentrate their minds on the home and domestic side of things. But this difference between men and women, instead of being a reason against their enfranchisement, seems to me the strongest possible reason in favour of it; we want the home and domestic side of things to count for more in politics and in the administration of public affairs than they do at present. We want to know how various kinds of legislative enactments bear on the home and on domestic life. And we want to force our legislators to consider the domestic as well as the political results of any legislation which many of them are advocating. We want to say to those of our fellow-countrywomen who, we hope, are about to be enfranchised, 'do not give up one jot or tittle of your womanliness, your love for children, your care for the sick, your gentleness, your self-control, your obedience to conscience and duty, for all these things are terribly wanted in politics. We want women, with their knowledge of child life, especially to devote themselves to the law as it affects children, to children's training in our pauper schools, to the question of boarding out, to the employment of children of tender years, and the bearing of this employment on their after life: to the social life of children and young persons of both sexes in the lower stratum of our towns and villages, to the example set by the higher classes to the lower, to the housing of the poor, to the provision of open spaces and recreation grounds, to the temperance question, to laws relating to health and morals, and the bearing of all these things and many others upon the home, and upon the virtue and the purity of the domestic life of our nation.'

Depend upon it, the most important institution in the country is the home. Anything which threatens the purity and stability of the home threatens the very life-blood of the country; if the homes of the nation are pure, if the standard of duty, of self-restraint and of justice is maintained in them, such a nation has nothing to fear; but if the contrary of all these things can be said, the nation is rotten at the core, and its downfall is only a question of time. Up to the present, my belief is that the home side and the political side of things have been kept too far apart, as if they had nothing to do with one another. We have before us the picture of the whole of Europe armed to the teeth, and the great neighbouring nations ready to spring like wild beasts at each other's throats, all for the sake of fancied political advantage, while the true domestic interests of the nations concerned would be almost as much injured by victory as by defeat. I confess that I think women are all too apt to forget their womanliness, even in such cases as this, and allow their aspirations to be guided by those of the masculine part of the society in which they find themselves. But by strengthening the independence of women, I think we shall strengthen their true native womanliness;[7] they will not so often be led away by the gunpowder and glory will-o'-the-wisp, which is really alien to the womanly nature, but will much more certainly than now cast their influence on whatever side seems to them to make for peace, purity and love.

A large amount of opposition to Women's Suffrage is based on the fact that to women has been given, by nature, the charge of the domestic and home side of things, and there is also the fear that contact with political life would blunt the gentler qualities of women. Let us look at these two objections separately. To women, it is said quite truly, has been given the charge of the home and the domestic side of things. That is to say, most women's lives are wholly or almost wholly devoted to work for their husband and children within their home. I will apply myself to meet the argument against Women's Suffrage based on the fact that the daily business of most women's lives lies in the routine of domestic affairs. For the proper discharge of these duties many very high and noble qualities are needed, and no insignificant amount of practical knowledge. Women who are immersed in domestic affairs should be good economists, knowing how to save and how to spend judiciously; they should know a good deal about the health and training of children, about education, about what influences character and conduct; no quality is more important in the management of servants and children than a strong sense of justice. In proportion as women are good and efficient in what concerns their domestic duties, they will, if they become voters, bring these excellent qualities to bear upon public affairs. Most men are as much taken up by some trade, business or profession in their everyday life as women are by their domestic duties, but we do not say that this man is so industrious and experienced in his business that it is a great pity that he should be admitted to the Franchise; we rather feel that all that makes him a useful member of society in his private life will also make him a good citizen in his public duties. I am well aware that there are some women who are not good for much in the home; in one class they think more of balls and fine clothes than of home duties; cases have been known, I grieve to say, in all classes, where they have broken up their homes through drunkenness and idleness; though for one home broken up and destroyed by a drunken woman there are probably three or four broken up and destroyed by a drunken man. These women who are not good for much domestically will most likely not be good for much politically; but exactly the same thing can be said of the existing male voters. Taking women in the mass, I believe it can be claimed for them that they are faithful and conscientious in the fulfilment of the duties already confided to them, and if this be so, it is the best assurance we can have that they will be faithful and conscientious in the new ones that may be entrusted to them.

I think we may surely claim for women in general a high standard of goodness and virtue. Most of us are probably fortunate enough to know many women who live up to the ideal described by the late Poet Laureate:

>Because right is right,
>To follow right were wisdom in the scorn
>Of consequence.[8]

In so far as conduct is a test of virtue, we have a rough test in the number of men and women respectively who are committed for trial, for serious offences against the law, and we find that the women thus committed are less than a fifth the number of the men, although women are more numerous than men by about four per cent. I do not stop now to enquire what the causes of this may be, but I think the bare fact is a strong evidence that the admission of women to the suffrage would raise rather than lower the average quality, as regards conduct, of the existing constituencies.

Duty is what upholds all the structure of national greatness; why then exclude from the responsibilities of citizenship a large number of women among whom the standard of duty as measured by their conduct is conspicuously high and pure?

Let us now consider the fear that has been expressed that contact with political life will blunt the gentler qualities of women. We know that a very similar fear has been expressed with regard to the extension of higher education to women. It was thought that if a woman knew Greek she would not love her children, and that if she learned mathematics she would forsake her infant for a quadratic equation. Experience has set these fears at rest. It was imagined that if women were admitted to the studies pursued by young men at Oxford and Cambridge, they would imitate the swagger and the slang of the idlest type of undergraduates. Experience has proved that these fears were baseless;[9] may we not also hope that the fears expressed by some of the effects of political life on womanly graces may prove to be equally unfounded? It seems to me very inconsistent and illogical to say with one breath Nature has made women so and so, and so and so, mentioning all kinds of graceful and delightful qualities, and then to add that all these qualities will disappear if a certain alteration takes place in the political constitution of the country. Nature is not so weak and ephemeral as this. All the Acts of Parliament that ever have been or ever can be passed cannot shake the rock upon which the institutions of Nature are founded. To think that we can upset the solemn edicts of Nature by the little laws of human invention is the most grotesque infidelity to Nature that has ever been dreamed of.

If you descend from these general considerations to look at the experience we have thus far had of the result of political activity upon the gentler qualities of women, I think we cannot do better than cite the example which has now for more than fifty years been given us by Queen Victoria. She has been from her early girlhood immersed in a constant succession of political duties and responsibilities, and yet no woman, as wife, mother or friend, has ever shown herself more entirely womanly in her sympathy, faithfulness and tenderness. I like very much the story told of the Queen in the early years of her reign, when one of her ministers apologised for the trouble he was giving her in regard to public business. 'Never mention that word to me again,' she replied, 'only tell me how the thing is to be done, and done rightly, and I will do it if I can.'[10] That is womanly in the best sense, and the very quality we want more of, not in politics only, but everywhere and in every department of life.

When we speak of womanliness and the gentler qualities of the feminine nature, we must be careful not to mistake true for false, and false for true. Is there anything truly feminine in fainting fits, or in screaming at a mouse or at a black beetle? Fifty years ago a female of truly delicate susceptibilities was supposed to faint on the slightest provocation; but there was, I venture to think, nothing truly and essentially womanly in this accomplishment: it was merely a fashion which has now happily passed away. Women don't faint now unless their heart or their digestion is out of order. Merely foolish foibles ought not to be dignified by the name of womanliness; their only advantage lies in their providing a cheap and easy means to persons of the other sex of establishing their own superiority. Those men who are not very sure, in the bottom of their hearts, of their own superiority, naturally like to be assured of it by finding a plentiful supply of women who go into hysterics if a mouse is in the room, know nothing of business except that consols[11] are things that go up and down in the city, or of history except that Alexander the Great was not the son-in-law of Louis XIV. The world would wag on if this kind of womanliness disappeared altogether; what we cannot afford to lose is the true womanliness, mercy, pity, peace, purity and love; and these I think we are justified in believing will grow and strengthen with all that strengthens the individuality and spontaneity of womanhood.

In conclusion, I will only add that I advocate the extension of the franchise to women because I wish to strengthen true womanliness in woman, and because I want to see the womanly and domestic side of things weigh more and count more in all public concerns. It is told in Nehemiah that when the walls of Jerusalem were rebuilt after the captivity, women as well as men shared in the work.[12] Our country now wants the hearts and brains of its daughters as well as the hearts and brains of its sons, for the solution of many perplexing and difficult problems. Let no one imagine for a moment that we want women to cease to be womanly; we want rather to raise the ideal type of womanhood and to multiply the number of those women of whom it may be said:

> Happy he
> With such a mother; faith in womankind

Beats with his blood, and trust in all things high
Comes easy to him, and though he trip and fall
He shall not blind his soul with clay.[13]

Transcribed from a copy in the University Library, University of Cambridge. No known copyright restrictions.

Notes

1. *Sussex Agricultural Express* 1888; *Brighton Gazette* 1888; *Hastings and St Leonards Observer* 1888; *Hampshire Telegraph and Sussex Chronicle* 1888; *Gloucestershire Chronicle* 1888. We have found no record of this speech given in London in 1888. It should be noted, though, that this was a theme Fawcett returned to: a similar speech was given in Cheltenham and Bath in 1894 (*Cheltenham Chronicle* 1894; *Bath Chronicle and Weekly Gazette* 1894).
2. A journal that was launched by leading American suffragist Mrs Victoria Woodhull Martin (1838–1927) alongside her daughter Zula Maud Woodhull (1861–1940) to support Woodhull Martin's ambitions to run again for the presidency of the United States as a humanitarian candidate (*Evening News and Post* 1892).
3. A lecture on the 'Electoral Disabilities of Women' to the Brighton Liberal Registration Association on 23 March 1870 at the Town Hall in Henry Fawcett's constituency (see Fawcett 1924, 91).
4. 'Following the Municipal Franchise Act of 1869 single women owners of property were able to vote in town elections. Then, from 1870 women with property could vote for the School Boards set up by the Forster Act, from 1875, for Poor Law Boards, from 1888 for the newly created County Councils, and from 1894 for the Parish and District Councils that were then established' (Heater 2006, 136).
5. By 1894 in the UK: the University of London was awarding degrees to women (since 1878); women were allowed to take the University of Cambridge Mathematical Tripos examinations (since 1881); College Hall had been opened by University College, London and the London School of Medicine for Women as the first hall of residence for women in the UK (1882); and Scottish universities opened degrees to women after the Universities (Scotland) Act 1889 (Dyhouse 1995).
6. James Russell Lowell (1819–91), American poet, critic and ambassador to Great Britain (1880–5), in a much-reported off-the-record interview printed in the *New York World* in December 1886 (see Knox 1956 for an overview of the scandal). 'The drift is in the direction of popular government' (reported in the *Brisbane Courier* 1886).
7. Fawcett's footnote: 'Mr R. L. Stevenson in one of his stories makes his hero refer to this, when a woman to flatter him repeats, parrot like, what she conceives to be the man's formula on love and honour. "My honour?" he repeated. "For a woman you surprise me . . . You speak, Madame von Rosen, like too many women, with a man's tongue," Prince Otto. P. 205' (Stevenson 1885, 205).
8. Tennyson (1842, 125).
9. Fawcett, with her long and successful involvement with Newnham College, speaks from experience, but it is worth noting that women were not awarded degrees at Cambridge until 1948. Women had studied at Oxford since the 1870s, but were only allowed to take degrees in 1920 (Dyhouse 1995).
10. Fawcett tells this anecdote at more length in her *Life of Her Majesty Queen Victoria* (1895, 38); the source is given as Mrs Jameson: presumably Anna Brownell Jameson (1794–1860), British writer.
11. Consolidated annuities or stock: government debt issues in the form of perpetual bonds.
12. Nehemiah 3:12. Only one set of daughters are named, amid a long list of men and their sons.
13. Tennyson (1847, 158–9).

18

The story of the opening of university education to women, 1894

Cheltenham Ladies' College Magazine. Spring 1894, 5–24.

By 1894, Fawcett had been promoting the education of women for over 25 years. This overview speech indicates her understanding of the political and social changes that were necessary to support women fully entering into higher education, but also discusses the people involved in the movement, particularly other female leaders, and the consistent and necessary support given by some senior academic men and politicians. The original notes it was 'Written for the Educational Conference at Chicago', an event also known as the International Congress of Education of the World's Columbian Exposition, which was held between 25 and 28 July 1893: the educational element of the Chicago World's Fair.[1] Many British teachers visited, subsidised by the UK government (Van Drenth and Van Essen 2004, 162), and Fawcett herself established the Royal Commission for the Chicago Exhibition Sub-Committee on Women's Education, which met in her Gower Street home, raising further funds from the London guilds to send women to the Congress (*Westminster Gazette* 1893). One of those supported with a £50 travel bursary was Miss Mary Louch,[2] head of the training department, Cheltenham Ladies' College[3] (*Globe* 1893).

Fawcett did not attend the Congress herself, but 'had been asked to produce something to show the value of University education for women' (Strachey 1931, 163). She collated a 'series of papers on the Education of Women in Great Britain and her colonies' following an invitation from the Hon. William T. Harris,[4] then commissioner of education of the United States, who was the general chairman of the Congress (National Education Association of the United States 1894, 853–914). Fawcett's paper was 'read by abstract'[5] by Miss E. P. Hughes[6] on 26 July, in a session that also featured a paper on the education of women written by Dorothea Beale,[7] principal of Cheltenham Ladies' College, 'read by abstract' by Miss Louch (United States Bureau of Education [USBE] 1895, 426).

Among the exhibits for the Congress,[8] Fawcett decided to send:

> 'a frame full of photographs of prize babies whose mothers are graduates. Some of the mothers I have asked to give me photographs of their babies,' she added in writing to a friend of this enterprise, 'are too plaguey genteel to let their babies appear in an exhibition; but I am beginning to get a nice collection' (Strachey 1931, 163).

She sent this with an explanation: 'The long row of beautiful children whose mothers have had a university education has the motto appended to it: *Non Angli sed angeli*.'[9] This intended to

> reassure the timid and to remind them that for 1,300 years the beauty of English children has passed into a proverb: so far, it has not been injured by educating their mothers. Experience, as far as it has gone, justifies the belief that education is not one of the things that harm distinctive womanhood[10] (Fawcett in USBE 1895, 1175).

Beale and Fawcett obviously knew each other, and Beale was friends with Elizabeth Garrett, Fawcett's sister.[11] Beale notes that they had compared their papers before the Congress.[12] Fawcett's speech was prepared for the proceedings of the event (Fawcett 1894), with this much-expanded version featuring in the *Cheltenham Ladies' College Magazine* (which was edited by Beale), presumably because of the positive mention of the College throughout. The article places the work of the school in its wider context but also builds on these links and shared messages and ambition for its readership. A shortened and revised version of Beale's speech was also featured in the magazine as a postscript to Fawcett's piece, framed to encourage her pupils to keep working towards a long-term goal, despite any difficulties they may face (Beale 1894b).

*

I propose to endeavour to trace in outline the development in England of one of the main branches of the Women's Movement – the claim to share in higher education.

The defective state of women's education in the first half of the century and still more in earlier times, it is difficult now to realize. Defoe had called attention to it in one of his Essays on Projects.[13] Mary Wollstonecraft had protested against it and against the mass of false theory and evil practice which supported it.[14] Sydney Smith had assailed it with the keen shafts of ridicule.[15] But very little had practically been done to place the education of women on a rational basis. The first definite piece of work in this direction was begun in 1846, and owed its initiative to the Rev. Frederick Denison Maurice,[16] who was then one of the Professors of King's College, London. The idea occurred to him that as it was part of his duty to teach young men at King's College, it would be right and suitable to provide classes for their sisters. The practical outcome of this idea was the foundation of Queen's College.[17] The Dowager Lady Stanley of Alderley[18] seconded Mr Maurice's efforts; he was also aided by Dr Trench, afterwards Archbishop of Dublin,[19] and by the Rev. C. G. Nicolay,[20] the first a professor and second a lecturer at King's College.

Classes for young women were opened in 1846; in 1848 a house was taken in Harley Street, and in 1853 a Royal Charter was obtained. The educational importance of the foundation of Queen's College is difficult to exaggerate. It opened a new life to those who profited by its instruction. Among its earliest pupils were Miss Buss, now Head Mistress of the North London Collegiate School for Girls,[21] and Miss Dorothea Beale, now Head of the Ladies' College, Cheltenham. These two ladies have devoted their whole lives to raise the standard of girls' education. Their schools afterwards served as models for the schools of the Girls' Public Day School Company, and have had a most important influence on development of education all over the United Kingdom.

Queen's College, being in a sense a sister establishment to King's College, was from its foundation a Church of England Institution, whereas Bedford College, founded mainly by Mrs Reid in 1849,[22] was entirely undenominational. As Queen's College is able to boast of Miss Buss and Miss Beale as among its earliest students, so Bedford College lays claim to the distinction of having provided part of the intellectual equipment of 'George Eliot'[23] and Barbara Leigh Smith, afterwards Madame Bodichon,[24] one of the founders of Girton College. After the foundation of Queen's and Bedford there was a long period of quiescence, when, if progress was made at all, it was so slow as to remind one of what Mr Russell Lowell once said of the movement of public opinion in England. He said it was like the movement of glacial drift: you could not see it move, but when you looked again after an interval, you found it had moved.[25] Possibly the slow rate of progress in the development of higher education for women after the foundation of Queen's and Bedford Colleges may be accounted for by the preoccupation of the national mind by the Crimean War[26] and the Indian Mutiny of 1854–6 and 1857–8. Times of national crisis, 'the glory and grief of battle won and lost',[27] may solder a race together, but the years thus occupied are not usually the years when social movements make rapid progress. Such times, however, are great tests of character, national and personal; in the presence of real danger, conventions and insincerities are at a discount; any one man or woman who can do a stroke of work for the country is urged to do it. The national necessities of England during the Crimean War gave Florence Nightingale[28] the opportunity of doing the work which her capacities, character and training had fitted her to do, and indirectly gave an impetus to another movement which has resulted, in England, in the opening of the medical profession and of University education to women. The train of ideas is not difficult to follow. If women can be of essential service to the sick as trained nurses, why should they not also be of essential service to them as doctors? To obtain medical education, women had to knock at the door of the Universities, and while they asked for medical education, they also asked for instruction in other branches of knowledge. In April 1862, my sister, Mrs Anderson, then Miss Elizabeth Garrett,[29] who was working with the aim of obtaining a medical qualification, memorialised the University of London to open its degrees to women. Her application was refused on legal grounds. On the last day of the same month, her father, Mr Newson Garrett, reopened the subject by again addressing the Senate of the University, begging for the reconsideration of his daughter's application and suggesting that a clause should be added to the Charter of the University expressly providing for the admission of women to its examinations and degrees. On May 7th, 1862, Mr Grote,[30] the historian, Vice-Chancellor of the University, moved a resolution favourable to the request of Mr Garrett's memorial. This was seconded by the Right Hon. Robert Lowe, MP (afterwards Lord Sherbrooke),[31] but after a protracted discussion the voting was equal, ten on each side, and the proposal was negatived by the casting vote of the Chancellor.[32] On this occasion the petitioner was able to appeal to the original charter of London University, where it was stated in the broadest possible terms that the University was founded with the object of holding forth 'to all classes and denominations without any distinction whatsoever an encouragement for pursuing a regular and liberal course of education'.[33] It appeared, however, that when this was written, in 1836, the greatest discovery of the nineteenth century, that women are human beings, had not been made. Women were told that though the University was for 'all classes and denominations whatsoever', it was not for them. In the autumn of 1862, a committee was formed to obtain for women admission to University Examinations.[34] The hon. secretary of this committee was Miss Emily Davies and the hon. treasurer was Louisa, Lady Goldsmid.[35] To Miss Davies more than any other single person, this branch of the women's education movement owed its inspiration and direction.

The committee began its work in what they wisely believed to be the line of least resistance. Very few people at that time were prepared to open the Honours and Tripos[36] Examinations of Oxford and Cambridge to women, but girls' schools were familiar and not terrifying objects even to the most timid. The first work undertaken by the committee was the effort to open for girls the University Local Examinations which had been established for boys in 1858.[37] Contemporaneously with this effort (1864), Miss Davies and Miss Bostock[38] were instrumental in preparing, independently of the committee, a memorial to the recently appointed Schools Inquiry Commission,[39] praying them to include girls' schools, and the application of endowments to girls' education, within the scope of their inquiry. The success of this application was one of the most important turning points in the struggle for the reform of girls' education. It gave the reformers a mass of evidence authenticated by the Royal Commission. It brought to light the almost entire exclusion of girls from the benefits of educational endowments, and had a very important bearing on the work that was subsequently done by the Endowed Schools Commissioners[40] in restoring to girls some of the educational endowments of which they had in previous generations been deprived.

It is true that some school mistresses, when the Schools Inquiry Commission was appointed, deeply resented its investigations. One replied that the questions were too inquisitorial for any woman of spirit to answer, and that every girl of spirit would leave the room on the appearance of the assistant commissioner in it.[41] Another replied to a letter asking permission to visit the school, 'I am sincerely sorry to find that Ministers have nothing better to do than to pry into the ménage of private families, as I consider my establishment, which has been in existence 30 years, and always held in the highest position.'[42] The Commission reported in 1868. It is unnecessary to dwell in detail on the character of the report as regards girls' schools.[43] It is sufficient to say that with but few exceptions, such as the Quakers' School at York, the North London Collegiate School and the Ladies' College, Cheltenham, hardly any girls' schools were reported upon as supplying their pupils with a liberal education. One of the chief causes of the defects in girls' schools was the want of suitable preparation for the profession of teaching on the part of governesses: 'my poverty and not my will consents'[44] might have been the motto of all but a very small proportion of the women who embarked upon this honourable and difficult profession. Another reason for the low standard of education in girls' schools was the indifference of parents and the public generally to anything in girls' education beyond what was showy and attractive. As a consequence of this want of interest in good education, nearly the whole of the educational endowments of the country had been appropriated for boys. The report of the Commission afforded a solid foundation of fact on which the reformers of girls' education have industriously built. Public attention was thoroughly aroused, and plans for improving the education of girls sprang up in a variety of directions. Very much was done to repair the injustice done to girls in the matter of endowments by the labours of the Endowed Schools Commission, now merged in the Charity Commission.[45]

Meanwhile Miss Davies' committee, formed in 1862, took up, as I have just said, as its first piece of work, the opening of the Local Examinations of the University of Cambridge to girls. These examinations, it is hardly necessary to say, are for young people of the school age: the Juniors must be under 16, and the Seniors under 18 (Oxford, 19): the examinations are held simultaneously in different local centres all over the country and in the colonies. When first established they were for boys only: in December 1863, an experimental examination for girls was held in London,[46] at which, with the consent of the Local Examinations Syndicate at Cambridge, all the regulations enforced in the case of boys were strictly observed. The next year a memorial signed by more than 1,000 teachers of girls and many other influential persons was addressed to the Vice-Chancellor of the University: the reply was favourable, but the matter had to be referred to a vote of the Senate. On March 12th, 1865, Miss Davies received a telegram from Mr Markby,[47] Secretary of the Cambridge Local Examinations Syndicate: 'Send up all you can to-morrow: voting at 12: opposition organised.'[48] On March 13th he wrote as follows: '55 to 51, so we are successful: it was a close contest. I got votes enough to turn the scale just before going into the Senate House.'[49] Cambridge was thus first in the field as regards English Universities to open its examinations to girls: it was several years before Oxford opened her local examinations also. The chief point to be remarked is that, owing chiefly to the strong views entertained on the subject by Miss Davies, exactly the same examination papers were used for boys and girls and exactly the same regulations were observed for both, except at first in the case of Cambridge the names of the girls examined were not given. Miss Davies has always been a very staunch opponent of any special University examinations for women, or of any variation, in the case of women, of what the University requires from the men who offer themselves for the Tripos examinations. Difference on this subject is the chief difference between those who have guided the fortunes of Girton and Newnham respectively.

The labours of Miss Davies' committee having been successful in opening the local examination to girls, they immediately afterwards began to project the idea of a College for women-students beyond the school age, where they could be prepared for University examinations of a more advanced character. The first list of subscriptions to the 'proposed college for women' is dated 1869, and amounts to nearly £3,000. The executive committee met in London, and the College when first opened in 1869, was situated at Hitchin, in Hertfordshire, about half-way between London and Cambridge.[50] In 1872 the College was transferred to handsome buildings specially erected for it at Girton, about two miles from Cambridge.

Having traced the development of one branch of the women's education movement as far as the opening of Girton College, I must now ask my readers to allow me to trace the development of another branch of the same movement which culminated in the foundation of Newnham College. I like to think of these two Colleges as sister stems of a beech tree, deriving their nourishment from the same root, but having an independent growth and differing from each other in some externals. The development of each presents some interesting examples of the inter-dependence or *solidarité* of the several parts of the women's movement.

The same energy that produced Girton also gave the first impulse to the opening of the medical profession for women in England, and also to the opening to women of University examinations of identically the same character as those provided for men.

The energy that produced Newnham produced also what is known as University Extension,[51] which in its turn led to the formation all over England of University Colleges in our principal centres of population, where men and women, not able to proceed to either of our ancient Universities, can obtain advanced education.

The promoters of Girton set before themselves, with unalterable determination, the aim of making the tests applied to University education for women exactly the same as for men. The promoters of Newnham approached the subject of the reform of women's education in a rather different spirit. They found it defective and sought to remedy its defects without desiring to follow exactly on the lines of men's education where they thought these were capable of improvement. Both in my judgment have been most useful; they have been complementary to each other. Girton has maintained for women the highest intellectual standard.

Newnham showed a greater power of adaptability to the then conditions of the educational problem, and had in view excellence of examination as an educational test, rather than identity of examination of women with men all through the University course.

Miss Anne J. Clough[52] was to Newnham all, and I may say, more than all, that Miss Davies was at Girton. She was not only the founder of the College and the originator of the movement from which the College sprang – Miss Davies was that to Girton – but Miss Clough was for the first twenty-one years of its existence its Principal. She, more than any other person, was, as a woman, the representative, in the University, of University Education for women; and she was the embodiment of wisdom, kindness, gentleness and tact; that won her not only the enthusiastic loyalty of her students and personal friends, but the cordial respect and consideration of University authorities. Her death last year was referred to in a University Sermon, preached by the Bishop of Peterboro', and in the annual address given by the Vice-Chancellor as one of the chief losses which the cause of Education has recently sustained. Her combination of sweetness, humour and determination made her a unique personality, to which much of her singular power of influencing other minds was due.

In 1866 Miss Clough was resident in Liverpool, and with the co-operation of Mrs Josephine Butler[53] formed the Liverpool Ladies' Educational Society.[54] This Society instituted courses of lectures for ladies, requiring steady work from those who attended them. After rather more than two years' successful work, the Society enlarged its aims. University lecturers were engaged, and other towns were invited to join in the scheme, so that the lecturers might go from town to town spreading the means of higher education for women in each. The inaugural meeting of this Society, which took the name of the 'North of England Council for the Higher Education of Women',[55] was called by Miss Clough at Mrs Butler's house in 1869. Manchester, Leeds and Sheffield joined, and the Ladies' Educational Council was formed with Mrs Butler as its president and Miss Clough as its secretary. This was the beginning of University Extension and ultimately of the University Colleges in many of our chief cities, and led indirectly to the foundation of Newnham College.

Among the Cambridge men who were in hearty sympathy with the efforts to spread education among women were Mr Henry Sidgwick;[56] and Mr James Stuart,[57] both of Trinity College. Mr (now Professor) Sidgwick, with the help of Miss Clough, undertook the direction of the movement for the Higher Education of Women in the University. Mr Stuart (now member for Shoreditch) directed or rather created the movement for University Extension. Time does not allow me to follow the history of this movement in any detail. It has had an important bearing on the higher education of women. Its principle is now well known. 'If Mahomet cannot go to the mountain, the mountain must go to Mahomet.'[58] To women in their homes, to clerks at their desks, to artisans at their work, even to the princess in the palace, Mr Stuart and his coadjutors said 'if you cannot go to the University, the University shall come to you'.

In consequence of Mr Stuart's efforts, University Extension has spread all over the English-speaking world. Chatauqua[59] in the United States has sprung from it. In England many of the towns that took the lead in welcoming the University Extension scheme were not long content with the visits of itinerant lecturers. The Firth College, Sheffield;[60] University College, Nottingham;[61] Yorkshire College, Leeds;[62] and the University Colleges of Liverpool,[63] Bristol[64] and Newcastle[65] sprang up in response to the demand for higher education that had grown up out of the University Extension movement.[66]

The University Colleges of Wales[67] and the Mason College, Birmingham,[68] are probably related to the same movement; and to these Colleges all over the country we certainly owe the establishment of the Victoria University.[69] It must be noted that the origin of the whole movement was in that meeting called by Miss Clough in Mrs Butler's house in 1862. Hence, as of so many other good things, we may truly say it 'Cherchez la femme',[70] and the consequence is that University Extension is one of the few really Democratic institutions in this country; it has been absolutely open and equal to all classes of men and women from the beginning. Women are admitted on equal terms to all the classes, either at Extension centres or at University Colleges (except when these latter include medical schools); and when Victoria University was founded by Royal Charter in 1880, all its degrees were as open to women as to men.[71] The slow and grudging recognition of the claims of women to higher education, which is a blot on the history of Owens College, Manchester,[72] is largely due to its being an older foundation, opened in 1851, before it had been discovered that the education of women was an important factor in national development. One other word must be added about University Colleges. They, and University College, London,[73] and the University Extension classes everywhere, are the only things in England we have to show in the way of mixed education. If we may still speak of this as an experiment, the experiment has been thoroughly successful: men and women sit together in the same class rooms, learn the same subjects, are tested by the same examinations, and the world has gone on much the same as it did before, only better – by giving men and women more points of sympathy and a larger number of common interests. Perhaps Mr Curzon, FRGS,[74] would say this is breaking down the barriers between the sexes. Possibly it is, but it must be remembered that Nature is a great sinner in this respect too. She breaks down the barriers between the sexes in a very effectual way, when she places men and women, as husbands and wives, brothers and sisters, together in the same family.

Going back now to the beginning of Newnham College, the Lectures established by the North of England Council for the Higher Education for Women led to a demand for an University examination of a higher grade than the Senior Local: and in 1868 the Higher Local Examination for women over 18 was established by the University of Cambridge.[75] Miss Davies and the Girton Committee opposed this as antagonistic to their main principle – identity of educational tests for men and women. Miss Clough, Mr Sidgwick and the other promoters of Newnham supported it as meeting a present need. Lectures for women *in* Cambridge, much on the same plan as those organised in Liverpool and other Northern towns by Miss Clough and Mrs Butler, were projected in 1869 and actually begun in 1870. Mr Henry Sidgwick was the originating mind of the whole scheme. I hope I may be pardoned a feeling of satisfaction in recalling the fact that the first meeting in Cambridge to discuss this plan was held in my house in December 1869;[76] and that the first document in the books containing the history of Newnham is the notice convening this meeting. The necessity of seeking the line of least resistance is apparent throughout this little document. The economy of having lectures for women delivered in Cambridge by lecturers already engaged in lecturing on the same subject in their respective Colleges is pointed out. There was perhaps another kind of economy in this method of stating our case. The circular also mentions that though the immediate object of the lecturers would be to afford means of higher education to women residing in Cambridge, yet if women from a distance, not having friends in Cambridge, 'should come here for the purpose of attending lectures', it would be necessary to provide 'some lodging or hall' for them! The word 'hall' was the only vestige of intrepidity in the circular. But I ask those who would point the finger of scorn at us to remember that if we had said we wished to establish a College for women at Cambridge, we might as well have said we wished to establish a College for women in Saturn. It was an absolute necessity to proceed with great caution. We made a good deal of use of the fact that the University had established an examination for women over 18, and that the Lectures for Women were designed with a view of providing the education which that Examination had been instituted to test.[77] We asked no recognition from the University further than what had already been given. The whole machinery of the lectures was voluntary. Several of the most distinguished professors had for many years past allowed the presence of ladies at their lectures. And many of these, besides some of the leading College lecturers, gave their support to 'the Lectures for Women'.[78] Our first list of friends contains the names of Professors Adams,[79] Cayley[80] and Maurice,[81] besides those of Messrs W. G. Clark,[82] Clifford,[83] Jebb,[84] Marshall,[85] Skeat[86] and Todhunter;[87] and the first series of lectures was delivered by men – many of whom had even then gained a world-wide reputation in their respective subjects. How much the whole movement owes these men, who befriended us at the very beginning of our efforts, I hope none of us will ever forget. In the Michaelmas Term, 1870, Mr John Stuart Mill and his step-daughter, Miss Taylor,[88] gave us a scholarship of £40 for two years. The same year, A. J. Balfour, MP,[89] gave us £20 towards a fund for a similar purpose. I mention these names as an illustration of the fact to which I shall presently refer – that the friends of women's education are not exclusively associated with any one political party. The numbers attending the lectures made satisfactory progress and the contingency which had been foreseen from the beginning became a reality: women from a distance, not having friends in Cambridge, desired to reside in the town for the purpose of attending the lectures; and in 1871 Miss Clough was invited by the Committee to come to Cambridge and open a house for these women students, of whom at first there were five only. This was the beginning of what is now Newnham College.

The plan pursued by Newnham and Girton in regard to the examinations of the University differed in one not unimportant respect. Newnham used the Higher Local Examination, established by the University for women over 18, as the first test of educational progress, proceeding afterwards by the permission of the examiners to enter the students for the Tripos examinations of the University. The view of the authorities of Newnham was that the Higher Local was a decidedly better educational test than the University examination for men known as 'the Little Go', and that it was also more suited to the needs of women. Girton, as I before explained, would have nothing to do with any special examination for women: every Girton student therefore had to pass 'the Little Go' before applying to the Examiners for leave to be examined in any of the Tripos Examinations. There were and are other minor differences between Girton and Newnham. Girton is founded on the principles of the Church of England, Newnham is completely unsectarian. Girton allows its students to study for the ordinary degree examinations. Newnham students only prepare for the Tripos examinations. If for any reason it is considered unsuitable to submit a student to the test of a Tripos, she is, at Newnham, encouraged to take various groups of the Higher Local. The ordinary, or 'Poll' examination, is not recommended. Girton is two miles out of Cambridge, and is governed by an Executive Committee which meets in London and is composed almost entirely of London people. Newnham is in Cambridge and is managed by a Council which meets at the College and consists almost wholly of Cambridge people.

In 1878, as the result of the long struggle for medical education, all the degrees of London University were thrown open to women.[90] This undoubtedly had a stimulating effect upon the friends of women's education in the University of Cambridge. The system represented by the London University would be unduly favoured if London gave perfect equality to its women students, while Cambridge merely suffered them to exist without giving them any claim to have their knowledge tested by University standards.

From the time of their foundation to the year 1881, Newnham and Girton students could only enter for University examinations, other than the Higher Local, by grace and favour of the examiners. There was no official recognition by the University of the women students. In 1880 a movement was initiated by Prof. and Mrs Steadman Aldis[91] of Newcastle, and supported by Miss Davies and the Girton Committee, to put an end to this state of things, and memorials were sent by them to the Senate of the University, praying that degrees might be opened to women who fulfilled the conditions of residence and of examination which the University demanded of its male students. Another memorial, promoted by Prof. Sidgwick, did not go so far as this. It was signed exclusively by members of the University and prayed that the arrangement by which the students of Girton and Newnham had been for the last 10 years informally admitted to University examinations should be placed on a formal and stable footing by receiving the sanction of the University. This proposal was carried by grace of the Senate by an overwhelming majority on the 24th February 1881.[92] From that time women had an assured position in the University; their claim to education was formally sanctioned. The success of the whole movement has from one point of view been very remarkable. The high places gained by women in the various tripos examinations is so well known as to require no emphasis.[93] There have been women senior in every tripos except those in Theology, Law and the Semitic Languages. This year at Newnham they have had 8 first classes, 18 second classes, 8 third classes and 2 students allowed the ordinary degree. But from another point of view there has been no progress. Women may take the highest honours that the University Examinations afford to either men or women: but they are not members of the University; they have no degree; the humblest poll man who has scraped through just sufficiently well to put BA after his name has a position superior to theirs. University prizes are not open to them for competition. And à fortiori [sic] none of the educational posts, which are of course reserved for members of the University. The whole education plant of the University is used by them on sufferance; threats have been heard that women will be desired not to occupy a seat in the library, because there are no more seats than enough for 'members of the University'.[94] At Oxford the women students are in a precisely similar position; they have no right to attend University lectures, and quite lately Mr Froude announced that he would in future lecture only to men[95] – that is to say to members of the University to whom he is paid to lecture. A gentleman of whom I know nothing but his name, Mr Mark Reed, commented with much satisfaction on this in *Macmillan's Magazine,* and spoke with the utmost contempt of 'girls playing at being undergraduates', and of the 'serious business of academical life being turned into an unseemly farce'[96] by the presence of ladies at University lectures. The intellectual distinction of many women students, and the scholarly work done by several of them after they have passed the Tripos examinations seem to have produced no effect in securing for them any approach to equality with members of the University. A series of memorials organised by Miss Davies, and very influentially signed, were presented to the Vice-Chancellor and Senate in 1887, asking that women might be admitted to degrees.[97] These memorials were not supported by Professor Sidgwick, who thought the time had not then come for raising the question of degrees. The Council of the University declined to appoint a syndicate to consider the question of opening degrees to women, and since that time no further effort has been made in this direction.

I have given the history of the Higher Education of women in the University of Cambridge at some length, because that has been the centre of the movement so far as England is concerned, and also because I am personally acquainted with its details, whereas I only know the history of Somerville, Lady Margaret and St Hugh's, Cheltenham, Holloway and Westfield Colleges and of the Welsh University Colleges at second-hand. But I will briefly mention what has been done for women's education at other University centres in various parts of the United Kingdom. The Association for the Education of Women in Oxford[98] provides the teaching for the Oxford Women's Colleges. The regulations of the University of Oxford in regard to women do not confine the examinations of the University to women who reside within its precincts. Students may be prepared for these examinations in their own homes, or at Colleges such as Cheltenham, Holloway and the Welsh University Colleges. This is the main distinction between Oxford and Cambridge so far as their connection with the women's education is concerned. The vote of the University of Oxford opening its examinations to women was passed in 1884.[99] Somerville was opened in 1879; Lady Margaret in 1879, its younger sister St Hugh's in 1886, St Hilda's in 1893. Westfield is a College for women in London, conducted on Church of England principles. It was founded in 1882 and prepares students for the degrees of the London University. The Royal Holloway College, the palatial buildings and endowment of which are due to the munificence of the late Thomas Holloway,[100] was opened by Her Majesty in the year of her Jubilee, 1887. It prepares students for the Oxford examinations and also for the London degrees. The Welsh University Colleges at Bangor, Aberystwyth and Cardiff all have Halls for women students, and women are admitted on equal terms to all their educational advantages. They prepare their students for the examinations of the Universities of Oxford and London, and in general for any University examinations where residence is not required. Though the limits of time at my disposal forbid me to do more than glance at the development of University examination for women in Scotland and Ireland, I cannot conclude without a brief reference to it. The Royal Commission appointed under the Universities of Scotland Act, 1889, had special powers bestowed upon it by the Act to enable each of the four Scottish Universities to 'admit women to graduation in one or more faculties and to provide for their instruction'.[101] The Commission acted on these powers, and on the 22nd February 1892, they issued an ordinance *enabling*, not compelling, each University to provide for the instruction and graduation of women. This was a culminating point after years of patient and persistent effort, the chief promoters of which have been, in Edinburgh, Professor Mason[102] and Miss Louisa Stevenson,[103] and in Glasgow, Mrs Elder,[104] Mrs Campbell (of Tulliechewan)[105] and Miss Galloway.[106] This ordinance lay for three months on the table of the House, and received the Queen's assent on June 28th, 1892. Each of the Scottish Universities has acted on its newly acquired powers. Edinburgh, St Andrew's and Aberdeen have opened their Science and Arts' Classes to women, and Glasgow has incorporated Queen Margaret College, a separate College for women, as an integral part of the University. 'The two systems of conjoint and separate teaching' for men and women 'have thus been inaugurated'.[107] Much excellent work has already been done by women-students of the Scottish Universities, and they have already borne away many University distinctions and prizes.

In Ireland one of the most important steps for the development of women's education was taken when it was decided in 1878, mainly through the efforts of Miss Isabella Tod,[108] of Belfast, with the Parliamentary assistance of the late Lord Iddesleigh,[109] to open the Intermediate Examinations to girls.[110] Previous to this, the Dublin and Queen's University Local Examinations had been open to girls, and the University of Dublin had instituted some special examinations for women. When the Queen's University, Ireland, was absorbed in the Royal University, in 1879,[111] all the examinations and degrees were thrown open to women. The Royal University, Ireland, it will be understood, occupies almost the same position as the London University does in England; that is, it is an examining not a teaching University. From the commencement it has had a considerable number of women graduates, and the proportion of distinctions and prizes taken by women has been very satisfactory, and the manner in which the women students have been received and welcomed affords a favourable contrast to scenes that have taken place in other parts of the United Kingdom. It will, perhaps, be remembered that an honorary degree in music was conferred by the authorities of the Royal University on the Princess of Wales, on the occasion of her visit to Ireland, a few years ago.[112] I believe this is the only instance of an honorary degree being given to a woman by any University.[113] The classes in Arts and Medicine at Queen's College, Belfast, are open to women. Alexandra College, Dublin (already referred to), and Victoria College, Belfast, are colleges for women only which prepare students for the Examinations of the Royal University.

Last year, when the tercentenary of Trinity College, Dublin, was celebrated, the occasion was used to present to the Fellows a memorial, most influentially signed, begging them to open their degrees to women.[114] The memorial was signed only by Irish men and women, and pointed out among other things that it would be most fitting, when the College was celebrating its foundation by the greatest of England's Queens, to extend the benefits of graduation to women. The College has as yet returned no definite answer to the memorialists, but I am informed that the matter is arousing a great deal of consideration, and that an answer may be expected during the autumn.[115]

When one looks back on what has been done within the limits of one generation to secure for women, in each part of the United Kingdom, the benefits of University Education, the wonder appears to me not that the progress has been so slow, but that with the materials at command, it has been so rapid. A comparison is often made by those who remember both movements, between the opening of University Education to Nonconformists[116] and its opening to Women. The two movements are alike in many important respects: each is in a sense an attack upon exclusiveness and privilege, not by levelling down but by levelling up. But the Nonconformists in their great struggle had the enormous advantage of possessing a large share of political power. Do you suppose that religious tests would have been abolished at our two ancient Universities when they were, if not one single Nonconformist throughout the country possessed a parliamentary vote? The friends of women's education have achieved a very large degree of success, but when we come to questions that require to be dealt with by legislation, the weakness of their position is only too manifest. Their clients have no votes and are unable to claim any of the time or attention of the Representative Chamber. They are entirely dependent on the accidental goodwill of enlightened individuals. It is difficult to make bricks without straw, and it is making bricks without clay for any mass of persons without votes to attempt to make a claim upon the time of the House of Commons. Not long ago the greatest of living Parliamentarians and the most powerful political personality of our times made a speech at the Distribution of Prizes in which, referring particularly to the educational position of women, he said they were subjected to 'gross injustice, flagrant injustice, shameful injustice';[117] but, alas, in his political addresses to his countrymen he makes no appeal to them, to enable him to remove these injustices.

    I am almost tempted to think that we have made as much progress as we can make without the lever of the Parliamentary vote. The peculiarity of our position in having no scintilla of political power has not however been wholly without its advantages. Neither party has ever been able to make any political capital by removing the injustices under which women labour, and therefore we have had no spectacle of the whole of one party clamouring for their removal, and the whole of the other enthusiastically endeavouring to preserve them. The friends of women's education have been found among the best and most enlightened men of all parties, as I think the names mentioned in the course of this address are sufficient to prove.

    In conclusion, I hope I am not overbold when I say that on looking backward on the past, and forward towards future prospects, we may fairly congratulate ourselves. We no longer resent Mr Lowell's comparison. The movement of glacial drift, though slow, is overwhelmingly powerful and so continuous as to almost baffle imagination. We may well be content that the renaissance of the 19th century, the awakening of women to a perception of the wonders of the old learning and the new science, should go on without haste and without rest.

Transcribed from a copy in Cheltenham Ladies' College Archives.
No known copyright restrictions.

Notes

1. The World's Columbian Exposition of 1893, or Chicago World's Fair, commemorated the 400th anniversary of Columbus' voyage to America by educating, entertaining and selling to 28 million visitors, featuring exhibitors from 46 nations over a six-month period (Bolotin and Laing 2002). Aside from the spectacle, it also became famous for the opportunities that it offered to women, including hosting the 'World's Congress of Representative Women' in May 1893, and for 'the much commented upon Woman's Building', which 'represented a highpoint in women's collective efforts to use the language of exhibition to praise their contribution to the social and moral economies of their respective nations' (Boussahba-Bravard and Rogers 2017, 15).
2. Mary Louch (1854–1947), head of the (teacher) training department at Cheltenham Ladies' College from 1888 to 1903 (*Cheltenham Chronicle and Gloucestershire Graphic* 1947), having previously undertaken the Cambridge Teacher Honours Certificate (presumably under Elizabeth Hughes: see note 6) (Cheltenham Ladies' College 1894).
3. Cheltenham Ladies' College is an independent school for girls aged 11 to 18 in Gloucestershire, England, founded in 1853 (Cheltenham Ladies' College 2020).
4. William Torrey Harris (1835–1909), educator and philosopher.
5. It is unclear what 'read by abstract' means, and the order in which the different versions of the paper were prepared, edited or expanded and published cannot be certain. In the Congress programme, they are given as 'Papers on the university education of women in England, prepared by Miss Fawcett [sic] and Miss Beale of London. Read by abstract by Miss E. P. Hughes and Miss. M. Louch, of London. Other papers prepared by foreign delegates for this department read by title or by abstract (and to be printed in full in the volume of proceedings)' (USBE 1895, 426). The shorter version of Fawcett's paper, in the proceedings of the Congress (Fawcett 1894c, 853), is simply titled 'University Education for Women in England'.
6. 'Miss E. P. Hughes, of Cambridge University, the accomplished daughter of Dr Hughes, of Barry . . . was amongst those who attended the World's Fair at Chicago' (*Barry Dock News* 1893). Elizabeth Phillips Hughes (1851–1925) was a student of Newnham who became a leading figure in education in Wales and the first head of the Cambridge Training College in 1885 (Gardner 1921, 76), which was later named Hughes Hall after her (Hughes Hall 2020).
7. Dorothea Beale (1831–1906), suffragist, educational reformer, author and principal of Cheltenham Ladies' College, 1858–1906. 'Miss Beale has received an invitation from Dr W. T. Harris, the Commissioner of Education of the United States, to attend the Congress of Education to be held at Chicago in July, to take part in the deliberations, and also to allow her name to be placed on the list of Honorary Vice-Presidents. She felt herself obliged to decline so long and fatiguing a journey, but she has sent some photographs and is writing a paper' (Cheltenham Ladies' College 1893, 153). Her speech, 'A Few Words of Retrospect and Forecast', is available in the proceedings of the Congress (Beale 1894a), and in a revised and shortened form in the college magazine (Beale 1894b).
8. The Woman's Education report, which aimed to exhibit 'as would form within certain limits a fair representation of English women's work in various fields of activity' (Fawcett, quoted in USBE 1895, 1174), included handicrafts, embroidery and needlework, and nursing and hygiene. Fawcett was responsible for 'Education, including medical' (p. 1175).
9. Meaning 'they are not Angles, but angels', reportedly spoken by St Gregory in the sixth century when he encountered pale English boys at a slave market, causing him to aim to convert then pagan Anglo-Saxon England to Christianity, as reported in Bede; see McClure and Collins (1999, 70–1).
10. Fawcett paraphrases Tennyson here: 'let her make herself her own / To give or keep, to live and learn and be / All that not harms distinctive womanhood', from *The Princess: A medley*, Part VII (Tennyson 1847, 156).
11. Beale and Garrett were both founding members of the Kensington Society, a women's discussion group founded in 1865 which was 'the location of the 1866 discussion of women's suffrage that led to the formation of an organized women's suffrage campaign' (Davies 2004, xxxiii).
12. 'When Mrs Fawcett and I came to compare notes we found that our papers covered much of the same ground. Mine had been written during the brief intervals of school work: hers was far more complete. I therefore willingly suppressed mine' (Beale 1894a, 862; Beale 1894b, 25).

13 'An Academy for Women' in Defoe (1697 [reprinted in 1969], 282–91).
14 In *A Vindication of the Rights of Woman* (Wollstonecraft 1792).
15 Rev. Sydney Smith (1771–1845), writer and Anglican cleric. See 'Female Education' (Smith 1810).
16 See Section 3, note 34.
17 An independent school for girls in London founded in 1848 by Maurice, and the first institution in Great Britain to award academic qualifications to women (Queen's College London 2020).
18 Henrietta Maria Stanley (née Dillon-Lee) (1807–95), Lady Stanley of Alderley, political hostess and campaigner for women's education.
19 Fawcett's footnote: 'Archbishop Trench afterwards became one of the chief promoters of Alexandra College, Dublin': Richard Chenevix Trench (1807–86).
20 Charles Grenfell Nicolay (1815–97), English clergyman, geographer and geologist.
21 Frances Mary Buss (1827–94).
22 Elizabeth Jesser Reid (1789–1866), social reformer and philanthropist, and founder of Bedford College. See Royal Holloway 2020.
23 Marian Evans (1819–80), better known as George Eliot, attended lectures in geometry at the Ladies' College in Bedford Square in 1851 (Ashton 2008).
24 Barbara Leigh Smith Bodichon (1827–91), artist and women's activist.
25 See Section 17, note 6.
26 October 1853–February 1856.
27 From Tennyson's *The Cup: A Tragedy* 1.2 (1884, 25).
28 Florence Nightingale (1820–1910), reformer of army medical services and nursing.
29 Elizabeth Garrett Anderson (see Introduction). See Manton 1958.
30 George Grote: see Section 11, note 21.
31 Robert Lowe (1811–92), Viscount of Sherbrooke.
32 Fawcett's footnote: 'It should perhaps be explained that the Chancellor, the late Lord Granville, was personally favourable to Miss Garrett's petition; he gave his casting vote as the chairman against it, in obedience to the general understanding that the casting vote of chairman should be given in such a way as not to disturb the *status quo*.'
33 University of London 2020.
34 See Wills (1951, 271) for an overview of the committee's establishment and work.
35 Louisa Sophia Goldsmid (1819–1908), feminist and promoter of women's education.
36 'A course of study leading to an honours degree at Cambridge University, where the student is required to pass two tripos examinations in order to be awarded their Bachelor of Arts. The name refers to the three-legged stool on which, in medieval times, graduates sat to deliver a satirical speech at their degree ceremony' (Oxford Reference 2020b).
37 See Kellaghan and Greaney (2019, 52).
38 Elizabeth (Eliza) Anne Bostock (1817–98), promoter of women's education.
39 'The Schools Inquiry Commission was the last of three Commissions appointed by the government between 1858 and 1864 to examine education in England and Wales and to make recommendations. Each dealt with the education of a particular social class . . . The Schools Inquiry Commission, chaired by Lord Taunton, was appointed in 1864 and reported in 1868 on schools for the middle classes . . . The Commissioners recommended the establishment of a national system of secondary education based on the existing endowed schools . . . The Commissioners were also profoundly concerned about the provision of education for girls' (Education in England 2020).
40 The Endowed Schools Act 1869 aimed to reform the charities on which schools were based: the commissioners 'were empowered to prepare schemes for the reorganization of governing bodies and the revision of charities, including their extension to the education of girls' (Lawson and Silver 1973, 304).
41 Schools Inquiry Commission (1868, 68).
42 Schools Inquiry Commission (1868, 69).
43 Original editor's note: 'This occupied twenty blue books. The reports on girls' schools and selections from the evidence were, by permission of the Commissioners, printed in one volume by Miss Beale; a few copies remain, and can be purchased from the secretary of this Magazine, price One Shilling. – [Editor.]'
44 *Romeo and Juliet* 5.1.
45 The Endowed Schools Commission was absorbed into the Charity Commission in 1874 (Lawson and Silver 1973, 304).

46 See British and Foreign School Society (1869, 21) for an account.
47 Rev. Thomas Markby (1824–70), fellow and classical lecturer of Trinity Hall, Cambridge, and supporter of women's education.
48 Stephen (1976, 99).
49 See Stephen (1976, 100): 'Miss Garrett's congratulations came promptly: "Your slip with the good news was most welcome. To win by ever so small a majority is delightful. This will be the stepping-stone to so much more."'
50 For the choice of Hitchin, see Stephen 1976. A combination of being between Oxford and Cambridge, affordability of renting a temporary house, the supportive Vicar of Hitchin, who was a senior wrangler at Cambridge, and Miss Davies's strong support were all factors, although many objections were raised about the distance from Cambridge, the time it would take to travel there, and the lack of museum and library facilities.
51 The organisation of courses in higher education for those who are not full-time students, including offering university-level lectures, teaching and examinations to those who are not university members. This activity is now commonly known in the UK sector as continuing education. The University Extension had its own movement which promoted and expanded related activities: see Adams 1900 for an overview and history.
52 Anne Jemima Clough (1820–92), first principal of Newnham College and promoter of women's education.
53 Josephine Elizabeth Butler (née Grey) (1828–1906), social reformer and women's activist.
54 See Clough (1897, 117–18).
55 In November 1867; see Clough (1897, 119–45) for its activities.
56 See Section 2, note 1.
57 James Stuart (1843–1913), professor of mechanism and applied mechanics and fellow of Trinity College.
58 A common saying, originating in Francis Bacon's 1625 essay 'Of Boldness' (quoted in Bacon 1908, 36).
59 A movement promoting adult education in the United States that was popular throughout the late nineteenth and early twentieth centuries; see Rieser 2003.
60 An arts and science college founded in 1879, it merged with other local colleges to become University College of Sheffield in 1897, which received its royal charter in 1905 to become the University of Sheffield (2020).
61 Opening in 1881 as the city's first civic college, it was awarded the royal charter in 1948, becoming the University of Nottingham (2020).
62 The Yorkshire College of Science was founded in 1874, and was open to all faiths and backgrounds. Combining with other colleges in Manchester and Liverpool to become the federal Victoria University in 1884, it was awarded its royal charter in 1904 to allow the city to have its own higher education institution: the University of Leeds (2020).
63 Opening in 1881, it received its royal charter in 1903, becoming the University of Liverpool (2007).
64 Opening to both male and female students in 1876, it was given a royal charter in 1901, becoming the University of Bristol (2020).
65 The Newcastle College of Physical Science was founded in 1871, becoming Durham College of Physical Science in 1883, Armstrong College in 1904, part of the University of Durham in 1908, King's College, Durham, in 1934 and the University of Newcastle upon Tyne in 1963 (Newcastle University 2018).
66 Fawcett's footnote: 'I have not ascertained the number of women students attending classes at all the various University Colleges: but I take the one at Nottingham as a fair example of the rest, and find on enquiry from Professor Symes, the Principal, that in the year just closed 200 women attended day classes, and 750 attended evening classes.'
67 The University of Wales was a federal university founded by royal charter in 1893 with three colleges: Aberystwyth (founded in 1872), Bangor (founded in 1884) and Cardiff (founded in 1883); Swansea was added in 1920. The university was reorganised in 1996, with constituent organisations awarding their own degrees from 2008 (Aberystwyth University 2020).
68 Mason Science College was founded in 1875, and became part of the newly founded University of Birmingham in 1900, the 'UK's first civic or "redbrick" University' (2020).
69 A short-lived federal university, established by royal charter in 1880, affiliating colleges throughout the north of England which went on to become the universities of Manchester, Liverpool and Leeds in the early 1900s (Charlton 1951).

70 A recently popular phrase, originating in Alexander Dumas' *Les Mohicans de Paris* (1859, 232).
71 Fawcett's footnote: 'The first examinations of Victoria University were held in 1881, when only men entered. Two women presented themselves for examination in 1883; in 1892 the number had increased to 30. There are now 44 women graduates of this University.'
72 Although the subject of intense debate from the late 1860s, Owens College did not admit women until 1883, after it had become a member of the federal Victoria University in 1880, whose charter stated that its university degrees would be open to both men and women (see University of Manchester Library n.d.b for an overview).
73 University College, London was founded in 1826, with women attending lectures by its professors from 1868 and classes and the ability to study towards University of London degrees officially open to men and women in 1878 (except those in the Faculty of Medicine) (Harte, North and Brewis 2018, 89).
74 George Nathaniel Curzon (1859–1925), later Marquess Curzon of Kedleston, Conservative statesman. Fawcett here is alluding to the controversy surrounding the proposal to admit women fellows to the Royal Geographical Society, opposed by Curzon in 1893 (although he 'presided over and actively supported the decision to admit women in 1913'); see Bell and McEwan (1996, 298) for an overview. Curzon became president of the National League for Opposing Woman Suffrage in 1912.
75 Fawcett's footnote: 'This examination was opened to men in 1873, but very few men avail themselves of it.'
76 Fawcett later wrote: 'I cannot forbear mentioning what I have always regarded as an honour, viz. that Professor Henry Sidgwick, the real founder of Newnham, asked me and my husband to lend our drawing-room for the first meeting ever held in Cambridge in its support . . . We were then occupying a furnished house which possessed a drawing-room of suitable size for such an occasion. I therefore recognize that the birth of Newnham under my roof was more or less accidental: nevertheless, such is human folly, I go on being proud and pleased about it. I know that Philippa was a little baby girl at the time, but was old enough to be brought in at the tea-drinking stage at the end of the proceedings and to toddle about in her white frock and blue sash among the guests. I thought in 1890 that no one but myself remembered this, but when Professor Sidgwick wrote to congratulate me on my daughter's place in the mathematical tripos of that year, he said, "Who would have thought, at the first meeting at your house, that the little girl who was trotting about would one day be above the Senior Wrangler?"' (1924, 73).
77 See Tullberg 1998 for the navigation of the politics and regulations which allowed women to study at Cambridge.
78 A prospectus, 'Merton Hall and the Cambridge Lectures for Women' (Clough 1873), is held in Newnham College Archives.
79 John Couch Adams (1819–92), Cambridge professor of astronomy, director of the Cambridge Observatory, and 'an early and active supporter of the provision of higher education for women . . . he was one of the first Cambridge professors to admit women to his lectures' (Hutchins 2004).
80 Arthur Cayley (1821–95), mathematician.
81 See Section 3, note 34.
82 William George Clark (1821–78), classical and Shakespearean scholar.
83 William Kingdon Clifford (1845–79), mathematician.
84 Sir Richard Claverhouse Jebb (1841–1905), classicist.
85 Alfred Marshall (1842–1924), economist.
86 Walter William Skeat (1835–1912), mathematician and philologist, and allegedly the first Cambridge professor to ride a bicycle (Sisam 2008).
87 Isaac Todhunter (1820–84), mathematician and historian of mathematics.
88 Helen Taylor (1831–1907), promoter of women's rights and amanuensis for John Stuart Mill.
89 Arthur James Balfour (1848–1930), 1st Earl of Balfour, Conservative politician and prime minister of the United Kingdom between 1902 and 1905.
90 Harte, North and Brewis (2018, 89).
91 William Steadman Aldis (1839–1928), professor of mathematics at the College of Physical Science at Newcastle, and his wife, Mary Steadman Aldis (née Robinson) (1837–97), promoters of women's rights and education, particularly in campaigning for women's education at Durham University.
92 Tullberg covers the history of admissions of women to examinations at Cambridge (1998, Chapter 5).

93 Original editor's note: 'The most remarkable of these successes was that obtained by Mrs Fawcett's daughter, who came out in the Mathematical Tripos above the Senior Wrangler.—[Editor.]'
94 'One major inconvenience was the restriction placed on their use of the University Library. In 1891, the teachers of the two colleges combined in a petition to the Library Syndicate for some relaxation of the rules that limited their use of the Library to the hours between 10 a.m. and 2 p.m. During these hours, the women were usually teaching and the Syndicate were "respectfully requested" that subject to payment of the necessary fee, the women might receive permission to use the Library from 10 a.m. to 4 p.m., an extension of two hours. Permission was refused' (Tullberg 1998, 86–7).
95 James Anthony Froude (1818–94), historian. In his inaugural professorial address at Oxford in autumn 1892, Froude stated 'the celibate seclusion of college life was gone, and ladies, to the horror of the scholastics, had invaded the sacred premises' (Markus 2005, 289), and in later lectures he announced he would lecture only to men (Reid 1892, 98).
96 'Historians of every school, all who hold the reputation of the universities dear – all indeed who have any respect for sense and the fitness of things – will rejoice to hear that [Froude] has set his face against what is fast growing to be a crying scandal. If girls wish to play at undergraduates, by all means let them do so; they might conceivably play at worse things . . . Neither Oxford nor Cambridge is in truth their proper playing-ground' (Reid 1892, 98). 'Reid' may be a pseudonym.
97 See Tullberg (1998, Chapter 6) for an account of the 1887 'damp squib'.
98 Founded in 1878, it was responsible for the administration of local student women at the University of Oxford from 1879 as the Society of Home Students, becoming St Anne's College in 1952 (St Anne's College n.d.).
99 See Mallet (1927, 433) for an overview of this process.
100 Thomas Holloway (1800–83), manufacturer of patent medicines and philanthropist.
101 Section 14, subsection 6, of the Universities (Scotland) Act, which 'gave power to the University Commissioners to enable each university to admit women . . . The Commissioners issued an ordinance, which, on June 28th 1892, became law, making it competent to the University Court of each university to admit women to graduation and to make provision for their instruction within the university in any or all of the subjects there taught' (Blaikie 1896, 289; Stevenson 1894, 875).
102 Fawcett's misspelling: David Mather Masson (1822–1907), literary scholar and editor and active member of the Edinburgh Association for the University Education of Women.
103 Louisa Stevenson (1835–1908), campaigner for women's rights.
104 Isabella Elder (née Ure) (1828–1905), benefactor and supporter of higher education for women, funding Queen Margaret College medical school in 1890.
105 Janet [Jessie] Campbell (née Black) (1827–1907), promoter of higher education for women in Scotland.
106 Janet Anne Galloway (1841–1909), promoter of higher education for women in Scotland.
107 Louisa Stevenson in another speech given at the World's Columbian Exposition in Chicago 1893, on 'Women Students in the Scottish Universities' (1894).
108 Isabella Maria Susan Tod (1836–96), campaigner for women's rights and writer.
109 Stafford Henry Northcote (1818–87), 1st Earl of Iddesleigh, Conservative politician who served on the educational royal commissions in the 1860s.
110 See Ó hÓgartaigh (2009) for an overview.
111 The Queen's University of Ireland had been founded in 1850, and was dissolved in 1882 and absorbed into the Royal University of Ireland, which was founded in 1879. In 1909 the Royal University of Ireland was dissolved, with the National University of Ireland taking over its functions, staff and students (2020).
112 Alexandra of Denmark (1844–1925), Princess of Wales, received a DMusic from the Royal University in May 1885, at the same time as her husband, Edward (later Edward VII, 1841–1910), received an honorary doctorate of laws (LLD) (Mollan 2007, 822).
113 Fawcett was given an LLD by the University of St Andrews in 1899 for her services to education; she wears her doctoral robes in Figures 7, 12, 13 and 22 in this volume. See also Rubinstein (1991, 106).
114 Trinity College Dublin was founded in 1592 (Trinity College Dublin 2019), so Fawcett refers to the 1892 celebrations, in which Alice Oldham (1850–1907) 'spearheaded a campaign to persuade Trinity College Dublin to open its degrees to women. Her campaign began with a memorial to the Board of Trinity College signed by 10,500 "Irish women of the educated classes" together with three other memorials, including two from Trinity lecturers' (Discovering Women in Irish History n.d.).

115 Women students were admitted to Trinity College for the first time in 1904 (Trinity College Dublin 2019).
116 See Section 6, note 8.
117 William Gladstone (then in opposition, after his final term as prime minister), in a speech given at the Distribution of Prizes at the Burlington School for Girls on Thursday, 17 July 1890. 'Enormous changes have taken place in your position, ladies, not only in your actual, but also in your prospective position, as members of society. It is almost painful to look back upon the state of women sixty years ago, upon the manner in which they were viewed by the law, and the scanty provision made for their welfare, and the gross injustice, the flagrant injustice, the shameful injustice, to which, in certain particulars, they were subjected' (*London Evening Standard* 1890). Fawcett was frustrated at Gladstone's lack of support: 'On the question of Women's Suffrage . . . Mr Gladstone had been, so to speak, "all over the place" about it' (Fawcett 1924, 111; see 111–15 for her opinions and experience of Gladstone).

19
Reporting Fawcett: Women's suffrage, London 1897

An address delivered at the Junior Constitutional Club, Piccadilly. Thursday, 11 November. London: McCorquodale and Co. Ltd, 1–18.

This report is of an invited speech Fawcett gave at the Junior Constitutional Club, a political London gentlemen's club for those with Conservative principles, founded in 1887 at 101 to 104 Piccadilly West (Dickens 1908). The Conservatives dominated the political landscape at the time, having won the 1895 election with Robert Gascoyne-Cecil, the 3rd Marquess of Salisbury,[1] as their leader. The Conservative approach to women's suffrage was linked to ideas of class:

> Those Conservatives who opposed women's suffrage very often did so not because they were against it in principle but because they feared that it would lead to universal suffrage. They reasoned that, if the register were weighted in favour of their party, the Liberals, when they returned to office, would introduce universal manhood suffrage. This, they believed, would almost certainly lead to revolution or worse (Maguire 1998, 50).

Even so, support for women's suffrage was growing: a second reading of the latest suffrage bill was passed on Wednesday, 3 February 1897, with a majority of 71 (*London Evening Standard* 1897a), leading to high hopes for the suffragists. On Wednesday, 7 July 1897, 'a large number of ladies congregated in the Central Lobby . . . under the impression that the Woman Suffrage Bill stood some chance of being proceeded with', but the bill was frustrated by Mr Labouchere,[2] who spoke for so long on the Verminous Persons Bill that there was no time left for the Women's Suffrage Bill (*London Evening Standard* 1897b). Fawcett co-signed a letter to the *London Evening Standard*:

> . . . the representatives of the people preferred to spend three hours in useless talk on an insignificant and repulsive subject, rather than be called upon to say Aye or No . . . Time is wasted, the dignity of Parliament is sacrificed, rather than give any attention to the wants and wishes of women . . . The events of last Wednesday will stimulate our Societies to renewed activity (Cooke et al. 1897, 3).

Indeed,

> . . . the suffragists . . . under Mrs Fawcett's leadership, braced themselves afresh after this fiasco. The two divided central societies, which had flown apart in the stress of party feelings in '85, were now reunited, and a scheme for the organisation of all the local societies into one National Union [of Women's Suffrage Societies] . . . was drawn up and adopted [in October 1897] (Strachey 1931, 178).

This talk, given shortly after the defeat of the suffrage bill, was the first scheduled address of the winter season organised by the Constitutional Club's political section. However, some members were 'very anxious it should be known that they have had nothing to do with the arrangement for Mrs Fawcett to arrange an address . . . In fact, they decidedly disapprove of it' (*Manchester Evening News* 1897), and it was described as being 'the suffragists, undismayed by their very rude rebuff . . . once more again upon the warpath' (*Birmingham Daily Post* 1897). Fawcett's speech is therefore one that is made to a potentially hostile audience that is suspicious of the ramifications of widening suffrage, in an attempt to persuade them to adopt it by appealing 'for a Conservative solution to the suffrage question' (Rubinstein 1991, 139) at the beginning of a new campaign. Fawcett makes her political affiliation clear: 'she was not herself a Conservative but a Liberal Unionist': a faction that broke from the Liberal Party in 1886 over their opposition to proposed Irish Home Rule, which in the future went on to amalgamate with the Conservatives. Her politics are therefore not irredeemably distant from her audience's, and she demonstrates her understanding of Conservative Party history and approach in a set of carefully chosen (but fairly strong) examples, and references to individuals, intended to persuade those listening that women's suffrage could benefit the Conservative cause. It was, however, not until 1904 that another suffrage bill was to come before Parliament: it was again talked out.

*

On Thursday Evening, November 11th, at the Junior Constitutional Club, Piccadilly, Mrs Henry Fawcett delivered an Address on the subject of the extension of the Parliamentary Franchise to Women, before a large and appreciative audience.

Mr J. T. Firbank, MP,[3] who presided, in introducing Mrs Fawcett to the meeting, remarked that although, no doubt, many of them in that room were unable to share the opinions held by that lady in regard to Women's Suffrage, he nevertheless hoped that they would give her a respectful and attentive hearing. As for himself, he had voted for the question when it was brought before the House of Commons, and it was therefore an additional pleasure to him to occupy the Chair on the present occasion.

Mrs Fawcett, who was received with applause, said she desired at the outset to thank them very sincerely for the kindness and hospitality with which she had been entertained in their Club that evening, and for the cordial welcome which had been extended to her by the Committee. Under the circumstances, she would be best showing her appreciation of their kindness if she at once plunged into the subject upon which she proposed to address them, viz. the admission of women to the Parliamentary franchise. It would be more convenient, perhaps, if she commenced by saying what it was not, rather than what it was, that they were asking for. They were not asking that every woman – or indeed that any woman – should become a Member of Parliament. She found that, even among well-informed gentlemen, some considerable misconception existed upon these very simple points. There was, as she had said, no proposal whatever that a man's wife, or that any woman, should have a seat in Parliament, or become a Minister of State – (laughter) – so that a great many of the foolish little squibs which they saw in the newspapers fell very wide of the mark. All that was proposed was that women who were householders or freeholders, or who otherwise fulfilled the qualifications which, if they were men, would entitle them to vote, should be allowed to vote in the election of Members of Parliament. They knew with very fair accuracy how many women would actually have the power of voting in the event of a change being made in the law in that respect. As they would doubtless remember, Sir Henry Fowler[4] moved for a return last session in the House of Commons giving the number of householders and occupiers – both men and women – throughout England and Wales, and from this it appeared that there were 729,000 women householders. Taking Scotland and Ireland at about the same proportion, she thought they would be justified in assuming that in the United Kingdom there would be a million women householders who were entitled to vote at Parliamentary elections, provided that a change in the law were brought about. She spoke, of course, subject to correction in the presence of so many gentlemen who were far better informed than herself, but she believed she was right in stating that there were about six million male voters in the United Kingdom; and therefore, if what they proposed were carried out, there would be approximately one million women voters to the six million men to whom that privilege was accorded. They would therefore see that a great many of the alarmist prognostications which were indulged in by some of their opponents to the effect that the men throughout the country would be simply out-voted by a horde and rabble of women were quite uncalled for. (Laughter.) There was really nothing so very terrible after all – even to the most timid of the stronger sex – (laughter) – in the thought that for every six men there was one woman who was entitled to vote at Parliamentary elections. That, then, was in brief what they were pressing forward, and endeavouring session after session to get brought before the House of Commons, in the hope that in time the good sense and good feeling of the people of England would back their proposals so that they might become law. Of course, many of them were aware that a large proportion of those 729,000 women householders, who were scattered over the country, were in business on their own account, or at the head of large establishments in which they employed a quantity of servants in various capacities. The male servants were entitled to vote, and yet those who, either through industry or fortune, were their employers, were held to be incapable of giving an intelligent vote at Parliamentary elections. That, in her opinion, was a most unsatisfactory state of things; but let them look for a moment how it worked out in some constituencies. She would take, for instance, the case of Bath, which she knew very well. Those of them who were familiar with the town would remember that Royal Crescent was one of the best and most prosperous residential quarters in the city. Now it was a fact that there were fewer names on the register of Parliamentary voters in the Royal Crescent than there were in many of the tenement houses in some of the lowest slums of the town. The reason for this was to be found in the fact that the great proportion of the inhabitants in that quarter of Bath were women, whereas in the poorer parts of the town every man who rented even a single room was entitled to vote. That, as she had already stated, was an exceedingly unsatisfactory condition of affairs, and one which she considered the members of the club would do well to think seriously about, and to see if it was not possible to find a remedy.

It would be useful, perhaps, if, in the first place, she ventured to reply as well as she was able to a few of the objections which were raised against their proposals. It was sometimes put forward as an argument that home was the best place for a woman. She did not object to that argument, in fact she heartily concurred in it[5] – but, on the other hand, if they accepted this view, home was surely the best place for a man also. (Laughter.) Her own opinion was that a woman who knew a great deal about the interests of home was all the more qualified to examine many of the measures which were brought before Parliament, and consider how they affected the home life, and so decide for whom she should record her vote at a Parliamentary election. So far from the home question being an argument against it, it was, in her view, one of the strongest in its favour. Another argument which she frequently heard brought forward was that women were so easily influenced, but perhaps that objection was best answered by another, which was that they were so obstinate that when once they took an idea into their heads the whole world could not get it out again. (Laughter.) Perhaps these two objections might be said to nullify one another. She was aware that there were many of her political opponents who were extremely nervous upon the subject, and declared that it would be most dangerous for women to have votes, seeing that they were so dreadfully influenced by the clergy. (Laughter.) Really she did not know that it was so very dreadful after all to be influenced by the clergy, for, as she had frequently pointed out,[6] there were clergymen of the Church of England as well as dissenting ministers, so that their respective influence was set off one against the other. On the other hand, it was sometimes forgotten that male electors occasionally obeyed other than purely political considerations in the exercise of their vote. (Laughter.) She once heard a couple of gentlemen discussing the respective merits of the candidates for a north country borough, and one of them strongly recommended a gentleman on the ground that his brother's dog had won the Waterloo Cup.[7] (Loud laughter.) She felt perfectly certain that similar considerations often entered into the choice of candidates for Parliamentary honours. She once had the pleasure of hearing an old postman in a country village who had been a soldier declare, when approached by the Conservative candidate, that he would vote for him because the candidate's grandfather and his own were wounded in the same battle. That, however, she could the more easily understand, for it was certainly far better than being influenced by unworthy considerations; but still, if it did not hold good as against a male elector, she could not imagine why it should absolutely disqualify women from having the vote granted to them. Then again, they heard a great deal from those who objected to the movement on the ground that women could not be soldiers. She once heard that objection raised by a gentleman who was about to go out to one of the Australian Colonies in the capacity of Governor, and she expressed the hope that before he left during his term of office he would have the honour, as the representative of the Queen, of giving her Majesty's assent to the passing of a Women's Suffrage Bill. He pointed out, in reply, that the question was a very serious one, and that women could never act as soldiers. To this she rejoined that if unfortunately war should be declared between Great Britain and any other Power, he himself might perhaps be equally incapable with herself of taking up arms in defence of their country, but that in all probability both he and she in very different degrees – he according to his wealth, and she in proportion to her poverty – would be called upon to help in some way towards the military defence of the country by putting their hands into their pockets and paying other people to fight for them. (Laughter.) In the next place it was impossible to doubt either the courage or the patriotism of women. And in regard to patriotism, had they not, as the Conservative party, called it forth over and over again when they sent women to perform the work in support of the maintenance of the principles which animated their party in connection with the organisation known as the Primrose League?[8] (Hear, hear.) Had they not seen the greatest possible sacrifices made by women in order to carry out the principles which they held to be so essential to the well-being and continued prosperity of their country? With regard to other well-known cases of the patriotism of women, she might mention that when General Gordon[9] was, in her opinion, most unfortunately and criminally abandoned, and when his fate was hanging in the balance, it was a lady who volunteered to send a force for his relief entirely at her own expense. That offer was not accepted by the Government of the day, but nevertheless it plainly showed that women were capable of possessing the highest feelings of self-devotion and patriotism, and were at the same time willing to make personal sacrifices in support of them. (Hear, hear.) It was hardly possible to speak upon this phase of her subject without recalling to mind with emotion the magnificent exhibition of courage which was displayed by the Duchesse d'Alençon at the lamentable fire which occurred last spring at the Paris Bazaar.[10] They would not need to be reminded how this noble lady, who was president of the Charity, absolutely refused to leave the burning building until she was satisfied that the poorest and humblest of the attendants had made their escape. That, she was sure they would all agree, was a most splendid example of courage, and one of which they had every reason to feel proud. (Applause.) Then there was the grand story of the behaviour of the Stewart child in connection with the murder of English and Scotch Missionaries in China some time ago.[11] But for the courage of this little girl, who was only 14 years of age, nearly the entire family would have been massacred. When she heard the murderers in the house, she at once hid her brother and sister under one of the beds and told them not to move. Then she got into bed herself, thinking that when the wretches entered the room they would be less likely to find the younger children, who were out of sight, if they massacred her first. As they would probably recollect, they came to the room and broke the poor girl's legs so that she was rendered lame for life, but the fact remained that by her marvellous courage and devotion she succeeded in saving the lives of her sister and brother.

There was another objection urged against the Women's Suffrage movement, and it was that politics had the effect of unsexing a woman. But there was a very simple reply to that argument, which was contained in the one word, the name of the Queen. (Hear, hear.) Her Majesty, as they knew, had been immersed in politics from the age of eighteen up to her present advanced age,[12] from early morning till late at night, and who could say that she was an unsexed woman? As wife, mother or friend, she had proved herself the most womanly of all women in all her dominions. One of those who were opposed to them on this question in the House of Commons – she alluded to Mr Samuel Smith[13] – said his objection to women having a vote was based on the ground that it would have a degrading influence upon the character of women. She candidly confessed that she felt that the argument came very badly from the hon. Member in question, seeing that he was a member of the party, a large part of whose reputation consisted in their having conferred political power upon those classes of the community who were previously without it, and if it really tended to degrade those who possessed the privilege, then she considered that the party to which Mr Smith belonged had acted wrongly in endeavouring to secure political power for those who had none. In her opinion there was a good deal of cant in objections of this kind; and in regard to Mr Gladstone's views on the question, as many of them would remember, the right hon. Gentleman urged the women of Midlothian to come out and help to win the seat, reminding them that so far from political work degrading their position as women, the fact of their having taken part in the election would gild their future years with sweet remembrances.[14] (Laughter.) But when at a later period women came to the House of Commons and asked Mr Gladstone and other members to help them to secure the power of giving a vote at Parliamentary elections, the right hon. Gentleman adopted a very different tone, remarking that he feared to trespass upon their delicacy and refinement and purity as women.[15] (Ironical laughter.) It was therefore plain that they could not resist coming to the conclusion that there was a great deal of cant displayed somewhere or other in regard to the question. Because if it were true that politics had a degrading influence upon women, she wondered how it was that the Conservatives as a party had been the foremost in advocating the active interference of women in political affairs. It was the Conservatives who first made an organised effort to enrol the sympathies and services of women in matters political,[16] and she did not believe there was a single gentleman among the Conservatives who would have done that if he had entertained the remotest belief that the influence of politics upon women was of a degrading character. Then again, it was urged by some of their opponents that women were altogether ignorant of politics, and in this she was reminded of the rejoinder made by Mrs Poyser, who said she was not denying that women were foolish, but that God Almighty made them to match the men.[17] (Laughter.) She was afraid, therefore, that if women were ignorant of politics, God Almighty made them so in order to match the men. (Renewed laughter.) In the course of her canvassing she had found that it would be difficult to beat the ignorance which was displayed by some of the electors. Upon one occasion – before the Jubilee – she came across a man who knew absolutely nothing about a Colony – indeed, he imagined it was a place from which coal was got. (Laughter.) In the House of Commons itself she had heard members when discussing this question ask what was the use of giving a vote to women when they did not understand the principles of bi-metallism.[18] (Loud laughter.) In this connection she had sometimes thought that if only those discussed the principles of this much-vexed question who thoroughly understood them, there would be less argument upon the matter in the columns of the public press.

In reference to the objection that women had nothing to do with politics, they might learn a good deal from a reply given to Napoleon by Madame De Staal, which was: 'Sire, we have this much to do with politics: we ought to know enough about them to understand why our heads are cut off!'[19] In regard to the events which had occurred in Ireland during the last fifteen years,[20] she could tell them that there were women in the sister island who wanted to know why they had been ruined, and why their fathers and husbands and brothers had been ruthlessly shot at, and, in some instances, murdered; and why, in less melancholy cases, having lived for many years on terms of good feeling with the tenantry in their respective neighbourhoods, they were suddenly met with nothing but black and surly looks. Those were matters which made the women of Ireland anxious to know something about politics, in order that they might understand the causes of these things.

Again, they heard a great deal about the thin edge of the wedge! (Hear, hear, and laughter.) Well, her own opinion was that the thin edge of the wedge had been in for a very long time past. It went in about 1,900 years ago, when, with the foundation of Christianity, the position of women gradually became very different to what it was in the heathen world. She referred to the opinion of Sir Henry Maine, who said that one might estimate the position occupied by the various countries of the world in the scale of civilisation by the measure of freedom which they accorded to women.[21]

She would now ask them to examine the matter from the point of view of actual experience. First of all, in their own country, they had had no less than twenty-seven years' experience of Women's Suffrage in local elections, such as the School Board, Boards of Guardians,[22] &c. In regard to the administration of the Poor Law, the results accruing from the influence of women – and especially in their own peculiar sphere – had been of the most satisfactory nature possible. If they compared the Poor Law Infirmaries,[23] for instance, of twenty-seven years ago with those which existed at the present day, they would recognise what enormous improvements had been effected; and this applied equally to the workhouse schools and the care of Poor Law children generally. (Hear, hear.) There was a time, as many of them would no doubt remember, when the return as to the number of children brought up in workhouses who proved to be failures was no less than fifty per cent, all of whom came back to the workhouse and contributed to swell the criminal population of the country. Since women, however, had had an opportunity of voting at Poor Law elections, a keen sense of responsibility in regard to the care of these children and other womanly tasks had been awakened, with the result that a great change for the better had taken place. At the present time it was a recognised fact that pauper children who were brought up in workhouses or boarded out were almost as successful in after life in becoming good and useful citizens as those who were not paupers. The achievement of this result was in large measure due to the zealous work which had been performed by women as guardians of the poor, and to the formation of various associations for the after-care of children. Then, if they turned to the School Boards, she need hardly do more than mention the benefits which had accrued to the girls in the various schools by the presence on those Boards of women in whom the female teachers were able to confide. They were just now on the brink of another election,[24] and in regard to the religious difficulty they would do well to bear in mind that the fight which was going on was not one between religious and secular instruction, but between two forms of religious teaching. The most representative members of the Progressive party did not advocate secular instruction, and she believed the reason was to be found in the fact that every candidate who sought election asked for the votes of a considerable number of women householders who, as a body, did not wish the children of this country to be brought up without receiving religious instruction. In other countries, where there were no women electors, the fight lay between the Secularists and those who wished for religious instruction.

From her own experience in going about the country, she had found a general idea prevailing that . . . once women were given a vote they would cease to enjoy such delightful entertainments as they had had that evening, that there would be an end at any rate to the enjoyment of all alcoholic beverages, and that there should be no more cakes and ale.[25] (Laughter.) She would ask them just to look for one moment at those countries where Women's Suffrage existed. For the past seventeen years, for instance, women had had the Parliamentary franchise in the Isle of Man.[26] (Ironical laughter.) Those who were responsible for the government of the island had been asked what the effect of this had been, more particularly in regard to the licensing question, and it had been found that no attempt whatever had been made to deal with it on the lines of prohibition;[27] in fact, the licensing system prevailing on the island was one which enabled lodging-house keepers to supply alcoholic drinks to be consumed on the premises to the people occupying their apartments. She had made enquiries into the matter, and had found that there was absolutely no wish or desire on the part of the inhabitants either to abolish the present licensing system or to prohibit the sale of intoxicating liquors. In America again there were three States where Women's Suffrage obtained,[28] and there were also several States where very severe prohibitionist laws were in force,[29] but, unfortunately for the arguments which were put forward, the States which had Women's Suffrage were not those where prohibition was enforced. In New Zealand, as they would probably recollect, there was both Women's Suffrage and a prohibitory liquor law,[30] but here again it was unfortunate for those who advanced the arguments which she was endeavouring to meet, that the law relating to the drink question was passed long before that conferred the franchise on women. Both Mr Seddon[31] and Mr Kingston,[32] who, as Premiers of New Zealand and South Australia, were present at the Jubilee festivities in London, spoke repeatedly of the success of Women's Suffrage in their colonies. The remarks of the first-named came, moreover, with peculiar force, seeing that he was at one time opposed to it, but having been Prime Minister during two Parliaments elected under Women's Suffrage, he had become entirely reconciled to it; his experience had been that so far from bringing to the front a set of noisy and excitable women politicians, the introduction of Women's Suffrage had been a complete success, and had caused women to take a greatly increased interest in the welfare of the colony. She might remind those, too, who put forward the thin edge of the wedge argument, that there had been no proposal either in Wyoming or the Isle of Man or in New Zealand to make women members of Parliament, although in the case of Wyoming and the Isle of Man the movement was thirty-two and seventeen years old respectively, and in New Zealand the Parliamentary franchise had been extended to women for upwards of six years.

Although she was not herself a Conservative but a Liberal Unionist,[33] she had, nevertheless, a great admiration for the element of stability and good sound common sense which characterised the Conservative party, and in this connection she could not help calling to mind the words of Tennyson, that 'he was the true Conservative who lopped the mouldering branch away'.[34] That was very true, and it was an axiom which the Conservative party had laid to heart. But it was necessary that they should look to the future. They must 'plant' as well as 'lop'. Their party was in a large majority at the present time, and it took a great deal to whittle away a majority of 152. But it was not in the nature of things that they would be in a majority for ever.[35] In the future, whether near or distant, they would be brought face to face with the question of one man one vote, and possibly that of universal suffrage. Where would they be, and what would be their attitude in regard to those questions? She thought they would be wise to strengthen their position by making an extension of the suffrage to those women who are householders, and who already fulfil the qualifications for the Parliamentary franchise. She did not want them to regard the question from a narrow party point of view. She thought she might remind them of the animus which was displayed by some of their opponents concerning the matter. They encountered their chief opposition in the House of Commons from Mr Labouchere. In regard to the leaders of the Liberal party generally, they never failed to exert themselves strenuously when the question was before Parliament to prevent a vote being taken upon it; and why did they adopt that attitude?

She was told that the opposition to the question of Women's Suffrage was almost the only subject upon which Lord Rosebery[36] and Sir William Harcourt[37] were agreed. (Laughter.) Whenever the question was brought forward in Parliament, and they seemed likely to be getting near a division, the Liberal party came out with a five-line whip against it, or else there was a strong speech from Sir William Harcourt, or a long printed letter from Mr Gladstone to Mr Samuel Smith.[38] (Renewed laughter). Although the heads of the Liberal party, with the addition of Mr Labouchere, were the most virulent and determined opponents of Women's Suffrage with whom they had to deal. As they would probably have noticed only quite recently, the question had been referred by the National Liberal Federation[39] to their various branches throughout the country, in order that they might express their opinion thereon. Very strenuous efforts had been made, of which she gave some details, to secure a hostile vote on the subject. She rather fancied that if they could read the motives of those Liberals who offered uncompromising hostility to the question, they would discover that their reason for so doing was the belief that if women householders received the Parliamentary franchise, it would not give added strength to their party. On the other hand, they were heartily grateful for the support which they had received from the leaders of the Conservative party; she did not only refer to the Earl of Beaconsfield,[40] who was a strong advocate of the principles which they espoused, or to men like Sir Stafford Northcote,[41] but more particularly to Lord Salisbury[42] and Mr Balfour,[43] who were known to be supporters of Women's Suffrage. Mr Balfour had spoken on the question in the House of Commons, whilst the Premier had repeatedly referred to it in terms of the warmest sympathy, and in private life had never hesitated to express his cordial adherence to the movement. In conclusion, she urged them very respectfully to take the matter up, arguing that if they did so, they would be acting in a truly Conservative spirit by endeavouring to give Constitutional expression to a social change which had already taken place; she also urged it because if they supported the movement, they would be given an opportunity of Constitutional expression to the patriotism and common-sense of women. (Loud applause.)

A short discussion followed, and the proceedings terminated with hearty votes of thanks to Mrs Fawcett for her Address and to the Chairman for presiding.

Transcribed from a copy in the Women's Library at LSE.
No known copyright restrictions.

Notes

1. See Section 3, note 11.
2. Henry Du Pré Labouchère (1831–1912), journalist, Liberal politician, 'wit, radical, and unscrupulous opponent of votes for women' (Rubinstein 1991, 135). Strachey reports: 'After one of Mrs Fawcett's slashing speeches delivered at Nottingham, the leader-writer of the local paper produced the following comment: "Mr Labouchere is taken to task by Mrs Fawcett for having had the audacity to say that we might as well extend the suffrage to rabbits as to women. Mr Labouchere, we are afraid, in this case has allowed his zeal to run away with his discretion. Rabbits, if possessed of the suffrage, might be trusted to do no great harm to the constitutional machine, but if we had a million women armed with such a weapon the result might be different"' (1931, 160).
3. Joseph Thomas Firbank (1850–1910), Conservative Party politician.
4. Henry Hartley Fowler (1830–1911), 1st Viscount Wolverhampton, solicitor and Liberal politician. Fowler was president of the Local Government Board, responsible for shaping the Local Government (England and Wales) Act 1894, under the terms of which it is widely quoted that 729,000 women became eligible to vote in local government elections, although the source for that statistic is unclear. Lord Rosebery had overseen an 1890 parliamentary return, which showed that 685,202 women would be eligible for the vote in England and Wales under the local government reforms (Rosebery 1890). A similar return from Scotland was compiled in 1891, giving a total of 116,123 women 'qualified to vote for County Councils and for Town Councils in each county and each borough' (Murray and Stark 2018a, 99), which gives a combined figure of 801,325. Qualified women in Ireland were not allowed to vote in local elections until 1898, where an additional '100,000 women' were registered (Murray and Stark 2018b, 128). Fowler refers to the 1890 return in Parliament on 20 March 1893 (HC Deb 1893) and 13 April 1894 (*Aberdeen Press and Journal* 1894).
5. See Sections 17 and 30.
6. See Section 3.
7. The largest hare-coursing event in the United Kingdom, running annually from 1836 to 2005.
8. The Primrose League, named after the favourite flower of the twice-serving Conservative prime minister Benjamin Disraeli, was founded in 1883 as an organisation for encouraging the spread of Conservative principles in the UK. Over the 'next two decades the Primrose League became a mass organization . . . central to the electoral fortunes of the Conservative Party' (Cooke 2011). Women were involved from the outset, and the Primrose League is credited with being 'the first political organization to give women the same status and responsibilities as men' (Cooke 2011) and claimed to be the 'first society to organise political education for women' (*Primrose League Gazette* 1918). Its 'involvement of upper- and middle-class women takes on a particular significance. It not only provided a (suitably domestic) political role for women, but also a political 'Society' which reinforced male association in the upper echelons of Westminster politics and local Conservative associations and clubs' (Green 1996, 98).
9. Major General Charles George Gordon (1833–85), British Army officer who served in the Crimea, China and Egypt, and (with growing celebrity) became governor-general of Sudan in 1877. In February 1884, he was sent to Khartoum to evacuate soldiers and citizens following a local Mahdist revolt against British and Egyptian control, but as well as coordinating the withdrawal of Egyptian women, children and wounded soldiers, Gordon rebelled against orders, setting up an embedded stronghold of 6,000 men, resulting in the almost year-long 'Siege of Khartoum'. There was much press coverage of the growing scandal and parliamentary debates regarding how to proceed. On 8 May 1884, the philanthropist Baroness Angela Georgina Burdett-Coutts (1814–1906) wrote to the *Times* from Paris, suggesting a public subscription for a volunteer movement to attempt the rescue of Gordon, lending her support to the cause. The letter describes 'the communications, or rather the entreaties, I have received from many personally unknown to me, to aid in the organizing by public subscription of a volunteer movement to attempt the relief of General Gordon. My correspondents are poor, but they offer to intrust to me all they can afford of their small means, and to raise their voices in unison with their wealthier fellow countrymen . . . which has united in a common indignation the French workman of Lyons, who offers you his 20f., with the English lady who, it is stated, has promised £5,000 for Gordon's defence.' The identification of this 'English lady' is never made clear (*Times* 1884). Burdett-Coutts may also have offered a suggested ransom of £200,000 for Gordon's return, which was not accepted (Healey 1978, 208–11). The Gordon Relief Expedition,

supported by the British government, was eventually dispatched in August 1884, but reached Khartoum in January 1885, two days after up to 10,000 inhabitants had been slaughtered, including Gordon. His posthumous reputation saw him become 'a figurehead for demotic imperialism' (Davenport-Hines 2008). An account of the siege was written by the young Winston S. Churchill (1899), following his voluntary posting to Sudan to fight the Mahdist forces in 1898.

10 Duchess Sophie Charlotte Augustine in Bavaria (1847–97), the Duchesse d'Alençon. She died on 4 May 1897 in the fire at the Bazar de la Charité, an annual charity event hosted by her and other French Catholic aristocracy, that was 'believed to have been due to the explosion of a lamp . . . The Bazar, being all wood and canvas, became a mass of flame in a very few minutes', eventually claiming 126 lives, including many notable society women (*Morning Post* 1897a). Sophie Charlotte refused to leave, insisting that visitors and girls working with her were saved first, and was last seen with 'her eyes lifted to Heaven. One would have said she was looking at a vision . . . had it not been for her noble thought of allowing the visitors to escape first she might easily have saved herself' (*Morning Post* 1897b). The Duchess's body was identified by her dentist (*L'Avenir de Roubaix-Tourcoing* 1897, 1), heralding the 'modern age of forensic odontology' – the 'use of teeth for legal purposes' (Taylor and Kieser 2016).

11 Now known as the Kucheng massacre of 11 Western Christians from the English, Irish, American and Australian Missions, which took place in Fujian, China, on 1 August 1895. Graphic accounts of the massacre were much featured in the press (*Globe* 1895). Fawcett here conflates the stories of Nellie (Eleanor) Saunders, who helped the children hide under the beds but was soon speared to death, and Mildred Stewart, whose knee was slashed but who survived: see Banks and Banks (2019, 17–19) for the grisly details.

12 In November 1887, Victoria would have been 68 years old.

13 Samuel Smith (1836–1906), Liberal politician and champion of social purity. Once 'in favour of extending the parliamentary suffrage to women householders' (Fawcett 1892b, 4), his opinion changed at Gladstone's request (see note 38). In April 1892, Smith publicly declared his intention to vote against the Women's Suffrage Bill of Sir Albert Rollit (1842–1922), in a letter issued to the press, reprinted as a pamphlet (Smith 1892). Fawcett deconstructed her view of the 'curious mixture in Mr S. Smith's mind of sentimental homage and practical contempt for, and distrust of, women' in a long letter to the '*Morning Post* and other papers' which itself was extended and reprinted in pamphlet form (Fawcett 1892b, 4).

14 Fawcett uses Gladstone's phrase from a speech in Edinburgh, urging women to aid the Liberal cause (*Scotsman* 1879, 6). In 1878, Gladstone confirmed he would not be standing again for Greenwich in the 1880 election; by early 1879 he would be standing, instead, for election in Midlothian (see Brooks 1985 for the background, reasoning and significance of this). Using modern political techniques, the Midlothian campaign saw him touring the country, delivering a series of long foreign and home policy speeches to large crowds, designed as media events 'with specific attention to the deadlines and operational requirements of the journalists covering it and crafted for maximum impact in the morning and evening papers' (Brighton 2014, 204), in a campaign which ultimately saw him returned, for the second time, as prime minister. Fawcett highlights Gladstone's appeal to women, during this campaign, at a time when they did not have the right to vote themselves: 'In the days of limited suffrage, influence could be exercised from below as well as above . . . Gladstone knew the value of winning over the unfranchised' (Brooks 1985, 61). For example, in a speech given at Dalkeith on 27 November 1879, 'Mr Gladstone addressed to the ladies present, who constituted the greater part of the audience, a most eloquent speech on the particular share the women ought to have in the crisis of the present time' (*Scotsman* 1879, 4). Fawcett was not enamoured with Gladstone's refusal to support the franchise: see Section 18, note 117.

15 'As this is not a party question, or a class question, so neither is it a sex question. I have no fear lest the woman should encroach upon the power of the man. The fear I have is, lest we should invite her unwittingly to trespass upon the delicacy, the purity, the refinement, the elevation of her own nature, which are the present sources of its power' (Gladstone 1892, 7).

16 See note 8.

17 Mrs Poyser in *Adam Bede* (Eliot 1859, 305).

18 Bimetallism is a monetary standard based upon the worth of two metals (usually gold and silver) rather than one. Britain had used a monometallic gold standard since 1821. In the 1870s, many other countries adopted a gold standard, including Germany, France and the United States. However, throughout the 1880s and early 1890s there was much debate, and a Currency Commission held, regarding whether Britain should move to a bimetal standard (see Reti 1963

for an overview). The Liberal MP Samuel Smith (see note 13) was one of the earliest and most vocal supporters of bimetallism. Smith had used his belief that 'women did not understand proportional representation and bimetallism' as an objection to voting for the Women's Suffrage Bill in 1892 (*Birmingham Daily Post* 1892). The laughter here is probably due to the fact that, as Sir Albert Rollit had suggested in the House of Commons, 'nobody understood the former problem . . . while the latter was a sealed book to everyone'.

19 Although Fawcett credits this to the author Marguerite Jeanne Cordier de Launay (1684–1750), baronne de Staal, de Launay was deceased before the birth of Napoleon di Buonaparte (1769–1821). This quip is usually attributed to the salon hostess Madame Sophie de Condorcet (1764–1822): 'Napoleon I, said to Madam Condorcet (an enthusiastic politician, the widow of the philosopher), "I *hate* women who meddle in politics!". She answered "Ah, mon Général! You men take a fancy now and then to cut off our heads, and we women have a natural curiosity to know what it is all about!"' (E. M. L. 1873, 4).

20 Referring to the attempt by the British government to create a devolved assembly for Ireland via the Government of Ireland Bill 1886, commonly known as the First Home Rule Bill. This led to renewed sectarian tensions in Belfast, and riots with loss of life and much damage of property with lasting economic consequences (Jackson 2003).

21 Sir Henry Maine (1822–88), comparative jurist and historian: 'the degree in which the personal immunity and proprietary capacity of women are recognised in a particular state or community is a test of its degree of advance in civilisation' (Maine 1873, 21).

22 See Section 17, note 4.

23 See Section 17, note 4, and also Ritch 2019.

24 The next British general election was 1900. Fawcett here is referring to the School Board elections of 1897, which took place on 25 November (*Morning Post* 1897c).

25 *Twelfth Night* 2.3.

26 Women in the Isle of Man who owned property in their own right were given the vote in 1881. See Hoy 2020.

27 'Women . . . have voted in the Parliamentary election for the Isle of Man, under a recent Act of enfranchisement, and they have cast their votes for beer' (*Isle of Man Times* 1897).

28 Women were enfranchised in Wyoming Territory in 1869 (Wyoming became a state with suffrage in 1890), Utah in 1870 (annulled by Congress in 1887), Montana in 1887 (in 1914 as a state), Colorado in 1893 and Idaho in 1896. It has been argued that western American states extended voting rights to women before those in the east due to the competitive political environment. In the west, 'fluid partisan politics and relatively strong mobilization produced early reform' (Teele 2018, 442).

29 Maine was the first to enact prohibition in 1851, and although that was repealed in 1858, it saw the start of the fight for national prohibition. The 18 states that 'held constitutional referenda' on prohibition 'during the 1880s were Kansas, Iowa, Ohio, Maine, Rhode Island, Michigan, Texas, Tennessee, Oregon, West Virginia, New Hampshire, Massachusetts, Pennsylvania, South Dakota, North Dakota, Washington, Connecticut and Nebraska' (Szymanski 2003, 219).

30 New Zealand was the first country to grant women the franchise, in 1893. 'Under an 1893 act voters could reduce the number of liquor outlets in their electorate, or ban them altogether, in referendums held every three years . . . Between 1894 and 1908, 12 out of 76 general electorates banned liquor sales' (Te Ara n.d.).

31 Richard John Seddon (1845–1906), radical Liberal politician and prime minister of New Zealand (1893–1906).

32 Charles Cameron Kingston (1850–1908), radical Liberal politician and premier of South Australia (1893–9).

33 A British political party formed in 1886 by a faction that broke from the Liberal Party in opposition to Irish Home Rule, forming an alliance with the Conservative Party in 1895 and amalgamating with it in 1912 (Cawood 2012).

34 'That man's the true conservative / Who lops the mouldered branch away' – from Tennyson's 'Hands All Round' (1881, 76).

35 The 1895 general election was won by the Conservatives, led by Lord Salisbury, who had formed an alliance with the Liberal Unionist Party (see note 33). They won 411 seats, giving a majority of 152 over the Liberal Party (177 seats), the Irish National Federation (70 seats) and the Irish National League (12 seats). No seats were won by the Independent Labour Party, or by other independents. That majority fell to 134 in the 1900 election, and was lost in the 1906 election, which was won by a landslide by the Liberal Party.

36 Archibald Philip Primrose (1847–1929), 5th Earl of Rosebery, 1st Earl of Midlothian, British Liberal politician, serving as prime minister from March 1894 to June 1895.
37 Sir William George Grenville Venables Vernon Harcourt (1827–1904), lawyer, journalist and Liberal politician, serving as chancellor of the exchequer under the Earl of Rosebery. 'After W. E. Gladstone retired, the history of the Liberal party became largely the struggle of two personalities, Lord Rosebery and Sir William Harcourt, for control of the leadership' (Gutzke 2007, 241). 'That Harcourt blamed Rosebery for popularising his unflattering nickname, "Jumbo", based on his apparent resemblance to a celebrated circus elephant, made relations between them increasingly fraught' (Freeman 2011, 10). Both opposed women's suffrage, with Harcourt 'rejoicing in the most antiquated views in regard to the place of women in society' (Gardiner 1923, 172).
38 In April 1892, Samuel Smith wrote to Gladstone for his endorsement of the Women's Suffrage Bill that was about to be presented to the House of Commons. In reply, Gladstone wrote a much-reproduced long letter (Gladstone 1892), in which he 'cannot but express the hope that the House of Commons will not consent to the second reading of the Bill for Extending the Parliamentary Suffrage to Women' (p. 3), setting out his objections to proposed changes to Female Suffrage, arguing that the wording and ramifications of the bill needed further consideration, given it excluded married women. Gladstone maintained that women were not suited to the responsibility of voting: Smith then opposed the 1892 bill, upon Gladstone's request. See also note 13: Fawcett wrote a scathing public letter to Samuel Smith about his changed opinion, and refusal to support women's suffrage (Fawcett 1892).
39 The National Liberal Federation was the union of the English and Welsh Liberal Associations. Formed in 1887, the Federation did not declare clearly in favour of women's suffrage until 1914 (Roy 1971, 55). It was replaced by the Liberal Party Organisation in 1936 (Dutton 2013, 306).
40 The honorary title given to Benjamin Disraeli (1804–81) by Queen Victoria. A Conservative politician who twice served as prime minister, Disraeli had long been a supporter of female enfranchisement, saying in the House of Commons in 1848: 'I say that in a country governed by a woman – where you allow women to form part of the other estate of the realm – Peeresses in their own right, for example – where you allow a woman not only to hold land, but to be a lady of the manor and hold legal courts – where a woman by law may be churchwarden – I do not see, where she has so much to do with State and Church, on what reasons, if you come to right, she has not a right to vote' (HC Deb 1848).
41 See Section 18, note 109.
42 See Section 3, note 11.
43 See Section 18, note 89.

20
Picturing Fawcett: Millicent Fawcett by Theodore Blake Wirgman, 1898

Figure 6: Millicent Fawcett, oil on canvas, by Theodore Blake Wirgman, 1898. Royal Holloway, University of London. Licensed for use.

This oil painting depicts Fawcett as a seated scholar, interrupted during reading, rather than a campaigner. 'Wirgman's portrait presents Fawcett in her middle years and shows a quieter, more introspective side' in the European tradition of depicting lone scholars in thought, a convention which had been successfully employed by Wirgman in a series of portraits of male sitters in the 1880s (Tedbury 2020b, 36). Fawcett's 'heart-shaped face, simply styled auburn hair and fine bone structure give her a rather youthful appearance. She does not yet wear the regalia of her LLD.[1] Instead she is dressed in the simple style that was favoured by female students and scholars at the end of the nineteenth century' (Tedbury 2020a).

The importance of the written word to her identity is represented by the reflection of the red-leather-bound book in the table, and 'a shelved book cabinet is visible behind her to the left'. The portrait probably dates from 1898, 'the year that Fawcett gave an important lecture at Bedford College on the future of women's education' (Tedbury 2020b, 36), meaning that she was approximately 51 years old at the time of painting.

This portrait was likely commissioned by Miss Dorothea Roberts (c. 1836–1922), an Irish suffragist, supporter of Irish Home Industries and 'old friend' of Fawcett's (Fawcett 1924, 98) whom she would have met on her lecture tours and at suffrage meetings: Fawcett spoke at a meeting of the Women's Suffrage Committee in London in 1881 that Roberts attended (*Northern Whig* 1881); Roberts spoke at Women's Liberal Unionist Association meetings in Ulster and Nottingham, which were linked to Fawcett, who became honorary secretary of the Nottingham association (*Northern Whig* 1889).

In 1890 Roberts's niece Mary Letitia Hollins (1850–1912) married the artist Theodore Blake Wirgman (1848–1925) (*Mansfield Reporter* 1889). Wirgman was born into a successful artistic family, training at the Royal Academy Schools from the age of 15, and then in Paris. On his return to London, he worked for John Millais (1829–96) (Bénézit 1924, 1072). He produced a variety of etched portraits for Victorian periodicals such as the *Graphic* and *Century Magazine* (National Portrait Gallery 2021b). Wirgman exhibited this portrait of Fawcett in the Royal Academy annual summer exhibition in 1898 (*Magazine of Art* 1898, 101). Roberts subsequently donated the portrait to Bedford College in 1899. There is no mention of Wirgman in Fawcett's recollections: he may have painted this from photographs, rather than a sitting, and this painting has similarities to some formal photographs taken of Fawcett around that time. However, Fawcett did write the memoriam notice to Wirgman's wife in 1912, so evidently knew them both well (*Common Cause* 1912d). In later life, Mary Wirgman hosted suffrage debates in her drawing room (*Common Cause* 1911a).

Bedford College was the first higher education college for women in the United Kingdom, founded in 1849 (see Section 18). Fawcett had a long relationship with Bedford College: her daughter Philippa had attended mathematics and chemistry classes there in the 1880s, prior to studying at the University of Cambridge. Fawcett was interested in the running of the college and may have been part of the governing body, being described as 'for many years a Governor' in a later fundraising campaign (*Common Cause* 1918). Fawcett 'on several occasions addressed student or other meetings with a wealth of historical and literary references' (Rubinstein 1991, 105), including an address opening the academic year of 1886 (*Times* 1886c) and 1897 (*Times* 1897), and at the 50th Anniversary 1899 Jubilee, which consisted of a variety of celebratory events including an exhibition of pictures in the art school (*Times* 1899e), although it cannot be ascertained whether this painting was shown there.

Bedford College merged with Royal Holloway in 1985. Until recently the portrait had been mistaken for that of Dame Emily Penrose (1858–1942), inaugural principal of Bedford College. In 2020, close examination of the painting while cataloguing Royal Holloway's portraits of women academics 'uncovered Wirgman's signature, a reference to Dorothea's gift was found in the college archives, and a reproduction of the portrait was located in the Royal Academy's illustrated catalogue' (Tedbury 2020a), properly attributing this significant painting.

Notes

1 The LLD was conferred one year after, in 1899, and the regalia is seen in the photograph of the 1908 NUWSS procession (Figure 7) and the Swynnerton and Ellis portraits (Figures 12, 13 and 22).

21
Women's suffrage, Manchester, 1899

A speech delivered to the Women's Debating Society, the Owens College, Manchester, on the 13th of February, 1899. Published by the North of England Society for Women's Suffrage. Manchester: Taylor, Garnett, Evans & Co. Ltd, 1–15.

Owens College, the foundational university college of what is now the University of Manchester, was established in 1851, although it had only admitted women to study in 1883.[1] A women's debating society had been established previously at the Manchester and Salford College for Women, and from 1883 it was presided over by the tutor for women students at Owens College, often inviting guest lecturers (University of Manchester Library n.d.a). By 1899, Fawcett was a well-known figure representing the NUWSS. She had been awarded an honorary law degree from St Andrews in January 1899, being one of the first women in the UK to have such an honour conferred upon them, and this was one of the first publications to describe her as 'Millicent Garrett Fawcett LLD': press coverage of the event (indicating which points of the speech generated applause and laughter) declares 'Mrs Dr Fawcett is an exceptional lady' (*Manchester Courier and Lancashire General Advertiser* 1899).

Manchester had been one of the important hubs of the UK suffrage movement since its inception in the late 1860s (Cooper 2018), as well as hosting the UK's first Trades Union Congress in 1868 (Trades Union Congress 2020). Fawcett tailors her speech on suffrage to an industrial audience, placing it in a long history of worker and trade union rights and stressing that women's progress has an economic and social basis in a 'peaceful revolution' that is the 'result not only of economic but of educational change'

(Rubinstein 1991, 138). Again, Fawcett stresses the need for support from leading men in moving towards winning suffrage, but also tears down the reasoning of popular figures who oppose suffrage. Fawcett's usual appeal, that suffrage would benefit women and their ongoing contribution to society 'without endangering the public safety', prevails.

*

I suppose there are very few persons in this room who have not given some thought, and some perhaps have given a great deal of thought and study, to the principles of representative government; and I hope there is no one who does not believe that, while displaying the faults and drawbacks which are to be found in all human institutions, it is on the whole the best form of government for the people of our own race in our present stage of political and social development. But even if there should be one or two who cling to what I regard as the wholly untenable position of the superior attractions of benevolent despotism, I would ask them from the practical point of view to concede what the facts make it necessary that they should concede, namely, that representative democratic government with certain checks and safeguards is what we actually have and are likely to have for as long a period of time as the human mind is capable of forecasting the future; whereas the benevolent despot is an airy abstraction with no probability of providing himself, in these islands, with a local habitation and a name.

With this brief preface I would ask you to consider for a moment the principles on which representative government is based. I take them to be these:

1. That the rights and interests of any and every person are only secure from being disregarded when the person interested is himself able, and habitually disposed, to stand up for them.
2. That the type of character and ideal of private and public duty evolved in a self-governed community are far higher than in one where people have nothing to do with the laws but to obey them, and nothing to do with the taxes but pay them.

With regard to the first of these, its truth has been demonstrated over and over again both in our long past and in our recent history. The rights and interests of individuals and of classes are only secure from being disregarded when they have the power and are habitually disposed to defend them; and of all means of defending those interests and rights, the most effectual and the most automatic and constitutional is the possession of the parliamentary franchise.

In an assembly such as this, numerous instances of this fact will spring in a moment to every mind. I need not remind anyone here that when the legislation in both Houses of Parliament was virtually exclusively in the hands of the landed aristocracy, a series of legislative enactments was passed with the object of protecting English agricultural products and of putting down industries of which the raw material was derived from other countries. Laws were passed with the object of fostering the woollen trade, while it was sought to destroy the cotton trade by the same means.[2] Again, from the Statutes of Labourers onwards till almost within our own memory, legislation has sought to keep down the wages of labour and to prevent, by various means, the working classes from increasing their share of the wealth which they assisted to produce.[3] Trade unions were till rather more than 20 years ago treated by the law as illegal associations, 'contrary to public policy and conspiracies in restraint of trade'.[4] With regard to agricultural labourers, I have frequently heard members of Parliament who sat in the House of Commons before 1884 say that agricultural questions were habitually discussed as if the only two classes that had any interest in them were the landowner and the farmer – the labourer was as totally ignored as if he did not exist.

I need not labour the point any more. The facts do not necessarily imply any great depravity. People see things from their own point of view so much more clearly than from the point of view of other people, and members of Parliament are not monsters of iniquity because they take more pains to inquire into and remedy the grievances of their constituents. For you must have observed that in all the cases I have quoted, the practical remedy was found *after* the class injured by the former state of things had been admitted to the parliamentary franchise. Thus we see free trade and a complete reform of our fiscal system following the first Reform Bill of 1832, which placed political power in the hands of the middle class; the legislation repressive and harassing to trade unions was repealed in 1871 and 1876,[5] following the Reform Bill of 1868,[6] which enfranchised workmen in towns; and there is no danger of the wants and interests of the agricultural labourer being neglected, since he too was enfranchised in 1884.[7] Since that date County Councils are providing him with technical education, Parish Councils are giving him a voice in the management of his own village affairs; he is invited to meet Prime Ministers at breakfast; the foremost champion of his cause sits in the House of Commons, and princes and countesses have discovered his existence and look upon him as a very interesting person. More important than any of these flattering attentions, politicians of all shades of opinion are now endeavouring to conduct his political education. Meetings are held at hours and places at which it will be convenient for the labourer to attend them. Speakers, papers and leaflets are diligently sought for which will appeal to him in a language sufficiently simple to be easily intelligible to him. Village sanitation is receiving an amount of attention it never received before.

It is easy to put forward the cynical and the ignoble side of this sequence of events; but surely it is worse than stupid to be blind to its nobler side. Is it not a splendid thing that the merchant, the mechanic and the labourer should feel that he has something beside his counting-house, his loom, or his plough: that he is the inheritor of all the past ages of England's greatness and glory, and that it rests in part with him to hand on that splendid heritage, not only unimpaired, but increased, to the generations yet to come? This is brought home to the enfranchised classes with a directness and force that the unenfranchised cannot, unless in a few exceptional cases, feel. This is why I want the franchise for women, even more than because I know their special rights and interests are often wholly disregarded for want of representation. I will give some special illustrations of this by-and-bye. But, personally, I care for the second of the two bases of democratic government more than for the first – viz. that the type of character and ideal of public and private duty evolved in a self-governed community is far higher than in one that is not self-governed. It is a great tonic to character, it tends to check the tendency to take a mean and too personal view of the interests of life, to know that you are intrusted with a share in the governing power of one of the greatest nations of the earth; that if it goes wrong it is in part your fault; that if it grows in wisdom and strength and righteousness, yours and your children's will be the glory. If we contrast the type of character evolved in the self-governing countries such as our own or the United States with the type evolved in autocracies such as Russia, or by pure despotisms such as are to be found in China and the East, it is impossible to hesitate as to the one to which preference should be given. I admit unreservedly that Englishwomen have benefited by the atmosphere of freedom in which they have lived. We are the children of our fathers just as much as men are; but still, when I contrast the general outlook on life of the great mass of middle-class women or of working class women, with the outlook on life of their brothers and fathers, I confess that I feel there is something wanting on the women's part. I feel they take a smaller and pettier view. Religion – real, deep, personal religion – when they have it, takes them out of this small way of looking at things. It gives them something really great, which puts things that are small in their proper proportion. But if they have not this – and, after all, in vivid intensity it is the gift of only a few – is it not almost a commonplace to say that they are apt not to see things in their true proportion, that the great with them is too often little, and the little great?

I expect that saying this I will be considered to have made a great concession to my opponents. But, on the other hand, why should we urge a change in the political status of women unless we believe that political responsibility tends to improve and lift up those who are intrusted with it? We want the electoral franchise not because we are angels oppressed by the wickedness of 'the base wretch man', but because we want women to have the ennobling influence of national responsibility brought into their lives. We have seen its good effects on our fathers, husbands and brothers, and we think, after all, we are not so degraded but that it would have a good effect upon us too, and that this boon might be granted us without endangering the public safety.

May I say a few words more on the general principles of representation? What is the object of representation? Surely it is to represent, not a part merely, but the whole of the nation. Not necessarily every individual, but every important section of the community; above all, that no one should feel himself or herself for ever hopelessly shut out from part or lot in the constitution. It is only when this is secured that you can ever be sure that Parliament really speaks with the voice of the nation. We have recently had experience, at the time of the Jubilee, and again more lately, of the tremendous moral effect produced when the nation is really united, when a Minister speaks, not for his own party merely, but for the whole people. This is only possible when the Government is broad based upon the people's will. We have experienced the benefits of extension of the franchise not once or twice, but many times when grave crises have arisen in our recent history. Those who feared that a democratic franchise would weaken the executive have seen their fears happily falsified. The executive have been all the stronger because they were acting for the masses as well as for the classes. The principle of extending the franchise to sections of society hitherto excluded has been tried and found to work well. Take a little courage, then, and venture to include the only important section still left out – the women of England.[8]

If I am asked on what basis I advocate the extension of the parliamentary franchise to women, I reply on the existing basis of household suffrage. The last time a Liberal Government was in power, Mr John Morley introduced a Bill dealing with the parliamentary franchise.[9] It was called a Registration Bill, but it was really partly an enfranchising and partly a disfranchising measure. He thus described its object in the House of Commons: 'They were not attempting to satisfy constitutional symmetry, but they were endeavouring to remove practical blots, *to turn into a reality the intention of Parliament that every inhabitant householder in the country should have a vote.*'[10] I have reminded you that before '84 questions affecting agriculture were constantly discussed in the House in a manner that might have led a visitor from Mars to imagine that there was no such person as the agricultural labourer. In the same spirit Mr Morley and most members of Parliament speak on questions dealing with representation as if no such a being as the woman householder had ever been observed to exist. His Bill, which aimed at turning into a reality the intention of Parliament that every inhabitant householder should have a vote, left the 729,000[11] women householders in England and Wales, the only important section of householders now excluded, exactly where it found them.

We know approximately the number of women householders in England and Wales from a Parliamentary Return moved for in the last Parliament by Sir Henry Fowler.[12] I have just mentioned that they are 729,000; if we take Scotland and Ireland in the proportion to their population, it may be calculated that a Women's Franchise Bill, based on household suffrage, would add about one million to the electorate of the United Kingdom.

I have not brought with me the text of the Women's Suffrage Bill which was read a second time in the House of Commons in 1897 by a majority of 73.[13] But it was a Household Suffrage Bill, and aimed at turning into a reality the intention of Parliament that every inhabitant householder should have a vote much more truly than Mr Morley's Registration Bill did.

The exact wording of any future Bill must necessarily be in the hands of our parliamentary advisers; but this is the general character of the Bill we have always advocated. You are no doubt aware that the existing electorate in the three kingdoms amounts to nearly 7,000,000 persons.[14] Therefore, if we had women's suffrage on a householding basis, we should have one woman voter to about seven men voters.

I promised just now that I would return to the subject with which I opened – namely, that the rights and interests of every person are only secure from being disregarded when the person interested is himself able and habitually disposed to stand up for them. I might have given my whole address on this theme if I were disposed to dwell on it. But it is almost unnecessary to point out that in nearly every particular where the rights and interests of men and women are supposed to be in conflict (I do not admit that they can really be in conflict), but where they are superficially in conflict, the law is still terribly unjust to women. I refer to the laws of divorce, of guardianship of children, of intestacy; to the different view taken by the law as regards the parentage of legitimate and illegitimate children. God gives every child two parents. The law thinks that one is sufficient, so it takes cognisance of the existence of one only. When the birth of a child brings happiness and blessing, the law recognises only the father; when the birth of a child means shame and misery, the law recognises only the mother. In both cases the law sets itself against the fact, and is, therefore, essentially immoral and false.

I have sometimes been tempted to think that the axiom that in an Act of Parliament the word man includes woman is only true when there is something to pay or some penalty to be exacted. Where it is a question of privilege, the word man is apt to bear the more restricted meaning of male person. This is a characteristic of the programmes of political parties. Not long ago at a meeting of one of the great parties, a programme was submitted for acceptance, and was accepted with the following items:

1. Pauper disqualification to be removed.
2. One man one vote.
3. Reduction of residence to three months.
4. Payment of members.
5. Throwing election expenses on the rates.

You will find my formula strictly applicable in each case. Where there is anything to get, it is for men only; where there is anything to pay, women are graciously allowed to help.

I might refer to other matters more under the control of custom than a legal enactment: the trade union exclusion of women from most of the better-paid employments. The Bishops voting to exclude women from being members of Church Councils. The inadequate share enjoyed by girls and women of the great educational resources of the country. The reluctance to allow women to be appointed to the more remunerative posts in the civil service, or in the local administration of the country. Appointments by Boards of Guardians of women to be (respectively) a relieving officer and a rate collector have recently been disallowed by the English and the Irish Local Government Boards. We fought and beat Mr Chaplin at the English Local Government Board;[15] but we have fought and been beaten by Mr Gerald Balfour at the Irish Local Government Board.[16] The crying want of women in the industrial and professional world is a larger field of better-paid employments. We who are fighting for this are fighting with one hand tied behind us as long as we are not allowed the parliamentary franchise. I cannot leave this branch of the subject without mentioning the outrageously light sentences too often passed upon wretches who have been guilty of criminal assaults on children and young girls. I shall be told that in our own generation there has already been a very great amelioration both of the law and of public opinion so far as the rights and interests of women are concerned. No doubt there has been, and it is so because there is a large and constantly increasing mass of women who are habitually disposed to stand up for these rights and interests, and a not perhaps very large, but a distinguished group of men who are habitually disposed to help us in our efforts. The possession and exercise of the parliamentary franchise is not the only way of standing up for one's rights and privileges. But it is *the* quiet and constitutional way, and the way that works automatically and without disturbance. As that way is not open to us, we must seek others – the platform, the press and, in short, all means of publicly proclaiming what we want and why we want it. There has been nothing embittering in our position, as there would have been if we had been actually powerless to improve the state of things. It has been rather exhilarating than otherwise to feel that year by year, with an occasional repulse here and there, we were making way and gaining ground, and to know that as long as life lasted we should always have a worthy object to work for. There is nothing like it for making life worth living:

> Things done are won;
> Joy's soul lies in the doing.[17]

But if you sympathise with and approve of the changes that have been brought about in the law and in public opinion thus far, I ask you to give us your help and encouragement in the fields where we have not yet conquered; especially help us to arm ourselves with the weapon of parliamentary representation. In Johnson's famous letter to Lord Chesterfield you will recall the well-known sentence: 'Is not a patron, my lord, one who looks with unconcern at a man struggling for life in the water, and when he has reached ground encumbers him with help?'[18] We have plenty of patrons; we need friends who will help us, if only by an encouraging voice, while we are still in deep waters. Above all, do not be alarmed by the silly old 'thin end of the wedge' argument. There is a deal of human nature in man,[19] as one of Dickens's characters observes, and in woman too. We need not be afraid of overthrowing the great institutions of nature by being just to women and by admitting them to stand within instead of without the portals of the constitution. The wedge is a very useful mechanical implement, but we do not rely upon any mechanical principle in this movement. We rely rather on the organic principle of growth. By every sign that we can read, this movement is one of living growth. We see it in one form or another in every country which enjoys the benefits of progressive civilisation – Russia, Scandinavia, Austria, Germany, Italy and France. Mechanical hindrances may check it or divert its course; but it has within it the vital spark of life, and will continue to make way, just as the tiny, tender shoots of a growing plant can thrust down a brick wall.

I have hitherto urged upon your acceptance the justice of the principle of women's suffrage without reference to the experience that has been gained of its practical working where it has been adopted. I might point out to you that in all local elections in the United Kingdom the principle of women's suffrage has been adopted.[20] It was first introduced into these elections about 30 years ago, and has worked so well, and with such an entire absence of the evils that were at one time predicted of it, that now it is included as a matter of course without one dissentient voice whenever any new representative body is created for the conduct of local affairs. Mr Theodore Roosevelt, the honest man *par excellence* in American politics, has lately proclaimed himself an advocate of women's suffrage.[21] He says he has observed its good effect in local matters, and therefore desires its extension to Imperial concerns.

I claim that, wherever women's suffrage has been put into practical operation, there has been similar extinction of all opposition to it. A few months ago the Hon. J. Cockburn, Agent-General for South Australia, was speaking on women's suffrage at a public meeting in Manchester.[22] He said that since it had been introduced into South Australia all opposition to it had ceased to exist. He claimed that experience had shown the influence of women in politics had been in the direction of moral and physical soundness for the whole people, and that it had given an impulse to social, sanitary, domestic and industrial legislation. He pointed out that his colony had followed the example of New Zealand, and that Victoria was about to follow the double example of New Zealand and South Australia; for that women's suffrage had been carried three times in the Lower House in Victoria, and lost in the Upper House, the last time by a majority of four only. With regard to women's suffrage in New Zealand, we have testimony as to its completely satisfactory working from men as diverse and distinguished as the late Right Hon. Sir George Grey, once Governor and afterwards Prime Minister of the colony;[23] Bishop Cowie, the Primate of New Zealand;[24] Dr Talmage;[25] the Right Hon. J. R. Seddon;[26] the present Prime Minister; Mark Twain[27] and the Agent-General, Mr Reeves.[28] All these men speak from their own knowledge and experience, in most instances lasting over many years. What have the opponents of women's suffrage to urge against this great cloud of witnesses in its support? A wild and random statement by the French gentleman who calls himself Max O'Rell that women's suffrage in New Zealand was such a complete failure that it had to be given up after six months' trial, having in that short time turned the fairest spot on God's earth into a wilderness.[29] It is unnecessary to reply to such statements, because they are absolutely destitute of the slightest foundation, in fact. You may probably remember the schoolboy's definition of a lie – a lie is an abomination unto the righteous, and a very present help in time of trouble.[30]

When I turn my attention away from those unworthy opponents, whose weapons consist almost wholly of misstatements and misrepresentations, it becomes the more necessary to endeavour to understand the position of worthier foes. I may perhaps find an example of these in Mr Goldwin Smith. He very frequently renews his attack upon Women's Suffrage, almost always reiterating his conviction that 'it means a revolution in the family as well as in the State' (*Times*, 17 Jan. 1899).[31] Let us examine this charge a little more closely. A revolution in the family! I venture to think that in the 25 years during which Mr Goldwin Smith has withdrawn himself from his own country in search of a more congenial atmosphere on the other side of the Atlantic, something that might without exaggeration be called a revolution in the family has taken place. I do not mean that family affection has been weakened or the sense of parental and filial duty undermined – on the contrary. But vastly greater independence, social, industrial and educational, has been achieved by the female members of the family group. The instruments of this peaceful revolution – evolution, it should perhaps rather be called – have been the enlarged employment of women, giving them economic independence, the immense improvement in education, the opening of colleges and universities in all parts of the United Kingdom, and the newly awakened desire on the part of women to drink of the fountain of knowledge;[32] and among the social instruments of this great change we ought not to omit to mention the sewing machine and the bicycle. Now I contend that what Mr Goldwin Smith calls a revolution in the family has already taken place, but so gradually and so peaceably that those affected by it are hardly conscious of it. The father of a family is no longer an autocrat –

> I'm the blessed Glendoveer:
> 'Tis mine to speak, and yours to hear[33]

– no longer describes his position in the domestic circle; and I feel I should be doing the fathers of England much less than justice if I did not say there is no one more delighted with the new independence and signs of strength and vigour on the part of their girls than they are. Unlimited monarchy has gone in the family, as surely as it has in the State; and as its disappearance has been marked in the State by the creation of a deeper sense of loyalty and patriotism, so I think its disappearance in the family has been and will be marked by a finer and stronger bond of mutual love and obligation between parents and children. If you will contrast the parental and filial sentiment between, say, Juliet and her father, old Capulet,[34] or between Clarissa Harlow and her father,[35] with the average every-day relationship between fathers and daughters now, you will appreciate how much the abolition of unlimited monarchy in the family has made for growth of a higher ideal in the relationship between father and child. An average father now wishes his children to be his friends, not his outwardly submissive, but perhaps inwardly insurgent subjects. If this be so, then the family revolution has taken place; and what I think the sensible politician should strive to bring about is an adaptation of the political machinery of the country to correspond with the social change that has already been accomplished. This would be done if women householders were admitted to parliamentary representation: this would be an adaptation of the political organism to correspond with changes that have already been accomplished in the social organism. It is by timely changes of this kind that our countrymen have repeatedly shown their genius for practical politics. We have a peculiar skill for inserting the graft of new ideas into the stem of old institutions, and this has given a continuity to our political history which has frequently received the tribute of respect and admiration from foreign observers. It has enabled us to achieve progress without revolution, to avoid all breaks with our past, while stretching forward to the new ideas and new life of the future. It is because an extension of the parliamentary franchise to women householders is in distinct accord with these national traditions that I urge its acceptance on you. I might add a long list of distinguished men and women who have supported it; but I prefer to argue the subject on its merits rather than by the weight of authority by which it is supported. To the women present this evening I would especially appeal to give this matter their earnest attention and support. The educational and many of the social advantages you now enjoy are a by-product of the movement on behalf of which I am addressing you. It is not very generous to enjoy the advantages of a movement and yet do nothing to help it forward. But I do not anticipate that we shall have cause to complain of any want of enthusiasm on your part. We shall perhaps have more reason to fear a too great impatience, a not altogether reasonable expectation that everything we desire to see done in the way of the improvement in the position of women shall be done in the course of a few months or a few years. If there are any here who are carried away by impatience at the slow growth of our work, I would remind them that all great events take time; and that to build securely it is almost always necessary to build slowly. All that we need are the commonplace English qualities of courage, patience and tenacity; if we have these, we shall make way with the task we have in hand, and we may be quietly confident that in due season we shall reap if we faint not.

Transcribed from a copy in the Women's Library at LSE.
No known copyright restrictions.

Notes

1. See Section 18, note 72.
2. Fawcett reaches back to the eighteenth century to make this argument: the 1700 and 1721 'Calico Acts' attempted to protect woollen manufacturing by prohibiting the sale of most cottons. The acts were repealed in 1774 (Parliament.uk n.d.e).
3. The Statute of Labourers, set by the English Parliament in the reign of Edward III in 1351, restricted wages and limited movement in order to regulate the labour movement at a time of shortage after the Black Death, although it was poorly enforced (Cohn 2007). After the second phase of industrialisation that began in the late 1840s, Britain had a period of stable economic growth. Six 'major pieces of factory/trade union/industrial relations legislation' passed after the 1867 Reform Act, when 'both Liberal and Tory governments showed interest in trade unions . . . The main consequence was that the status of trade unions, although not their power, was enhanced. The Employers and Workmen Act 1875 modified the old Master and Servant Law so that employers too could be sued for breach of contract. The 1874 Factory Act set a ten-hour limit on the working day – the unions were campaigning for eight. The 1871 Trade Union Act recognised unions as legal entities as corporations and as such they were entitled to protection under the law . . . The question as to whether unions could in practice take effective strike action by picketing the workplace was the subject of much controversy. Interestingly, it was a Liberal government which criminalised picketing (1871 Criminal Law Amendment Act), and a Tory government which de-criminalised it (1875 Conspiracy and Protection of Property Act) . . . Therefore by the 1880s, a strong, although narrowly based trade union movement had been created' (Davis n.d.).
4. 'Conspiracy in restraints of trade' is a common legal phrase referring to the vague common law 'which made it criminal for two persons to agree to do what would not be criminal if done by one, and what, apart from agreement, had no criminal element in it', which was repealed in 1875, in an Act that defined this more closely, meaning 'the long struggle between employers and employed as to trade combinations was closed' (Harrison 1890). Fawcett here is perhaps alluding to a letter that appeared in the *Times* in 1897 about shipping rings who were charged 'with having compassed an indictable conspiracy in restraint of trade and against public policy' (Clarke 1897), although these are words also used in combinations elsewhere.
5. See note 3.
6. The Reform Bill was passed in 1867, rather than 1868 (Parliament.uk n.d.g).
7. See Parliament.uk n.d.g for an overview of the reform acts, and the changing rights of the working and middle classes in respect to the franchise.
8. Of course, the women of Scotland, Ireland and Wales were also excluded from the franchise.
9. The previous Liberal government had been in power from 1892 to 1895. John Morley had introduced his registration bill for electoral reform in 1894, which proposed to reduce the period of qualification for electors and called for half-yearly registration of voters. An amendment was tabled that would extend the suffrage to women, following the formation of

a Special Appeal Committee in 1892 and a petition which had gathered 248,000 signatures in favour of the extension of the franchise to women by March 1894 (Crawford 2001a, 648–9). The bill was defeated by 298 votes against 292 on 4 May 1894 (Maccoby 1953, 185).

10 John Morley (1838–1923), Liberal politician and Chief Secretary for Ireland, on the first reading of the Registration Bill in the House of Commons on Friday, 13 April 1894: 'They were not attempting to satisfy Constitutional symmetry, but they were endeavouring to remove practical blots, to turn into a reality the intention of Parliament that every inhabited householder in the country should have a vote, and to secure that the voice of a constituency, instead of being adulterated and multiplied by out-voters, should find its own expression' (*Evening Express* 1894).

11 See Section 19, note 4.

12 Henry Fowler refers, in Parliament, to Lord Rosebery's 1890 parliamentary return on 20 March 1893 (HC Deb 1893) and 13 April 1894 (*Aberdeen Press and Journal* 1894).

13 The Women's Suffrage Bill was introduced by the Conservative MP Ferdinand Faithful Begg (1847–1926), following the petition presented to Parliament after the Special Appeal (see note 9). Even though the majority of MPs voted for it, it did not become law, due to the 'Conservative Government's refusal to allocate further time to the bill' (Smith 2007a, 20). The majority was actually 71, not 73.

14 A parliamentary return requested shortly after this speech gives the total voters in 1899 in England and Wales, Scotland and Ireland as 6,600,283. This rose to 6,732,613 in 1900 (Home Office 1900, 25).

15 The Women's Local Government Society campaigned to both press and Parliament for the right for women to fill such offices, supplying information regarding women holding similar posts in England, encouraging private correspondents to write in support and interviewing members of Parliament. They also drew attention to anomalies in poor law administration in Ireland (see note 16) (Crossman 2006, 201).

16 'There were no women relieving officers or rate collectors in the nineteenth century, although . . . [in Ireland] the Clogher Board fought a long and ultimately unsuccessful campaign to appoint a woman rate collector in 1898–99' (Crossman 2006, 184; see 199–208 for the campaign to support Ann Eliza Magill in her application to become a rate collector).

17 *Troilus and Cressida* 1.2; see also Figure 14.

18 On 7 February 1755, Dr Samuel Johnson (1709–1784), poet, writer and lexicographer, wrote his famous letter to Philip Dormer Stanhope (1694–1773), 4th Earl of Chesterfield. Although Chesterfield had been the patron of the original *The Plan of a Dictionary of the English Language* (1747), he had given little support to Johnson over the eight years of writing. Johnson objected when Chesterfield described himself as the principal patron of the work shortly before publication (see Bate 1977, 256–8, 270).

19 This is a quote from the travel memoir of Charles Kingsley (see Section 3, note 31). In *At Last: A Christmas in the West Indies*, the 'wise Yankee' says: 'There is a great deal of human nature in man' (1871, 39), which is presumably a reference to earlier nineteenth-century American literature, featuring the problematic trope of wise slaves using this phrase, as featured in the *Casket* (1829, 129). Dickens uses this phrase in quotation marks in a column on Zulu nursery tales in *All the Year Round* (Dickens 1874).

20 'Following the Municipal Franchise Act of 1869 single women owners of property were able to vote for the School Boards set up by the Forster Act, from 1875, for Poor Law Boards, from 1888 for the newly created County Councils, and from 1894 for the Parish and District Councils that were then established' (Heater 2006, 136).

21 Theodore Roosevelt Jr (1858–1919), president of the United States 1901–9 and, at the time of this speech, 33rd governor of New York. 'Despite his instinct to acknowledge the strength of women, Roosevelt's views on suffrage remained indefinite for many years. In an 1898 letter to Susan B. Anthony he said "I have always favoured allowing women to vote, but . . . I do not attach the importance to it that you do. I want to fight for what there is the most need of and the most chance of getting". By the next year he must have sensed an increase in public demand because he recommended women's suffrage on school related topics during his inaugural address as governor of New York. Within five years, however, Roosevelt's willingness to work on the issue had all but faded. He even admitted that he had become only "lukewarm" in support of women's suffrage because he did not believe it an important issue that Congress would pass' (Jenkins 2020, 212). It was not until 1912 that his Progressive Party chose to endorse women's suffrage as part of the presidential campaign, setting them apart from both Republicans and Democrats,

being the first time a major party had supported women's suffrage in the United States.
22 Sir John Alexander Cockburn (1850–1929), premier of South Australia from 1889 to 1890, was the guest speaker at the annual meeting of the National Union of Women's Suffrage Societies on Wednesday, 16 November 1898, at Manchester's Association Hall, chaired by Fawcett. 'He came from a country where women had exercised the franchise for some years [since 1894], and they had got so much used to it that it seemed very strange to come to a country where one's wife had not got a vote' (*Manchester Courier and Lancashire General Advertiser* 1898).
23 Sir George Grey (1812–98), British soldier and colonial administrator. Grey gave a supportive, and emotive, speech at the annual meeting of the Central Committee of the National Society for Women's Suffrage in London on 6 July 1894, showing the success of women's suffrage in New Zealand: 'This new species of modes of action will undoubtedly stir men up, and those who oppose women doing these things are enemies of their country and not friends to the human race in whatever part of the world' (Grey 1894, 3).
24 William Garden Cowie (1831–1902), bishop of the Anglican Diocese of Auckland and elected primate of the Anglican Church of New Zealand in 1895. 'Asked if the granting of the franchise to the women had been in any way a disappointment, Bishop Cowie emphatically declared that it had not. The generality of women, he claimed, were interested in the moral character of men. He laughed heartily when reminded of Max O'Rell's prediction that the short trial of the experiment in New Zealand had resulted in a fervent desire for the immediate undoing of it, and exclaimed "There was never a greater delusion. I am not speaking of Auckland only, for my duties take me all over New Zealand, and there is only one opinion"' (*Star* 1897).
25 Dr Thomas De Witt Talmage (1832–1902), American preacher, prominent Presbyterian and social reformer. In a tour of New Zealand in 1894, he reported 'The women in New Zealand have already done well, for while in the United States and Europe the women are discussing in parlors and on the platform how they shall get their rights at the ballot box that castle has already been stormed and taken by the women here' (*Poverty Bay Herald* 1894).
26 Richard John Seddon (1845–1906). 'A women's suffrage clause was contained in the 1893 Electoral Bill, introduced by Premier Seddon', although he himself initially opposed this. It was not until 1896 that he welcomed women's electoral participation, in gratitude for their votes for the Liberal Party, 'signalling the fact that all future governments would have to take the women's vote into consideration' (Brookes 2016, 138 and 143).
27 Mark Twain, the pen name of Samuel Langhorne Clemens (1835–1910), American writer and publisher, who had long been vocally supportive of women's suffrage: 'We brag of our universal un-restricted suffrage; but we are shams after all, for we restrict when we come to the women' (1875, quoted in Paine 1912, 542). He gives an account of women's suffrage in New Zealand in his memoirs from his world tour: 'Men ought to begin to feel a sort of respect for their mothers and wives and sisters by this time. The women deserve a change of attitude like that, for they have wrought well . . . In the New Zealand law occurs this: "The word *person* wherever it occurs throughout the Act includes *woman*"' (Twain 1897, 299–301).
28 William Pember Reeves (1857–1932), New Zealand politician, author and social reformer. Reeves wrote an account of women achieving the vote in New Zealand from his perspective later in 1903: 'So, one fine morning of September 1893, the women of New Zealand woke up and found themselves enfranchised. The privilege was theirs – given freely and spontaneously, in the easiest and most unexpected manner in the world, by male politicians, whose leaders, for the most part, had been converted to faith in the experiment by reading the English arguments so gallantly but unavailingly used by Mill and others in controversies on the other side of the earth. Brief had been the season through which New Zealand women had to struggle or agitate. No franchise leagues had fought the fight year after year, no crowded meetings had listened to harangues from eloquent and cultured women with intellects and powers of expression protesting even more effectually than their words against the political subjections of their sex' (Reeves 1903, 112).
29 Max O'Rell was the pseudonym of the French author Léon Paul Blouet (1847–1903), a celebrity of the day, selling vast quantities of books and gaining a reputation as an entertaining lecturer, undertaking a two-year world tour to the United States, Canada, Australia, New Zealand and South Africa from 1894. His most successful lecture was 'Her Royal Highness, Woman' in which he 'presented ready-made clichés of gender relations' (Verhoeven 2010, 7). A section of this lecture was published under the title 'Petticoat Government' in 1896, in which he remarks 'I know of one country only where the government by woman was given a real trial, and that is New Zealand. The law was passed and the experiment was made. The law, I believe, had to be

repealed after six months. The Government had taken such a tyrannical form that that loveliest of spots on the earth was on the eve of a revolution, of a desperate struggle for liberty' (O'Rell 1896, 101). Fawcett uses this as an example of anti-suffrage sentiment in *Women's Suffrage: A short history of a great movement* (1912a, 39).

30 Fawcett here splices Proverbs 29:27 with Psalm 46:1.
31 Goldwin Smith (1823–1910), British historian and journalist who lived in North America from 1868, teaching at Cornell until the university admitted women in 1871 (Conable 1977, 76–7). 'Female suffrage is a subject hardly less momentous than Home Rule, since it means a revolution in the family as well as in the State' (*Times* 1899a).
32 See Section 18.
33 A glendoveer is a 'kind of semi-divine spiritual being', from the Sanskrit *gandharva* (OED 2020a). This quote is taken from 'The Rebuilding', one of the poems in the then immensely popular *Rejected Addresses: or the New Theatrum Poetarum*, first published in 1812, that parodied famous authors of the time (Smith and Smith 1841, 41). The authors refer to the soon-to-be poet laureate Robert Southey (1774–1843)'s *Curse of Kehama*, a poem attempting to depict Indian spiritual life, as a source (Southey 1810).
34 *Romeo and Juliet*. Lord Capulet is a tyrannical father (3.5).
35 Referring to *Clarissa, or the History of a Young Lady* (Richardson 1748). James Harlowe, Clarissa's father, restricts her access to the outside world, attempts to force her to marry a chosen match and refuses to forgive her for her perceived betrayal.

22
The white slave trade: its causes, and the best means of preventing it, 1899

Paper read June 1899. International Congress, 1–8.

'The White Slave Trade is the traffic in girls for immoral purposes' (National Vigilance Association 1899, 4): today we would call this human trafficking for the purposes of sexual exploitation. The International Congress on the White Slave Trade was held in London from 21 to 23 June 1899, at the invitation of the National Vigilance Association (NVA) and Central Vigilance Society for the Repression of Criminal Vice and Public Immorality (NVA 1899, 2). Fawcett's ongoing concern for public morality (see Section 12) had seen her involved with the NVA, which was the most prominent organisation in the fight against sex trafficking, since it was formed in 1885: in 1910 she recalled, 'We were looked on with some suspicion, and I think we were regarded as about half crazy and wholly undesirable' (Fawcett, in Rubinstein 1991, 90).[1] Leading the NVA's Preventive and Rescue Sub-Committee, which 'was especially concerned with preventing girls and women from becoming prostitutes and with rescuing those who had done so', she was elected an NVA vice-president in 1891, serving on the committees until 1893 (Rubinstein 1991, 90–1); this was closely linked to her work opposing children being employed in theatres (see Section 14). Fawcett believed that the insufficient legislation and legal loopholes surrounding legal consent, prostitution and incest 'were the result of political expediency' as a direct outcome of women's lack of suffrage and therefore lack of voice in the House of Commons (Rubinstein 1991, 91).

The Congress was well attended, with more than a hundred delegates, and decided on a 'modest programme for immediate legal and diplomatic reform by the improvement of codes and extradition treaties' (NVA 1899, 11–12). Fawcett's paper was read on 22 June, in a session with papers from Germany, Norway, Denmark and America (NVA 1899, 14). Published in the proceedings of the conference (Fawcett 1899a), it was also issued, unrevised, as a stand-alone pamphlet.

While the tactics and approach of the NVA did lead to progress in the domestic and international fight against sex trafficking, many of the ideas and policies it, and Fawcett, espoused 'ultimately had a detrimental effect upon its self-professed agenda'. The NVA assumed British superiority, hindering international cooperation, and

> operated its domestic anti-trafficking initiatives according to a gendered, class-based xenophobia, which was founded on the tacit exaltation of the 'respectable (male) British citizen', and distinctions between the 'deserving' and the 'undeserving' foreign poor [with a] focus of its antipathy and suppressive actions . . . on that foreign female population [endorsing and often extending prejudices] towards 'the foreigner' and 'the prostitute' that had currency in the culture of the day, [setting an] unfortunate example for . . . the global anti-trafficking movement (Attwood 2015, 329).

Fawcett herself also never perceived of her vigilance work as curtailing any liberties: 'Some . . . appear to think that any curtailment of liberty of vice is an unjustifiable curtailment of the liberty of the subject . . . I think that *freedom* in vice is an unjustifiable curtailment of the liberty of the subject' (Fawcett 1893c). However, there are some aspects of Fawcett's thoughts on purity that many modern feminists find difficult to reconcile with her recent standing as a feminist icon (Jeffreys 1982; Bland 1992).

*

The evil we have met to consider and endeavour to cope with is probably one that has existed for a very long time, and in all countries. It is not singular in this. Its grim companions are murder, theft and fraud, and it must be observed that it partakes of the character of all these. The sufferers by the crime we are considering are worse than murdered morally, and very often their actual physical life is destroyed: the worst of thefts is the theft of the innocence and purity of the youth – male and female – of a nation; and as for fraud, the crime we are considering lives and moves and has its being in an atmosphere of fraud. The great peculiarity of the crime is that, known to exist as it is in nearly all countries, and whilst, of course, it is in the highest degree abhorrent in the eyes of every decent man and woman, I believe that up to the present moment no concerted international effort has been made to grapple with it and render it more difficult and dangerous. We have extradition treaties with nearly all civilized countries to enable us to pursue and arrest criminals who fly from justice,[2] and this particular crime, under the name of abduction, kidnapping or false imprisonment, is among extraditable offences. But the peculiarity of the crime is that it is often begun in one country, carried a step further in another, and actually completed in a third; and perhaps in no one country has what amounts to a criminal offence been committed. The fact must be faced that this crime is more internationally organized than any other, and therefore a specially organised international machinery for its suppression and punishment, and the protection of its victims, is called for. What that special international machinery should be, and how it should be worked, is the question which this International Conference has been called together to consider. It is very largely a matter for experts in international and criminal law. But the causes which have produced the crime, and the extraordinary and abnormal toleration of it in most countries, are subjects that should awaken in every intelligent citizen, man or woman, the strongest interest and concern.

The fact that the crime exists is not questioned by those who know anything about the darker side of human nature – that is to say, over a very large part of the world, women and girls can be bought and imprisoned, and used by the men who have bought them for immoral purposes as a source of income; that they can be shipped from country to country like so many head of cattle; and that when once they have passed into the clutches of the men who live on the proceeds of their infamy, they are all but powerless to escape.

I will illustrate what I mean by an example. An advertisement appears in an English paper that a lady of rank residing near Paris desires a young English girl as a companion for her only daughter, salary no object, and so on. Of course there would be hundreds of replies, and many girls might be foolish or inexperienced enough to keep an appointment to meet the advertiser without any protection: they might thus find themselves in the clutches of a bad man or woman who would certainly have made a careful study of the criminal law of the country they were in, so as to avoid bringing himself or herself within its provisions. The miscreants who engage in this trade would have been able to select, from among the numerous answers they had received to their false advertisement, those who were most friendless and helpless. They could deliberately select girls who were ignorant of the language of the country to which they were going; who were poor, who were presumably without influential and energetic relatives. Thus, the poorer and more ignorant and miserable the condition of the young female part of the population in any country, the more they are exposed to the evil machinations of the men who live on this nefarious trade. The cruel persecution of the Jews in Russia has, I am informed, been the cause of a terrible increase in the number of Russian Jewesses who have been the victims of the white slave trade.[3] Deported in the first instance from Odessa to Constantinople, they are from the city sent to all parts of the world as the organisation of the ghastly trade may direct. When Mr Coote[4] was in Russia, he was informed by a gentleman who had been Russian Consul at Buenos Ayers [sic] for three years that he estimated there were 3,000 European women enslaved and imprisoned in the 'tolerated houses'[5] of that city, and that he believed at least half of them to be Russians, many of them Jewesses. He added that the price of a woman varied from 3 to 500 roubles (about £30 to £50).[6]

I do not refer to these things in any spirit of self-righteousness as far as our own country is concerned. We have no cause for self-complacency. It is less than a year since a law was passed in England making it a punishable offence in a man to live on the earnings of prostitution.[7] Thus we had, till 1898, a law which provided punishment for the offence of solicitation on the part of the woman, but provided no punishment for the man who lived on her earnings. The Vagrancy Law Amendment Act put an end to that absurdity, and made the law about solicitation much more nearly equal as between the two sexes. It is cheering to learn that, within a few months of the new Act being passed in England, a similar Act was adopted in Cape Colony,[8] and I have recently received cuttings from a Cape paper giving an account of the first prosecution under the new Act. It appears from this report that in punishing one villainy the Cape police unearthed another, and that other is the crime we are considering to-day how best to thwart. The man who, in Cape Town, was prosecuted for living on the earnings of prostitution, one George Terry, an Englishman born in France, was astounded at his arrest. He claimed that his was one of the best-conducted bad houses in Cape Town, and said, 'I paid £50 for that girl you saw in the kitchen. I bought her at "So-and-so" without a skirt or a stitch of clothes. The other one I bought in Johannesburg, and paid £100 for her.' The man could, of course, only be punished for the offence with which he was charged, but the magistrate inflicted the heaviest penalty which the law allowed, £20 fine, or three months' hard labour. But here we have, in an English colony, sharing, no doubt, to the full all the English traditions of personal liberty, an example of the white slave trade flourishing, and only discovered accidentally in the course of the pursuit of another crime. The pretence on which the man claimed his victim was the one with which every one who has given even a casual attention to this subject is familiar, that of owning all the clothes in which the girl was attired; any attempt at flight is then represented as theft, theft of the clothes the victim is wearing at the time of her departure. When I was writing this paper I had the opportunity of conversation with an English lady who had lived many years in Italy. I told her what I was doing. She at once saw the connection of the subject with that of 'tolerated houses', as they exist in France, Italy, Belgium and other countries; she informed me that the female inmates of these houses in Italy are not allowed to go out, except under charge of their keepers; they are virtually imprisoned for life. The only means of escape which they have is if some man, touched by their miseries will either promise to marry them or be responsible for them for life. My informant told me she had, from time to time, heard in Italy of heart-breaking scenes taking place within the walls of these 'tolerated houses'; of one of their inmates imploring and craving a man, who came for immoral purposes, to deliver her and take her out.

It seems, therefore, at whatever point we come to close quarters with this trade in human beings, we are brought forcibly to the conviction that it is closely associated with what is called ordinary immorality: that legal enactments and punitive measures, though they are necessary and right in every well-ordered State, yet will never really cut at the root of the evil with which we desire to contend if they are unaccompanied by an elevation in the moral tone. What is wanted above all is a higher moral standard in the community at large, and especially a higher moral standard among men; an abandonment of the false theory that vice is a necessity for men, and that, therefore, Governments are bound to make provision for it; and that the action or course of conduct which is social death to a woman is to be tolerated and excused in a man. For years and years, good men and women, who have tried to stem the flood of national immorality, have too much concentrated their efforts upon the reform of one sex, and that, probably, of the two, the least guilty. We hear a great deal of rescue and preventive work among women: admirable societies are at work in this country, and, no doubt, in other countries, with the object of awakening the moral sense in young women,[9] of warning them of possible dangers, of sheltering and protecting them at critical moments. Many societies which may not have a direct moral purpose of this kind in view, yet very frequently subserve the same end, and by opening educational opportunities to women and extending the field for their employment by raising their wages and ameliorating their industrial conditions, make the position of the woman in honest industry more attractive and desirable, thereby lessening the economic temptation held out by a life of vice. All these various efforts are most valuable, and have done and are doing a vast amount of good. Still, how far are we from reaching any goal where we may sit down content! If this Conference is to do good we must dwell, not so much on our measure of success – such as it is – but upon the causes of failure.

I think the most obvious source of failure is the comparative absence of direct moral training and teaching for boys and men on this matter, and the low tone of public opinion as regards sexual immorality in men. In the home and in the school there is not, it is to be feared, among most parents and teachers, a sufficiently keen sense of their responsibility for starting the boy and the young man upon sound lines on this matter. Almost as soon as a child is old enough to think, observe and speak, he asks questions of his parents which bear on the most fundamental of human relations. What does birth mean, what is motherhood, and what is fatherhood? In all probability the answer given him is a lie: and this is considered even by fairly truthful people not only as excusable, but as absolutely necessary. In this way the child is started wrong from the first. If he has average intelligence he knows that his parents have told him an untruth; he is puzzled and bewildered, and he is left to gather the truth from the chance ribaldry of a companion or playfellow only a little less ignorant than himself. I do not mean that it is necessary or desirable to stimulate a child's curiosity in these matters; but generally the curiosity is there, and whatever the child learns should be told it seriously, and if it is not the whole truth, what is said should at least be true as far as it goes.

If we follow the child's life from home to the school, too often we know that he is placed in terribly unwholesome surroundings as regards sexual morality. Too young and ignorant to know what he is doing, he is very likely left to establish habits and a mode of thought that poisons domestic life at its source. Every now and then a terrible scandal startles society. A man with perhaps a well-known name and position is convicted of criminal vice.[10] Hands are held up in horror: certain names must never again be mentioned. But why is it not asked 'Where were these habits contracted? What is the source and origin of the evil? If boys at school have their minds poisoned and their bodies ruined, what is to be expected of the man a few years later?'

That schoolmasters, especially the younger generation of schoolmasters, are facing these problems, and endeavouring to solve them, is one of the most encouraging signs of the times. But their efforts should be backed up by the influence of parents and of society in general if it is to prove truly effectual.

Another great engine of national education or of national degradation is the army. Especially is this the case in those countries which have universal military service. We know that in a book recently published in

France, M. Gohier stated that in the barracks the young Frenchman learns lying, tale-bearing, low debauchery, moral cowardice and drunkenness;[11] that he is made to believe that drunkenness and debauchery are the glorious prerogatives of manhood. We, in England, have no means of judging whether these charges are true or not: but we know that M. Gohier has been prosecuted for libelling the army, and that he has been acquitted by a jury of his countrymen. But let us not fix our eyes on what is happening in other countries where the judgments we are able to form are very likely to be arrived at without sufficient knowledge. Let us look at home and ask what sort of school the English army has been to the young Englishmen who enter it. The *Times*, on Monday, June 5th, less than three weeks ago, contained a telegraphic account of a ghastly outrage perpetuated upon a respectable Burmese woman in Rangoon, close to the public highway, not by a solitary man (any body of men may contain a scoundrel), but by twelve or sixteen men, and with some twenty-five or thirty others looking on. Forty men in all were implicated.[12] The Burma Government has offered a reward of 1,000 rupees for the detection of the offenders; and the Viceroy of India has ordered that no expense or trouble shall be spared to bring the offenders to justice; but the fact that such an outrage has been committed, and for a long time remained unpunished, is an illustration of the bad social influences often brought to bear on young men who enter the army. It is no good going on with rescue and preventive work for women while the other half of the nation are given over to a state of mind which looks upon low debauchery, and cowardly villainy, as manly.

From 1868 to 1886, English Governments, Liberal as well as Conservative, passed laws, and had them carried out, which were based on the assumption that it was part of the duty of Parliament and of the military authorities to provide for the army physical safety in the indulgence of sexual vice.[13] It has been conclusively proved that the military authorities had undertaken an impossibility; that the physical dangers could not be removed by the laws which had been passed, and that the disease in question was increased by their influence, because they led men to depend upon a security which did not exist. These bad laws were repealed thirteen years ago, and in the last published report of the Army Medical Department for the year 1897 we find the following satisfactory passage: 'The decline in venereal diseases, which commenced in 1886, and which has continued practically without interruption ever since, is again observed in 1897 . . .' – *Times*, March 3rd, 1899.[14]

We note with satisfaction a very great change for the better in the tone in which some of the military authorities in this country deal with this and kindred subjects, and although we have not universal military service, the change is of great importance to the whole population, for the tone of the army has an immense influence either for good or evil on the tone of civil society. The army may be looked upon as a vast school through which many thousands of our countrymen pass year by year. If they come out of the army better men all round than they went in, the whole community benefits, while there is no need to point out that the whole community suffers if the reverse is the case. Now what did Commander-in-Chief, General Lord Wolseley,[15] say on this point, about a year ago? In a memorandum which he addressed to the officers of the army in April 1898, he said, 'Nothing has probably done more to deter young men who have been respectably brought up from entering the army than the belief, entertained by them and their families, that barrack-room life is hell; that no decent lad can submit to it without loss of character or self-respect.' He goes on to express his desire that in making recommendations for promotion, regard should be had not only to professional efficiency but also to personal character, and that 'no man, however efficient in other respects, should be considered fit to exercise authority over his comrades if he is of notoriously vicious and intemperate habits'.[16] We know that a general order, quite on the same lines, was addressed, a few months earlier, by the late Commander-in-Chief of India, General Sir George White,[17] to the officers of the Indian Army. We are very thankful for this evidence that the Heads of the Army are beginning to make a serious endeavour to raise the tone of the officers and men on this subject, and that they see that the army suffers if its low reputation keeps men of good character from joining it. It will make things much easier for those who are longing for a higher tone throughout society in sexual morality if the army should become a help instead of a hindrance. There is reason for hopefulness, but there is also reason for deep humiliation. Hope may be derived from noting what had already been done with regard to the closely allied subject of drunkenness. Can we not, many of us, remember the time when it seemed almost as much a matter of course that a soldier should be a drunkard as that he should wear a red coat? People were considered to be foolish fanatics when they wished to start army temperance associations; now there are large numbers of these societies:[18] there are 22,000 total abstainers in the Indian Army; and in twenty years the fines for drunkenness had diminished by about half.[19] The reproach of drunkenness is very largely removed from the army, and the army authorities, from the Secretary of State and Commander-in-Chief downwards, lose no opportunity of encouraging sobriety among all ranks in the army.

There is another important and influential section of society from whom, in times gone by, the question of sexual morality received little help, but among whom in recent years a better tone has prevailed, and from whom, in the future, I believe great things may be expected. Is it necessary to say that I refer to the medical profession? Here, again, is a case in point, where a contrast of the present with the past gives a new hope for the future. How often in years that are past have medical men taught their male patients that the laws of health were at variance with the laws of morality, and that immorality was a necessity, to which it was absolutely inevitable that a certain number of women should be sacrificed – that the harlot was therefore a public benefactor, screening by her personal sacrifice the innocence and purity of home? The death-blow to this ghastly falsehood has been given by such leaders of the medical profession as Sir James Paget,[20] Sir Andrew Clark,[21] Dr Barlow[22] and others.

If I am asked what moral agencies we have in England endeavouring to cope with this evil, of which the culminating horror is the white slave trade, instead of enumerating the names of philanthropic societies, the object of which is to patch together again the human wreckage caused by immorality, rather would I call attention to the growth of a sounder state of feeling in the home, in the school, in the university, in the barracks, and in the consulting-room.

There are also two social movements of comparatively recent growth which are, I believe, purifying influences. We know that in the physical world the greatest of deodorisers and antiseptics are light and air. We observe a similar thing in the moral world. The evil deeds we want to make war upon love the darkness because they are evil. To drag them into the light is going a long way towards annihilating them. May I recall to you for a moment a memorable correspondence which took place in 1861 between Thackeray and Elizabeth Barrett Browning on this point? She had offered him for publication in the *Cornhill*, a poem which he felt bound, with very great reluctance, to refuse.[23] 'Not', he wrote to her, 'that the writer is not pure, and the moral most pure, chaste and right, but there are things my squeamish public will not hear on Monday, though on Sunday they listen to them without scruple . . . Though you write pure doctrine and real modesty and pure ethics, I am sure our readers would make an outcry and so I have not published the poem.'

She replies,

Also I confess that from your Cornhill standpoint (*pater familias* looking on), you are probably right ten times over. From mine, however, I may not be wrong, and I appeal to you as the deep man you are, whether it is not the higher mood which on Sundays bears with the plain word . . . I don't like coarse subjects or the coarse treatment of any subject. But I am deeply convinced that the corruption of our society requires not shut doors and windows, but light and air; and that it is exactly because pure, prosperous women choose to *ignore* vice, that miserable women suffer wrong by it everywhere. Has *pater familias*, with his oriental traditions and veiled female faces, very successfully dealt with a certain class of evil? What if *mater familias*, with her quick sure instincts and honest, innocent eyes, do more towards their expulsion by simply looking at them and calling them by their names?

There is a vast deal more openness in dealing with these subjects than there was when Mrs Browning wrote nearly forty years ago. No one will deny that there are drawbacks connected with this development of plain speaking; but also, I think, no one can deny that on the whole the change has been for good.

One other social change which has made great progress during the present generation, and has proved a moral agency in coping with the powers of darkness, is the growing movement towards equality between men and women. Most men have heretofore exacted a higher standard of conduct (in sexual matters) from women of their families than they have attempted to act up to themselves. It is a result of the highest importance of the women's movement, that women are now beginning to ask men to practice as well as preach; not 'to show the steep and thorny path to heaven whilst . . . himself the primrose path of dalliance treads, and recks not his own rede'.[24] It is characteristic of Shakespeare's insight into human nature that as soon as Ophelia says this, Laertes, who up to then had seemed to have ample time to give moral advice to his sister, exclaims hurriedly, 'Oh fear me not. I stay too long.'

I believe that some among my audience may fear that this growing tendency to apply the same moral standard to men and women has its drawbacks, that there is a danger that we shall level down instead of levelling up. No one ought to leave this danger out of account. But if we are duly on our guard against it, I believe that the only true road towards a permanently higher and purer state of things is the universal recognition of one moral law for men and women. Then our civilisation will no longer be disgraced by the entrapping and imprisoning of women for the gratification of the cupidity and other evil passions of men.

Transcribed from a copy in the Women's Library at LSE.
No known copyright restrictions.

Notes

1. Rubinstein (1991, 90) quotes from Coote 1916.
2. The Extradition Act of 1870 placed British extradition upon a statutory basis: prior to that, a cumbersome process of individual treaties had been in place (Booth and Sells 1980, LVII).
3. 'Jewish women were recruited from impoverished families in Eastern Europe. The extreme poverty of many of the Jewish communities in the Russian Pale of Settlement at the end of the nineteenth century . . . worsened even more by the effects of the Russo-Japanese War and World War I . . . This situation became the source of wealth for unscrupulous Jewish white-slave traffickers . . . At the turn of the century the traffic in Jewish women, mainly from Russia and Rumania, had reached, among other places, Johannesburg, Cape Town, Pretoria, the Philippine Islands, Alexandria, Cairo, Constantinople, Damascus, Bombay, Rio di Janeiro and Buenos Aires' (Mirelman 1984, 147–8).
4. William Alexander Coote (1842–1919), moral reform campaigner and foundational co-secretary of the NVA. After a divine vision, he resolved to travel widely throughout Europe to establish an international policing network (Coote 1910, 21).
5. Brothels. The Criminal Law Amendment Act 1885 outlawed these in England (Scott 2013, 111).
6. According to the National Archives' Currency Converter, this would equate to £2,345–£3,908 in 2017.
7. The Vagrancy Act 1898; see Scott (2013, 252).
8. This had a link to Fawcett, as it was implemented by her cousin Edmund Garrett (1865–1907), who had been the charge of Fawcett's sister Miss Agnes Garrett; Fawcett lived with them in Gower Street following Henry Fawcett's death. Edmund Garrett was, by then, the editor of the *Cape Times* in South Africa, becoming a member of Parliament in the Cape Legislative Assembly from 1898. He 'grafted several new clauses' to the Police Offences Act 'on the lines of the English Criminal Law, with procuration and other offences of a like kind by men. Garrett described his tactics and their success in a letter . . . To Mrs Fawcett . . . "*Your* Act on the Statute Book of Cape Colony is, or should be, a useful bit of work. I merely adapted to Cape conditions the English Act which you sent, and read your *Times* extract to the House to drive it through . . . On this peg I hung all your proposal"' (Cook 1909, 147).
9. 'From 1885 social purity groups became increasingly active and numerous. Various societies were formed, ranging from the London Council [for the Promotion of Public Morality], the Moral Reform Union, the Social Purity Alliance, the White Cross Army and the Church of England Purity Society, the Friends' Association for the Promotion of Social Purity through to the historically notorious National Vigilance Association' (Bartley 2000, 155).
10. Fawcett is referring here to Oscar Wilde's trial and conviction for gross indecency in 1895 (Adut 2005).
11. Urbain Gohier (1862–1951), French lawyer, author, anarchist and anti-Semite, was tried for defaming the French Army in his 1898 pamphlet *L'armée contre la nation* (The Army Against the Nation). A translation of the 'most striking passages' appeared in the *Pall Mall Gazette*: 'The army is merely the school of all the crapulous vices of laziness, lying, sneakishness, shamelessness, filthy debauchery, moral cowardice and drunkenness . . . The barracks are rotting France through and through with alcoholism and disease' (*Pall Mall Gazette* 1898). He was acquitted in March 1899 (*Standard* [London] 1899).
12. *Times* 1899d. The 40 men were from the West Kent Regiment: the assault was carried out by British soldiers. The telegraph, of course, had transformed the speed of news transmission in the Victorian period: Burma (now Myanmar) had been connected to the 'Further India' British telegraphic network since 1860 (Beauchamp 2001, 97). The correspondent's column was dated 4 June: only the day before.
13. 'In the later 1860s a series of Contagious Diseases Acts attempted to control sexually transmitted diseases in the armed services by eliminating prostitution in garrison towns and ports. The Acts were the result of campaigns by various groups concerned with public health. However, a strong protest movement grew up – the Ladies' National Association led by the social reformer Josephine Butler – which argued that it was the men who frequented prostitutes who needed to be punished. The Acts were eventually suspended in 1883, and repealed in 1886' (Parliament.uk n.d.i).
14. Fawcett does not complete the sentence: 'the greatest decrease being in primary venereal sores' (*Times* 1899b).

15 Field Marshal Garnet Joseph Wolseley (1833–1913), 1st Viscount Wolseley, admired British army general.
16 Although issued on 26 April, it was later presented as a parliamentary paper in August; see *Times* 1898.
17 Field Marshal Sir George Stuart White (1835–1912), 'late' because he was commander-in-chief of India from April 1895 until March 1898. In July 1897, he sent out a general order to the Indian Army regarding behaviour, focusing 'on the question of venereal disease in the army' (*Union Signal* 1897, 9).
18 The temperance movement had transitioned to a mass movement by the late 1870s, and in 1888 the Liberal politician William S. Caine (1842–1903) established the Anglo-Indian Temperance Association (Carroll 1976, 418). By 1889 'there are according to [its] last quarterly report . . . 280 Temperance Societies working in India. These are spread over the length and the breadth of the country and are trying to develop in the national mind a real interest in this noble cause' (Indian National Congress 1900, 78).
19 Fawcett's note: '*Times*, May 16th, 1899. Meeting of Army Temperance Association'. Fawcett does not quote the rest of the report made by Sir George White on figures from 1894: 'Drunkenness and its effects were at the bottom of nearly all the crime in our Indian Army' (*Times* 1899c). The total strength of the British Army in India 'in 1887 was about 230,000 men of all arms, of whom 73,000 were British' (Strachey 1888, 64); by 1899 'out of 70,000 English soldiers located in India, 24,000 are total abstainers' (Indian National Congress 1900, xxiv).
20 Sir James Paget (1814–99), surgeon, after whom many diseases are named, including Paget's disease of the nipple and areola (Paget 1874).
21 Sir Andrew Clark (1826–93), physician. Clark had tended to Henry Fawcett's severe illness in 1882 (Fawcett 1924, 134), and was doctor to (and a supporter of) Elizabeth Garrett Anderson.
22 Sir Thomas Barlow (1845–1945), physician known for his research on scurvy in infants, and physician to Queen Victoria in her last two years, from 1899 to 1901.
23 The *Cornhill* was one of the most important monthly Victorian literary journals, established in 1860, under the editorship of the popular novelist William Makepeace Thackeray (1811–63). In 1861, Thackeray rejected Elizabeth Barrett Browning's poem 'Lord Walter's Wife' on 'grounds of respectability'; see Scott (1999, 269–70) for an overview and the source of this correspondence.
24 *Hamlet* 1.3.

23
The concentration camps in South Africa, 1901

Westminster Gazette. Thursday, 4 July 1901, 1–2.

The South African War (or Second Boer War) was fought between Great Britain and the two Boer[1] (Afrikaner) republics – the Orange Free State and the South African Republic – between 11 October 1899 and 31 May 1902, ultimately resulting in British victory. It was a large, destructive and costly war, causing 'an almost complete suspension of work for Women's Suffrage' (Fawcett 1924, 149). The British armies operated a scorched-earth policy, destroying farms, while the Boers reverted to guerrilla warfare. Survivors were rounded up into segregated concentration camps that were poorly run, overcrowded and unhygienic, leading to contagion and high mortality rates, particularly for women, children and the elderly (Krebs 1992). 'Over 4,000 women and 22,000 children died when a succession of major epidemics – particularly measles, diarrhoea, enteritis, typhoid and pneumonia – occurred, spread when people were moved from one concentration camp to another, to be closer to their original homes' (Stanley and Wise 2006). In December 1900 the English social worker Emily Hobhouse (1860–1926) travelled to South Africa on a charity mission and to investigate the conditions in the camps. The resulting reports on the inhumane conditions (Hobhouse 1901), initially published in the *Manchester Guardian* (1901), achieved wide publicity and, ultimately, led to an improvement in conditions (Hobhouse 1902).

In this newspaper column, Fawcett presents a jingoistic rebuttal to Hobhouse's findings, showing her faith in the British establishment and its approaches. Fawcett approved of the Boer War, and believed the camps to be 'part of the fortune of war'. Eleven days after the publication of this article, 'the War Office was asked in the House of Lords to appoint a commission of enquiry, to visit the concentration camps and report on their conditions' (Rubinstein 1991, 122). Fawcett was assigned to assemble this committee of six ladies, having 'no credentials in either public health or colonial matters, but she was efficient, she believed in the necessity for the way, and she was well-known for being an advocate of women's rights. In addition, Fawcett had made up her mind that the camps were necessary before she set off for South Africa' (Krebs 1992, 46). 'I at once consented to go, and . . . I could be ready to start in a week or less' (Fawcett 1924, 153). Hobhouse was rejected for the committee and refused permission by the War Office to return to the camps (Rubinstein 1991, 122): she was considered by many to be a 'violent pro-Boer' (Strachey 1931, 192).[2]

Fawcett sailed on 22 July 1901 with her daughter Philippa as a companion; she arrived in South Africa on 10 August and went on to spend four months there (Fawcett 1924, 153–74; Strachey 1931, 179–205; Rubinstein 1991, 123–7). The Commission visited 'all the concentration camps except the one at Fort [Port] Elizabeth, of which even the pro-Boer ladies at Cape Town had no complaint to make' (Fawcett 1924, 166), but did not visit any of the camps which held African prisoners (Krebs 1992, 52; Lally 2015, 47). The Fawcett Commission issued recommendations in late 1901 and published its report in full in 1902 (Concentration Camps Commission 1902). It ultimately upheld Hobhouse's findings but was critical of the Boer women for their own lack of responsibility, blaming the high mortality rate on the Boers' own lack of hygienic practices: 'Fawcett's advocacy of women's rights in Britain did not, as Hobhouse noted, lead her to sympathise with women in South Africa' (Krebs 1992, 49; see Krebs 1992 and Lally 2015 for an intersectional analysis of gender, race and class within the reports).[3] Fawcett's feminism here is 'white and middle class' (Dalley 2021, 13), and the reference to the lack of hygiene of the imprisoned Boer women and children in the camps is a colonialist trope used to justify systems of supremacy, oppression and internment (Vaughan 1991; Bashford 2004; Denness 2012).

The British authorities implemented the Commission's recommendations within a few weeks of having them, which did improve camp conditions: 'Men had been blamed for the conditions in the camps, and women were credited for the reforms' (Krebs 1992, 53). However, this episode and Fawcett's judgemental approach to those who were not English (see also Section 33) are the most problematic and disturbing aspects of her career, and must now be squared with her recasting as a feminist icon. A combined total of both Black and White deaths in the camps by the end of hostilities 'approache[d] 40,000' (Smith 2007b).

The camps were closed at the end of the war. Fawcett's beliefs about the behaviour of the British Forces in the South African War, and the camps themselves, never changed: shortly before her death in 1929, she wrote a letter to the *Times Literary Supplement* correcting 'the aspersions cast by the late Miss Hobhouse on the management and administration', praising the 'British soldier' for being 'the best of peacemakers' and noting the 'lesson in practical kindness' in seeing troops settling a family 'in their neat little tent in the concentration camp' (Fawcett 1929a, 436).

*

During the past fortnight I, in common with most other people, have read many newspaper summaries of Miss Emily Hobhouse's Report[4] on the condition of the concentration camps for women and children in South Africa, but it is only within the last few days that I have had the opportunity of reading the Report itself, and there are some features in it which appear not to have been given sufficient prominence in the summaries and extracts which have been made. To these I desire to call the attention of your readers.

First, I would note Miss Hobhouse's frequent acknowledgements that the various authorities were doing their best to make the conditions of camp life as little intolerable as possible. The opening sentence of the Report proper is: 'January 22. – I had a splendid truck given to me at Capetown through the kind co-operation of Sir Alfred Milner[5] – a large double covered one, capable of holding twelve tons.' In other places she refers to the help given her by various officials. The commandant at Aliwal North[6] had ordered £150 worth of clothing and had distributed it; she undertook to forward some of it (p. 6). At Springfontein[7] 'the commandant was a kind man, and willing to help both the people and me as far as possible' (p. 9). At Mafeking[8] the superintendent was a Scotchman, 'thoroughly capable and suitable, but, alas! likely to be removed ere long' (p. 11). Other similar quotations might be made.

Miss Hobhouse acknowledges that the Government recognise that they are responsible for providing necessary clothes, and she appears rather to deprecate the making and sending of further supplies from England. I will quote her exact words on this point. The italics are mine: 'The demand for clothing is so huge that it is hopeless to think that the private charity of England and Colonial working parties combined can effectually cope with it. *The Government recognise that they must provide necessary clothes*, and I think we all agree that, having brought these people into this position, it is their duty to do so. *It is, of course, a question for English folk to decide how long they like to go making and sending clothes.* There is no doubt they are immensely appreciated; besides, they are mostly made up, which the Government clothing won't be' (p. 8). Miss Hobhouse says that many of the women in the camp at Aliwal North had brought their sewing-machines. If they were set to work to make clothes, it might serve a double purpose of giving them occupation and the power of earning a little money, and it would also ensure the clothes being made sufficiently large. Miss Hobhouse says people in England have very incorrect notions of the magnificent proportions of the Boer women. 'Blouses which were sent out from England intended for women could only be worn by girls of twelve and fourteen: they were much too small for the well-developed Boer maiden, who is really a fine creature. Could an out-out woman's size be procured?' (p. 9).

It must be remembered that when Miss Hobhouse saw the camps for the first time – it was in January, the hottest month in the South African year – the difficulty of getting supplies along a single line of rails, often broken by the enemy, was very great. The worst of the camps she saw was at Bloemfontein,[9] the worst features of this worst camp were:

1. Water supply was bad.
2. Fuel was very scarce.
3. Milk was very scarce.
4. Soap was not to be had.
5. Insufficient supply of trained nurses.
6. Insufficient supply of civilian doctors.
7. No ministers of religion.
8. No schools for the children.
9. Exorbitant prices were demanded in the shops.
10. Parents had been separated from their children.

Within the Report itself, either in footnotes or in the main body of the Report, Miss Hobhouse mentions that active steps had already been taken to remedy these evils. Tanks had been ordered to boil all the water (p. 7). She left money to buy another, and supplied every family with a pan to hold boiled water. Soap was being given out with the rations. 'Moreover, the Dutch are so very full of resource and so clever, they can make their own soap with fat and soda' (p.7). The milk supply was augmented; during the drought fifty cows only yielded four buckets of milk daily. 'After the rains the milk supply was better' (p. 5, note). An additional supply of nurses were on their way. 'The Sister has done splendid work in her domain, battling against incessant difficulties . . . and to crown the work she has had the task of training Boer girls to nurse under her' (p. 8). Ministers of religion are in residence, and schools, under Mr E. B. Sargant, the Education Commissioner, are open for boys and girls (p. 6). Children have been reunited to parents, except that some girls, through Miss Hobhouse's kind efforts, have been moved away from the camps altogether into boarding-schools. Even in this Bloemfontein camp, notwithstanding all that Miss Hobhouse says of the absence of soap and the scarcity of water, she is able to write: 'All the tents I have been in are exquisitely neat and clean, except two, and they are ordinary' (p. 5). Another important admission about this camp is to be found in the last sentence of the account of Miss Hobhouse's second visit to Bloemfontein. She describes the iron huts which have been erected there at a cost of £2,500, and says: 'It is so strange to think that every tent contains a family and every family is in trouble – loss behind, poverty in front, privation and death in the present. But they are very good, and say they have agreed to be cheerful and make the best of it all' (p. 8).

There can be no doubt that the sweeping together of about 63,000, men, women and children[10] into these camps must have been attended by great suffering and misery, and if they are courageously borne it is greatly to the credit of the sufferers. The questions the public will ask, and will be justified in asking, are:

1. Was the creation of these camps necessary from the military point of view?
2. Are our officials exerting themselves to make the conditions of the camps as little oppressive as possible?
3. Ought the public at home to supplement the efforts of the officials and supply additional comforts and luxuries?

The reply to the first question can only be given by the military authorities, and they have answered it in the affirmative. Put briefly, their statement is that the farms on the veldt were being used by small commandos of the enemy as storehouses for food, arms and ammunition; and, above all, they have been centres for supplying false information to our men about the movements of the enemy and correct information to the enemy about the movements of the British.[11] No one blames the Boer women on the farms for this; they have taken an active part on behalf of their own people in the war, and they glory in the fact. But no one can take part in war without sharing in its risks, and the formation of the concentration camps is part of the fortune of war. In this spirit 'they have agreed', as Miss Hobhouse says, 'to be cheerful and make the best of it all'.

The second question – 'Are our officials exerting themselves to make the camps as little oppressive as possible?' – can also be answered in the affirmative, judging from the evidence supplied by Miss Hobhouse herself. This does not imply that at the date of Miss Hobhouse's visit, or at any time, there were not matters capable of improvement. But it is confessed even by very hostile witnesses that our Government had a very difficult task and that its officials were applying themselves to grapple with it with energy, kindness and goodwill. Miss Hobhouse complains again and again of the difficulty of procuring soap. May I quote, as throwing light upon the fact that the Boer women were no worse off in this respect than our own people, that Miss Brooke-Hunt, who was in Pretoria to organise soldiers' institutes a few months earlier than Miss Hobhouse was at Bloemfontein, says in her interesting book *A Woman's Memories of the War*: 'Captain — — presented me with a small piece of Sunlight soap, an act of generosity I did not fully appreciate till I found that soap could not be bought for love or money in the town.'[12] A Boer woman of the working class said to Miss Brooke-Hunt: 'You English are different from what I thought. They told us that if your soldiers got inside Pretoria they would rob us of everything, burn our houses, and treat us cruelly; but they have all been so kind and respectable. It seems a pity we did not know this before.'[13] Miss Hobhouse supplies some rather similar testimony. On page 11 of her Report she says: 'The Mafeking camp folk were very surprised to hear that English women cared a rap about them or their suffering. It has done them a lot of good to hear that real sympathy is felt for them at home, and I am so glad I fought my way here, if it is only for that reason.' In what sense, except against heat and fatigue, Miss Hobhouse had to fight her way to the camps does not appear, for she acknowledges the kindness of Lord Kitchener and Lord Milner in enabling her to visit them (pp. 3 and 14); we must therefore suppose that they provided her with a pass. But the sentence just quoted is enough in itself to furnish the answer to the third question – 'Is it right for the public at home to supplement by gifts of additional comforts and luxuries the efforts of our officials to make the camp life as little intolerable as possible?' All kinds of fables have been told to the Boer men and women of the brutality and ferocity of the British. Let them learn by practical experience, as many of them have learnt, that the British soldier is gentle and generous, and that his women-folk at home are ready to do all in their power to alleviate the sufferings of the innocent victims of the war. I know it will be said, 'Let us attend to the suffering loyalists first.' It is a very proper sentiment, and if British generosity were limited to the gift of a certain definite amount in money or in kind I would be the first to say,

'Charity begins at home, and our own people must come first.' But British generosity is not of this strictly measured kind. By all means let us help the loyal sufferers by the war; but let us also help the women and children of those who have fought against us – not with any ulterior political motive, but simply because they have suffered and are bound to suffer much, and wounded hearts are soothed and healed by kindness. Mr Rowntree[14] has spoken publicly of the deep impression made on the Boer women by the kindness shown them by our men. One said she would always be glad to shake hands with a British soldier; it was because of the kindly devices they had invented to make over their rations to the women and children during the long journey when all were suffering severe privations. Another Boer girl, referring to an act of kindness shown her by a British officer, remarked quietly, 'When there is so much to make the heart ache it is well to remember deeds of kindness.' The more we can multiply deeds of kindness between Boer and Briton in South Africa, the better for the future of the two races, who, we hope, will one day fuse into a united nation under the British flag.

Transcribed from a copy in the British Library.
No known copyright restrictions.

Notes

1. A Dutch-speaking, or later Afrikaans-speaking, White farmer in South Africa.
2. The dislike of Hobhouse by the imperialist Garretts continued for years after: see Crawford (2002, 210) for an account of this entering the domestic sphere.
3. To understand the power dynamics at play and the intersections of feminism, race and empire, see also Bhavnani 2001, Theron 2006, Midgley 2007 and Gouws 2017.
4. See *Manchester Guardian* 1901 for the newspaper summary and Hobhouse 1901 for the published report.
5. Alfred Milner (1854–1925), Viscount Milner: public servant, politician, governor of the Cape Colony and high commissioner of South Africa from 1897.
6. A camp established in 1900 in the Orange River Colony. See British Concentration Camps of the South African War n.d.a.
7. A camp in operation by 1901 in the grasslands of the southern Free State. See British Concentration Camps of the South African War n.d.f.
8. A camp in the Cape Colony that was possibly the first to be established and which, for a period, had the highest death rate of any camp. See British Concentration Camps of the South African War n.d.c.
9. One of the largest camps to be established, used as a holding camp, in the Free State. See British Concentration Camps of the South African War n.d.b.
10. This figure is low. At the war's end 'the British official history shows the number of white Afrikaners in concentration camps as 116,572, with 47,150 in the Transvaal camps' (Scott 2007, 2). Approximately 25,000 White and 15,000 Black deaths are recorded and verified in the camps (Smith 2007b).
11. See Surridge 1998 for an overview.
12. Brooke-Hunt (1901, 174).
13. Brooke-Hunt (1901, 173–4).

14 The Quaker member of Parliament Joshua Rowntree (1844–1915) was sent to South Africa to investigate mortality rates in camps at the end of 1900, but his reports were largely ignored (Hewison 1989, 205–6). Both of these quotes are taken from a speech he gave after his return, in Lancaster on Thursday, 20 June 1901, which was reported in the *Times*: 'While desolation was behind, despair was in front of these unhappy people' (*Times* 1901).

24
Why we women want votes, 1906

Daily Mail. Tuesday, 20 November 1906, 6.

In 1906, women's suffrage returned to the political agenda. Following a period of social unrest after the South African War, the Liberal Party won a landslide majority in the February 1906 general election, with the Conservatives losing more than half their seats. For the first time, the majority of MPs were nominally in favour of women's suffrage.[1] The campaign itself was also gathering pace and attention, although using different tactics. In 1903, the Women's Social and Political Union (WSPU) was founded as a women-only political movement and militant organisation by Emmeline Pankhurst (1858–1928) and her daughter Christabel Pankhurst (1880–1958), becoming known for civil disobedience and direct action. In 1906, the term 'suffragettes' was coined in a *Daily Mail* article (1906a) to belittle women campaigning for the vote: however, this was a term the militants embraced (and one that also differentiated them from the constitutional suffragists), and with their increased and often scandalous activities, the subject of votes for women again became newsworthy. In October 1906, 11 suffragettes were jailed after a protest in the House of Commons lobby. In a letter to the *Times*, Fawcett wrote: 'I hope the more old-fashioned suffragists will stand by them; and I take this opportunity of saying that in my opinion, far from having injured the movement, they have done more during the last 12 months to bring it within the region of practical politics than we have been able to accomplish in the same number of years' (Fawcett 1906a).

A Women's Enfranchisement Bill was introduced by the Labour MP Keir Hardie (1856–1915) on 7 November 1906 (HC Deb 1906b). Fawcett's article in the *Daily Mail* came in the same week that the prime minister, Henry Campbell-Bannerman (1836–1908), had 'said he was afraid it was impossible to find time during the present session for the passing of the

Local Authorities (Qualification of Women) Bill', which was framed as a 'Blow to Suffragettes' (*Daily Mail* 1906b). Fawcett sets out recent legislative advances for, and barriers to, women for a popular audience, drawing on very recent events. Alluding to the suffragettes' 'unusual things by way of protest', she stresses the 'non-revolutionary' aspect of asking for voting rights, being of the opinion that it would bring 'into harmony the political status of women with changes which have already taken place in their industrial and educational status'. Unfortunately, the Women's Enfranchisement Bill, although introduced in March 1907, would run out of time before it became law.

*

When people sometimes ask 'Why do women want the franchise?', the obvious reply is: 'For exactly the same reasons that men want it: to secure the attention of Parliament to their various wants and wishes.'

As long as the parliamentary franchise was very much restricted, so that practically only the upper and middle classes were represented, women were in a relatively less disadvantageous position than they are now; they were excluded from citizenship, but so were the great mass of the artisans and labourers of the country. Now the only other classes which share with women an invidious distinction of disfranchisement are felons, idiots, paupers and Peers. But Peers are compensated by having a House of their own; felons, idiots and paupers suffer only temporary disfranchisement; women, and women alone, are permanently and for ever shut out from all share in controlling the laws by which they are governed.

An anomalous position

A woman may pay hundreds a year in taxation; she may be the head of a large establishment giving employment to dozens of persons; she may be the source of wholesome influence and kindly common sense in her immediate neighbourhood; she may be regarded with affection and esteem by a whole country side, and her advice may be sought in practical affairs by men and women far and near. But when it comes to electing a member of Parliament for the place where she lives, she is in a lower political position than any drunken, illiterate ne'er-do-weel man who is not fit to black her boots.

There are people who affect surprise that women regard such a state of things as insulting and degrading. As Hosea Bigelow puts it:

> Some folks seem to think it's natur'
> To take sarse and not be riled.
> Who'd expect to see a tater
> All on end at being biled?[2]

That women should be angry, that some of them should even be excited and do unusual things by way of protest seems to some complacent critics the height of folly and vulgarity, if not of sheer indecency. But the exclusion of women from all power of influencing the course of legislation is very far from being a merely sentimental grievance. By long years of patient work, capable and devoted women succeeded in opening to their sex positions of public usefulness, such as membership of school boards.[3] Many women were elected by their fellow citizens, men and women, to sit on these boards. By the universal testimony of those who worked with them on the boards and under them as teachers in the elementary schools, they did their work splendidly: they had no axes of their own to grind, they were hard-working and they brought to their work a knowledge of education, of the practical needs of the parents and children, and an understanding of the problems and difficulties of the teachers which made their aid in the educational administration of the country of the utmost value.

By the Education Act of 1902[4] new education authorities were created on which women were ineligible to be elected. It is true that the borough and county councils are compelled by law to co-opt upon their education committees at least one woman; but this is a very inferior substitute for the women who were formerly placed upon the boards by the electorate. The final authority and the power of the purse rests with the whole council, on which the co-opted members may not sit.

No real security

The history of the Education Act of 1902 has made all women who have worked for women's freedom feel that not one of the points of vantage they have gained as the result of years of effort during the last half-century is really secure without the protection of the parliamentary franchise. No represented class could have been treated as the women of England were treated by the Act of 1902. When the Liberals came in, Mr Birrell[5] expressed the greatest sympathy with our point of view in this matter, and Sir Henry Campbell-Bannerman told the deputation which waited upon him in May[6] that his whole Cabinet were unanimous in desiring to pass the Local

Government (Qualification of Women) Bill,[7] which would render women eligible for election on borough and county councils.

But they have managed to restrain their ardour in the matter with great success. The Education Bill of the present year leaves the grievance untouched, and no time is found in this autumn session to deal with the Bill, which would effectually remove it.

Bills that have voting power behind them, such as the Trade Disputes Bill,[8] are pushed through by the very same men who a few months earlier were denouncing its principles, because the Labour vote must at any cost be conciliated. Bills without voting power behind them, such as the Women's Local Government Bill, even when the Cabinet unanimously approve them, are postponed and neglected.

The Trade Disputes Bill illustrates another of the practical injustices which women have to endure under a so-called representative system, which represents everybody except half the nation. The clauses which legalise picketing make the industrial position of working women still more precarious than heretofore. It is well known that the trade unions have been in the past bitterly hostile to the entrance of women into the skilled trades. The physical intimidation of women workers has been resorted to in known instances in the past. This Bill will go far to make such intimidation legal in the future. The professors of law in the Universities of Oxford and Cambridge have protested most strongly against the Bill from this point of view among others. Professor Dicey, in a powerful article in the *National Review* for October, said if this Bill passes, 'every woman's right to support herself as she pleases will depend not on the law of the land but on the policy of trade unions'.[9] Professor Westlake[10] has said the same.

The only remedy

They might as well have whistled to the wind. The men's trade union vote had to be secured; and the possibility of the industrial freedom of women (without votes) being imperilled was not even, I believe, referred to when the Bill was in Committee in the House of Commons. Sir A. Acland-Hood, however, did point out that if the Bill passes, the women who last summer sought to 'peacefully persuade' Mr Asquith to hear their views on women's suffrage and were sent to prison for six weeks for doing so have only to form themselves into a trade union and their future proceedings will be under the aegis of the law.[11]

There is only one really sufficient remedy against legislative neglect and injustice – the extension of the parliamentary franchise to women on the same terms as those enjoyed by men. Every women's suffrage society is founded for this single purpose. We decline to be led away on the false scent of adult suffrage. If the suffrage were extended to women on the same terms as men, probably 1,500,000 to 2,000,000 women would be added to the existing electorate of about 7,000,000.[12] More new electors would be added to the register than were enfranchised by the Reform Bill of 1832.[13]

The change we are asking for is great and important, but it is meeting with an ever-increasing support on the part of the public.[14] It is essentially non-revolutionary in character because it brings into harmony the political status of women with changes which have already taken place in their industrial and educational status. That a woman such as the late Miss Beale,[15] who created for her own sex a magnificent educational establishment like the Ladies' College, Cheltenham, with a thousand pupils, ranging from the kindergarten to the university, should be held to be incapable of giving a vote in a parliamentary election, is the greatest and most glaring of electoral anomalies.

Transcribed from a copy in the British Library.
No known copyright restrictions.

Notes

1. Fawcett maintained that 'the Parliament elected in January 1906 . . . contained more than 400 members, belonging to all parties, who were pledged to the principle of women's suffrage. A considerable number of these had expressed their adherence to the movement in their election addresses' (Fawcett 1912a, 70).
2. Hosea Biglow was a fictional creation of the American poet, essayist and critic James Russell Lowell (1819–91). In a series of satirical poems and letters first published in 1848, Lowell expressed his opposition to the Mexican-American War, seeing it as an attempt to extend slavery. Hosea Biglow is a young New England farmer and rustic poet, commenting in Yankee dialect. Fawcett mis-transcribes slightly: 'We being to think it's nater / To take sarse an' not be riled; – / Who'd expect to see a tater / All on end at being biled?' (Lowell 1859, 4).
3. See Section 18.
4. 'By the 1890s, over 2,500 new school boards had been created in England and Wales under the 1870 legislation . . . In 1902 Parliament passed a new Education Act . . . which radically reorganised the administration of education at local level. It abolished the school boards in England and Wales. All elementary schools were placed in the hands of local education authorities . . . The Act also, for the first time, made significant provision for secondary and technical education' (Parliament.uk 2020). The School Boards created under the 1870 Education Act permitted women to be elected as members (and in fact Elizabeth Garrett and Emily Davies were two of the first women to be elected to the London School Board). However, the 1902 Act abolished School Boards and did not allow women to be elected to the county and borough councils that were to run the new Local Education Authorities.
5. Augustine Birrell (1850–1933), Liberal politician, president of the Board of Education and Cabinet minister, who was 'said to be' a strong supporter 'of the cause' (Rover 1967, 64).
6. Sir Henry Campbell-Bannerman (1836–1908), Liberal politician, leader of the Liberal Party from 1899 to 1908 and prime minister of the United Kingdom from 1905 to 1908. On Saturday, 19 May

1906, a large demonstration by advocates of the franchise for women was held on Victoria Embankment and in Trafalgar Square. Organised by the NUWSS and representing 26 organisations (Fawcett 1924, 180), a deputation of 400 persons waited for Campbell-Bannerman at the Foreign Office, with 40 members of Parliament also there. In his speech, although congratulating women on their contribution to society, 'He had only one thing to preach to them, and that was the virtue of patience (loud cries of "No, no") . . . he was content with giving that very limited encouragement (some hissing) . . . There was a distinct feeling of disappointment at the character of the answer to their demands' (*London Evening Standard* 1906).

7   The Qualification of Women (County and Borough Councils) Act 1907 clarified the right of women ratepayers to be elected to borough and county councils in England and Wales. One of the first to be elected in 1907 was Elizabeth Garrett Anderson, in Aldeburgh, becoming the UK's first female elected mayor in 1908 (Keen, Cracknell and Bolton 2018, 11).

8   Trade Disputes Act 1906, a fundamental statute that provided trade unions with immunity from liability for any actions that arise from strike actions (Kidner 1982).

9   Albert Venn Dicey (1835–1922), jurist and professor of English law at Oxford, then LSE (Dicey 1906a, 220), who was by then a strong anti-suffragist, despite holding these views on trade unions.

10 John Westlake (1828–1913), professor of international law at Cambridge, who had been a strong and active supporter of women's suffrage since the movement started. On Monday, 19 November, the *Times* printed letters from both Dicey and Westlake opposing the Trade Disputes Bill (Dicey 1906b; Westlake 1906).

11 Sir Alexander Fuller-Acland-Hood (1853–1917), Conservative Party politician. 'If this Amendment was defeated he sincerely trusted that the suffragettes would form a trade union, and endeavour to peacefully persuade every Member of the present Government' (HC Deb 1906a).

12 See Section 19, note 4.

13 '. . . immediately before the Reform Bill more than 400,000 Englishmen held a franchise of some sort . . . The Great Reform Act expanded the overall electorate to more than 650,000, a precise number after 1832 because of the imposition of a national system of registration' (Phillips and Wetherell 1995, 413–14).

14 'Those who thought that these unusual proceedings would strike the Women's Suffrage Movement dead were soon proved to be wrong. The very reverse was the case. The secretaries and other active members of the older Suffrage Societies were worked off their feet; every post brought applications for information and membership. Women's Suffrage was the topic of conversation in every household and at every social gathering; the newspapers, too, were full of it' (Fawcett 1924, 184).

15 Dorothea Beale, principal of Cheltenham Ladies' College; see Section 18, note 7.

25
The prisoners of hope in Holloway Gaol, 1906

Contemporary Review. December 1906, 820–6.

Throughout 1906, the militant tactics of the WSPU continued, as it escalated its campaign of civil disobedience and direct action. High-profile demonstrations and lobbies of Parliament and individual members of the Cabinet led to much media coverage. Exasperation from the establishment encouraged further protest, leading to arrests and imprisonment in Holloway, London's female-only prison. In this piece, Fawcett acknowledges the benefit of the WSPU's militant actions, in that they were generating support for and interest in women's suffrage, meaning that 'the question of Women's Suffrage has become a living issue of practical politics'. Fawcett places its tactics within a wider history of direct action which caused social change, equating its stance with major historical protests. At the same time, Fawcett continues to request unity, asking that all the different campaigning groups should peacefully work together 'in asking for the franchise for women, now, on the same terms in which it is or may be granted to men', and showing the personal relationship that she had with those in the WSPU.

It was not until 1907 that 'both the militant groups abandoned the plan which for the first few years they had worked – that of suffering violence, but using none' (Fawcett 1912a, 63), and it was at that point that Fawcett's opinion of the militants changed (see Section 28).

*

Almost exactly seventy-five years ago, on October 29th, 1831, one whole district of the city of Bristol was laid in ashes, hundreds of men were killed, the Mansion House, the Bishop's Palace and the Gaol were broken into, looted and burnt.[1] A contemporary, Charles Greville, wrote that for 'brutal ferocity and wanton, unprovoked violence' the Bristol riots vied with some of the worst scenes of the French Revolution.[2] About the same time, Nottingham Castle was burned down by an infuriated mob.[3] In Derby, where some rioters had been sent to gaol for window-breaking, the mob attacked the prison, released the prisoners, and several lives were lost.[4] Miss Martineau wrote in her *History of the Peace* that in London many people believed revolution to be inevitable,[5] and brave men wrote 'our day here was tremendously alarming. Many windows were broken, several peers were insulted in the streets, and Lord Londonderry was struck insensible from his horse by the blow of a stone.'[6]

All this riot and bloodshed had been provoked by the Lords having thrown out the Reform Bill of 1831,[7] which would have swept away the rotten boroughs and created something like a rational system of popular representation.

Nothing marks the immense social progress attained during the three-quarters of a century between 1831 and 1906 more than the mildness of the measures now required to rouse the public to a sense that representation is still incomplete when it leaves out half the nation. The burning, pillage and massacres of Bristol, Derby and Nottingham are seen no more; they are now unnecessary, because the whole nation has attained a higher level of general morality, education, courage and self-restraint. It is shameful indeed that any form of violence is needed to enforce the claims which are admitted by the Prime Minister to be conclusive and irrefutable. But the degree of violence is mildness itself compared with what was needed in earlier times. The unrepresented can now appeal to the represented to do them justice. But John Bull, a still unburied old gentleman, as Mr George Meredith has said,[8] is slow to move in the direction of reform unless something in the nature of an external stimulus be administered to him. Yet how mild was the demonstration in front of Mr Asquith's house in June, for which four women suffered six weeks' imprisonment;[9] and the scene in the Lobby on October 23rd, which was followed by the imprisonment for two months of Mrs Cobden Sanderson and her comrades.[10] For waving flags and making speeches in the Lobby in 1906 seem to have been as effectual in rousing public opinion and overcoming opposition as murder and pillage were in 1831.

The older Suffragists have worked for forty years always on constitutional lines. They have shown persistence and patience. I am one of them, and I do not care to blow their trumpet. On side issues, such as married women's property, the guardianship of children, education, the opening to women of professional and other occupations, they have achieved much. On the Suffrage question they have broken the ground and sowed the seed. They have helped to create a social change which makes the withholding of the Suffrage an absurdity. But John Bull still will not move without something in the nature, I will not say of a kick, but an electric shock. We older workers were plodding but not magnetic; we could not give the requisite electric shock. Then our young friends came along and did what we could not do. They have applied the electric battery, and the question of Women's Suffrage has become a living issue of practical politics.

Something has happened which has touched the heart and imagination of the English people. A group of women of all classes, from the gently reared and cultivated lady to the factory hand, have agreed to go to prison for an ideal – the ideal of justice and liberty for their sex. They have committed no moral crime; there is no blood upon their hands; but they have within the walls of Parliament itself demonstrated that women are not prepared to wait patiently for the crumbs that may some day be thrown from the rich man's table. They were committed to prison for two months as ordinary offenders for refusing to enter upon their own recognisances not to do the same again. They neither grumble nor whine. They bear with cheerfulness the cheerless prison, the solitude and the privations of the dimly lighted cell, the coarse food and clothing and the absence of what to some of them throughout their lives have been the everyday necessaries of comfort and cleanliness. They even refuse to accept a higher class treatment, although such acceptance is urged upon them by trusted friends. The result is that the electric shock has been applied; what seemed more than half dead is living and active. The seed we have been sowing all these years is coming up. The secretaries and other active members of the older Suffrage societies are worked off their feet; new members pour in; every post brings applications for information and literature; Women's Suffrage is the topic of conversation in every household and in every social gathering. Money comes too in unexpected and sometimes amusing ways. Where the societies were formerly receiving half-crowns and shillings, they are now receiving £5 and £10 notes. One lady sends the latter sum as conscience money for not having worked as she ought to have done for Women's Suffrage in the past. Another, from Ireland, of whom I had ordered my usual autumn supply of bulbs, writes, 'I do not send a bill; give the money to those good women who are persecuting the Government.' Every women's suffrage meeting is filled to overflowing. The people are coming in hundreds where they used to come in tens. At one of these meetings, which was so full that an overflow was necessary, the local MP, a friend of Women's Suffrage, was present. He spoke in subdued and chastened tones of recent events and of the 'very mistaken tactics which we so greatly deplore', and expressed his belief that the prisoners in Holloway had 'deeply injured the cause we all have at heart'. Whereupon a working man's voice came from the back of the meeting, 'They've rose the country, sir.' That voice expressed the political instinct of the people. The prisoners have roused the country and Women's Suffrage has become practical politics.[11]

    I have heard some ladies say that they would not so particularly object to a few months' imprisonment; it would be very quiet and restful, they remarked; and the observation is perhaps not unnatural to those who are working almost beyond their strength and have never realised the conditions of prison life. I visited Mrs Cobden Sanderson[12] in Holloway Prison on November 13th. I asked to be allowed to go to her in her cell, but this was not permitted, so I saw her in the visitors' room in the presence of one of the warders. She was in the coarse and clumsy prison dress marked with the broad arrow. Her pocket handkerchief was to all intents and purposes a duster, that is it was as dark coloured and coarse as the ordinary duster. One a week is the allowance served out. She laughed heartily at my exclamation on noticing it, and said it was lucky she had not had a cold. I had brought her a few flowers; she was not allowed to accept them, but she enjoyed handling them and smelling them while we were together. She is a vegetarian and her dinner in prison consists of three baked potatoes; but the doctor has recently ordered her two ounces of butter daily. 'That makes an enormous difference,' she said cheerfully. She looked and seemed well, and did not utter a syllable of grumbling. I thought of:

> As shines the moon in cloudy skies
> She in her poor attire was seen.[13]

One word would open her prison door and set her free: that word she will not speak. She believes it would injure the cause of women's freedom. There was a light in her eye, a self-forgetting enthusiasm in her voice which cheered and refreshed me. Great is the power of self-sacrifice. Like faith, it moves mountains. Mrs Cobden Sanderson had noted all that happened in July when Miss Kenny, Miss Billington, Mrs Knight and Mrs Sbarborough[14] were sent to prison for six weeks for endeavouring to 'peacefully persuade'[15] Mr Asquith to give them an interview on the subject of Women's Suffrage. These four were all working women; and she resolved, when a method of agitation was determined on by the Social and Political Union[16] which would probably again involve imprisonment of those who carried it out, that the working women should not be left to bear the brunt of it alone. So she stood with them and went to prison with them quite deliberately and fearlessly.[17] I have been asked several times whether the noisy tactics practiced in Cavendish Square in the summer and in the Lobby of the House of Commons in October do not make me feel ashamed of being a woman. What curious things some people are ashamed of and not ashamed of; they can be ashamed of self-sacrificing enthusiasm for the cause of freedom, but not of vanity, snobbishness, self-seeking and petty meannesses! The columns headed 'Women's Interests' and so forth in the daily Press, treating of such thrilling subjects as 'Should Matrons wear White?'[18] or 'The Famine in Valenciennes Lace';[19] new papers for women floated upon the journalistic sea on the inflated bladders of pure and undiluted snobbishness; advertisements betraying an undisguised appetite for grinding the faces of the poor; such things as these may tempt one sometimes to be ashamed of being a woman. But unconventional daring, generous self-sacrifice, even if the wisdom of the methods and their application be open to reasonable objection, will always stir the blood and quicken and deepen the sense that life, after all, is not a slough of vulgar self-seeking.

Frankness compels me to acknowledge that if I had known beforehand what Mrs Cobden Sanderson and the others intended to do on October 23rd, I should have implored them to desist, but I see now that I should have been wrong. One of the most respected and influential clergymen in London, the Rev. R. J. Campbell,[20] writes to me that he is in the same position, and he adds, 'It seems to me that the methods adopted have been more potent in impressing the public mind with the justice of claims for Women's Suffrage than any adopted heretofore. Great reforms have usually been effected by some amount of law-breaking.' The last statement is not an opinion so much as a well-known historical fact. Mr Gladstone said that the explosion at Clerkenwell Prison brought the disestablishment of the Irish Church within the region of practical politics.[21] On another occasion, speaking in more general terms in defence of Mr Chamberlain, who had threatened in 1884 to march 100,000 men from Birmingham to London to overawe the opposition of the House of Lords to the Reform Bill of that year,[22] he said, 'If no instructions had ever been addressed in political crises to the people of England except to remember to hate violence and to love order and to exercise patience, the liberties of this country would never have been accomplished.'[23]

Historians teach us the same lesson. Lord Acton's recently published lectures show that he believed that the world owes religious liberty to the

Dutch Revolution, constitutional government to the English, federal republicanism to the American and political equality to the French and its successors.[24] Nevertheless, up to the present it has been the boast of the women's movement that its victories have been won without violence. Mark Twain has pointed out that women are the only people who have accomplished their transition from serfdom to the borders of complete civil liberty without bloodshed and physical violence.[25] Some people seem to think this is easily explained by the lower degree of physical strength possessed by women. They have forgotten the Parisian *pétroleuses* of 1871[26] and the *harridans* of the French revolution of the eighteenth century.[27] Even quite lately, during a strike of miners in South Wales, women showed an appalling degree of ferocity and brutality; men who refused to join the strike went in peril of their lives. They were black-leaded, their clothes torn off their backs and they were dragged through the streets by gangs of infuriated women. These things were duly reported in the newspapers of September 6th and 7th, 1906,[28] but they were not made the subjects of hysterical outburst in leading articles and offensive cartoons in the illustrated papers. For these wild and misguided women were not fighting for anything for themselves; they were acting the 'womanly' part of backing up their husbands' trade union. It is curious to contrast the mildness of the comments of the press on the disgraceful scenes at Maesteg and Pontlottyn in September with the unmeasured violence of the attacks made on the women who waved flags and made speeches in the Lobby in October. In the latter case physical violence was used, but it was used against the women to eject them forcibly from the Lobby. In the South Wales case, physical violence was used by the women to terrorise the men who were not supporting the union. The comparatively mild comments of the press upon the subject may probably be accounted for by the desirability, to which all political parties are equally alive, of not alienating the trades union and labour vote.

The continued withholding from women of that which ever-growing numbers of them regard as their just due is converting into rebels women whom nature never intended to be rebels. There is now a want of harmony between the political status of women and their social and educational status. The first has remained stationary and rigid: in some respects even it has retrograded; but in every department of human activity which is outside legislative control, the status of women during the last half century has made enormous advances. It is unnecessary to repeat the well-known tale. Two examples will suffice. At one end of the scale the greatest scientific discovery of the age is due to the genius of a woman,[29] and at the other end of the scale by far the larger half of the textile operatives of this country are women.[30] These last are impertinent enough to wish to know why, when they provide the income of Labour members, they should not also be fit to vote for them.

Fundamentally, women are intensely law-abiding; it is a part of their physical constitution to be so, and bitter, indeed, is their sense of wrong before they can be driven to any extra constitutional courses. Those who are now prepared for unconstitutional forms of agitation are a small minority. The great majority of us feel that every constitutional form of agitation must be exhausted before we resort to illegality in any form. Constitutional agitation is not exhausted. There are means, strictly legal and constitutional, by which women can show their power of damaging the political prospects of the man or party who refuses to do them justice. Unrepresented masses of people have always in the past obtained their enfranchisement by making it obvious that the consequences of their continued exclusion would be more disagreeable than their admission to political rights. And women can do this in either or both of two ways without infringing the bounds of constitutional agitation. The first is by active opposition to Government candidates at bye-elections, as long as the Government abstains from giving any pledge to enfranchise women. Organized bands of workers can be sent to every bye-election and endeavour to compass the defeat of the Government candidate. This is a method which has the recommendation of not requiring large pecuniary resources, and, as most women are poor, this is an important consideration. The second plan is to run candidates of our own at bye-elections who will promise to make Women's Suffrage their first object if returned to Parliament. This method would be more expensive than the first, and great care would be needed in the selection of suitable candidates; but these are difficulties which could be overcome. The Labour Party have built up their power to a large extent through the capacity they have shown to run Labour candidates.[31] One experiment of this kind was made by Women Suffragists at the General Election. The Women Textile Workers' Union ran a Women's Suffrage candidate at Wigan. He did not get in, but after only a fortnight before the constituency he polled 2,205 votes, a very satisfactory result, showing what good work and enthusiasm could do.[32] Half or a quarter of that number of votes detached from the poll of a Government candidate would be enough in many elections to keep an enemy out. Our first aim would be to get our own candidate in, but the next would be to keep an enemy out, or to weaken a Government which has shown no disposition to be our friend.

We must make it quite clear that the Women's Suffragists of all sections are united in asking for the franchise for women, now, on the same terms in which it is or may be granted to men. After women are enfranchised, let those in favour of universal adult suffrage agitate for it. To ask for adult suffrage now[33] is in reality to oppose Women's Suffrage. The extension of the suffrage to women on the same terms as those on which men enjoy it would enfranchise more electors than were enfranchised by the Reform Bill of 1832, a sufficiently important electoral reform. There are about 7,000,000 male electors now;[34] probably the women with the same electoral qualification would be as many as 1,500,000.[35] There would thus be a leaven of women voters in every constituency; but adult suffrage would mean the creation at one blow of an electorate consisting in every constituency of more women than men, and the demand for this would put off Women's Suffrage to the Greek Kalends.[36] Men have had nearly a century of the education which is a corollary of gradual political emancipation. Let women enjoy the same advantage. The adult suffrage cry is a trap into which we decline to enter. The voices which recommend it to us are voices which we know already to belong to active opponents of our enfranchisement. In vain the net is spread in the sight of any bird. Our aim is clear and simple, and recent events have placed it within measurable distance of realisation.

Some of our friends say we must not ask for Women's Suffrage now because a new electorate would involve a new election, and no one can expect a party which has been twenty years in the wilderness to court an immediate appeal to the constituencies. The suggested difficulty is more apparent than real. Great political changes are very seldom accomplished in the first year a Government takes them in hand. And every Women's Suffragist would gladly agree, in the event of the present Government undertaking to introduce their Bill, to support a clause suspending its actual operation until this Parliament dies a natural death, commits *felo de se*[37] or falls before the attacks of the Opposition. Some lawyers are of opinion that the removal of a disability would not, like the lowering of the franchise, render an immediate appeal to the constituencies a constitutional propriety. Whether they are right or not, the suggested difficulty is not substantial, and there would be many easy ways of meeting it.

Transcribed from a copy in the British Library.
No known copyright restrictions.

Notes

1. See Eagles 1832.
2. Charles Cavendish Fulke Greville (1794–1865), clerk of the Privy Council and social diarist, in his journal on 11 November 1832: 'The country was beginning to slumber after the fatigues of Reform, when it was rattled up by the business of Bristol, which for brutal ferocity and wanton, unprovoked violence may vie with some of the worst scenes of the French Revolution, and may act as a damper to our national pride. The spirit which produced these atrocities was generated by Reform, but no pretext was afforded for their actual commission; it was a premature outbreaking of the thirst for plunder, and longing after havoc and destruction, which is the essence of Reform in the mind of the mob' (Greville 1888, 214).
3. See Martineau (1877, 447).
4. See Martineau (1877, 447).
5. Harriet Martineau, sociologist. 'Men saw now that the word "revolution", so often in the mouths of the anti-reformers, might prove to be not so inapplicable as had been supposed; that, if the peers should not come immediately and voluntarily and by the light of their own convictions, into harmony with the other two powers of the government, it would prove true that, as they were themselves saying, "the balance of the constitution was destroyed". Was it not already so? it was asked' (1877, 455).
6. Fawcett here embellishes a quote: 'Several peers were insulted in the streets and Lord Londonderry was struck insensible from his horse by a stone' (Balmforth 1900, 30).
7. Although the distribution of the population throughout the UK had changed extensively in the eighteenth and nineteenth centuries, particularly caused by industrialisation, the old system of representation in Parliament remained: many new towns and their populations were unrepresented, and only a small percentage of the populace were entitled to vote. Electoral reform had been discussed for decades, and became a major campaign issue in the 1830 and 1831 elections. The pro-reform Whigs won a majority in 1831, and a Reform Bill was finally passed in September of that year. However, the House of Lords rejected the Bill after a series of memorable debates, leading to rioting across the country. The First Reform Bill was finally passed in 1832 (Erskine May 1865, 221–8).
8. George Meredith (1828–1909), English novelist and poet, in a letter to the *Times* on 'The Suffrage for Women': 'The mistake of the women has been to suppose that John Bull will move sensibly for a solitary kick. It makes him the more stubborn, and such a form of remonstrance with him alienates the decorous among the sisterhood, otherwise not adverse to an emancipation of their sex. It cannot be repeated, if the agitating women are to have the backing of their sober sisters. Yet it is only by repetition of this manner of enlivening him that John Bull (a still unburied old gentleman, though not much alive) can be persuaded to move at all. Therefore we see clearly that the course taken by the suffragists was wrong in tactics' (Meredith 1906). John Bull is a fictitious personification of the United Kingdom, found in political cartoons since the eighteenth century.
9. The WSPU's militant campaign gathered pace in 1906, with a focus particularly on Liberal Cabinet members. Herbert Henry Asquith (1852–1928) was then chancellor of the exchequer. The WSPU had requested a personal interview with Asquith following the forceable ejection of their members from a speech of his in Nottingham: he replied that 'his rule was not to receive any deputation unconnected with his office', to which Sylvia Pankhurst wrote again to say 'the enfranchisement of women . . . is intimately bound up with the duties of your office'. Receiving no answer to this, the WSPU 'wrote to him saying that a small deputation would call at his house, No. 20 Cavendish Square, on the morning of Tuesday, June 19th' (Pankhurst 1911, 82–4). Teresa Billington (1877–1964, later Billington-Greig), Annie Kenney (1879–1953, misspelled by Fawcett in this piece), Adelaide Knight (1871–1950) and Jane Sbarborough (1842–1925) were sentenced to imprisonment in Holloway for the resulting affray (Pankhurst 1911, 82–7).
10. (Julia Sarah) Anne Cobden Sanderson (1853–1926), socialist and suffragette, imprisoned in Holloway following a protest at Westminster on 23 October 1906, the day Parliament reassembled for the autumn session. The government had allowed only 20 women in the Lobby; these women sent for the Chief Liberal Whip to ask 'whether he proposed to do anything to enfranchise the women of the country during the session . . . The Liberal Whip soon returned with a refusal to hold out the very faintest hope . . . On hearing this . . . They therefore decided

to hold a meeting, not outside in the street, but just there, in the Lobby of the House of Commons . . . in the twinkling of an eye dozens of policemen sprang forward' (Pankhurst 1911, 101–2). George Bernard Shaw wrote to the *Times* regarding Cobden Sanderson: 'nobody in the world really wishes to see one of the nicest women in England suffering from the coarsest indignity and the most injurious form of ill-treatment that the law could inflict on a pickpocket' (Bernard Shaw 1906). Fawcett herself wrote to the *Times* to say 'I have known Mrs Cobden-Saunderson [sic] for 30 years. I was not in the police-court on Wednesday . . . but I find it absolutely impossible to believe that she bit, or scratched, or screamed, or behaved other-wise than the refined woman she is' (Fawcett 1906a).

11   This section is recycled in *What I Remember* (Fawcett 1924, 184). The MP is not identified.
12   See note 10.
13   Tennyson, in *The Beggar Maid*: 'As shines the moon in clouded skies, / She in her poor attire was seen' (1872, 72).
14   See note 9.
15   See Section 24, note 11.
16   The Women's Social and Political Union.
17   Cobden Sanderson refused to acknowledge the power of the court over her 'so long as I have no word and no part in making the laws which I am supposed to obey' (*Manchester Courier and Lancashire General Advertiser* 1906).
18   'Should Matrons Wear White? A pathetic appeal has just appeared in the columns of the *Frankfurt Gazette*, and though it comes from a German woman to Germans, it cannot fail to move every feminine heart, of any nationality whatsoever. "Why" runs the appeal "may not German ladies of a certain age wear white blouses without incurring the ridicule of their more youthful sisters?"' (*Bombay Gazette* 1906).
19   'A famine in Valenciennes lace is not the unreasonable result of the phenomenal demand for lace edging this season. Months ago, when it first became known that La Mode had decided to smile on the frilly hat . . . preparations were made on a large scale to meet the anticipated demand' (*Walsall Advertiser* 1906).
20   Reginald John Campbell (1867–1956), non-conformist congregational minister of the City Temple in London, famed for preaching to large audiences.
21   On 13 December 1867, the Irish Republican Brotherhood (nicknamed the 'Fenians') attempted to rescue a senior Republican arms dealer, Richard O'Sullivan-Burke (1838–1922), from Clerkenwell Prison, London, by blowing a hole in the wall while the inmates were taking exercise. The resulting explosion killed 12 members of the public, leaving many others injured and destroying local property. The only person found responsible, Michael Barrett (1841–68), was hanged in the last public execution in Britain (*Victorianist* 2011). Gladstone, then the Liberal leader in opposition, declared that the Anglican Church of Ireland should be disestablished (separating church from state). Later, in his Midlothian speeches of 1879, Gladstone 'went on to speak of the circumstances under which the Irish was disestablished in 1869, and of his own declaration only four years before that the question was out of the range of practical politics, and he added what follows: "Now, it is come to this: a gaol in the heart of the Metropolis was broken open in circumstances which drew the attention of the English people to the state of Ireland . . . the whole country became alive to the question of the Irish Church – it came within the range of practical politics"' (*Sheffield Daily Telegraph* 1879).
22   Fawcett extrapolates here. In a speech on 4 August 1884 at a Liberal demonstration in Birmingham, Joseph Chamberlain had reflected on the 1832 Reform Bill riots: 'In 1832 . . . it was after a conflict which brought this country almost to the verge of a revolution. They had read that there were 100,000 men in Birmingham and the surrounding district who had sworn to march on London (– a voice; "We shall do it again,") in defence of their liberties . . . he had hoped they had left these days of disorder far behind them . . . [but t]hey were told that when the bill was sent again to the Lords they would stand firm and reject it. In that case this agitation must and would go on to the bitter end' (*Western Daily Press* 1884).
23   Mr Gladstone in the House of Commons on Wednesday, 29 October 1884 (*Evening Mail* 1884).
24   John Emerich Edward Dalberg-Acton (1834–1902), 1st Baron Acton, historian and Liberal politician, quoted from his posthumously printed Inaugural Lecture of 1895, given at Cambridge: 'Here we reach a point at which my argument threatens to abut on a contradiction. If the supreme conquests of society are won more often by violence than by lenient arts, if the trend and drift of things is towards convulsions and catastrophes, if the world owes religious liberty to the Dutch Revolution, constitutional government to the English, federal republicanism

to the American, political equality to the French and its successors, what is to become of us, docile and attentive students of the absorbing Past? The triumph of the Revolutionist annuls the historian' (Dalberg-Acton 1906, 13–14).

25 'The women deserve a change of attitude . . . in forty-seven years they have swept an imposingly large number of unfair laws from the statute books of America. In that brief time these serfs have set themselves free – essentially. Men could not have done so much for themselves in that time without bloodshed – at least they never have; and that is argument that they didn't know how. The women have accomplished a peaceful revolution, and a very beneficent one; and yet that has not convinced the average man that they are intelligent, and have courage and energy and perseverance and fortitude. It takes much to convince the average man of anything' (Twain 1897, 315).

26 Female supporters of the Paris Commune, accused of deliberately burning much of Paris in May 1871, using bottles full of petroleum, when Paris was being recaptured by the Versailles troops. No women were convicted of arson, and recent research has concluded that no incidents of deliberate arson were caused by *pétroleuses* (Gullickson 1996).

27 Women in France had traditionally had no role outside of household affairs: militant activism during the French Revolution, including the Women's March to Versailles and the Demonstration of 20 June 1792, helped convey that women's rights should be part of the revolution, leading to the Declaration of the Rights of Woman and of the Female Citizen in 1791 (Beckstrand 2009).

28 'Women are playing a prominent part in the colliery strike in the Maesteg district of South Wales, where 4,000 colliers are "out". They have in many cases attacked non-union men . . . A crowd of women seized two young non-union miners at Maesteg, dragged them into the street, tore off their upper garments, and blackleaded their faces' (*Daily Mirror* 1906). 'An attack by women upon a non-unionist is reported at Pontlottyn. The women dragged him into the street, tore off his waistcoat and shirt, and savagely pulled his hair and beard. Other women took his part, and the two parties indulged in a lively wordy encounter' (*Westminster Gazette* 1906, 6).

29 Presumably, Fawcett is referencing Marie Skłodowska Curie (1867–1934), Polish and naturalised-French physicist and chemist, who shared the 1903 Nobel Prize in Physics with her husband Pierre Curie (1859–1906) and physicist Henri Becquerel (1852–1908) for their work on the theory of radioactivity. A banner highlighting the work of Marie Curie was carried in NUWSS processions.

30 'In textile manufacturing, the vast majority of jobs [1891–1914] were light, relatively unskilled and performed under conditions deemed "suitable" to the grade of female labour needed. Women, accordingly, constituted an ideal labour supply. Firstly, they were considered more economical to use than men . . . Secondly, women of the required grade found little reason not to accept the work. Its conditions met their standards of respectability, its low pay relative to "men's industries" was in keeping with their financial expectations, and no other work that paid substantially more or had substantially better working conditions was open locally to women of their labour grade' (Hogg 1967, 130).

31 The Labour Representation Committee, a centre-left party formed as an alliance of trade unionists and democratic socialists, was founded in 1900. In the 1906 general election, they won 29 seats, although this was also due to a pact made by the Liberal Party to not split the progressive vote in 30 seats, to ensure that the Conservatives were kept out (Hinton 1983, 73–5).

32 'Among the special features of this General Election . . . for the first time in English political life a candidate stood for Parliament in the interest of the Working Women of Lancashire and Cheshire with the avowed object of obtaining for them the Parliamentary franchise' (*Labour Leader* 1906). Thorley Smith (1873–1940) of Wigan came second to the Conservative Sir Francis Sharp Powell (1827–1911), who received 3,573 votes.

33 All adult men in the UK were eventually enfranchised by the Representation of the People Act 1918, also known as the Fourth Reform Act.

34 See Section 21, note 14.

35 See Section 19, note 4.

36 A humorous phrase for 'never', 'since the Greeks used no calends in their reckoning of time' (OED 2020c).

37 Suicide: Latin for 'felon of himself', which was still a crime.

26
Picturing Fawcett: NUWSS procession, 1908

Figure 7: NUWSS procession, 13 June 1908. From front left to right: Lady Frances Balfour, Millicent Fawcett, Ethel Snowden, Emily Davies and Sophie Bryant. The Sport and General Illustration Co. From the Women's Library at LSE. No known copyright restrictions.

Large-scale meetings were central to proving public support for the female vote and drawing attention to the cause. This is a photograph of one of the many large processions that took place between 1907 and the outbreak of World War I. Enumerating those staged by the NUWSS, Fawcett wrote: 'In February 1907, 3000 women marched in procession in London, from Hyde Park to Exeter Hall. In October 1907, 1,500 women marched in procession through Edinburgh. In October 1907, 2,000 women marched in procession through Manchester. In June 1908 [see Figure 7], 15,000 women marched in procession in London to the Albert Hall' (Fawcett 1912a, 86). 'Our object was to let the man in the street and the club windows see that women of all classes were demanding this reform and were in deadly earnest in doing so' (Fawcett et al. 1908).

At the start of May 1908, the NUWSS announced a large-scale demonstration on Saturday, 13 June, intended to convince the recently appointed Liberal prime minister, Herbert Asquith, that there was majority support for female suffrage:

> we wish to show that there are also thousands of essentially law-abiding women who deeply resent the absolute refusal to their whole sex of the most elementary right of citizenship . . . Professional women, University women, women teachers, women artists, women musicians, women writers, women in business, nurses, members of political societies of all parties, women trades unionists and co-operative women all have their own organizations and will be grouped in the procession under their own distinctive banners, which have been specially designed for the occasion by the Artist's League for Women's Suffrage (Fawcett et al. 1908).

Specially chartered trains brought women to London, 'and for an hour and a half the stream of women, with bands and banners, flowed through the main thoroughfares . . . Spectators thronged the line of route' (*Western Chronicle* 1908). 'The sun shone upon us and I believe we made a really favourable impression on the crowd of onlookers . . . I believe few more beautiful street scenes can have been witnessed in London than this procession afforded' (Fawcett 1924, 191). Pictured here from left to right are Lady Frances Balfour (1858–1931, a member of the executive committee of the NUWSS and president of the London Society for Women's Suffrage between 1896 and 1919), Millicent Fawcett in her doctoral robes (see Figures 12, 13 and 22), Mrs Ethel Annakin Snowden (1881–1951), feminist and socialist activist, Emily Davies (who in 1866 had handed the first women's suffrage petition to John Stuart Mill with

Elizabeth Garrett) and Sophie Bryant (1850–1922, headmistress of North London Collegiate School). They are marching beneath a banner representing East Anglia, an area in the east of England comprising the counties of Norfolk, Suffolk and Cambridgeshire: Fawcett's hometown was Aldeburgh on the Suffolk coast.

Fawcett recalled the Albert Hall bedecked with the banners as a 'fairy palace of beauty' (1924, 191). Unknown to her,

> the marchers had provided themselves with bunches of summer flowers; and when she came on to the platform to preside over the vast meeting, the young girls who were acting as stewards came forward and heaped them at her feet, until she was almost buried behind them. 'I felt like Freia behind the mass of the *Niebelungen* treasure' she said afterwards; but everyone could see that she was moved, and found it difficult to open the meeting (Strachey 1931, 230).

Reportage of the event covers her brief speech:

> From floor to topmost corner and further angle of the huge galleries the interior was alive with women and bright with colour, especially the platform, which had as its background the banners grouped in brilliant array. Mrs Fawcett, who opened the meeting, was greeted with tremendous cheering. Her remarks were short and to the point. She said that as a chairman she had intended to make a speech, but that time was getting on and there were other speakers: and as some of those present, who had come from all parts of England, had trains to catch and tea to get before that, she would omit a chairman's speech, and merely give them a message, which was that theirs was the greatest cause in the world, and she asked all present to dedicate their lives to it. (Cheers.) (*Western Chronicle* 1908).

The procession was featured in much news coverage: see Crawford 2008 for an overview of the march, and the banners designed by the Artists' Suffrage League.

27
Picturing Fawcett: Millicent Fawcett, 1908

Figure 8: Millicent Fawcett, 1908, matte bromide print by O. and K. Edis. © National Portrait Gallery, London.

(Mary) Olive Edis (1876–1955) was a self-taught, pioneering photographer. Along with her sister Katherine (1880–1963), she maintained a studio in London (for portraits) and one in Sheringham, Norfolk (where the sisters photographed fishermen, local views and visiting celebrities). They had a family connection to Fawcett: Fawcett's sister Elizabeth was married to James George Skelton Anderson (1838–1907), whose cousin Mary Edis (née Murray, 1853–1931) was Olive and Katherine's mother. Katherine married Robert Legat in 1907, and is no longer credited on company photographs from the mid-1910s: it is likely that this photograph of Fawcett was taken by Olive. Olive's London portraits saw her capture many from the Votes for Women movement, including Elizabeth Garrett Anderson (National Portrait Gallery 2021e), Agnes Garrett (National Portrait Gallery 2021f) and Emmeline Pankhurst (National Portrait Gallery 2021g, 2021h). In 1918 Edis became the first official British female war artist, commissioned by the Imperial War Museum 'to record war work by the British women's services in France and Flanders' (Neale 2004). Edis's signature portraiture style utilises only natural light and shadow (Murphy and Elmore 2016).

Taken in the first-floor room of Fawcett's Gower Street home, this striking, honest portrait shows a modern woman at work. Another from the same sitting appears in the *Sketch*, credited to 'O. and K. Edis' (*Sketch* 1908). Strachey describes Fawcett's methods:

> It was her habit, when she had an important speech to make, first to work over it at her desk, taking notes and arranging her ideas, and then to sit down somewhere else with a piece of needlework in her hands and go over it again carefully in her head . . . The facts on which she built up these important speeches she collected for herself. She read the papers without the aid of Press-cutting agencies, and never allowed anyone to 'devil' for her. She still answered every letter personally, and was punctual for every appointment. She rose early in the mornings, and sat at her desk writing terse postcards for hours every day, always carefully punctilious to inform her colleagues of every important fact which she thought they should know, and always remembering her scores of private friends (Strachey 1931, 229).

28
National Union manifesto, 1908

Women's Franchise. Thursday, 19 November 1908, 237.

The NUWSS, which had supported peaceful and legislative efforts towards women's enfranchisement since 1897, was reconstituted in 1907 with an elected executive, and Fawcett was made its president (Rubinstein 1991, 137). However, different approaches towards campaigning for the vote continued to emerge. Mrs Emmeline Pankhurst, a one-time member of the North of England Suffrage Society (a constituent of the NUWSS), formed the WSPU in order to promote direct and militant action in pursuit of the vote (see Section 25). In 1907, a small group of prominent members left the WSPU in protest at the Pankhursts' undemocratic approach to leadership, forming the Women's Freedom League (WFL), which adopted non-violent forms of militant protest, such as non-cooperation with the census and resistance to taxation, rather than attacks on people and property (Eustance 1993).

Throughout 1907 and 1908, the frequency, size and popularity of disparate protests for women's suffrage increased. On 9 February 1907, the NUWSS organised their first large procession, consisting of 3,000 women from 40 suffragist societies, marching from Hyde Park to Exeter Hall. It had 'mud, mud, mud, as its predominant feature, and it was known among us afterwards as the "mud march"' (Fawcett 1924, 190). On 12 February 1907, the WSPU held their first 'Women's Parliament': 57 women and 2 men were arrested for storming the Houses of Parliament (Pankhurst 1914, 83). A second WSPU Women's Parliament on 20 March saw similar arrests (Pankhurst 1914, 86). On 21 June 1908, the WSPU's 'Women's Sunday' rally in Hyde Park saw 30,000 women march, viewed by a quarter of a million spectators (Pankhurst 1914, 112–15). Ignored by the prime minister, the next week suffragettes smashed windows in

Downing Street (Pankhurst 1914, 118). On 11 October 1908, Emmeline Pankhurst urged the audience of a suffrage rally in Trafalgar Square, ahead of the reopening of Parliament, to 'rush' the House of Commons: she was then arrested and sentenced to three months in Holloway Prison (Pankhurst 1914, 119–30).

On 28 October 1908, three WFL members unfurled a banner from the Ladies' Gallery in the House of Commons, with two (Matters and Fox) chaining themselves to a grille; the grille had to be removed with the suffragettes still attached.[1]

Concerned by these displays of 'performative and spectacular' militancy (Nym Mayhall 2003, 46), Fawcett felt it necessary to set out the constitutional approach of the NUWSS to distinguish their actions from those of the WSPU and the WFL. The NUWSS

> endeavoured to steer an even keel. They never weakened in their conviction that constitutional agitation was not only right in itself, but would prove far more effective in the long run than any display of physical violence, as a means of converting the electorate, the general public and, consequently, Parliament and the Government, to a belief in women's suffrage (Fawcett 1912a, 62).

The *Women's Franchise* was a weekly newspaper published between 1907 and 1911 by John E. Francis (1874–1941), owner of the Athenæum Press and a prominent member of the Men's League for Women's Suffrage (Crawford 2001a, 461). The paper acted as a bulletin board[2] for all the major groups within the suffrage movement, and therefore was an appropriate venue for communicating and stressing the NUWSS position against militant or 'suffragette' tactics to all interested parties.

*

Two years ago I came forward in defence of what have since become known as 'Suffragette' tactics,[3] and said I thought it was the duty of the old Suffragists to stand by the women, then in prison, who were at the moment the objects of very severe criticism from the press and the public. I do not go back from what I then said. In a circular letter dated November 1906, to old Suffrage friends, I used the following expressions:

> I need hardly say that I am convinced that the work of quiet persuasion and argument form the solid foundation on which the success of the Woman's Suffrage movement will be reared, and I, in common with the great majority of Suffrage workers, wish to

continue the agitation on constitutional lines; yet I feel that the action of the prisoners has touched the imagination of the country in a manner which quieter methods did not succeed in doing.

Since that time, however, many circumstances have changed: the methods of violence have become more violent, their popularity has increased; and I feel now that the Societies standing for lawful and constitutional methods of agitation only should definitely and deliberately say so. We do not sit in judgment on the motives of those who believe that injustice can best be met by violence. We acknowledge – I have constantly and publicly acknowledged – their courage and self-sacrifice; but when they adopt methods which we believe to be wrong in themselves, we are compelled to dissociate ourselves from them.

All the various Suffrage Societies are at one in the object sought, viz.: the extension of the Franchise to women on the same terms as it is or may be granted to men, but they differ as to methods of attaining that object, and it is right that the difference should be clearly expressed, so that those who are invited to join our Society, or any other, should know exactly what their membership implies.

The document printed below was drawn up by the Executive Committee of the National Union of Women's Suffrage Societies, and it was resolved by them to send it in the first place to Members of Parliament and afterwards to the Press.

MILLICENT GARRETT FAWCETT.

Letter from the Executive Committee.

To the Members of the House of Commons.

GENTLEMEN. On behalf of the National Union of Women's Suffrage Societies, we desire to address you with regard to the present position of the movement for the extension of the Franchise to women. We do so more particularly because of the recent disturbances in the Ladies' Gallery and the Strangers' Gallery of the House of Commons, and outside the Palace of Westminster.[4] We wish to place on record our strong objection to all these and similar disturbances and breaches of the peace. We deeply regret them, and are convinced that our great cause, the basis of which is justice and not force, does not require such methods for its advocacy. They are completely at variance with the policy of the National Union of

Women's Suffrage Societies, which is one of steadfast adherence to lawful and constitutional methods of agitation.

We appeal now, as we have appealed in the past, to reason, justice and experience; the result of this appeal has been the gradual conversion of large numbers of men and women to our cause, so that at the General Election more than half of the House of Commons, including two-thirds of the present Government, were returned as pledged supporters of Women's Enfranchisement.[5] We are unwilling to believe that arguments thus accepted and pledges thus given will be cast aside because other methods have been adopted by what are known as the 'militant' societies. The justice and expediency of any cause is not affected by the unwisdom of some of its advocates; nor should the steady, argumentative agitation of forty years be now ignored because in the disappointment of long deferred hopes, methods of anger and impatience, and even of violence, have been resorted to. While, therefore, we feel assured that Members will not change their opinions, nor abstain from voting because of the disorder that has occurred, we should not be candid if we did not state that the deepest disappointment exists in our Union at the long delay which has occurred in placing a measure for the extension of the Parliamentary Franchise to women upon the Statute Book. The refusal of the Closure in 1907,[6] the failure to make any further progress with Mr Stanger's Bill this Session in spite of its great majority on the second reading,[7] and the absence of any apparent effort in the House have caused many workers almost to despair and in so far have given encouragement to the militant movement; for it must be remembered that the refusal of justice has often led to methods of violence and disorder.

We urge our friends in the House of Commons to make every effort next session to carry a Women's Suffrage Bill into law. Such a measure would be more satisfactory than waiting for the chances of the moving of an amendment to the Government Reform Bill,[8] and would give positive proof of the sincerity of members who are pledged to our cause. The pledge, however, given by the Prime Minister is distinct,[9] and while it does not satisfy us because we desire that the Government should itself include Women's Suffrage in its Reform Bill, we still accept it, knowing that it will be adhered to and that the House will be left free from any Government opposition to insert Women's Suffrage in the Reform Bill.

The Ministry have advised HM the King to promise to his Indian subjects a wider measure of representative institutions than has hitherto prevailed in our great dependency.[10] They have done so because they believe it to be in harmony with social changes which have already taken place among the vast populations of India, and therefore just and right. They have not been deterred from this course by the fact that the unrest in India has been accompanied by crimes of violence compared with which the unconstitutional action of the militant Suffragists fades into insignificance.[11]

Believing in the justice of our cause, we appeal to you to increase your efforts on its behalf, and we assure you, on our side, that the patience, perseverance, self-sacrifice and hard work on constitutional lines which have brought us within measurable distance of success will be steadfastly adhered to by our societies.

We are, on behalf of the National Union of Women's Suffrage Societies,

Your obedient servants,
MILLICENT GARRETT FAWCETT, President.
BERTHA MASON, Treasurer.[12]
FRANCES HARDCASTLE, Hon. Secretary.[13]

Transcribed from a copy in the British Library.
No known copyright restrictions.

Notes

1 See note 4.
2 The aim of the *Women's Franchise* was 'to afford an outlet in print to all those interested in woman suffrage', with all profits 'devoted to the cause of women suffrage . . . the object of the publication is propaganda, and not profit' (Francis 1908, 8). As the main groups launched their own papers, demand for the *Women's Franchise* publication fell away. The NUWSS published the weekly *Common Cause* between 1909 and 1920, which was succeeded by the *Woman's Leader*. The WFL published the *Vote* weekly between 1909 and 1933. The WSPU published *Votes for Women* from 1907 and the *Suffragette* between 1912 and 1915. *Votes for Women* continued to be published, under the editorship of Emmeline and Frederick Pethick-Lawrence (1867–1954 and 1871–1961 respectively) until February 1918, although from October 1912 it was no longer associated with the WSPU. These, plus *Jus Suffragi*, the journal of the International Woman Suffrage Alliance (IWSA), published between 1906 and 1938, became the main sources of information about the movement.
3 Section 25.
4 Originally, women wanting to watch the House of Commons proceedings had to do so via a ceiling ventilation shaft, but after the 1834 fire the Ladies' Gallery was added by the architect Charles Barry (1795–1860) in his redesign. The Ladies' Gallery had apertures covered with heavy metal grilles that became both a physical and metaphorical symbol of women's exclusion, as Fawcett later explained: 'One great discomfort of the grille was that the interstices of the heavy brass work were not large enough to allow the victims who sat behind it to focus it so that both eyes looked through the same hole. It was like using a gigantic pair of spectacles which did not fit, and made the Ladies' Gallery a grand place for getting headaches' (Fawcett 1920a,

166). On 28 October 1908, three WFL members undertook a protest which is now known as 'The Grille Incident'. During a debate on the Licensing Bill, Muriel Matters (1877–1969), journalist and educator, Violet Tillard (1874–1922) and Helen Fox unfurled a banner from the Ladies' Gallery, with two (Matters and Fox) chaining themselves to a grille covering the aperture (little is now known about Fox). Below, in the visitor's gallery, which was known at that time as the Strangers' Gallery, sympathetic men threw leaflets. The authorities had to wait for a blacksmith to remove both grille and women, allowing Matters to deliver a campaign speech, which (although not recorded in Hansard) is considered to be the first delivered by a woman in the House of Commons. The 'women refused to produce keys of the padlocks, and the chains had accordingly to be filed off. The three women were then escorted off the premises by the police.' At the same time, disturbances also occurred outside St Stephen's Hall, with 15 arrests for forced entry (*Times* 1908b). The public galleries were subsequently closed until 1909. The grille itself is now in the Museum of London (2021).
5 See Section 24, note 1.
6 On 8 March 1907, Willoughby Hyett Dickinson (1859–1943), Liberal MP, introduced to Parliament the second reading of a Women's Enfranchisement Bill, but it was 'talked out', where opponents debate beyond the allocated voting time, leading to the failure of the bill. 'The Women's Enfranchisement Bill is dead. Amid scenes of extraordinary excitement it was ungallantly "talked out" by Mr Rees, the Liberal member . . . Mr Dickinson, who had charge of the measure, made three attempts during the last five minutes of the sitting to get the closure, but the Speaker refused to accept it. An extraordinary hurricane of cheers and counter-cheers greeted the Speaker's decision. The closing moments of the sitting were intensely dramatic' (*Daily Mirror* 1907).
7 On 28 February 1908, Henry Yorke Stanger (1849–1929), Liberal MP, brought a private member's bill on women's enfranchisement to the House of Commons for a second reading, which it passed with a substantial majority of 179, despite attempts to talk it out (*Women's Franchise* 1908a). However, the bill failed to make any further substantial progress, stalling with Asquith's pledge (see note 9).
8 Fawcett here is certain of future reform by legislative measures: although the 1907 Women's Enfranchisement Bill was timed out before becoming law (see note 6), there was much debate around the topic, and Asquith's pledge (see note 9) had meant that 'all the organs of public opinion without exception recognised that this promise advanced the movement for women's suffrage to a higher place in practical politics than it has ever before occupied' (Fawcett 1911, 70).
9 On 20 May 1908, the Liberal prime minister, Herbert Henry Asquith, made 'an important announcement . . . in reply to a deputation from the Women's Liberal Federation . . . The advocates of Women's Suffrage were told by Mr Asquith that before the close of the present Parliament it would be the duty of the Government to pass a comprehensive measure of Electoral Reform. He did not promise that the Bill, as drafted, would contain provisions extending the Parliamentary franchise to women, inasmuch as he remained unconverted to the expediency of such a course. But he has an open mind on the subject, and if an amendment were submitted favouring Women's Suffrage on democratic lines, the Government would not oppose it' (*Western Times* 1908a). However, 'the advanced army of Suffragettes' were 'not satisfied . . . They are afraid there is some sinister motive in the background . . . and that his conditions imply a great deal more than is openly expressed' (*Western Times* 1908b).
10 Just a few weeks earlier, on 2 November, Edward VII had issued a new proclamation 'of the King, Emperor of India, to the princes and peoples of India' (Parliamentary Papers 1908), marking 50 years since Queen Victoria 'took upon herself the government of the territories administered by the East India Company' following the Indian Rebellion of 1857. In this proclamation, patterned on one in a similar format made by Victoria in 1858, Edward VII stated that 'From the first, the principle of representative institutions began to be gradually introduced, and the time has come when, in the judgement of my Viceroy and Governor-General and others of my counsellors, that principle may be prudently extended. Important classes among you, representing ideas that have been fostered and encouraged by British rule, claim equality of citizenship, and a greater share in legislation and government' (*Times* 1908c).
11 The revolutionary movement for Indian independence had organised increasingly armed and militant rebellion against British rulers from the early twentieth century: 'In 1908 political crime in western Bengal amounted to eight dacoities, seven attempted murders and bomb explosions, eleven murders and two conspiracy cases (at Alipore and Midnapore). At the end of 1908 the terrorists began a new phase of their campaign, aimed at assassinating police

officers and their families, and intimidating the judiciary' (Popplewell 1995, 108). NB. A 'dacoity' was the name given to a robbery by an armed gang in India.

12 Bertha Mason (see Section 11, note 12), campaigner for suffrage and temperance, was active in the Manchester National Society for Women's Suffrage, acting as chairperson when it became the North of England Society for Women's Suffrage. Moving to London in 1904, she took on the treasurer role of the NUWSS. Her 1912 book *The Story of the Women Suffrage Movement* provides another account of the long road to enfranchisement.

13 Frances Hardcastle (1866–1941), mathematician educated at Girton College, Cambridge; Bryn Mawr College, Pennsylvania; and the University of Chicago, before becoming a graduate student at Girton. She worked 'for a year as a joint secretary, with Frances Sterling, for the NUWSS . . . before moving to Newcastle where she served as secretary of the North-Eastern Federation of Women's Suffrage Societies' (Davis 2004).

29
Picturing Fawcett: A woman speaking at the Oxford Union for the first time, 1908

Figure 9: 'A woman speaking at the Oxford Union for the first time'. Illustration by Samuel Begg. *Illustrated London News* (November 1908, 745). © Illustrated London News Ltd/Mary Evans Picture Library.

On 20 November 1908, Fawcett became the first woman to speak at the Oxford Union (*Oxford Chronicle and Reading Gazette* 1908).

> Invitations of an unusual nature reached me to speak on Votes for Women. One was from the President . . . to put the case for the political enfranchisement of women before the Society . . . I am not sure that I appreciated at the time the degree to which the invitation to speak at the Oxford Union was an innovation: but an article . . . on the Centenary of the Union published in December 1923 describes the President's father, adding 'It was the only time I ever heard a non-resident or a stranger speak at the Union.' When to the disqualifications of being neither a resident, nor a graduate, nor an undergraduate, I added the further damning fact of being of the wrong sex, I can appreciate now, better than I did at the time, the generosity which prevailed among the young men who gave me so warm a welcome to the Society . . . the debate went off with perfect order and good temper. I heard no new arguments either for or against Suffrage, but it was very cheering to see the hall and galleries packed and to witness the great interest our question was arousing in the University . . . When the voting came, the Ayes were 329 and the Noes 360; therefore we were defeated in a House of nearly 700 members by 31, and almost everyone who spoke to me on the subject assured me that this majority, such as it was, did not represent undergraduate feeling, but that a considerable number of the older members of the University who are entitled to be present, although they very seldom avail themselves of the privilege, had turned the scale by their votes. If undergraduates only had voted, I was assured there would have been a considerable majority for Women's Suffrage. I was glad to learn that youth had been on our side. But, in fact, the result appeared to please everyone, and when the figures were read out there was much cheering and counter-cheering: everyone was pleased (Fawcett 1924, 196–7).

This relief halftone tear sheet of the event was illustrated by Samuel Begg (1854–1936), a staff member of the *Illustrated London News*.

30
Men are men and women are women, 1909

Reprinted as pamphlet by permission from the *Englishwoman*. Vol. 1, No. 1 (February 1909), 17–30.

This article appeared in the first issue of the *Englishwoman*, a new monthly magazine 'intended to reach the cultured public, and bring before it, in a convincing and moderate form, the case for the Enfranchisement of Women'. The editorial committee[1] shared Fawcett's non-militant views: 'constitutional methods, and no other methods, will be officially advocated in the paper' (Balfour et al. 1909).

Fawcett, here, confronts not the militant suffragettes but another party in the fray: the 'organised opposition by women to women's suffrage in England' under the leadership of Mrs Humphry Ward (Fawcett 1912a, 43). Mary Augusta Ward (1851–1920) was a British novelist and philanthropist who worked to improve education for both women and the poor, establishing the Passmore Edwards Settlement (along the lines of Toynbee Hall: see Section 17) for the working classes in Gordon Square, London. Ward had been a significant and passionate campaigner against women having the right to vote, instigating 'An Appeal against Female Suffrage', which garnered 104 distinguished signatories in 1889 (Stanley et al.), while simultaneously defending women's abilities, virtues and achievements. Fawcett's measured 'Reply' to 'An Appeal' (1889) set her firmly in a 30-year oppositional, public dialogue with Ward. Fawcett consistently argued that the anti-suffrage stance was a 'fundamental absurdity' given their complete 'favour of every improvement in the personal, proprietary, and political status of women that had already been gained, *but against any further extension of it*' (Fawcett 1912a, 45).

The anti-suffragists may have opposed the parliamentary franchise, but they supported women's votes in local and municipal elections.

Organised campaigns against women's suffrage increased when militant tactics were adopted by the suffragettes and became increasingly vocal, benefitting 'from widespread gender conservatism across all social classes' (Bush 2018). In July 1908, the anti-suffragists formed themselves into a society, the Women's National Anti-Suffrage League (WNASL), with Mrs Humphry Ward as founding president. Early 1909 saw them preparing for a 'vigorous campaign . . . reinforced by a new organisation called the Men's Committee for Opposing Female Suffrage', with 43 branches in action and public meetings planned throughout Great Britain (*Western Times* 1909). 'A weekly paper was published [the *Anti-Suffrage Review*, from 1908 to 1918], and for many years Mrs Fawcett was one of its constant readers, drawing much entertainment and many useful arguments from its absurdities' (Strachey 1931, 233).

The article here, responding to the growing activities of the anti-suffragists, emphasises that their case was based on their belief that men and women had fundamentally different qualities, and that being involved in politics would 'unsex' them (Rubinstein 1991, 139). Instead, Fawcett reappropriates their commonly used phrase, which attempted to politically differentiate the sexes, to argue that although men and women were different in experiences, nature, education and opportunities, *both* would benefit when women obtained the vote. This was a theme that had long been present in her speeches and columns.[2]

Shortly after the publication of this essay, on 26 February 1909, Fawcett debated Mrs Humphry Ward at the Passmore Edwards Settlement 'on women's suffrage'.[3] Fawcett won 235 votes to Mrs Humphry Ward's 74, in front of an 'enthusiastic audience'. In the debate, Mrs Humphry Ward referred spikily to the *Englishwoman* as 'Mrs Fawcett's own newly-started review' (*Times* 1909a).

In 1910 the Anti-Suffrage League amalgamated with the Men's League for Opposing Woman Suffrage, forming the National League for Opposing Women's Suffrage. Their activities waned with the outbreak of the war in 1914, but continued until 1918, when limited suffrage was granted (Bush 2007). Fawcett later described the anti-suffrage activities as 'frothy nonsense' (1924, 123).

*

For the first time in the forty-two years of the Women's Suffrage movement, its advocates have to face an organised and manifestly influential opposition. Englishmen, in physical warfare, are said often to fall into the error of under-estimating and disregarding the strength of the forces opposed to them. Do we not all remember the young officers, in 1899 and 1900, who left England for South Africa almost weeping, because they were so dreadfully afraid the war would be over before they had any chance, poor lads, of taking their part in it?[4] Suffragists must beware of falling into a similar error. The arguments of the anti-suffragists can easily be shown to be in reality either reasons for supporting the extension of the franchise to women, or to belong to the category of assertions which have no relation to the facts of human life. But the anti-suffragists are a power notwithstanding their arguments; they are a power because they appeal to innate prejudice, to the vested interests of the present monopolists of political power and to all those excellent, well-meaning persons who believe that change of any kind, especially political change, is contrary to the designs of Providence, and that 'Nature herself is the first and greatest of anti-suffragists'.[5]

That the opponents of women's suffrage have frequently shown their entire incapacity for estimating the forces with which they are contending should serve not as an example, but as a warning. The *Spectator*, for instance, in the summer of 1906, proclaimed that the Women's Suffrage movement in England was practically annihilated because of the demonstration of a group of militant suffragists on Mr Asquith's doorstep.[6] Yet, in the summer of 1908, this same *Spectator* discovered that women's suffrage, as a political force, was not dead at all, but that organised opposition to it was a matter of urgency, and it complacently congratulated the 'wiser women' who agree with the *Spectator* and have formed an organisation 'powerful through weight and numbers' to proclaim the tremendous discovery that women are not men and that men are not women.[7] Another and even more recent blunder of the same kind, made by the most distinguished of the anti-suffragists, should also be a warning to us not to do likewise. By voice and pen Mrs Humphry Ward assured the public last summer as the result of her own knowledge, gathered during a recent four month visit to the United States, that women's suffrage in the United States had become almost extinct, owing to the organised opposition of women themselves.[8] Immediately came replies from leading American suffragists which recalled Mark Twain's famous cable to his friends, 'Report of my death greatly exaggerated.'[9] The veteran authoress Mrs Julia Ward Howe,[10] President of the New England Woman Suffrage Association, and Dr Anna Shaw,[11] President of the National American Woman Suffrage Association, replied to Mrs Humphry Ward in letters which must have convinced every unprejudiced reader that a very great error had been made when it was said that women's suffrage had been extinguished as a living political movement in the United States.[12] But if more proof of this were needed, it came to hand in two long cabled communications in the *Times* of November 28th and December 7th on Woman Suffrage in the United States. The first of these pointed out that the greatest weapon against women's suffrage in America is not the anti-suffrage associations, but the force which upholds and profits by political corruption. Politicians who are identified with 'graft', and in the last resort use even murder to enforce their peculiar political system, look with horror upon women voting, and are just as much opposed to it in municipal as in State and federal elections.[13] The second of the *Times* cables bears testimony to the vitality of the Women's Suffrage movement in the United States. Ladies prominent in New York Society, such as Mrs Clarence McKay[14] and Mrs W. K. Vanderbilt,[15] are interesting themselves in the movement. Mrs Taft,[16] the wife of the new President, is said to be favourable to it. A gigantic meeting had been held at Carnegie Hall on December 4th. 'Society ladies, mistresses of millions . . . are placing their means and influence at the disposal of the suffrage movement.' 'There is no doubt at all that the movement is assuming large proportions . . . and after Friday's reconnaissance it really appears as though the movement in this country were going to be as impressive as in England.'[17] The correspondent attributes a good deal of the present strength of the suffrage movement in America to the attacks made upon it in the *Times* by Mrs Humphry Ward and others.

> The strong impetus given to the Woman Suffrage movement here . . . was due to the *Times* and Mrs Humphry Ward. It may surprise you that your leading articles commenting on Mrs Ward's and other letters to you in the summer regarding the position of woman suffrage in this country should have had this effect, but it is the fact. Mrs Humphry Ward, perhaps, in this case, should have 'let sleeping dogs lie'.[18]

Now it is not for one who, like myself, has never been in the United States[19] to say whether the *Times* correspondent is right in attributing the present activity of the Women's Suffrage movement in America to the irritation produced on being told by an English visitor that the movement was dead; but I do happen to know something about another cause to which the *Times* correspondent attributes it. 'The American Suffragettes', he says, 'are jealous that English women should have been before them as pioneers.'[20] He calls this motive 'pleasingly human and – feminine.' One is tempted to retort with –

> Alas! The good man little knew
> All that the wily sex could do.[21]

One of the last things of which it is possible to convince the average man is that women can ever act in thorough loyalty to each other; but this is one of the good things that men have got to learn. Almost at the same moment in which this curious interpretation of the motives of the American movement was given in the *Times*, I received a letter from Mrs Chapman Catt,[22] President of the International Women's Suffrage Alliance, to explain a postponement of her expected visit during December to England. In this letter she said she was remaining in the United States to help in the great women's demonstration in the Carnegie Hall on December 4th, because she felt that in this way, and in helping to promote the gigantic petition to Congress which will be presented in January,[23] she would best be helping the English movement. So well do suffragists in every country understand that what helps one helps all, and what hurts one hurts all. The work has taught us loyalty to each other.

The foregoing illustrations are designed to enforce my moral, that we make a great mistake in under-estimating the forces opposed to us, even when we are not impressed by the weight of their arguments or by the accuracy of their appeals to historical or economic fact. I have selected as the title of this paper a specimen of startling epigram dear to the hearts of the anti-suffragists, and made to pass muster with them as an argument. 'Men are men and women are women' is the form they usually prefer;[24] but sometimes, to show that age cannot wither nor custom stale their infinite variety, they put it in another form, and say 'Women are not men, and men are not women.'[25] The 'wiser women', they say, realise this momentous fact, but the misguided and anarchic women, who claim that the object of national representation should be to represent the nation, and not merely half of the nation, are oblivious of it, and are even in antagonism to what is one of the plainest facts of every-day life. This curiously perverse attitude of mind on the part of the anti-suffragists shows that they have not even used their intelligence sufficiently to grasp the main outlines of the case for women's suffrage. They go on repeating their catchword that 'Men are men and women are women', meaning thereby that the point of view, the experience of life, the sphere of activity of women differ in many important respects from those of men, without seeing that these very facts are among the strongest and most irrefutable of the reasons for urging that no representative system is complete or truly national which entirely leaves out the representation of women. 'Women', they urge in one of their publications (*Why an Educated Working*

Woman Opposes Woman's Suffrage), 'have different duties, different capacities, the woman's being in the spheres of Home, Society, Education, Philanthropy.' One would think that the obvious conclusion from this must be that when Parliament is dealing with legislation which concerns the home, society, education or philanthropy, it would be well if there were some constitutional means of enabling the influence and experience of the average women of the country to make themselves felt.

When the question of the enfranchisement of the working men of this country was under consideration in the 'fifties' and 'sixties',[26] was it considered an argument against their admission to a place in the constitution that their duties, experience of life and industrial interests were not identical with those of their employers and the wealthier sections of society which then monopolised all Parliamentary representation? Certainly not. It was the direct reverse. So far as the working man had interests, experience, duties and capacities different from those of the middle and upper classes, so far was it felt that these differences strengthened his claim to representation. If in all respects his immediate and obvious interests were identical with those of the classes already represented, he did not suffer from the want of representation. What represented them also represented him. It was where they differed that the shoe pinched and that he felt his want of a constitutional means of causing his point of view to be taken into consideration by Parliament.

Before the enfranchisement of the working classes, Trades Unions were illegal combinations; a defaulting treasurer or secretary of a trade's union could not be prosecuted.[27] In the year 1834, a group of Dorsetshire labourers, who endeavoured to persuade some of their fellow working men to join a trades union and to take an oath in connection with the ceremony of enrolment, were sentenced to seven years' transportation.[28] The wages of labourers in Dorsetshire at the time were only 7*s.* or 8*s.* a week; bread was twice its present price. These unhappy men, therefore, lived in continual sight of starvation, yet they were subjected to an incredibly cruel punishment, worse almost than death, for endeavouring, by what was then an illegal means, to improve their industrial position. Notwithstanding these well-known facts, we see reported in the papers speeches of almost inconceivable ignorance by anti-suffragists to-day that the right to vote has done nothing in the case of men to improve their industrial condition.

The ignorance of women is indeed a stone that is often thrown at us by the anti-suffragists, and they certainly give plenty of illustrations of it. The ignorance of the working classes was perpetually urged as a reason for depriving them of representation; but one of the first results of the Reform Act of 1867[29] was the Education Act of 1870;[30] and immediately after the extension of household suffrage to counties in 1884,[31] which enfranchised the agricultural labourer, efforts were for the first time made to afford him the means of political education. The various political parties saw to it that he was supplied with suitable political literature. Political meetings were held at hours and in places which suited his convenience. Sometimes condescending politicians unrolled their stores of political knowledge in a manner which recalled that of De Quincey's elder brother lecturing in the nursery: 'I hope I have made this clear to the meanest understanding' – with a polite and comprehensive bow all round the assembled auditory – 'to the most excruciatingly mean of understandings.'[32] When this happened, the agricultural labourer, armed with the vote and the ballot, let it be known that this style of oratory did not please him, and a different and more pleasing kind of eloquence was very quickly supplied. The possession of a vote all round greatly improves manners as between class and class. When women are enfranchised, the possession of a vote will in itself be a means of combating ignorance. Women are, as a rule, conscientious with regard to any responsibility with which they are entrusted. It must also be remembered that a large number of women who would be enfranchised would be amongst the most thoughtful and best-educated members of the community. At the present time, speaking generally, such women stand altogether outside political life. If they were enfranchised, they would naturally take their part in it, and their influence in politics, coloured as it would be by high character, intelligence and knowledge of the real basis of national greatness, could not but have an elevating influence on political life and conduce to the welfare of the nation. How often have I conversed with such a woman, the head of a school perhaps, well educated, not only in book knowledge, but wise and sagacious in respect of everything that goes to form character and strengthen the will for good ends, and reflected, 'What a thousand pities that this refined and powerful intelligence is shut out from direct influence on current politics.' Such women are, of course, under any political system, an invaluable national asset. But is the nation making all the use of them it should make when it shuts, bangs and bolts the door of direct political power in their faces and says in effect, as far as politics are concerned, 'We have no need of such as you'?

The concluding paragraphs of the recently published memorial of 538 medical women of the United Kingdom to the Prime Minister in support of women's suffrage emphasises the point that the vote will exercise a stimulating effect on women;[33] encouraging them in larger numbers to undertake work in branches of public service where the co-operation of women is especially needed, and fostering among both men and women the sense of citizenship and of national responsibility.

'The educated working woman' who writes a leaflet for the anti-suffragists veils her identity and remains anonymous – no one can tell how far she has earned the title she gives herself; but the registered medical women of the United Kingdom deserve to be called educated working women if anyone does, and it is not a little significant and encouraging to find that out of 553, no fewer than 538 support women's suffrage, and only 15 are against it.

The anti-suffragists seem very shy of any allusions to the practical working of women's suffrage in Australia and New Zealand;[34] if they had been able to quote any evil result from it in those countries, they would have made good use of it. But no such evil results being to hand, they content themselves with the obvious comment that the conditions of life in Australia and New Zealand are different from those in this country. There are undoubtedly important differences between the home country and her daughter nations across the seas; but the differences are not all in a direction making women's suffrage less desirable here than there. The Englishwoman at home is at least as mentally active, as well educated, as conscious of responsibility to the community, as fertile in resource in dealing with social problems as her sisters in Australia. We are perhaps more prepared for the suffrage than they were when they received it. But every responsible New Zealand and Australian statesman has borne evidence of the good results of women's suffrage in their respective countries.[35] The sense of national responsibility has been strengthened. New Zealand, the first great British Colony to enfranchise its women, was also the first great daughter state to place herself by the side of the mother country in the blackest moment of the South African War.[36] The women who are the most truly womanly have deeply implanted in them the twin principles of love and duty. Then what more natural than that the women of New Zealand should be keen to make their sacrifice in the hour of national peril to the mother country, and to send out their sons to stand side by side with ours on the battle-fields of South Africa?

Again, Mr Deakin, when he was here for the Colonial Conference of 1907,[37] said in one of his public speeches that the result of women's suffrage in Australia had been to deepen the sense of national responsibility among men; for he reminded his audience that it was *after* women had been enfranchised in Australia that the men of Australia had for the first time faced their national responsibilities in the matter of making due preparation for national defence.

Touching the question of the relations of women's suffrage to war and peace, Mrs Humphry Ward has said that women might by their votes be responsible for causing a war, but would not have to pay, in their own persons, the physical suffering and loss of life which every war necessitates; there would therefore, she argued, be a divorce between power and responsibility.[38] Mrs Ward does not make any observation on the fact that this is exactly what happens now under the existing political system. The British soldier has no share in the political entanglements and intrigues which precede and lead up to war; his share in empire, as Mr Rudyard Kipling has said, is 'to salt it down with his bones'.[39] The Chancellors, the Secretaries of State, the Quai d'Orsay, Wilhelmstrasse, the Ballplatz, Downing Street and their presiding geniuses, for the time being, make war when it seemeth them good. Tommy pays the price in life and limb. The politicians make war, soldiers pay the price and make peace. The real authors of the South African war were not the men who actually fought in it, although the Boers had a system of universal service. Kruger[40] and Leyds,[41] on the Boer side, Chamberlain[42] and Milner,[43] on the British side, were more responsible for the war than any soldiers. The soldiers had merely to do, or try to do, what the politicians told them, and often to die in the attempt.

As far as suffering is concerned, the stay-at-homes, women included, possibly suffer even more acutely than those who do the actual fighting. It costs a father and mother more anguish to part with a beloved son to fight in a war which may cost his life, than it does a high-spirited young man to drink delight of battle with his peers. The sickening suspense, the watching for the lists of killed and wounded, is a too recent experience of many sorrow-stricken parents among us to be forgotten yet. Many more people died of the South African war than were slain by bullets or by enteric.[44] 'He never recovered from the loss of his son in the Boer war' is a very frequent answer to inquiries about what seemed the premature death of a man who ought to have had many years of useful activity before him. And what is true of the father is no less true of the stricken mother. The bullet pierces another heart than that of its immediate victim. This is not necessarily to condemn war, but to take account of its cost to non-combatants as well as to combatants.

Another favourite argument of the anti-suffragists is that the ultimate basis of law is physical force, and physical force is male and not female. This argument was used, on a recent occasion, by an unwary orator, who illustrated it by pointing to the policeman at the entrance of the hall where he was speaking. He had not remembered that his illustration refuted his argument. For the policeman, the representative of the physical force by which law is carried out, was the servant of a municipality elected by male and female voters. Therefore, the illustration showed that the physical force necessary in the last resort for the carrying out of the law is a tool or instrument in the hands of the executive authority, and that for the efficiency of that physical force it is a matter of indifference whether the executive is elected by men only or by both men and women. Nay, it is a matter of indifference whether the executive be elected at all or not. The police force and the army support in the last resort the decrees of an autocrat just as they do those of a democratically elected government. Dr Whitehead, of Cambridge, has pointed this out in an excellent paper. That the ultimate direction of affairs must be vested in those who in their own persons possess the fighting strength of the nation is an argument that goes far.

> In fact it goes much too far, for it proves that the vast majority of governments that have ever existed were impossible. It proves that the government of Louis XIV of France was impossible, because in his own person he was unable to coerce the French nation. It proves that any despotism is impossible, and that any oligarchy is impossible. When I contemplate these results of the argument I wish it were true; but, unfortunately, it is manifestly false.[45]

This *reductio ad absurdum* of the physical force argument speaks for itself. It has very seldom happened, and never did happen until the advent of democracy, that the executive government of any country was identified with the balance of physical force in the same country. Even now in England, though we are far advanced towards democracy, the representative system does not secure that the majority of men who possess the superiority of physical force obtains the majority of voting power. Lord Avebury has recently pointed out that at two recent general elections the minority of voters obtained a majority of representatives in the House of Commons, and consequently the control of the executive government.[46] This is obviously an electoral anomaly; but according to the exponents of the 'physical force' argument against women's suffrage, the majority of men, out-manoeuvred at the polls, ought to have risen in rebellion against the minority who had secured the balance of power, and with it the choice of the executive in the House of Commons. Of course, nothing of the kind happened. The executive government, whether elected by a majority or a minority of the men of the country, retains the control of the police and the army, and is bound to use them, if necessary, in support of its constitutional authority. Before 1867[47] there was never even an approach to an identity between the physical strength and the voting strength of the nation.

But the refutation of the physical force argument is complete on yet another ground. The more reckless of its exponents express it bluntly by saying that 'Law in its ultimate issue rests on physical force.' The reply is a direct negative. Law, in all civilised communities, does not rest in its ultimate issue on physical force, but on justice. To maintain the contrary is, when the argument is followed out, to maintain the doctrine of a military despotism. The appeal of those who seek to change the laws is not to brute force, but to justice and reason. There are communities in which brute force is the 'ultimate' basis of government. According to what we read in the newspapers, the negro republic of Hayti is one of them. A daily paper recently reported that Alexis, the late President, had been driven out of the island, and had barely escaped with his life from a mob which threatened to tear him to pieces. The paragraph continues, 'There are several military candidates for the succession, but General Simon, having the largest armed force, proposes to elect himself.'[48] This is an excellent example of the sort of government which rests ultimately on physical force. The Czar of Russia attempts to build his Government on 'the ultimate basis' of physical force. The control of the army is his; his officials have besides organised 'black bands' which pursue the ends favoured by the Government by means of massacre and unspeakable horrors and abominations. The number of persons executed year by year and month by month is enormous;[49] the prisons are kept in so insanitary a state that 60 per cent of the prisoners die of preventable diseases. Transportations to Siberia, executions, artificially produced diseases, these are the supports of the Czar's Government.[50] Can anyone say that such a foundation is firm and strong? Is it not universally believed that this state of things is unstable, temporary? it cannot possibly last.[51] The appeal uttered by Count Leo Tolstoy just before his eightieth birthday is to justice, to reason.[52] They must prevail at last, or Russia must cease to exist as a civilised power.

In Mons. Paul Sabatier's lectures on Modernism, delivered, if my memory does not deceive me, at the Passmore-Edwards Settlement, in the spring of 1908, under the aegis of Mrs Humphry Ward, occurs this passage:

> At a low stage of development men are obedient only to force, but little by little behind brute force there opens out the idea of moral force; the tyrant himself puts his tyranny under the protection of a greater power than himself: it is by God (as he says) that he has been invested with authority. Mankind does not stop there when in order to reverence the law, it has no need to believe it to have descended from Sinai, and when the law binds us, even where it cannot compel, it is simply because it answers to our best selves.[53]

In the religious evolution of mankind, the idea of justice as tempering even omnipotence very early indeed found an expression in the foremost minds of the ancient world. Dr Adam's lectures on 'The Religious Teachers of Greece' constantly reiterate the seeking of the leaders of Greek thought after the idea of justice as the very basis of divine government.[54] If there be a religion which is based on the idea of force uncontrolled by any ethical restraint, it is the religion described by Browning in his 'Caliban on Setebos'.

> Thinketh such shows nor right nor wrong in Him,
> Nor kind, nor cruel. He is strong and Lord.
> And strong myself compared to yonder crabs . . .
> Doth as He likes, or wherefore Lord? So He.[55]

That is the religious conception of Caliban. 'Law resting, in its ultimate basis, on physical force.' It is not Christianity. Nineteen hundred years ago, the Roman soldiers, egged on by the Jewish priests, crucified the Founder of the Christian religion.[56] Pilate, Herod and the Priests represented physical force: the marred and wounded body hanging on the cross represented an idea. Which proved the stronger of the two? The question requires no answer. It has not happened once but hundreds of times that the still small voice appealing to what is high and noble is stronger than armies, and speaks louder and more penetratingly than drums and trumpets. Mr J. R. Green's *Short History of the English People* has a preface which sets forth what he aimed at in writing his book; he gave less space, he said, than most historians to military achievements and the campaigns of great captains, because he had to find more space than most historians for figures

> . . . little heeded in common history, the figures of the missionary, the poet, the printer, the merchant, the philosopher. In England more than elsewhere constitutional progress has been the result of social development . . . I have endeavoured to point out how much of our political history is the outcome of social changes.[57]

This last sentence exactly describes the position of the women's suffrage movement at the present time. Social development has enormously changed the social position of women, and calls for a corresponding change in their political position. The responsibilities and duties of citizenship are keenly felt by constantly increasing numbers of women; they are asking for the most elementary rights of citizenship, a share in controlling the laws under which they live. It is a mere playing with this demand to say that law is based on physical force which women are incapable of either supplying or resisting. All governments need the use of physical force just as they need the use of money and other material objects; but our ultimate appeal is to justice, and to the answer that must be given to the question, 'Will enfranchisement of women be a power that will work for the good of the community?' All experience which has been gained of the working of women's suffrage in our own and other countries leads to the conclusion that this question may confidently be met with an affirmative. Even Mrs Humphry Ward herself appeals to the usefulness of the women's vote in municipal elections, and urges that it should be organised to secure the success of one of the philanthropic schemes with which her name is honourably associated.[58] If the women's vote in municipal elections should be organised to secure a good object, why should not the women's vote in Parliamentary elections be used for a similar purpose? The hand-and-fast line between what is municipal and what is Parliamentary exists only in imagination. Even Mr Gladstone said it passed the wit of man to draw the dividing line between local and imperial concerns.[59] Our friends, the anti-suffragists, ought to choose which horse they are going to ride; but, instead of making their choice and sticking to it, they show extraordinary agility, worthy of circus-riders, in skipping from one horse to another. Now they are altogether satisfied with every extension of municipal voting and eligibility to women: but when the Women's Local Government Qualifications Bill was before the House of Lords eighteen months ago, it had no more inveterate opponent than one of the leaders of the anti-suffragists, Lord James of Hereford. With his trained legal intellect he saw the consequences involved, and said if this Bill passed, it would be difficult to find the man who would be able to argue against the extension of the Parliamentary franchise to women.[60] The whole position is, in fact, absurd: that a woman is eligible for the highest municipal offices and is at the same time unable to give a simple vote for a Member of Parliament. Our appeal is to common sense, supported by justice and experience.

Transcribed from a copy in University of Glasgow Archives and Special Collections. No known copyright restrictions.

Notes

1. The committee was comprised of Jane Maria Strachey (1840–1928) and Frances Balfour (1858–1931), two long-time members of the NUWSS and friends of Fawcett, as well as the artist Mary Lowndes (1857–1929), the writer Cicely Hamilton (1872–1952) and Elisina Grant Richards (1878–1959), wife of the publisher Franklin Thomas Grant Richards (1872–1948), whose company published the magazine (Balfour et al. 1909, 1).
2. See Section 17.
3. See Fawcett (1924, 198–200) for her delight in winning, and Trevelyan (1923, 234–5) for Mary Ward's recollection of the event.
4. See Section 23 for Fawcett on the South African War and her staunch belief in the project. Large numbers of troops embarked from the UK from November 1899, often sent off with enthusiastic parades and cheering crowds (*Times* 1899f), with 'the general absence of poignant emotion both on ship and on shore. There must have been sore hearts in the crowd, but they have known how to conceal their wounds in public, and the superficial aspect has been one of cheerful gaiety, with just a touch of restrained feeling here and there' (*Times* 1899g).
5. Fawcett here is paraphrasing the arguments often used by the anti-suffragists. Mrs Ward had said that women's 'ignorance is imposed by nature and [is] irreparable' (Ward 1908, 349), which was a quote much repeated by Fawcett (1912, 45).
6. *Spectator* (1906, 820–1).
7. 'The wiser women of Britain, the women opposed to the extension of the Parliamentary franchise to women, are doing the right thing in the right way' (*Spectator* 1908, 117–18).
8. '... after half a century of agitation, the Woman Suffrage movement is obviously declining, put down by the common sense of women themselves. They certainly could have got it if they had ultimately determined upon it' (Ward 1908b).
9. In 1897 Twain had famously said 'The report of my death was an exaggeration' in response to a rumour that he was dying in poverty in London (Marshall White 1897).
10. Mrs Julia Ward Howe (1819–1910), American poet and author, best known for 'Battle Hymn of the Republic'.
11. Dr Anna Howard Shaw (1847–1919), preacher, physician and a leader of the American women's suffrage movement.
12. On 30 June 1908, following a four-month trip to the US and Canada, a letter from Mrs Humphry Ward was published in the *Times*. The letter argued that woman suffrage was not inevitable, and that 'the movement has not only failed; it has checked the legitimate development of women's influence in the spheres which most truly belong to them', asking the women of England to likewise defeat it (Ward 1908a). A reply from Dr Anna Shaw (writing from New York) was published on 8 July, giving counter-arguments, stating that Mrs Ward 'has written from that very biased point of view which is inevitable when one hears but one side of a story, and only half of that' (Shaw 1908). On 1 September, the *Times* published Mrs Humphry Ward's response to 'Some Suffragist Arguments', stating that the 'suffrage agitation attributes an entirely fictitious importance to the Parliamentary vote' and that women's lives had progressed without it. Mrs Humphry Ward suggests that the majority of women in both the US and the UK do not want the vote, giving examples and statistics of the situation in America (Ward 1908b). A reply from Julia Ward Howe (in New England) was published in the *Times* on 1 October, providing counter-statistics to show that Mrs Ward was 'seriously misinformed' (Ward Howe 1908). Mrs Humphry Ward replied on 10 October, arguing that suffrage in America 'since 1896 ... has scored no success of any importance anywhere; and that the general feeling about it in the suffrage camp is a feeling of despondency' (Ward 1908c).
13. *Times* 1908c.
14. Katherine Alexander Duer Mackay (1878–1930), New York socialite and suffragist who founded the Equal Franchise Society in 1908.
15. Alva Belmont (1853–1933), socialite and prominent figure in the American women's suffrage movement. She was married to William Kissam Vanderbilt (1849–1920) from 1875 to 1895, but married Oliver Belmont (1858–1908) in 1896.
16. Helen Louise 'Nellie' Taft, née Herron (1861–1943), wife of William Howard Taft, First Lady of the United States from 1909 to 1913 and supporter of suffrage (National First Ladies' Library, n.d.).
17. *Times* 1908f.

18 *Times* 1908f.
19 See Section 18 for Fawcett sending a speech to be read at the Chicago World's Fair in 1893.
20 *Times* 1908f.
21 A misquoted line from a popular Irish air, 'By the Lake Whose Gloomy Shore' by Thomas Moore (1779–1852), on St Kevin: 'Ah! The good Saint little knew / what the wily sex can do' (Moore 1852, 204).
22 Carrie Chapman Catt, president of the National American Woman Suffrage Association (NAWSA) from 1900 to 1904 (and later from 1915 to 1920) and founder of the IWSA, of which Fawcett was a member, in 1904.
23 Under Carrie Chapman Catt, NAWSA had coordinated the first petition to the Senate and House of Representatives of the United States for 'an amendment to the National Constitution which will enable women to vote' (NAWSA 1909) in a form which appeared in local newspapers throughout the United States. The petition of 'about 500,000 names, divided more or less evenly between men and women and coming from all parts of the country' (*Sun* [New York] 1910) was finally presented to Congress at the suffrage hearing on 18 April 1910, in a suffragist parade to the Capitol.
24 This phrase appears in the medical literature of the mid-nineteenth century, but crosses over to discussion of women's progression in society. In a piece supporting Fawcett's 'Education of Women of Middle and Upper Classes' (see Section 2), the Reverend John Llewelyn Davies (1826–1916) explains the major objection to providing women's colleges: 'Nature is thought to protest against this plan of identical studies for the two sexes. Men are men, and women are women; therefore the studies of men should be manly, and the studies of women womanly' (Davies 1868, 174). The phrase then appears in Bushnell's *Women's Suffrage: The reform against nature* (1869, 102) and is used commonly thereafter.
25 See City Branch (1900, 10).
26 See Section 3, note 5.
27 See Section 11, note 8.
28 The Tolpuddle Martyrs; see Marlow 1971.
29 See Section 6, note 7.
30 See Section 14, note 5.
31 See Section 11, note 1.
32 Fawcett here misquotes from the memoir of the author Thomas de Quincey (1785–1859), *Autobiographic Sketches* (1853), recalling lectures from his domineering older brother, William. 'He had been in the habit of lowering the pitch of his lectures with ostentatious condescension to the presumed level of our poor understandings . . . he flattered himself he had made the point under discussion tolerably clear; "clear" he added, bowing round the half circle of us, the audience, "to the meanest of capacities"; and then he repeated, sonorously, "clear to the most excruciatingly mean of capacities". Upon which, a voice . . . retorted "No, you haven't: it's as dark as sin"; and then . . . a second voice exclaimed, "Dark as night"' (De Quincey 1853, 45–6).
33 In 1908, Elizabeth Garrett Anderson and colleagues in the Association of Registered Medical Women wrote 'to all the registered medical women residing in the United Kingdom asking whether or not they are in favour of woman suffrage. The results of this inquiry are as follows: In favour, 538; against, 15 . . . the enfranchisement of women is essential to their well-being' (*Times* 1908g, 6).
34 See Section 21, note 22; and Section 19, note 30.
35 See Section 21, notes 23 and 24.
36 See Section 23 for Fawcett's support of the South African War and Hall 1949 for New Zealand's involvement.
37 Alfred Deakin (1856–1919), Australian politician and second prime minister of Australia. The 1907 Imperial Conference was one of a set of periodic gatherings in London of leaders from colonies and dominions of the British Empire between 1887 and 1937.
38 See 'Why I Do Not Believe in Woman Suffrage' (Ward 1908d, 251–6).
39 Fawcett here repurposes critical verse from the poet Rudyard Kipling (1865–1936). 'The Sons of the Widow' in *Barrack Room Ballads* is critical of the Queen, safe at home in Windsor, while 'the men an' the 'orses what makes up the forces', who have won Victoria ''alf of creation she owns: / We 'ave bought 'er the same with the sword an' the flame, / An' we've salted it down with our bones. (Poor beggars! – it's blue with our bones!)' (Kipling 1890, 96).
40 Stephanus Johannes Paulus Kruger (1825–1904), South African politician and president of the South African Republic between 1883 and 1900.

41 Willem Johannes Leyds (1859–1940), Dutch lawyer and state secretary of the South African Republic, serving as the Republic's special envoy in Brussels in the South African War.
42 Joseph Chamberlain, British politician and secretary of state for the colonies during the South African War.
43 Alfred Milner, colonial administrator who was governor of the Cape Colony and high commissioner for Southern Africa during the South African War.
44 Intestinal illness, or more specifically typhoid or paratyphoid fever.
45 Alfred North Whitehead (1861–1947), British mathematician and theologian, then fellow of Trinity College, Cambridge, in a speech at the annual meeting of the Cambridge Women's Suffrage Association (1906).
46 On Thursday, 3 December 1908, a 'Mimic Election' was held by the Proportional Representation Society in an imaginary election at London's Caxton Hall, to show the practical implications of electoral reform, inviting the public to respond: 21,690 sent in filled-in voting papers. Many MPs attended, and Lord Avebury's speech pointed out the 'mockery of representation. It could not be alleged that the present Government had been sent to power by a minority, but it could be said with truth that they and their friends had 130 seats more than the votes cast for them at the last General Election entitled them to' (*Morning Post* 1908c).
47 The Second Reform Act; see Section 3, note 5.
48 On 2 December 1908, the self-proclaimed 'President for Life' of Haiti, Pierre Nord Alexis (1820–1910), fled Port-au-Prince (*Times* 1908e, 7) following a famine in the country that had led to food riots. The rebellion was led by François C. Antoine Simon (1843–1923), army general, who succeeded Alexis as president. The closest quote to Fawcett's that has been found is in *Pearson's Weekly*: 'General Simon, having the large armed force, proposes to elect himself President of Haiti. No "Simple Simon" this' (1908).
49 Fawcett's note: 'See daily papers, December 17th, 1908.' See *Times* 1908h.
50 Exile to Siberia as a punishment had a long history in Russia; see Pallot, Piacentini and Moran (2012, 47–8).
51 The Russian Tsarist autocracy were overthrown in 1917, in a political and social revolution that concluded with the establishment of the Soviet Union in 1923.
52 The Russian author Leo Tolstoy (1828–1910) celebrated his 80th birthday in August 1908, although the 'Governors-General of Moscow and Warsaw [had] forbidden all public celebrations on Count Tolstoy's birthday in those cities' (*Morning Post* 1908b) following his internationally published article against capital punishment, and his condemnation of both its use by the Russian government, and the Russian society that tolerated it (Tolstoy 1908).
53 Charles Paul Marie Sabatier (1858–1928), French clergyman and historian, who gave three lectures in London in 1908 at Ward's Passmore Edwards Settlement: this is a quote from the third lecture, given on 10 March (Sabatier 1908, 137; *Morning Post* 1908a).
54 James Adam (1860–1907), senior tutor in Classics of Emmanuel College, Cambridge, in his lectures published in 1908 illustrating 'the substitution of harmony and justice for discord and violence in the divine government of the world' (Adam xii).
55 Browning (1864, 127).
56 See Mark 15:1–40; Matthew 27:1–55; Luke 23:1–50; John 19:1–25.
57 John Richard Green (1837–83), English historian. *A Short History of the English People* was a bestselling text (1875, vi).
58 Ward argues that if more women took advantage of their recent access to positions in local government, many of the issues surrounding social deprivation and disability with the schools she was involved with could have been addressed: 'a hundred things could have been done for children, if voters and organizers had so willed it', but women 'have not shown any great zeal' in coming forward. She uses this as a reason for arguing against the vote: 'good brains and skilled hands are being diverted from women's real tasks to this barren agitation for equal rights' (Ward 1908d, 261).
59 The local concern, in this case, was Ireland, in an 1886 discussion of a bill to amend the provision for its future government: 'in this House, we can draw for practical purposes a distinction between affairs which are Imperial, and affairs which are not Imperial. It would not be difficult to say in principle that, as the Irish Legislature will have nothing to do with Imperial concerns, let Irish Members come here and vote on Imperial concerns. All depends on the practicability of the distinction. Well, Sir, I have thought much, reasoned much, and inquired much with regard to that distinction. I had hoped it might be possible to draw a distinction, and I have arrived at the conclusion that it cannot be drawn. I believe it passes the wit of man; at

any rate, it passes not my wit alone, but the wit of many with whom I have communicated' (HC Deb 1886, 1056). This, shortened to an approximation of 'it passed the wit of man to devise a separation between purely Irish and Imperial concerns', was much quoted in later debates by other members of both Houses (*Times* 1886a).

60 Fawcett writes about Henry James (1828–1911), 1st Baron James of Hereford: 'In 1898, when the London Borough Councils were established in the place of the Vestries, an amendment was moved and carried in the House of Commons rendering women eligible for the newly created bodies as they had been on the old ones. When the Bill came to the House of Lords, this portion of it was vehemently opposed by the late Lord James of Hereford (afterwards one of the vice-presidents of the Anti-Suffrage League), and his opposition was successful, notwithstanding a powerful and eloquent speech by the late Lord Salisbury, then Prime Minister, in support of the eligibility of women on the new Borough Councils. Again, when in 1907 the Bill rendering women eligible for Town and County Councils reached the House of Lords, it had no more sincere and ardent opponent than Lord James. He saw its bearing upon the question of women's suffrage, and the absurdity involved in a state of the law which allows a woman to be a Town or County Councillor, or even a Mayor, and in that capacity the returning officer at a Parliamentary election, but does not permit her to give a simple vote in the election of a member of Parliament. "If", said Lord James, "their Lordships accepted this measure making women eligible for the great positions that had been specified in great communities like Liverpool and Manchester, where was the man who would be able to argue against the Parliamentary franchise for women?" The Bill became an Act, notwithstanding Lord James's opposition, and within twelve months he had become a vice-president of the League for Opposing Women's Suffrage and for "Maintaining the Representation of Women on Municipal and other Bodies concerned with the Domestic and Social Affairs of the Community"' (Fawcett 1912a, 49–50).

31
Picturing Fawcett: International Woman Suffrage Alliance Congress, 1909

Figure 10: IWSA Congress, London, April 1909, with Millicent Fawcett, first vice-president, seated centre. Top row from left: Thora Daugaard (Denmark), Dr Louise Qvam (Norway), Dr Aletta Jacobs (Netherlands), Annie Furuhjelm (Finland), Zinaida Ivanova [pseud. Zinaida Mirovich] (Russia), Dr Käthe Schirmacher (Germany), Klara Honegger (Switzerland), unidentified. Bottom row from left: unidentified, Anna Bugge Wicksell (Sweden), Rev. Dr Anna Shaw (USA), Millicent Fawcett (first vice-president, UK), Carrie Chapman Catt (president, USA), Fredrikke Marie Qvam (Norway), Dr Anita Augsburg (Germany). From the Nasjonalbiblioteket/National Library of Norway. No known copyright restrictions.

In 1902, although not physically in attendance, Fawcett was elected as second vice-president of the International Woman Suffrage Committee, which was established at the annual convention of the National American Woman Suffrage Association (NAWSA) in Washington, USA (Crawford 2001a, 301). The resulting organisation, the IWSA, was founded in 1904 to act as an international body to stimulate individual national women's associations to achieve enfranchisement, representing the pacifist voice and bringing together eight national societies. At that meeting, 'Mrs Fawcett was made a Vice-President . . . and served upon the Board of Officers from that time onwards, attending every meeting with regularity; and after the office was opened in London she became personally responsible for the greater part of the work' (Strachey 1931, 243). The fifth conference of the IWSA was held in various locations throughout London from 26 April to 1 May 1909, with delegates from 21 countries engaged in discussions, concerts, visits and a conference presided over by Carrie Chapman Catt,[1] an American women's suffrage leader (IWSA 1909). Fawcett, by then first vice-president, chaired various sessions of the convention and reported on UK suffrage – and militant – tactics: 'Our business as women asking for justice is not to rely upon physical force but in the eternal principles of right and justice. Law-abiding methods alienate no-one, while methods of violence and disorder create anti-Suffragists by the hundred' (Fawcett in IWSA 1909, 104).

> The highest point of the proceedings was reached with a procession of workers, from University women in their brilliant robes to industrial women in their overalls, and cotton-operatives earning four shillings as weekly wage for sixty hours. All this vast crowd of women, with banners and emblems, marched into the Albert Hall to the sound of jubilant greetings from the women of all nations . . . Renewed acquaintance with the most prominent suffrage leaders was of great value to the delegates, who saw in them the women who shrank from no sacrifice for their ideals (Deutsch 1929, 16).

The organisation is still in existence today as the International Alliance of Women,[2] an international non-governmental organisation that promotes women's rights around the world.

Notes

1. See Section 30, notes 22 and 23.
2. http://womenalliance.org.

32
Picturing Fawcett: Mrs Henry Fawcett, LLD, president of the National Union, 1909

Figure 11: Mrs Henry Fawcett, LLD, president of the National Union, 1909. Elliott & Fry, London. No known copyright restrictions.

Fawcett is 62 years old in this photograph. A portrait from the same sitting was featured on the front page of the *Common Cause* in October 1909: 'It will scarcely be necessary to tell our readers that Mrs Fawcett, whose portrait adorns our front page, is President of the National Union of Women's Suffrage Societies, whose oldest affiliated society was founded in 1867' (*Common Cause* 1909b, 350). The NUWSS had been a loose federation of suffrage societies without centralised leadership until January 1907, when 'a new constitution was adopted which provided for elected officers, an executive committee and a quarterly policy-making council'. Although by then Fawcett 'had achieved a unique position in suffrage circles', the presidency was not elected until the 1907 council meeting. 'With its new structure and the new prominence which militancy had given to the suffrage cause, the union was clearly going to exert a much greater impact on the political scene than in its first decade' (Rubinstein 1991, 153–4).

The photography studio of Elliott & Fry, founded in 1863 by Joseph John Elliott (1835–1903) and Clarence Edmund Fry (1840–97), 'was one of the most important in the history of studio portraiture in London', capturing portraits of many leading Victorian politicians, scientists, artists, celebrities and social figures, as well as royalty. Posed simply with few props in the naturally lit 'glass-room' in Baker Street, sitters 'could choose from a selection of fifteen painted backgrounds. Sittings were charged at a guinea, which entitled the sitter to 18 *cartes-de-visite* (visiting card size) or six of the larger "cabinet portrait" photographs. This was twice the sum for the best theatre seats and was deemed by many followers of fashion as "an amusement a la mode"' (National Portrait Gallery 2006). However, 'Many sitters . . . did not pay. Instead they sat so that the company could sell prints commercially, giving the sitters additional publicity and Elliott & Fry useful income' (Hannavy 2008, 480). Fawcett sat for them at various times in her professional career. Here, in this assured, formal pose, Fawcett is aligned with those other Victorian luminaries photographed by the famed studio, as an established leader of recognisable significance.

33
Reporting Fawcett: Wanted: a statesman, 1909

Address delivered at the Athenaeum Hall, Glasgow, 22 November.[1] Privately published, 1–11.

In March 1909 a bill that aimed to confer the franchise on all men and women of full age was defeated on its second reading (*Morning Post* 1909). Throughout the summer, the suffragettes intensified their violent campaign, with many of those sentenced to Holloway going on hunger strike (Grant 2011); force-feeding began that September (Crawford 2001a, 571). Arguments for the vote were becoming popularly associated with these actions, and NUWSS meetings were becoming rowdy and were often disrupted (Strachey 1931, 231–2; Rubinstein 1991, 160). Fawcett remained keen to distance the NUWSS from militant action, refusing to cooperate with the WSPU (Strachey 1931, 220–5; Rubinstein 1991, 164). In the last months of 1909, Fawcett travelled widely to make her constitutional case for women's suffrage, being scheduled to speak in Cardiff, Manchester, London, Shrewsbury, Chester, Manchester (again), Sussex, Kent, Glasgow, Edinburgh and again in Kent (Rubinstein 1991, 170). In late November, a large meeting was held by the Glasgow and West of Scotland Association for Women's Suffrage (GWSAWS) (*Scotsman* 1909), featuring Fawcett and Dr Elsie Inglis[2] as the principal speakers (*Common Cause* 1909d). These invited speeches provided an opportunity for local suffragists to publicise both the cause and their approach: two-and-a-half thousand handbills advertising this event, and two thousand copies of the resulting speech, sold for one penny, were printed for broad circulation (GWSAWS 1909).

Fawcett shows here her mounting frustration with the political leadership's response to the impasse between militant, suffragist and government action. This is a speech of Empire: Fawcett includes pointed reference to the violent protests in India, where 'native' men were being included in discussions to resolve tensions, while women were not allowed to do the same in the UK. Note also Fawcett's views on suffrage for 'native' men in South Africa, the first realisation of the growing military threat in Germany and the response of the UK colonies. However, the speech also includes undercurrents of a debate happening in the NUWSS itself regarding potential support for universal suffrage, to which Fawcett was at this time, for tactical reasons, opposed (see Rubinstein 1991, 159).

*

At a public meeting in support of Women's Suffrage, held at the Athenaeum, Glasgow, on November 23, 1909 – Mr C. Cameron Corbett, MP,[3] in the chair – Mrs Fawcett, LLD, said:

MR Cameron Corbett, Ladies and Gentlemen – I must first of all thank the Chairman for his very kind references to myself and my association with the Suffrage movement,[4] and I should like, if I may, briefly to refer to what he has said with regard to some excesses and some acts of violence which have been committed by those who are called the militant Suffragists.[5] I regret and condemn these actions, but I should like to add that I have no sympathy at all with those who withdraw their support from our movement because they disapprove of and discountenance violence. It is scarcely necessary to point out that if those who believed in the righteousness and justice of a cause withdrew from it because they disapproved of the conduct of some of its advocates, we should find ourselves in a very awkward position indeed in regard to almost everything we hold dear. Take the position of religion itself. I do not want to go into detail, but if we were to abandon Christianity because we disapprove, highly disapprove, of some of the things done by those who advocate Christianity – done for the sake, as they thought, of advancing Christianity – we should be in the same position as those who are prepared to abandon their advocacy of Women's Suffrage because they disapprove of the excesses of certain extremists. (Hear, hear.) I suppose there are few people now in any part of the world who would justify such action as that which characterised the administration of the Inquisition in Spain and in Holland and different parts of Europe in the fifteenth and sixteenth centuries.[6] We look on that as a great crime and a great blot on the history of Christianity, but we should be unpardonably lacking in our Christian duty if, because of anything that was done in the name of religion at that time, we assumed an attitude of indifference regarding the spread of the Christian faith.

I should like, in moving this resolution, which I have great pleasure in doing, to explain first of all what it is exactly we are asking for, because I find, notwithstanding that we are constantly explaining what our principles are, a great many people imagine we are asking for a great deal more than we are in fact asking for. We are not asking that every woman should have the suffrage. That would be an enormous and an unwieldly change in our Constitution. It would immediately place about eleven million persons on the registers.[7] We are not proposing to do anything so extravagant. We are only asking that those who fulfil the qualifications that entitle men to vote should not be debarred from voting simply from the fact of their being women. (Applause.) If effect were given to that principle, it would entail a very moderate addition to the existing register. There are at the present time all over the three kingdoms of England, Scotland and Ireland, 7½ millions of men upon the register. If what we ask were granted, it is reckoned there would be an addition to the existing register of not more than 1½ to two million women. Speaking roughly, it would be an addition of one woman to every four men. (Hear, hear.) I do not think, therefore, the most timid need become alarmed by the addition of such a proportion of women to the register as this. There would be four of you to one of us, even if the worst, as you may so regard it, should happen. (Laughter.) We are not proposing to overwhelm you by a horde of women voters.

Then we are sometimes attacked from the opposite point of view. It is said that what we are asking for is simply adding to the representation of the wealthy and propertied classes. This is also an entire misrepresentation and misunderstanding. We have carefully analysed the registers, which we are able to do from the fact of women being on the municipal registers, and we have analysed them in a large number of constituencies. Mr Philip Snowden,[8] the well-known Labour Member – who is not likely to be misled into under-estimating the representation of property – has stated in his place in the House of Commons that he has examined these registers himself, and he is convinced that if what we ask for were granted, the women added to the electorate would belong in an overwhelming majority to the working classes. He stated they would be in as large a majority as 84 per cent of the whole.[9] We are asked sometimes why we do not work for something more extensive than this. I have tried to meet that objection by saying that, in my opinion, adult suffrage is both undesirable and unnecessary at the present time. Lord Crewe, when the Liberal women waited upon him, also stated on behalf of his party that they are not prepared to advocate adult suffrage.[10] It is not a question of practical politics at all, so that you need not be frightened at the prospect of seeing the men out-voted. Ours, I may here remark, is a non-party Society. We belong to all parties. We have Conservative friends, Liberal friends and Radical friends. It would be suicidal mania on our part as a Society if we adopted the cry for adult suffrage. We should immediately lose the support of every Conservative and Unionist, a loss we could not contemplate without enormous regret. I noticed the other day Mr Winston Churchill, when speaking on Women's Suffrage, said he was of the same opinion as that expressed by Mr Cameron Corbett – namely, that the Women's Suffrage movement had been greatly thrown back by the recent disorders that have taken place – and he said that he himself was not prepared to take any part at all in advocating Women's Suffrage until those disorders had ceased. And he said something more than that. He said no responsible Government could possibly take up the question in a practical manner until these disorders, which we regret and condemn, had ceased to take place.[11] Well I don't think that is the attitude of a practical statesman. (Applause.) It seems to me it is very much like a physician who, if called in to see a patient who was raving in a delirium, turned round and said, 'He is in dreadful condition; I will do nothing whatever for him until he is tranquil and quiet. As soon as he has recovered you can send for me again.' (Laughter.) These disorders are a symptom of social and political unrest. They should be dealt with by statesmen in a statesmanlike manner. Members of the Government should not shut their eyes to them, but should seek to discover the causes of these disturbances, and should remove the causes from which they spring if it is within their power to do so. (Applause.) Mr Winston Churchill is doubtless a very interesting and versatile young man[12] – (laughter) – I was about to call him a statesman, but I don't think I can apply to him that expression. I happened to be in Manchester at the time he was seeking re-election for North-west Manchester, and I took part with the Women Suffragists of Manchester in a deputation to him eighteen months ago to ask him his views on Women's Suffrage. He had been in Parliament then a good many years, but he had never given any really active support to the movement. We were anxious to extract from him a definite and explicit statement. I was there as representing the National Union, but there were many ladies with me who belonged to Manchester and who had taken an active part in former elections in promoting the success of the party to which Mr Churchill belongs. Hitherto that gentleman had been very careful and circumspect in his answers, and when now interrogated he assumed a most profoundly solemn demeanour and exclaimed: 'Ladies, I am your friend. I will be your friend in the Cabinet.'[13] (Laughter.) The Licensing Bill was then before Parliament, and he said the Government were going to rise or fall with the fate of that Bill. He said he had inquired from his friends at the Colonial Office what had been the practical influence of Women's Suffrage in New Zealand[14] and Australia,[15] and he said, with an intense solemnity which I can hardly convey to you, that he had been informed, on the highest authority, that Women's Suffrage had been a great power, especially in the cause of temperance. We could have told him that without this special inquiry of his friends at the Colonial Office, or this waiting for cables from New Zealand and Australia. (Hear, hear.) But times have changed. Why is it that Mr Churchill now says he can do nothing for Women's Suffrage? Would it not be still a power for the promotion of temperance? Is not temperance as important a cause now as it was eighteen months ago? I do not understand the position of a politician who will trim his sails with every wind in that way. (Applause.) In April 1908, Mr Churchill expressed himself about Women's Suffrage in highly flattering terms. He was at that time anxious to conciliate the good opinion of a large number of women in Manchester who had been accustomed to work in support of the party to which he belongs. He said, 'I will try my best as and when occasion offers, because I do sincerely think the Women Suffragists have a logical case, and one in respect of which there is a great popular demand amongst the women.'[16] But what a very different attitude is that which he now takes up! He now says he can do nothing for Women's Suffrage, and that no responsible Government can have anything to do with it until all Women Suffragists are perfectly quiet, tranquil and well-behaved. (Laughter.) He treats us as if we were a group of naughty children:

> Until I see that again you have smiled
> I will not take the trouble to nurse such a child.[17]

(Laughter.) I would contrast with this attitude of Mr Churchill the attitude that has been taken up by men who really deserve the name of statesmen. I would mention particularly the name of Lord Morley with regard to the disorders and unrest that have been manifested in our great dependency of India during the last few years.[18] (Applause.) There are a group of people in India – not a very large one, perhaps, but still an important one – who are earnestly demanding to have a larger share in the government of their own country. We all grieve that that demand has been accompanied by a most terrible series of crimes and attempted crimes. Only a few days ago we were startled to see an attempt had been made on the life of the Viceroy, Lord Minto, and his wife when they were driving to a public place in India,[19] and last summer public feeling was outraged by the murder of that well-known man, Sir Curzon Wyllie, at the Imperial Institute.[20] The disorders and crimes which have marked the political movement in India might, in the view of some persons, be thought to justify the withdrawal of all official sympathy and assistance from the cause itself. But what has been the attitude of Lord Morley and other statesmen? They have not said, 'We will do nothing until India is perfectly tranquil, content and quiet.' No, they have grappled with the difficulty before them in a statesmanlike manner. (Applause.) Lord Morley, before he introduced the legislation which has gone through both Houses of Parliament,[21] gathered together around him a number of people in London responsible, as civil servants and in other capacities, for the government of India, and he put the whole case before them in a statesmanlike manner. In the course of his address he said, 'We are in India in the presence of a living movement, and a movement for what? For objects which we ourselves have taught them to think are desirable objects; and unless we can somehow reconcile order with the satisfaction of those ideas and aspirations, the fault will not be theirs; it will be ours; it will be the breakdown of British statesmanship.'[22] (Hear, hear.) I would apply that to our own movement. We have here a living movement. No one can doubt it; ours is a living movement and a movement for objects which every great and far-seeing English statesman has taught us to think are desirable objects – the right to a share in self-government and in the citizenship of our country. We say that if the Government cannot somehow reconcile order with the satisfaction of our reasonable demand, the fault will not be ours; it will be theirs; it will mark the breakdown of British statesmanship. (Applause.)

Then again, we had Mr Asquith speaking at the Lord Mayor's banquet, referring with justifiable complacency to the recent political settlement in South Africa and drawing attention to the fact, familiar to us all, that the two white races lately at each other's throats, burning and slaying with all the marks of enmity and antagonism between them, are now reconciled, and have drafted the Constitution of a United South Africa loyal to the British throne. In referring to the adjustment of this serious difficulty and to the promulgation of the new Constitution, Mr Asquith said, 'Great is the magic, as all our history proves, of free institutions.'[23] Yes, but why not try that magic on us? (Applause.) We are as much entitled to have that magic tried on us as the Boers and the British are in South Africa.[24] (Hear, hear.) After saying this, Mr Asquith made an appeal to the future Parliaments of United South Africa to remember the position of the native races, and he expressed 'confidence that the same width of outlook, the same liberality of temper, which has made possible the Union will be exercised as widely and as promptly as policy and prudence may allow in extending to the broadest possible limits both the rights and privileges of citizenship'. The Prime Minister drew the attention of the coming South African Parliament[25] to the desirability of making provision for the natives of South Africa to have some direct share in the government of their country. But he uttered not a syllable in regard to women either in South Africa or here. No magic of free institutions for us! Why not apply the same principles here in Great Britain in regard to the position of women? It is a startling thing to those of us who have spent any time in a great colony like South Africa or in India, and found ourselves in the position of being one of a handful of white people surrounded by a great mass of coloured population, to remember that by the admission of natives to the franchise in South Africa – and they are admitted in Cape Colony[26] – every British woman is placed in a position of inferiority to that occupied by the Kaffirs[27] of Cape Colony, as she is also to that of the Maori women of New Zealand,[28] who have more power in developing and moulding the future of the Empire than we have in England. (Hear, hear.) Why should the Maori women be in a superior position politically to that held by the women of England? (Applause.)

Our old friends – the anti-Suffragists[29] – are never tired of saying women ought not be admitted to the franchise because women are not practically familiar with the intricacies of international trade, with naval and military questions, and so forth. I wonder if they have ever taken part in political elections and seen what sort of knowledge of international trade or of naval and military problems is possessed by the ordinary man who goes to the poll. (Laughter.) It is an entire misconception of the very ground-work of representative institutions to think that this knowledge is called for from the ordinary elector. We do not expect the ordinary elector to be an expert on all these great and difficult questions. It is the work of a man's lifetime to grasp even one of them. Even an ordinary member of Parliament is not called upon to be an expert in banking and international trade. It is enough for him to be able to grasp certain great principles so that he may be guided to appreciate a difficulty sufficiently to decide him which party he shall support. (Hear, hear.) On the other hand, there are a considerable number of questions in which women may be considered as experts. I think women are experts in a great many questions which deal with the welfare of the home; they are experts upon questions affecting the upbringing of those children who are to be the future citizens of the Empire, and they have made themselves experts to a large extent in matters concerning the administration of the poor law, nursing and so forth, questions which will have an important influence on the preservation of infant life, on housing and temperance and things of that kind. (Applause.) All these are great and important questions which must be dealt with by legislation. Is it right and wise to exclude from all power of influencing the decisions of Parliament on these questions – to totally exclude – the women of the country, when it is they who know more about them than any other section of the population? (Applause.) I would refer for a moment to a very important question, which is important in the eyes of a very large number of men, and important, I think, in the eyes of nearly all women – I mean the place of religion in education. It is a great and important subject, and it is dealt with from time to time by Parliament in a manner which is not altogether satisfactory to the great mass of women of this country. (Hear, hear.)

The mothers of the children are the last people to be consulted as to what kind of religious instruction should be given to the children in the schools which the State provides. We see what has happened in countries like France and Italy, where democracy has been developed on exclusively masculine lines, and where there is universal suffrage for men and no suffrage at all for women,[30] who are shut out from all share in the public affairs of the nation. Women are there more rigidly excluded than they are in England, because here we have local franchises, and women have the power of sitting on the local educational bodies.[31] In France, however, there is no representation of women at all in these respects, and in both France and Italy religion is absolutely excluded from the public education that is granted by the State. Two remarkable letters appeared in the *Times* last week on this very question, and it was shown in them that so rigidly and absolutely is all reference to religion excluded from the education of the children that in the reading books in French schools such expressions as 'Thank God' and 'God forbid' are rigorously shut out lest the children should ask to what Being these exclamations referred. One of the French ministers boasted, 'We have put out in the Heavens the lights that will never be lit again.'[32] Can you imagine that if the mothers had their chance of influencing the Government of the country such words as these and such actions as these would have been permitted? I don't think it possible that such would have been the case. (Applause.) If you go to the churches in France, you see women of all classes joining in worship, but you see very few men indeed. There is this great gap in thought between the men, who are Freethinkers, and the women, who are religious-minded.[33] Religion there is almost entirely in the hearts and minds of the women, and it is not a desirable thing there should be this great chasm between the men and women, and that the women should have no chance of influencing the way in which their children should be educated. (Hear, hear.)

Mrs Humphry Ward had said we make a great mistake in imagining we could not without Women's Suffrage get a reform of the laws that are unjust to women.[34] True, after much toil and labour, the Married Women's Property Act[35] and the Guardianship of Children Act[36] have been placed on the statute Book. The Guardianship of Children Act is, however, a very imperfect measure. It does not give a married woman any legal guardianship over her child in the lifetime of her husband. The law recognises but one parent – the father – except in those unhappy cases where the child is born out of wedlock, and there the only parent recognised by the law is the mother.[37] That is a great blot on our marriage laws; and we know there are others which ought to be removed and which we lack the motive power to get dealt with in Parliament because we have not the women's vote behind it. (Applause.) Then there is the question of the administration of the law, the great severity with which offences from which men are the chief sufferers are punished compared with the leniency towards offences from which women and girls are the chief, or indeed the only sufferers. Three and five years' penal servitude for blackmailing, and only three months, with the alternative of a fine, for injuries to children, which most women regard as worse than murder. But it is not only for the sake of better laws and juster administration that I care for Women's Suffrage. If the King would appoint a Royal Commission[38] with instructions to so alter and modify the legal system of this country as to place both sexes on an equality, I should be pleased, because I should be certain that such a Commission would never be appointed unless the suffrage were on the threshold. I do not desire Women's Suffrage simply because of what women would get in the way of justice before the law; I desire it also on account of what it would help women to be, on account of its influence in moulding and developing the characters of women themselves. (Applause.) It is not good for women and it is not good for men that women should be encouraged to think they have no part or lot in the great affairs of the nation. The home is a great and important national interest. I want women to realise that, and also that they should take a real and keen interest in national affairs, that they should have a sense of citizenship and look to their duties in the home as sacred duties which are as truly work for the nation as any which men may be called upon to perform. (Applause.) We have it that in the Colonies, where women have the power of making their voice heard and their influence felt, the effect has been a great gain to the men as well as to the women. It has, we are assured, deepened the sense of responsibility in men, and it was after women got the vote in Australia that men grappled seriously with the difficult problem of national defence.[39] That is exactly the sort of thing which I think any reasonable person would expect to see take place. Women and men do not live in water-tight compartments. They are husbands and wives, brothers and sisters. What influences one must influence the other, and it is to the advantage of the entire nation if one-half of it is lifted up to a higher sense of national responsibility. (Hear, hear.) I am getting almost to the end of my time, but I should like to refer to one other thing before I sit down. I have already referred to the influence of Women's Suffrage in Australia and New Zealand. We are constantly getting testimony to it from those who have had political experience of its working. Not long ago, Mr Price, the Premier of South Australia, was over in England, and, in reply to a question he said, 'Women Suffrage has done exactly what we expected it to do. It has purified politics. No man with a shady reputation can hope to be returned. Moral and social questions receive careful and serious attention, and education is watched and encouraged. I put that down to the silent, sensible, and sober influence of the women.'[40]

The anti-Suffragists say that they dread Women's Suffrage because they fear that women would have no care for the Imperial greatness of our country. Have they forgotten already that in the black week of the South African War, New Zealand, the first Colony to give women the suffrage, was also the first Colony to send its sons to stand side by side with the sons of Great Britain in the battlefields of South Africa?[41] Then, again, this last spring, when we were all startled to hear of the rapid development in Germany of her naval equipment, a cable immediately came from New Zealand which offered a Dreadnought as a free gift to the Mother Country in that crisis.[42] (Applause.) There was no bargaining or asking, 'If we do this for you, what are you going to do for us?' but simply a cable offering a Dreadnought, followed by a similar cable from Australia. I did feel proud that those two Colonies that had given the suffrage to women were the first to come forward with these generous offers. (Applause.)

Before I sit down, let me make an earnest appeal to the men who are here to use the electoral power that they have to insist on Parliament dealing seriously with the Women's Suffrage question. (Hear, hear.) You have a power given to you – the vote; we, on the other hand, find it very difficult to get the serious attention of Parliament, because we have no voting power behind us. As *Punch* has very humorously put it, 'Women cannot get the suffrage because they have not got the vote.'[43] (Laughter.) Men should use their electoral power to forward the cause of Women's Suffrage. It is no use saying, 'I am in favour of it; I suppose it will come,' and then doing nothing to make it come. I attribute a great deal of these regrettable disorders to the fact that the men in favour of Women's Suffrage have not exerted themselves as they ought to get a practical measure passed through Parliament. (Hear, hear.) Members of Parliament pay attention to those who have votes rather than to those who have not. Use your electoral power and our enfranchisement will be near at hand. (Applause.) I make an earnest appeal to the women also to come and help on this movement. We are bound to win, and we want not only to win, but to win in the right way. We are engaged in a cause that should call for the very best powers of heart and mind that any of us may possess. It is a cause in which, as a great writer has said, 'not to have been by instinctive choice on the right side is to have failed in life.'[44] (Loud applause, during which Mrs Fawcett resumed her seat.)

Transcribed from a copy in University of Glasgow Archives and Special Collections. No known copyright restrictions.

Notes

1. Although the pamphlet is dated 22 November, the lecture was delivered on 23 November 1909 (*Common Cause* 1909c, 395).
2. Elsie Maud Inglis (1864–1917), physician and surgeon, and honorary secretary of the Edinburgh National Society for Women's Suffrage.
3. Archibald Cameron Corbett (1856–1933), Scottish Liberal Party and then Liberal Unionist Party politician, MP for Glasgow Tradeston, and 'one of the staunchest friends to the suffrage' (*Common Cause* 1909e, 478), serving on the committee of the National Union of Suffrage Societies. Note the mistake made in his initials in the published pamphlet.
4. In his opening remarks, Cameron Corbett 'said that his own belief, and it was a very profound one, was that no man or woman could ever adopt any method which he or she believed to be ugly in itself, either for personal or political ends, without being the worse for it. This movement was a right movement. If any man or woman had turned aside from the Suffrage movement, which was based on justice, by the conduct of some of its advocates, then that was an unworthy turning aside from duty' (*Common Cause* 1909d, 458).
5. See Sections 25 and 28.
6. The Inquisition was a group of separate institutions within the Catholic Church intended to maintain Catholic Orthodoxy, regulating faith and combating heresy in response to the Protestant Reformation (Peters 1989).
7. The Third Reform Act of 1884, although it had established a uniform franchise throughout the country, still only allowed approximately 60 per cent of men in the UK to vote (see Section 11, note 1). Estimations of the size of the existing vote, and the effect proposed reforms would have on it, were regularly used in Parliament (see the *Times* 1909c). The number of names on the parliamentary register for the whole of the UK on 1 January 1910 was 7,695,717, and the estimated male population at that time was 11,911,618 (Rosenbaum 1910, 473). Fawcett presumably extrapolates her estimated size of the 'eligible' female vote from figures such as these.
8. Philip Snowden (1864–1937), Viscount Snowden, elected Labour MP for Blackburn in 1906.
9. Snowden said 'at least 82 per cent of the women enfranchised would belong to the working classes' (HC Deb 1908, cols 267–70).
10. Robert Offley Ashburton Crewe-Milnes (1858–1945), 1st Marquess of Crewe, Liberal politician, then leader of the House of Lords. On Saturday, 4 September 1909, Crewe-Milnes met a deputation

of the Warwick and Leamington Branch of the NUWSS prior to a Budget demonstration in Victoria Park, Leamington Spa. A full account is available in the *Leamington Spa Courier* 1909.
11 On Monday, 18 October 1909, a deputation of nine of the WFL waited for Churchill after his address to a meeting of the Dundee Women's Liberal Association, asking him to give a definite pledge to forefront the question of women's enfranchisement at the next election. In his 'candid and truthful' reply, he said, 'I am quite sure that, while these tactics of silly disorder and petty violence continue, there is not the slightest chance of any Government that will be called into power, or of any House of Commons which is likely to be elected, giving you the reform which you seek' (*Times* 1909f, 10).
12 Churchill was a week short of his 35th birthday at the time of the speech, and had served in the House of Commons first as a Conservative MP (1901–4), then as a Liberal (1904–8), then as president of the Board of Trade and the youngest Cabinet member since 1866 (Jenkins 2001, 129). Newly appointed Cabinet members had to seek re-election, but Churchill narrowly lost the Manchester North West by-election to a Conservative candidate in May 1908, later succeeding in the safer seat of Dundee.
13 The meeting took place on Tuesday, 14 April 1908, at the offices of the Liberal Federation. A report at the time describes Churchill's demeanour: '"We never expected Mr Churchill would do anything," said a prominent member of this organisation [NUWSS] when spoken to yesterday, "as he is rather a shuffler"' (*Manchester Courier and Lancashire General Advertiser* 1908; see also *Southern Echo* 1908).
14 See Section 21, note 27.
15 See Section 21, note 22.
16 On Wednesday, 15 April, Churchill held a meeting, where questions were raised (around brewers and barmaids and working conditions) followed by a question on suffrage (*Dundee Courier* 1908). Churchill's reply in full is featured in *Votes for Women* 1908.
17 A reference to the poem 'For a little girl that did not like to be washed' in the popular *Rhymes for the Nursery* by Jane and Ann Taylor, first published in 1806 and available in many editions: 'What! cry when I wash you, not love to be clean! / Then go and be dirty, not fit to be seen: / And till you leave off, and I see you have smiled, / I can't take the trouble to wash such a child' (Taylor and Taylor 1806, 52).
18 The Liberal politician John Morley (1838–1923; see Section 21, note 10) was made secretary of state for India in 1905, retaining the post in Asquith's new Cabinet of 1908. When rioting had occurred in the Punjab and Bengal in 1907, he countenanced patience and compromise, appointing an Indian politician, Satyendra Prasanno Sinha (1863–1928), to the viceroy's council in 1909, and aimed to achieve practical reforms within the Indian provincial context (Hamer 2004).
19 On 13 November 1909, Gilbert John Elliot-Murray-Kynynmound (1845–1914), 4th Earl of Minto, viceroy of India (1905–10), and his wife, Mary Caroline, née Gray (1858–1940), were visiting Ahmedabad when bombs were thrown at their car, but the bombs did not explode: 'a sergeant who was riding by the side of the carriage knocked the first bomb aside with his sword . . . the second bomb struck the wrist of a servant who was holding an umbrella over Lady Minto' (*Times* 1909h).
20 Sir William Hutt Curzon Wyllie (1848–1909), army officer serving in India from 1867, then as an official of the British Indian government, holding a variety of senior posts including that of agent to governor-general in central India. Returning to the UK in 1901, he was the political aide-de-camp for the secretary of state for India. On Friday, 1 July 1909, 'While attending, with Lady Wyllie, an entertainment given to Indians by the National Indian Association at the Imperial Institute, South Kensington, London . . . Wyllie was assassinated, almost under the eyes of his wife, by Madan Lal Dhingra, a Hindu extremist student, whom Wyllie had helped, who suddenly fired at him with a revolver, killing him instantly . . . These crimes were precursors of terrorist crimes in India' (Brown 2004).
21 The Indian Councils Act of 1909, also referred to as the Morley–Minto reforms, introduced a series of measures reforming the principles of membership of imperial and local councils in India, allowing Indian representatives limited rights (Metcalf and Metcalf 2006, 160–1).
22 Lord Morley (see note 18) gave an after-dinner speech as a guest of the Indian Civil Service Dinner Club, at the Trocadero Restaurant, on Thursday, 11 June 1908 (*Times* 1908a). Fawcett reused this example, and quote, in an open letter to the chancellor of the exchequer in 1911, after a week where hundreds of militant suffragettes rioted in the vicinity of the House of Commons and disrupted a speech by the prime minister at the City Temple (*Times* 1911f).

23 For Asquith's full speech at the Guildhall banquet on Tuesday, 9 November 1909, see *Times* 1909g. The draft constitution led to the South Africa Act 1909, ratifying the union of four colonies (Cape of Good Hope, Natal, Orange River Colony and Transvaal) into South Africa (Brand 1909).
24 See Section 23 for Fawcett's relationship to the South African War.
25 The South African Union Parliament first sat on 4 November 1910, after parliamentary elections held in September (*Times* 1910b, 5–7).
26 The vote had been open to men of all races who met the required £25 property franchise in Cape Colony since 1872. The Franchise and Ballot Act 1892 raised the property qualification, disenfranchising poorer voters, including large proportions of non-White men (Evans et al. 2018).
27 A historical name for the Nguni people of south-eastern Africa, now historical and offensive: it was already derogatory by the time it was used here (OED 2020b).
28 The 1893 Electoral Act had given all New Zealand women the vote, including Māori, although voting was segregated, with general and Māori voting taking place on different days until 1951 (Brookes 2016, 199).
29 See Section 30.
30 Women were enfranchised in France in 1944 and achieved partial suffrage in Italy in 1925, with full suffrage in 1945.
31 See Section 17, note 4.
32 Eugène Tavernier (1854–1928), French journalist, writing in the *Times* of the 'Religious Question in France', reports on comments by René Viviani (1863–1925), then socialist minister of labour, on efforts to 'root out all religious belief' (1909a). This was followed up by a column regarding the organisation of the anti-religious 'free-thinkers' (1909b, 5).
33 Fawcett had previously made this over-simplified statement about secularisation regarding the men and women of Belgium; see Section 11, note 20.
34 See Section 30.
35 See Section 11, note 14.
36 The Children and Young Persons Act 1908; see Pickard (2014, 28).
37 'Unless the husband is disqualified by misconduct, desertion or cruelty he it is who, in the last resort, determines the child's domicil, religion, education and upbringing' (Greig 1924, 239). A feminist campaign led by NUSEC from 1919 eventually resulted in the 1925 Guardianship of Infants Act, which established equality between mothers and fathers in relation to rights over children (Brophy 1985, 45–7).
38 A royal commission is an ancient mechanism to establish 'an ad hoc advisory committee appointed by the government (in the name of the Crown) for a specific investigatory and/or advisory purpose'. These were popular during the Victorian era, with 'some 388 commissions . . . established between 1830 and 1900'. They have become less frequent since World War II (Barlow 2013).
39 The first Australian federal army unit was established in 1899, and the new Australian Army founded in 1901 (Palazzo 2001): Fawcett reaches here to connect this directly to women's suffrage.
40 Thomas Price (1852–1909), South Australian United Labor Party leader and premier of South Australia 1905–9, on a visit to London in April 1908 (*Women's Franchise* 1908b).
41 See Section 30, note 36.
42 In March 1909 it became clear that Germany was putting in place the manufacturing infrastructure capable of 'extraordinary growth' that would soon allow them 'a navy more powerful than any at present in existence', and that Great Britain must take action 'if we are to retain the supremacy in rapidity and volume of construction' (*Times* 1909b). There were suggestions that Canada and Australia should offer the cost of a Dreadnought to Great Britain (the predominant type of battleship in the early twentieth century, named after the successful HMS Dreadnought, launched in 1906; *Times* 1909d). However, it was New Zealand who first gave a concrete offer: 'With feelings of pride and satisfaction I transmit to your lordship following message. Begins. Government of New Zealand offer to bear cost of immediate building and arming by the British Government of one first-class battleship of the latest type. If subsequent events show it to be necessary will also bear cost of second warship of the same type. Ward, Prime Minister. Ends' (*Times* 1909e).
43 An anonymous poem that appeared in the satirical magazine *Punch*, titled 'Any Premier to Any Suffragette': 'Dear Lady, while your aims / Have my sincere approval, / And while I own your grievance claims / Immediate removal; / Yet since your cause and you / The frivolous make

nought of, / And that might risk a vote or two – / It isn't to be thought of! / So, lady, it is plain / While at your claim one man shies, / Until you have a vote 'tis vain / To ask us for the franchise' (*Punch* 1906).

44 Walter Pater (1839–94) in his 1885 novel *Marius the Epicurean*: 'Surely, evil was a real thing; and the wise man wanting in the sense of it, where not to have been, by instinctive election, on the right side, was to have failed in life' (Pater 1885, 239).

34
Picturing Fawcett: Dame Millicent Fawcett, CBE, LLD, by Annie Louisa Swynnerton, c. 1910

Figure 12: Dame Millicent Fawcett, CBE, LLD, by Annie Louisa Swynnerton. Preparatory oil painting, likely painted c. 1910. Sold at Christie's London in 1959 (when the photograph was taken), Sotheby's in 1970 and Christie's again in 1973. Current whereabouts unknown. Picture from negative held at the National Portrait Gallery. Permission given for use by the National Portrait Gallery.

Figure 13: Dame Millicent Fawcett, CBE, LLD, by Annie Louisa Swynnerton. Exhibited 1930, likely painted c. 1910. Oil on canvas. © Tate, London 2020. Licensed for use.

Manchester-born Annie Louisa Robinson Swynnerton (1844–1933) was a pioneering figure painter, the first woman to be elected an associate member of the Royal Academy of Arts in 1922 and a strong advocate of women's rights (Thomson 2018). She had close connections to prominent figures in the women's movement, including the Garrett family, painting Agnes Garrett in 1885 (see Crawford 2002, 292–6).

Fawcett is 'rosy cheeked and quizzical' (Crawford 2002, 295) in her honorary degree robes: in 1899 she was the first woman to be given an honorary degree (Doctor of Laws, LLD) by the University of St Andrews, for 'her splendid services in the cause of women's education' (Blackburn and Mackenzie 1899), and from then on, she regularly campaigned in her doctoral attire (see Figure 7). This portrait may have been painted to mark or foreground that achievement (Herrington and Milner 2019, 104), although, based on comparison to photographs of Fawcett, it is likely to be dated c. 1910. It is not mentioned in Fawcett's memoir (1924) or Strachey's biography (1931), and is undated. In 1930 it was described as having been 'painted, I believe, some twenty years ago for an admirer of Mrs Fawcett, who, however, did not appreciate its rare art quality' (J. B. 1930b).

The location is 'very likely the first-floor back room of 2 Gower Street' in front of the fireplace designed by Rhoda and Agnes Garrett: 'natural light is excluded, the sitter is lit by the glow from the fire and from candles. The painting places the sitter, despite the formality of the attire, in a very comfortable domestic scene' (Crawford 2002, 296). The traditional chiaroscuro technique used is reminiscent of Swynnerton's earliest figure paintings, and continues her 'remarkable faithfulness to the unadorned appearance of her middle-aged female sitters' (Herrington and Milner 2019, 104). In the preparatory portrait Swynnerton foregrounds the red buttons of the St Andrews gown, but she omits them from the final version. The quill in the preparatory sketch is removed to favour a less formal arrangement of hands, and the placement of the high (perhaps Japanese) screen adjusted.

In May 1930, a few months after Fawcett's death, the finished portrait was included in the Royal Academy's *Portraits of Distinguished Men and Women* exhibition, described as 'The Late Dame Millicent Fawcett C.B.E, LL. D'. It received a positive reception: 'if there is a picture in the Academy which deserves to be called important it is this one' (Bury 1930); 'one of the finest examples of [Swynnerton's] art, and a memorial to the great leader of the women's suffrage cause in her most vital personality' (J. B. 1930b; see also Konody 1930 [*Daily Mail*]; J. B. 1930a [*Manchester Guardian*]; and the *Times* 1930). Other commentators were not so emphatic: 'while we admire the painting as a picture, it is not our

Dame Millicent which it portrays' (*Woman's Leader* 1930). Shortly after the exhibition, it was purchased by the Trustees of the Chantrey Bequest (a legacy fund left by the sculptor Sir Francis Chantrey [1781–1841] to obtain artworks made in Britain for a public national collection of British fine art) and presented to the Tate Gallery, where it has remained since (*Vote* 1930b). This was only 16 years after the suffragette Mary Wood attacked a John Singer Sargent portrait with a meat cleaver in the Royal Academy's annual Summer Exhibition (Bonett 2013). The previous year, a 1927 portrait of the militant suffragette Mrs Emmeline Pankhurst (1858–1928) by Miss Georgina Brackenbury (1865–1949) had been accepted by the National Portrait Gallery (*Woman's Leader* 1929d; National Portrait Gallery 2021d): these decisions by the galleries indicating the changing views towards and acceptance of the women's movement by general public and establishment.

The unframed, preparatory copy is likely the one in Swynnerton's own collection at the time of her death: 'Portrait of Dame Millicent Fawcett in academical gown, 29 in. by 24 in.' (Christie, Manson and Woods 1934, 12). This was sold at auction by Order of the Executors on Friday, 9 February 1934, with Swynnerton's 'artistic effects of the Studio'. Although the preparatory study has appeared in various London auctions since, its whereabouts are unknown, and this 1959 negative held in the National Portrait Gallery archives is its only pictorial record.

35
Broken windows – and after, 1912

London Daily News. Saturday, 9 March 1912,[1] 4.

The period between 1909 and 1912 saw both further violence from the militants and frustrated parliamentary attempts to move towards women's suffrage. In January 1910, the anti-suffragist Liberal prime minister, H. H. Asquith, had promised in his general election campaign to introduce a Conciliation Bill which would extend suffrage to property-owning women. A hung Parliament resulted, but a non-partisan Conciliation Committee of 36 members of Parliament was established, chaired by Lord Lytton,[2] proposing legislation that was supported by the suffrage societies and both front benches (*Times* 1910a). Parliamentary time was scheduled to discuss this women's franchise bill, which passed its first and second readings, but Asquith prevented it from proceeding, calling another general election on 18 November. The WSPU saw this as a betrayal, and the resulting protest march to Parliament became known as 'Black Friday', when police and male bystanders subjected 300 suffragettes to humiliating physical and sexual violence (Solomon 1911), changing the relationship between the militant suffrage movement and the police (Crawford 2001a, 560).

In May 1911 the Second Conciliation Bill won a majority of 167 in the House of Commons (*Times* 1911b), but was dropped by Asquith in November 1911 in favour of a manhood suffrage bill (*Times* 1911d), with few believing 'that the House of Commons would accept at present an amendment which would institute womanhood as well as manhood suffrage – an amendment, that is to say, which by a stroke of the pen would make the majority of the electors in the country women': this had 'blown the Conciliation Bill into the air' (*Times* 1911e). February 1912 saw a Third Conciliation Bill introduced that would establish a household qualification for women occupiers, of whom there were approximately one and a half to two million[3] in the United Kingdom. A second reading was planned in late March (*Times* 1912b). The WSPU opposed this, demanding a return to a bill giving votes to women on equal terms with men (*Votes for Women* 1912).

In this newspaper column, written at the start of March 1912, Fawcett reasserts her constitutional approach to suffrage in the face of escalating threats, violence, and protests from the militants. There is a sense of hope, here – while also a plea for calm and a distillation of her argument, presented in 'Wanted: A Statesman',[4] for adequate political leadership to see and support their cause in advocacy of the upcoming vote, despite the violent actions of a minority.

Fawcett believed that achieving the vote was near, writing:

> Women's Suffrage has been debated again and again in Parliament, and no bill has been defeated on second reading since 1886. The majority in 1910 was 110; in 1911 it was 167. It will be an outrage which will be deeply and permanently resented if the result of all this continuous work and effort is to give more representation to men and none at all to women (Fawcett 1912g, 333–4).

On 28 March, the Third Conciliation Bill was defeated by an adverse majority of 14: Irish Nationalists had voted against the bill due to concerns that a vote for women would be used to prevent Irish Home Rule (*Times* 1912e). 'Our disappointment was intense. We had thought that now, at least, after nearly forty years of work, we had a definite prospect of success' (Fawcett 1924, 202). Privately, Fawcett wrote in July 1912, 'We suffragists have had a time of great trial just lately seeing our good cause sullied & driven back by the criminal folly of a few fanatics. It is no good reasoning with them. They are not open to reason' (Fawcett 1912h, 1).

*

There has been an undoubted crisis in the Suffrage movement since last Friday, caused by the intense indignation naturally aroused by the window-smashing raids of a small group of the so-called Suffragettes on that day[5] and subsequently.[6] The anti-Suffragists are exploiting this feeling of indignation for the benefit of anti-Suffragism.[7] This is natural and unavoidable. The errors of Suffragists are the meat and drink of the anti-Suffragists. But although we recognise that the anti-Suffragists are entitled to their glee, and though we may feel in a measure

> This is your hour and the power of darkness,[8]

yet I think we may call upon them to restrict themselves within the somewhat prosaic limits of fact. Their joy is so hysterical that they have given rein to their fancy and are circulating many inventions. For instance, in an evening paper I read yesterday, March 6th: 'Mrs Fawcett is in despair'; and a few lines further on that Mr Birrell[9] had said 'he had finished with Woman's Suffrage for ever'.[10] As I knew I was not in despair, and had never uttered a syllable to justify anyone in saying I was, the new *obiter dictum* attributed to Mr Birrell did not disturb me; and this morning I am not surprised to see that he characterises the statements attributed to him as 'absolute bunkum'.[11]

Another instance of the hysteria of the anti-Suffragists at the present moment is found in their attitude to the Conciliation Bill. The window-smashing suffragists are dead against the Conciliation Bill; they have adopted the line of 'all or nothing'.[12] Therefore, say the anti-suffragists, we are so angry with them that we will give them what they want and destroy the Conciliation Bill which they have been opposing for the last four months.

Evil for evil

And now a few words on our own position and attitude. One never turns to the Bible without finding something that is a staff to lean upon, and on looking up the exact wording of a passage that was running in my head I came upon: 'See that none render evil for evil unto any man . . . Rejoice evermore. In everything give thanks . . . Prove all things; hold fast that which is good . . . Faithful is He that calleth you Who also will do it.'[13] These words suffice for our marching orders for the present. What are we suffragists striving for? A natural recognition that the woman is as necessary to the successful building of a well-ordered State as she is necessary to the building up of the family. Some suffragists, not a very numerous group,[14] have temporarily lost all faith in human honour, in human sense of justice, and are attempting to grasp by violence what should be yielded to the growing conviction that our demand is based on justice and common sense, and that the continued exclusion of women from the representative system of the country is false to the facts of human life.

We have made immense progress. The number of our societies, which was 211 a year ago, is now 365. The number of our subscribing members has run up in the same interval from over 21,000 to over 30,000.[15] The whole tone of the country about our question has changed in the direction which we desire. There is no cause for despair; there is every cause for confidence and hope. The National Union of Women's

Suffrage Societies, of which I am the president, has held fast all through its career, now extending to more than 40 years, to peaceful and law-abiding methods of work. We have no relish for the task of condemning the methods pursued by other suffragists, but we have on three several occasions in 1908,[16] 1909[17] and 1911[18] categorically condemned methods of violence not for the sake of imputing blame, but to make our own position and methods clear, and we have had the satisfaction of seeing the methods of order becoming more and more widely accepted.

Seek the causes

There is another point of view which should not be left out of sight. Statesmen are the physician of the body politic.[19] When things go wrong, when, for instance, women, who are by nature gentle and refined, take to conduct which is condemned, and in my opinion justly condemned, as characterised by insensate violence, these disorders are symptoms of a social disease to the cure of which statesmen should apply themselves. Punishment, of course, will be meted out; the funds of the offending society may quite properly be charged with the cost of the actual damage done. But all this, natural and inevitable as it is, only touches the symptoms and not the cause. Force is no remedy. Statesmen must seek the causes and endeavour to remove them. The causes are similar to the causes which produced the unrest in India; the social and educational status of large masses of the population have changed without being accompanied by a corresponding change in their political status. In India, as Lord Morley said, the leaders of the unrest were striving for objects which we ourselves had taught them were desirable objects, 'and unless we can somehow reconcile order with the satisfaction of those ideas and aspirations, the fault will not be theirs; it will be ours: it will be the breakdown of British statesmanship'.[20]

When Lord Morley's plan for extending some measure of representation to the people of India was before the country,[21] the air was thick in India and in London with crime and attempted crime. The lives of the Viceroy, Lord Minto, and his wife, were attempted in India;[22] and Sir Curzon Wyllie and an Indian gentleman were murdered in cold blood by a fanatic at the Imperial Institute at the very moment when the Indian Bill was before the House of Lords.[23] Did this cause Lord Morley to withdraw the measure by which he hoped to combine the maintenance of order with the satisfaction of those ideals of self-government which educated natives of India had learned from Western civilization? The question needs no answer. Lord Morley's advice to the House of Lords and through that House to the country was 'Stick to your guns', do not be frightened away from prosecuting to their completion measures which you have deliberately advocated as necessary to produce a harmony where there is now discord. It may be hoped that British statesmanship will see that similar reasoning applies to the present situation. The crimes and errors committed by the women are far less serious than the crimes committed in connection with India. But surely the path of wisdom is the path which Lord Morley adopted with regard to India. This, at any rate, is the manly and courageous course.

Transcribed from a copy in the British Library.
No known copyright restrictions.

Notes

1. See also a letter from Fawcett published in the *Times* on the same day, on 'Constitutional Suffragists and the Militants' (Fawcett 1912d).
2. Victor Alexander George Robert Bulwer-Lytton (1876–1947), 2nd Earl of Lytton, Conservative member of the House of Lords and member of the Men's League for Women's Suffrage.
3. See Section 33, note 7.
4. Section 33.
5. On Friday, 1 March 1912, the 'militant section of the woman suffrage party embarked . . . on an unprecedented campaign of wanton destruction of property in the West-end of London . . . some hundreds of women sallied forth carrying large muffs in which hammers were concealed, and at a given moment . . . went up to the plate-glass windows of shops and deliberately smashed them . . . Along the Strand, in Cockspur-street, in the Haymarket and Piccadilly, in Coventry-street, in Regent-street, in part of Oxford-street and in Bond-street . . . the large plate-glass windows of traders of all kinds . . . were ruined in this ruthless way . . . The police . . . made many arrests, amounting, it is said, in all to 124 . . . An attack was also made on the Prime Minister's house in Downing-street . . . "This is a demonstration" [Christabel Pankhurst] said, "simply to show that we are determined in our militant tactics to get the vote"' (*Evening Mail* 1912).
6. On Monday, 4 March, there was further window-smashing in Kensington High Street, Knightsbridge and Brompton Road. Lord Cromer's house was attacked, Post Office windows were broken, and there was an attempt that evening to raid Westminster (*Times* 1912d).
7. An anti-suffrage meeting had been held in the Albert Hall on Wednesday, 28 February 1912, and it was thought the militants had carried out their window-smashing in response: many of the speakers had used the violent tactics of the militants as a reason to oppose women's suffrage (*Times* 1912c). A column describing the aftermath of the events of Friday, 1 March, in the *Anti-Suffrage Review* personally attacks Fawcett, describing the 'unctuous rectitude in the Public Press' of those who have washed their 'hands of allied militancy and pleaded for a clear distinction between militants and non-militants . . . All this attitudinizing, however, comes too late in the day. It is moreover insincere. So long as it suited their purpose, the so-called constitutional Suffragists made common cause with the militants . . . The utterances and acts of the "stars" of Suffragedom – Mrs Fawcett, Lady Betty Balfour and Lady Selborne – show that no hard and fast dividing line can be drawn between professing non-militants and professing militants' (*Anti-Suffrage Review* 1912, 68).

8   Luke 22:53.
9   Augustine Birrell, British Liberal Party politician, then chief secretary for Ireland, who was opposed to the tactics used by the militants.
10 'One thing is becoming plain – namely, that the militant Suffragists have, for the time being . . . killed the chance of Women's Suffrage . . . It is no wonder that the temperate advocates of the principle, such as Mrs Fawcett, who was labouring for the cause when Miss Christabel Pankhurst was in her cradle, are in despair to see their life's work undone in a day' (*Pall Mall Gazette* 1912a). See also the *Daily Express* 1912 for the original source of Birrell's quote.
11 Fawcett paraphrases: 'A Statement on the suffrage position attributed to Mr Birrell appeared in the *Daily Express* yesterday . . . This statement was, I understand, brought to the notice of Mr Birrell today, and the Chief Secretary promptly denied that he ever used such words to any one. Further, he repudiated the implication that he has ever associated himself with the Suffragette propaganda' (*Pall Mall Gazette* 1912b, 3).
12 The WSPU stated that a government plan to abandon 'the Manhood Suffrage Bill in favour of a Plural Voting Bill, and inviting Suffragists to place their hopes once again upon the Conciliation Bill . . . would meet with the uncompromising and militant opposition of the Women's Social and Political Union. We of this Union have decided finally and firmly that we will not rely upon the Conciliation Bill or any other private Member's measure for Woman Suffrage . . . As self-respecting women we demand the withdrawal of the Manhood Suffrage Bill: but we demand with equal vigour the introduction in its stead of another Government Bill giving votes to women on equal terms with men' (*Votes for Women* 1912).
13 1 Thessalonians 5:15–24.
14 By August 1907 there were 70 WSPU branches (Rosen 2013, 88). The WSPU 'never divulged total membership figures and claimed not to keep a membership list' but it has been calculated that approximately 12,400 new members joined between 1909 and 1912 (Rosen 2013, 211), and of those, 'the minority of members who remained "militant" rather than "feminist" . . . probably numbered about 1000' (Purvis 1994, 323). In 1914 the WFL had 53 branches, but only 4,000 members (Smith 2007a, 44). In total, between 1905 and 1914, approximately 1,000 women (mostly, but not all, WSPU members) and 40 men were imprisoned as a result of the various 'deeds' they undertook for the cause.
15 See Section 37, note 2.
16 See Section 28.
17 'The National Union of Women's Suffrage Societies strongly condemns the use of violence in political propaganda, and being convinced that the true way of advancing the cause of Women's Suffrage is by energetic, law-abiding propaganda, reaffirms its adherence to constitutional principles, and instructs the Executive Committee and the Societies to communicate this resolution to the Press' (*Common Cause* 1909a, 341).
18 Fawcett publicly condemned violence at various points in 1911: 'force is no argument. We shall win, I believe, through steadfast courage and persistent work in proving to men and women all over the country that what we are asking is reasonable and would promote the well-being of the nation' (Fawcett 1911). See also *Common Cause* (1911c, 633) for a later statement: 'Mrs Fawcett, who moved the resolution [to adhere to constitutional methods, at the NUWSS council meeting on Friday, 8 December], said that it was necessary in view of the misapprehension existing in the minds of many people to make it clear that the National Union had never been associated with methods of violence.' Fawcett probably refers here to the open letter she sent David Lloyd George (1863–1945, then chancellor of the exchequer) in early December 1911: 'I regret and deplore the disgusting scenes . . . The National Union has always condemned methods of violence. My Suffrage friends are constantly asking me, Can nothing be done to stop them?' (*London Daily News* 1911b).
19 See Section 33.
20 See Section 33, note 22.
21 See Section 33, note 21.
22 See Section 33, note 19.
23 See Section 33, note 20.

36
Picturing Fawcett: Millicent Garrett Fawcett, 1912

Figure 14: Millicent Garrett Fawcett, bromide print by Lizzie Caswall Smith, 1912, with Fawcett's signature and quote from *Troilus and Cressida*.[1] From the Women's Library at LSE. No known copyright restrictions.

Although this image featured in *What I Remember* with a note stating that it was taken in 1918 (Fawcett 1924, 247), a head-and-shoulders portrait from the same sitting appears on the front page of the *Common Cause* on Thursday, 22 February 1912, depicting the 64-year-old Fawcett as 'President: National Union of Women's Suffrage Societies' (1912b), attributed to Lizzie Caswall Smith of 309 Oxford Street. Another head-and-shoulders portrait from the same sitting is used in the *Common Cause* in a 'Personalities of the Pilgrimage' spread on 25 July 1913, attributed to Miss Lizzie Caswall Smith: 'Mrs Fawcett, President of the National Union of Women's Suffrage Societies (with 450 Societies and nearly 50,000 members) who has been on Pilgrimage for three weeks' (*Common Cause* 1913h). A popular photograph, this full-body portrait was used for Fawcett's obituary in the *Vote* (1929a) and attributed to Caswall Smith a few weeks later (*Vote* 1929b, 271).

Lizzie Caswall Smith (1870–1958) was a noted and exhibited studio photographer in the early 1900s, specialising in theatre and society subjects. She was likely trained by her brother, John Caswall Smith (1867–1902), whose business she inherited on his early death (National Portrait Gallery 2021c). Caswall Smith's Gainsborough Studio on Oxford Street, operating from 1902 to 1920, was a short walk from Fawcett's Gower Street home. As well as photographing many famous actors, 'Smith was a supporter of the suffrage movement and photographed many suffragettes including Christabel Pankhurst and Flora Drummond, images that were made into postcards' (National Portrait Gallery 2021c). Two different photographs of Fawcett taken by Caswall Smith 'appear on postcards with the caption "President of the National Union of Women's Suffrage Societies"' (Crawford 2001a, 563): at least one of them was from this sitting. Such photographs were a necessary part of promotional messaging for the Suffrage campaign, and Fawcett regularly 'consented to be photographed . . . on purpose to give us the pleasure of having a new postcard of her'; these postcards were then sold by the NUWSS Literature Department at 2d. each to raise funds for the cause (*Common Cause* 1912e).

Notes

1 Characteristically, Fawcett slightly misquotes: 'Things won are done; joy's soul lies in the doing' (1.2.173). See also Section 21, note 17.

37
Who's for us? For him are we, 1912

'The friends of women's suffrage'.
Daily Citizen, Manchester. Monday,
4 November 1912, 4.

Throughout the late nineteenth and early twentieth centuries, the franchise was not the only topic that took up much parliamentary discussion time. Another was the campaign for Irish self-government, or 'Home Rule', which dominated discussions of Irish nationalism, from the founding of the Home Government Association pressure group in 1870 through to the eventual founding of the Irish Free State in 1922, accomplished alongside mounting protests, armed insurrection, rebellion and the Irish War of Independence (Jackson 2003).

Fawcett had a long association with Ireland: since the 1870s she had 'visited Ireland repeatedly, and made many firm and lifelong friends there, and she did a great deal of very effective speaking against the Home Rule proposals' (Strachey 1931, 127). She undertook many speaking tours for the Unionist cause, and was engaged with the proposed admission of women to degrees at Trinity College Dublin (Fawcett 1924, 94–102; Strachey 1931, 150; Rubinstein 1991, 119). Ever the imperialist, Fawcett fervently believed that the best course for Ireland was to remain part of the Union, stating:

> For Ireland, the issue of this struggle will involve the maintenance or the destruction of civil and religious liberty, not for the loyal minority only, but for the whole country. For England, the issue of the struggle will involve the destruction or the maintenance of her greatness and honour; whether she shall capitulate to men who boast their hatred of her, or defy them and stand true and steadfast

to those loyal Irish men and women who know, from bitter experience, that all they most value in life depends upon their remaining under the protection of the Parliament of the United Kingdom (*Cambridge Chronicle and Journal* 1892; see also Rubinstein 1991, 116).

Although the protests for Home Rule and the women's franchise were contemporaneous, Fawcett noted the difference in treatment by the authorities:

> There is a certain element of humour afforded by the spectacle of those who condoned every kind of ferocity and crime in pursuit of Irish Home Rule being driven almost beside themselves by the much milder degree of criminality which has been perpetrated by the suffragettes (Fawcett 1909c, 147).

The political machinations of these two campaigns interacted at a crucial point for women's suffrage (Crawford 2003). By 1910 Home Rule had looked increasingly possible: after the 1910 election the Irish Nationalists held the balance of power in the House of Commons, and concessions were made to them. The failure of the Third Conciliation Bill by a slim majority against in March 1912 was caused by the Irish Parliamentary Party, who believed that votes for women would result in the defeat of their own cause (see Section 35). A few weeks after, in April 1912, a Home Rule Bill was introduced that would grant Ireland self-government (*Irish Independent* 1912): women would not be entitled to vote in Home Rule Ireland.

In this newspaper column, we see how this continued to play out throughout 1912. From 1910 onwards all Labour MPs had voted in support of women's suffrage, and in early 1912 the NUWSS and the Labour Party formed an electoral alliance, with the Labour Party becoming the first major political party pledging to include votes for women in their manifesto and the NUWSS establishing an 'Election Fighting Fund to sustain Labour candidates and to defeat the Liberals' (Bartley 1998, 53). Fawcett made much of this relationship, even though she herself was a Liberal Unionist, showing how politically flexible she was prepared to be. In August 1912 she described Labour as 'The Best Friends of Women's Suffrage' (Fawcett 1912e): finally she had support from the 'statesmen' that she had argued for (see Section 33). In November 2012 a Labour MP, Philip Snowden, attempted to introduce an amendment to the Home Rule Bill that would include women's suffrage:

Fawcett here argues for its support, but it failed a few days later. One further attempt was made in May 1913 to give women the vote, in a Representation of the People Bill: this was again blocked by Irish Nationalists (HC Deb 1913a, 1913b). These were the last attempts made to win female suffrage before World War I.

*

This line of George Meredith's, 'Who's for us? for him are we',[1] is a precise and accurate statement of the election policy of the National Union of Women's Suffrage Societies. It appears to me the only consistent political policy which a non-party, non-militant organisation like ours could take up. Our union consists of over 400 societies spread all over England, Wales and Scotland,[2] and includes women of all classes and of all parties, as well as a good proportion who have separated themselves from party alliances because the party to which their inclinations would lead them to belong cannot make up its mind to say 'yea' or 'nay' to the fundamental question whether representative government ought to represent the whole population or only half of it. With these differences, what binds us together is our enthusiasm for women's Suffrage, and we unite, as our democratic representative organisation enables us to do, in supporting in elections the best friend of women's suffrage. Everybody knows that the two main parties, Liberals and Conservatives, are divided on the question of women's votes,[3] and the Irish Party is temporarily, at all events, actively hostile,[4] while the Labour Party stands out as the only party definitely and officially pledged to the great cause for which the National Union of Women's Suffrage Societies exists.[5]

The National Union Executive Committee, after consultation with all its societies represented in council meetings, has resolved to take note in future political actions of this divergence of view between the Labour Party and all other parties, to recognise the fact that the Labour Party has made our cause its cause, and is pledged up to the hilt, if words have any meaning, to take advantage of any and every opportunity which the vicissitudes of political life may afford, to remove from the women of this country the stigma of complete political disfranchisement.[6] This is why we of the National Union advise our friends throughout our societies to support the party which supports us. Not that we do even this with a hard and fast absolutism. We shall not support any Labour candidate who is not personally satisfactory on the suffrage question. And there are men not a few in the other parties who have shown by staunch and steadfast friendship to our cause that they can stand by us, even under all the malign influence of party pressure exercised against us. Never under any circumstances will the National Union oppose these tried and trusted friends. But with these two exceptions, when Labour men are standing in a contested election, we regard them, other things being equal, as the best friends of suffrage because they have the support of their party behind them, which the candidates belonging to other parties have not.

England behind Denmark

A parallel to our case exists at the present moment in Denmark and Sweden. About a year ago, as the result of a General Election, the Liberal Party in Sweden was returned to power.[7] The gentleman who became Premier was a member of the Men's League for Women's Suffrage.[8] One of the first bills given notice of by his Government was a Women's Suffrage Bill, which was accordingly announced in the King's speech at the opening of the Swedish Parliament last February.[9] A somewhat similar political situation exists in Denmark. A Liberal Government has been returned to power,[10] and one of its first acts has been to give notice of the introduction of a Women's Suffrage Bill.[11] What should be the action of all suffragists in Sweden and Denmark? To this question it seems to me there can be but one answer. It is obvious that they should support the party which has espoused their cause, which in this case happens to be the Liberal Party. If their own party preferences are so vehement that they cannot do this, let them confess it honestly; but do not let them attack those who are comparatively free from party bias as political partisans because they can honestly and enthusiastically give political support to the party which has made the great principle for which they contend – namely, political rights for women – a plank in its platform.

Let no one suppose that the National Union is so devoid of political sense as to send down to a constituency in support of a Labour candidate workers and speakers who are out of sympathy with the Labour movement. We have between 35,000 and 40,000 members,[12] some of whom are Liberal, some Conservative, and some supporters of the Labour Party. We have therefore an ample field of selection, and we naturally choose those among our workers who are thoroughly in sympathy with the Labour Party to support Labour candidates in contested elections.

Miss Courtney's letter, which has recently appeared in the columns of the *Daily Citizen*, sufficiently emphasises the complete disagreement of the National Union of Women's Suffrage Societies with the recently announced election policy of the Women's Social and Political Union.[13] This seems to be 'Who's for us? Against him are we.' The WS and PU single out for special attack the one party which has, from its formation, supported votes for women, and calls upon the Labour Party to do what it is obviously impossible they should do, i.e., vote against everything they have been returned to Parliament by their constituents to support in order to defeat the Government. Our line of policy is a very different one. We support the best friends of suffrage everywhere; and because among parties the Labour Party has shown itself the best friend to suffrage, we give special support to the Labour Party. It is unnecessary here to repeat for the thousandth time that the Labour Party have, of their own initiative and in pursuance of their own principles, given their support as a party to women's enfranchisement. What we expect of them is that they all keep the promises and pledges which they have given, not secretly to the National Union, but openly and publicly to their own followers again and again, to the effect that no Franchise Reform Bill will be acceptable to them which excludes women from voting, and that they will fight for the women's cause when the Bill is in Committee, clause by clause,[14] with all the strength that is in them.

Votes for Irish women

An occasion has arisen which will give the Parliamentary Labour Party an immediate opportunity of showing the strength of their convictions upon the question of women's enfranchisement. This will be when Mr Snowden's[15] amendment to include the women now on the municipal register in the Irish electorate is reached next Tuesday.[16] A parrot cry will be set up that this is a question which ought to be left to an Irish Parliament to decide.[17] But if this is a sound argument, why was the Franchise Reform Bill introduced at all? It profoundly modifies both by enfranchisement and disfranchisement the existing electorate, and whatever the electorate is in Great Britain will also be the electorate for the Irish Parliament.[18] It is impossible to have it both ways. Whether the Parliament in Westminster has the right to alter the existing franchise for all three kingdoms[19] or it has not; but there is manifest absurdity in saying it may set up manhood suffrage without consulting the Irish Parliament, but must not admit women to any share of representation at all. Numbers of petitions have been received from Irish borough and county councils, including those of Dublin, Cork and Limerick, in favour of women's suffrage.[20] How many Irish public representative bodies have petitioned Parliament in favour of manhood suffrage? I have never heard of one. On Wednesday last, Mr Asquith announced that after the first nominated Senate of the Irish

Parliament, the Government would recommend that all future Senates should be elected by proportional representation, the areas being the four provinces and not the counties.[21] This important decision on an absolutely new principle is taken without consultation with the Irish Parliament and apparently to the complete surprise of the Irish members;[22] and yet we shall probably hear member after member with his tongue in his cheek saying, when Mr Snowden's amendment comes on, that the enfranchisement of Irish women is a question which must be sacredly reserved for the decision of the Irish Parliament.

If the Labour Party stand firm on their fundamental principle of suffrage for both sexes, they can secure the passing of Mr Snowden's amendment, or such a big reduction in the normal Government majority as will amount to a moral victory. It is absolutely erroneous to regard the amendment as hostile to Home Rule. Mr Snowden is a convinced Home Ruler.[23] The Women's Liberal Federation are ardent Home Rulers to a woman,[24] and kept the Home Rule flag flying when many who are now actively waving it were inclined to put it in the background. The Women's Liberal Federation passed a resolution at a recent representative council meeting urging the Government to make provision for the inclusion of women voters in the electorate for the proposed Irish Parliament.[25] What we expect 'the best friends of women's suffrage' to do this week is to support Mr Snowden's amendment and secure that Irish women shall be among the electors of the new Irish Parliament.

Transcribed from a copy in the British Library.
No known copyright restrictions.

Notes

1. George Meredith (1828–1909), English novelist and poet. This is an apt quote of the repeated refrain from 'A Ballad of Fair Ladies in Revolt' (1883, 130–53), in which, while evoking nostalgic chivalry, Meredith voices the aspiration of women to be treated as equals alongside men, and the need for men to support women in achieving representation. 'We may be blind to men, sir: we embrace / A future now beyond the fowler's nets. / Though few, we hold a promise for the race / That was not at our rising: you are free / To win brave mates; you lose but marionettes. / He who's for us, for him are we' (Meredith 1883, 141).
2. Formed in 1897 when many suffrage societies around Britain combined, the NUWSS was the largest organisation campaigning for votes for women. By 1909 it had 13,429 members from 130 societies; in 1910 that had increased to 21,571 members from 217 societies; in 1911 there were 26,000 members (Crawford 2001a, 439). By late 1912, its membership was growing by 1,000 members a month (Hume 1982, 190).
3. The position of the main parties on the question of women's suffrage was not clear, given the complex variety of opinions which existed within the parties (see Bartley 1998, 67–71). The NUWSS published pamphlets that compiled often conflicting statements made by leading politicians on the subject (NUWSS 1912 and 1913).

4   See Section 35.
5   Unfortunately, 'Labour was too insignificant a party to have much effect at all', having only 42 MPs at the time (Bartley 1998, 84).
6   This was a view shared by many fighting for the cause: 'The Labour Party, at its great meeting in the Albert Hall [in February 1912], pledged itself up to the hilt to do its uttermost to secure votes for women on the same terms as men. Mr Ramsay MacDonald, when asked whether he was prepared to turn the Government out on this issue, replied with an uncompromising, emphatic "Certainly!". This pledge is the most valuable asset we possess – outside our own invincible determination not to be tricked or put off any longer' (*Vote* 1912).
7   The general election was held in Sweden between 3 and 24 September 1911: importantly, this was the first election there with universal male suffrage. The Free-Minded National Association, a liberal party led by Karl Albert Staaff (1860–1915), obtained 40 per cent of the vote (*London Daily News* 1911a).
8   Staaff joined the recently formed MFKPR (the Swedish Men's League for Women Suffrage) in 1911 (Boheman 1911; Rönnbäck 2004, 103). The MFKPR was affiliated to the National Association for Women's Political Suffrage (*Landsföreningen för kvinnans politiska rösträtt*, LKPR) formed in 1901. The MFKPR was founded in 1911 and welcomed many esteemed politicians into its membership, ensuring that the LKPR had its own representatives in the Swedish Parliament (Backlund and Sjödahl Hayman 2011, 47).
9   At the opening of Parliament on 16 January 1912, the Swedish King said, 'Electoral reform had eliminated all distinctions between citizens based on conditions of wealth. The time had now come when in all justice the same privileges should be extended to women' (*Times* 1912a). However, women did not succeed in getting the vote in Sweden until 1919.
10 In the 1910 Danish Folketing election, Venstre, Danmarks Liberale Parti (literally 'Left, Denmark's Liberal Party'), a conservative-liberal party, was elected. It was only in power for one term, until 1913 (Nohlen and Stöver 2010, 524).
11 By the end of June 1910, 'a Bill giving women full suffrage and making them eligible for Parliament' had 'passed the lower house' (*Votes for Women* 1910). However, women did not succeed in getting the vote in national parliamentary elections in Denmark until 1915.
12 See note 2.
13 Dame Kathleen D'Olier Courtney (1878–1974) was the honorary secretary of the NUWSS from 1911 to 1915: 'Sir, The discussion on the relations between suffragists and the Labour Party which has recently taken place . . . reveals considerable misunderstanding of the actual position . . . It must be a matter for profound regret that suffrage societies should differ, not only as regards methods, but as regards policy: but the divergence of opinion between the National Union and the Women's Social and Political Union is so important that it is necessary to insist upon it . . . The National Union, with all other suffrage societies, stands for equal suffrage, but is willing to accept any measure of enfranchisement for women which can secure a majority in the House of Commons: it is unalterably opposed to any extension of the franchise to men which does not include women' (Courtney 1912).
14 This is a pointed reference to the dropping of the Second Conciliation Bill in May 1911 in favour of a Male Suffrage Bill (see Section 35), although Asquith indicated that an amendment to it could give some women the vote (see note 18).
15 Philip Snowden, 1st Viscount Snowden (see Section 33, note 8), Labour politician and supporter of women's suffrage, who married Ethel Annakin (1881–1951), feminist and socialist activist (see Figure 7).
16 Under Snowden's amendment, 100,000 Irish women would have been enfranchised. He maintained that 'the Imperial Legislature could not divest itself of the responsibility of providing for the representation of every class and interest in Ireland'. The amendment was rejected after a short debate on 5 November 1912, with 314 votes against and 141 in favour (*Times* 1912j).
17 The Government of Ireland Act 1920 created the Northern Ireland and Southern Ireland parliaments (Jackson 2003, xxvii).
18 The Franchise Bill was introduced on 17 June 1912, and aimed to substitute 'a simple continuous franchise for the mass of inconsistent provisions resulting from successive tinkerings in the law', abolishing plural voting in multiple constituencies and the university franchise, thus removing an estimated 525,000 existing votes, as well as redistributing seats and adding 2,500,000 male voters qualified by residence or occupation to the register (*Times* 1912g). Although the House of Commons initially voted in favour of the introduction of the

bill, it was dropped in January 1913 when the Speaker of the House of Commons ruled that it could not be amended to give votes to women (*Times* 1913a). This led to further and escalating militant action throughout the year, including window-smashing, arson, bombs and the cutting of major telephone wires (*Suffragette* 1913b, 258).

19 The Parliament at the time was the Parliament of the United Kingdom of Great Britain and Ireland, under the Acts of Union 1800: it had the right to change the franchise for England (including Wales), Scotland and Ireland.

20 In early summer 1912 a petition asking for the parliamentary vote for Irishwomen was organised by the Irishwomen's Suffrage Federation, a constitutional suffragist organisation, with support from the *Common Cause*. Gathering 3,000 names from across Ireland, it was presented to Mr Asquith in July (*Common Cause* 1912f, 275–6).

21 *Times* 1912h.

22 See the debate in the House of Commons on Thursday, 31 October 1912 (*Times* 1912i).

23 The day after this column appeared, Snowden said in the House of Commons, 'I have so far . . . given consistent support to the Home Rule Bill' (HC Deb 1912, 1061).

24 The Women's Liberal Federation, as part of the Liberal Party, had supporting Home Rule as one of its founding principles: 'Mr Gladstone in the election of 1886 had openly expressed his desire that women should assist in the carrying of home rule for Ireland. Women's Liberal associations were quickly formed all over the country and a general federation of these associations was constituted' (Sewall 1894, 416). By 1907, there were 613 affiliated associations, with an approximate membership of 83,000, and the Federation had as one of its objects 'To promote just legislation for women (including the local and Parliamentary franchise . . .)' (Liberal Publication Department 1908, 6). Fawcett had long thanked the Women's Liberal Federation 'for their convictions in regard to women's suffrage' (NUWSS 1892, 75), and held the view that 'their co-operation was of great and obvious importance' in 'uniting their efforts with those of the suffrage societies' (Fawcett 1911, 78).

25 *Times* 1912f.

38
Picturing Fawcett: Millicent Fawcett's Hyde Park address, 1913

Figure 15: Millicent Fawcett's Hyde Park address on 26 July 1913. Postcard. Photograph taken by Central News Agency, originally featured in the *Daily Telegraph* on 28 July (1913), reprinted in the *Common Cause* on 1 August (1913i) and the *Illustrated London News* (1913) on 2 August. From the Women's Library at LSE. No known copyright restrictions.

The summer of 1913 saw public spectacles from both suffragettes[1] and suffragists. On 26 July 1913, a rally of 50,000 supporters of the NUWSS met in Hyde Park: the culmination of a five-week, nationwide non-militant Women's Suffrage Pilgrimage (Crawford 2001a, 549–53; Robinson 2018).

This 'march of non-militant Suffragists from every part of England and Wales, converging on London on a given day' (Fawcett 1924, 209), had set out on 18 June, travelling along six main routes. Fawcett joined the pilgrimage herself on the Great North Road, a week before it reached London (Fawcett 1913b).

> The whole thing caught on to a tremendous extent . . . once people understood that we had no desire to hurt anybody nor to damage anything, they gave us a most cordial reception. The final demonstration was held in Hyde Park . . . There were nineteen platforms, representing our nineteen Federations (Fawcett 1924, 209).

> The largest crowd surrounded the central platform, where Mrs Fawcett, the president . . . described the pilgrimage as the biggest piece of work their organisation had yet called upon its members to undertake . . . 'A great deal is generally heard of the militants' she proceeded, 'but we have brought home to the villages and towns throughout the country that there are large masses of women pledged definitely to non-militantism. We are determined and as devoted to the cause of women's suffrage as any other women.' At the dispersal from this platform Mrs Fawcett was escorted by a cheering crowd (*Scotsman* 1913).

Fawcett later recalled, 'It was all like a wonderful dream' (1924, 210). The following day, there was a special service in St Paul's Cathedral, and Fawcett reflected in a letter written to Dr Jane Walker that evening, 'We have got on at a really wonderful pace when we remember what a tremendously difficult job we have tackled without an ounce of direct political power to back us up' (Strachey 1931, 270). Afterwards, promotional and collectible 'Postcards of the Pilgrimage' such as this were sold to raise funds for the NUWSS, and were 'in demand' (*Common Cause* 1913j).

Notes

1   See Section 46 for the suffragette processions following the death of Emily Wilding Davison in June 1913.

39
To the members of the National Union, 1914

Common Cause. Friday, 7 August 1914, 376.

On 28 July 1914, the Austro-Hungarian state declared war against the Kingdom of Serbia, followed at the start of August by the German Empire declaring war against the Russian Empire, Belgium and France. The British Empire declared war against the Germans on 4 August: World War I had begun (Hart 2014). In this letter, Fawcett immediately writes to members of the NUWSS about balancing their peaceful, constitutional support for women's suffrage with the needs of the nation at war.

The NUWSS executive committee decided the following day that 'ordinary political work will have to be suspended during the war', opting for a scheme by which it 'as a Union may make itself of use at this period of national crisis', focusing on the relief of distress and the provision of comfort, using the staff at headquarters as 'a bureau for receiving, classifying, and distributing offers of help' (*Common Cause* 1914c). Other suffrage societies took a similar line: the Women's Freedom League (WFL), at an emergency meeting on 10 August, reaffirmed 'the urgency of keeping the Suffrage flag flying' but decided their 'chief object will be to render help to the women and children of the nation' (*Vote* 1914). The Women's Social and Political Union (WSPU) temporarily suspended 'all activities', including dismissing organisers and ceasing publication of the *Suffragette*, although Mrs Pankhurst argued that this was because militancy must be 'rendered less effective by contrast with the infinitely greater violence done in the present war' (*Votes for Women* 1914c). Although the period from 1913 until the outbreak of war had seen extreme violence from the militants (*Suffragette* 1913b, 258), the government announced that all those imprisoned for 'crimes connected with the suffrage agitation' were to be released unconditionally (*Western Mail* 1914). The campaign for votes for women was therefore at a halt, but as Fawcett made clear, 'while they give themselves without sparing to the common weal, they must never forget the full dignity of their womanhood: there must be an absolute determination not to go back after the war is over to the old position of subordination' (*Votes for Women* 1914b).

Fawcett's final sentence in this letter is an attempt to remind members not only of the core aims of the NUWSS in pursuing women's suffrage, but also that they must now work together supporting a war which they had had no voice in declaring. The front page of the 14 August 1914 edition of the *Common Cause* quoted this final sentence in large font, with 'Women! Your Country Needs You!' (*Common Cause* 1914b).

*

August 5, 1914.

The greatest crisis known in all our national history is upon us. Nearly all Europe is at war, and our country is involved.

I have often made appeals to you to render services involving much hard work and self-sacrifice for the sake of the great cause which binds us all together. I have never asked in vain. I now make another and a different appeal. Let us members of the National Union bind ourselves together for the purpose of rendering the greatest possible aid to our country at this momentous epoch.

As long as there was any hope of peace, most members of the National Union probably sought for peace and endeavoured to support those who were trying to maintain it.[1] But we have another duty now. Now is the time for resolute effort and self-sacrifice on the part of every one of us to help our country; and probably the way in which we can best help it is by devising and carrying through some well-thought-out plan which can be worked at continuously over many months, to give aid and succour to women and children brought face to face with destitution in consequence of the war.

We have already appealed to our 500 Societies to make suggestions as to how best work of this kind could be done,[2] and we have received many letters from individual members of the NU expressing a hope that some plan on these lines will be devised and recommended by the NU as a whole.

The Executive Committee will be considering these plans to-morrow, and our Societies will be communicated with as soon as possible.[3]

In the midst of this time of terrible anxiety and grief, it is some little comfort to think that our large organisation, which has been carefully built up during past years to promote Women's Suffrage, can be used now to help our country through this period of strain and sorrow. 'He that findeth his life shall lose it, and he that loseth his life for My sake shall find it.'[4] Let us show ourselves worthy of citizenship, whether our claim to it be recognised or not.

Transcribed from a copy in the British Library.
No known copyright restrictions.

Notes

1. At the end of July, when war looked imminent, Fawcett had coordinated a manifesto from the IWSA that was delivered to the Foreign Office and foreign embassies in London: 'We women of twenty-six countries, having banded our-selves together . . . with the objective of obtaining our political means of sharing with men the power which shapes the fate of nations, appeal to you to leave untried no method of conciliation of arbitration for arranging international differences which may help to avert deluging half the civilised world in blood' (Fawcett and Macmillan 1914, 680).
2. The NUWSS mobilised quickly: 'At two days' notice a decision had to be arrived at whether or no [sic] to help organising a public platform in London upon which women of various Societies could voice the women's claim to be heard on questions of peace and war'. It filled the Kingsway Hall on Tuesday, 3 August, 'with nearly its full complement of two thousand women', discussing 'women's attitude to war in general, their earnest desire for peace, and their determination to use their utmost efforts to alleviate the inevitable misery that must follow' in 'accordance with the fundamental principles of Suffragism – that women have an equal right with men to speak and to be heard' (*Common Cause* 1914a). In addition, the NUWSS had begun to collect suggestions of help: 'We could not summon our six hundred societies to a Council, the railways were wanted for other work than ours, but we consulted our societies by post and laid before them our views' (Fawcett 1924, 217). 'A large number of such offers have already been made spontaneously, either by letter or in person, and a system of card indexes has been started. The authorities have been approached on this subject, and if they accept help of this kind, the work may assume large proportions' (*Common Cause* 1914c).
3. *Common Cause* (1914c).
4. Matthew 10:39.

40
Picturing Fawcett: Millicent Garrett Fawcett, 1914

Figure 16: Millicent Garrett Fawcett by Lena Connell, 1914, with Fawcett's signature. From the Women's Library at LSE. No known copyright restrictions.

Lena Connell (1875–1949) was a successful professional photographer (who only employed women). A member of the WSPU, she photographed many suffrage leaders, as well as artists, musicians and actors, in her London studio (*Vote* 1910). Portraits from this sitting appear on the front cover of the April 1914 *Woman's Kingdom* exhibition programme (NUWSS 1914), in the November 2014 *Ladies' Field* (Fawcett 1914b) and in a feature on Fawcett in the *Matron* as 'Matron of the Month' for June 1915 (p. 5).

Fawcett wears a gold and enamel pendant given to her in appreciation by the NUWSS in March 1913 (*Common Cause* 1913a), which she regularly wore at official events. A heraldic interpretation of 'National', 'Women' and 'Suffrage', it is based on the Royal Coat of Arms of the United Kingdom, with quadrants representing each country, displayed here on a lozenge, the traditional shape of the shield borne by unmarried (and therefore independent) women. The 'suffrage' colours of the NUWSS – red, white and green – surround this, in the form of garnets, pearls and green enamel. In heraldic convention, the ivy leaves represent strong and lasting friendship, and the white Tudor rose represents England, as well as love, purity and hope. The Arms on the brooch are slightly incorrect, as the tinctures of the second (Scotland) and fourth (England) quarters are inverted, which was probably a small mistake by the jeweller. There is no maker's mark, so this remains an anonymous piece (Cook 2021). Such creative use of heraldic convention was popular, and encouraged, on Artists' Suffrage League banners (Lowndes 1909): this is not a registered coat of arms (Petrie 2021). The values that Millicent Fawcett's co-workers appreciated in her – 'Steadfastness and Courage' (Crawford 2016c) – are engraved on the back of the brooch. The quoted phrase is taken from a message Fawcett gave to members of the National Union (Fawcett 1913a).

Fawcett can be seen wearing the pendant in Ellis's 1928 portrait (see Figure 22), and it also features on the 1932 memorial plaque to her in Westminster Abbey (see Section 55), retaining the characteristic colourway of Fawcett's pendant. It also appears on the left lapel of Wearing's 2018 statue, providing a unifying visual and representational link to the NUWSS throughout these photographs, artworks and memorials. Wearing portrays Fawcett in 1897, although she never received the brooch until 1913. The pendant/brooch itself was recently discovered in a locked drawer of a Fawcett Society desk: 'presumably Philippa Fawcett had returned the pendant to the London Society for Women's Service, the precursor of the Fawcett Society, and as time went by its existence and meaning had been forgotten' (Crawford 2016c).

It appeared on the *Antiques Roadshow* 'Pioneering Women Special' in 2018, marking the centenary of the first women in the UK winning the right to vote (BBC 2018), and in March 2020 it went on permanent display at the Museum of London (2020).

41
Life's cost, 1915

Conservative and Unionist Women's Franchise Review. October–December 1915, 41.

As early as 1870, Fawcett had criticised the suggestion that men and women should have different political rights because they possessed differences in strength (see Section 3): the 'physical force objection' (Brown 2018). She had since argued for suffrage along constitutional lines, decrying violent protest (see Section 35). However, her political position was to advocate for the use of force in Empire (see Section 23). World War I highlighted the tension between these stances and 'actual fighting and its corollary, national defence' (Fawcett 1914b, 7). While the immediate crisis of 1914 had seen the NUWSS suspend 'ordinary political work', pausing their peaceful campaign for suffrage in order to provide practical support to the nation at a time of crisis (see Section 39),[1] a debate then raged between pacifist and non-pacifist NUWSS leaders regarding how appropriate it was that an organisation which had sold itself as being non-violent and constitutional in action should be seemingly so supportive of war.

The commitment of the suffrage movement to the war effort was far from simple, with some NUWSS members avowed pacifists, some proposing a negotiated peace, some 'objecting to any activity which could be considered as promoting the continuance of the war' (Strachey 1931, 285) and some supportive of the government; with these differences of opinion, the NUWSS 'never at this time came near to offering unconditional support' (Newberry 1977, 416). This caused great strain within the movement, as Fawcett herself 'could not distinguish between the many shades of opinion . . . and it was a very serious blow to her to find them now following a course of action which was violently opposed to her sense of what was right' (Strachey 1931, 286).

In order to support the war effort, Fawcett insisted on making public pro-war utterances, including a speech at the February 1915 NUWSS Council meeting, where she declared, 'Until the German army is driven from France and Belgium . . . I believe it is akin to treason to talk of peace' (Strachey 1931, 289; see also *Common Cause* 1915a). This led to an immediate split in the NUWSS, with the resignation of all the other officers and 10 members of the executive committee (Newberry 1977, 419; Rubinstein 1991, 219–23). The result proved to be either a failure of or (at least) 'a great test of her leadership, and a matter whose outcome was of deep importance to the suffrage cause . . . complicated as they were by the strain under which everyone was living, and by the sundering of many ties of personal friendship and affection' (Strachey 1931, 285). Fawcett later avoided confronting these difficulties in her own published accounts and reminiscences of the suffrage movement. 'The painful events of the spring of 1915 . . . are really the only part of my fifty years' work for women's suffrage which I wish to forget' (Strachey 1931, 296).

Despite this personal price, Fawcett continued to argue that war was 'an imperative national duty' (1915b, 194–5). In 'Life's Cost', she 'draws the distinction between force and brute force which the pacifist fanatic is unable to make' (*Common Cause* 1915b).

*

I have read of some extreme pacifists, in their passion of opposition to the use of physical force, saying that they would rather be left to the mercy of an invading army than be protected by armed forces of any kind.[2] One is tempted to retort that they have never tried it and that they might possibly revise their position if they were brought out of the region of theory into the presence of actual facts. They, however, within the security and tranquillity of our Island home, invite one or other of the countries of the world – our own included, no doubt – to become a 'martyr nation',[3] and deliberately allow itself to be devastated and ruined by a merciless invader without offering the least resistance.

In so far as this attitude of mind is sincere and has been thought out to its foundations, it is worthy of respect, though it will probably command little assent, at least not enough assent to render it practically dangerous. The United States, for example, is far removed from the intrigues and quarrels of Europe.[4] While England is guarded by the silver streak, the United States of America is guarded by thousands of miles of ocean. Their people and Government are pacifists in a high degree and also idealists; their armed forces, whether by sea or land, are, compared with the armed forces of Europe, almost negligible.[5] But they have realised within the last twelve months that even thousands of miles of ocean are not a sufficient guard for their liberty and independence, unless they also have the use and control of physical force to protect them and safeguard their right to develop their own form of civilisation in their own way. Recent events have awakened them to the insecurity of their position; they show no disposition whatever to become a 'martyr nation'. On the contrary, we hear that the American Cabinet are taking steps to raise a national militia of half a million men and also to strengthen their navy and coast defence. Mr Garrison, their Minister of War, has stated that 'America in setting an example of pacifism to the entire world for many years, seemed justified at the time, but that events in Europe and the Far East have not justified such pacifism and indeed have reduced this country to a state of impotence'.[6]

As long as man consists both of body and spirit, men and governments must have all use and control of physical force and of other material things. Mind is greater than matter, we shall all agree, but to allow the more brutal among the family of nations to overcome and destroy the less brutal does not promote the rule of spiritual forces: rather it shows brutal materialism triumphant.

May I invite a brief consideration of what the policy of pacifist fanatics would involve?

In the first place, whether they like it or not, they are receiving at this moment the protection of the British Navy and Army against the invading hordes which let loose rapine and lust over helpless Belgium a year ago. We and they sleep tranquilly in our beds, night after night, giving no more consideration to the visits of aeroplanes than we give to other possible but not probable unpleasantnesses. We receive our daily supply of food unrestricted except by a slight increase in its cost.[7] All this is due to the protection we receive from the Navy. Besides the grand Fleet which everyone knows about,[8] there are the hundreds of men trawling for mines all round our coasts.[9] They work day and night for us, carrying their lives in their hands. Their work is to make the approach to our ports safe for the hundreds of ships which, week by week, bring us supplies of food from all quarters of the globe.

Let me describe one little incident of recent occurrence. Two ladies living at an east coast watering place planned a visit in a small boat to a fleet of seven trawlers, each carrying ten men, who had been working within a few miles of the shore ever since the war began. The ladies arrived at a thrilling moment. One of the trawlers had just been torpedoed. The other boats had rescued and brought in the crew, all except one poor fellow, who was drowned. The ladies saw the rescued men, white and cold with the shock. They will not forget easily what they saw, nor all that we owe to the unwearying vigilance and self-sacrifice of their work. Do we enough realise it? Are we sufficiently grateful for it?

However sincerely the more violent pacifists proclaim their abhorrence of receiving protection by means of armed force, they and we are, one and all, receiving it every moment that we live. It is part of life's cost. It is difficult to conceive how any of us can avoid continuing to receive it. We, pacifists and all, in peace as well as in war, are protected from burglary and murder and other inconveniences by a well organised police force. If all physical force is to be deprecated, this also is to be taken account of. Why not face the fact that physical force is not only harmless but useful and necessary. But like other useful and necessary things, like fire or alcohol, it has to be kept in its place. It is the servant and not the master. It must not, to quote Mr Asquith, be allowed to become 'the governing factor in regulating the relations between States',[10] or, as we suffragists add, 'between individuals'. We do not admit that because an average man could knock down an average woman, therefore he is fit to be a citizen and have a share in the government of the country, and she is not.

This indicates the essential resemblance between the anti-suffrage philosophy and the German philosophy of politics. Mrs Humphry Ward and her followers used to say, in days which now seem before the Flood, that 'the State is founded on physical force and physical force is male'.[11] We were wont to reply to this by a direct negative: 'The State is not founded on physical force but on Law and moral force, and physical force is both male and female.'[12] Now every one all over Great Britain, including the Prime Minister, is saying what the suffragists said. Not long ago at the Guildhall he said that the issue of this war was, 'Is right or is force to dominate mankind?'[13] What we were up against on a smaller scale as suffragists, we are now all up against on a larger scale as a Nation, struggling to preserve its ideals of liberty and Right against brute force. It is worth any price that can be exacted for it.

Transcribed from a copy in the British Library.
No known copyright restrictions.

Notes

1 Fawcett details what she believed the role of the NUWSS should be in wartime in a special supplement of *Ladies' Field*: 'The National Union of Women's Suffrage Societies, and doubtless other women's societies as well, have been approached from many quarters with the view of inducing them to use their organisation to promote recruiting; but we feel that our right line of activity is not in lecturing men upon their duty to their country, but in encouraging women to do theirs . . . At the present crisis, therefore, it seems to me that women's societies should

concentrate on those activities which seek to minimise, as far as possible, the damage to the race caused by the war. Hence, in the National Union we are encouraging our 600 societies and branches to co-operate with local relief committees to save the children and women from destitution, to watch over expectant mothers, and encourage, under a scheme originated by the Women's Co-operative Guild, local authorities to establish maternity centres to give effectual aid before, during and after childbirth to necessitous mothers' (Fawcett 1914b, 7–8).

2   Organised opposition to the war saw both conscientious objection and the founding of several associations in 1914, such as the Fellowship of Reconciliation and the No-Conscription Fellowship, whose members spoke publicly on pacifism, aiming to build 'solidarities of resistance' (Mitchell 2014, 47). There was much coverage of these types of arguments in the press.

3   This was a phrase commonly used to refer to Belgium, a neutral country which was invaded by Germany on 4 August 1914, suffering great atrocities as the German armed forces passed through it to outflank the French army: 'Soldiers fallen in vast numbers on the field of battle, innocent creatures massacred, towns and villages burnt to the ground, monuments destroyed, populations exiled: such are the horrors that made Belgium the Martyr Nation, and stirred the compassion of all noble hearts' (*Western Daily Press* 1914).

4   At the outbreak of war, the United States had adopted a policy of neutrality, which was fiercely debated (*Evening Mail* 1914). They did not enter the war until 1917 (*Evening Mail* 1917b).

5   'General Wood, Chief of General Staff . . . declared that if the troops were sent to war as they now are, without guns or ammunition, it would be absolute slaughter . . . The War Department believed that in the case of war with a first class Power an army of half a million would be needed' (*Londonderry Sentinel* 1914).

6   Lindley Miller Garrison (1864–1932), lawyer and secretary of war, in a telegram to the *Daily Telegraph* (1915). Fawcett lightly edits.

7   The policy of 'business as usual' dominated in the early years of the war, although government controls were introduced around the trade of foodstuffs, followed by rationing in 1918 (Paxton and Hessler 2012, 85).

8   The Grand Fleet was designed first as a deterrent, and also in readiness for an encounter with Germany's High Seas Fleet (the largest naval battle between them occurring in 1916, at the Battle of Jutland). It had approximately 160 naval ships; the size of the Grand Fleet varied throughout the war, with the number of battleships increasing over time. There was much coverage of the strength and spectacle of the Grand Fleet in newspapers throughout 1915; see, for example, the series of articles in the *Times* by the American war correspondent Frederick Palmer (1873–1958) from 16 October onwards (Palmer 1915).

9   'Upwards of 6000' fishermen 'were employed with their trawlers and drifters in the perilous work of mine-sweeping' (*Times* 1915b).

10 On 25 September 1914, seven weeks after the UK declared war upon Germany, the prime minister addressed a large crowd at the Dublin Mansion House in a recruiting meeting called by the Lord Mayor (following similar speeches in London and Edinburgh). 'It seems to me to be now at this moment as good a definition as we can have of our European policy – the idea of public right. What does it mean when translated into concrete terms? It means first and foremost, the clearing of the ground by the definite repudiation of militarism as the governing factor in the relation of States and of the future moulding of the European world' (*Times* 1914, 10).

11 Fawcett summarises here: the WNASL manifesto gave the main reasons why they opposed the concession of the parliamentary vote to women, including 'Because the complex modern State depends for its very existence on naval and military power, diplomacy, finance, and the great mining, constructive, shipping and transport industries, in none of which women can take any practical part. Yet it is upon these matters, and the vast interests involved in them, that the work of Parliament largely turns' (Ward 1908, 257).

12 Again, Fawcett paraphrases. She had opposed the physical force objection to women's suffrage since 1870; see Section 3 and Brown 2018.

13 In June 1915 Asquith inaugurated 'a national campaign in support of the War Loan and to initiate a concerted national movement for war economy': this was his closing argument (*Times* 1915a).

42
Lift up your hearts, 1916
Englishwoman. Vol. 29 (January 1916), 5–15.

By 1916, the effect of World War I on the working population was becoming apparent to all. A relaxation of trade union rules in 1915 had allowed women to undertake industrial work, with women being substituted for men across all industries: 'there was not a paper in Great Britain that by 1916–17 was not ringing with praise of the courage and devotion of British women in carrying out war work of various kinds, and on its highly effective character from the national point of view' (Fawcett 1924, 226).[1] As a result, democracy was also beginning to include women in its scope, and even the most reluctant of political leaders were beginning to change their views towards women.

Fawcett's speeches and articles on women's work in wartime both documented and extolled women's capabilities, while highlighting the lack of previous opportunities for women and the poor employment practices that contributed to their disempowerment. In 'Lift up Your Hearts',[2] Fawcett's unwavering patriotism shines through, but also her 'chief purpose', being 'the practical one of building on what women had achieved to improve their conditions in the post-war years'[3] (Rubinstein 1991, 234). Throughout, she maintains the moral argument for use of force in wartime, her dismissal of the pacifist approach and her support of the government (see Section 41). Strachey's ever-supportive view was that this was 'both tactically wise and politically expedient. The attitude of the National Union in turning its strength to the service of the country put its leaders into a very strong position when the suffrage question again came forward' (1931, 300–1). In actuality, there was a 'complex matrix' of suffrage organisations, taking various pacifist and non-pacifist approaches to the war effort, all of which added to the momentum of growing rights for women (Smith 2016, 93).

*

> These times strike monied worldlings with dismay:
> Even rich men, brave by nature, taint the air
> With words of apprehension and despair:
> While tens of thousands, thinking on the affray,
> Men unto whom sufficient for the day
> And minds not stinted or untilled are given,
> Sound, healthy children of the God of heaven,
> Are cheerful as the rising sun in May.[4]

These lines, which Wordsworth wrote in 1803, are applicable to our position in 1916; while rich men, 'brave by nature, taint the air with words of apprehension and despair', the men in the trenches and men and women at home earning their bread by daily toil, 'sound, healthy children of the God of heaven, are cheerful as the rising sun in May'. The gossip of the clubs and of the lobbies and smoking-rooms of the House of Commons finds no echo among the great mass of the workers, whether at home or abroad, whether men or women. These see clearly the national task which lies before them, and are determined to put it through by self-sacrificing labour in the trenches, in the mine or the factory.

Some of the 'Intellectuals', conceiving it their task to instruct other people in the first principles of national duty, inform mankind from time to time that they are prepared to guide the nation how to think and what to think about the war. If they could only see it, the relations of teacher and scholar should be exactly reversed. The sound political sense of the nation at large is much more to be trusted than is that of its would-be superior people. But we cannot expect the 'Intellectuals' to see this. They take the chair for one another at small meetings, and the chairman recommends the lecturer, or the lecturer the chairman, as 'a man who has raised hostility by making English people think about the war';[5] or they announce their readiness 'to educate the nation'[6] on the real principles on which a permanent peace can be secured. Nobody takes much notice, because every one has been thinking about the war all the time; and every one would be only too delighted if these wise men of Gotham[7] could produce a receipt for making war impossible. Many great and wise men, philosophers such as Plato and Immanuel Kant, warriors such as Henri IV and Napoleon, men of world-wide fame such as Dante, Erasmus, Grotius, Sir Thomas More, Bentham and Rousseau, have cudgelled their brains to find it and have failed. Let it be at once acknowledged that no such failure is final. It must indeed be remembered that the failure, such as it is, is only a comparative failure. As Miss Campbell Smith says in her introduction to Kant's *Essay on a Perpetual Peace*:

> War used to be the rule: it is now an overwhelming and terrible exception . . . It must never be forgotten that war is sometimes a moral duty, that it is ever the natural sequence of human passion and human prejudice. An unbroken peace we cannot and do not expect; but this is what we must work for. As Kant says, we must keep it before us as an ideal.[8]

There is, therefore, every reason why continuous effort should be made to find a basis of permanent peace, but the search should be conducted in a spirit of humility, and the self-appointed teachers should show a readiness to learn of their predecessors. If they would impress their fellow-countrymen, some of them must reconcile themselves to the painful fact that they themselves are ignorant and fallible in almost the same degree as those whom they seek to instruct. If they have been thinking about the war for seventeen months, so has every one else; if they are prepared 'to educate the nation', they must give some proof that they have some of the qualifications for doing so, that they know something or feel something which the mass of mankind has neither known nor felt. Up to the present there is little sign of anything of the kind, and thus their educational offers fall on stony ground.

It is a relief to get away from the atmosphere created by the gossipers and pessimists into that of the 'sound, healthy children of the God of heaven' – the mass of the people, men and women, who are working for their country either in the mine, the factory or the field.

Every one who returns from the Front brings tales of the matchless spirit, the undaunted courage and confidence of our men. Less has perhaps been heard of the same spirit which exists, in no less degree, in the factory and the workshop. It is my desire in these pages, while recognising to the full the splendid work, both military and industrial, done by men, to draw particular attention to what the nation owes at the present time to the magnificent adaptability, the industrial efficiency and the patriotism of women. Every fighting man needs the incessant labour of six to eight non-fighting men and women in order to keep him equipped with all the necessaries of military service;[9] and as more and more men are drafted away to military service, their places are being filled by women, who are working as never before. Lord Kitchener said in his appeal to the workers, which is posted in every factory, that

> In carrying out the great work of providing the Army with its equipment, employers and employees alike are doing their duty to their King and country equally with those who have joined the Army for service in the Field.[10]

This appeal has been answered by a spirit of sustained, untiring effort never before seen and most admirable. Miss Anderson,[11] the chief Lady Inspector of Factories, quotes again and again, in her recent report, from her staff of inspectors, one and all speaking in terms of the highest appreciation of the patriotic spirit in which the women have worked:

> This spirit [says Miss Squire][12] has accomplished what the mere prospect of increased wages has failed to do; it is a truism among managers that girls, even on piece-work, cannot be induced to exceed a pace which enables them to earn what they consider a normally sufficient wage; but during the last few months the motive, 'our soldiers need it', has made them work at top speed.[13]

Another lady inspector, Miss Slocock,[14] writes:

> It is only by visiting the factories that one can realise the extent to which the equipment and comfort of the troops in the field depends upon the work of the women and girls at home, and the amount of overtime worked has, I believe, only been possible without injurious effects because the workers have been so glad to help. In one factory I found them singing for joy because . . . they had started on a Government order.

Another lady inspector says that she has been surprised to find so little complaint or ill-effect from long hours, and adds:

> This may be partly due to the better standard of living that the overtime money makes possible, but I think it is mainly due to the ideal for which the women are now working. It would revolutionise industry if some ideal other than money could be inspired in times of peace.

Again and again the report speaks of the new power of resistance to fatigue showing itself in industrial women comparable in a way with the spirit of the men at the front. Miss Anderson and her staff have also much that is interesting to say in praise of the industrial competence and adaptability of women in factories in spite of the general absence in the past of openings for them through technical schools or skilled trade training. In a previous number of the *Englishwoman* (September 1915) a quotation was given from the *Engineer* giving the highest possible praise to women working in many of the munition factories, and stating that after a very short training they were turning out work of which any skilled artisan might feel proud.[15] Miss Anderson's report gives many other examples of the high industrial capacity of women. In the work of soldering Government tins, in which special care and uniformity is required, girls who were put on to learn it made progress at an astonishing rate, and passed through the learners' to the expert stage very quickly. Up to the present year the great want of industrial women has been the degree to which they were jealously excluded from means of learning the more skilled parts of industrial work. This has been borne in upon every one who has studied the position of the industrial woman as a whole, and is especially emphasised in the excellent tract No. 178, published in March 1915, by the Fabian women's group under the title of *The War: Women and Unemployment*. One quotation must suffice:

> The present provision of technical education for girls by local authorities is extremely inadequate . . . outside London it hardly exists. Now is the time to provide more schools and classes, teaching new trades and promoting efficiency in trades already followed, which will make women competent wage-earners in the future.[16]

The same point is also brought into clear relief in the Report on Women's Employment drawn up for the British Association, 1915 (Draft Interim Report of the Conference on Outlets for Labour after the War). It is there pointed out that there is a permanent shortage of skilled labour in proportion to unskilled in the whole field of industry, and that this disproportion is exceptionally large among women. There is never any lack of unskilled workers, but the amount of unskilled labour which can be employed depends upon the proportion of skilled labour which can be obtained to lead and guide it. 'In the case of men the lack of training and experience is all too general; *amongst women it is with rare exceptions the universal rule*' (p. 7).[17] Now the experience gained since the outbreak of war conclusively proves that the absence of skilled workers among women was due to no eternal and immutable law of nature, but to prejudice, both male and female, and also to masculine power and privilege. Of the women in the textile trades (and women are better organized in this trade than in any other) it is found that men and women working the same machines are paid at different rates, because women as a rule cannot 'tune' or 'set' their machines. One hears this repeated over and over again; but one is very seldom told that the reason why women could not, before the War, 'tune' or 'set' their machines is that they were not allowed to be taught how to do so.

It has taken a European War to break down this wall of prejudice, so destructive of the resources of the nation, and wasting to a large degree the industrial capacity of the female half of the population. Now that millions of men have left industrial occupations to defend the principles of liberty and self-government in this great War, the nation has learned that it must use its women workers and encourage them to employ every ounce of skill which their natural faculties enable them to acquire. Accordingly, women are pouring in thousands into trades and occupations from which hitherto they have been excluded. This change which many (the National Union of Women's Suffrage Societies among the number) foresaw from the beginning of the War,[18] and urged the Government in vain to take definite steps to provide for, has now come with a tremendous rush.

The newspapers are full of the new demand for women's labour. Women are now employed as tramway drivers or conductors in many of our large towns, including London, Manchester, Salford, Liverpool, Sheffield, Leeds, Edinburgh, Cardiff and Birmingham. Many hundreds of women are employed on railways. The London, Brighton and South Coast Railway has opened a school for giving them systematic training. Eight hundred women applied to enter the school, a far larger number than could be admitted. That they are doing their work well may be gathered from the sentence, 'All the Stationmasters speak well of the women.' As carriage-cleaners they naturally excel, and are spoken of as doing the work much more thoroughly than the men previously employed.[19] The Great Central Railway has taken on an exceptionally large number of women, variously estimated in the press at between 700 and 1,300. The newspapers announce that the Great Western Railway is employing women not only as ticket collectors and ticket clerks, but in very responsible posts in the office of the superintendent of the line, the chief goods manager and the general manager. These ladies are university graduates. Their work is mainly secretarial. One of them controls an important section of the work in the rates and taxes department.[20]

Women are being trained and employed in large numbers as motor-drivers and electricians. Hunting women are turning their knowledge of horses to account, and are in charge of War Office depots for horses; as acetylene welders women will shortly become indispensable in the manufacture of aeroplanes. The London Society of the NUWSS has done splendid work in selecting women for many of these new occupations and putting them in the way of suitable training.[21]

The War Office has also employed women as judges[22] and forwarders of hay.[23] The splendid work done by women in munition factories has been so fully and so recently described in the press that it is unnecessary here to repeat the high praise bestowed upon it, especially as some remarkable expressions of appreciation were quoted in the December number of the *Englishwoman*.[24] The number of women thus engaged is at present a matter of conjecture. Miss Mary MacArthur, in a recent article, says that it runs into six figures.[25] Lord Derby has said that 'the response of women to the call of duty has been simply magnificent'.[26] If I mistake not he is entirely free from any predisposition to overestimate the value of women's work. Other authorities quote the extraordinary effort now being made by women and girls in munition work. In Birmingham a signed article by Mr W. T. Massey states that practically every available man and woman in one district is helping the Allied armies by supplying them with munitions: he says that the women are earning good money, but that 'patriotism more than money is the motive'. From our men, he adds, we expect much in the hour of trial. 'It is the women who surprise us.'[27] Like Mr Asquith, he apparently did not know that women were prepared to make sacrifices for their country.[28] But evidently the War has taught him what he did not know before, and again he says, 'Patriotism is the oil which makes the machine work smoothly.' He says, 'Quite out of the limelight, there are scores of thousands of women toiling night and day on tasks for which their lives would be quite unsuited but for an unquenchable desire to do something for their country.' He describes a factory run entirely with women's labour, and quotes its manager as saying that there was not a slacker in the whole establishment. The women thought far less of the amount of money they drew at the end of the week than of the number of shells which had passed through their hands. If the supply of material ran out, they did not wait till it was brought to them, but went at once and fetched it themselves. He spoke with equal enthusiasm of their skill after a very short period of training.

Now all this appreciation of women's work, the opening to them of skilled employments, the great improvement in their scale of wages, must be welcomed with deep thankfulness by all who have been trying for years to find some means of lifting up the industrial status of women. But we must not shut our eyes to certain dangers connected with the present state of things. First, there is now such a keen demand for women's work that the great importance of training is apt to be neglected.

One hears of schemes for giving three weeks' training to young women who are seeking work as clerks and secretaries, in banks, business houses, government and municipal offices, etc.;[29] another scheme, still more audacious, proposes a fortnight's free instruction to women in farm work! The subjects comprised milking, cleaning and bedding-down of cattle, calf-feeding, the getting-in of roots, straw, etc., the mixing and grinding of food for cattle, poultry-rearing, etc.[30] Now, this sort of thing may be looked at from two points of view. It may be regarded as an enormous compliment which men pay to women to imagine that they can learn in a fortnight or three weeks arts and crafts which men take years to acquire. But as women have been little accustomed to the language of compliment as regards their professional or industrial efficiency, one is forced to regard it from another point of view, and recognise it as the result of hurry and scramble, the want of prevision as to the nation's needs at this time of crisis which has characterised so much of the national organization of the country. So far as this very short period of training and preparation becomes general, it is almost certain to bring women's work into disrepute. Employers will compare the woman 'complete agriculturalist' after a fortnight's training with the ordinary farm-labourer, and will say that they would rather have one man (probably with years of experience behind him) than three women. The same remark applies to the too hastily trained girl clerk or secretary. Heads of offices who take on raw schoolgirls of seventeen or eighteen with the merest smattering of training, say contemptuously that it takes three girls to do a man's work. If they took boys under similar conditions, everybody would recognise the inevitable consequences. It must be strongly insisted upon that if women and girls are to be fitted to do skilled work they must go through a proper training for it. They may, as so many young men do, train for their work by doing it under skilled direction; but in this case it should be recognised that they are in training, and their wages and status as regards responsibility will be accommodated to their position of apprenticeship.

Secondly, there is a very real danger that the patriotic enthusiasm of women will be exploited by unscrupulous employers, and the women will be paid very much lower wages than the value of their work justifies. We already hear of Government offices offering twenty-five shillings a week to women for really skilled work requiring professional training; such work, for example, as map-drawing to scale. Some Labour leaders have gone so far as to predict the outbreak of a serious sex-war in this country when the war with the Germans is over, because they say that the men who will then get their discharge from the Army will find the work to which they were accustomed before the war being done by women for less than half the wages which the men had received.[31] There can be little doubt that there are elements of danger in this situation, and that, as far as possible, the principle of the same wages for the same work must be insisted upon.

The difficulty of the situation has been increased by the policy which has been pursued by trade unions for so many years of keeping women out of the skilled and therefore better-paid industries,[32] and thus forcing them down into the lower ranks of industry. The true policy for the unionists would have been to welcome the women in and either admit them to the men's unions or help them to form unions of their own. The wages of the sweated man vary round about one pound a week; but the wages of the sweated woman vary round about less than half that sum.[33] The difference probably far exceeds the value of their respective output, and forms a constant temptation to the employer to use the woman to undercut the man.

I feel very strongly that the whole nation owes a deep debt of gratitude to the trade unionists and the leaders of the Labour Party for the strenuous and self-sacrificing efforts they have made for years to raise the standard of living for their class. They are the great majority of the nation, and it is of really immeasurable national importance that they should enjoy the material elements of a civilised existence. The effect upon physical health, upon infant mortality,[34] upon other insidious evils eating into the very life-blood of the nation are part and parcel of this great heroic struggle to raise and maintain at a high level the general standard of living. If the masses are ground down to the position, unhappily occupied by many women before the War, of receiving less than subsistence wages, it is not possible to have a nation that can be honestly described as 'sound, healthy children of the God of heaven'.[35]

I do not myself believe in the possibility of a sex-war. We should have had one long ago if it had been a possibility; there have been evils great enough to provoke it, the cruel injustice of many of the laws relating to women; the measureless ocean of contempt for women expressed in nearly all classical literature in which the youth of many men is steeped; unlimited political authority on the one side and unlimited subjection on the other.[36] But there have always been the real things to keep us straight: the love of husband and wife, of father and daughter, of mother and son; the causes that we have worked for together, a common patriotism, a common agony in hours of national disaster and strain, a common uplift at the signs of national greatness and unity. Women have not worked as they have during the last seventeen months with any ulterior aim of winning thereby their own claim to citizenship. They have worked for their country from the strongest of all motives, love for her. But men and women, when the end of the War comes, will feel that they have each borne a part in a titanic struggle; they have been 'up against the real things', life and death, heroic self-sacrifice for all we hold most dear; and I believe that the nation will realise, as it never has before, that the women of the country are worthy to be recognised as free, self-governing citizens.

> Transcribed from a copy in the Women's Library at LSE.
> No known copyright restrictions.

Notes

1. 'Mrs Fawcett once described . . . how her years of familiarity with the movement had taught her to pick out the word "woman" from a page of the *Times* the instant she opened the paper. It had been a faculty not very often called into requisition . . . But after 1915 it had plenty of exercise, and her daily study of the newspapers became a very different matter when there were all these hopeful and encouraging eulogies to read and enjoy' (Strachey 1931, 304).
2. A reference to a popular hymn written in 1881 by Henry Montagu Butler (1833–1918): '"Lift up your hearts!", We lift them, Lord, to thee' (Church of England 1906, 343–4).
3. See also Fawcett 1916e.
4. 'October, 1803', a sonnet by Wordsworth, published in 1807 (Wordsworth 1882, 380).
5. Fawcett is referring in particular to George Bernard Shaw (1856–1950), Irish playwright, critic and political activist. Shortly after the outbreak of World War I, he published his tract *Common Sense about the War* (1914), initially in the *New Statesman*, but republished due to its popularity elsewhere, which argued that warring nations were all culpable in a controversial rejection of patriotism which claimed 'no British Government within my recollection has ever understood the nation' (p. 23). Nearly a year after this controversy in October 1915, 'Mr Bernard Shaw broke his long silence . . . when he lectured on "the Illusions of the War"' in Covent Garden, in a Fabian Society address. He was introduced by the pacifist public intellectual Bertrand Russell (1872–1970), who described him as the 'man who has raised hostility by making English people think about the war' (*Liverpool Echo* 1915).
6. Paraphrasing Shaw's style in *Common Sense about the War* (1914).
7. A phrase meaning foolish ingenuity: medieval villagers in Gotham, England, had reportedly feigned imbecility to avoid a visit from King John (*Encyclopædia Britannica* 1911).
8. Mary Campbell Smith (1869–1938), Scottish writer and academic based in Germany (Kant 1903, 104–5).
9. The ratio of military personnel needed to supply each combat solider is known as the 'tooth-to-tail' ratio. It is unclear where Fawcett sourced these statistics. See McGrath 2007 for quantification methods regarding troop resourcing from the early twentieth century onwards.
10. Horatio Herbert Kitchener (1850–1916), 1st Earl Kitchener, secretary of state for war, organised a large volunteer army and the production of materials for the war effort. His appeal from 1914 (*Cotton Factory Times* 1914) was posted in factories 'and helped to stimulate the women to work long hours without complaint' (Andrews 1918, 114).
11. Adelaide Anderson (1863–1936), Elizabeth Garrett Anderson's niece by marriage.
12. Rose Squire (1861–1938), factory inspector and member of the Health of Munition Workers' Committee during World War I.
13. All three quotes are from HM Factory Inspectorate (1914, 40).
14. Emily Slocock (1874–1964).
15. A substantial quote from the 20 August edition of the *Engineer* appears in the *Englishwoman* (1915a, 276–8).
16. Women's Group Executive (1915, 9).

17 See Kirkaldy (1915, 74).
18 See Section 39, Introduction.
19 *Social Gazette* 1915.
20 *Times* 1915c.
21 See Fawcett 1914b.
22 *Sunday Mirror* 1915.
23 'Their duties are to check the quantity and quality of the hay and straw purchased by the War Office, and to superintend its despatch' (*Reading Observer* 1915).
24 The *Englishwoman* 1915b quotes once from the *Times* and thrice from the *Manchester Guardian*.
25 Miss Mary Macarthur (1880–1921), Scottish supporter of universal adult suffrage, trade unionist and secretary of the Women's Trade Union League: 'The Munitions Act . . . affects at least a hundred thousand women and girls in the factory and workshop, and I am afraid it would have been a poor look out for them were it not for the fact that many thousands have joined the National Federation of Women Workers' (Macarthur 1916, 5).
26 Edward George Villiers Stanley (1865–1948), 17th Earl of Derby, Conservative politician, then secretary of state for war, in a letter read at a Young Men's and Young Women's Christian Associations event, raising funds for munition workers (*Sheffield Daily Telegraph* 1915). He was not a vocal supporter of suffrage for women.
27 Presumably a version of Massey 1915: William Thomas Massey (1870–1947) was a war correspondent, and later news editor of the *Daily Telegraph*.
28 In April 1915 Asquith made a speech at Newcastle, praising women's contribution and work in munition factories (*Scotsman* 1915): it was argued that this was his first vocal support for the women's movement (*Votes for Women* 1915). In October 1915, speaking in the House of Commons on the heroic death of the British nurse Edith Cavell (1865–1915), he said, 'in this United Kingdom and throughout the Dominions of the Crown there are thousands of such women, and a year ago we did not know it' (*Evening Mail* 1915). Fawcett remarked, 'Pathetic blindness! Especially as a great deal of it must have been wilful' (1924, 229).
29 London County Council ran this popular and successful scheme (*Western Daily Press* 1916).
30 An experimental scheme training 300 women in milking and light farm work was established in late 1915 (*Chester Chronicle* 1915).
31 *Leeds Mercury* 1915.
32 See Braybon 2013 for the complexity of this statement: 'It is not possible to describe the views of the labour movement *en masse* to the influx of women's workers. Unions had varying policies on the matter of women . . . the fact that a union opposed women workers and did not allow them to join its ranks did not mean that individual workmen were not kind and helpful . . . although some writers at the time condemned unions as a whole for their response to women, a division can be made between the reactions of the general labour unions, or those which included a large number of less skilled men, and of craft unions' (p. 68).
33 In 1912, the average wage of men working in industrial trades was just under 30 shillings a week, although women earned approximately 12 shillings per week (Barnes 1912, 2–3).
34 Infant mortality rates fell before and during World War I due to complex, interlocking reasons regarding access to steady income, reform in working conditions and improvements in preventative medicine; see Braybon 2013, Chapter 5. The press often reposted 'the complaints of the Women's Trade Union League regarding long hours, low pay, and poor conditions, and space was often given to the discussion of possible cases of exploitation, particularly where women were working with such dangerous substances as aircraft dope or TNT' (p. 114).
35 See note 4.
36 Fawcett's note: 'As I wrote these lines I received a letter from a young married woman: her husband is "somewhere in France", and she is going daily to a city office to work as a clerk, thereby setting free another man for the army. One sentence of this letter runs, "When I look back and remember how I wept with sheer wretchedness at the thought of turning out every morning to spend the day in a city office, I can hardly believe I was so stupid. It was the most heartening thing you can imagine to see the eagerness of the men clerks to help us and correct our mistakes." – Not much sex-war about this.'

43
An immense and significant advance, 1917

Englishwoman. Vol. 33, No. 99 (March), 193–7.

The war changed discussions about the franchise.

> Compulsory military service for men had been adopted, and this strengthened the demand for manhood suffrage on the very reasonable ground that if a man could be compelled to offer his life for his country, he should at least have some influence, as a voter, in controlling the policy which might cause such a sacrifice to be called for . . . We made some unsuccessful efforts . . . to define . . . service as to include the services of women (Fawcett 1920a, 126).

On 4 May 1916 the NUWSS 'addressed a careful letter to Mr Asquith on the points raised by the obsolete register and the necessity for a new one, and also for a new qualification for the franchise' (Fawcett 1920a, 126–7). It argued as follows:

> When the Government deals with the franchise, an opportunity will present itself of dealing with it on wider lines than by the simple removal of what may be called the accidental disqualification of a large body of the best men in the country, and we trust that you may include in your Bill clauses which would remove the disabilities under which women now labour (Fawcett 1916d).

An immediate reply from Asquith was 'very much more encouraging than any previous letter we had received' (Fawcett 1920a, 128). Fawcett wrote at the time that this was the outstanding Suffrage event of the week. It marks an important stage in our progress towards our goal . . . The war has had a wonderful effect on people's minds. They have come away from the world of words and phrases, and have come up against the world of real things. Conventions and shams have been dropped; and Anti-suffragism was almost wholly built upon conventions and shams (Fawcett 1916c).

Parliamentary discussions on voter reform continued throughout 1916 (Fawcett 1920a, 129–33). In August, Mr Asquith vocally supported the principle of women's suffrage, which 'in effect made the Liberal Party into a Suffrage Party' (Fawcett 1920a, 134). Fawcett explained:

> The only real obstacle which now confronted us was the plausible plea that, however desirable women's suffrage was in itself, it was not the time during the most gigantic war in history to raise this great question of constitutional reform. It was our business to show that *now was the time* when such a reform was not only desirable, but absolutely necessary (Fawcett 1920a, 135–6).

Difficult questions of electoral reform required further discussion, and an Electoral Reform Conference was established: 'an all-party committee intended to produce an agreed report on suffrage reform, of which votes for women was the most contentious issue' (Rubinstein 1991, 238; see also Rolf 1979). During this phase of discussions, Asquith was replaced by Lloyd George[1] as prime minister, which was of major assistance to the suffragists. Although rumours swirled that the Speaker's Conference would not recommend votes for women, its report, published at the end of January 1917, proposed 33 drastic reforms to the franchise (*Evening Mail* 1917a, 5), including recommending 'by a majority a form of women's suffrage which, though excluding youthful war workers, would enfranchise millions of women' (Rubinstein 1991, 238). The NUWSS had planned a 'women's worker's demonstration to support the inclusion of any Electoral Reform Bill', at which Fawcett, presiding, said 'The result of the Speaker's Conference was an illustration of the deathless energy and vitality of the Suffrage movement . . . though the brew seemed distinctly anti-Suffrage, when the tap was turned – Suffrage came out!' She urged the government 'without delay to introduce a Bill based on the lines of the report' (*Common Cause* 1917c). This column, written shortly after the NUWSS meeting, recounts the changing political landscape and the developments over the previous few months, while being infused with hope that women's suffrage was now within reach.

*

The National Union of Women's Suffrage Societies Meeting on February 20th, in the Queen's Hall, was the first large meeting they had called for two years.[2]

It was planned just at the time when the Press was full of confident assertions that the Report of the Speaker's Conference, then recently concluded but unpublished, contained no satisfactory reference to women's suffrage.[3] If this had been true, the meeting would have been one of indignant protest. This protest would have been directed against the Conference for evading the duty which had been laid upon it by the House of offering solutions upon various problems (Women's Suffrage being by far the most important) which in pre-war days had long disturbed the peace and harmony of the country. But most fortunately the prevalent rumours turned out to be untrue, so that protest was unnecessary, and the whole tone of the meeting was one of confidence and hope. It is, of course, well known that the Conference was not unanimous in its suggested solution of the women's claim.[4] This could hardly have been expected, seeing that some of the most extreme and, as we consider, bigoted[5] of our opponents had been included among its numbers. But although not unanimous, the Conference decided by a majority, rumour says a large majority,[6] that some measure of women's suffrage should be conferred; and it suggested as its most practical form what in 1912–13 we used to call the Dickinson basis – i.e., the giving of the Parliamentary franchise to every woman on the Local Government Register and to the wife of every man who is on that register.[7] It also suggested that women graduates of Universities having parliamentary representatives should be entitled to vote as University electors.[8] In mitigation of the satisfactory character of these suggestions, the Conference proposed that women, whether as University graduates or as qualified on the Dickinson basis, should not be allowed to exercise the Parliamentary franchise until they had attained the age of thirty or thirty-five.[9]

These proposals do not of course fulfil the demand of the Suffrage Societies. One and all we have consistently asked for the enfranchisement of women on the same terms as men – and the foregoing comes far short of this, especially as the Conference recommended for men a very near approach to manhood suffrage.[10] We therefore shall not have attained our goal if the Government should adopt the Conference recommendations and pass them into law.

Notwithstanding this, however, we shall have gained a great deal. First and foremost, the destruction, once and for all, of the sex disability.

In the vehement days of youth I used to say that I would welcome any bill which conferred the franchise even only on one woman, because that in itself would destroy the disqualification resting upon half the nation;[11] and everything else we desired could have been made to follow. But the proposals of the Speaker's Conference – even if the absurdly high age limit is confirmed by Parliament – would place on the Parliamentary Register 6,000,000 women. This at least is the calculation of Mr W. H. Dickinson, MP, a member of the Conference and a very warm friend of our cause.[12] He points out that the Conference has recommended certain modifications in the Local Government Register – namely, that in substitution for all existing franchises,

> Every person who for a period of six months immediately preceding the 15th January and the 15th July in any year has occupied as owner or tenant any land or premises in a Local Government area in England and Wales, shall be entitled to be registered and to vote as a Local Government elector in that area.[13]

This clears away many obstacles in the way of women getting on the Local Government Register in England and Wales; for, as the law now stands, women can only vote as occupiers and not, as men can, also as owners, lodgers or service voters. The new regulations recommended by the Conference would place women on an equality with men so far as the Local Government register is concerned; and almost all women lodgers could register as tenants if they had complete control over the rooms or room in which they lived. The reduction of the period of occupation from one year to six months also tells in the direction of a more generous measure of enfranchisement.

I think I am justified in saying that the universal feeling among suffragists is one of profound satisfaction that the Speaker's Conference, by a large majority, has recommended the destruction of the electoral disabilities of half the nation, and I think it is also true to say that there is unanimity among suffragists in the opinion that complete justice to women will not be attained until women vote upon the same terms as men. But when this is said and duly weighed, I believe there is an enormous preponderance of feeling not only in the National Union, but among suffragists generally, that we should support the recommendations of the Conference, and do everything in our power to urge the Government to make them, without delay, the general basis for legislation. For it must be remembered that the report is the result of a carefully balanced compromise. All parties and all opinions were represented in the

Conference, and no one section obtained, in the finally resulting report, all its own way. As in all compromises, there had to be give and take on both sides; the suffragists got the abolition of the sex disqualification, but had to yield on the question of equality of qualification. It is obvious that when agreement has been achieved under those circumstances, it might be fatal for us to come in from the outside and say we won't have this and we won't have that. Such a course might very well bring the whole delicately balanced structure about our ears. An 'all or nothing' party might argue that this would be no disadvantage, but very probably forget that it might simply induce the Government to take no action whatever. There is a general agreement to avoid contentious matters, and there is a considerable group in the Government who are arguing that the present register, imperfect as it is, is still quite fairly representative of the country. These are already urging the desirability of taking a General Election upon it.[14]

The NUWSS and practically the whole of the other suffrage organizations are determined to put no obstacle whatever in the way of getting 6,000,000 women on the register before the next General Election.[15] The industrial interests of women, though not so fully safeguarded as we could wish by the new proposals, are far more fully safeguarded than they would be if there were not any women among the electorate.

The friends of suffrage for women have a unique opportunity at the present time, and I think the great majority of them are clear-sighted enough to perceive it. The tide of public opinion now runs strongly in favour of our movement. Instances of the conversion of well-known anti-suffragists pour in, in an ever-increasing tide.[16] But tides have a way, after running strongly in one direction, of turning and running strongly in another. Our policy should be to float our vessel on the tide that is now running strongly towards the success of our cause. We never had such a good chance as at this moment. What can be more significant than the very history of the Speaker's Conference itself? It was suggested by one anti-suffragist, sanctioned by another, presided over and appointed by a third;[17] and yet, when the report comes out, it recommends by a majority that some measure of Women's Suffrage should be conferred, and proceeds to formulate suggestions which would make women about a third of the entire electorate.

I do not like to conclude this brief review of the situation without a few words of very cordial thanks and appreciation to those Members of Parliament who so skilfully and ably conducted the case for women's suffrage inside the Conference. They had a difficult and delicate task. They were members of different parties not, in general, accustomed to act together. But under very able guidance and with a deep sense of responsibility, not only to the women who were anxiously watching and waiting, but to the whole country which evidently keenly desires a settlement of a fifty-year-old struggle, they were able to achieve a practical agreement on a long-unsettled controversy and to render it not only possible but probable that women will be on the register before the next General Election. It will be an extraordinary sign of the deep strength and vitality of the principle of free representative government in this country if the administration is able to pass an important scheme of electoral reform even in the midst of this great war. It will emphasise the truth of what has been declared over and over again: that this war is a war of freedom, that it is a struggle between the opposing principles of autocracy and self-government. Sir John Simon said in his speech at Kingsway Hall on February 10th:

> We have the strongest ground for expecting the Government to introduce such a Bill, and it has a better prospect of passing into law than any previous Bill. I am confident that no such Bill could be introduced by the Government unless it contained proposals for Women's Suffrage. That is an immense and significant advance.[18]

Transcribed from a copy in the Women's Library at LSE.
No known copyright restrictions.

Notes

1 David Lloyd George, Liberal politician and prime minister of the United Kingdom from 1916 to 1922.
2 *Common Cause* 1917c.
3 On Wednesday, 17 January, the *Westminster Gazette* (1917a) reported that the Speaker's Conference had ended, but 'The Committee was not able to come to any agreement on the vexed question of Women Suffrage', leading to widespread coverage and a requirement for newspapers to state 'that certain reports which have appeared in the Press purporting to represent the recommendations of the Speaker's Conference on Electoral Reform are wholly unauthorized, inaccurate, and misleading' (*Times* 1917a).
4 The 'recommendation represents the opinion of the majority' (HC Deb 1917, 468): this was widely reported.
5 Fawcett later said 'the conference was proposed by one antisuffragist (Mr Long), supported by another (Mr Asquith), and presided over by a third (the Speaker)' (Fawcett 1920a, 138). Walter Long (1854–1924) was a Unionist politician, and then secretary of state for the colonies. He had proposed the Speaker's Conference in August 1916 (*Birmingham Daily Post* 1916), although he was known for being 'hostile' in his attitude to women's suffrage (*Lichfield Mercury* 1912). For Asquith's antipathy to women's suffrage, see Section 35. The Speaker, James William Lowther (1855–1949), was a Conservative politician with 'a high reputation for fairness, for great personal tact and courtesy, for humour, and all which it stands for in the management of men, but he was believed to be a strong antisuffragist' (Fawcett 1920a, 137).

Lowther had made a controversial ruling on women's suffrage in 1913, deciding it could not be added to a male suffrage bill, which led to its failure (*Penrith Observer* 1913). For further discussion of the 'thirty-two representatives of various political persuasions and individual points of view' who sat on the committee, see Rolf (1979, 44).

6 'There is authority for stating (says the Exchange Telegraph Company) that the Speaker's conference . . . has decided, by a considerable majority, in favour of the general principle of Woman Suffrage, but that there was a small minority against granting the vote on equal terms' (*Westminster Gazette* 1917b, 6).

7 '. . . moved by Mr (now Sir) W. H. Dickinson, also a very stalwart friend' (Fawcett 1920a, 45). See Section 28, note 6.

8 University constituencies represented the members of institutions rather than residents of a geographical area. In 1948 the university constituencies in the UK were abolished, taking effect from the dissolution of Parliament in 1950 (Registrar General 1954, 175).

9 On this topic, Lady Frances Balfour, president of the London Society for Women's Suffrage, wrote in the *Weekly Dispatch*, 'The age of thirty or thirty-five has always been a popular one in feminine computation of their census or service age. The conference, in recommending it and including married women of that age, has no doubt signified its view that women have then reached the period when they are beyond the influences of "fear or favour" in casting their vote . . . Men are to receive the franchise at twenty-one, and a woman is to receive it at thirty-five. Better late than ever [sic], but that age limit will cut out many women who at a far earlier age have given themselves "body, soul and spirit" to the service of the nation . . . The conference had to accept a compromise, for it could not yet unite in a finding which trusted the people' (Balfour 1917).

10 One man, one vote. 'Their proposals do not amount to manhood suffrage, though in practice they will come very near it. It may be that the Conference has deliberately avoided actual manhood suffrage in order to avoid the demand for complete womanhood suffrage which would then represent "equal terms with men"' (*Votes for Women* 1917).

11 See Section 3.

12 The 6,000,000 figure was calculated with regard to Dickinson's 1913 amendment (see note 7) and used thereafter to estimate the effect of giving women the vote under the same terms as men (*Pall Mall Gazette* 1913, 1).

13 Directly quoted from the Conference recommendations; see the *Evening Mail* (1917a, 6).

14 Discussions about the timing of electoral reform in relation to the forthcoming general election were undertaken in the House of Commons on 19 July 1916 (*Times* 1916). The next general election was not called until November 1918, immediately after the armistice with Germany.

15 Articles in the *Common Cause* stressed the need for compromise: 'The acceptance of the principle of Women's Suffrage with the prospect of immediate adoption . . . are gains too great to be hazarded for the chance of getting more . . . The rising tide of a great national effort is sweeping away the cross-currents which used to neutralise and paralyse all attempts at forward movement . . . It rests with us to take advantage of the tide' (*Common Cause* 1917a, 9).

16 *Common Cause* 1917b. There were many public statements made on a changed opinion of suffrage; see, for example, James Louis Garvin (1868–1947), the editor of the *Observer*: 'Before the war I opposed their claim unwillingly on the sole ground that when Armageddon came only men could maintain the State. Now I see that men alone could never have maintained it . . . If I am a convert on this point, I am a glad convert. After Armageddon nothing can be the same again . . . For all the better purposes of that epoch, a wide enfranchisement of women holds the key' (*Reading Observer* 1917).

17 See note 5.

18 John Allsebrook Simon (1873–1954), who had served as home secretary with Asquith, then in opposition. For coverage of his speech see the *Reading Observer* (1917).

44
Sing, rejoice and give thanks, 1918
Common Cause. Friday, 15 March 1918, 572.

Following the Electoral Reform report published in January 1917 (see Section 43), Parliament voted on the next steps, resulting in a 'majority of 341 to 62 on March 28th for the introduction of legislation on the lines of the Speaker's Conference', which became the Representation of the People Bill, and voting 'of 329 to 40 on May 23rd for the Second Reading of the Bill' (Fawcett 1917b). Fawcett reminded her readers, though, that

> Women's Suffrage is not safe until it is on the Statute Book. The Bill has to go through all its remaining stages in the Commons and all its stages in the Lords, then to come back to the Commons for the consideration of the Lords' amendments. There are, therefore, many stages before the Bill becomes an Act. Still, we are justified in feeling very confident: for this reason; Women's Suffrage now has behind it an immense volume of support from all parties all over the country (Fawcett 1917b).

Fawcett was right to be cautious. Amendments were proposed, with the NUWSS urging 'the Government to apply to women local government electors the same principle which had already been adopted by the House in regard to the parliamentary vote – namely, to admit to the register not only those women who were qualified in their own right, but also the wives of men similarly qualified', and although some 'held out no hope that the Government would accept the amendment', the government withdrew its opposition on 20 November, with the report stage and third reading of the bill concluded in the House of Commons on 7 December (Fawcett 1920a, 147).

The next stage 'had to be fought in the House of Lords, where we had far more formidable opponents than in the House of Commons' (Fawcett 1920a, 148), and there were hostile speeches.

> The real fight in the Lords began when committee stage was reached, on 8th January 1918. As a preliminary step the antisuffragists moved the elimination from the Bill of all clauses which had not been unanimously recommended by the Speaker's conference. This was aimed at Clause IV, which enfranchised women, but was opposed by the Government and withdrawn. Then came the more direct attack, the deletion of the parliamentary franchise from Clause IV. This gave rise to a full-dress debate, lasting three days (Fawcett 1920a, 149–50).

Fawcett wrote an impassioned, direct appeal (against a proposed amendment to take the matter of Women's Suffrage to a referendum) to members of the House of Lords, when they began sitting to discuss on 8 January:

> I beg your Lordships . . . to consider the effect upon the Bill as a whole of any of the changes you contemplate . . . Strife between the two Houses would immediately result, and strife of a kind most dangerous to the political peace . . . I appeal, therefore, to those members of the House of Lords who are faint-hearted to consider whether they need really fear their countrywomen . . . This is a Representation of the People Bill. Why leave half the People out of it? (Fawcett 1918a, 502).

A vote on 10 January went against the amendment, adopting women's suffrage by 134 votes to 71 (*Northern Whig* 1918). 'The antisuffragists were white with rage; the suffragists were flushed by the certainty of victory . . . The Royal Assent was given to the Bill on February 6th 1918. Thus ended our parliamentary struggle' (Fawcett 1920a, 152–3).

'Sing, Rejoice and Give Thanks' gives Fawcett's reflection on the final stages of parliamentary discussion, and the eventual passing of the bill on 6 February, couching the relief after years of campaigning and hope for the future in Christian terms, while coming to the realisation that the campaign had finally succeeded, giving the vote to women over the age of 30 who met a property qualification. Having had further time to reflect, Fawcett commented shortly after:

I most devoutly believe that the Suffrage movement, all through its fifty years' existence as practical politics, has made continuous and fairly rapid progress. I have gone as far as to say, when incited to describe the 'ups and downs', that I could not do this because it had had all 'ups' and no 'downs'. That is how it really looked to me at the time, and how, even more plainly now, it looks to me in perspective. There were moments, no doubt, of disappointment; one was when the Conciliation Bill was defeated in 1912,[1] when we knew we had a majority of MPs in the House of Commons definitely pledged to support it. But those of us whose disposition and training led us to take long views never doubted for a moment that ultimate success was certain . . . Looking back over the last fifty years' work for women, I can truly say it has been a joyful and exhilarating time: punctuated by victory after victory. What we were able to do without the Suffrage is in the highest degree encouraging for the outlook of our successors. They, with the franchise to back their efforts, will be able to do much more than we. One great drawback in the old unenfranchised days lay in the length of time, the concentration of *personnel*, energy and money necessary to accomplish what we were aiming at . . . I can only hope that those who are beginning their work now may have as joyful a fifty years before them as I and many dearly loved colleagues have to look back upon (Fawcett 1918c).

*

The sixth of February will ever be a red-letter day in Suffrage annals, for on that day the Representation of the People Bill passed its final stages and received the Royal Assent.[2]

A few of us watched its progress to the very last, and to the very last we were thrilled by excitement and uncertainty.[3] The doubt arose out of the disagreement of the Commons with the Lords' amendments. The Lords suggested a reasonable and harmless compromise; the Government accepted it, and it ought to have gone through quite easily,[4] but Mr Austen Chamberlain[5] worked himself up to a white-hot passion against it, and endeavoured to work up the House of Commons to share his rage. His speech was greeted by cheers which came ominously from all parts of the House. If he had succeeded in carrying the House with him, the Bill would have been lost. But the Government stood firm. Mr Bonar Law announced on their behalf that they would use their whole machinery to bring the conflict to an end and save the Bill;[6] and, as we all know, on the motion that the House agree to the Lords' Amendment, the numbers were:

For the motion	....	224
Against	....	114
Majority	....	110

Within half an hour from this division, the Bill had been carried to the House of Lords and had received the Royal Assent, and 6,000,000 women[7] were added to the electorate, and will take part in the next General Election.

My feelings can only be expressed by the words of the 126th Psalm.[8] All through the fifty years of the struggle I have believed absolutely and confidently in success; but now that success has come, I can hardly realise it.

Let not any Suffragist belittle the greatness of our victory. The Bill establishes what is virtually household suffrage for women, coupled with the high age-limit of thirty, which we have protested against and dislike.[9] The object, however, was quite obvious – namely, to reduce the number of women voting to a figure which would allay the terror of the most timid of the other sex. There will accordingly be 6,000,000 women voters to 10,000,000 men voters. It must be remembered that the addition to the electorate is far larger than that made by any previous Reform Bill. The additional number of voters created by the Bill of 1832 was only half a million;[10] by the Bill of 1867, one million;[11] by the Bill of 1884, two million;[12] but by the Bill of 1918, it is eight million, of whom six million are women. What do these figures show? They show that men were more than fifty years in getting the principle of Household Suffrage fully accepted for themselves; we have succeeded in getting Household Suffrage for women after a struggle of practically the same duration. And it surely is something to be proud of that we have been able to accomplish this without a vote between us and on non-party lines. We have not appealed to party passion, but always and constantly to the common sense of all parties, to the lessons of experience and to the principles of liberty and self-government on which the whole of our national life has been founded.[13] Every other great Reform Bill has been carried only after a tremendous party conflict, which has split the country into rival factions, breathing forth hatred and suspicion against one another. Our Bill, as we are proud to call it, has been carried by the consent and active co-operation of all parties. In the House of Commons it was supported by every leader of each of the great political parties. There has never been anything like it before, and we may perhaps look upon it as a happy omen of a new spirit which women may bring into politics.

Transcribed from a copy in the British Library.
No known copyright restrictions.

Notes

1. See Section 35.
2. *Times* (1918a, 8).
3. Fawcett 1918a.
4. See the *Times* 1918a. The amendments regarded alternative votes and proportional representation.
5. Sir Joseph Austen Chamberlain (1863–1937), Conservative politician, then member of the War Cabinet.
6. Andrew Bonar Law (1858–1923), Conservative politician, then chancellor of the exchequer, in his rousing speech that closed the debate (*Times* 1918a).
7. See Section 43, note 12.
8. The title of this piece is from Psalm 98: 'Shew yourselves joyful unto the Lord, all ye lands: sing, rejoice, and give thanks' (Society for Promoting Christian Knowledge 1916, 96). Psalm 126 is one of relief and celebration after toil: 'When the Lord turned again the captivity of Sion: then were we like unto them that dream / Then was our mouth filled with laughter: and our tongue with joy. / Then said they among the heathen: The Lord hath done great things for them. / Yea, the Lord hath done great things for us already: whereof we rejoice. / Turn our captivity, O Lord; as the rivers in the south. / They that sow in tears: shall reap in joy. / He that now goeth on his way weeping, and beareth forth good seed: shall doubtless come again with joy, and bring his sheaves with him' (Society for Promoting Christian Knowledge 1916, 131).
9. 'I do not lose sight of one very important drawback to the present Act, namely the absurdly high age limit imposed on women voters. A boy, if he has served in the Navy or Army, may vote at the age of 19; no woman may vote in Parliamentary elections below the age of 30. It is wholly unreasonable and I am convinced will not be maintained for more than a few years. But the reason why it was imposed is quite obvious; it was intended to calm the fears of those who were afraid of creating a register in which the majority of the voters were women' (Fawcett 1918c).
10. See Parliament.uk n.d.g for an overview of the Reform Acts, and the changing rights of the working and middle classes in respect of the franchise. See also Section 25, note 7.
11. See Section 11, note 16.
12. See Section 33, note 7.
13. See Section 28.

45
Still in thy right hand carry gentle peace, 1918

Common Cause. Friday, 20 December 1918, 427.

The armistice of 11 November 1918 ended war between the Allied Powers and Germany. A general election was immediately called in the UK for 14 December: the first in which some women over the age of 30, and all men over the age of 21, were eligible to vote. Fawcett wrote this column in the *Common Cause* a few days after the general election, when the results were not yet known, since votes from those serving overseas still had to be tallied. The Eligibility of Women Act had been passed on 21 November 1918, which

> rendered the election of women to the House of Commons a possibility . . . Owing to the very short time between the passing of the Act and the General Election the opportunity for women to select constituencies and work up their candidature was very inadequate. Nevertheless, there were seventeen women candidates, one of whom, in Ireland,[1] was elected (Fawcett 1920, 170).

In this column, Fawcett reflects on the nature of peace and power and the place of women and, in particular, the suffrage movement during the war, while looking ahead hopefully to a political landscape fully involving the suffragist approach of the peaceful 'eternal feminine'. Shortly after, she commented:

> I feel deeply thankful to have been privileged to live in such a wonderful time as this. If we approach the great problems of the day in a broad and generous-minded spirit, with appreciation of what

has been done by all ranks and classes of our fellow countrymen and women in the great struggle through which we have now passed, if we look forward to seeing the same spirit guiding them in the future as in the past, I believe that that spirit will be blessed to us. We are the same men and women now as we were in the most arduous time in the struggle. Great Britain is the same country now as she was then, and I believe that the great qualities displayed then will be shown in the future, and we shall come out of this tremendous struggle a greater and purer nation than we went into it. Now that we have the power of the vote behind us to back up the improvement in the position of women, I see nothing dismal in the outlook, but everything seems full of promise and hope, and a real certainty of a greater and better time to come (Fawcett 1919).

*

The year just closing will ever be memorable as the year which brought to an end the greatest and most destructive war in history. It is the year of the Great Peace; and it is also the year of the enfranchisement of women.[2] It seems to me not extravagant to trace a connection between these two events.

In the first place, the eyes of men have been opened and their hearts have been softened by the way in which both men and women instantly, at the outbreak of the war, sprang forward to offer all they had and were for the service of their country; and as the years of war went on, their zeal and desire to serve never waned. It is my purpose here to speak of the women. Those who were trained, the doctors and the nurses, were the first to offer themselves; the work of the nurses was, of course, accepted at once and gladly; the work of the women doctors was rejected in this country, but accepted by France, Belgium and Serbia, and that is why so many first-class hospitals officered by British women were placed under the French, Belgian and Serbian, and not under the British Red Cross.[3]

Suffragists at the outbreak of the war had an advantage over most other women from the fact that they were organised in their several Societies; it was the work of only a few hours to transfer our machine from the purposes of peace to the purposes of war.[4] We had a big organisation in our hands with a skilled staff of experienced women, and we were therefore ready instantly to set this machine to work in various ways to sustain our country during the tremendous struggle. The services of women in different kinds of war work have been amply and generously recognised on a thousand platforms.[5] I do not wish to represent that this transfer of our work from peace to war uses went through without dislocation of some of our machinery.[6] But so strong was the current bearing women along to national service that we often found that members of our Staff who left us on account of their pacifist proclivities soon sought and obtained employment in organising and directing the work of women in the manufacture of munitions and other warlike activities.[7]

There can be no doubt that the excellence of woman's work for the country, their adaptability and efficiency not only astonished the Man-in-the-Street, but converted him into a Suffragist. The foremost example is that of Mr Asquith, who acknowledged in 1917 that in former years his mind had been 'clouded by fallacies and sealed by illusions'.[8] Even the President of the Anti-Suffrage League, and the representative of the Government in the House of Lords, Lord Curzon, though not converted from his errors, was not prepared to back them by his vote,[9] with the result that the woman's clause in the Reform Bill was carried in the Upper House by nearly two to one.

And so, in a very real sense, War, with its horrors and desolations, brought us our birthright of free citizenship, and already many other birthrights have followed in the train of this one essential thing. What I desire to consider now is whether we are justified in hoping and believing that the citizenship of women will strengthen the foundations of peace. Shall we, in our right hands, carry gentle peace?[10] The answer to this question is not quite plain and simple. Many women are extremely quarrelsome and vindictive; they are as capable as men are of hatred, and of the blindness which hatred brings. If Hamlet could say of himself: 'I am very proud, revengeful, ambitious',[11] could not many women, when they look into their own hearts, say the same? Out of such passions war is born. Can we hope that human nature will ever be so much changed and purified that this monstrosity will never be brought to birth again. I have been to a good many election meetings lately, and the women present have roared for the Kaiser's blood as loudly as the men. They also have as keen a desire that their own personal losses should be wiped out by German gold. A woman caught hold of me at one of the meetings and said, 'I have lost three sons in the war; I shouldn't mind if Germany is made to pay every penny the war has cost.' I tried, but, I fear with scant success, to make her pause and realize what she was saying. Such things make one's heart sink. Did she really mean that her sons' lives could be paid for with £ s. d.? Had we really won the war only to lose our own soul? This is the darker side of the question we are considering. Let us look now at some of its brighter aspects.

Throughout the animal creation, man not excepted, the male is the fighting sex. Birds in their little nests do not agree. All male creatures struggle with one another. And therefore to leave practically the whole of the control and government of the world in the hands of the fighters to the exclusion of the non-fighters must increase the risks of war.

Looking again at the chief protagonists in the great war just closed, one thing comes out clearly. The countries where the social and political power of women is greatest are Great Britain, the United States and France; the countries where the social and political power of women is the lowest are Germany, Austria and Turkey.[12] And it is these last, without a shadow of doubt, which planned and provoked the war. The blood-guiltiness is on the heads of those nations, and among them, especially on Prussia, where the general subjection, both political and social, of women, was carried to its utmost depths.[13]

This looks as if in those countries where women had a fair chance of developing their own special gifts and qualities the risks of war are diminished.

May I take specific instances in illustration of this view? I remember being so very much struck by a scene I witnessed in the Town Hall of Oldham on the day when Mrs Lees was installed in office as Mayor.[14] Before she appeared, there was a most acrimonious quarrel, conducted with considerable want of restraint and with a complete absence of dignity, by members of the Town Council about the next succession to the Mayoralty. It was a squalid scene, full of pettiness and of lengthy discussion upon points of no real consequence to anyone. Then suddenly a complete change was witnessed. With almost magical rapidity the storm subsided, smiles succeeded frowns and sneers. Mrs Lees entered, was decorated with the robes and chain of office, and proceeded to give her inaugural address. It was a change from howling to music, from empty wrangling over things that did not matter to a thoughtful consideration of the things that did matter: the health of the town, the welfare of the children, the creation of municipal amenities calculated in various ways to make Oldham, if not beautiful, at any rate less depressingly the reverse of beautiful.[15] And, I thought, if the entrance of women into municipal politics can create this blessed change, what may we not hope from the future when the women in every sphere of activity will really come into their own.

I can give another example from Mrs Oliver Strachey's election campaign[16] in Brentford and Chiswick.[17] On December 12th, an article appeared in the *Times* with the head lines, 'Eggs at Brentford. Mrs Oliver Strachey's Popularity'.[18] My first thought was, 'Heavens! Have they been pelting her with rotten eggs?'[19] But I was wrong, as usual, as the White Queen said.[20] At the end of a most charming article, written I know not by whom, but I venture to say by a literary artist, 'the eggs at Brentford' were explained to be not the traditional election egg, stale and evil-smelling, but presents of fresh eggs from unknown sympathisers sent to convey good wishes and to aid the woman candidate in holding out.[21] Could there be a more delightful contrast between the ancient and modern use of eggs in elections? If this is the eternal feminine in politics, shall we not all welcome it with enthusiasm, and hope that as women more and more become a power in politics, they will in their right hands carry gentle peace.

Transcribed from a copy in the British Library.
No known copyright restrictions.

Notes

1. Constance Georgine Markievicz (1868–1927), Irish Sinn Féin politician and revolutionary. Given Sinn Féin's abstentionist policy, she refused to take her seat in the House of Commons (Pašeta 2017).
2. See Section 44.
3. For example, Flora Murray (1869–1923) and Fawcett's niece, Louisa Garrett Anderson (1873–1943), established a hospital in Paris with the support of the French Red Cross (F. Murray 1920). In 1914, the surgeon Elsie Inglis (1864–1917) set up the Scottish Women's Hospitals for Foreign Service committee, which aimed to provide all-female-staffed hospitals. When the Red Cross refused to support this initiative, Inglis used her connections with the NUWSS (and Fawcett) to fundraise. Scottish Women's Hospitals sent units to service in France, Serbia, Corsica, Salonika, Romania, Russia and Malta (Lawrence 1971; see also Fawcett 1920a, 95–105).
4. See Sections 39, 41 and 42.
5. See Section 42.
6. See Section 41 regarding the resignation of the officers and executive members of the NUWSS.
7. It is not clear who Fawcett is referring to here. An honorary secretary of the NUWSS, Kathleen D'Olier Courtney had both worked full-time at national headquarters between 1911 and 1914, and resigned in April 1915. Courtney then 'worked for the Serbian Relief Fund in Salonika, took charge of a temporary Serbian refugee colony in Bastia, Corsica, and was decorated by the Serbian government' (Grenier 2004). Clara Dorothea Tabor Rackham (1875–1966) resigned in autumn 1915 to take up work as a factory inspector (*London Gazette* 1915).
8. Asquith, in a statement in the House of Commons on the results of the Electoral Reform Conference (see Section 43) and his reasons for now supporting votes for women (*Times* 1917b).
9. Lord Curzon (see Section 18, note 74) was by then leader of the House of Lords. Although personally opposed to the Representation of the People Act, he knew the repercussions of ignoring the Commons majority would be significant (House of Lords Debate [hereafter HL Deb] 1918, 508–24).
10. The fall of Cardinal Wolsey in *Henry VIII* 3.2: 'Still in thy right hand carry gentle peace, / To silence envious tongues. Be just, and fear not: / Let all the ends thou aim'st at be thy country's, / Thy God's, and truth's.'
11. *Hamlet* 3.1.
12. Women obtained the right to vote in Germany on 30 November 1918 (although this was later restricted in the 1930s under the National Socialists) (Hannam, Auchterlonie and Holden 2000, 114). In Austria, women gained the right to vote in December 1918 (p. 29). In Turkey, women did not get the right to vote until 1931 for local elections and 1934 for national elections (p. 297).

13 Women in Prussia (and some other German states) were not permitted to engage in politics until 1908 (Palatschek and Pietrow-Ennker 2004, 236; see also Parlow 1908).
14 Dame Sarah Anne Lees (1842–1935), English Liberal politician, first female councillor elected in Lancashire (1907–19) and the first female mayor in Oldham (1910–11), making her the second woman mayor in England after Fawcett's sister Elizabeth Garrett Anderson in 1908.
15 Fawcett is alluding to the 'Beautiful Oldham Society' founded by Lees in 1903 in an attempt to improve the town's environment (Crawford 2001a, 337).
16 Rachel (Ray) Pearsall Conn Strachey (1887–1940), feminist activist and writer, close friend and biographer (see Strachey 1931) of Fawcett. Strachey stood as an independent candidate in the 1918, 1920 and 1922 elections, 'but expressed great delight when she was defeated' (Caine 2011).
17 Strachey stood as an independent candidate for Brentford and Chiswick in 1918, particularly as an opponent to the coalition candidate Colonel Walter Grant Morden (1880–1932), who had said that 'a women's place is to rule the home' (*Times* 1918b). Although Strachey was described as 'the favourite in the contest' (*Times* 1918c), Grant Morden won, with 9,077 votes to Strachey's 1,263. Two thousand, six hundred and twenty votes went to the Labour candidate, William Haywood (*Yorkshire Telegraph and Star* 1918).
18 *Times* 1918b.
19 On the Great Pilgrimage in 1913 (see Figure 15), suffragists had been pelted with eggs and dead rats (*Common Cause* 1913g).
20 Said by the Red Queen, in *Through the Looking-Glass, and What Alice Found There* (Carroll 1872, 191).
21 'Mrs Strachey is constantly receiving presents of fresh eggs from unknown admirers. At a time when eggs are so scarce and dear, could there be a more remarkable proof of popularity?' (*Times* 1918b).

46
Courage calls to courage everywhere, 1920

The Women's Victory – and After: Personal reminiscences, 1911–1918. London: Sidgwick and Jackson Ltd, 66–7.

In March 1919, at the age of 71, and having seen 'the whole feminist movement . . . stand on ground which is firmer and stronger than any ground we have stood on before', Fawcett stood down as president of the NUWSS (Fawcett 1919), which in April 1919 renamed itself the National Union of Societies for Equal Citizenship (NUSEC). In the latter part of 1919 and into early 1920 (Rubinstein 1991, 257–8), she wrote a memoir covering the recent history of gaining the vote for women and the role of the NUWSS in achieving it: *The Women's Victory – and After: Personal reminiscences, 1911–1918*. Throughout her political life, Fawcett had argued for the vote along non-violent, constitutional lines. Yet it is in a rare and passing reflection in her memoir upon a specifically militant suffragette action that Fawcett's most famous phrase is to be found: 'Courage calls to courage everywhere' (Fawcett 1920a, 66).

On Wednesday, 4 June 1913, the militant suffragette and WSPU member Emily Wilding Davison (1872–1913) was mortally wounded as she ran out in front of the King's horse, Anmer, at the Epsom Derby (*Globe* 1913, 11). Davison died from her injuries four days later. Although her motives and purpose remain unclear (Morley and Stanley 1988; Crawford 2014a), the WSPU was quick to describe her as a martyr: 'she has taught the world that there are women who care so passionately for the vote and all it means that they are willing to die for it' (*Suffragette* 1913a). On Saturday, 14 June, a 'great and imposing funeral procession' for Davison weaved across London, comprised of hunger strikers, followed by representatives of many suffrage organisations, and 'throngs of people . . . lined the route' (*Votes for Women* 1913, 553). She was buried at home in Morpeth on Sunday, 15 June, when 'thousands of people . . . lined the streets to watch several hundred suffragettes and the hearse take nearly two hours to go the half mile from the railway station to the parish church . . . the last in the line of great suffragette shows of strength and presence' (Morley and Stanley 1988, 173).

At the time, Fawcett did not publicly comment[1] or attend the funeral procession or burial. She was in Europe, in preparatory meetings for the International Woman Suffrage Alliance (IWSA) Congress, and heard the news in Vienna on either 11 or 12 June (*Common Cause* 1913c). An anonymous tersely worded column on 'Responsibility', condemning the leadership of the WSPU, appeared in the NUWSS's *Common Cause* of Friday, 13 June, to 'record with deep regret the death of Miss Emily Wilding Davieson [sic]. It is impossible not to put the question – who is responsible for this piteous waste of courage and devotion?' (*Common Cause* 1913e). Fawcett was in Budapest attending the IWSA Congress on the day of Davison's funeral procession (*Common Cause* 1913f). Although 'many NUWSS members turned out' in the pageant,

> at a national level the NUWSS failed to take part or even to send a wreath. Ray Strachey, then Assistant Secretary to the London Union, wrote to an inquiring member that 'we' deplored Emily Davison's action, however much it might have been done in good faith, for it alienated otherwise sympathetic people (Morley and Stanley 1988, 172–3).

The NUWSS had already planned its own march, the Great Pilgrimage, which began on 18 June and saw 50,000 suffragists (including Fawcett herself from mid-July) walking to London from all over the UK, culminating in a rally in Hyde Park on 26 July (see Figure 15). Planned to draw attention to the moderate constitutionalist approach in the face of militant violence, the beginning of the Pilgrimage, at least, was overshadowed in the newspapers by the event at Epsom and its sensationalist aftermath.

Fawcett finally mentioned Davison's death seven years later in *The Women's Victory – and After*, at the close of a chapter about the summer of 1913 focusing on the NUWSS Pilgrimage. Fawcett points out that the volunteers pledging to serve the army in a true 'principle of self-sacrifice' had won Britain the war. This short passage remains dismissive of Davison's actions and the suffragettes' framing of her as a martyr:

'a woman was capable of throwing away her life on the chance that it might serve the cause of freedom'. Fawcett's view of the suffragettes' tactics had not mellowed over time;[2] however, there is a concession, however fleeting,[3] to the public response to militant action and its role in feminist conscience-raising: 'Courage calls to courage everywhere, and its voice cannot be denied.'

Fawcett is not a writer who regularly serves the reader pithy epithets, but 'Courage calls to courage everywhere' has become her defining phrase. This is despite the fact that original sales of *The Women's Victory – and After* were poor[4] (Rubinstein 1991, 257–8). From the late 1970s, the quote, denuded of context, started to appear in compilations of feminist, twentieth-century and inspiring quotations (McPhee and Fitzgerald 1979, 239; Donadio et al. 1992, 245; Setzer 1994, 52; Zadra 1999, 101). The quote was repeated by the radical feminist philosopher Mary Daly (1928–2010) (1984, 281 and 302; 1998, 103). It has circulated online as motivational inspiration since at least the early 2000s.[5] 'Courage calls to courage everywhere' has become a part of popular culture since its use on the 2018 statue of Fawcett by Gillian Wearing (b. 1963), which was unveiled to mark the centenary of the Representation of the People Act 1918.

On 21 October 2015, Daniel, Lord Finkelstein, wrote an editorial in the *Times* stating, 'Breaking the law didn't win votes for women; it was moderate, law-abiding suffragists and male MPs – not militant suffragettes – who did most to secure victory . . . So here's my proposal. In 2018, the centenary of votes for women, why not have a statue of Millicent Fawcett in Parliament Square?' (Finkelstein 2015). On 8 March 2016 (International Women's Day), Caroline Criado Perez (b. 1984) launched a petition, followed by an online campaign, to put the first statue of a woman in Parliament Square (Criado Perez 2016; Dico 2016; Criado Perez and Cohen 2016). On 11 May 2016, the Mayor of London, Sadiq Khan (b. 1970), announced as 'a proud feminist in City Hall . . . he is keen to explore a suitable high-profile site for a statue' (Khan 2016). Criado Perez's campaign originally called for a statue of a suffragette. However, on 7 June 2016, it was revealed that the proposed statue would be of Millicent Fawcett, a suffragist (Cohen 2016; Harris 2016). Very suitably, the announcement was made at an event hosted by the Fawcett Society, held in the Speaker's House State Rooms, to commemorate the 150th anniversary of the first women's suffrage petition being presented to Parliament in 1866 (Crawford 2016b).[6] Shortly after, promotional material for a memorial lecture to Millicent Fawcett, organised by the Fawcett Society and held on 6 July to commemorate the 150th anniversary of the first suffrage petition, used the phrase 'Courage calls to courage everywhere.'[7]

On 2 April 2017, the UK government announced that Millicent Fawcett had officially been chosen to be remembered by a statue as part of the funded celebrations[8] to mark the centenary of the Representation of the People Act 1918, stressing that she 'led the peaceful campaign for women's suffrage' (Ministry of Housing, Communities and Local Government 2017). On 13 April 2017, it was announced that Gillian Wearing had been commissioned by the Mayor of London, making her the first female sculptor to have a piece in Parliament Square (Greater London Authority 2017a). Wearing is known for her use of signs in her artworks (Phaidon 2018). The artist's statement for 'Courage Calls' submitted for planning permission explains:

> The sign Fawcett holds bears her own words . . . The text has been selected to encourage viewers to think of others who are selfless and courageous. Fawcett's words were written in response to the death of Suffragette Emily Davidson,[9] who was trampled to death by the King's horse at Epsom Derby. Davidson put her own life on the line in order to protest the right to women's voices being heard. Fawcett, who as a non-militant Suffragist did not align herself with the Suffragettes, did however understand that the Suffragettes played an important role in securing the vote for women. The viewing public will not need to know the full context of this quote, as the words speak on a much wider level. However, the words embed a relationship and connection between the two groups (Wearing 2017).

Planning permission was submitted on 21 June 2017 and granted on 19 September 2017 (Greater London Authority 2017b), at which point the designs were unveiled, with the statue and its wording receiving much press coverage (BBC 2017b, *Guardian* 2017, *Huffington Post* 2017).[10] Work began immediately.[11] The statue was unveiled on 24 April 2018 (NPR 2018).

This excerpt from *The Women's Victory – and After* gives the full context of the now-famous quote. Fawcett highlights the peaceful nature of the Great Pilgrimage, and its successes, before briefly reflecting at the chapter's close on the militant activities that had also taken place that summer, and the institutional and public responses to them. Although making a comparison between Davison's death and the sacrifice made since then by others in the service of their country, and the attention given to both suffragist and suffragette activities, the quote is not quite so clearly congratulatory regarding militant action as the modern meaning now projected onto it.

*

Again and again, on all possible occasions, we urged that the redress of grievances was the true remedy for disorder. We recognized, along with very large numbers of people hitherto uninterested in our movement, the courage and power of self-sacrifice of the militants, but we felt that the use of the weapon of physical force was the negation of the very principle for which we struggled: it was denying our faith to make our faith prevail.

In the early summer of 1913, an incident occurred which deeply touched the popular imagination and placed the principle of self-sacrifice as illustrated by the militants on a hill-top from which it was seen not only all over our own country, but throughout the world. Courage calls to courage everywhere, and its voice cannot be denied.

The race for the Derby was held on the last Wednesday of May.[12] The King's horse was the favourite. Crowds even more enormous than usual gathered to witness it; among them, a young woman, a militant suffragist, Emily Davidson,[13] of Morpeth in Northumberland, had managed to place herself close to the winning-post against the rope barrier which kept the crowd off the actual track. As the King's horse swept by at a tremendous speed, Emily Davidson threw herself in front of it. Down came the horse with fearful violence; the jockey was, of course, thrown and seriously injured; and there lay Emily Davidson, mortally injured.[14] She had deliberately sacrificed her life[15] in order, in this sensational way, to draw the attention of the whole world to the determination of women to share in the heritage of freedom which was the boast of every man in the country. The King enquired for the jockey; the Queen enquired for the injured woman.[16] In a day or two it was announced that she was dead. She never recovered consciousness. She had died for her cause. After one of the military disasters which accompanied the early development of Risorgimento in Italy, the historian writes that young Italy had, at least, shown that it knew how to die.[17] Emily Davidson had shown that she, too, knew how to die. I happened to be in Vienna at the time, and I shall not easily forget the awed solemnity with which a Viennese with whom I had had some halting conversation in German on the suffrage question came to me and said, 'Miss Davidson ist todt.'

It is said that the urgency of the suffrage problem in Great Britain was one reason which induced the ex-Kaiser and his advisers to consider England a decadent power;[18] if this is true, it is only an example of the way in which he misread every sign of the times and totally misunderstood this country. That a woman was capable of throwing away her life on the chance that it might serve the cause of freedom might have taught him to expect what happened about fourteen months later, when over 5,000,000 young Englishmen voluntarily joined the army in order to preserve the principles of liberty and self-government throughout the world.

Transcribed from editor's own copy. No known copyright restrictions.

Notes

1. There is a common misconception that Fawcett's phrase 'Courage calls to courage everywhere' is 'taken from a speech she gave after the death in 1913 of campaigner Emily Wilding Davison at the Epsom Derby' (BBC 2017b). See also the use of this phrase in various news outlets, including the *Guardian* 2017, *Huffington Post* 2017 and *NPR* 2018. It is also seen on the Google Arts and Culture site documenting the creation of Wearing's statue (2018a). This can be traced back to an error in the Mayoral Press Release confirming planning permission had been granted (Greater London Authority 2017b). It is worth stressing that no such 1913 speech from Fawcett exists: 'Those words were not written at the turbulent time of Davison's death, when Fawcett made no public comment, but in the relative safety of 1920' (Purvis 2018).
2. In 1928 she commented, 'I do not share . . . admiration of the militant movement, for I have always been opposed to absolute autocracy, and have believed in the educative effects of freedom and responsibility' (Fawcett 1928d).
3. See also Section 25: Fawcett had been sympathetic to the civil disobedience of the WSPU, and the benefits of direct action, until they turned violent.
4. 'Sales had been poor, despite generally favourable press notices . . . it would be necessary to obtain support . . . if the book was to be saved from commercial failure' (Rubinstein 1991, 257). See Strachey (1920, 158) for an overview, suggesting that Fawcett's focus on the political framework, including 'so few personal reminiscences', and the fact that audiences were no longer interested in the concluded struggle were the reasons behind the low sales: 'how picturesque it was! The Pilgrimage: the Banners: the Processions: Hyde Park on a Sunday, and the rotten eggs at street corners! Gone are all those pleasures, and in their place the vote'.
5. The earliest extant use of 'Courage Calls to Courage Everywhere, and its Voice Cannot Be Denied' as an online motivational quote found so far is a digital image indexed by Google from PictureQuotes.com on 1 February 2001: http://www.picturequotes.com/courage-calls-to-courage-everywhere-and-its-voice-cannot-be-denied-quote-370791.
6. See Introduction.
7. Fawcett Society 2016.
8. The statue was 'Commissioned by the Mayor of London with 14-18 NOW, Firstsite and Iniva to commemorate the Centenary of the Representation of the People Act 1918, through the Government's national centenary fund' (1418now.org 2018). 14–18 NOW was the UK's arts programme for the World War I centenary.
9. Note Wearing's misspelling of Davison, following Fawcett's spelling.
10. See note 1 regarding the accuracy of the press coverage. No twenty-first-century newspaper coverage featuring 'courage calls to courage everywhere' has been found prior to the Mayoral Press Release (Greater London Authority 2017b).
11. See Google Arts and Culture 2018b for the making of the statue.
12. The Epsom Derby was on the first Wednesday in June, rather than the last in May (*Globe* 1913).
13. Note Fawcett's misspelling. Davison was also not a 'young woman', being 41 at the time of the Derby.
14. See *Globe* (1913, 11) for a detailed account. A newsreel from *Pathé News*, of both Derby and funeral procession, survives (British Pathé 2011).
15. It is not known if she did intend to do so: 'Emily Davison's masterstroke was to have met her death without leaving any specific indication of her intent, this absence a *tabula rasa* on which may be inscribed any number of theories', creating 'a tangle of fictions, false deductions, hearsay,

conjecture, misrepresentation and theory'. These include martyrship, misadventure and deliberate positioning and purpose, although conclusions remain inconclusive: 'While not setting out purposely to kill herself she did knowingly put herself in the way of harm' (Crawford 2014a). The *Emily Wilding Davison Centenary Exhibition* from LSE Digital Library contains more information: https://digital.library.lse.ac.uk/exhibitions/emily-wilding-davison-centenary.

16 'Immediately after the accident the King ordered inquiries to be made as to the nature of his jockey's injuries . . . Before the King and Queen left Epsom they received a reassuring report from the doctor and were also informed of the condition of Miss Davison . . . The Queen sent a messenger later in the evening to Epsom Hospital to inquire for Miss Davison' (*Times* 1913b).

17 The Risorgimento was the unification of states of the Italian Peninsula into the Kingdom of Italy in the nineteenth century. The Italian nationalist Emilio Attilio (1811–44) had written 'in one of his letters . . . "And if we do lose our lives, what matters? Italy will never live till Italians learn to die"' (Mario 1909, 80).

18 This was a common belief. In her 17 November 1914 speech at Plymouth Guildhall, where suffragism was abandoned for the patriotic cause, Emmeline Pankhurst remarked, 'one of the mistakes the Kaiser made, one among many, was that he thought under all circumstances the British people would continue their internal dissensions' (Pugh 2000, 9).

47
Picturing Fawcett: Dame Millicent Fawcett, 1925

DAME MILLICENT FAWCETT, D.B.E.

Figure 17: Fawcett photographed outside her home at 2 Gower Street, London, on the day of her investiture as Dame Grand Cross of the Order of the British Empire (GBE) on Thursday, 12 February 1925. The Topical Press Photographic Agency, 1925. In Lang (1929, 91). No known copyright restrictions.

In 1917, the newly created Order of the British Empire allowed women to receive chivalric honours (Crown Office 1917), and there followed complaints that Fawcett had not yet been awarded this recognition (*Manchester Guardian* 1924). In the 1925 New Year Honours she was appointed Dame Grand Cross of the Order of the British Empire (GBE) (*London Gazette* 1925). The *Illustrated London News* commented, 'the Dameship proffered to Mrs Fawcett, that wonderful champion of Women's Causes, who has done more for the acquisition of the vote than all the militant suffragettes, is a tardy recognition of a great Englishwoman' (*Illustrated London News* 1925). The *Woman's Leader* celebrated the achievement, chided the prime minister for taking so long, and asked for more: 'we should have been tempted by our better knowledge of Dame Millicent Fawcett's political wisdom and greatness of character to create her not a Dame of the Grand Cross, but a Duchess in her own right' (1925a).

With this honour, Fawcett transcended from establishment figure to celebrity. Tickets were sold for a crowded afternoon tea at Claridge's Hotel on Tuesday, 10 February, for the three women featured in the 1925 honours: Fawcett, the actress Dame Ellen Terry (1847–1928) and the surgeon Dame Louisa Aldrich-Blake (1865–1925) (*Yorkshire Post and Leeds Intelligencer* 1925).[1] The actual ceremony took place on 12 February 1925. A cropped version of this cheerful photograph of Fawcett aged 77, taken on her doorstep, was featured in the *Daily Mail* (1925, 16): 'Dame Millicent Fawcett leaving for her investiture by the King at Buckingham Palace yesterday.' 'Many people assembled outside the Palace in the hope of seeing these ladies, but they obtained only the most cursory glance, seeing that they arrived and left in motor-cars' (*Leeds Mercury* 1925). Mrs Henry Fawcett was known afterwards as Dame Millicent Fawcett.

This picture was later reused as a headshot in *Reynolds's Illustrated News*, where Fawcett was described as 'the veteran suffragist who is near to seeing the fruition of her life's work' (1927).

Notes

1 A picture of the three dames appeared on the front page of the *Birmingham Daily Gazette* 1925. Fawcett is wearing the same hat as she wore to the investiture.

48
Picturing Fawcett: Dame Millicent Fawcett at NUSEC garden party, 1925

Figure 18: Dame Millicent Garrett Fawcett speaking in the garden of Aubrey House at a party organised in her honour by NUSEC on Thursday, 23 July 1925. From the Women's Library at LSE. No known copyright restrictions.

To celebrate Fawcett's investiture as Dame (see Figure 17), a 'wholly delightful garden party' was organised by the National Union of Societies for Equal Citizenship (NUSEC, the new name adopted by NUWSS after the close of World War I, having achieved votes for some women). For the party, NUSEC 'resolved itself temporarily into the National Union of Women's Suffrage Societies' and many luminaries of the suffrage movement 'spoke from a platform backed by banners which had seen service in many processions' (*Woman's Leader* 1925c): on the right is an old London banner, on the left, Edinburgh. Seated next to Fawcett is Miss Eleanor Rathbone (1872–1946), the campaigner for women's rights who had taken over the presidency after Fawcett's retirement in 1919. The event was attended by many involved in the movement:

> Who was there? It is impossible for us to give a complete list, space forbids. Nor is it easy to make a rational selection since every person there played a notable part, prominent or obscure, in the movement which Dame Millicent led . . . including distinguished guests from Australia, Canada, Switzerland and other countries, as well as representatives of Societies of the National Union scattered throughout the country . . . But of this at least we are certain: the spirits of Miss I. O. Ford, and Dr Elizabeth Garrett Anderson, and Mrs Osler, Mrs Harley, and Dr Elsie Inglis were there – for how, when so many of their old friends were gathered together and wanting them so badly, could they have failed to come? (*Woman's Leader* 1925c).

The location, Aubrey House, 'the most glorious of gardens, on Campden Hill', in Holland Park, London, was a 'garden familiar to Kensington suffragists as the scene of many old encounters', and 'Dame Millicent, in an interesting reminiscent speech which provoked much laughter on occasion, told the audience why Aubrey House was to her a place full of pleasant memories' (*Vote* 1925): it was at a party there in April 1865 that Millicent had first met Henry Fawcett (Fawcett 1924, 53; see Figure 1), and it was also the house in which Millicent Fawcett worked with other committee members of the early London suffrage society in 1867 (*Vote* 1925).

49
What the vote has done, 1926 and 1927
NUSEC, London: Gwen M. Parry, Chandos House.

Fawcett had a busy retirement. She travelled, including a trip to Cairo and four trips to Palestine (Fawcett 1926b; Rubinstein 1991, 263). She became a magistrate (*Manchester Guardian* 1920). From 1920 until 1925 she was chairman of the *Woman's Leader and Common Cause* (a new paper which subsumed the *Common Cause* and was close to, but not the official publication of, NUSEC) (Rubinstein 1991, 259), which serialised her autobiography. These memoirs were published as *What I Remember* (1924). She attended various NUSEC meetings and other conferences, dinners and public events. She continued to publish articles, reviews and letters in newspapers. Throughout, she kept up to date with the changing political landscape, and her concerns remained with women's emancipation, particularly focusing on internationalisation, continuing her association with the IWSA and being elected vice-president of the nascent League of Nations Union (Rubinstein 1991, 255).

Towards the end of *The Women's Victory – and After*, Fawcett had noted a comment made in the House of Lords that 'the mere fact women have a right to vote makes no difference at all',[1] and began to keep a tally of the successes women's enfranchisement had wrought (1920a, 156–68). These were also summarised in her final article in the *Englishwoman* (Fawcett 1920b). An updated account was released as a series of pamphlets which 'first appeared as a brief single-page leaflet. It has now grown, augmented year by year, as new Acts have been carried' (Fawcett 1927e, 112). These were sold at the price of 2d. to fundraise for NUSEC, firstly in 1922 (4 pages), then 1924 (4 pages), 1925 (6 pages), 1926 (6 pages) and the final revision in 1927 (8 pages). These were 'not simply a celebration of the women's vote' (Rubinstein 1991, 264) but aimed to point out inequalities that affected women while also providing a map of the concerns of NUSEC and where they were focusing their energies in lobbying since the granting of the franchise to some women in the United Kingdom in 1918 (see Section 44). As Fawcett wrote in the *Chambers's Encyclopedia* entry regarding Women's Rights, 'The movement towards the emancipation of women is one from status to contract' (1927d, 693).

Here the full text of the 1926 edition of the pamphlet is provided, plus the additions made in the 1927 edition, particularly indicating the developing political discussions on extending the franchise to all women. References are given throughout to key discussions in the *Common Cause* and *Woman's Leader*, showing the interest the suffrage movement had in key legislative initiatives, broadly framed, and how they affected women.

*

Before women were enfranchised it was possible, after years of hard work and persistent effort, to get through Parliament changes in the law favourable to the position of women. But this process was not rapid; and it absorbed the labour of a large number of able women. During the first eighteen years of the present century, four such measures were carried, or one in every four and a-half years, whereas in the seven years since women have had the vote the rate has been speeded up in a rather remarkable degree. I wish, however, to emphasise not merely the number and value of the Acts that have been passed since women had the vote, but the completely different and improved atmosphere that has been created as regards the sphere of women in national life and its responsibilities. Those of us who had worked in the Lobbies and Committee Rooms of the House of Commons for bettering the legal position of women were conscious of this improvement from the very moment when the Representation of the People Act, 1918, received the Royal Assent.[2] We were no longer there on sufferance, but by right.

Below will be found a list of many of the changes in the law favourable to women, which have been made in the United Kingdom since the passing of the Representation of the People Act in February 1918.

1918

The Parliamentary (Qualification of Women) Act renders it possible for a constituency to choose a woman as its representative in the House of Commons. This Act went through almost unopposed.[3] But as it was passed only three weeks before the General Election of 1918 took place, it is not surprising that no woman was elected.[4] Nearly all the constituencies had already selected their candidates. Notwithstanding this, 16 women stood for election,[5] among them one who had been a leading opponent of Women's Suffrage. Viscountess Astor[6] (C.), stood at a by-election for Sutton, Plymouth, in 1919, and was elected, while Mrs Wintringham[7] (L.), at another by-election at Louth, in 1921, was elected. In the General Election of November 1922, there were 25 women candidates, but only the 2 who had already been in Parliament were successful. In May 1923, another by-election, at Berwick-on-Tweed, resulted in the return of a third woman to Parliament – Mrs Philipson,[8] as a Conservative, who had the immense majority of more than 6,000 votes over her opponent. In the General Election of December 1923, there were 34 women candidates, of whom 8 were successful, 3 belonging to the Conservatives, 3 to the Labour and 2 to the Liberal parties respectively. The 3 women who had already sat in the House of Commons were re-elected – in the case of 2 of them, by largely increased majorities. It was a proud moment when, in 1924, 2 women were appointed members of the Government – Miss Margaret Bondfield[9] as Parliamentary Secretary to the Ministry of Labour, and Miss Susan Lawrence[10] as one of the Parliamentary Private Secretaries to the Board of Education. After the General Election of October 1924, in spite of the disappointment felt at the defeat of all but 4 of the 41 women candidates, an examination of the circumstances makes it plain that they merely shared the fate of their respective Parties. Miss Ellen Wilkinson,[11] indeed, won the seat for her Party. The presence of women members of the Government was maintained by the appointment of the Duchess of Atholl[12] to the Parliamentary Secretaryship of the Board of Education.

1918

The Registration of Midwives Amending Act removes some of the defects of the previous Act passed in 1902, which was placed on the Statute Book only after 12 years' hard work, and included several obvious defects, because it was feared that their removal would jeopardise its passing. In 1918, the Amending Act was adopted as a Government measure and passed almost unopposed.[13]

1918 to 1923

The Affiliation Orders (Increase of Maximum Payment) Act 1918 (England and Wales) amended the Bastardy Laws Act of 1872, which fixed 5s. a week as the maximum which the father (whatever his wealth) could be made to pay towards the maintenance of an illegitimate child, by increasing this sum to 10s. a week. It will be noted that this important change in the Law was passed through both Houses of Parliament in the very year that women were enfranchised, and it should also be noted that four years later, in 1923, a new **Bastardy Act** in charge of Captain Bowyer[14] was passed which, among other things, raised the maximum amount which could be paid under an affiliation order to 20s.[15]

1919

The Sex Disqualification (Removal) Act. In November 1918, immediately before the General Election, Mr Lloyd George[16] and Mr Bonar Law[17] promised, if returned to power, to introduce legislation 'to remove all existing inequalities in the law between men and women'. They were returned to power by an immense majority, but the King's speech at the opening of Parliament gave no indication of any intention to fulfil this pledge. In 1919 the Labour Party introduced and carried through all its stages in the Commons, notwithstanding Government opposition, a measure called the Women's Emancipation Bill, and this roused the Government. The Bill of the Labour Party was torpedoed in the House of Lords, and the Government passed through all its stages in both Houses the Sex Disqualification (Removal) Act. The Government measure was not so complete as that of the Labour Party, as it made no reference at all to the franchise, but it gave an important instalment in the direction of fulfilling the pledge quoted above. It opened the legal profession in both its branches to women; it enabled women to sit on Juries and to act as Magistrates, and it made it clear to the Universities of Oxford and Cambridge that they were free to open their membership, degrees and all other privileges to women. Oxford availed itself of these powers without delay. Under the Sex Disqualification (Removal) Act, more than 1,000 women have been appointed as Magistrates.[18]

1919

Nurses Registration Act. Trained nurses, without the vote, had been working for registration for 32 years but without success; one year after the enfranchisement of women, the principle of registration was accepted by the Government and the Act embodying it was passed into law.[19]

1919 to 1925

League of Nations. The Charter of the League of Nations contains a clause rendering women equally eligible with men for all appointments in connection with the League, including the Secretariat.[20] This clause has not remained a dead letter. Dame Rachel Crowdy[21] has been put in charge of the section dealing with Public Health, and the Traffic in Women and Children, and many other women have been given responsible positions in the International Labour Bureau and within the Secretariat of the League. Great Britain has not as yet appointed a Woman Delegate to the Assembly of the League, but each year since 1922, a woman has been appointed as substitute-delegate. In 1922 it was Mrs Coombe Tennant, JP;[22] in 1923, Dame Elizabeth Lyttelton;[23] in 1924, Mrs Swanwick;[24] and this year the appointment was held by the Duchess of Atholl, DBE, LLD, MP. Miss Bondfield was appointed as the British Government Representative to the 21st Session of the Governing Body of the International Labour Office in Geneva in 1924.

1920 to 1925

Women in the Civil Service. The position in the Civil Service is still very far from being completely satisfactory. Major Hills, MP,[25] succeeded in May 1920 in passing without opposition a resolution in the House of Commons favourable to the adoption of equal conditions for women as Civil Servants, and in August 1921 a notable Parliamentary victory was won, when the Government would certainly have been defeated if they had not made important concessions to the claims of women to be admitted to the Home Civil Service under the same regulations which govern the admission of men. The question of the remuneration of women was postponed for three years, but unfortunately when, in 1924, this was considered, a Treasury Inquiry reported against giving of Equal Pay on the grounds of expense. In 1925 the first examination was held for admission to the administrative classes of the Service, and was open to men and women alike.[26]

1920

Married Women's Property Act (Scotland) gives a married woman the same rights over her property as a single woman, and brings the Scottish legislation into line with the English on this subject.[27]

1920

Maintenance Orders (Facilities for Enforcement) Act makes it possible for sums payable under Maintenance Orders to be recovered from men who have gone to any other part of the Empire. Reciprocal legislation, without which the British Act is a dead letter, has now been passed in most of the Dominions and Colonies except India and Canada.[28]

1922

Married Women (Maintenance Act) (England and Wales) provides that under a Separation Order a sum up to 10s. for each child shall be allowed to a wife in addition to a maximum sum of 40s. for herself.[29]

1922

The Infanticide Act provides that a woman should not be accused of murder if, having killed her infant child, it can be shown that she was still suffering from the effects of confinement.[30]

1918 to 1925

Women Police. In 1918, the Metropolitan Policewomen Patrols were established and by 1921 numbered 111. The Sex Disqualification (Removal) Act 1919 legalised the appointment of women as police, and their inclusion in the Police Pensions Act 1921 further stabilised their position. In 1922, 80 of the Patrols were dismissed, but in 1924 the numbers were increased to 50 and they were established as police constables with full powers. Two Home Office Committees of Inquiry, in 1920 and 1924, strongly recommended their employment.[31] This Autumn, Miss Ellen Wilkinson will introduce, under the ten minutes rule, a Bill making it compulsory on Watch Committees of Boroughs under the Municipal Corporations Act to appoint women constables.

1922 to 1925

Nationality of Married Women. A Bill providing that a British woman should, on marriage, have the same right to change or retain her nationality as has a man, was put before the House in 1922. The Joint Select Committee of both Houses of Parliament which was set up on this Bill failed to agree on a report. In February 1925, however, a resolution in favour of this principle was passed by the House of Commons, and although the Government has as yet done nothing in the matter except to inform the Dominions and to ask their opinion, the support of the House of Commons should do much to bring about this reform.[32]

1922

Criminal Law Amendment Act. As a result of the long struggle for the protection of the young girl, the passing of the Criminal Law Amendment in July 1922 must be regarded as a triumph. Criminal Law Amendment Bills of various kinds have been introduced year after year. In 1922, as a result of great pressure mainly from women's organisations, the Government introduced its own Bill, and even this did not get through without difficulty. The most important clauses of the Act are those which:

(A) Raise the age of consent for indecent assault from 13 to 16.
(B) Take away the plea of reasonable cause to believe that a girl is under the age of 16 except in the case of young men of 23 and under on the occasion of the first offence.
(C) Extend the time-limit during which proceedings can be taken in a case of criminal assault from six to nine months after the offence.[33]

1922 to 1925

The Law of Property Act 1922 recants the intestacy laws of England and Wales. In cases of intestacy in future, a husband or wife will inherit equally the property of the other; mothers are put in the same position as fathers as to inheriting the property of intestate children or grandchildren; daughters and younger sons are given an equal share with the elder son in unsettled land left by an intestate ancestor. This same Act, while in some cases it puts widows in a worse position than they are now, does improve the position of the widow of an intestate husband who leaves a very small estate, because of the provision which increases the share she takes in his property, before any division is made to other beneficiaries, from £500 to £1,000, together with household goods.

The Law of Property Act 1925 provides that a husband and wife are to be treated as two persons for all purposes of acquisition of interest in property under a disposition whereas in some cases, at present, if property is left to a husband and wife, and another, the husband and wife take only the half instead of two-thirds.[34]

1923

The Matrimonial Causes Act (England and Wales) promoted by the NUSEC provides that a wife may divorce her husband on the same grounds as a husband his wife, viz. adultery. The Members of the Royal Commission on Matrimonial Causes 1923 reported unanimously in favour of this reform, which obviously promotes an important advance towards an equal moral standard between the two sexes.[35]

1923

Intoxicating Liquor (Sale to persons under 18) Act was piloted through its Parliamentary career very skilfully by Lady Astor. It provides that no intoxicating liquor shall be sold to any person under 18 for consumption on licensed premises except when beer, etc., is sold with a meal. It also forbids the treating of persons under 18.[36]

1925

Guardianship of Infants Act 1925, which was in many respects based on the Guardianship of Infants Bills which had been promoted by the NUSEC in five successive Parliaments, amends the 1886 Guardianship of Infants Act. It lays down in the Preamble that it is expedient that equality between the sexes should obtain with respect to the guardianship of infants and the rights and responsibilities conferred thereby. Amongst the more important provisions of the Act are the following:

(1) That in any dispute affecting the child, mothers and fathers have the same right to appear before a Court, and that the decision shall be given solely in accordance with what is for the welfare of the child.
(2) Equal rights to both parents with regard to appointment of guardians after death.
(3) The right of the mother to obtain a maintenance order for the child, as well as an order for custody.
(4) The right to bring cases under the Act before a Summary Court.[37]

1925

Summary Jurisdiction (Separation and Maintenance) Act 1925 (England and Wales), which also included certain points from a larger Bill promoted by the NUSEC in 1922, was finally passed into law after being held up by three successive General Elections. It adds to the grounds on which a separation order can be given for both husband and wife: (1) cruelty to children and (2) habitual drunkenness. It enables a woman to obtain a separation order from her husband if he has enforced cohabitation when suffering from venereal disease, or has forced her to submit herself to prostitution. It removes the condition that a wife has to leave her husband first before applying for a separation order on the grounds of habitual cruelty or failure to maintain, and modifies the law relating to the rescinding of maintenance orders when a separated wife has been guilty of adultery.[38]

1925

Widows, Orphans and Old Age Contributory Pensions Act 1925, which represents a great extension of the principle of Social Insurance in this country, provides that pensions at the rate of 10s. a week should be given to the following:

(1) Widows of insured men who die after January 1926.
(2) Existing widows of insured men with children under the age of 14½.
(3) Insured men or women between 65 and 70, or the wives of over 65 of such men.

(*Note*. On reaching the age of 70, these classes of persons will receive an Old Age Pension without the restrictions contained in the Old Age Pensions Act.) It further provides for Children's Allowances of 5s. for the eldest child and 3s. for each subsequent child to be paid to the children of both existing widows and future widows until they are 14½ years old, or until 16 if they are receiving full-time instruction at a day school. Orphan's Pensions of 7s. 6d. a week are paid to the children of insured men or insured women after both the parents are dead, with the same age limits as above. The Act comes into force in January 1926 for purposes of contributions and for the payment of pensions to widows and their children and to orphans.

Unrestricted Old Age Pensions will be given to the old insured people over 70 from July 1926, and Old Age Pensions between 65 and 70 from January 1928. Special conditions are laid down with respect to exempt persons, persons in exempted employments and voluntary contributors. For ordinary insured persons, the additional contributions over and above those at present required for Health Insurance amounts to 4d. a week for men, and 2d. a week for women, to both employer and employee.[39]

Postscript: Legislation still pending, 1926

Legitimacy Bill (England and Wales) 1925. Bills providing for the legitimisation of children on the subsequent marriage of their parents have been before Parliament for four successive Sessions, but, three years running, such Bills have, by the dissolution of Parliament, been prevented from reaching the Statute Book. This year the Government measure on these lines has passed all its stages in the House of Lords, and will probably pass its stages in the House of Commons before the end of the year.[40] It excludes from the benefits of the Bill those children either or both of whose parents was married to someone else at the time of their birth.

Equal Franchise. Attempts have been made in Parliament almost every year since 1918 to provide for the extension of the franchise to women on the same terms as to men, and in 1919[41] and 1920[42] Equal Franchise Bills passed their second readings in the House of Commons. In 1922[43] and 1923[44] Bills were introduced under the Ten Minutes Rule, but went no further. In 1924 the Representation of the People Act (1918) Amendment Bill, with Equal Franchise for its principal object, was introduced by a private member of the Labour Party and adopted by the Labour Government, which, however, went out of Office before all the stages of the Bill could be taken.[45]

In 1925, a Representation of the People Act (Amendment) Bill, with Equal Franchise for its main object, was again introduced by private members of the Labour Party, but was opposed by the Government on the grounds that Mr Baldwin[46] had promised to set up a conference of members of all parties to arrive at an 'Agreed Measure' on Equal Franchise.[47] It was announced that this conference would be appointed in 1926.[48] We must await developments with regard to it, but we cannot rest content until full equality between men and women has been reached as regards the franchise, the most elementary of all rights of citizenship.

Additions in 1927 edition

Adoption of Children Act 1926 (England and Wales) should prove a valuable measure in safeguarding the interests of the three parties concerned in an adoption: the child, the real parents and the adopting parents.[49] The court will now have to sanction adoptions, and to satisfy itself that the real parents understand what is implied in the total surrender of their child, and that the adopters provide a suitable home and are prepared to assume the rights and responsibilities of parenthood.[50]

1926

Public Health (Smoke Abatement) Act 1926. This small Act deals with a subject very close to the heart of women: the elimination of dirt caused by smoke. It provides that smoke will in future come within the rigours of the law not only if it is black, as previously, but whatever hue it chooses to favour. Increased penalties are also laid upon smoke producers. Unfortunately, far too much power is given to the Ministry of Health to exclude certain processes of industry, and no attempt is made to include dwelling houses or sea-going ships.[51]

Postscript—Legislation still pending, 1927

Equal Franchise. Attempts have been made in Parliament almost every year since 1918 to provide for the extension of the franchise to women on the same terms as to men, and in 1919 *the Women's Emancipation Bill* and in 1920 the *Representation of the People Bill* passed their second readings in the House of Commons. In 1922 and 1923, Bills were introduced under the Ten Minutes Rule, but went no further. In 1924 the *Representation of the People Act (1918) Amendment Bill*, with Equal Franchise for its principal object, was introduced by a private member of the Labour Party and adopted by the Labour Government, which, however, went out of Office before all the stages of the Bill could be taken.

In February 1925 a *Representation of the People Act (Amendment) Bill* with Equal Franchise for its main object was again introduced by private members of the Labour Party, but was opposed by the Government on the grounds that Mr Baldwin had given the following pledge, which was to be carried out before the end of this Parliament:

> The Unionist Party is in favour of equal political rights for men and women, and desire that the question of the extension of the franchise should, if possible, be settled by agreement.[52]

The Home Secretary stated:

> I have the authority of my right hon. friend (the Prime Minister), who is by my side, to say, as all the House knows would be the case, that he stands by that pledge . . . There is no dispute whatever as to the Prime Minister's pledge or its meaning and intention, and we do mean to carry out that pledge. We do mean to give equal political rights to men and women.[53]

On April 13th 1927, Mr Baldwin announced his intention to place on the Statute Book next session legislation giving the vote to women on the same terms as men and from the age of 21,[54] and repeated and emphasised it at the Annual Conference of the National Union of Conservative and Unionist Associations at Cardiff on October 6th, 1927.[55]

Our long struggle for a complete measure of Women's Suffrage seems to be nearing its close.[56] The addition of five million women voters to the electorate will, we hope, mean not only that practically all women will be able to play their part in matters concerning the community generally, but also that the point of view of women, and legislation with regard to matters in which they and their children are specially concerned, will play an even greater part on the parliamentary stage than ever before.

The Public Places (Order) Bill (England and Wales), provides that there should be no special legislation against prostitutes, but that laws relating to order and decency in the streets should be applied to men and women equally, and that police evidence alone should not be considered sufficient proof of annoyance. This Bill has been introduced into both Houses of Parliament two years running, as a result of which a Government committee has been appointed to enquire into the whole subject.[57]

Parliament (Qualification of Peeresses) Bill has been introduced three years running by Lord Astor.[58] The first two Bills provided for the right for Peeresses in their own right to sit and vote in the House of Lords. This year's Bill asked for less, viz. that the Crown should be allowed to exercise discretion to alter or to make letters patent for Peeresses to sit. The Bill was withdrawn in view of the Government's proposal to tackle the whole question of reform of the House of Lords.[59]

Perhaps I may be permitted to add, without offence, that having had opportunities of observing manners in the House of Commons, and comparing them over a period of nearly 60 years, I see an enormous, almost an incredible improvement in this respect in recent years. Democracy is a great teacher of manners. Women felt the difference and the improvement almost immediately after February 1918.

1926 edition transcribed from a copy in the Women's Library at LSE.
1927 edition transcribed from a copy in the Nancy Astor Collection,
University of Reading Special Collections. No known copyright restrictions.

Notes

1. James Bryce (1838–1922), Liberal politician, in discussion of the Representation of the People Bill: 'In the United States the grant of woman suffrage has made no difference whatever. The general administration is no better and it is no worse ... Where legislation is passed it is passed under the influence of public opinion, and the mere fact that women have a right to vote makes no difference at all' (HL Deb 1917, 188).
2. See Section 44.
3. *Common Cause* (1918, 334–6).
4. This is not true: Constance Markievicz was elected but did not take her seat; see Section 45, note 1.
5. See Reeves 2020 for an overview.
6. Nancy Witcher Langhorne Astor (1879–1964), Unionist politician and first woman seated as a UK member of Parliament, in 1919.
7. Margaret Wintringham (1879–1955), Liberal politician.
8. Mabel Philipson (1886–1951), actress then Conservative politician.
9. Margaret Grace Bondfield (1873–1953), Labour politician and women's rights activist.
10. Arabella Susan Lawrence (1871–1947), Labour politician.
11. Ellen Cicely Wilkinson (1891–1947), British Labour Party politician; see Wilkinson 1925.
12. Katharine Marjory Stewart-Murray (1874–1960), Scottish Unionist Party politician.
13. See Dale and Fisher 2009 for an overview.
14. George Edward Wentworth Bowyer (1886–1948), Conservative politician.
15. See McFadyean 1945 for an overview.
16. See Section 43, note 1.
17. See Section 44, note 6.
18. Fawcett 1920c.
19. *Common Cause* 1919d.
20. *Common Cause* 1919c. The Charter of the League of Nations was signed on 28 June 1919 as Part I of the Treaty of Versailles (Northedge 1986). The commitment to gender equality is in Article 7.
21. Rachel Eleanor Crowdy (1884–1964), English nurse and member of the British National Committee for the Suppression of the White Slave Trade.
22. Winifred Coombe Tennant (1874–1956), suffragist, Liberal politician, spiritualist and Justice of the Peace (*Manchester Guardian* 1921).
23. Fawcett's error: Dame Edith Balfour Lyttelton (1865–1948), novelist, activist, spiritualist and Justice of the Peace (*Vote* 1923, 273).
24. Helena Swanwick (1864–1939), pacifist feminist, member of the NUWSS and editor of the *Common Cause* from 1909 to 1912.
25. John Waller Hills (1867–1938), Liberal Unionist and Conservative politician.
26. See Zimmeck 1984 for an overview. The topic of women in the British Civil Service was returned to often in the *Woman's Leader* over this period.
27. E. Murray (1920).
28. *Woman's Leader* 1920b.
29. The Married Women (Maintenance) Act was updated in 1920, with a Separation and Maintenance Orders Bill in 1922 (*Woman's Leader* 1921, 1922c).
30. *Woman's Leader* 1922d.
31. See Carrier 1983 for an overview. The topic of women police was returned to often in the *Woman's Leader* over this period.
32. Macmillan (1921, 323–4). The 'unordered state of affairs was remedied by the 1948 British Nationality Act, which provided finally that marriage had no effect on the nationality of British women' (Baldwin 2001, 553).
33. *Woman's Leader* 1922d.
34. *Woman's Leader* 1922d.
35. *Woman's Leader* 1923a.
36. See the *Woman's Leader* (1923b, 39) and the *Times* 1923.
37. Hubback (1925b, 284).
38. Hubback (1925b, 284).

39 'Widow's Pensions at last! As we write the words we rub our eyes and wonder if it is really true that the reform for which we have laboured so long has at last found its way onto the Statute Book' (*Woman's Leader* 1925d). See also the *Times* 1925b.
40 See Picton-Turbervill 1924. The bill received Royal Assent on 15 December 1926 (*Times* 1926).
41 *Vote* 1919.
42 *Woman's Leader* (1920a, 325).
43 *Woman's Leader* (1922b, 41).
44 *Woman's Leader* 1923c.
45 *Woman's Leader* (1924, 66).
46 Stanley Baldwin (1867–1947), Conservative politician and prime minister.
47 Hubback (1925a, 390), *Times* 1925a.
48 William Joynson-Hicks (1865–1932), Conservative politician and home secretary: 'We are so busy that I am afraid we cannot set up a conference this session. My idea is to set up a conference in 1926 – it will take some few months to go into all the questions' (*Times* 1925a).
49 Added and changed from the paragraph in the 1926 edition ending '2*d*. a week for women, to both employer and employee'. The text prior to this is the same in the 1927 edition, except the section on pending legislation. The new text from the 1927 edition is appended, from pages 7–8.
50 See the *Woman's Leader* 1926a and the *Times* 1927a.
51 See Mason (1926, 146). The bill received Royal Assent on 15 December 1926, coming into play on 1 July 1927; see the *Times* 1927c.
52 Hubback (1925a, 390).
53 William Joynson-Hicks in a House of Commons debate on 20 February 1925. See also the *Times* (1925a, 7).
54 *Woman's Leader* 1927b, *Times* 1927b.
55 *Woman's Leader* 1927c. See also: 'To pretend that equal franchise means anything but an equal franchise at 21 is to delude yourselves, and to make that fatal mistake on the part of the Tories to try and score by being clever. (Laughter.)' *Times* (1927d, 8).
56 The Representation of the People (Equal Franchise) Act 1928 was introduced in March, receiving Royal Assent on 2 July 1928; see Figures 19 and 20.
57 See the *Woman's Leader* 1925b. The Macmillan Committee on Street Offences report, 'published in 1929, was largely sympathetic to feminist criticisms and to the case for repeal of the solicitation laws', but 'no legislation was advanced. After the Macmillan Committee reported, the issue faded' (Breitenbach and Wright 2014, 409–10).
58 Waldorf Astor (1879–1952), 2nd Viscount Astor, politician, newspaper proprietor and husband to Nancy Astor.
59 See *International Woman Suffrage News* (1925, 154), Hubback 1926 and the *Woman's Leader* 1927a.

50
How University College, London led the way in the education of women, 1927

Woman's Leader. Friday, 29 July 1927, 200.

In the spring of 1925 Fawcett stood down as the chairman of the board of directors of the *Woman's Leader,* and also as an individual member of NUSEC itself (following a disagreement about the principle of family allowances), although she remained on friendly terms with Eleanor Rathbone and other NUSEC leaders, maintaining contact with them particularly regarding the continuing campaign for equal franchise (Rubinstein 1991, 271). Fawcett still attended mass demonstrations: a few weeks before writing this column, and a month after her 80th birthday, Fawcett joined a meeting of over 40 organisations in Trafalgar Square on 16 July welcoming 'the Prime Minister's promise of a Bill giving votes to women from 21 and on the same terms as men', although she turned down an invitation to speak (*Vote* 1927). Throughout this period, and despite stepping away from NUSEC, Fawcett's letters, articles and reviews on a variety of topics, including her travels, continued to appear in the *Woman's Leader*. This particular column is an account of 'the substance of a "talk" by Dame Millicent which was broadcast on Thursday June 23rd from 2LO', the second BBC radio station,[1] then transmitting across the UK every evening (Fawcett 1927c; *Northampton Chronicle and Echo* 1927).

Fawcett's earliest writings focus on the need for education for women (see Section 2), and this was a theme she had campaigned on throughout her career (see Section 18). After the death of Henry in 1884, Fawcett (and Philippa) moved into the home of her sister Agnes Garrett (1845–1935), a Georgian townhouse at 2 Gower Street, Bloomsbury, London (Fawcett 1924, 20). Agnes had moved there in 1875 with the sisters' cousin

Rhoda Garrett (1841–82) shortly after Agnes and Rhoda had established their interior design company (Crawford 2002, 193). Fawcett lived with Agnes at Gower Street for the rest of her life.[2] Six hundred metres along the same side of the street to the north lies the main entrance to the campus for what is now University College London (UCL), established as the radical London University in 1826, and changing to University College, London in 1836. In 1878 UCL's supplemental charter made it the first British university allowed to award degrees to women (Harte, North and Brewis 2018, 89). Between 1900 and 1876 it was known as University of London, University College, before adopting the modern University College London (UCL) in 1976.

It is fitting, if perhaps coincidental, that in the latter half of her life Fawcett lived in close vicinity to a university enacting the educational principles she had long argued for, and she was aware of and involved in activities at University College, London. For example, Philippa had attended mathematical classes there (Fawcett 1887a; Fawcett 1924, 135–6); Fawcett wrote the obituary for Rosa Morison (1841–1912), the lady superintendent of women students at University College between 1883 and 1912, that appeared in the *Common Cause* (Fawcett 1912b); activities at and research from University College, London were often reported in NUWSS publications (for example, the *Common Cause* 1912c, 779; 1913b; Rees 1922); Fawcett chaired events there (for example, *Woman's Leader* 1922a); members of the National Federation of Women Teachers were also present at many demonstrations, such as the 16 July Trafalgar Square meeting, including representatives from the Institute of Education and University College (UCL Institute of Education Archives n.d.); and Fawcett was joined on air for the 23 June 2LO talk about women's education by Miss Margaret Murray (1863–1963), the Egyptologist who had worked at University College since 1894 and was by then assistant professor in Egyptian archaeology (*Northampton Chronicle and Echo* 1927; Mallowan 2004). The 'substance' of Fawcett's radio broadcast talk, reproduced in the *Woman's Leader*, revisits major figures in the history and development of women's education (with Fawcett paraphrasing and directly quoting from her 1889 book, *Some Eminent Women of Our Times: Short biographical sketches*), before concluding by praising her nearby institutional neighbours for their achievements and support for women's education.

*

I had the privilege, now many years ago, of hearing Lord Rosebery[3] give the address at St Andrews in celebration of the 600th anniversary of the founding of the University.[4]

He drew attention to the contrast between the permanence of the 'little lamp of learning' which was lighted then and the fleeting character of other contemporary features of the civilization which existed six centuries ago. Where, he asked, are the fighting barons and bishops with their battles and their burnings? They have clean gone off the face of the earth, 'their place knoweth them no more'.[5] But 'the little lamp of learning' not only continues in existence, but burns clearer and brighter century after century, and fills a far more important place in the national life of Scotland and Great Britain than when it was first lighted.

University College, London has also been a 'lamp of learning'; and it was lighted by those who had at heart the inclusion within its radiance of all those to whom the so-called 'national' universities offered nothing.

Among the excluded classes were what one may almost call 'Jews, Turks, and heretics',[6] and to these must be added 'women'. The idea that women were capable of benefiting by University education was born early in the nineteenth century. Its godfather, perhaps its parent, was Sydney Smith, who contended in the *Edinburgh Review* in 1810 that women would be 'none the worse for sense and knowledge';[7] but he went much further than this, because he had to convince the British public in general that they were mistaken in supposing that if women were permitted to eat of the tree of knowledge, the rest of the family would soon be reduced to the same kind of aerial and unsatisfactory diet; or that the care and perpetual solicitude which a mother feels for her children depended upon her ignorance of Greek and mathematics, and that the latter study would cause her to desert her infant for a quadratic equation.

When I spoke of the Rev. Sydney Smith as the father of the movement for women's education in this country, I should have said the *modern* movement; for there were splendid forerunners in the same field at a much earlier time, such as Sir Thomas More,[8] Roger Ascham,[9] Defoe (who wrote as wittily on it as Sydney Smith),[10] Mary Astell,[11] who *nearly* succeeded in persuading Queen Anne to found a college for the higher education of women; and there was also, a little later, in 1726, Elizabeth, Lady Godolphin, who, actually out of her own fortune founded and endowed a first-rate school for girls at Salisbury – a school which still flourishes and celebrated its second centenary in Westminster Abbey last year.[12] Lady Godolphin's first thought had been to make the Dean and Chapter of Salisbury her trustees, and to leave the guidance of the school in their hands, but they rejected her gift with contumely and would have nothing to do with such an undertaking, which they regarded not only as useless, but as actually mischievous. Therefore, Lady Godolphin, quite undismayed by clerical opposition, placed her gift in the charge, as trustees, of the

Mayor and Corporation of the City, and with them it remains to this day.

Sydney Smith's witty words did not fall on a barren soil; moreover, the Quakers had long set a good example in the sound education they provided for their girls and boys alike. Elizabeth Fry was the child of a wealthy Quaker family, the Gurneys of Norwich, who had given their children, girls as well as boys, a thoroughly good education, including instruction in Latin and mathematics. Mrs Fry's great work for prison reform began about 1813, when she was 33 years of age. Her husband thoroughly sympathized with her public work; but there were people even among the Quakers who protested that a married woman had no duties except to her husband and children. Neither did popular feeling wholly sympathize with Mrs Fry's efforts.[13] Hood's ballad, 'Keep your school out of Newgate, Mrs Fry',[14] is probably symptomatic of a widely diffused prejudice against her work.

Mary Carpenter[15] was another forerunner of the best type of educated woman. And she, too, had been prepared for her work by a thoroughly sound education. It may interest our listeners to know that in 1877, within a month of her death, she signed the memorial to the Senate of the London University in favour of the admission of women to degrees.[16]

Mrs Somerville[17] is another example of a woman profiting largely from the educational opportunities accidentally open to her. Early in the nineteenth century, she attended the lectures of University Professors in Edinburgh and was awarded a silver medal by one of the Mathematical Societies of that day. She was very materially helped in her work by her second husband, and she wrote of this in a spirit that is a credit to them both:

> The warmth with which my husband entered into my success deeply affected me; for not one in ten thousand would have rejoiced in it as he did; but he was of a generous nature, far above jealousy and he continued through life to take the kindest interest in all I did.[18]

Harriet Martineau's[19] education benefited in consequence of a rather curious combination of circumstances. Her family, which was of Huguenot descent, had settled in Norwich and had become Unitarians. Early in the nineteenth century, the Rev. Isaac Perry, the head of a leading boys' school in Norwich, became a Unitarian, with the consequence of losing nearly all his pupils. The Unitarians in Norwich thereupon felt it their duty to rally round him and support him to the utmost of their power.[20] Hence those, like the Martineaus, who had children, sent them, girls as well as boys, to Mr Perry's school, so that the little Harriet had, from her earliest childhood, the advantage of being under a thoroughly competent teacher.

The education of women no longer depends upon the fortuitous grouping of lucky accidents. And one of the first great steps towards this desirable end was taken 100 years ago by University College. It began to have women students very soon after its foundation,[21] and to-day, among its 3,200 students, 1,074, a little more than a third, are women.[22]

Transcribed from a copy in the British Library.
No known copyright restrictions.

Notes

1. No known recording of this exists, and Rubinstein does not note Fawcett's radio appearances in *A Different World for Women* (1991). 2LO was the first British Broadcasting Company radio transmitter, which began nationally broadcasting in 1922, 'when radio listening changed from a specialist hobby to a national pastime' (Stanley 2012). Fawcett had previously been interviewed in the London Studio on Friday, 14 November 1924 (*Radio Times* 1924, 303). The British Broadcasting Company became the British Broadcasting Corporation in 1927.
2. In 1954 a blue plaque was erected by London County Council: 'Dame Millicent Fawcett 1847–1929 pioneer of women's suffrage lived and died here' (OpenPlaques.org 2009).
3. See Section 19, note 36.
4. The University of St Andrews was founded in 1413: Fawcett means the 500th anniversary, which was celebrated from 12 to 15 September 1911 (Special Collections 2012). Lord Rosebery was installed as rector on 14 September: Fawcett paraphrases from his rectorial address (*Times* 1911c).
5. Psalm 103:16.
6. A common phrase that can be traced back to early Baptist teachings from 1611/12: 'For men's religion to God is between God and themselves . . . Let them be heretics, Turks, Jews, or whatsoever, it appertains not the earthly power to punish them in the least measure': Thomas Helwys (1550–1616), in Helwys (1998, 53).
7. See Section 18, note 15. Fawcett paraphrases.
8. See Section 16, note 5.
9. Roger Ascham (1515–68), English scholar, in *The Scholemaster* (1570).
10. 'An Academy for Women' in Defoe (1697 [reprinted in 1969], 282–91).
11. Mary Astell (1666–1731), writer and philosopher who outlined plans for a women's educational establishment (Perry 2009).
12. Goodman 2006. Fawcett had a close relationship with her sister-in-law, Sarah Maria Fawcett (1830–1923), who was a governor of Godolphin School for 30 years (Howells 2021).
13. Elizabeth Fry (1780–1845) (Fawcett 1889c, 1–8; de Haan 2017).
14. Hood 1825.
15. Mary Carpenter (1807–77), educationist and penal reformer (Fawcett 1889c, 9–17; Prochaska 2004).
16. This sentence is taken directly from Fawcett (1889c, 17).
17. Mary Somerville (1780–1872) (Fawcett 1889c, 35–45; Creese 2009).
18. Somerville (1874, 176), quoted in Fawcett (1889c, 40).
19. See Section 25, note 5, and Fawcett (1889c, 57–68).
20. This sentence is taken directly from Fawcett (1889c, 58).
21. London University was founded in 1826, changing to University College, London in 1836. The admission of women into University College was gradual, with University College professors lecturing to classes for the independently run Ladies Educational Association in 1868, their classes moving onto college premises in 1871, and all classes in the college open to both men and women by 1878, when women were able to study for University of London degrees (Harte, North and Brewis 2018, 89).
22. The proportion of women was even higher than Fawcett thinks here: 'By the session 1925–6 women numbered 1,074 out of a total of 2,426 full time students' (Harte, North and Brewis 2018, 171).

51
The end crowns all, and that old common arbitrator, Time, will one day end it, 1928

Woman's Leader. Friday, 6 July 1928, 175.

Although the Representation of the People Act 1918 had given the parliamentary vote to women in the UK over the age of 30 who met property qualifications, continued suffrage campaigning and pressure on Parliament were needed to push through changes that would give women the vote on the same terms as men (Law 1997). From 1919, various private members' bills were introduced, although they could not proceed without the support of the government. The Labour minority government which came to power in 1924 had pledged commitment to equal political rights, although the legislation timed out before the 1924 general election, which returned a large majority for the Conservatives, who had not included equal franchise in their manifesto. However, the new prime minister, Stanley Baldwin,[1] made a pledge in favour of equal political rights, and by 1925 it was presumed it was government policy (Takayanagi 2018). The Equal Political Rights Campaign Committee (a coalition of women's organisations) organised demonstrations, published widely and maintained pressure upon the government and individual MPs (Law 1997, 214–17). In 1926, the Equal Franchise Cabinet Committee was formed to investigate the issue, deciding on 12 April 1927 that the government position would be to support the vote being given to 21-year-old women, therefore allowing them the same rights as men. Women's organisations continued to raise awareness and maintain pressure. The government finally made a formal commitment to equal franchise in the King's Speech on 7 February 1928, with the second reading of the Representation of the People (Equal Franchise) Bill taking place on 29

March 1928, passing with 387 ayes and 10 noes after a seven-hour debate (Takayanagi 2018). The bill received Royal Assent and passed into law on 2 July 1928 (*Western Daily Press* 1928).

Throughout the final phase of the campaign for equal franchise, Fawcett was in her late seventies and early eighties, and had retired from the movement, not being involved in any meaningful way in the leadership and organisation of lobbying and protest. However, she remained interested in progress, and 'in letters to the Press and in interviews with reporters, as well as in private talk with young and old alike, she eagerly praised and defended the young women of the new generation' (Strachey 1931, 347). Fawcett was travelling at the time the confirmation of success came through.

> My friends at home will easily picture to themselves my delight in receiving from Miss Macadam[2] last Friday evening the welcome telegram 'Second Reading carried: immense majority.' This good news reached me just twelve hours before I was leaving Jerusalem on my way home. I only sent in reply the one word: 'Hallelujah.' (Fawcett 1928a).

Later, on the occasion of the Royal Assent, came the time for reflection on the collective work necessary to achieve this victory:

> 'Equal Franchise Bill. Le Roy le veult.'[3] These words brought to an end a long struggle, ardently and, I think I may say, skilfully conducted for more than sixty years by Englishwomen to gain political freedom. There are many who commiserate with us on this account; they speak and write of 'sixty years in the wilderness',[4] and regard those who went through it as objects of pity and compassion. Well, the 'wilderness blossomed as the rose'.[5] I, who was in the struggle ever since Mill's speech in the House of Commons in 1867,[6] maintain, from my own personal experience, that it was a time of steadily growing confidence in the success of our cause, and also that our process of working for it was all along joyful and hopeful. For a very large proportion of those sixty years were punctuated by some distinct step forward in the movement to which we were pledged (Fawcett 1928b).

In 'The End Crowns All' (a quote taken from *Troilus and Cressida* 4.5), Fawcett stresses that success was dependent on winning support from the great men of politics – an approach that she had taken throughout her 60 years of constitutional lobbying for women's emancipation.

*

For sixty years we have thought and worked and prayed for this free citizenship for women, and now we have it, at least as far as political conditions can give it to us.

Well! Looking back, as I can, over these sixty years, I can say that they have been happy years; we have felt from year to year that our cause has made way towards our ultimate goal. Of course, there have been ups and downs, but still we could always feel that we were making steady progress: a sure source of happiness. But we have had still another, in the scores of friends we have made, of every shade in politics and comprising all sorts and conditions of men and women. I can remember, of course, and remember gratefully, the great people who have befriended us: Prime Ministers, Secretaries of State, Bishops and commercial magnates, and also the leaders of the Labour party, especially as it was a dozen years ago.

I do not think there has ever been a great political reform which has been carried through from its inception to its complete success with such a minimum of physical violence. Even when the 'militants' were at the height of their militancy, they shed no blood either of man or beast;[7] such physical suffering as was involved in their strategy, they bore themselves, they did not inflict it on others. They showed in more than one instance that they were prepared to lay down their lives for the cause of women's freedom.[8]

For this at anyrate we 'sing, rejoice, and give thanks'.[9]
Mark Twain once wrote of the women suffragists of his own country:

> in 40 years they have swept away an increasingly large number of unfair laws from the Statute Books of America. In this brief time these serfs have set themselves free – essentially. Men could not have done as much for themselves in that time without bloodshed; at least, they never have, and that is an argument that they didn't know how.[10]

The great blot of negro slavery[11] could not be or at least was not removed from the American nation without the cost of four years of civil war and the death of one of the greatest leaders and statesmen that America or any other country has ever known. This fact has sunk so deeply into the political mind that I have heard the text: 'Without the shedding of blood there is no remission of sin'[12] quoted as if it proved that bloodshed was a necessary preliminary to any great advance in national wellbeing. The Quakers have all through their history stood out for the opposite theory in politics and social organization, and I think I may fairly say that they have proved their case a great deal more successfully at any rate than the promoters of reform by violence have proved theirs.[13] Nevertheless, the two policies of Reform by violence and Reform by peaceful persuasion will probably continue to make their several appeals.[14] I was at a suffrage meeting at the height of the militant activity and one of our Parliamentary friends was firing away in strong condemnation of the militants, when the voice of a working man came from the far end of the hall: 'They've rose the country, Sir',[15] and I think we all felt that he had hit the nail on the head.

The extent of the work of conversion which was needed to bring the leaders of the Liberal party to a belief in their own principles[16] was the more remarkable because when we went among the rank and file in the constituencies, we found much more support of women's franchise from the Liberals than from the Conservatives. The ordinary Liberal in the constituencies gave us help and encouragement. What was the miasma which changed him into an enemy when he entered into the charmed circle of the leaders of the party? We can perhaps infer what it was from such books as the letters of Lady Frederick Cavendish, which was published about a year ago. She was living in Mr Gladstone's family almost as an adopted child. She was his niece and by her marriage became the daughter-in-law of the then Duke of Devonshire. We can see from her letters that she could see nothing in the demand of women for the protection of Parliamentary representation but what was 'entirely odious and ridiculous'.[17] How she arrived at this opinion has not been clearly revealed; but there can be little doubt that she reflected the dominant tone of the family in which she was an adopted child; and this tradition of hostility to the enfranchisement of women was handed on in official Liberalism until it was broken by Mr Lloyd George and Lord Grey. In the Conservative party, the tone of its upper circles was entirely different. Family circumstances caused the late Lord Salisbury (the great Prime Minister) to have to earn his living by his pen.[18] This withdrew him a great deal from the ease and luxury of the very rich and probably produced a life-long impression on his character and outlook on life. He, and also the Conservative Prime Minister who had preceded him, Benjamin Disraeli, had known what it was to be poor,[19] and I cannot help feeling that this was part of their political education and that it helped them to understand what the industrial and social problem of women often was, and how their exclusion from even the least scrap of political power added to their difficulties. These two, often at variance on other matters, were allied in their support of the enfranchisement of women, and they were followed by three other Conservative Prime Ministers all of whom have given our cause their constant and most valuable support. To have had five

Conservative Prime Ministers in succession, all supporting our cause, had been a really great asset in the later stages of our work.

Transcribed from a copy in the British Library.
No known copyright restrictions.

Notes

1. See Section 49, note 46.
2. Elizabeth Macadam (1871–1948), a NUSEC officer and editor of the *Woman's Leader*.
3. 'Le Roy le veult' is a Norman French phrase, meaning 'the King wills it', which signifies a bill has received Royal Assent, with the reigning monarch approving an act of legislature in the Parliament of the United Kingdom. Fawcett narrowly missed hearing these words spoken in the context of the Equal Franchise Bill, because the timing of parliamentary business was changed and she arrived less than a minute late: 'I know it is only a form, but I should have liked to have heard it' (*Leeds Mercury* 1928).
4. Drawing a parallel with the 'forty years in the wilderness' of Deuteronomy 29:5.
5. Isaiah 35:1.
6. See Fawcett (1928c, 175); see also Introduction, pp. 3–4.
7. The target of militant violence was property, including empty residential properties, hotels, farm buildings, sports pavilions, churches, railway stations and other public buildings: it was not the intention to cause injury or death to others (*Suffragette* 1913b; Bearman 2005). However, both humans and horses died or were injured because of these attacks (Bearman 2005, 374).
8. Emily Wilding Davison's death in 1913 is the most well-known death of a suffragette (see Section 46), although the WSPU blamed the deaths of the suffragettes Mary Jane Clarke (1862–1910), Emmeline Pankhurst's younger sister) and Henria Leech Williams (1867–1911) on their treatment by police in the Black Friday protests of 1910 (Williams 1911; see Section 35).
9. From Psalm 98: see Section 44, note 8.
10. Twain (1897, 310).
11. This is the strongest statement Fawcett has made so far to demonstrate her views on transatlantic enslavement (Fawcett was born 14 years after the Slavery Abolition Act 1833, and there is no evidence that either the Garrett or Fawcett families inherited monies from this trade or the Slave Compensation Act 1837). Fawcett more routinely referred to prostitution as a form of slavery (see Sections 12, 16, 22). In the foreword to a 1916 reissue of an 1886 pamphlet by the physician Elizabeth Blackwell (1821–1910), *Purchase of Women: The great economic blunder*, Fawcett equates Blackwell's experience as 'a witness of the death struggle on human slavery' in the USA and Blackwell's view of the 'degrading effect of slavery on slaves and slave-owners' to her own views on prostitution (Fawcett 1916a, x). It was Fawcett's lament on hearing of the death of Abraham Lincoln that first drew her to Henry Fawcett's attention; see Figure 1.
12. Hebrews 9:22.
13. It is interesting to consider the modern conception of votes for women being won by the militant suffragettes, rather than the peaceful suffragists, in this context (Finkelstein 2015).
14. See Section 46.
15. Also mentioned in Section 25 and Fawcett (1924, 184).
16. 'Our worst enemies all through our long struggle were the official Liberals. Every Liberal Prime Minister (with one exception) between 1870 and 1916 was fiercely antagonistic to our claim. The exception was Sir Henry Campbell-Bannerman, and he unfortunately died after a very short tenure of his great office. It was in 1906, if I remember rightly, that he received a large deputation representative of the whole Suffrage party. When their various representatives had spoken, Sir Henry declared his conviction that "they had made out a conclusive and irrefutable case", but that he could do nothing to promote the success of the cause for which they had pleaded. He did not state his reason, but there could not be any doubt that it was to be found in the then unconquered hostility of his colleagues in the Cabinet' (Fawcett 1928a; see Section 24, note 6).

17. Lucy Caroline Cavendish, née Lyttelton (1841–1925), in a diary entry of '*January 15th*, 1867. The subject of female suffrage (odious and ridiculous notion as it is) is actually beginning to be spoken of without laughter, and as if it was an open question. I trust we are not coming to that' (Cavendish 1927, 22). Later in life she became a pioneer of women's education. This possibly drew Fawcett's attention, given that, as well as her marriage, 1867 saw her join her first suffrage organisation (Fawcett 1924, 117) and attend debates on the topic in Parliament, including hearing Disraeli and John Stuart Mill's speeches (Fawcett 1924, 64).
18. Robert Arthur Talbot Gascoyne-Cecil (1830–1903), 3rd Marquess of Salisbury, who was prime minister on three separate occasions. Estranged from his family upon his marriage, from 1850 to the 1880s Cecil supplemented the family income through his journalism (Smith 2011).
19. Disraeli had a privileged background, but in his early twenties lost a fortune speculating on South American mining companies in an attempt to establish the financial independence necessary for a literary career (Parry 2011).

52
Picturing Fawcett: Royal Assent to the Equal Franchise Act, 1928

Figure 19: 'Officers and members of the National Union of Societies for Equal Citizenship, after the Royal Assent to the Equal Franchise Act', 2 July 1928. Postcard. From the Women's Library at LSE. No known copyright restrictions.

Figure 20: 'Dame Millicent Fawcett, Miss Fawcett, Miss Garrett and Mrs Strachey after the Royal Assent to the Equal Franchise Act', 2 July 1928. Postcard. From the Women's Library at LSE. No known copyright restrictions.

On 2 July 1928, the Representation of the People (Equal Franchise) Act 1928, giving women electoral equality with men, became law.

> The picturesque formal ceremony which took place . . . was the final scene of a long drama enacted on the Parliamentary stage off and on for a period of over sixty years. Dame Millicent Fawcett, Miss Agnes Garrett, Mrs Despard were present with representatives of the National Union of Societies for Equal Citizenship (*Woman's Leader* 1928b).

'Dame Millicent was eager to be present on this, the very last of all the Women's Suffrage occasions, and took great pains to find out the exact time of the ceremony' (Strachey 1931, 249), although unfortunately 'the time for the ceremony was advanced' and 'she was less than a minute too late' (*Leeds Mercury* 1928). 'In the lobby afterwards there were quiet friendly congratulations and outside the last suffrage demonstration took place – a mild, gentle, but happy close to a stormy story – when the little group was photographed' (*Woman's Leader* 1928b). Later that day, Fawcett gave a speech to 'a large unseen audience' on the British Broadcasting Corporation's 2LO radio station;[1] 'suffragists who were present in the House of Lords or listened to Dame Millicent must have felt a well of thanks-giving springing up their hearts for the recognition at long last of their hopes' (*Woman's Leader* 1928b). The text of Fawcett's radio broadcast speech was reproduced the following week:

> The Royal Assent has been given to an Act which at last gives the vote to women on the same terms as men. For those of us who have been working for this all our lives, it is a historic occasion. People used to talk about the fifty years struggle from 1868 to 1918 as our 'fifty years in the wilderness'.[2] But it was far from being a wilderness. We had gains in many directions; and as a matter of fact we took just two years less than men to win household suffrage. We worked for the vote with ardour and passion because we believed that it would benefit not women only, but the whole community. It is a remarkable fact – though it is no surprise to me – that in the short time women have had the vote, social questions have received much more attention in Parliament than they have ever received before. It is therefore with hope and confidence that we look forward to the results of the new Reform Act. Surely the problems facing the world to-day will need the best service that men and women can give as intelligent citizens, and not least the enthusiasm of the younger generation (Fawcett in *Woman's Leader* 1928c, 184).

Fawcett's message was featured in the *Woman's Leader* alongside the picture taken on 2 July, with the caption:

> Members of the National Union of Societies for Equal Citizenship and Women's Freedom League attended the House of Lords to hear the Royal Assent of the Equal Franchise Bill. Photo shows: Some of the members at the House of Lords. The group includes Dame Millicent Fawcett, Miss Garrett, Miss Courtney, Miss Philippa Fawcett, Miss Macadam, Miss Chrystal Macmillan, Miss Catherine Marshall, Mrs Strachey, Mrs Swanwick and Miss Ward (*Woman's Leader* 1928c, 184).

These postcards became popular keepsakes. A later advertisement in the *Woman's Leader* offered for sale:

> Equal Franchise – A memento. Readers will remember the photograph, reproduced in this paper, of a group of N.U.S.E.C. members outside the Houses of Parliament on the occasion of the granting of the Royal Assent to the Equal Franchise Act. This interesting group makes a clear and excellent picture, printed post card size: at the same time a very delightful photograph was taken of Dame Millicent Fawcett, with her sister Miss Agnes Garrett, and her daughter, leaving Westminster in Mrs Oliver Strachey's car. These two photographs form a very charming memento of a great and historic occasion: members desirous of obtaining copies (price 6d. each) may do so on application to Headquarters (*Woman's Leader* 1928d).

Notes

1. For 2LO see Section 50, note 1. No known recording of this exists. This speech does not appear in the bibliography compiled by Rubinstein (1991, 291–302).
2. See Section 51, note 4.

53
Picturing Fawcett: Dame Millicent Fawcett at the Victory Breakfast, 1928

Figure 21: Dame Millicent Fawcett at the Victory Breakfast, Hotel Cecil, Thursday, 5 July 1928. From the Women's Library at LSE. No known copyright restrictions.

On 5 July 1928 the WFL hosted a Victory Breakfast for 250 invited guests at the Hotel Cecil in the Strand, London. 'It was a great reunion of old workers in the suffrage cause, and of members of all societies working for equal suffrage', including many from both the militant and constitutional arms of the movement and various politicians, with many giving speeches (*Vote* 1928a, 221). The event recalled 'the breakfasts we used to have in the old days when the prison gates were unbarred' (*Vote* 1928a, 222), referring to the breakfasts held by the militant suffrage societies to celebrate the release of their members from prison. A picture of the wider room with Fawcett in the background, which allowed identification of this photograph, appeared in the *Daily Mirror* (1928), and Fawcett's menu card and programme, signed by many speakers, is in the Women's Library at LSE (WFL 1928).

Dame Millicent Fawcett, then 81 years old, was 'outstandingly honoured by all present'. She said that:

> they had all had a joyful time and did not need commiseration. Year after year their work had been punctuated by victories of one sort or another. She expressed gratitude to the Labour Party for its support, but said that less gratitude was due to the Liberals because they were so behindhand in their support. Gratitude was due to the present Government for standing by its promise to women. 'We expect great things of the women of the future', continued Dame Millicent; 'they are not pledged to us, we are pledged to them.' She recalled a meeting at the Albert Hall some years ago, when a speaker was having a very lively reception.[1] Being on the platform, she said to him: 'Go-on – go on – go on.' He drew out the big organ stop of his voice and succeeded in making himself heard. 'To the women of the future,' said Dame Millicent, 'I say, "Go-on – go on – go on!"'[2] (*Vote* 1928a, 222).

Notes

1 Referring to the speech of the Labour politician Arthur Henderson (1863–1935) at the NUWSS meeting on 14 February 1914 (Fawcett 1924, 216; see also *Votes for Women* 1914a).
2 Strachey notes this was Fawcett's usual encouragement to 'new younger ones who were coming into the movement' (1931, 350).

54
Picturing Fawcett: Dame Millicent Fawcett, by Lionel Ellis, 1928

Figure 22: Dame Millicent Garrett Fawcett, oil on canvas, by Lionel Ellis, 1928. Now in Newnham College, University of Cambridge. Orphan work, due diligence undertaken, permission granted by Newnham College for inclusion.

Sitting again in her graduate robes from St Andrews (see Figures 7, 12 and 13), this frailer portrait emphasises the vivid red of the hood and buttons, drawing out the details of the NUWSS pendant (see Figure 16): Fawcett is presented as learned and experienced. In June 1928 NUSEC announced it wished

> to celebrate the passing of the Representation of the People (Equal Franchise) Bill in a lasting way by having a portrait of Dame Millicent Fawcett of such a quality that it may ultimately find a place in a public gallery . . . a small deputation of representatives . . . visited Dame Millicent and obtained her consent (*Woman's Leader* 1928a).

The commissioned artist was Lionel Ellis (1903–88), an unknown young painter who had studied at the Plymouth School of Art and the Royal College of Art. In February 1928 one of his paintings was featured to public acclaim in Sir Joseph Duveen's successful *British Artist's Exhibition*, a scheme to encourage lesser-known British artists, at Plymouth Museum and Art Gallery (*Western Morning News and Mercury* 1928a). Lady Nancy Astor,[1] the MP for Plymouth Sutton, had opened the exhibition, and immediately commissioned him to undertake a portrait of her daughter, the Hon. Nancy Phyllis Louise Astor (1909–75) (*Western Morning News and Mercury* 1928a).

Strachey describes how 'many hours . . . were taken up by the sittings for the portrait which her friends had absolutely insisted on having painted. Dame Millicent disliked the idea of this very much indeed; but when it came to be done she found much entertainment in it, and made great friends with the young artist' (1931, 351). Ellis himself recalled:

> It was with a considerable amount of nervousness that I first entered Dame Millicent's house to arrange about the sitting for the portrait I was to paint. At once, however, all these emotions were dispelled, and I discovered why this noble lady was so much loved. With sympathetic interest she sat daily for what to her must have been long, weary hours, but which to me were all too short, so happy was I listening to her words. Often she spoke of Disraeli, and of her meeting with Garibaldi, and it was only then that, with a shock, I realized her great age. I say a shock, because as I was concerned with portraying her character, the qualities which struck me most were strength and undiminished desire for further achievement. It was difficult to conceive that a long and active life lay behind.

She would often relate stories of her childhood . . . The time passed quickly with her breezy conversation, and the hilarity and accompanying gestures often played havoc with the sleeve or hood she wore for the sittings. Then with a winning charm that was so youthful, she would promise to remember not to speak with the hands in the future. It was with regret that I finished the painting – so much so that I suggested another portrait – but I was privileged to visit her a number of times afterwards (Ellis, in the *Woman's Leader* 1929e).

Ellis's portrait was presented on Wednesday, 12 December 1928, at Lady Astor's home at 4 St James's Square. 'A large and enthusiastic gathering of old friends took part in this very delightful ceremony, and it was felt to be very felicitous that it should be in the house of the first woman to sit in the House of Commons' (*Woman's Leader* 1928e). 'This portrait of Dame Millicent . . . makes her look unfamiliarly austere, and this was at once realised when Dame Millicent briskly rose to thank her fellow workers and to assure them that she had always thoroughly enjoyed her work among them' (*Vote* 1928b). 'In spite of the fact that she had to listen once more to all sorts of variants of the theme of her praises, and then to make a speech of her own, Dame Millicent enjoyed the occasion' (Strachey 1931, 352).

Rather than being displayed in London, the portrait found a home at Newnham College, Cambridge, which Fawcett had co-founded in 1871,[2] although it is not clear when it was accepted there. Ellis exhibited from 1927 to 1933, then became a master at Wimbledon School of Art from the late 1930s to the 1960s, while working as an artist and book illustrator (Carter 2015). Works of his known to be in a UK collection include the portrait securing his early fame (ArtUK 2021), a 1938 drawing in the British Museum (n.d.) and illustrations and woodcuts in various books. A large collection of oil paintings from his estate sold at auction in 2021 (Ewbank's Auctions 2021).

Notes

1 See Section 49, note 6.
2 See Section 2, note 2.

55
Can women influence international policy? 1929

'Influence on foreign affairs'. *Times of India*. Monday, 19 August 1929, 8.

Fawcett's final article appeared two weeks after her death. The last few months of her life were busy and happy: travelling with her sister Agnes to Ceylon in January 1929, where she lectured (*International Woman Suffrage News* 1929); laying the foundation stone of the new buildings of the London and National Society for Women's Service[1] in Marsham Street in April (*Woman's Leader* 1929a); visiting Canterbury in May, and Brighton in June (Rubinstein 1991, 282–4). Her last public appearance was on 18 July 1929, 60 years and a day after her first suffrage speech, as guest of honour at a NUSEC luncheon to 'celebrate the advent of the first woman Cabinet Minister,[2] and the return to Parliament of fourteen women MPs' (Rathbone 1929, 209). Shortly after, a cold developed into double pneumonia. Concern for her was such that her condition was widely and regularly reported in the press (*Dundee Evening Telegraph* 1929; *Sunderland Echo and Shipping Gazette* 1929; *Western Mail* 1929). She died on Monday, 5 August 1929, aged 82, at home at Gower Street, with Philippa and Agnes at her side (Rathbone 1929, 209).

Fawcett's funeral was held on Thursday, 8 August, at Golders Green Crematorium, London, with a great number of family members in attendance and representatives from numerous organisations from every side of the women's rights movement: 'It was a sad company mourning the loss of a very dear friend and almost worshipped leader, but there was nevertheless an atmosphere of peace and thanksgiving for a long and beautiful life, unusually rich not only in completed public achievement but in personal loyalties, friendships, and affection' (*Woman's Leader* 1929c).

There was a suggestion made by many suffragists that Fawcett should be interred at Westminster Abbey (*Western Morning News and Mercury* 1929), although this quietly did not proceed,[3] and no public announcement was made regarding the final resting place of her ashes. A sold-out memorial service was held in Westminster Abbey on 19 November, which Ray Strachey detailed afterwards at 6.30 p.m. on BBC Radio (*Radio Times* 1929):

> The Abbey was thronged to the doors with men and women of all kinds, assembled from all over the country to do honour to one who was a great pioneer and a great statesman ... There were, of course, the great public men of the day ... the women were more striking still. For they were the living evidence of the work of her life ... representing over 80 great national organisations – political societies, professional societies, women teachers, civil servants, nurses, engineers, and all sorts, young women just entering on their new opportunities, older women who had seen the struggle at its height, medical women and representatives of the great women colleges in their robes and scarlet gowns – more than a thousand of them, typifying and actually proving Dame Millicent's life work (Strachey 1929).

On 12 March 1932, a memorial to Dame Millicent Fawcett was unveiled in St George's Chapel in Westminster Abbey[4] (Westminster Abbey 1932, 2021). It consists of bronze wreathed roundels[5] placed on either side of Henry Fawcett's 1887 memorial.[6] Her inscription reads 'Dame Millicent Garrett Fawcett 1847–1929. A wise constant and courageous Englishwoman. She won citizenship for women' (Westminster Abbey 1932, 2021; *Woman's Leader* 1932). Attached to one of the roundels is a representation of the coat of arms of the NUWSS, also featured in the brooch/pendant presented to Fawcett in 1913 (see Figure 16), which is worn on Wearing's 2018 statue of Fawcett in Parliament Square, providing a link between the memorial in the Abbey and the statue nearby. The other roundel in the Abbey has a representation of the insignia of the Dames Grand Cross[7] of the Most Excellent Order of the British Empire, with its pale blue enamelled cross and crimson rings.

Fawcett's final newspaper column, 'Can Women Influence International Policy?', was taken from quotes 'in an interview', although it is not known when this was conducted.[8] Fawcett had long been interested in international aspects of the suffrage movement, attending the International Congress of Women in London in 1899 (Rubinstein 1991,

137), being elected second vice-president of the IWSA 'at the inaugural congress in Berlin in 1904 . . . and first vice-president at the London congress in 1909' (Rubinstein 1991, 203; see Figure 10) and, in her later years, being involved in the League of Nations Union (Rubinstein 1991, 255). It is fitting that her final newspaper article considers how the extension of women's suffrage will go on to affect the UK government's policies in the widest sense: Fawcett characteristically looks to the future, and women's increasingly important place in it.

*

Throughout the ages, the conduct of international policy has been controlled by men. Women have had little or nothing to do with such matters. By tradition, and by the limitation of their spheres of activity by men, they have largely confined their energies to domestic affairs – to the management of a household, the care of their children and the making of a home. In comparatively recent years, as their education has advanced and their outlook widened, they have more or less forced men to concede to them the right to share in the control and direction of affairs which were previously considered a masculine prerogative. They have taken their place in industry, in art, literature and science, in municipal government, and are now fighting for a firm foothold in national government and, through national government, for a voice in the conduct of international affairs. How any man with any political sense can ever entertain the idea that the extension of womanhood suffrage will not materially affect the conduct of English policy I cannot imagine! It is going to make an enormous difference – provided of course that the new women voters use their power in a reasonable and enlightened manner – as I think they will – and are not swayed by masculine eloquence and prejudice.

Working for peace

There is little doubt, I think, but that this recent extension of the franchise to the women of England is going to result in the introduction of a better spirit in international affairs. We have already several organisations which work for the emancipation of women throughout European countries,[9] and I must say that we have received consistent support and good comradeship from the women of America.[10] Women's influence in international policy will always be directed towards the furtherance of peace and the establishment of amicable relations between the nations of the world. That is what we must work for. I do not think there is anyone, neither man nor woman, who can regard the awfulness and the desolation of the last Great War without coming to the conclusion that war is a monstrosity in this civilised age, an anachronism which must never be allowed to recur. Women, probably more so than men, are strong in their determination to prevent the catastrophe of future wars. That is why they have always supported so wholeheartedly the ideals of the League of Nations.[11] I am not able to give, offhand, the percentage of women in the membership of the League,[12] but I know from conversations I have had with Lord Cecil[13] and other leaders that their numerical strength in the League is very great and that they do exercise a tremendous influence.

Need for organisation

These opportunities will not come by magic: they must be made; and to make opportunities, women will have to organise their forces not only in England, but in all other countries, and, indeed, on an international basis. As I have said, there are a great many organisations in existence which are working for the education of women in order that they may be fitted to make the best use of opportunities that arise. Of course, women cannot act separately from men, as men in the past have acted separately from women with little or no regard for feminine views. Women will always be associated with men, but now in England and America they share equally with men in the election of those whose work it will be to direct international policy, and they are at length in a position to influence that policy. We do not lack leaders of our cause and exponents of our principles. There is, for instance, Miss Maude Royden[14] in England, who is one of the most forceful speakers in the country and who has done noble work in furthering the rights of women and bringing feminine influence to bear on national policy.

Feminism in France

In France there are several outstanding women, but in that country the political influence of women, and their consequent influence on international relationships, is exercised less directly. Women there have succeeded in obtaining very prominent and influential positions in various walks of life, but in political life they do not appear to be taking a very obvious place. There have been several international conferences of women in Paris,[15] and they have been marked by extraordinary enthusiasm and splendid speaking, and I have no doubt that their influence on European policy will be for the good. The subject of the feminine movement in France, however, and its influence on political policy, is very difficult. As far as I have been able to ascertain, French women are more or less satisfied without having any direct influence on politics. Many of them, however, run big businesses and hold splendid positions in industry and commerce, and it is through that sphere that they seem to work.

An obsolete law

The position of French women under the laws of the Code Napoleon[16] is, of course, a source of considerable discontent. Under that code married women are not allowed to receive gifts or to make gifts – or even to send or to receive letters – without the express permission of their husbands. Such a position appears intolerable, and at a meeting of women which I attended in Paris some time ago, the most passionate indignation was expressed at such a state of affairs. One particular instance may be given, and that is of the wife of a French soldier who had been bequeathed a legacy, but was unable to take it because the whereabouts of her husband could not be ascertained. The woman was in straightened [sic] circumstances and had several children to care for, but nevertheless the law would not permit her to take advantage of the gift. I believe the matter was eventually remedied, but as far as I know the restrictions of the Code Napoleon are still in operation. This case merely proves the need for women to organise and to work for equality of status with men, not only in France but in all countries.

Transcribed from a copy in the British Library.
No known copyright restrictions.

Notes

1 'The London and National Society for Women's Service (renamed thus in 1926) grew out of a previous sequence of women's suffrage groups: it had previously been known as The London Society for Women's Service (1919), prior to this it had been the London Society for Women's Suffrage (1907), which in turn grew out of the Central Society of Women's Suffrage ... In 1953 it became the Fawcett Society'. In 2000 the Westminster School purchased Millicent Fawcett Hall, which had been at the heart of the new London and National Society for Women's Service (LNSWS) building, and refurbished it as a theatre for use in the school's drama activities, retaining the name Millicent Fawcett Hall when it reopened in 2001 (Historic England n.d.). See Introduction, p. 6, for Fawcett's relationship to the LNSWS.

2   Margaret Grace Bondfield (1873–1953), Labour politician and trade unionist. An MP for Northampton and then Wallsend, she served as minister of labour from June 1929 until August 1931.
3   There is no record in the Deanery files, nor in the Chapter minutes or service files, that this discussion took place with Westminster Abbey (Payne 2021).
4   In 2013 the memorial was moved from its position on the chapel's south wall to its west side (Westminster Abbey 2021).
5   Millicent's memorial was by Sir Herbert Baker (1862–1946) in collaboration with Arthur George Walker (1861–1939) and Laurence Arthur Turner (1864–1957) (*Woman's Leader* 1932). Walker created the 1930 statue of Emmeline Pankhurst now in Victoria Tower Gardens (*Vote* 1930a, 81). Turner was known for his work on other memorials, and in particular for decorative carved elements (*Country Life* 1912, 23).
6   Henry Fawcett's memorial was by Sir Alfred Gilbert (1854–1934).
7   See Figure 17.
8   Likewise, a final book review for the *Woman's Leader* was found on her desk and published on 16 August (*Woman's Leader* 1929b), although it is not known when it was written. Remaining with the international theme, Fawcett reviews *Being the Life of Saroj Nalini, Founder of the Women's Institute Movement in India* (Dutt 1929; Fawcett 1929b, 219).
9   Ruiz and Marín 2012.
10 Bolt 2014.
11 Northedge 1986; see also Section 49, note 20.
12 See Miller 1994 for women's involvement in the League of Nations. 'There were only six women out of 177 total delegates at the 1922 General Assembly, a figure which climbed to 14 in 1930. As late as 1936, when 50 countries sent delegations to the League Assembly, there were still only a mere 12 women included' (Rees 2020). Fawcett probably means here the individual UK memberships, as part of the League of Nations Union, which she was involved in (Rubinstein 1991, 255). By 1931 there were 406,868 paid UK subscribers (Thompson 1977, 951).
13 Edgar Algernon Robert Gascoyne-Cecil (known as Lord Robert Cecil, 1864–1958). Conservative, then independent conservative, politician and peace campaigner (and son of Robert Arthur Talbot Gascoyne-Cecil, who had served as prime minister). Cecil became leader of the League of Nations Union in 1918 (Ceadel 2011). Lord Cecil unveiled the memorial to Fawcett in Westminster Abbey on Saturday, 12 March 1932 (*Vote* 1932).
14 (Agnes) Maude Royden (1876–1956), suffragist, renowned preacher and member of the League of Nations Union (*Coming Day* 1920). In 1928, 'pressing the Christian cause of peace and the need for the League of Nations . . . her tour extended from the USA to New Zealand and Australia; thence to Japan and China and India' (Fletcher 2004).
15 Fawcett attended a meeting of peace negotiators in Paris in 1919 with a group of women from the Allied countries to urge the case for improvement in women's conditions (Rubinstein 1991, 252; Strachey 1931, 331–2), and the 1926 IWSA Congress in Paris (Rubinstein 1991, 280). There were other Paris meetings reported in the *Common Cause*, such as the 1912 Congres Permanent du Féminisme Internationale (*Common Cause* 1912g), and the 1913 Tenth International Women's Conference (*Common Cause* 1913d, 131).
16 The legal framework in France establishing a coherent set of laws in post-revolutionary France. See Herchenroder 1938 for the lack of women's rights: 'the Code placed married women on no higher plane than minors and lunatics' (p. 196).

Bibliography

All URLs were correct when checked on 15 January 2022.

1418now.org, 2018. 'Gillian Wearing: Millicent Fawcett'. https://www.1418now.org.uk/commissions/millicent-fawcett/.

Abdela, Lesley, 1992. 'Safe as houses?'. *Guardian*. Tuesday, 11 February 1992, 16.

Aberdeen Press and Journal, 1894. 'Imperial Parliament, House of Commons, Friday. The Registration Bill. The government proposals. Criticism by Mr Balfour'. Saturday, 14 April 1894, 5.

Aberystwyth University, 2020. 'History of Aberystwyth University'. https://www.aber.ac.uk/en/about-us/history/.

Adam, James, 1908. *The Religious Teachers of Greece. Gifford lectures delivered at Aberdeen University 1904–06*. Aberdeen: Aberdeen University.

Adam Matthew Digital, 2021. 'Women's suffrage collection from Manchester Central Library'. http://www.ampltd.co.uk/collections_az/WomSuf-MCL2/highlights.aspx.

Adams, Herbert Baxter, 1900. 'University extension in Great Britain'. Chap. XVIII. *Report of the Commissioner of Education for 1898–99*. Washington: United States Bureau of Education (USBE), 957–1055.

Adut, Ari, 2005. 'A theory of scandal: Victorians, homosexuality, and the fall of Oscar Wilde'. *American Journal of Sociology*. Vol. 111, No. 1, 213–48.

Anderson, Nancy F., 1982. 'The "Marriage with a Deceased Wife's Sister Bill" controversy: Incest anxiety and the defense of family purity in Victorian England'. *Journal of British Studies*. Vol. 21, No. 2 (Spring 1982), 67–86.

Andrews, Irene Osgood, 1918. *Economic Effects of the War Upon Women and Children in Great Britain*. Preliminary Economic Studies of the War, Carnegie Endowment for International Peace. New York: Oxford University Press.

Anonymous, 1875a. 'Mrs Fawcett's novel'. *Examiner*. Saturday, 22 May 1875, 581–3.

Anonymous, 1875b. 'Janet Doncaster'. *Times*, London. Friday, 25 June 1875, 4.

Anonymous, 1875c. 'Janet Doncaster'. *British Quarterly Review*. October 1875, 556–7.

Anti-Suffrage Review, 1912. 'Militants and non-militants'. No. 41 (April 1912), 68.

Arnold, Matthew, 1869. *Culture and Anarchy: An essay in political and social criticism*. London: Smith, Elder and Co.

Arnold, Matthew, 1990. 'The last word'. Super, Robert Henry (ed.), 1990. *The Complete Prose Works of Matthew Arnold*, Vol. 11. Ann Arbor: University of Michigan Press.

ArtUK, 2021. 'Lionel Ellis'. https://artuk.org/discover/artists/ellis-lionel-19031988#.

Ascham, Roger, 1570. *The Scholemaster*, edited by Edward Arber, 1895. London: Westminster and Co.

Ashton, Rosemary, 2008. 'Evans, Marian [*pseud.* George Eliot]'. *Oxford Dictionary of National Biography*. Oxford: Oxford University Press. https://doi.org/10.1093/ref:odnb/6794.

At the Circulating Library, 2020. 'Author information: BTAO "Anonyma"'. *At the Circulating Library: A database of Victorian fiction, 1837–1901*. http://www.victorianresearch.org/atcl/show_author.php?aid=2856.

Attwood, Rachael, 2015. 'Stopping the traffic: The National Vigilance Association and the international fight against the "white slave" trade (1899–c. 1909)', *Women's History Review*. Vol. 24, No. 3, 325–50. https://doi.org/10.1080/09612025.2014.964064.

L'Avenir de Roubaix-Tourcoing, 1897. 'Catastrophe, Bazar de charité. Les Morts: Reconnaissanse de la duchesse d'Alençon'. Vendredi 7 Mai 1897, 1. https://www.bn-r.fr/presse/pdf/PRA_AVE/PDF/1897/PRA_AVE_18970507_001.pdf.

Backlund, Berith, and Sjödahl Hayman, Anna, 2011. *Kvinnohistoria i Sverige*. Göteborg: Göteborgs universitetsbibliotek. http://hdl.handle.net/2077/28027.

Bacon, Francis, 1908. *The Essays or Counsels Civil and Moral of Francis Bacon*. Ed. Fred Allison Howe, 1908. Boston: D. C. Heath and Co.

Bakewell, Joan, 2004. 'Just 70: Burials, scattered ashes, memorials . . . the new mantra of consumer choice now even applies to death'. *Guardian*. Friday, 9 July 2004, 12.

Baldwin, M. Page, 2001. 'Subject to empire: Married women and the British Nationality and Status of Aliens Act'. *Journal of British Studies*. Vol. 40, No. 4, 522–56.

Balfour, Frances, 1917. 'When is woman old enough to vote? The 35-year age-limit in the new scheme'. *Weekly Dispatch*, London. Sunday, 4 February 1917, 5.

Balfour, Frances, Strachey, Jane Maria, Hamilton, Cicely, Lowndes, Mary, Grant Richards, Elisina, 1909. 'Preface'. *Englishwoman*. No. 1 (February 1909), 1–2.

Balmforth, Ramsden, 1900. *Some Social and Political Pioneers of the Nineteenth Century*. London: Swan Sonnenschein & Co., Ltd.

Banks, Linda, and Banks, Robert, 2019. *Through the Valley of the Shadow: Australian women in war-torn China*. Eugene, OR: Pickwick Publications.

Barbauld, Anna Letitia, and Aikin, Lucy, 1826. *The Works of Anna Lætitia Barbauld. With a memoir by Lucy Aikin*, Vol. 1. New York: Carvill and Co.

Barlow, Pepita, 2013. 'The lost world of royal commissions'. *Institute for Government Blog*. 19 June 2013. https://www.instituteforgovernment.org.uk/blog/lost-world-royal-commissions.

Barnes, George Stapylton, 1912. 'To the secretary of the board of trade. December 1912'. In British Parliamentary Papers (1913), *Report of an Enquiry by the Board of Trade into the Earnings and Hours of Labour of Workpeople of the United Kingdom*, vol. 8, 1913. London: Darling and Son, 1–3.

Barry Dock News, 1893. 'Mrs Grundy's jottings'. 22 December 1893, 4.

Bartley, Paula, 1998. *Votes for Women, 1860–1928*. Oxford: Hodder and Stoughton.

Bartley, Paula, 2000. *Prostitution: Prevention and reform in England, 1860–1914*. London: Routledge.

Bashford, Alison, 2004. *Imperial Hygiene: A critical history of colonialism, nationalism and public health*. Houndmills: Palgrave Macmillan.

Bate, Walter Jackson, 1977. *Samuel Johnson*. New York: Harcourt Brace Jovanovich.

Bath Chronicle and Weekly Gazette, 1894. 'Women's suffrage meeting'. Thursday, 15 March 1894, 5.

Batorowicz, Krzysztof, 2012. 'The vision of a university in the British tradition: Reflecting on the Universities Tests Act 1871: What have we developed and what are we losing?' In *The British World: Religion, memory, society, culture. Refereed proceedings of the conference hosted by the University of Southern Queensland, Toowoomba, July 2nd–5th, 2012*. Ed. Marcus K. Harmes, Lindsay Henderson, Barbara Harmes and Amy Antonio. Toowoomba, Australia: University of Southern Queensland, 405–14.

BBC, 1936. 'Louisa wants a bicycle: Or the fight for woman's freedom'. BBC Northern Ireland. Tuesday, 8 September 1936, 8.55 p.m. In *Radio Times*, Friday, 4 September 1936, 4.

BBC, 1946. 'Queen Victoria was furious'. BBC Home Service. Sunday, 5 May 1946, 7 p.m. In *Radio Times*, Friday, 3 May 1946, 6.

BBC, 1954. 'I knew her: Mary Stocks talking about Dame Millicent Fawcett'. *Home for the Day*, Light Programme. Sunday, 7 February 1954. In *Radio Times*, Friday, 5 February 1954, 11.

BBC, 1989. 'Down your way: Millicent Garrett Fawcett'. BBC Radio 4. Sunday, 12 November 1989, 5 p.m.

BBC, 2000. 'Missing persons: Millicent Garrett Fawcett'. BBC Radio 4. Saturday, 6 May 2000, 2.30 p.m.

BBC, 2002. 'Women's Library finds home'. *BBC News*. Friday, 1 February 2002. http://news.bbc.co.uk/1/hi/entertainment/1794220.stm.

BBC, 2004. 'Footlight fairies'. BBC Radio 4. Wednesday, 14 April 2004, 11 a.m.

BBC, 2006. 'Great lives: Millicent Garrett Fawcett'. BBC Radio 4. Tuesday, 19 December 2006, 4.30 p.m. https://www.bbc.co.uk/programmes/p00gj7nf.

BBC, 2017a. 'Bodelwyddan Castle's portrait gallery exhibition to close'. *BBC News*. Monday, 13 March 2017. https://www.bbc.co.uk/news/uk-wales-north-east-wales-39253282.

BBC, 2017b. 'Millicent Fawcett statue gets Parliament Square go ahead'. *BBC News*. 20 September 2017. https://www.bbc.co.uk/news/uk-england-london-41330508.

BBC, 2018. 'Pioneering women special'. *Antiques Roadshow*. Series 41. Part of the BBC 'Hear Her' season. BBC One, Sunday, 10 June 2018, 8 p.m. https://www.bbc.co.uk/programmes/b0b6vj13. See the episode at https://www.dailymotion.com/video/x6vsk3h.

Beale, Dorothea, 1894a. 'A few words of retrospect and forecast'. In *Proceedings of the International Congress of Education of the World's Columbian Exposition, Chicago July 25–28, 1893*. New York: National Education Association, 862–4.

Beale, Dorothea, 1894b. 'Cheltenham Ladies' College, 1894'. Postscript to Mrs Fawcett's Paper. *Spring College Magazine*, 5–24.

Bearman, Christopher J., 2005. 'An examination of suffragette violence'. *English Historical Review*. Vol. 120, No. 486, 365–97.

Beauchamp, Kenneth George, 2001. *A History of Telegraphy: Its technology and application*. Stevenage: The Institution of Engineering and Technology.

Beckstrand, Lisa, 2009. *Deviant Women of the French Revolution and the Rise of Feminism*. Cranbury, NJ: Associated University Presses.

Begum, Tahmina, 2018. 'Tatty Devine X Fawcett Society necklaces are our new feminist jewellery crush'. *Huffington Post*. 25 May 2018. https://www.huffingtonpost.co.uk/entry/feminist-jewellery-fawcett-society_uk_5b07d679e4b0fdb2aa525947.

Belfast News Letter, 1928. 'Queen Elizabeth. Only contemporary likeness in statuary. Discovered in London church'. Wednesday, 1 August 1928, 12.

Bell, Morag, and McEwan, Cheryl, 1996. 'The admission of women Fellows to the Royal Geographical Society, 1892–1914: The controversy and the outcome'. *Geographical Journal*. Vol. 162, No. 3, 295–312.

Bénézit, Emmanuel, 1924. *Dictionnaire Critique et Documentaire des Peintres, Sculpteurs, Dessinateurs & Graveurs de Tous les Temps et de Tous les Pays*, Vol. 3, L–Z. Paris: Ernest Gründ.

Bennett, Mary, 2010. *Ford Madox Brown: A catalogue raisonné*, Vol. 2. New Haven and London: Yale University Press for Paul Mellon Centre for Studies in British Art.

Bentley, Michael, 1987. *The Climax of Liberal Politics: British liberalism in theory and practice, 1868–1918*. Baltimore, MD: Edward Arnold.

Bhavnani, Kum-Kum, 2001. *Feminism and Race*. Oxford: Oxford University Press.

Birmingham Daily Gazette, 1925. 'A reception was given in London yesterday'. Wednesday, 11 February 1925, 1.

Birmingham Daily Post, 1871. 'Woman's suffrage'. Wednesday, 6 December 1871, 5.

Birmingham Daily Post, 1883. 'The Bright celebration: Banquet in the Town Hall, Speeches by Earl Granville and Mr Bright'. Friday, 15 June 1883, 5.

Birmingham Daily Post, 1892. 'Parliamentary notes, House of Commons, Wednesday'. Thursday, 28 April 1892, 4.

Birmingham Daily Post, 1897. 'London correspondence'. Tuesday, 26 October 1897, 5.

Birmingham Daily Post, 1916. 'Mr Walter Long's appeal'. Thursday, 17 August 1916, 3.

Blackburn, Eileen, 1996. 'If not Ben, why not Milly or Liz?' Letters to the editor. *Guardian*. Tuesday, 30 July 1996, 14.

Blackburn, Helen, and Mackenzie, Antoinette M., 1899. *Englishwomen's Review of Social and Industrial Questions*, Vol. 30, January to December 1899. London: Williams and Norgate. 2017 Kindle edition, Advisory editors J. Horowitz Murray and M. Stark. Abingdon: Routledge.

Blaikie, W. Garden, 1896. 'Woman's battle in Great Britain'. *The North American Review*. Vol. 163, 282–95.

Bland, Lucy, 1992. '"Purifying" the public world: Feminist vigilantes in late Victorian England'. *Women's History Review*. Vol. 1, No. 3, 397–412.

Boheman, Ezaline, 1911. 'Sweden'. *Jus Suffragii*. Sunday, 15 October 1911, 17.

Bolotin, Norm, and Laing, Christine, 2002. *The World's Columbian Exposition: The Chicago World's Fair of 1893*. Champaign, Illinois: University of Illinois Press.

Bolt, Christine, 2014. *The Women's Movements in the United States and Britain from the 1790s to the 1920s*. Abingdon: Routledge.

Bombay Gazette, 1906. 'Should matrons wear white?' Wednesday, 1 August 1906, 6.

Bonett, Helena, 2013. '"Deeds not word": Suffragettes and the Summer Exhibition'. Royal Academy, July 2013; republished June 2018. https://www.royalacademy.org.uk/article/deeds-not-words-suffragettes-and.

Booth, V. E. Hartley, and Sells, Peter, 1980. *British Extradition Law and Procedure*, Vol. 1. Germantown, MD: Sijthoff and Noordhoff.

Boswell, James, 1791. *The Life of Samuel Johnson, LL. D. Comprehending an account of his studies, and numerous works in chronological order*. London: Jones & Co.

Boussahba-Bravard, Myriam, and Rogers, Rebecca, 2017. 'Introduction: Positioning women in the World's Fairs, 1876–1937'. In *Women in International and Universal Exhibitions 1876–1937*, edited by Myriam Boussahba-Bravard and Rebecca Rogers. London: Routledge, 1–24.

Bradford Daily Telegraph, 1869. 'Friday July 30, 1869'. Friday, 30 July 1869, 2.

Brand, Robert Henry, 1909. *The Union of South Africa*. Oxford: Clarendon Press.

Braybon, Gail, 2013. *Women Workers in the First World War*, 3rd edition. London: Routledge.
Breitenbach, Esther, and Wright, Valerie, 2014. 'Women as active citizens: Glasgow and Edinburgh c. 1918–1939'. *Women's History Review*. Vol. 23, No. 3, 401–20.
Brighton, Paul, 2014. *Original Spin: Downing Street and the press in Victorian Britain*. London: I. B. Tauris.
Brighton Gazette, 1888. 'Public notices'. Thursday, 19 January 1888, 1.
Brighton Guardian, 1868. 'Brighton election'. Wednesday, 18 November 1868, 5.
Brisbane Courier, 1886. 'Mr Lowell on England (*Pall Mall Gazette*). A repudiated interview by Mr Julian Hawthorne'. Wednesday, 29 December 1886, 3.
British and Foreign School Society, 1869. *The Educational Record with the Proceedings of the British and Foreign School Society*, Vol. 7, January 1867 to July 1869. London: Printed for the Society.
British Athletics, 2018. 'First ever Millicent Fawcett mile to be held at Müller Anniversary Games'. https://www.britishathletics.org.uk/news-and-features/first-ever-millicent-fawcett-mile-to-be-held-at-muller-anniversary-games/.
British Concentration Camps of the South African War, n.d.a. 'Aliwal North'. https://www2.lib.uct.ac.za/mss/bccd/Histories/Aliwal_North/.
British Concentration Camps of the South African War, n.d.b. 'Bloemfontein'. https://www2.lib.uct.ac.za/mss/bccd/Histories/Bloemfontein/.
British Concentration Camps of the South African War, n.d.c. 'Mafeking'. https://www2.lib.uct.ac.za/mss/bccd/Histories/Mafeking/.
British Concentration Camps of the South African War, n.d.d. 'Springfontein'. https://www2.lib.uct.ac.za/mss/bccd/Histories/Springfontein/.
British Museum, n.d. 'drawing. Drawn by Lionel Ellis. Female figure walking to left'. 1938,0212.1. https://www.britishmuseum.org/collection/object/P_1938-0212-1.
British Pathé, 1928. 'A Queen cleaned – Dame Millicent Fawcett unveils only contemporary statue of Queen Elizabeth . . . repaired, repainted and restored as it was in the 16th century'. Pathé Newsreels, Film ID 736.12. https://www.britishpathe.com/video/a-queen-cleaned/.
British Pathé, 2011. 'Emily Davison throws herself under the Kings Derby Horse 1913'. https://www.britishpathe.com/video/emily-davison-throws-herself-under-the-kings-derby.
British Philatelic Bulletin, 2008. 'Women of distinction. Royal Mail honours the achievements of six outstanding women'. Vol. 45 (July 2008), 340–1.
Brooke-Hunt, Violet, 1901. *A Woman's Memories of the War*. London: James Nisbet & Co.
Brookes, Barbara, 2016. *A History of New Zealand Women*. Wellington, New Zealand: Bridget Williams Books.
Brooks, David, 1985. 'Gladstone and Midlothian: The background to the first campaign', *Scottish Historical Reviews*. Vol. 44, 1, No. 177 (April 1985), 42–67.
Brophy, Julia Anne, 1985. 'Law, state and the family: The politics of child custody'. PhD dissertation, University of Sheffield. http://etheses.whiterose.ac.uk/1795/1/DX185403.pdf.
Brown, Frank Herbert, 2004. 'Wyllie, Sir (William Hutt) Curzon'. *Oxford Dictionary of National Biography*. Revised by Roger T. Stearn, 23 September 2010.
Brown, Heloise, 2018. 'The physical force objection to women's suffrage'. In *'The Truest form of patriotism': Pacifist feminism in Britain, 1870–1902*. Manchester: Manchester University Press, 13–25.
Browning, Robert, 1864. 'Caliban upon Setebos: Natural theology in the island'. *Dramatis Personae*. London: Chapman and Hall.
Buck, Louisa, 2018. '"Courage calls to courage everywhere": Suffragist sculpture unveiled in London'. *The Art Newspaper*. 24 April 2018. https://www.theartnewspaper.com/interview/courage-calls-to-courage-everywhere-gillian-wearing-s-suffragette-sculpture-unveiled-in-london.
Bury, Adrian, 1930. 'The Royal Academy'. *Saturday Review*. 10 May 1930, 581.
Bush, Julia, 2007. *Women against the Vote: Female anti-suffragism in Britain*. Oxford: Oxford University Press.
Bush, Julia, 2018. 'The anti-suffrage movement'. Votes for Women. British Library, 5 March 2018. https://web.archive.org/web/20180326122211/https://www.bl.uk/votes-for-women/articles/the-anti-suffrage-movement.
Bushnell, Horace, 1869. *Women's Suffrage: The reform against nature*. New York: Charles Scribner and Company.

Caine, Barbara, 2011. 'Strachey [*née* Costelloe], Rachel Pearsall Conn [Ray]'. *Oxford Dictionary of National Biography*. https://www.oxforddnb.com/view/10.1093/ref:odnb/9780198614128.001.0001/odnb-9780198614128-e-38017?rskey=SSEwK4&result=2.

Calcutta Review, 1870. 'Article III: Woman'. Vol. 52, 227–65.

Cambridge Chronicle and Journal, 1892. 'Presentation of An Address to Mrs Fawcett'. *The Cambridge Chronicle and University Journal, Isle of Ely Herald, and Huntingdon Gazette*. Friday, 10 June 1892, 7.

Carrier, John Woolfe, 1983. 'The acceptance and statutory recognition of women as police officers in England and Wales with special reference to the Metropolitan Police, 1914–1931'. PhD Thesis, London School of Economics and Political Science.

Carroll, Lewis, 1872. *Through the Looking-Glass, and What Alice Found There*. London: Macmillan and Co.

Carroll, Lucy, 1976. 'The temperance movement in India: Politics and social reform'. *Modern Asian Studies*. Vol. 10, No. 3, 417–47.

Carter, David E., 2015. *Plymouth's Forgotten Prodigy*. Lulu.com.

Casket, 1829. *From the Mass. Journal: Philosophy and independence. The Casket. Flowers of literature, wit and sentiment for 1829*. Philadelphia: Sam C. Atkinson, 129.

Cavendish, Lucy, 1927. *The Diary of Lady Frederick Cavendish*, Vol. 2, edited by John Bailey. New York: Frederick A. Stokes.

Cawood, Ian, 2012. *The Liberal Unionist Party: A history*. London: I. B. Tauris.

Ceadel, Martin, 2011. 'Cecil, (Edgar Algernon) Robert Gascoyne- [*known as* Lord Robert Cecil], Viscount Cecil of Chelwood'. *Oxford Dictionary of National Biography*. https://www.oxforddnb.com/view/10.1093/ref:odnb/9780198614128.001.0001/odnb-9780198614128-e-32335?rskey=h9j2oo&result=2.

Chambers's Encyclopaedia, 1876. *Chambers's Encyclopaedia: A dictionary of universal knowledge for the people with maps and numerous wood engravings*, Revised edition, Vol. 2. London: W. and R. Chambers.

Charlton, Henry Buckley, 1951. *Portrait of a University, 1851–1951: To commemorate the centenary of Manchester University*. Manchester: Manchester University Press.

Cheltenham Chronicle, 1894. 'Mrs Fawcett in Cheltenham: Women's suffrage'. Saturday, 17 March 1894, 6.

Cheltenham Chronicle and Gloucestershire Graphic, 1947. 'Formerly on Ladies' College staff: Death of Miss M. Louch'. Saturday, 18 January 1947, 4.

Cheltenham Ladies' College, 1893. *Spring College Magazine*.

Cheltenham Ladies' College, 1894. *Spring College Magazine*.

Cheltenham Ladies' College, 2020. 'History of College'. https://www.cheltladiescollege.org/about-clc/history-of-college/.

Cherry, Bridget, and Pevsner, Nikolaus, 2002. *London 4: North*. The Buildings of England. London: Yale University Press.

Chester Chronicle, 1915. 'Farm notes'. Saturday, 4 December 1915, 7.

Christ's Hospital, 2020. 'History of the school'. https://www.christs-hospital.org.uk/about-ch/history-of-the-school/.

Christie, Manson, and Woods, 1934. *Catalogue of the Remaining Works of the Late Annie L. Swynnerton A. R. A. and The Artistic Effects of the Studio Removed from 1a The Avenue, 76 Fulham Road, S.W.3* (Sold by Order of the Executors). https://archive.org/details/1934-02-09-Annie-Swynnerton-Catalogue-PDF/mode/2up.

Church of England, 1906. *The English Hymnal*. Oxford: Oxford University Press.

Churchill, Winston S., 1899. *The River War: An historical account of the reconquest of the Soudan*, Vol. 1. London: Longmans, Green and Co.

City Branch, 1900. *Labour Laws for Women: Their reason and their results*. London: City Branch, Independent Labour Party.

Clark, Jessica P., 2020. *The Business of Beauty: Gender and the body in modern London*. London: Bloomsbury Visual Arts.

Clarke, H. H., 1897. 'Shipping rings'. Letters to the editor. *Times*, London. Friday, 15 October 1897, 5.

Clerkenwell News, 1871. 'London Daily Chronicle and Clerkenwell News'. Tuesday, 2 May 1871, 4.

Clough, Anne Jemima, 1873. 'Merton Hall and the Cambridge lectures for women', 22 October 1873, Newnham College Archives.

Clough, Blanche Athena, 1897. *A Memoir of Anne Jemima Clough*. London: Edward Arnold.

Cohen, Claire, 2016. 'Suffragette statue campaign calls on Parliament to honour Millicent Fawcett'. *Daily Telegraph*. 7 June 2016. https://www.telegraph.co.uk/women/politics/suffragette-statue-campaign-calls-on-parliament-to-honour-millic/.
Cohn, Samuel, 2007. 'After the Black Death: Labour legislation and attitudes towards labour in late-medieval western Europe'. *Economic History Review*. Vol. 60, No. 3, 457–85.
Collier, Martin, 2003. *Italian Unification, 1820–71*. Portsmouth, NH: Heinemann.
Coming Day, 1920. 'Miss Maude Royden at the City Temple. Women and the League of Nations'. Sunday, 15 February 1920, 99.
Common Cause, 1909a. 'The quarterly council meeting'. Thursday, 14 October 1909, 341.
Common Cause, 1909b. 'Our portrait'. Thursday, 21 October 1909, 350.
Common Cause, 1909c. 'Forthcoming meetings'. Thursday, 4 November 1909, 394–5.
Common Cause, 1909d. 'Glasgow'. Thursday, 2 December 1909, 458.
Common Cause, 1909e. 'A good friend in Glasgow'. Thursday, 16 December 1909, 478.
Common Cause, 1911a. 'Forthcoming meetings'. Thursday, 2 March 1911, 771.
Common Cause, 1911b. 'Portrait of Mr and Mrs Fawcett'. 20 July 1911, 262.
Common Cause, 1911c. 'Special council meeting, December 8th 1911'. Thursday, 14 December 1911, 632–3.
Common Cause, 1912a. 'Mrs Fawcett'. Thursday, 25 January 1912, 714.
Common Cause, 1912b. 'The speakers at the Albert Hall, Friday February 23rd'. Thursday, 22 February 1912, 777.
Common Cause, 1912c. 'Infant mortality and the employment of mothers'. Thursday, 22 February 1912, 779–80.
Common Cause, 1912d. '"In memoriam", Mary Letitia Wirgman'. Thursday, 22 February 1912, 785.
Common Cause, 1912e. 'Literature department'. Thursday, 7 March 1912, 820.
Common Cause, 1912f. 'Irishwomen's Suffrage Federation. Petition to Mr Asquith'. Thursday, 25 July 1912, 275–6.
Common Cause, 1912g. 'A permanent women's conference in Paris'. Thursday, 3 October 1912, 451.
Common Cause, 1913a. 'London society's reception'. Friday, 7 March 1913, 818.
Common Cause, 1913b. 'Professor Geddes at University College'. Friday, 18 April 1913, 21.
Common Cause, 1913c. 'The international congress at Buda-Pesth'. Friday, 16 May 1913, 86.
Common Cause, 1913d. 'International women's suffrage'. Friday, 6 June 1913, 131.
Common Cause, 1913e. 'Responsibility'. Friday, 13 June 1913, 152.
Common Cause, 1913f. 'Congress at Buda Pesth'. Friday, 13 June 1913, 159.
Common Cause, 1913g. 'Latest news from our pilgrims. Mrs Fawcett joins the march!' Friday, 11 July 1913, 237.
Common Cause, 1913h. 'Personalities of the pilgrimage'. Friday, 25 July 1913, 275.
Common Cause, 1913i. 'Mrs Fawcett in Hyde Park'. Friday, 1 August 1913, 293.
Common Cause, 1913j. 'How to conduct a suffrage stall'. Friday, 17 October 1913, 486.
Common Cause, 1914a. 'Notes and comments, women's meeting'. Friday, 7 August 1914, 371.
Common Cause, 1914b. Front cover. Friday, 14 August 1914, 385.
Common Cause, 1914c. 'Executive committee'. Friday, 14 August 1914, 390.
Common Cause, 1915a. 'National Union meeting at Kingsway Hall. Mrs Fawcett's speech'. Friday, 12 February 1915, 712.
Common Cause, 1915b. 'Reviews'. Friday, 15 October 1915, 336.
Common Cause, 1917a. 'A bill without delay'. Friday, 16 February 1917, 8–9.
Common Cause, 1917b. 'With the tide'. Friday, 23 February 1917, 2.
Common Cause, 1917c. 'Women worker's suffrage demonstration'. Friday, 2 March 1917, 7.
Common Cause, 1918. 'The Millicent Fawcett scholarships, Bedford College for Women, University of London'. Friday, 15 March 1918, 636.
Common Cause, 1919a. 'Women's service'. Friday, 28 February 1919, 551.
Common Cause, 1919b. 'Mrs Fawcett's address to the council'. Friday, 21 March 1919, 606.
Common Cause, 1919c. 'Women and the League of Nations'. Friday, 2 May 1919, 22.
Common Cause, 1919d. 'The Nurses State Registration Bill'. Friday, 28 November 1919, 425.
Conable, Charlotte Williams, 1977. *Women at Cornell: The myth of equal education*. Ithaca: Cornell University Press.
Concentration Camps Commission, 1902. *Report on the Concentration Camps in South Africa, by the Committee of Ladies Appointed by the Secretary of State for War: Containing report on the camps in Natal, the Orange River Colony, and the Transvaal*. London: Printed for his Majesty's Stationery Office by Eyre and Spottiswoode.

Connell, L., 1914. Millicent Garrett Fawcett. LSE Library. https://www.flickr.com/photos/lselibrary/28828469812/.

Cook, Beverley, 2021. 'Research question regarding Millicent Fawcett's Brooch', email to Melissa Terras. Wednesday, 26 May 2021.

Cook, Edward Tyas, 1909. *Edmund Garrett: A memoir*. London: Edward Arnold.

Cooke, Alistair, 2011. 'Founders of the Primrose League'. *Oxford Dictionary of National Bibliography*. 19 May 2011. Oxford: Oxford University Press. https://doi.org/10.1093/ref:odnb/42172.

Cooke, M. M. Russell, Fawcett, Millicent Garrett, Hallett, Lilias Ashworth, Lyttleton, Kathleen, McLaren, Priscilla Bright, 1897. 'The House of Commons and women's suffrage: To the editor of the *Standard*'. *London Evening Standard*. Monday, 12 July 1897, 3.

Cooper, Glynis, 2018. *Struggle and Suffrage in Manchester: Women's lives and the fight for equality*. Barnsley: Pen and Sword History.

Coote, William Alexander, 1910. *A Vision and Its Fulfilment: Being the history of the origin of the work of the National Vigilance Association for the suppression of the White slave traffic*. London: National Vigilance Association.

Coote, William Alexander, 1916. *A Romance of Philanthropy: Being a record of some of the principal incidents connected with the exceptionally successful thirty years' work of the National Vigilance Association*. London: National Vigilance Association.

Cotton Factory Times, 1914. 'Kitchener and clothiers. Message in Hebden Bridge work-shops'. Friday, 4 December 1914, 5.

Country Life, 1912. 'Country homes gardens old and new: Headley Court Epsom. The residence of Mr Walter Cunliffe'. Vol. 32, No. 809 (6 July 1912), 18–25.

Courtney, K. D., 1912. 'Women and the Labour Party, attitude of Chief Suffrage Society'. *Daily Citizen*, Manchester. Tuesday, 29 October 1912, 3.

Coustillas, Pierre, 2008. 'Gissing's pacifism; A temperament in the light of history'. *Gissing Journal*. Vol. 44, No. 2. April 2008. http://estminst-studies.net/gissing/newsletter-journal/journal-44-2.pdf.

Cox, Pamela, and Hobley, Annabel, 2015. *Shopgirls: True stories of friendship, hardship and triumph from behind the counter*. London: Random House.

Cox, Paul, 2021. 'RE: Question about Henry Fawcett; Dame Millicent Fawcett by Ford Madox Brown (1872)', email to Melissa Terras. Tuesday, 4 May 2021.

Crawford, Elizabeth, 2001. *The Women's Suffrage Movement: A reference guide 1866–1928*, Paperback edition. London: Routledge.

Crawford, Elizabeth, 2002. *Enterprising Women: The Garretts and their circle*. London: Francis Boutle Publishers.

Crawford, Elizabeth, 2003. 'Suffrage stories: "We believe that the rousing of the Irish people had best be left to Irish women"'. Paper given at The Suffragette and Women's History Conference, University of Portsmouth. *Women and Her Sphere*. 11 October 2003. https://womanandhersphere.com/2014/04/29/suffrage-storieswe-believe-that-the-rousing-of-the-irish-people-had-best-be-left-to-irish-women/.

Crawford, Elizabeth, 2008. 'Suffrage stories: An army of banners – designed for the NUWSS Suffrage Procession 13 June 1908'. *Woman and Her Sphere*. June 2008. https://womanandhersphere.com/2014/11/26/suffrage-stories-an-army-of-banners-designed-for-the-nuwss-suffrage-procession-13-june-1908/.

Crawford, Elizabeth, 2014a. 'Emily Wilding Davison: Centennial celebrations'. *Women's History Review*. Vol. 23, No. 6, 1000–7.

Crawford, Elizabeth, 2014b. 'Suffrage stories: The 1866 suffrage petition – and the geyser'. *Woman and Her Sphere*. 13 May 2014. https://womanandhersphere.com/2014/05/13/suffrage-stories-the-1866-suffrage-petition-and-the-geyser/.

Crawford, Elizabeth, 2016a. 'Suffrage stories: Suffragette statues: Or why does the present take no interest in the past?' *Woman and Her Sphere*. 10 May 2016. https://womanandhersphere.com/2016/05/10/suffrage-stories-suffragette-statues-or-why-does-the-present-take-no-interest-in-the-past/.

Crawford, Elizabeth, 2016b. 'Suffrage stories/collecting suffrage: The 1866 women's suffrage petition'. *Woman and Her Sphere*. 7 June 2016. https://womanandhersphere.com/2015/09/15/suffrage-storiescollecting-suffrage-countdown-to-12-october-and-release-of-the-film-suffragette-the-1866-womens-suffrage-petition/.

Crawford, Elizabeth, 2016c. 'Suffrage stories: Fawcett Society wreath-laying service for Millicent Garrett Fawcett, St George's Chapel, Westminster Abbey'. *Woman and Her Sphere*. 2 July 2016. https://womanandhersphere.com/2016/07/04/suffrage-stories-fawcett-society-wreath-laying-service-for-millicent-garrett-fawcett-st-georges-chapel-westminster-abbey-2-july-2016/.

Crawford, Elizabeth, 2020. 'The Women's Printing Society'. Women, British Library Exhibition 2020. https://www.bl.uk/womens-rights/articles/the-womens-printing-society.

Crawford, Elizabeth, 2021. 'Millicent Fawcett (1847–1929): The making of a politician'. In *The British Women's Suffrage Campaign: National and international perspectives*, edited by June Purvis and June Hannam. Abingdon: Routledge, 10–24.

Creese, Mary R. S., 2009. 'Somerville [*née* Fairfax; *other married name* Greig], Mary'. *Oxford Dictionary of National Biography*. https://www.oxforddnb.com/view/10.1093/ref:odnb/9780198614128.001.0001/odnb-9780198614128-e-26024.

Criado Perez, Caroline, 2016. 'Put a statue of a suffragette in Parliament Square to mark 100 years of female suffrage'. 8 March 2016. https://www.change.org/p/westminster-council-put-a-statue-of-a-suffragette-in-parliament-square.

Criado Perez, Caroline, and Cohen, Claire, 2016. 'Emma Watson is calling on Sadiq Khan to put a suffragette outside Parliament – and you can too'. Women, *Daily Telegraph*. 10 May 2016. https://www.telegraph.co.uk/women/politics/emma-watson-is-calling-on-sadiq-khan-to-put-a-suffragette-outsid/.

Criminal Law Amendment Act 1885. https://www.swarb.co.uk/acts/1885Criminal_Law_AmendmentAct.shtml.

Crossman, Virginia, 2006. *Politics, Pauperism and Power in late Nineteenth-Century Ireland*. Manchester: Manchester University Press.

Crown Office, 1917. 'Central chancery of the orders of knighthood'. *London Gazette*. Second supplement. Friday, 24 August 1917, 8791–3.

Daily Express, 1912. 'Mr Birrell disgusted. "I have finished with them forever"'. No. 3, 716. Wednesday, 6 March 1912, 1.

Daily Mail, 1906a. 'Mr Balfour and the "suffragettes". Hecklers disarmed by the ex-premier's patience'. From our Special Correspondent. Wednesday, 10 January 1906, 5.

Daily Mail, 1906b. 'Blow to suffragettes'. Thursday, 15 November 1906, 7.

Daily Mail, 1925. 'Dame Ellen Terry and Buckingham Palace. The Queen's dolls' house at Olympia'. Friday, 13 February 1925, 16.

Daily Mirror, 1906. 'Welsh Amazons. Women blacklead and "frog-march" non Unionists in colliery strike'. Thursday, 6 September 1906, 4.

Daily Mirror, 1907. 'Suffrage bill talked out. Mr J. D. Rees kills Votes for Women measure'. Saturday, 9 March 1907, 3.

Daily Mirror, 1928. 'Suffragettes celebrate granting of flapper vote'. Friday, 6 July 1928, 7.

Daily Telegraph, 1913. 'Scenes and speeches. Mrs Fawcett's platform'. Monday, 28 July 1913, 5.

Daily Telegraph, 1915. 'America's army. War minister's scheme. 500,000 trained soldiers'. Saturday, 14 August 1915, 7.

Dalberg-Acton, John Emerich Edward, 1906. 'Inaugural lecture on the study of history'. In *Lectures on Modern History*. London: Macmillan and Co, 1–30.

Dale, Pamela, and Fisher, Kate, 2009. 'Implementing the 1902 Midwives Act: Assessing problems, developing services and creating a new role for a variety of female practitioners'. *Women's History Review*. Vol. 18, No. 3, 427–52.

Dalley, Lana L., 2021, 'Confronting "white feminism" in the Victorian literature classroom'. *Nineteenth-Century Gender Studies*. Vol. 17, No. 1 (Spring 2021). http://m.ncgsjournal.com/issue171/dalley.html.

Daly, Mary, 1984. *Pure Lust: Elemental feminist philosophy*. Boston: Beacon Press.

Daly, Mary, 1998. *Quintessence . . . Realizing the archaic future: A radical elemental feminist manifesto*. Boston: Beacon Press.

Damrosh, Leo, 2005. *Jean-Jacques Rousseau: Restless genius*. New York: Mariner Books.

Davenport-Hines, Richard, 2008. 'Gordon, Charles George'. *Oxford Dictionary of National Biography*. Oxford: Oxford University Press. https://doi.org/10.1093/ref:odnb/11029.

Davies, Emily, 2004. *Emily Davies: Collected letters, 1861–1875*, edited by Ann B. Murphy. Charlottesville: University of Virginia Press.

Davies, John Llewelyn, 1868. 'A new college for women'. *Macmillan's Magazine*. Vol. 18 (May–October 1868), 168–75.

Davies, John Llewelyn, 1885. 'The weakness of the law'. Letters to the editor. *Times*, London. 4 August 1885, 6.
Davis, Ann Elizabeth Leighton, 2004. 'Hardcastle, Frances'. *Oxford Dictionary of National Biography*. Oxford: Oxford University Press. https://doi.org/10.1093/ref:odnb/64021.
Davis, Mary, n.d. 'Trade Union congress history, Timeline, 1850–1880. The Union makes us strong'. TUC History Online. http://www.unionhistory.info/timeline/1850_1880.php.
Defoe, Daniel, 1969. *An Essay Upon Projects*. Scolar Press Facsimile. Menston: Scolar Press Limited.
Denness, Zoë, 2012. 'Women and warfare at the start of the twentieth century: The racialization of the "enemy" during the South African War (1899–1902)'. *Patterns of Prejudice*. Vol. 46, Nos 3–4, 255–76. https://doi.org/10.1080/0031322X.2012.701497.
Denney, Colleen, 2017. *Women, Portraiture and the Crisis of Identity in Victorian England: My lady scandalous reconsidered*. Abingdon: Routledge.
Derby Daily Telegraph, 1928. 'Modern Girl: Alert brain beneath shingled hair. Developed at 21'. Monday, 16 January 1928, 3.
Deutsch, Regine, 1929. *The International Woman Suffrage Alliance: Its history from 1904 to 1929*, by Regine Deutsch on behalf of the Board of Alliance. Hertford: Stephen Austin and Sons Ltd.
Dicey, Albert Venn, 1906a. 'A protest against privilege'. *The National Review*. No. 284 (October 1906), 209–24.
Dicey, Albert Venn, 1906b. 'The Trade Disputes Bill, to the editor of the Times'. Monday, 19 November 1906, 5.
Dickens, Charles, 1837. *The Posthumous Papers of the Pickwick Club*. London: Chapman and Hall.
Dickens, Charles, 1839. *The Life and Adventures of Nicholas Nickleby*. London: Chapman and Hall.
Dickens, Charles, 1844. *The Life and Adventures of Martin Chuzzlewit*. London: Chapman and Hall.
Dickens, Charles, 1848. *The Haunted Man and the Ghost's Bargain*. Edinburgh: T. and A. Constable.
Dickens, Charles, 1850. *The Personal History, Adventures, Experience, and Observation of David Copperfield the Younger of Blunderstone Rookery*. London: Bradbury and Evans.
Dickens, Charles, 1853. *Bleak House*. London: Bradbury and Evans.
Dickens, Charles, 1855. 'The Boots'. *Household Words*. 15 December 1855, 18–22.
Dickens, Charles, 1856. *The Holly-Tree Inn. In seven chapters*. Philadelphia: T. B. Peterson.
Dickens, Charles, 1858. *The Poor Traveller: Boots at the Holly-Tree Inn, and Mrs Gamp*. London: Bradbury and Evans.
Dickens, Charles, 1874. 'Zulu nursery tales'. *All the Year Round*. 7 February 1874, 352.
Dickens, Charles Junior, 1908. *Dickens Dictionary of London*, c. 1908 edition. Quoted in Victorian London. https://www.victorianlondon.org/entertainment/juniorconsitutionalclub.htm.
Dico, Joy Lo, 2016. 'How would Emily vote on the EU?'. *Evening Standard*. Wednesday, 9 March 2016, 16–17.
Discovering Women in Irish History, n.d. 'Trinity College campaign'. http://womeninhistory.scoilnet.ie/content/unit4/tcd.html.
Donadio, Stephen, Smith, Joan, Mesner, Susan, and Davison, Rebecca, 1992. *The New York Public Library Book of Twentieth-Century American Quotations*. New York: Stonesong Press.
Downey, William, and Downey, Daniel, 1890. *The Cabinet Portrait Gallery, 1st Series*. Cassell and Company, London.
Van Drenth, Annemieke, and van Essen, Mineke, 2004. 'The position of Dutch and American women in early twentieth-century educational sciences: Different roots but similar outcomes'. In *Scholarly Environments, Centres of Learning and Institutional Contexts 1560–1960*, by Alasdair A. Macdonald and Arend H. Huussen. Leuven: Peeters, 151–67.
Dumas, Alexander, 1859. *Les Mohicans de Paris*. Calmann-Lévy, 1885. Paris: Ancienne Maison Michel Lévy Frères.
Dundee Advertiser, 1871. 'The great jewel robbery'. Friday, 3 March 1871, 6.
Dundee Courier, 1908. 'Mr Churchill and free trade. Mr Churchill and women's suffrage'. Thursday, 16 April 1908, 5.
Dundee Evening Telegraph, 1929. 'Dame Millicent Fawcett's illness'. Monday, 29 July 1929, 4.
Dutt, Guru-Sadaya, 1929. *A Woman of India: Being the life of Saroj Nalini (founder of the Women's Institute movement in India)*. London: Hogarth Press.
Dutton, David, 2013. *A History of the Liberal Party since 1900*, 2nd edition. Basingstoke: Palgrave Macmillan.
Dyhouse, Carol, 1995. *No Distinction of Sex? Women in British Universities 1870–1939*. London: UCL Press.

Eagles, John, 1832. *The Bristol Riots, Their Causes, Progress, and Consequences*. Bristol: Gutch and Martin.
Edgeworth, Maria, 1801. *Moral Tales for Young People*, 1866 edition, Vol. 2. Leipzig: Bernhard Tauchnitz.
Edgeworth, Maria, 1809. *Tales of Fashionable Life*. In three volumes. London: J. Johnson.
Edinburgh Evening News, 1884. 'Mr Valentine Baker'. Thursday, 15 May 1884, 3.
Education in England, 2020. *Taunton Report (1868), Report of the Schools Inquiry Commission*. http://www.educationengland.org.uk/documents/taunton1868/index.html.
Eliot, George, 1859. *Adam Bede*, Vol. 3. Edinburgh and London: William Blackwood and Sons.
Eliot, George, 1863. *Romola*. London: Smith, Elder and Co.
Eliot, George. 1868. *The Spanish Gypsy*. London: William Blackwood and Sons.
Eliot, George, 1871. *Middlemarch*. London: William Blackwood and Sons.
Ellerton, Nerida F., and Clements, M. A. Ken, 2014. *Abraham Lincoln's Cyphering Book and Ten Other Extraordinary Cyphering Books*. Berlin: Springer Science & Business Media.
E. M. L. (Lynch, Eliza Matilda), 1873. 'A few words on women's suffrage'. Reprinted with additions, by the kind permission of the Proprietors from the *Englishwoman's Review*. Dublin: R. D. Webb and Son, Printers.
Encyclopædia Britannica, 1911. 'Gotham, Wise men of', 11th edition. Cambridge: Cambridge University Press, 271.
Englishwoman, 1915a. 'Echoes'. Vol. 27, No. 81, 275–81.
Englishwoman, 1915b. 'Echoes'. Vol. 28, No. 84, 276–7.
Erickson, Amy Louise, 2002. *Women and Property in Early Modern England*. Abingdon: Routledge.
Erskine May, Thomas, 1865. *The Constitutional History of England since the Accession of George the Third 1760–1860*, 2nd edition, Vol. 2. London: Longman, Green, Longman, Roberts & Green.
Eustance, Claire Louise, 1993. '"Daring to be free": The evolution of women's political identities in the Women's Freedom League, 1907–1930'. Doctoral dissertation, University of York, Centre for Women's Studies. http://etheses.whiterose.ac.uk/2516/1/DX178742.pdf.
Evans, Julie, Grimshaw, Patricia, Philips, David, and Swain, Shurlee, 2018. 'South Africa: Saving the White voters from being "utterly swamped"'. In *Equal Subjects, Unequal Rights*. Manchester: Manchester University Press, 157–81.
Evening Express, 1894. 'The Registration Bill. Read the first time in the Commons on Friday'. Saturday, 14 April 1894, 4.
Evening Mail, 1884. 'Parliamentary intelligence'. Friday, 31 October 1884, 6.
Evening Mail, 1912. 'Suffragist outrages. Wholesale window smashing in London. Attack on the Prime Minister's house'. London. Monday, 4 March 1912, 5.
Evening Mail, 1914. 'United States neutrality, remarkable statement by former ambassador'. Friday, 6 November 1914, 3.
Evening Mail, 1915. 'Confidence of king and country'. Wednesday, 3 November 1915, 7.
Evening Mail, 1917a. 'Electoral reform. An agreed plan. Report of Speaker's Committee. Questions of the franchise'. Wednesday, 31 January 1917, 5–6.
Evening Mail, 1917b. 'The United States at war'. Friday, 6 April 1917, 4.
Evening News and Post, 1892. 'Who's who'. London. Friday, 22 July 1892, 2.
Ewbank's Auctions, 2021. 'Rare horse paintings come to auction at Ewbank's, 33 years after artist Lionel Ellis's death'. https://www.ewbankauctions.co.uk/News-Blog/rare-horse-paintings-come-to-auction-at-ewbank-s-33-years-after-artist-lionel-ellis-s-death.
Express and Echo, 1871. 'Extraordinary robbery'. Monday, 16 January 1871, 1.
Fawcett, Henry, and Fawcett, Millicent Garrett, 1872. *Essays and Lectures on Social and Political Subjects*. London: Macmillan and Co.
Fawcett, Millicent Garrett, 1868. 'The education of women of middle and upper classes'. *Macmillan's Magazine*. Vol. 17 (November 1867–April 1868), 511–17.
Fawcett, Millicent Garrett, 1870a. *Political Economy for Beginners*. London: Macmillan and Co.
Fawcett, Millicent Garrett, 1870b. 'The electoral disabilities of women'. *Fortnightly Review*. May 1870, 622–32.
Fawcett, Millicent Garrett, 1871. 'Electoral disabilities of women'. A lecture delivered at the New Hall, Tavistock, March 11th 1871. Printed for the Bristol & West of England Society for Women's Suffrage. Tavistock: Tavistock Printing Company, 1–23.
Fawcett, Millicent Garrett, 1872. 'Mrs Fawcett on women's suffrage'. A speech delivered in the Town Hall, Birmingham, December 6th 1872. Reprinted from the *Birmingham Morning News*. Birmingham: C. N. Wright, 1–8.

Fawcett, Millicent Garrett, 1873a. 'Mr Fitzjames Stephen on the position of women'. *Examiner*. Saturday, 24 May 1873, 539–41.
Fawcett, Millicent Garrett, 1873b. *Mr Fitzjames Stephen on the Position of Women*. London: R. Clay and Sons, and Taylor.
Fawcett, Millicent Garrett, 1873c. 'His influence as a practical politician'. In *John Stuart Mill: His life and works. Twelve sketches by Herbert Spencer, Henry Fawcett, Frederic Harrison and other distinguished authors*. Boston: James R. Osgood and Company, 81–7.
Fawcett, Millicent Garrett, 1874. *Tales in Political Economy*. London: Macmillan.
Fawcett, Millicent Garrett, 1875. *Janet Doncaster*. London: Smith, Elder and Co.
Fawcett, Millicent Garrett, 1877. 'Communism'. *Encylopædia Britannica*, 9th edition, Vol. 6, 211–19.
Fawcett, Millicent Garrett, 1883. 'Women and representative government'. *Nineteenth Century*. August 1883, 285–91.
Fawcett, Millicent Garrett, 1884a. 'The New Forest. I. Picturesque'. *Magazine of Art*. October 1884, 1–8.
Fawcett, Millicent Garrett, 1884b. 'The New Forest. II. Historical'. *Magazine of Art*. November 1884, 45–52.
Fawcett, Millicent Garrett, 1885a. 'Burnham Beeches'. *Magazine of Art*. September 1885, 485–92.
Fawcett, Millicent Garrett, 1885b. 'Italy': 140–53, and 'European cities': 154–78. In *Orient Line Guide*, edited by William John Loftie, 2nd edition. London: Sampson Low.
Fawcett, Millicent Garrett, 1885c. 'The protection of girls: Speech or silence'. *Contemporary Review*. September 1885, 326–31.
Fawcett, Millicent Garrett, 1887a. 'Letters to Pearson regarding [her daughter] Philippa Fawcett's preparations to study mathematics at Cambridge; and seeking Pearson's opinion of various mathematics coaches'. UCL Special Collections, PEARSON/11/1/6/8.
Fawcett, Millicent Garrett, 1887b. 'Employment for girls. The civil service (the Post Office)'. *Atalanta*. Vol. 1, No. 3, 174–6.
Fawcett, Millicent Garrett, 1888a. 'The employment of children in theatres: How the factory acts and education acts have worked'. *Echo*. 10 December 1888, 2.
Fawcett, Millicent Garrett, 1888b. 'The employment of children in theatres: What the teachers of the children say'. *Echo*. 12 December 1888, 2.
Fawcett, Millicent Garrett, 1888c. 'The employment of children in theatres: What theatrical people say'. *Echo*. 15 December 1888, 2.
Fawcett, Millicent Garrett, 1888d. 'The employment of children in theatres: The economic difficulty'. *Echo*. 18 December 1888, 1.
Fawcett, Millicent Garrett, 1888e. 'Naples': 77–98; 'Cities of Italy': 99–114; and 'Germany': 115–22. In *Orient Line Guide*, edited by William John Loftie, 3rd edition. London: Sampson Low.
Fawcett, Millicent Garrett, 1889a. 'The appeal against female suffrage: A reply'. *Nineteenth Century*. No. 149 (July 1899). London: Kegan Paul, Trench and Co.
Fawcett, Millicent Garrett, 1889b. 'The employment of children in theatres'. *Contemporary Review*. December 1889, 822–9.
Fawcett, Millicent Garrett, 1889c. *Some Eminent Women of Our Times: Short biographical sketches*. London: Macmillan.
Fawcett, Millicent Garrett, 1890. 'Letter to W. T. Stead', 17 August 1890. Stead Papers, Churchill College, Cambridge. Quoted in Rubinstein (1991, 38).
Fawcett, Millicent Garrett, 1891. 'Introduction'. In *A Vindication of the Rights of Woman*, by Mary Wollstonecraft, New edition. London: T. Fisher Unwin Ltd, 2–30.
Fawcett, Millicent Garrett, c. 1892a, 'MGF to the Society for Psychical Research'. Society for Psychical Research Collections, Cambridge University Library, CUL SPR 24/13.
Fawcett, Millicent Garrett, 1892b. 'A reply to the letter of Mr Samuel Smith, M.P. on women's suffrage by Mrs Fawcett. Reprinted, with additions, from the *Morning Post* and other papers'. Central Committee of the National Society for Women's Suffrage, 10 Great College Street, Westminster. London: Women's Printing Society, 1–11. Available from https://digital.library.lse.ac.uk/objects/lse:lij464nez/read/single#page/85/mode/1up.
Fawcett, Millicent Garrett, 1892c. 'Politics in the home'. *Albemarle, A monthly review*. Vol. 1, No. 6 (June 1892), 195–200.
Fawcett, Millicent Garrett, 1893a. 'Politics in the home'. *Humanitarian, A monthly review of sociological science* (London, July 1893), 43–9.
Fawcett, Millicent Garrett, 1893b. 'Politics in the home'. *Literary Digest*. Vol. 7 (May–October 1893), 310–11.

Fawcett, Millicent Garrett, 1893c. 'The vigilance record, June'. Quoted in Bland, Lucy, 1992. '"Purifying" the public world: Feminist vigilantes in late Victorian England'. *Women's History Review*. Vol. 1, No. 3, 397–412. https://doi.org/10.1080/09612029200200013.

Fawcett, Millicent Garrett, 1894a. 'Home and politics'. An address delivered at Toynbee Hall and elsewhere, 4th edition. London: Women's Printing Society, 1894, 1–8.

Fawcett, Millicent Garrett, 1894b. 'From Gibraltar to Naples'. In *Orient Line Guide*, edited by William John Loftie, 5th edition. London: Sampson Low, 61–74.

Fawcett, Millicent Garrett, 1894c. 'University education for women in England'. In *National Education Association of the United States, 1894. Proceedings of the International Congress of Education of the World's Columbian Exposition, Chicago July 25–28, 1893*. New York: National Education Association, 853–62.

Fawcett, Millicent Garrett, 1894d. 'The story of the opening of university education to women'. Cheltenham Ladies' College, 1894. *Spring College Magazine*, 5–24.

Fawcett, Millicent Garrett, 1895. *Life of Her Majesty Queen Victoria*. London: W. H. Allen.

Fawcett, Millicent Garrett, 1897. 'Women's suffrage'. An address delivered at the Junior Constitutional Club, Piccadilly, Thursday November 11th 1897. London: McCorquodale and Co. Ltd, 1–18.

Fawcett, Millicent Garrett, 1899a. *Women's Suffrage, A Speech Delivered to the Women's Debating Society, The Owens College, Manchester, 13th February 1899*. North of England Society of Women's Suffrage. Manchester: Taylor, Garnett, Evans and Co. Ltd, 1–15.

Fawcett, Millicent Garrett, 1899b. 'United Kingdom'. By Mrs Henry Fawcett LLD. In *National Vigilance Association, 1899. The White Slave Trade: Transaction of the International Congress on the White Slave Trade, held in London on the 21st, 22nd and 23rd June 1899, at the invitation of the National Vigilance Association*. London: Wertheimer, Lea and Co, 139–47.

Fawcett, Millicent Garrett, 1899c. 'The white slave trade: Its causes, and the best means of preventing it'. Paper read June 1899. International Congress, 1–8.

Fawcett, Millicent Garrett, 1901a. *Life of the Right Hon. Sir William Molesworth, Bart., M.P., F.R.S.* London: Macmillan.

Fawcett, Millicent Garrett, 1901b. 'London to Marseilles and Naples': 49–60; and 'Cairo': 92–6. In *Orient Line Guide*, edited by William John Loftie, 6th edition. London: Sampson Low.

Fawcett, Millicent Garrett, 1901c. 'The concentration camps in South Africa'. *Westminster Gazette*. Thursday, 4 July 1901, 1–2.

Fawcett, Millicent Garrett, 1903. 'Impressions of South Africa, 1901 and 1903'. *Contemporary Review*. November 1903, 635–55.

Fawcett, Millicent Garrett, 1904. 'Openings for women in South Africa. I. Gardening'. *Imperial Colonist*. March 1904, 28–30.

Fawcett, Millicent Garrett, 1905. *Five Famous French Women*. London: Cassell.

Fawcett, Millicent Garrett, 1906a. 'The imprisoned suffragists'. *Times*, London. Saturday, 27 October 1906, 8.

Fawcett, Millicent Garrett, 1906b. 'Why we women want votes'. *Daily Mail*. Tuesday, 20 November 1906, 6.

Fawcett, Millicent Garrett, 1906c. 'The prisoners of hope in Holloway Gaol'. *Contemporary Review*. December 1906, 820–6.

Fawcett, Millicent Garrett, 1908. 'National Union manifesto'. *Women's Franchise*. Thursday, 19 November 1908, 237.

Fawcett, Millicent Garrett, 1909a. 'Men are men and women are women'. Reprinted as a pamphlet, by permission from the *Englishwoman*. Vol. 1, No. 1 (February 1909), 17–30.

Fawcett, Millicent Garrett, 1909b. 'Wanted: A statesman. Address delivered at the Athenaeum Hall, Glasgow, November 22nd, 1909'. Privately published, 1–11.

Fawcett, Millicent Garrett, 1909c. 'The women's suffrage movement: Statesmanship or coercion?' *Englishwoman*. Vol. 4, No. 11 (December 1909), 144–51.

Fawcett, Millicent Garrett, 1911. 'Mrs Fawcett's opinion of the procession on June 17th. To the editor of the *Common Cause*'. *Common Cause*. 4 May 1911, 60.

Fawcett, Millicent Garrett, 1912a. *Women's Suffrage: A short history of a great movement*. London: T. C. & E. C. Jack.

Fawcett, Millicent Garrett, 1912b. 'In memoriam: Miss Rosa Morison'. *Common Cause*. Thursday, 15 February 1912, 5.

Fawcett, Millicent Garrett, 1912c. 'Broken windows – and after'. *London Daily News*. Saturday, 9 March 1912, 4.

Fawcett, Millicent Garrett, 1912d. 'Constitutional suffragists and the militants. Mrs Fawcett's position, to the editor of the *Times*'. *Times*, London. Saturday, 9 March 1912, 7.

Fawcett, Millicent Garrett, 1912e. 'The best friends of women's suffrage'. Reprinted from the *Standard*. London: National Union of Women's Suffrage Societies. https://digital.library.lse.ac.uk/objects/lse:soy666pik/read/single#page/43/mode/1up.

Fawcett, Millicent Garrett, 1912f. 'Who's for us? For him are we. The friends of women's suffrage'. *Daily Citizen*, Manchester. 4 November 1912, 4.

Fawcett, Millicent Garrett, 1912g. 'How British women are organized in politics'. In *The Woman's Athenæum: The woman of affairs, business, professions, public life*, Vol. 9. New York: The Woman's Athenæum, 333–6.

Fawcett, Millicent Garrett, 1912h. Autograph letter signed to Miss Gibson. Lot 242, Forum Auctions, London. The Saleroom, 30 September 2021. https://web.archive.org/web/20210910144323/https://www.the-saleroom.com/en-gb/auction-catalogues/forumauctions/catalogue-id-forum-10282/lot-a68e42df-b53c-4f15-838e-ad9e00c09544.

Fawcett, Millicent Garrett, 1913a. 'Message from Mrs Fawcett to members of the National Union'. *Common Cause*. Friday, 31 January 1913, 735.

Fawcett, Millicent Garrett, 1913b. 'Courage!'. *Common Cause*. Friday, 11 July 1913, 227.

Fawcett, Millicent Garrett, 1914a. 'To the members of the National Union'. *Common Cause*. Friday, 7 August 1914, 376.

Fawcett, Millicent Garrett, 1914b. 'Women and the war'. *Ladies' Field*. Supplement: The Woman Suffrage Movement and the War. 21 November 1914, 7–8.

Fawcett, Millicent Garrett, 1915a. 'Life's cost'. *Conservative and Unionist Women's Franchise Review*. October–December 1915, 41.

Fawcett, Millicent Garrett, 1915b. 'The National Union of Women's Suffrage Societies and the Hague Congress'. *Englishwoman* (June 1915), 193–200.

Fawcett, Millicent Garrett, 1916a. 'Foreword'. *Purchase of Women: The great economic blunder: Part 1*, Elizabeth Blackwell, 1886. London: G. Bell, ix–xi. https://www.loc.gov/resource/mss12880.mss12880-045_0296_0349/?sp=32.

Fawcett, Millicent Garrett, 1916b. 'Lift up your hearts'. *Englishwoman*. Vol. 29 (January 1916), 5–15.

Fawcett, Millicent Garrett, 1916c. 'Mr Asquith's letter'. *Common Cause*. Friday, 19 May 1916, 82.

Fawcett, Millicent Garrett, 1916d. 'The letter sent to Mr Asquith'. *Common Cause*. Friday, 19 May 1916, 84.

Fawcett, Millicent Garrett, 1916e. 'The war conscience in time of peace'. *Englishwoman*. Vol. 96 (December 1916), 196–209.

Fawcett, Millicent Garrett, 1917a. 'An immense and significant advance'. *Englishwoman*. Vol. 33, No. 99 (March 1917), 193–7.

Fawcett, Millicent Garrett, 1917b. 'To the National Union of Women's Suffrage Societies. A message from Mrs Fawcett'. *Common Cause*. Friday, 22 June 2017, 1.

Fawcett, Millicent Garrett, 1917c. 'The problem of venereal diseases'. *Review of Reviews*. Vol. 55 (February 1917), 155–8.

Fawcett, Millicent Garrett, 1917d. 'The war's effect on woman's work'. *War Illustrated*. 6 January 1917, 482–4.

Fawcett, Millicent Garrett, 1918a. 'The Representation of the People Bill in the House of Lords. A plea for peace'. *Common Cause*. Friday, 11 January 1918, 501–2.

Fawcett, Millicent Garrett, 1918b. 'Sing, rejoice, and give thanks'. *Common Cause*. Friday, 15 March 1918, 572.

Fawcett, Millicent Garrett, 1918c. 'Looking backward'. *Common Cause*. Friday, 15 March 1918, 632.

Fawcett, Millicent Garrett, 1918d. 'Still in thy right hand carry gentle peace'. *Common Cause*. Friday, 20 December 1918, 427.

Fawcett, Millicent Garrett, 1919. 'Mrs Fawcett's address to the council'. *Common Cause*. Friday, 21 March 1919, 606.

Fawcett, Millicent Garrett, 1920a. *The Women's Victory – and After: Personal reminiscences, 1911–1918*. London: Sidgwick and Jackson Ltd.

Fawcett, Millicent Garrett, 1920b. 'The difference suffrage has made'. *Englishwoman*. Vol. 45, No. 133 (January 1920), 1–7.

Fawcett, Millicent Garrett, 1920c. 'The future of the women's movement'. *Woman's Leader and the Common Cause*. Friday, 6 February 1920, 4.

Fawcett, Millicent Garrett, 1921. 'Six weeks in Palestine. Spring 1921'. London: Women's Printing Society.
Fawcett, Millicent Garrett, 1922. 'Our second visit to Palestine. Spring 1922'. London: Women's Printing Society.
Fawcett, Millicent Garrett, 1924. *What I Remember*. London: T. Fisher Unwin Ltd.
Fawcett, Millicent Garrett, 1926a. *What the vote has done*. National Union of Societies for Equal Citizenship. London: Gwen M. Parry, Chandos House, 1–6.
Fawcett, Millicent Garrett, 1926b. *Easter in Palestine, 1921–1922*. London: T. Fisher Unwin Ltd.
Fawcett, Millicent Garrett, 1927a. *What the vote has done*. National Union of Societies for Equal Citizenship. London: Gwen M. Parry, Chandos House, 1–8.
Fawcett, Millicent Garrett, 1927b. 'Palestine, 1927'. *Woman's Leader*. Friday, 6 May 1927, 105.
Fawcett, Millicent Garrett, 1927c. 'How University College, London led the way in the education of women'. *Woman's Leader*. Friday, 29 July 1927, 200.
Fawcett, Millicent Garrett, 1927d. 'Women's rights', New edition. *Chambers's Encyclopedia*. Philadelphia: J. B. Lippincott Company, 693–8.
Fawcett, Millicent Garrett, 1927e. 'The new feminism. What has the women's vote accomplished for the country?'. *Good Housekeeping*. May 1927, 23 and 112.
Fawcett, Millicent Garrett, 1927f. 'First Women's Suffrage Committee'. To the editor of the Manchester Guardian. *Manchester Guardian*. Tuesday, 21 June 1927, 20.
Fawcett, Millicent Garrett, 1928a. 'Retrospect'. *Woman's Leader*. Friday, 20 April 1928, 87.
Fawcett, Millicent Garrett, 1928b. 'Equal franchise. Victory after sixty years'. *Manchester Guardian*. Friday, 6 July 1928, 20.
Fawcett, Millicent Garrett, 1928c. 'The end crowns all, and that old common arbitrator, Time, will one day end it'. *Woman's Leader*. Friday, 6 July 1928, 175.
Fawcett, Millicent Garrett, 1928d. 'Foreword'. In *Towards Citizenship: A handbook of women's emancipation*, by Phyllis Crawhall Challoner and Vera Laughton Mathews. London: P.S. King & Son, 7.
Fawcett, Millicent Garrett, 1929a. 'Miss Hobhouse'. *Times Literary Supplement*. Thursday, 30 May 1929, 436.
Fawcett, Millicent Garrett, 1929b. 'A woman of India'. *Woman's Leader*. Friday, 16 August 1929, 219.
Fawcett, Millicent Garrett, 1929c. 'Can women influence international policy? Influence on foreign affairs'. *Times of India*. Monday, 19 August 1929, 8.
Fawcett, Millicent Garrett, Balfour, Frances, Mason, Bertha, and Ford, Isabella O., 1908. 'Woman suffrage procession. To the editor of the Times'. *Times*. Friday, 8 May 1908, 22.
Fawcett, Millicent Garrett, and Macmillan, Chrystal, 1914. 'International manifesto of women'. *Votes for Women*. Vol. 7, No. 335. Friday, 7 August 1914, 680.
Fawcett, Millicent Garrett, and Turner, Ethel M., 1927. *Josephine Butler: Her work and principles and their meaning for the twentieth century*. London: Association for Moral & Social Hygiene.
Fawcett Society, 2016. 'JULY 6TH: Millicent Fawcett 150th anniversary memorial lecture'. https://www.webarchive.org.uk/wayback/en/archive/20170215153513/http://www.fawcettsociety.org.uk/2016/06/millicent-fawcett-150th-anniversary-lecture/.
Fawcett Society, 2020. 'Our history'. https://www.fawcettsociety.org.uk/our-history.
Fife Free Press, 1874. 'Lecture on women of modern fiction', Kirkcaldy. Saturday, 5 December 1874, 3.
Fifeshire Journal, 1874. 'Leven'. Thursday, 19 November 1874, 5.
Finkelstein, Daniel, 2015. 'Breaking the law didn't win votes for women: It was moderate, law-abiding suffragists and male MPs – not militant suffragettes – who did most to secure victory'. *Times*. Wednesday, 21 October 2015, 31.
Finn, Margot, 1996. 'Women, consumption and coverture in England, c. 1760–1860'. *Historical Journal*. Vol. 39, No. 3, 703–22.
Fisher, Lucy, 2018. 'Celebrate the vote, then tackle trolls, minister urges'. *Times*. Wednesday, 7 February 2018, 10.
Fletcher, Sheila, 2004. 'Royden, (Agnes) Maude'. *Oxford Dictionary of National Biography*. https://www.oxforddnb.com/view/10.1093/ref:odnb/9780198614128.001.0001/odnb-9780198614128-e-35861.
Ford, Ford Madox, 1896. *Ford Madox Brown: A record of his life and work*. London: Longmans.
Fordyce, James, 1775. *Sermons to Young Women, in Two Volumes*. London: S. Crowder, C. Ware and T. Payne.

Francis, John E., 1908. 'Woman suffrage, Conservative and Unionist Women's Franchise Association'. *Times*. Thursday, 19 November 1908, 8.
Freeman, Nicholas, 2011. *1895: Drama, disaster and disgrace in Late Victorian Britain*. Edinburgh Critical Studies in Victorian Culture. Edinburgh: Edinburgh University Press.
Gardiner, Alfred George, 1923. *The Life of Sir William Harcourt*, Vol. 2. London: Constable and Company Ltd.
Gardner, Alice, 1921. *A Short History of Newnham College Cambridge*. Cambridge: Bowes and Bowes.
Gayle, Damien, and Mohdin, Aamna, 2021. 'Parliament Square crowd protests against policing of Sarah Everard vigil'. *Guardian*. Sunday, 14 March 2021. https://www.theguardian.com/uk-news/2021/mar/14/parliament-square-crowd-protest-policing-sarah-everard-vigil.
Ghazi, Polly, 1992. 'Suffragette citadel under attack from council bulldozers'. *Observer*. Sunday, 19 January 1992, 5.
Gladstone, William E., 1892. 'Female suffrage. A Letter from the Right Hon. W. E. Gladstone, M.P. to Samuel Smith, M.P'. London: John Murray.
Glasgow and West of Scotland Association for Women's Suffrage (GWSAWS), 1909. 'Minutes, 3rd November and 22nd December 1909'. In Rubinstein (1991, 171).
Gleadle, Kathryn, 1995. *The Early Feminists: Unitarians and the emergence of the women's rights movement, 1831–51*. London: Palgrave Macmillan.
Glenny, Misha, 2012. *The Balkans: Nationalism, war, and the great powers, 1804–2011*. New York: Penguin.
Globe, 1893. 'Sending teachers to Chicago'. Monday, 22 May 1893, 8.
Globe, 1895. 'The massacre in China. Details of the outrages. More missions attacked'. Thursday, 8 August 1895, 4.
Globe, 1913. 'Drama of the Derby. Woman's mad deed. Striking narratives by eye-witnesses. To spoil the race'. Thursday, 5 June 1913, 11.
Gloucester Journal, 1875. 'Trial of Colonel Valentine Baker: Conviction and sentence'. Saturday, 7 August 1875, 6.
Gloucestershire Chronicle, 1888. 'The suffrage for women. Public meeting in Gloucester – address by Mrs Fawcett'. Saturday, 11 February 1888, 3.
Godwin, William, 1798. *Memoirs of Mary Wollstonecraft*, 1969 reprint of 1927 edition. New York: Haskell House Publishers.
Gohier, Urbain, 1898. *L'armée contre la nation*. Paris: La Revue Blanche.
Goldman, Lawrence (ed.), 2003. *The Blind Victorian: Henry Fawcett and British liberalism*. Cambridge: Cambridge University Press.
Goodman, Joyce F. 2006. 'Godolphin, Elizabeth'. *Oxford Dictionary of National Biography*. https://www.oxforddnb.com/view/10.1093/ref:odnb/9780198614128.001.0001/odnb-9780198614128-e-95354.
Google, 2018. 'Millicent Fawcett's 171st Birthday'. https://www.google.com/doodles/millicent-fawcetts-171st-birthday.
Google Arts and Culture, 2018a. 'Millicent Fawcett Statue'. https://artsandculture.google.com/exhibit/millicent-fawcett-statue/iQLSQacRKlFMKw.
Google Arts and Culture, 2018b. 'Making the Fawcett Statue'. https://artsandculture.google.com/exhibit/making-the-fawcett-statue/TQLyKb4yfu-KJQ.
Gordon, Eleanor, and Nair, Gwyneth, 2003. *Public Lives: Women, family, and society in Victorian Britain*. New Haven: Yale University Press.
Gouws, Amanda, 2017. 'Feminist intersectionality and the matrix of domination in South Africa'. *Agenda*. Vol. 31, No. 1, 19–27.
Grant, Jane, 2016. *In the Steps of Exceptional Women: The story of the Fawcett Society 1866–2016*. London: Francis Boutle Publishers.
Grant, Kevin, 2011. 'British suffragettes and the Russian method of hunger strike'. *Comparative Studies in Society and History*. Vol. 53, No. 1, 113–43.
Graphic, 1872. 'Women's rights – A meeting at the Hanover Square Rooms'. Saturday, 25 May 1872, 484.
Greater London Authority, 2017a. 'Gillian Wearing announced as artist of Suffragist statue'. Mayoral Press Release, 13 April 2017. https://www.london.gov.uk/press-releases/mayoral/gillian-wearing-to-create-suffragist-statue.
Greater London Authority, 2017b. 'Green light for Millicent Fawcett statue in Parliament Square'. Mayoral Press Release, 19 September 2017. https://www.london.gov.uk/press-releases/mayoral/green-light-for-millicent-fawcett-statue#.

Green, Ewen Henry Harvey, 1996. *The Crisis of Conservatism: The politics, economics and ideology of the British Conservative Party, 1880–1914*. London: Routledge.

Green, John Richard, 1875. *A Short History of the English People*. London: Macmillan and Co.

Gregory, John, 1774. *A Father's Legacy to His Daughters*. Dublin: Thomas Ewing.

Greig, James W., 1924. 'The joint and equal guardianship of infants in various legal systems'. *Journal of Comparative Legislation and International Law*, 3rd series. Vol. 6, No. 4, 238–44.

Grenier, Janet E., 2004. 'Courtney, Dame Kathleen D'Olier'. *Oxford Dictionary of National Biography*. https://www.oxforddnb.com/view/10.1093/ref:odnb/9780198614128.001.0001/odnb-9780198614128-e-37316?rskey=V4hubM&result=2.

Greville, Charles C. F., 1888. *The Greville Memoirs: A journal of the reigns of King George IV. King William IV. And Queen Victoria, by the late Charles C. F. Greville, Esq*., edited by Henry Reeve, A New Edition, Vol. 2. London: Longmans, Green and Co.

Grey, George, 1894. *Speech by the Right Hon. Sir George Grey, K.C.B., At the Annual Meeting of the Central Committee of the National Society for Women's Suffrage, July 6th, 1894*. London: Central Committee of the National Society for Women's Suffrage. https://digital.library.lse.ac.uk/objects/lse:qed905gid/read/single#page/62/mode/1up.

Grosvenor Papers, 1870. *Female Suffrage: An answer to Mrs Fawcett, on the electoral disabilities of women*. London: Darton.

Grote, George, 1854. *A History of Greece, Vol. I., Legendary Greece, Grecian history to the reign of Peisistratus at Athens*, 4th edition. London: John Murray.

Guardian, 2017. 'Artist unveils design for Parliament Square suffragist statue'. Wednesday, 20 September 2017. https://www.theguardian.com/artanddesign/2017/sep/20/artist-gillian-wearing-unveils-design-parliament-square-statue-suffragist-leader-millicent-fawcett.

Gullickson, Gay, 1996. *Unruly Women of Paris*. Ithaca: Cornell University Press.

Gutzke, David W., 2007. 'Rosebery and Campbell-Bannerman: The conflict over leadership reconsidered'. *Bulletin of the Institute of Historical Research*. Vol. 54, No. 130 (November 1981), 241–50.

Gwynn, Stephen Lucius, 1917. *The Life of the Rt. Hon. Sir Charles W. Dilke*. London: John Murray.

de Haan, Francisca, 2017. 'Fry [*née* Gurney], Elizabeth'. *Oxford Dictionary of National Biography*. Oxford: Oxford University Press. https://doi.org/10.1093/ref:odnb/10208.

Hall, Davis Oswald William, 1949. *The New Zealanders in South Africa, 1899–1902*. Wellington, New Zealand: War History Branch, Department of Internal Affairs.

Hamer, David, 2004. 'Morley, John, Viscount Morley of Blackburn'. *Oxford Dictionary of National Biography*, 23 September 2004. https://doi.org/10.1093/ref:odnb/35110.

Hamilton Advertiser, 1874. 'Bothwell'. Saturday, 19 December 1874, 1.

Hampshire Telegraph and Sussex Chronicle, 1888. 'Entertainments, etc'. Saturday, 21 January 1888, 4.

Hannam, June, 1989. *Isabella Ford*. Oxford: Basil Blackwell.

Hannam, June, Auchterlonie, Mitzi, and Holden, Katherine, 2000. *International Encyclopedia of Women's Suffrage*. Santa Barbara: ABC-CLIO Inc.

Hannavy, John, 2008. *Encyclopedia of Nineteenth-Century Photography*. Abingdon: Routledge.

Harris, Sarah Ann, 2016. 'Millicent Fawcett "should be given statue in Parliament Square" on 150th anniversary of women's vote petition'. *Huffington Post*. 7 June 2016. https://www.huffingtonpost.co.uk/entry/millicent-fawcett-statue-parliament-square-150th-anniversary-womens-vote-petition_uk_57557ebde4b04a0827f1ea2a.

Harris, William. 1885. *The History of the Radical Party in Parliament*. London: Kegan, Paul, Trench and Co.

Harrison, Brian, 1987. *Prudent Revolutionaries: Portraits of British feminists between the wars*. Oxford: Clarendon Press.

Harrison, Frederic, 1890. 'The law of conspiracy in England and in Ireland'. *Pall Mall Gazette*. Thursday, 10 April 1890, 2.

Hart, Peter, 2014. *The Great War: 1914–1918*. London: Profile Books.

Harte, Negley, North, John, and Brewis, Georgina, 2018. *The World of UCL*, 4th edition. London: UCL Press.

Hastings and St Leonards Observer, 1888. 'Public notices'. Saturday, 21 January 1888, 4.

Hauswedell, Tessa, Nyhan, Julianne, Beals, Melodee H., Terras, Melissa, and Bell, Emily, 2020. 'Of global reach yet of situated contexts: An examination of the implicit and explicit selection criteria that shape digital archives of historical newspapers'. *Archival Science*. Vol. 20, 139–65.

Hazlitt, W. Carew, 1874. *Mary and Charles Lamb: Poems, letters and remains: Now first collected, with reminiscences and notes*. London: Chatto and Windus.
Healey, Edna, 1978. *Lady Unknown: Life of Angela Burdett-Coutts*. Basingstoke: Sidgwick and Jackson Ltd.
Heater, Derek, 2006. *Citizenship in Britain: A history*. Edinburgh: Edinburgh University Press.
Helwys, Thomas, 1998. *A Short Declaration of the Mystery of Inquiry (1611/12)*, edited by Richard Groves. Macon, GA: Mercer University Press.
Herchenroder, M. F. P., 1938. 'The capacity of married women in French law'. *Journal of Comparative Legislation and International Law*, 3rd series. Vol. 20, No. 1, 196–203.
Herrington, Katie J. T., and Milner, Rebecca, 2019. *Annie Swynnerton: Painting light and hope*. Manchester: Manchester Art Gallery.
Hewison, Hope Hay, 1989. *Hedge of Wild Almonds. South Africa, the 'pro-Boers' and the Quaker conscience 1890–1910*. London: James Currey.
Hinsliff, Gaby, 2004. 'Westminster "sisters" split on pardon for suffragettes'. *Observer*. 25 July 2004, 11.
Hinton, James, 1983. *Labour and Socialism: A history of the British labour movement 1867–1974*. Amherst: University of Massachusetts Press.
Historic England, n.d. 'Millicent Fawcett Hall'. *Historic England Research Records*. Heritage Gateway. https://www.heritagegateway.org.uk/Gateway/Results_Single.aspx?uid=1009665&resourceID=19191.
HM Factory Inspectorate, 1914. *Annual Report of the Chief Inspector of Factories and Workshops for the Year 1914*. Report of the Inspectors of Factories to Her Majesty's Secretary of State for the Home Department. London: William Spottiswoode.
Hobhouse, Emily, 1901. *Report of a Visit to the Camps of Women and Children in the Cape and Orange River Colonies*. London: Friars.
Hobhouse, Emily, 1902. *The Brunt of the War and Where it Fell*. London: Methuen and Co.
Ó hÓgartaigh, Margaret, 2009. 'A quiet revolution: Women and second-level education in Ireland, 1878–1930'. *New Hibernia Review*. Vol. 13, No. 2 (Samhradh/Summer 2009), 36–51.
Hogg, Sallie Heller, 1967. 'The employment of women in Great Britain 1891–1921'. Doctoral Thesis, University of Oxford.
Holmes, Ann S., 1997. 'Fallen mothers: Maternal adultery and child custody in England, 1886–1925'. In *Maternal Instincts: Visions of motherhood and sexuality in Britain, 1875–1925*, edited by Ann S. Holmes and Claudia Nelson. Houndmills: Macmillan Press, 37–57.
Holton, Sandra Stanley, 1986. *Feminism and Democracy: Women's suffrage and reform politics in Britain, 1900–1918*. New York: Cambridge University Press.
Home Office, 1900. *Parliamentary Constituencies (Electors, &c.) (United Kingdom). Return to an Address of the Honourable the House of Commons, dated 31 January 1900, for 'Return showing, with regard to each PARLIAMENTARY CONSTITUENCY in the UNITED KINGDOM, the Total Number, as far as possible, the Number in each Class of ELECTORS on the Register now in force; and also showing the Population and Inhabited Houses in each Constituency (in continuation of Parliament: Paper, no 78, of Session 1899)'*. London: Printed for Her Majesty's Stationery Office by Eyre and Spottiswoode.
Hood, Thomas, 1825. 'A *friendly* address to Mrs Fry, in Newgate'. In *Odes and Addresses to Great People*, 2nd edition. London: Baldwin, Cradock and Joy, 23–32.
House of Commons Debates (HC Deb), 1848. 'National representation'. 20 June 1848, Vol. 99, col. 950. https://hansard.parliament.uk/commons/1848-06-20/debates/688659fb-1ca8-4908-a8f1-3cab1085e13c/NationalRepresentation.
House of Commons Debates (HC Deb), 1867a. 'Factory Acts (Educational Clauses) – resolution'. 26 February 1867, Vol. 185, cols 1066–88. https://hansard.parliament.uk/Commons/1867-02-26/debates/6f894336-a623-4253-b852-d332202786cb/FactoryActs(EducationalClauses)—Resolution.
House of Commons Debates (HC Deb), 1867b. 'Clauses 3, 4 progress May 17'. 17 May 1867, Vol. 187, col. 832. https://hansard.parliament.uk/Commons/1867-05-20/debates/c38e8bdb-704c-4952-9375-e33d7967a5a4/Clauses34ProgressMay17.
House of Commons Debates (HC Deb), 1867c. 'Committee progress June 18'. 18 June 1867, Vol. 188, col. 199. https://hansard.parliament.uk/Commons/1867-06-20/debates/44c3013d-3524-449e-9a3d-28afa8e0d268/CommitteeProgressJune18.

House of Commons Debates (HC Deb), 1871a. 'Women's Disabilities Bill, Second Reading'. 3 May 1871, Vol. 1871, col. 94. https://api.parliament.uk/historic-hansard/commons/1871/may/03/second-reading#column_94.

House of Commons Debates (HC Deb), 1871b. 'Trades Unions Bill. First Reading'. 14 February 1871, Vol. 204, cols 257–73. https://api.parliament.uk/historic-hansard/commons/1871/feb/14/leave-first-reading-2.

House of Commons Debates (HC Deb), 1876. 'Medical Act Amendment (Foreign Universities Bill)'. 5 July 1876, Vol. 230, col. 1019. https://api.parliament.uk/historic-hansard/commons/1876/jul/05/second-reading-1#column_1019.

House of Commons Debates (HC Deb), 1883. 'Parliamentary Franchise (Extension to Women)'. 6 July 1883, Vol. 281, cols 664–724. https://api.parliament.uk/historic-hansard/commons/1883/jul/06/resolution.

House of Commons Debates (HC Deb), 1885. 'Parliament – Business of the House – Infants Bill'. 14 August 1885, Vol. 301, col. 37. https://api.parliament.uk/historic-hansard/commons/1885/aug/14/parliament-business-of-the-house-infants#S3V0301P0_18850814_HOC_14.

House of Commons Debates (HC Deb), 1886. 'Government of Ireland Bill. Motion for leave [first night.]'. 8 April 1886, Vol. 304, cols 1036–141. https://api.parliament.uk/historic-hansard/commons/1886/apr/08/motion-for-leave-first-night.

House of Commons Debates (HC Deb), 1889. 'Cruelty to Children Prevention Bill (No. 308)'. 10 July 1889, Vol. 338, cols 31–3. https://api.parliament.uk/historic-hansard/commons/1889/jul/10/cruelty-to-children-prevention-bill-no.

House of Commons Debates (HC Deb), 1893. 'Electoral disqiulification [sic]'. 20 March 1893, Vol. 10, cols 513–15. https://api.parliament.uk/historic-hansard/commons/1893/mar/20/electoral-disqiulificaton.

House of Commons Debates (HC Deb), 1906a. 'Trade Disputes Bill'. 2 November 1906, Vol. 163, col. 1485. https://api.parliament.uk/historic-hansard/commons/1906/nov/02/trade-disputes-bill.

House of Commons Debates (HC Deb), 1906b. 'Women's enfranchisement'. 7 November 1906, Vol. 164, cols 571–3. https://api.parliament.uk/historic-hansard/commons/1906/nov/07/womens-enfranchisement.

House of Commons Debates (HC Deb), 1908. 'Women's Enfranchisement Bill'. 28 February 1908, Vol. 185, cols 212–87. https://api.parliament.uk/historic-hansard/commons/1908/feb/28/womens-enfranchisement-bill-1.

House of Commons Debates (HC Deb), 1912. 'Clause 9 (Composition of Irish House of Commons)'. 5 November 1912, Vol. 43, cols 1060–131. https://api.parliament.uk/historic-hansard/commons/1912/nov/05/clause-9-composition-of-irish-house-of.

House of Commons Debates (HC Deb), 1913a. 'Representation of the People (Women) Bill'. 5 May 1913, Vol. 52, cols 1704–819. https://api.parliament.uk/historic-hansard/commons/1913/may/05/representation-of-the-people-women-bill.

House of Commons Debates (HC Deb), 1913b. 'Representation of the People (Women) Bill'. 6 May 1913, Vol. 52, cols 1887–2005. https://api.parliament.uk/historic-hansard/commons/1913/may/06/representation-of-the-people-women-bill.

House of Commons Debates (HC Deb), 1917. 'Mr Speaker's services'. 28 March 1917, Vol. 92, cols 462–524. https://api.parliament.uk/historic-hansard/commons/1917/mar/28/mr-speakers-services.

House of Commons Debates (HC Deb), 1925. 'Official report'. Friday, 20 February 1925, Vol. 180, cols 1500–3. Quoted in House of Commons Debates, 1928. 'Representation of the People (Equal Franchise) Bill'. Thursday, 29 March 1928, Vol. 215, cols 1359–481. https://api.parliament.uk/historic-hansard/commons/1928/mar/29/representation-of-the-people-equal.

House of Lords Debates (HL Deb), 1917. 'Representation of the People Bill'. Monday, 17 December 1917, Vol. 27, cols 163–220.

House of Lords Debates (HL Deb), 1918. 'Representation of the People Bill'. 10 January 1918, Vol. 27, cols 465–527. https://api.parliament.uk/historic-hansard/lords/1918/jan/10/representation-of-the-people-bill.

Howarth, Janet, 2007. 'Fawcett, Dame Millicent Garrett [née Millicent Garrett]'. *Oxford Dictionary of National Biography*. https://www.oxforddnb.com/view/10.1093/ref:odnb/9780198614128.001.0001/odnb-9780198614128-e-33096?rskey=PiO06N&result=2.

Howells, Jane, 2021. 'Sarah Maria Fawcett'. *Her Salisbury Story*. https://hersalisburystory.com/stories/historic/sarah-maria-fawcett-12830-1923/.

Hoy, Mike, 2020. 'The story – Votes for women in the Isle of Man'. *Tynwald, The Parliament of the Isle of Man*. http://www.tynwald.org.im/education/women/Pages/VotesForWomen-IOM.aspx.

Hubback, Eva, 1925a. 'The woman's political year'. *Woman's Leader and the Common Cause*. Friday, 2 January 1925, 389–90.

Hubback, Eva, 1925b. 'Mother and fathers'. *Woman's Leader and the Common Cause*. Friday, 2 October 1925, 284.

Hubback, Eva, 1926. 'The political year'. *Woman's Leader and the Common Cause*. Friday, 31 December 1926, 414.

Huffington Post, 2017. 'Parliament Square to get its first female statue as Millicent Fawcett monument gets go-ahead'. Wednesday, 20 September 2017. https://www.huffingtonpost.co.uk/entry/parliament-square-millicent-fawcett-monument_uk_59c24acde4b0f22c4a8ddb15.

Hughes Hall, 2020. 'History. The University and the Colleges'. https://www.hughes.cam.ac.uk/about/history/.

Hume, Leslie Parker, 1982. *The National Union of Women's Suffrage Societies, 1897–1914*. London: Garland Publishing, Inc.

Hutchins, Roger, 2004. 'Adams, John Couch'. *Oxford Dictionary of National Biography*. https://doi.org/10.1093/ref:odnb/123.

Ibsen, Henrik, 1889. *A Doll's House: A play in three acts*. London: Fisher Unwin.

Illustrated London News, 1872. 'Metropolitan news'. Saturday, May 18 1872, 471.

Illustrated London News, 1913. '"Better is wisdom than weapons of war": Non-militant suffragists in Hyde Park'. Saturday, 2 August 1913, 177.

Illustrated London News, 1925. 'The world of the theatre. Three honours'. Saturday, 17 January 1925, 30.

Indian National Congress, 1900. *Report of the Fifteenth Indian National Congress held at Lucknow, on the 27th, 28th, 29th and 30th December, 1899*. Lucknow: Methodist Publishing House.

International Woman Suffrage Alliance (IWSA), 1909. *Report of the Fifth Conference and First Quinquennial, London, England. April 26, 27, 28, 29, 30, May 1, 1909*. London: Sidders & Co.

International Woman Suffrage News, 1925. 'Parliament Qualifications of Peeresses Bill'. Friday, 3 July 1925, 154.

International Woman Suffrage News, 1929. 'Dame Millicent Fawcett in Ceylon'. Friday, 1 March 1929, 90.

Irish Independent, 1912. '"The Irish Home Rule Bill". Many views on it'. 15 April 1912, 5.

Irish Times, 1870. 'The audience which assembled last night in the Molesworth Hall'. Tuesday, 19 April 1870, 4.

Isle of Man Times, 1897. 'News summary'. Tuesday, February 23 1897, 2.

J. B., 1930a. 'The Royal Academy. John at his best. Big portrait year'. *Manchester Guardian*. 3 May 1930, 11.

J. B., 1930b. 'The Chantrey purchases. Some comments'. *Manchester Guardian*. 8 May 1930, 5.

Jackson, Alvin, 2003. *Home Rule: An Irish history, 1800–2000*. Oxford: Oxford University Press.

Jeffreys, Sheila, 1982. '"Free from all uninvited touch of man": Women's campaigns around sexuality, 1880–1914'. *Women's Studies International Forum*. Vol. 5, No. 6, 629–45.

Jenkins, Jessica D., 2020. *Exploring Women's Suffrage through 50 Historic Treasures*. London: Rowman and Littlefield.

Jenkins, Roy, 2001. *Churchill*. London: Macmillan Press.

Jeune, Mary, 1889. 'Children in theatres'. *English Illustrated Magazine*. Vol. 7 (1889–90), 7–14. Available at https://babel.hathitrust.org/cgi/pt?id=mdp.39015056059655&view=1up&seq=22.

Joannou, Maroula, and Purvis, June, 1998 (eds). *The Women's Suffrage Movement: New feminist perspectives*. Manchester: Manchester University Press.

Johnson, Samuel, 1747. *The Plan of a Dictionary of the English Language: Addressed to the Right Honourable Philip Dormer, Earl of Chesterfield, one of His Majesty's principal secretaries of state*. London: J. and P. Knapton, T. Longman and T. Shewell, C. Hitch, A. Millar, and R. Dodsley.

Jones, Lloyd, 1919. *The Life, Times, and Labours of Robert Owen*. New York: George Allen & Unwin.

Jordan, Ellen, 2001. *The Women's Movement and Women's Employment in Nineteenth Century Britain*. Routledge Research in Gender and History, 2nd edition. London: Routledge.

Kant, Immanuel, 1903. *Perpetual Peace, A Philosophical Essay*, translated by M. Campbell Smith. London: Swan Sonnenschein and Co.

Karnie, Jim, 1874. 'Social science at Glasgow, pen-and-ink sketches by our special artist'. *Pictorial World*. 24 October 1874, 153.

Karnie, Jim, 1875. 'Millicent Fawcett's lecture on the female characters of Dickens, Thackeray, and George Eliot at the Unitarian Church, Glasgow'. *Pictorial World*. Saturday, 2 January 1875, 360.

Keen, Richard, Cracknell, Richard, and Bolton, Max, 2018. *Women in Parliament and Government. Briefing Paper, No. SN01250, 20th July 2018*. House of Commons Library. https://education.niassembly.gov.uk/sites/userfiles/UK%20Parliament%20%20-%20Women%20in%20Parliament%20.pdf.

Kegan Paul, Charles, 1879. 'Prefatory memoir'. In *Letters to Imlay, With Prefatory Memoir By C. Kegan Paul*, by Mary Wollstonecraft. London: C. Kegan Paul and Co, v–lxiii.

Kellaghan, Thomas, and Greaney, Vincent, 2019. *Public Examinations Examined*. Washington, DC: World Bank Group.

Khan, Sadiq, 2016. 'Sadiq Khan's response'. Change.org, 11 May 2016. https://www.change.org/p/westminster-council-put-a-statue-of-a-suffragette-in-parliament-square/responses/34643.

Kidd, Benjamin, and Maywood, Henry John, 1884. *Guide to Female Employment in Government Offices*. London: Cassell and Co.

Kidner, Richard, 1982. 'Lessons in trade union law reform: The origins and passage of the Trade Dispute Act 1906'. *Legal Studies, The Journal of the Society of Public Teachers of Law*. Vol. 2, 34–52.

Kingsley, Charles, 1871. *At Last: A Christmas in the West Indies*. London: Macmillan and Co.

Kipling, Rudyard, 1890. *Departmental Ditties, Barrack Room Ballads and Other Verses*. New York: John W. Lovell Company.

Kirkaldy, Adam W. (ed.), 1915. Chapter III: 'Outlets for labour after the war'. In *Credit Industries and the War. Being reports and other matter presented to the section of economic science and statistics of the British Association for the Advancement of Science*. London: Sir Isaac Pitman and Sons Ltd, 68–192.

Knox, George, 1956. 'The Hawthorne-Lowell affair'. *New England Quarterly*. Vol. 29, No. 4 (December 1956), 493–502.

Konody, Paul, 1930. 'The critic's view. The brilliant and the commonplace.' *Daily Mail*. Saturday, 3 May 1930, 14.

Korn, Naomi, 2016. 'Checklists: Rights, risks and rewards'. Naomi Korn Associates. https://naomikorn.com/2016/07/22/checklists-rights-risks-and-rewards/.

Krebs, Paula M., 1992. 'The last of the gentlemen's wars: Women in the Boer War concentration camp controversy'. *History Workshop Journal*. Vol. 33, No. 1, 38–56.

Labour Leader, 1906. 'The women's suffrage candidate'. Friday, 2 February 1906, 10.

Lally, Erica, 2015. 'Race and racism: British responses to civilian prison camps in the Boer War and the Kenya Emergency'. *UCLA Historical Journal*. Vol. 26, No. 1. https://escholarship.org/uc/item/0h5760fh.

Lang, Elsie M., 1929. *British Women in the Twentieth Century*. London: T. W. Laurie.

Law, Cheryl, 1997. *Suffrage and Power: The women's movement, 1918–1928*. London: I. B. Tauris.

Lawrence, Margot, 1971. *Shadow of Swords. A biography of Elsie Inglis*. London: Joseph.

Lawson, John, and Silver, Harold, 1973. *A Social History of Education in England*. London: Methuen & Co. Ltd.

Leamington Spa Courier, 1909. 'Lord Crewe and the suffragists'. Friday, 10 September 1909, 6.

Leeds Mercury, 1915. 'Women and war problems. Prospects of a sex conflict. At the cross-roads'. Tuesday, 19 October 1915, 4.

Leeds Mercury, 1925. 'The Queen chats with Ellen Terry'. Friday, 13 February 1925, 1.

Leeds Mercury, 1928. 'Little tragedy of women's votes. Dame Millicent Fawcett misses last stage. Too late to hear the Royal Assent'. Tuesday, 3 July 1928, 1.

LeGeyt, Alice Bell, 1871. 'Our English letter'. *Women's Journal* (USA). 12 August 1871, 256.

Leicester Journal, 1872. 'Summary of news'. Friday, 17 May 1872, 3.

Lesthaeghe, Ron, and Lopez-Gay, Antonio, 2013. 'Spatial continuities and discontinuities in two successive demographic transitions: Spain and Belgium, 1880–2010'. *Demographic Research*. Vol. 28, 77–136.

Liberal Publication Department, 1908. *The Liberal Year Book for 1908*, Fourth Year. London: The Liberal Publication Department.

Lichfield Mercury, 1912. 'The political parties and women's suffrage'. Friday, 12 January 1912, 4.

Lieven, Dominic (ed.), 2015. *The Cambridge History of Russia. Vol. 2, Imperial Russia, 1689–1917*. Cambridge: Cambridge University Press.

Liverpool Echo, 1915. 'The New Shaw'. Wednesday, 27 October 1915, 4.

London Daily News, 1911a. 'Result of proportional representation in Sweden'. Thursday, 28 September 1911.
London Daily News, 1911b. '"Disgusting scenes." National Union condemns militant methods'. Mrs Fawcett and Mr Lloyd George. Tuesday, 5 December 1911, 2.
London Evening Standard, 1890. 'Mr Gladstone on female education'. Friday, July 18 1890, 2.
London Evening Standard, 1897a. 'Parliamentary notes'. Thursday, 4 February 1897, 5.
London Evening Standard, 1897b. 'Parliamentary notes'. Thursday, 8 July 1897, 5.
London Evening Standard, 1906. 'Women and the vote, Counsel of the Prime Minister, virtue of patience'. Monday, 21 May 1906, 9.
London Gazette, 1915. 'Factory and Workshop Acts 1901 to 1911'. 29 October 1915, 10648.
London Gazette, 1925. 'Central chancery of the orders of knighthood'. Supplement to the *London Gazette*. 1 January 1925, 5.
Londonderry Sentinel, 1914. 'United States army scandal, staff officer's warning'. Saturday, 10 January 1914, 3.
Lowell, James Russell, 1848. *The Biglow Papers*. 4th American edition, 1859. London: Trübner and Co.
Lowndes, Mary, 1909. *Banners and Banner-Making*. London: Artist's Suffrage League.
Lyden, Anne M., 2014. *A Royal Passion: Queen Victoria and photography*. Los Angeles: J. Paul Getty Trust.
Macarthur, Mary R., 1916. 'Women in munition work'. *The Woman Worker*. No. 1, New series. London: National Labour Press, 5–7.
Maccoby, Simon, 1953. *English Radicalism 1886–1914*. London: George Allen & Unwin. 2002 Reprint, London: Routledge.
Macmillan, Chrystal, 1921. 'The imperial cabinet and the nationality of married women'. *Woman's Leader and the Common Cause*. Friday, 24 June 1921, 323.
Magazine of Art, 1898. 'Royal Academy Pictures 1898, Illustrating the Hundred and Thirtieth Exhibition of the Royal Academy, Being the Royal Academy Supplement of "The Magazine of Art"'. London: Cassell and Company Limited. https://archive.org/details/in.ernet.dli.2015.97164/page/n5/mode/2up.
Maguire, Gloria E., 1998. *Conservative Women: A history of women and the Conservative Party, 1874–1997*. St Antony's Series. London: Palgrave Macmillan
Maine, Henry Sumner, 1873. *The Early History of the Property of Married Women, as Collected from Roman and Hindoo Law: A lecture delivered at Birmingham, March 25 1873*. Manchester: A. Ireland and Co., Printers.
Mallet, Charles Edward, 1927. *A History of the University of Oxford. Vol. III: Modern Oxford*. Reprinted 1968. New York: Barnes and Noble.
Mallowan, Max, 2004. 'Murray, Margaret Alice'. *Oxford Dictionary of National Biography*. Revised by R. S. Simpson. https://www.oxforddnb.com/view/10.1093/ref:odnb/9780198614128.001.0001/odnb-9780198614128-e-35169.
Manchester Courier and Lancashire General Advertiser, 1898. 'Women's Suffrage. Meeting in Manchester'. Thursday, 17 November 1898, 8.
Manchester Courier and Lancashire General Advertiser, 1899. 'Mrs Fawcett or Mrs Dr Fawcett'. Tuesday, 14 February 1899, 6.
Manchester Courier and Lancashire General Advertiser, 1906. 'Suffragette scenes'. Friday, 26 October 1906, 5.
Manchester Courier and Lancashire General Advertiser, 1908. 'The women's campaign. "Winston the Shuffler." The Jewish suffragists'. Thursday, 16 April 1908, 9.
Manchester Evening News, 1897. 'London Letter [by our own private wire]'. Tuesday, 9 November 1897, 4.
Manchester Guardian, 1901. 'The concentration camps. Miss Hobhouse's report'. Wednesday, 19 June 1901, 10.
Manchester Guardian, 1920. 'Women magistrates: Names approved by the Lord Chancellor'. Tuesday, 20 July 1920, 6.
Manchester Guardian, 1921. 'Our London correspondence: The Supreme Council. Woman parliamentary candidates'. Monday, 8 August 1921, 4.
Manchester Guardian, 1924. 'Mr Baldwin's honours list'. Monday, 18 February 1924, 4.
Manchester Guardian, 1929. 'Dame Millicent Fawcett'. Monday, 5 August 1929, 14.
Mansfield Reporter, 1889. 'Crumbs'. Friday, 29 November 1889, 5.
Manton, Jo, 1958. *Elizabeth Garrett Anderson*. London: Adam and Charles Black.

Mario, Jessie White, 1909. *The Birth of Modern Italy: Posthumous papers of Jessie White Mario*, edited by Duke Litta-Visconti-Arese. London: T. Fisher Unwin.

Marks, Sylvia Kasey, 1983. 'A brief glance at George Eliot's "The Spanish Gypsy"'. *Victorian Poetry*. Vol. 21, No. 2, 184–90.

Markus, Julia, 2005. *J. Anthony Froude: The last undiscovered Great Victorian: A biography*. New York: Scribner.

Marlow, Joyce, 1971. *The Tolpuddle Martyrs*. London: History Book Club.

Marshall White, Frank, 1897. 'Mark Twain amused. Humorist says he even heard on good authority that he was dead. Cousin, not he, sick'. *New York Journal and Advertiser* (2 June 1897), 1. https://www.loc.gov/resource/sn83030180/1897-06-02/ed-1/?sp=1&q=twain&r=0.182,0.652,0.508,0.405,0.

Martineau, Harriet, 1877. *A History of the Thirty Years' Peace, A.D. 1816–1846*, Vol. 2. London: George Bell and Sons.

Martineau, Harriet, 1885. *Autobiography*, Vol. 1. Boston: James E. Osgood and Company.

Mason, Bertha, 1912. *The Story of the Women's Suffrage Movement*. London: Sherratt and Hughes.

Mason, Bertha, 1926. 'Local government matters'. *Woman's Leader and the Common Cause*. 28 May 1926, 146.

Massey, W. T., 1915. 'Munition making. Woman's part. Patriotism at the Lathe'. *Liverpool Daily Post and Mercury*. Wednesday, 17 November 1915, 3.

Matron, 1915. 'The matron of the month, Mrs Garrett Fawcett'. June 1915, 5.

Mazzini, Joseph, 1862. *The Duties of Man*. London: Chapman & Hall.

McClure, Judith, and Collins, Roger, 1999. *Bede: The ecclesiastical history of the English people*. Oxford: Oxford University Press.

McDonald, Lynn, 2005. *Florence Nightingale on Women, Medicine, Midwifery and Prostitution*, Vol. 8. Collected Works of Florence Nightingale. Waterloo, Ontario: Wilfrid Laurier University Press.

McFadyean, Kenneth, 1945. 'The need for reform in statutes affecting illegitimacy'. *Medico-Legal and Criminological Review*. Vol. 13, No. 2, 62–75.

McGrath, John J., 2007. *The Other End of the Spear: The tooth-to-tail ratio (T3R) in modern military operations*. Fort Leavenworth, Kansas: Combat Studies Institute Press.

McPhee, Carol, and FitzGerald, Ann, 1979. *Feminist Quotations: Voices of rebels, reformers and visionaries*. New York: Thomas Y. Crowell.

Meredith, George, 1883. *Poems and Lyrics of the Joy of Earth*. London: Macmillan and Co.

Meredith, George, 1906. 'The suffrage for women, to the editor of the Times'. *Times*. Thursday, 1 November 1906, 12.

Metcalf, Barbara D., and Metcalf, Thomas R., 2006. *A Concise History of Modern India*, 2nd edition. Cambridge: Cambridge University Press.

Midgley, Clare, 2007. *Feminism and Empire: Women activists in Imperial Britain, 1790–1865*. Abingdon: Routledge.

Mill, John Stuart, 1869. *The Subjection of Women*. London: Longmans, Green, Reader, and Dyer.

Mill, John Stuart, 1972. *The Later Letters of John Stuart Mill 1849–1873*, edited by Francis E. Mineka and Dwight N. Lindley. Toronto, Ontario: University of Toronto Press.

Miller, Carol, 1994. '"Geneva – The key to equality": Inter-war feminists and the League of Nations'. *Women's History Review*. Vol. 3, No. 2, 219–45.

Ministry of Housing, Communities and Local Government, 2017. 'Millicent Fawcett to be honoured with first statue of a woman in Parliament Square'. Press Release, 2 April 2017. https://www.gov.uk/government/news/millicent-fawcett-to-be-honoured-with-first-statue-of-a-woman-in-parliament-square.

Mirelman, Victor A., 1984. 'The Jewish community versus crime: The case of white slavery in Buenos Aires'. *Jewish Social Studies*. Vol. 46, No. 2 (Spring 1984), 145–68.

Mitchell, Angus, 2014. '1914–18 and the war on peace'. *History Ireland*. Vol. 22, No. 4. Special Issue, Ireland and WWI (July/August 2014), 46–9.

Mollan, Charles, 2007. *It's Part of What We Are. Science and Irish culture, No. 3. Some Irish contributors to the development of the chemical and physical sciences. Volume 1: Richard Boyle (1566–1643) to John Tyndall (1820–1893)*. Dublin: Royal Dublin Society.

Moore, Thomas, 1852. *Irish Melodies with Symphonies and Accompaniments by Sir John Stevenson and Characteristic Words by Thomas Moore*, New edition, edited by J. W. Clover. Dublin: James Duffy.

More, Thomas, 1516. *Utopia. Utopia by Sir Thomas More*, 1909 edition. Harvard Classics. New York: P. F. Collier and Son Company.

Morley, Ann, and Stanley, Liz, 1988. *The Life and Death of Emily Wilding Davison: A biographical detective story*. London: Women's Press.

Morley, John, 1878. *Rousseau*. London: Chapman and Hall.

Morning Post, 1883. 'The Bright celebration'. Thursday, 14 June 1883, 3.

Morning Post, 1897a. 'Terrible calamity in Paris. Fire at a charity bazaar. Loss of over 100 lives'. Wednesday, 5 May 1897, 7.

Morning Post, 1897b. '"The Paris disaster. Latest details from our correspondent." Paris, May 6'. Friday, 7 May 1897, 3.

Morning Post, 1897c. 'The school board elections. Arrangements for polling'. Thursday, 25 November 1897, 6.

Morning Post, 1908a. 'Arrangements for this day'. Tuesday, 10 March 1908, 7.

Morning Post, 1908b. 'Count Tolstoy. (From our own Correspondent)'. Saturday, 5 September 1908, 5.

Morning Post, 1908c. 'Proportional representation. A mimic election'. Friday, 4 December 1908, 5.

Morning Post, 1909. 'Imperial Parliament. Adult suffrage and votes for women. Franchise Bill shelved'. Saturday, 20 March 1909, 4.

Murphy, Alistair, and Elmore, Elizabeth, 2016. *Fishermen and Kings: The photography of Olive Edis*. Norwich: Norfolk Museums Service.

Murphy, Gillian, 2016. 'The Women's Library at 90'. Wednesday, 15 June 2016. https://blogs.lse.ac.uk/lsehistory/2016/06/15/the-womens-library-at-90/.

Murray, Eunice G., 1920. 'The differences in Scottish and English law regarding women'. *Woman's Leader and the Common Cause*. Friday, 17 September 1920, 721.

Murray, Flora, 1920. *Women as Army Surgeons. Being the history of the Women's Hospital Corps in Paris, Wimereux and Endell Street, September 1914–October 1919*. London: Hodder and Stoughton.

Murray, Janet Horowitz, and Stark, Myra (eds), 2018a. *The Englishwoman's Review of Social and Industrial Questions: 1891*. London: Routledge.

Murray, Janet Horowitz, and Stark, Myra (eds), 2018b. *The Englishwoman's Review of Social and Industrial Questions: 1899*. London: Routledge.

Museum of London, 2020. 'Millicent Fawcett's "Steadfastness and Courage" brooch to go on permanent display for the first time', 11 March 2020. https://www.museumoflondon.org.uk/news-room/press-releases/millicent-fawcetts-brooch-on-display-first-time.

Museum of London, 2021. 'Panel, About this object'. Collections Online. https://collections.museumoflondon.org.uk/online/object/545198.html.

Nation and Athenaeum, 1929. 'Now Complete. The New Edition of *Chambers's Encyclopaedia*'. Autumn Literary Supplement. Vol. 46, No. 6, 227.

National American Woman Suffrage Association (NAWSA), 1909. 'Petition to the Senate and House of Representatives of the United States'. *Progress* (January 1909). Manuscript/Mixed Material. https://www.loc.gov/item/rbcmiller002060/.

National Archives, 2017. 'Currency Converter: 1270–2017'. https://www.nationalarchives.gov.uk/currency-converter/.

National Education Association of the United States, 1894. *Proceedings of the International Congress of Education of the World's Columbian Exposition, Chicago July 25–28, 1893*. New York: National Education Association. Available at https://archive.org/details/addressesproce1893natiuoft/.

National First Ladies' Library, n.d. 'First Lady biography: Helen Taft'. *National First Ladies' Library*. http://www.firstladies.org/biographies/firstladies.aspx?biography=27.

National Portrait Gallery, 2006. 'Elliott and Fry. Victorian photographs by Elliott and Fry'. December 2006. https://www.npg.org.uk/about/press-old/elliott-and-fry.

National Portrait Gallery, 2018. 'National Portrait Gallery reveals how a painting of its founder was slashed with a cleaver by a suffragette'. News release. Monday, 29 January 2018. https://www.npg.org.uk/assets/files/pdf/press/2018/Rebel-Women-season-and-display.pdf.

National Portrait Gallery, 2021a. 'Dame Millicent Fawcett, by Henry Joseph Whitlock'. https://www.npg.org.uk/collections/search/portrait/mw159845/Dame-Millicent-Fawcett?LinkID=mp01548&role=sit&rNo=2.

National Portrait Gallery, 2021b. 'Theodore Blake Wirgman'. https://www.npg.org.uk/collections/search/person/mp07746/theodore-blake-wirgman?role=art.

National Portrait Gallery, 2021c. 'Lizzie Caswall Smith'. https://www.npg.org.uk/collections/search/person/mp60354/lizzie-caswall-smith?role=art.

National Portrait Gallery, 2021d. 'Emmeline Pankhurst'. https://www.npg.org.uk/collections/search/portrait/mw04857/Emmeline-Pankhurst.
National Portrait Gallery, 2021e. 'Elizabeth Garrett Anderson'. https://www.npg.org.uk/collections/search/portrait/mw179218/Elizabeth-Garrett-Anderson?LinkID=mp10088&role=art&displayNo=60&rNo=53.
National Portrait Gallery, 2021f. 'Agnes Garrett'. https://www.npg.org.uk/collections/search/portrait/mw162108/Agnes-Garrett?LinkID=mp10088&role=art&displayNo=60&rNo=20.
National Portrait Gallery, 2021g. 'Emmeline Pankhurst'. https://www.npg.org.uk/collections/search/portrait/mw16893/Emmeline-Pankhurst?LinkID=mp03440&role=sit&rNo=14.
National Portrait Gallery, 2021h. 'Emmeline Pankhurst'. https://www.npg.org.uk/collections/search/portrait/mw18790/Emmeline-Pankhurst?LinkID=mp03440&role=sit&rNo=15.
National Society for Women's Suffrage, 1892. 'Conversazione'. In *Occasional Paper*, May 1892. London: Vacher & Sons, Westminster, 72–5.
National Society for Women's Suffrage, 1894. 'Some publications issued by the Central Committee'. In *Report of the Executive Committee Presented at the Annual General Meeting held in the Westminster Town Hall, July 6th, 1894*. London: Women's Printing Society Limited, 23.
National Trust, n.d. 'Dame Millicent Garrett Fawcett (1847–1929) and her husband Prof. Henry Fawcett, M.P. (1833–1884)'. http://www.nationaltrustcollections.org.uk/object/1288088.
National Union of Women's Suffrage Societies (NUWSS), 1912. *To Men and Women of the Liberal Party*. B.10, March 1912. London: National Union of Women's Suffrage Societies. https://digital.library.lse.ac.uk/objects/lse:soy666pik/read/single#page/74/mode/1up.
National Union of Women's Suffrage Societies (NUWSS), 1913. *Ministers' Pledges*. B.90, January 1913. London: National Union of Women's Suffrage Societies. https://digital.library.lse.ac.uk/objects/lse:soy666pik/read/single#page/48/mode/1up.
National Union of Women's Suffrage Societies (NUWSS), 1914. *Woman's Kingdom. Souvenir & Handbook of the Exhibition. Organised by the National Union of Women's Suffrage Societies*. Olympia: 11–30 April 1914. In Rubinstein (1991, 201).
National University of Ireland, 2020. 'History of the NUI'. http://www.nui.ie/about/history.asp.
National Vigilance Association (NVA), 1899. *The White Slave Trade: Transaction of the International Congress on the White Slave Trade, Held in London on the 21st, 22nd and 23rd June 1899, At the Invitation of the National Vigilance Association*. London: Wertheimer, Lea and Co.
Neale, Shirley, 2004. 'Edis [married name Galsworthy], (Mary) Olive'. *Oxford Dictionary of National Biography*. https://www.oxforddnb.com/view/10.1093/ref:odnb/9780198614128.001.0001/odnb-9780198614128-e-54348?rskey=yyy4CC&result=1.
New York Times, 1929. 'Dame M. Fawcett, suffragist, dead'. 5 August 1929, 21.
Newberry, Jo Vellacott, 1977. 'Anti-war suffragists'. *History*. Vol. 62, No. 206, 411–25.
Newcastle University, 2018. 'History of Newcastle University'. https://www.ncl.ac.uk/who-we-are/history/.
Newnham College, 2020. 'History'. https://www.newn.cam.ac.uk/about/history/.
Nohlen, Dieter, and Stöver, Philip, 2010. *Elections in Europe: A data handbook*. Baden-Baden, Germany: Nomos.
Northampton Chronicle and Echo, 1927. 'Daventry to-day.' Thursday, 23 June 1927, 2.
Northedge, Frederick Samuel, 1986. *The League of Nations: Its life and times*. Leicester: Leicester University Press.
Northern Echo, 1874. 'North Country news'. Wednesday, 2 December 1874, 4.
Northern Whig, 1881. 'Ladies' letter'. Thursday, 14 May 1891, 6.
Northern Whig, 1889. 'Liberal Unionism in Nottingham. Formation of a women's association'. Wednesday, 6 March 1899, 3.
Northern Whig, 1918. 'Lords and woman suffrage, hostile amendment rejected, A large majority'. Friday, 11 January 1918, 6.
NPR, 2018. 'London's Parliament Square gets its first statue honoring a woman'. Tuesday, 24 April 2018. https://www.npr.org/sections/I-way/2018/04/24/605242498/londons-parliament-square-gets-its-first-statue-honoring-a-woman.
Nym Mayhall, Laura E., 2001. 'Household and market in suffragette discourse, 1903–14'. *The European Legacy*. Vol. 6, No. 2, 189–99.
Nym Mayhall, Laura E., 2003. *The Militant Suffrage Movement: Citizenship and resistance in Britain, 1860–1930*. Oxford: Oxford University Press.
O'Rell, Max, 1896. 'Petticoat government'. *The North American Review*. Vol. 163, No. 476 (July 1896), 101–14.

Oakley, Ann, 1983. 'Millicent Garrett Fawcett: Duty and determination'. In *Feminist Theorists: Three centuries of key women thinkers*, edited by Dale Spender. New York: Pantheon Books, 184–202.

OpenPlaques.org, 2009. 'Dame Millicent Garrett Fawcett 1847–1929 pioneer of women's suffrage lived and died here'. https://openplaques.org/plaques/186.

Oppenheim, Maya, 2019. 'Migrant women protest in Westminster over controversial domestic abuse bill'. *Independent*. Thursday, 13 June 2019. https://www.independent.co.uk/news/uk/home-news/domestic-abuse-bill-protest-migrant-women-parliament-a8957536.html.

Oxford Chronicle and Reading Gazette, 1908. 'Mrs Fawcett at the Oxford Union. A verdict and an impression'. Friday, 27 November 1908, 7.

Oxford English Dictionary (OED), 2020a. 'Glendoveer'. *Oxford English Dictionary Online*. March 2021. Oxford University Press. https://www.oed.com/view/Entry/78890?redirected From=glendoveer&.

Oxford English Dictionary (OED), 2020b. 'Kaffir, n. and adj'. *Oxford English Dictionary Online*. December 2020. Oxford University Press. https://www.oed.com/view/Entry/102330?redirected From=Kaffir.

Oxford English Dictionary (OED), 2020c. 'calends | kalends, n.'. *Oxford English Dictionary Online*. September 2020. Oxford University Press. https://www.oed.com/view/Entry/26319?redirected From=kalends.

Oxford Reference, 2020a. 'Horace Walpole 1717–97'. https://www.oxfordreference.com/view/10.1093/acref/9780191826719.001.0001/q-oro-ed4-00011269.

Oxford Reference, 2020b. 'Tripos: Overview. Quick Reference'. https://www.oxfordreference.com/view/10.1093/oi/authority.20110803105752761.

Paget, James, 1874. 'On disease of the mammary areola producing cancer of the mammary gland'. *St Bartholomew's Hospital Reports*, 10, 87–90.

Paine, Albert Bigelow, 1912. *Mark Twain, A Biography. The personal and literal life of Samuel Langhorne Clemens*, Vol. 2. New York: Harper & Brothers.

Paisley Herald and Renfrewshire Advertiser, '1874'. Saturday, 14 November 1874, 1.

Palatschek, Sylvia, and Pietrow-Ennker, Bianka (eds), 2004. *Women's Emancipation Movements in the Nineteenth Century, A European Perspective*. Stanford, CA: Stanford University Press.

Palazzo, Albert, 2001. *The Australian Army: A history of its organisation 1901–2001*. Oxford: Oxford University Press.

Pall Mall Gazette, 1885. 'The maiden tribute of Modern Babylon – I. The report of our secret commission'. Vol. 42, No. 6336. Monday, 6 July 1885, 1–6.

Pall Mall Gazette, 1886. 'Mrs Fawcett on women's suffrage'. Monday, 29 March 1886, 6.

Pall Mall Gazette, 1898. 'The prosecution of Urbain Gohier. The incriminating passages of the book'. Tuesday, 13 December 1898, 6.

Pall Mall Gazette, 1912a. 'Notes of the day'. Wednesday, 6 March 1912, 6.

Pall Mall Gazette, 1912b. 'Political notes'. Thursday, 7 March 1912, 3.

Pall Mall Gazette, 1913. 'Votes for wives. What the Dickinson amendment will do'. Wednesday, 22 January 1913, 1.

Pallot, Judith, Piacentini, Laura, and Moran, Dominique, 2012. *Gender, Geography, and Punishment: The experience of women in Carceral Russia*. Oxford Geographical and Environmental Studies. Oxford: Oxford University Press.

Palmer, Frederick, 1915. 'With the grand fleet'. *Times*. Saturday, 16 October 1915, 9.

Pankhurst, E. Sylvia, 1911. *The Suffragette: The history of the women's militant suffrage movement 1905–1910*. Boston: The Woman's Journal.

Pankhurst, E. Sylvia, 1931. *The Suffragette Movement: An intimate account of persons and ideals*. London: Longmans, Green and Co.

Pankhurst, Emmeline, 1914. *My Own Story*. London: Eveleigh Nash.

Parliamentary Papers, 1908. 'East India (proclamations). Return to an address of the Honourable House of Commons, dated 9 November 1908; copies of the proclamation of the King, Emperor of India, to the princes and peoples of India, of the 2nd day of November 1908, and the proclamation of the late Queen Victoria of the 1st day of November 1858, to the princes, chiefs, and people of India, LXXV'.

Parliament.uk, n.d.a. 'Disestablishment'. https://www.parliament.uk/about/living-heritage/evolutionofparliament/legislativescrutiny/parliamentandireland/overview/disestablishment/.

Parliament.uk, n.d.b. 'Later factory legislation'. https://www.parliament.uk/about/living-heritage/transformingsociety/livinglearning/19thcentury/overview/laterfactoryleg/.

Parliament.uk, n.d.c. 'Second Reform Act 1867'. https://www.parliament.uk/about/living-heritage/evolutionofparliament/houseofcommons/reformacts/overview/furtherreformacts/.

Parliament.uk, n.d.d. 'The 1870 Education Act'. https://www.parliament.uk/about/living-heritage/transformingsociety/livinglearning/school/overview/1870educationact/.

Parliament.uk, n.d.e. 'The growth of textile manufacturing'. Living Heritage, Industry and Community. https://www.parliament.uk/about/living-heritage/transformingsociety/tradeindustry/industrycommunity/overview/textileindustries/.

Parliament.uk, n.d.f. 'The Reform Act 1832'. https://www.parliament.uk/about/living-heritage/evolutionofparliament/houseofcommons/reformacts/overview/reformact1832/.

Parliament.uk, n.d.g. 'The Reform Acts and representative democracy'. Living Heritage. https://www.parliament.uk/about/living-heritage/evolutionofparliament/houseofcommons/reformacts/.

Parliament.uk, n.d.h. 'Third Reform Act 1884'. https://www.parliament.uk/about/living-heritage/evolutionofparliament/houseofcommons/reformacts/overview/one-man-one-vote/.

Parliament.uk, n.d.i. 'Regulating sexual behaviour: the 19th century'. https://www.parliament.uk/about/living-heritage/transformingsociety/private-lives/relationships/overview/sexualbehaviour19thcentury.

Parliament.uk, 2020. 'Further reform, 1902–14. Living and learning, Going to school, Overview'. https://www.parliament.uk/about/living-heritage/transformingsociety/livinglearning/school/overview/reform1902-14/.

Parliament.uk, 2021. 'Ballot Act, 1872'. https://www.parliament.uk/about/living-heritage/transformingsociety/electionsvoting/elections-and-voting-in-the-19th-century/reforming-election-methods/from-the-parliamentary-collections/election-petitions211/.

Parlow, Maud, 1908. 'The German party congress and the women's movement'. *Social Democrat*, Vol. 12, No. 10 (15 October 1908), 441–6. Marxists Internet Archive 2008. https://www.marxists.org/history/international/social-democracy/social-democrat/1908/10/german-congress.htm.

Parry, Jonathan, 2011. 'Disraeli, Benjamin, earl of Beaconsfield'. *Oxford Dictionary of National Biography*. https://www.oxforddnb.com/view/10.1093/ref:odnb/9780198614128.001.0001/odnb-9780198614128-e-7689?rskey=s7zf3Z&result=3.

Pašeta, Senia. 2017. 'Markievicz [*née* Gore-Booth], Constance Georgine, Countess Markievicz in the Polish nobility'. *Oxford Dictionary of National Biography*. https://www.oxforddnb.com/view/10.1093/ref:odnb/9780198614128.001.0001/odnb-9780198614128-e-37472?rskey=MMDqKl&result=2.

Pater, Walter, 1885. *Marius the Epicurean, His Sensations and Ideas*, Vol. 1. London: Macmillan and Co.

Paxton, Robert O., and Hessler, Julie, 2012. *Europe in the Twentieth Century*, 5th edition. Boston: Wadsworth.

Payne, Matthew, 2021. 'Question about Westminster Abbey History – Millicent Fawcett', email to Melissa Terras. Thursday, 20 May 2021.

Pearson's Weekly, 1908. 'Our little shafts, by Robin Hood'. Thursday, 24 December 1908, 3.

Pederson, Joyce S., 1999. 'Love, politics, and the Victorians: Liberal feminism and the politics of social integration'. *The European Legacy*. Vol. 4, No. 6, 42–57.

Pennell, Elizabeth, 1884. *Life of Mary Wollstonecraft*. Boston: Roberts Brothers.

Penrith Observer, 1913. 'Chairman's ruling on amendments'. Tuesday, 28 January 1913, 3.

Perry, Ruth, 2009. 'Astell, Mary'. *Oxford Dictionary of National Biography*. https://www.oxforddnb.com/view/10.1093/ref:odnb/9780198614128.001.0001/odnb-9780198614128-e-814.

Peters, Edward, 1989. *Inquisition*. Berkeley and Los Angeles: University of California Press.

Petrie, John, 2021. 'College of arms enquiry', email to Melissa Terras. Friday, 21 May 2021.

Phaidon, 2018. 'Why Gillian Wearing put a sign on her Millicent Fawcett statue'. https://www.phaidon.com/agenda/art/articles/2018/april/24/why-gillian-wearing-put-a-sign-on-her-millicent-fawcett-statue/.

Phillips, Edward, 1694. *The Poetical Works of John Milton, to which is Prefixed a Biography of the Author, by his Nephew, Edward Phillips*, 1868 edition. New York: D. Appleton and Co.

Phillips, John A., and Wetherell, Charles, 1995. 'The Great Reform Act of 1832 and the political modernization of England'. *The American Historical Review*. Vol. 100, No. 2 (April 1995), 411–36.

Pickard, Sarah, 2014. 'Anti-social behaviour in Britain. Victorian and contemporary perspectives'. New York: Palgrave Macmillan.

Picton-Turbervill, Edith, 1924. 'The Legitimacy Bill'. *Woman's Leader and the Common Cause*. Friday, 14 March 1924, 51.
Pictorial World, 1875. 'Coverage of lecture on women of modern fiction', Glasgow. Saturday, 2 January 1875, 358.
Platt, Verity, 2020. 'Why people are toppling monuments to racism'. Behaviour and Society. *Scientific American*. 3 July 2020. https://www.scientificamerican.com/article/why-people-are-toppling-monuments-to-racism/.
Pope, Alexander, 1735. *Of the Characters of Women: An epistle to a lady*. London: Lawton Gilliver.
Popplewell, Richard James, 1995. *Intelligence and Imperial Defence: British intelligence and the defence of the Indian Empire, 1904–1924*. London: Frank Cass.
Poverty Bay Herald, 1894. 'Dr Talmage on New Zealand'. Vol. 21, No. 7141 (25 November 1894), 4.
Preston Chronicle, 1872. 'The atrocious outrage of a wife at Preston. Verdict of manslaughter'. Saturday, 20 April 1872, 5.
Primrose League Gazette, 1918. 'Women and the vote: Socialist propaganda', Vol. 26 (June 1918), 5.
Prochaska, Frank, 2004. 'Carpenter, Mary'. *Oxford Dictionary of National Biography*. https://www.oxforddnb.com/view/10.1093/ref:odnb/9780198614128.001.0001/odnb-9780198614128-e-4733?rskey=SciNTV&result=1.
Pugh, Martin, 2000. *Women and the Women's Movement in Britain, 1914–1999*, 2nd edition. Houndmills: Macmillan Press.
Punch, 1906. 'Charivaria'. 30 May 1906, 384. In *Punch Vol. CXXX*. January–June 1906. London: Bradbury, Agnew and Co.
Purvis, June, 1994. 'A lost dimension? The political education of women in the suffragette movement in Edwardian Britain'. *Gender and Education*. Vol. 6, No. 3, 319–27.
Purvis, June, 2018. 'Letters. Misgivings over new statue and old portrait of Millicent Fawcett'. *Guardian*. Wednesday, 25 April 2018. https://www.theguardian.com/politics/2018/apr/25/misgivings-over-new-statue-and-old-portrait-of-millicent-fawcett.
Queen's College London, 2020. 'A proud history'. https://www.qcl.org.uk/about-us/a-proud-history.
De Quincey, Thomas, 1853. *Autobiographic Sketches*, Vol. 1. London: James Hogg and Sons.
Radio Times, 1924. 'Wireless programme – Friday (Nov 14th)'. 7 November 1924, 303.
Radio Times, 1929. 'A great feminist'. Tuesday, 19 November 1929. 2LO London & 5XX Daventry. Vol. 25, No. 320 (15 November 1929), 488.
Rathbone, Eleanor F., 1929. 'A completed life. Millicent Garrett Fawcett. 11th June 1847–5th August 1929'. *Woman's Leader*. Friday, 9 August 1929, 209–10.
Reading Observer, 1915. 'Women's work'. Saturday, 2 October 1915, 2.
Reading Observer, 1917. 'Women's work'. Saturday, 24 February 1917, 6.
Rees, Gwendolen, 1922. 'Library work as a profession for women'. *Woman's Leader*. 23 June 1922, 164.
Rees, Yves, 2020. 'The women of the League of Nations'. News. 10 January 2020. La Trobe University. https://www.latrobe.edu.au/news/articles/2018/opinion/the-women-of-the-league-of-nations.
Reeves, Rachel, 2020. *Women of Westminster: The MPs who changed politics*. London: Bloomsbury Publishing.
Reeves, William Pember, 1903. *State Experiments in Australia and New Zealand*, Vol. 1. New York: E. P. Dutton and Co.
Registrar General, 1954. *The Registrar General's Statistical Review of England and Wales for the Five Years 1946–1950*. London: Her Majesty's Stationery Office.
Reid, Mark, 1892. 'Our young historians'. *Macmillan's Magazine*. Vol. 67 (November 1892), 91–8.
Reilly, Claire, 2019. 'Google Doodle celebrates International Women's Day 2019'. Cnet.com. 8 March 2019. https://www.cnet.com/news/google-doodle-celebrates-international-womens-day-2019/.
Reti, Steven P., 1963. *Silver and Gold: The political economy of international monetary conferences, 1867–1892*. London: Greenwood Press.
Reynolds's Illustrated News, 1927. 'Full adult suffrage at last'. Sunday, 16 October 1927, 2.
Richardson, Samuel, 1748. *Clarissa, or the History of a Young Lady, Comprehending the Most Important Concerns of Private Life, and Particularly Shewing the Distress that May Attend the Misconduct both of Parents and Children in Relation to Marriage*. London: Printed for S. Richardson.
Rieser, Andrew, 2003. *The Chautauqua Moment: Protestants, progressives, and the culture of modern liberalism*. New York: Columbia University Press.

Ritch, Alistair, 2019. *Sickness in the Workhouse: Poor Law medical care in provincial England, 1834–1914*. Rochester Studies in Medical Health. Rochester: University of Rochester Press.

Rix, Kathryn, 2019. 'Women and the municipal franchise'. *The History of Parliament Blog*, 2 August 2019. https://thehistoryofparliament.wordpress.com/2019/08/02/women-and-the-municipal-franchise/.

Roberts, Ursula, 1912. *The Cause of Purity and Women's Suffrage*. London: The Church League for Women's Suffrage, 1–11.

Robinson, Jane, 2018. *Hearts and Minds: The untold story of the Great Pilgrimage and how women won the vote*. London: Transworld Publishers.

Roderick, Gordon, 2016. *Victorian Education and the Ideal of Womanhood*. London: Routledge.

Rolf, David, 1979. 'Origins of Mr Speaker's conference during the First World War'. *History*. Vol. 64, No. 210, 36–46.

Rönnbäck, Josefin, 2004. *Politikens genusgränser: Den kvinnliga rösträttsrörelsen och kampen för kvinnors politiska medborgskap 1902–1921*. Stockholm: Bokförlaget Atlas.

Rose, Lizzie, 2021. 'Thousands attend Sisters Uncut and Reclaim the Fight protests against police violence'. *The Tab*. Monday, 15 March 2021. https://thetab.com/uk/london/2021/03/15/thousands-attend-sisters-uncut-and-reclaim-the-fight-protests-against-police-violence-39625.

Rosebery, The Lord, 1890. *Woman's Suffrage (Local Government). Return to an Address of the House of Lords, Dated 16th May 1889, for Return Showing the Number of Women in England and Wales Who are Qualified to Vote for County Councils and for Councillors in Municipal Boroughs, Indicating in each Case What is the Qualification Which Entitles a Woman to Be Placed on the Register*. Ordered to be printed 13 February 1890. London: Henry Hansard and Son, and Eyre and Spottiswoode.

Rosen, Andrew, 2013. *Rise Up, Women!: The militant campaign of the Women's Social and Political Union, 1903–1914*. Abingdon: Routledge.

Rosenbaum, Simon, 1910. 'The general election of January, 1910, and the bearing of the results on some problems of representation'. *Journal of the Royal Statistical Society*. Vol. 73, No. 5 (May 1910), 473–528.

Rousseau, Jean-Jacques, 1762. *Emile, or Education*, translated by Barbara Foxley 1921. London & Toronto: J. M. Dent and Sons, 1921.

Rover, Constance, 1967. *Women's Suffrage and Party Politics in Britain 1866–1914*. London: Routledge and Kegan Paul.

Roy, Douglas, 1971. *The History of the Liberal Party, 1895–1970*. London: Sidgwick and Jackson.

Royal Holloway, 2020. 'Our origins as education pioneers: Our founders'. https://www.royalholloway.ac.uk/about-us/our-history/our-founders/.

Rubinstein, David, 1989. 'Victorian feminists: Henry and Millicent Garrett Fawcett'. In *The Blind Victorian: Henry Fawcett and British Liberalism*, edited by L. Goldman. Cambridge: Cambridge University Press, 70–85.

Rubinstein, David, 1991. *A Different World for Women: The life of Millicent Garrett Fawcett*. Columbus, OH: Ohio State University Press.

Ruiz, Blanca Rodriguez, and Marín, Ruth Rubio, 2012. *The Struggle for Female Suffrage in Europe: Voting to become citizens*. Leiden: Brill.

Sabatier, Paul, 1908. *Modernism: The Jowett lectures, 1908*. New York: Charles Scribner's Sons.

Sanghani, Radhika, 2015. 'The uncomfortable truth about racism and the suffragettes'. *Telegraph*. 6 October 2015. https://www.telegraph.co.uk/women/womens-life/11914757/Racism-and-the-suffragettes-the-uncomfortable-truth.html.

Schools Inquiry Commission, 1868. Vol. 7. *General Reports by Assistant Commissioners. Southern Counties*. Presented by both Houses of Parliament by command of Her Majesty. London: George E. Eyre and William Spottiswoode, for Her Majesty's Stationery Office.

Scotsman, 1874a. 'Professor Flint on the Late John Stuart Mill'. Wednesday, 18 February 1874, 4.

Scotsman, 1874b. 'Philosophical institution: The women of modern fiction'. Monday, 30 November 1874, 1.

Scotsman, 1879. 'Edinburgh'. Thursday, 27 November 1879, 4–6.

Scotsman, 1909. 'Mr A. Cameron Corbett, M. O., and militant suffragists'. Thursday, 25 November 1909, 12.

Scotsman, 1913. 'Great suffrage demonstration in Hyde Park'. Monday, 28 July 1913, 8.

Scotsman, 1915. 'The prime minister at Newcastle. Appeal for munitions of war. Great reception by Tyneside workers'. Wednesday, 21 April 1915, 10.

Scott, George Ryley, 2013. *A History of Prostitution from Antiquity to the Present Day*. Abingdon: Routledge.

Scott, John L., 2007. 'British concentration camps of the Second South African War (the Transvaal, 1900–1902)'. Master's Thesis, Florida State University. https://diginole.lib.fsu.edu/islandora/object/fsu:176437/datastream/PDF/view.

Scott, Rosemary, 1999. 'Poetry in the "Cornhill Magazine": Thackeray's influence'. *Victorian Periodicals Review*. Vol. 32, No. 3 (Fall 1999), 269–74.

Setzer, Claudia, 1994. *The Quotable Soul. Inspiring quotations crossing time and culture*. New York: John Wiley and Sons, Inc.

Sewall, May Wright (ed.), 1894. *The World's Congress of Representative Women*, Vol. 1. Chicago: Rand McNally & Company.

Shaw, Anna H., 1908. 'To the editor of the Times'. *Times*. Wednesday, 8 July 1908, 10.

Shaw, George Bernard, 1906. 'Woman suffrage, to the editor of the Times'. *Times*, London. Wednesday, 31 October 1906, 8.

Shaw, George Bernard, 1914. 'Common sense about the war'. In *New York Times* (1914), *Current History of the European War: What men of letters say*, Vol. 1, No. 1. New York: New York Times, 11–60.

Sheffield Daily Telegraph, 1870. 'Mr Bright seriously ill'. Thursday, 10 February 1870, 2.

Sheffield Daily Telegraph, 1872. 'Domestic'. Saturday, 7 December 1872, 2.

Sheffield Daily Telegraph, 1879. 'Mr Gladstone's method of legislation'. Friday, 28 November 1879, 3.

Sheffield Daily Telegraph, 1915. 'Lord Derby's appeal for help to workers'. Friday, 5 November 1915, 8.

Shields Daily Gazette, 1872. 'A ladies meeting on woman suffrage'. Saturday, 11 May 1872, 2.

Sisam, Kenneth, 2008. 'Skeat, Walter William'. Revised by Charlotte Brewer. *Oxford Dictionary of National Biography*. https://doi.org/10.1093/ref:odnb/36116.

Sketch, 1908. 'Small talk'. Wednesday, 17 June 1908, 296.

Smith, Angela K., 2016. *Suffrage Discourse in Britain during the First World War*. Abingdon: Routledge.

Smith, Harold L., 2007a. *British Women's Suffrage Campaign, 1866–1928*, 2nd edition. London: Routledge.

Smith, Horatio, and Smith, James, 1841. *Rejected Addresses; or The New Theatrum Poetarum*, 3rd American edition, from the 19th London edition. Boston: William D. Ticknor.

Smith, Iain R., 2007b. *Morbidity and Mortality in the Concentration Camps of the South African War (1899–1902)*. Centre for the History of Medicine, University of Warwick. https://warwick.ac.uk/fac/arts/history/chm/research/archive/morbidity/outcomes/.

Smith, Paul, 2011. 'Cecil, Robert Arthur Talbot Gascoyne-, third marquess of Salisbury'. *Oxford Dictionary of National Biography*. https://www.oxforddnb.com/view/10.1093/ref:odnb/9780198614128.001.0001/odnb-9780198614128-e-32339.

Smith, Samuel, 1892. 'Letter from Samuel Smith, M.P.'. 24 April 1892 [Pamphlet] 7 Delaney Street, Westminster. In *Women's Suffrage and Party Politics in Britain 1866–1914*, by Constance Rover, 1967. London: Routledge & Kegan Paul, 180.

Smith, Sydney, 1810. 'Female education'. Edinburgh Review, 1810. In *The Works of the Rev. Sydney Smith*, by Sydney Smith, 1839, Vol. 1. London: Longman, Orme, Brown, Green and Longmans, 231–56.

Social Gazette, 1915. 'Things we hear'. Saturday, 12 June 1915, 2.

Society for Promoting Christian Knowledge, 1916. *Prayer-Book Psalter. Revised in accordance with the proposals of a Committee appointed by the Archbishop of Canterbury*. London: Society for Promoting Christian Knowledge.

Soderlund, Gretchen, 2013. *Sex Trafficking, Scandal, and the Transformation of Journalism, 1885–1917*. London: University of Chicago Press.

Solomon, Georgiana, 1911. 'Black Friday'. *Votes for Women*, No. 76. London: Women's Social and Political Union.

Somerville, Martha, 1874. *Personal Recollections from Early Life to Old Age of Mary Somerville, with Selections from Her Correspondence. By her daughter, Martha Somerville*. Boston: Roberts Brothers.

Southern Echo, 1908. 'Winston Churchill, and the suffragists at Manchester'. Thursday, 16 April 1908, 3.

Southey, Robert, 1810. *The Curse of Kehama*. London: Longman, Hurst, Rees, Orme and Brown.

Special Collections, 2012. 'The most enormous party – when we were 500!' *University of St Andrews Special Collections Blog*. Friday, 9 March 2012. https://special-collections.wp.st-andrews.ac.uk/2012/03/09/the-most-enormous-party-when-we-were-500/.

Spectator, 1906. 'Woman suffrage'. 26 May 1906, 820–1.

Spectator, 1908. 'The Women's National Anti-Suffrage League'. 25 July 1908, 117–18.

Spencer, Herbert, 1850. *Social Statics: Or the conditions essential to human happiness specified, and the first of them developed*. London: John Chapman.

St Anne's College, n.d. 'Established 1879: History'. https://www.st-annes.ox.ac.uk/this-is-st-annes/history/.

St James's Gazette, 1883. 'The Cobden Club Dinner'. 2 July 1883, 11.

St James's Gazette, 1888. 'The pantomime child'. 17 December 1888, 6.

Standard (London), 1899. 'The military libel case'. Wednesday, 15 March 1899, 5.

Stanhope, Philip, 1774. *Letters Written by the Late Right Honourable Philip Dormer Stanhope, Earl of Chesterfield, to his son, Philip Stanhope, Esq.; Late Envoy Extraordinary at the Court of Dresden*. London: J. Dodsley.

Stanley, Henrietta Maria (and 103 other signatories), 1889. 'An appeal against female suffrage'. *Nineteenth Century*. Vol. 25 (January–June 1889), 781–8. London: Kegan Paul, Trench and Co.

Stanley, Liz, and Wise, Sue, 2006. 'Putting it into practice: Using feminist fractured foundationalism in researching children in the concentration camps of the South African War'. *Sociological Research Online*. https://doi.org/10.5153/sro.1121.

Stanley, Will, 2012. 'This is 2LO, London Broadcasting Station Calling!' *Science Museum Blog*, 14 November 2012. https://blog.sciencemuseum.org.uk/this-is-2lo-london-broadcasting-station-calling/.

Stanton, Elizabeth Cady, Anthony, Susan B., and Gage, Matilda J., 1887. *History of Woman Suffrage*, Vol. 3, 1876–1885. New York: Susan B. Anthony.

Star, 1897. 'Bishop Cowie on women's suffrage'. 29 January 1897, 1. https://paperspast.natlib.govt.nz/newspapers/TS18970129.2.14.3.

Star, 1929. 'Obituary: Dame Millicent Fawcett, death of famous suffragist leader, womanly woman'. Monday, 5 August 1929. In Steinbach (2008, 322).

Steinbach, Susie L. (ed.), 2008. *Millicent Garrett Fawcett*. Lives of Victorian Political Figures, Part III, Vol. 4. London: Pickering and Chatto.

Steinbach, Susie L., 2016. *Understanding the Victorians: Politics, culture and society in nineteenth-century Britain*. Abingdon: Routledge.

Stephen, Barbara Nightingale, 1976. *Emily Davies and Girton College*. Westport, CT: Hyperion Press.

Stephen, James Fitzjames, 1873. *Liberty, Equality, Fraternity*. New York: H. Holt and Co.

Stephen, Leslie, 2011. *Life of Henry Fawcett*. Cambridge Library Collection. Cambridge: Cambridge University Press.

Stevenson, Hew, 2013. 'Who gets credit for universal female suffrage?' Letters to the editor. *Daily Telegraph*. Monday, 4 February 2013, 19.

Stevenson, Louisa, 1894. 'Women students in the Scottish universities'. By Miss Louisa Stevenson, Honorary Secretary of the Edinburgh Association for the University Education of Women. In *National Education Association of the United States, 1894. Proceedings of the International Congress of Education of the World's Columbian Exposition, Chicago July 25–28, 1893*. New York: National Education Association, 877–9.

Stevenson, Robert Louis, 1885. *Prince Otto: A romance*. London: Chatto and Windus.

Stott, Mary, 1978. 'Cause for celebration'. *Guardian*. Wednesday, 15 February 1978, 11.

Strachey, John, 1888. *India: Pictorial and descriptive*. London: Kegan Paul, Trench & Co.

Strachey, Ray, 1920. '"The woman's leader" in literature. The women's victory – and after'. *Woman's Leader*. Friday, 19 March 1920, 158.

Strachey, Ray, 1928. *The Cause: A short history of the women's movement in Great Britain*. London: G. Bell and Sons.

Strachey, Ray, 1929. 'Westminster Abbey Memorial Service'. *Woman's Leader*. Friday, 22 November 1929, 324.

Strachey, Ray, 1931. *Millicent Garrett Fawcett*. London: John Murray.

Sturge, Eliza Mary, 1872. *On Women's Suffrage*. Birmingham: White and Pike. Available at https://digital.library.lse.ac.uk/objects/lse:yag818yac/read/single#page/257/mode/1up.

Suffolk and Essex Free Press, 1869. 'Selections'. Thursday, 1 April 1869, 6.

Suffragette, 1913a. 'A review of the week. Miss Emily Wilding Davison'. Friday, 13 June 1913, 571.

Suffragette, 1913b. 'A Year's Record. The following are the more serious attacks on property which have been attributed to Suffragettes during the year 1913'. Friday, 26 December 1913, 258.
Sun (London), 1834. 'London'. Tuesday, 19 August 1834, 2.
Sun (New York), 1910. 'Women hiss the president'. Friday, 15 April 1910, 1–2.
Sunday Mirror, 1915. 'Women judges. Assessors in women's cases at munitions tribunals'. Sunday, 12 December 1915, 2.
Sunday Times, 1988. 'Matching faces to places: New homes for portraits'. Sunday, 17 July 1988.
Sunderland Echo and Shipping Gazette, 1929. 'Dame Millicent Fawcett'. Thursday, 1 August 1929, 12.
Surridge, Keith Terrance, 1998. *Managing the South African War, 1899–1902, Politicians v. Generals*. Studies in History. Woodbridge, Suffolk: The Boydell Press.
Sussex Agricultural Express, 1888. 'Eastbourne'. Saturday, 28 January 1888, 5.
Sutherland, Gill, 2006. *Faith, Duty, and the Power of Mind: The Cloughs and their circle, 1820–1960*. Cambridge: Cambridge University Press.
Szymanski, Anne-Marie E., 2003. *Pathways to Prohibition: Radicals, moderates, and social movement outcomes*. Durham, NC: Duke University Press.
Takayanagi, Mari, 2018. 'Women and the vote: The parliamentary path to equal franchise, 1918–28'. *Parliamentary History*. Vol. 37, No. 1, 168–85.
Tavernier, Eugène, 1909a. 'The religious question in France. I. A French Catholic's view'. *Times*, London. Saturday, 6 November 1909, 5.
Tavernier, Eugène, 1909b. 'The religious question in France. II. A French Catholic's view'. *Times*, London. Monday, 8 November 1909, 5–6.
Tavistock Gazette, 1871. 'The electoral disabilities of women'. Friday, 17 March 1871, 4.
Taylor, Jane A., and Kieser, Jules A., 2016. *Forensic Odontology: Principles and practice*. Oxford: John Wiley & Sons.
Taylor, Jane, and Taylor, Ann, 1806. *Rhymes for the Nursery*, 1849 new illustrated edition. Philadelphia: George S. Appleton.
Te Ara, n.d. 'Page 2. The temperance influence'. Story: Liquor laws. *Te Ara: The encyclopedia of New Zealand*. https://teara.govt.nz/en/liquor-laws/page-2.
Tedbury, Imogen, 2020a. 'Vote winner – a newly discovered portrait of Millicent Fawcett is a significant find'. *Apollo Magazine*. 12 May 2020. https://www.apollo-magazine.com/millicent-fawcett-new-portrait-discovery-london/.
Tedbury, Imogen, 2020b. *Modern Portraits for Modern Women. Principals and pioneers from the Royal Holloway and Bedford New College Art Collection*. Understanding British Portraits. London: Royal Holloway and Bedford New College.
Teele, Dawn Langan, 2018. 'How the West was won: Competition, mobilization, and women's enfranchisement in the United States'. *The Journal of Politics*. Vol. 80, No. 2, 442–61.
Tennyson, Alfred, 1842. *Œnone. Poems by Alfred Tennyson*, Vol. 1. London: Edward Moxon.
Tennyson, Alfred, 1847. *The Princess: A medley*. London: Edward Moxon.
Tennyson, Alfred, 1872. *Songs etc, From the Published Writings of Alfred Tennyson*. London: Strahan and Co.
Tennyson, Alfred, 1881. *Alfred Tennyson: His life and works*, edited by Walter E. Wace. Edinburgh: MacNiven and Wallace.
Tennyson, Alfred, 1884. *The Cup and the Falcon*. London: Macmillan and Co.
Thackeray, William M., 1848. *Vanity Fair*. London: Bradbury and Evans.
Theron, Bridget, 2006. 'Victorian women, gender and identity in the South African War: An overview'. *African Historical Review*. Vol. 38, No. 1, 3–24.
Thompson, J. A., 1977. 'Lord Cecil and the pacifists in the League of Nations Union'. *Historical Journal*. Vol. 20, No. 4, 949–59.
Thomson, Susan, 2018. *The Life and Works of Annie Louisa Swynnerton*. Manchester: Manchester Art Press.
Thorpe, Jennifer R., 2018. '6 feminist road trips to take with your squad this summer'. *Bustle*. 2 June 2018. https://www.bustle.com/p/6-feminist-road-trips-to-take-with-your-squad-this-summer-9245051.
Times, 1872a. 'Yesterday four unhappy men suffered the last'. Wednesday, 14 August 1872, 9.
Times, 1872b. 'It is fortunate that we are not often called upon'. Tuesday, 16 April 1872, 6.
Times, 1884. 'General Gordon: To the editor of the Times, from Burdett-Coutts'. Saturday, 10 May 1884, 7.
Times, 1886a. 'Parliamentary intelligence'. Friday, 20 August 1886, 6.

Times, 1886b. 'Popular lectures in the East-End'. Monday, 11 October 1886, 6.
Times, 1886c. 'Bedford College'. Thursday, 14 October 1886, 7.
Times, 1888a. 'The social progress of women'. Wednesday, 11 March 1888, 4.
Times, 1888b. 'Mrs Fawcett on men and women'. Monday, 26 November 1888, 6.
Times, 1897. 'Prospective arrangements'. Saturday, 25 September 1897, 10.
Times, 1898. 'Naval & military intelligence'. Thursday, 25 August 1898, 4.
Times, 1899a. 'The Liberal leadership, to the editor of the Times'. Tuesday, 17 January 1899, 8.
Times, 1899b. 'Naval and military intelligence'. Friday, 3 March 1899, 11.
Times, 1899c. 'Army Temperance Association'. Tuesday, 16 May 1899, 13.
Times, 1899d. 'Burma. From our correspondent'. Monday, 5 June 1899, 7.
Times, 1899e. 'The Jubilee of Bedford College'. Thursday, 15 June 1899, 7.
Times, 1899f. 'The war. The military situation, by a military correspondent'. Saturday, 4 November 1899, 8.
Times, 1899g. 'Embarcation of troops (from our special correspondent)'. Thursday, 9 November 1899, 7.
Times, 1901. 'The concentration camps'. Saturday, 22 June 1901, 12.
Times, 1908a. 'Lord Morley on India'. Friday, 12 June 1908, 11.
Times, 1908b. 'Political notes, suffragist demonstration'. Thursday, 29 October 1908, 10.
Times, 1908c. 'The King-Emperor and India. Imperial message to princes and peoples'. Monday, 2 November 1908, 10.
Times, 1908d. 'Woman suffrage in the United States. The progress of the movement. From our own Correspondent, Nov 27th'. Saturday, 28 November 1908, 5.
Times, 1908e. 'The revolution in Haiti'. Friday, 4 December 1908, 7.
Times, 1908f. 'The woman-suffrage movement. Meetings in New York. (From our own Correspondent, Dec 6th)'. Monday, 7 December 1908, 8.
Times, 1908g. 'Woman suffrage. Medical women and the prime minister'. Monday, 14 December 1908, 6.
Times, 1908h. 'The problem of Haiti'. Monday, 14 December 1908, 10.
Times, 1909a. 'Debate between Mrs Humphry Ward and Mrs Fawcett'. Saturday, 27 February 1909, 9.
Times, 1909b. 'House of Commons. Accelerated German construction'. London. Wednesday, 17 March 1909, 6.
Times, 1909c. 'Review of Parliament, House of Commons'. London. Saturday, 20 March 1909, 12.
Times, 1909d. 'The dominions and the navy. London'. Monday, 22 March 1909, 7.
Times, 1909e. 'House of Commons. New Zealand and the navy'. London. Thursday, 25 March 1909, 7.
Times, 1909f. 'Woman suffrage. Mr Churchill on suffragist tactics'. London. Tuesday, 19 October 1909, 10.
Times, 1909g. 'Guildhall banquet. Speech by the prime minister'. London. Wednesday, 10 November 1909, 7.
Times, 1909h. 'Imperial and foreign intelligence. Attempt on the life of Lord Minto. Bombs thrown at Ahmedabad'. Monday, 15 November 1909, 5.
Times, 1910a. 'Woman suffrage'. London. Friday, 27 May 1910, 10.
Times, 1910b. 'The making of the union. A retrospect'. London. Friday, 4 November 1910, 5–7.
Times, 1911a. 'Sir Charles Dilke's will. Bequests to public institutions'. Thursday, 30 March 1911, 10.
Times, 1911b. 'Parliament, House of Commons, Friday, May 5. Private business. Women's Enfranchisement Bill'. Saturday, 6 May 1911, 14.
Times, 1911c. 'Lord Rosebery at St. Andrews. A vision of the past. The lighthouse of learning'. Friday, 15 September 1911, 7.
Times, 1911d. 'Manhood suffrage. Government Bill next session. Statement by Mr Asquith'. Wednesday, 8 November 1911, 8.
Times, 1911e. 'Women and the Bill. The legislative programme'. Wednesday, 8 November 1911, 8.
Times, 1911f. 'Suffragist violence. Mrs Fawcett's appeal to cabinet ministers'. Tuesday, 5 December 1911, 7.
Times, 1912a. 'Opening of the Swedish Riksdag'. Wednesday, 17 January 1912, 5.
Times, 1912b. 'Political notes. Woman suffrage'. Tuesday, 20 February 1912, 7.
Times, 1912c. 'The anti-suffrage demonstration'. Friday, 29 February 1912, 9.
Times, 1912d. 'Further suffragist outrages'. Tuesday, 5 March 1912, 8.

Times, 1912e. 'The Conciliation Bill rejected. Adverse majority of fourteen. A nationalist coup. Commons and the militant outbreaks'. Friday, 29 March 1912, 9.
Times, 1912f. 'Women Liberals and the Reform Bill'. Thursday, 6 June 1912, 7.
Times, 1912g. 'The Franchise Bill'. Tuesday, 18 June 1912, 9.
Times, 1912h. 'The prime minister's explanation'. Thursday, 31 October 1912, 11–12.
Times, 1912i. 'The Home Rule Bill. The Irish senate'. Friday, 1 November 1912, 12–14.
Times, 1912j. 'Woman suffrage in Ireland. Labour proposal defeated'. Wednesday, 6 November 1912, 10.
Times, 1913a. 'Franchise Bill dropped'. Tuesday, 28 January 1913, 6.
Times, 1913b. 'The suffragist scene. His Majesty's jockey injured'. Thursday, 5 June 1913, 8.
Times, 1914. 'Ireland in the fighting line. Enthusiasm in Dublin. Mr Asquith's call to the volunteers'. Saturday, 26 September 1914, 9–10.
Times, 1915a. 'Save and lend. Prime minister's appeal. Opening of thrift campaign. Large war loan applications'. Wednesday, 30 June 1915, 9–10.
Times, 1915b. 'Our debt to the fishermen. Devoted work of mine-sweepers. A patriotic record, by our naval correspondent'. Friday, 2 July 1915, 12.
Times, 1915c. 'Women railway clerks'. Monday, 13 December 1915, 5.
Times, 1916. 'House of Commons'. Thursday, 20 July 1916, 10.
Times, 1917a. 'The electoral reform conference'. Thursday, 18 January 1917, 9.
Times, 1917b. 'House of Commons. Electoral reform. Mr Asquith's statement'. Thursday, 29 March 1917, 8.
Times, 1918a. 'The Lord's "P. R." proposal. Home secretary's statement'. Thursday, 7 February 1918, 8.
Times, 1918b. 'Eggs at Brentford. Mrs Oliver Strachey's popularity. From our special correspondent'. Thursday, 12 December 1918, 10.
Times, 1918c. 'Babies and gardens at Brentford. Mrs Strachey's campaign. From our special correspondent'. Saturday, 14 December 1918, 10.
Times, 1923. 'Lady Astor's Bill'. Saturday, 14 July 1923, 10.
Times, 1925a. 'Parliament. Women and the franchise. The Labour Bill rejected. Government measure promised'. Saturday, 21 February 1925, 7.
Times, 1925b. 'The new pensions scheme'. Wednesday, 6 May 1925, 17.
Times, 1926. 'Closing of the session. Legitimacy Bill third reading'. Tuesday, 14 December 1926, 14.
Times, 1927a. 'Adoption of Children Act'. Monday, 3 January 1927, 14.
Times, 1927b. 'Women to vote at 21. Prime minister's statement. Bill next session'. Thursday, 14 April 1927, 14.
Times, 1927c. 'Smoke abatement'. Friday, 1 July 1927, 16.
Times, 1927d. 'Prime Minister at Cardiff. The government policy. Lords' reform and franchise'. Friday, 7 October 1927, 7–8.
Times, 1929. 'Dame Millicent Fawcett'. Tuesday, 6 August 1929, 11.
Times, 1930. 'The Royal Academy. (By Our Art Critic)'. Saturday, 3 May 1930, 13.
Times, 2001. 'Stony broke'. City Diary. Tuesday, 10 April 2001, 29.
Tolstoy, Leo, 1908. 'I cannot be silent. The frequency of executions in Russia provokes a denunciation of government that spares neither Czar, Church, nor Duma'. *New York Times*. Sunday, 19 July 1908, 31.
Trades Union Congress, 2020. 'Our History'. https://www.tuc.org.uk/about-the-tuc/our-history.
Trevelyan, Janet Penrose, 1923. *The Life of Mrs Humphry Ward*. London: Constable and Company.
Trinity College Dublin, 2019. 'About Trinity – History'. https://www.tcd.ie/about/history/.
Trollope, William, 1834. *A History of the Royal Foundation of Christ's Hospital*. London: William Pickering.
Tullberg, Rita McWilliams, 1998. *Women at Cambridge*. Cambridge: Cambridge University Press.
Twain, Mark, 1897. *Following the Equator: A journey around the world*. New York: Doubleday & McClure.
Tylor, Edward Burnett. 1873. *Primitive Culture: Researchers into the development of mythology, philosophy, religion, language, art and custom*, 2nd edition, Vol. 1. London: John Murray.
Union Signal, 1897. 'Indian Army mortality'. *Union Signal; A journal of social welfare*. Thursday, 21 October 1897.

United States Bureau of Education (USBE), 1895. *Report of the Secretary of the Interior Being Part of the Message and Documents Communicated to the Two Houses of Congress at the Beginning of the Second Session of the Fifty-Third Congress. Volume V. Part II: Education and the World's Columbian Exposition, 423–1749*. Washington: Government Printing Office. Available at: https://books.google.co.uk/books?id=myFHAQAAIAAJ&pg.

UCL Institute of Education Archives, n.d. 'Trafalgar Square demonstration 1927'. UCL Institute for Education, UWT/D/1/69/.

Universities (Scotland) Act 1889. http://www.legislation.gov.uk/ukpga/Vict/52-53/55.

University of Birmingham, 2021. 'A brief history'. https://www.birmingham.ac.uk/university/about/history/index.aspx.

University of Bristol, 2020. 'History and heritage'. https://www.birmingham.ac.uk/university/history-and-heritage/index.aspx.

University of Leeds, 2020. 'Heritage'. https://www.leeds.ac.uk/info/5000/about/133/heritage.

University of Liverpool, 2007. 'History of the university'. http://www.liv.ac.uk/about/history/, archived at https://web.archive.org/web/20070902011543/http://www.liv.ac.uk/about/history/.

University of London, 2020. 'Royal Charter'. https://london.ac.uk/about-us/history-university-london.

University of Manchester Library, n.d.a. 'Description of "Manchester and Salford College for women miscellaneous society, University of Manchester women students' Debating Society Archive, 1882–1905. University of Manchester Library. GB 133 WDS" on the Archives Hub website'. https://archiveshub.jisc.ac.uk/data/gb133-wds.

University of Manchester Library, n.d.b. 'Description of the Archive of the Manchester and Salford College for Women'. *Jisc Archives Hub*. https://archiveshub.jisc.ac.uk/data/gb133-mcw.

University of Nottingham, 2020. 'A brief history of the university'. https://www.nottingham.ac.uk/about/history/abriefhistoryoftheuniversity.aspx.

University of Sheffield, 2020. 'History and heritage'. https://www.sheffield.ac.uk/about/history.

Varty, Anne, 2008. *Children and Theatre in Victorian Britain*. London: Palgrave Macmillan.

Vaughan, Megan, 1991. *Curing Their Ills: Colonial power and African illness*. Stanford, CA: Stanford University Press.

Verhoeven, Jana, 2010. '"The biggest thing in years": Max O'Rell's lecture tour in Australasia'. *Explorations*. Vol. 44, No. 3. http://isfar.org.au/wp-content/uploads/2016/10/44_JANA-VERHOEVEN-The-Biggest-Thing-in-Years-Max-ORells-Lecture-Tour-in-Australasia.pdf.

Victorianist, 2011. '. . . "Four killed and forty wounded was the tally, and indignation raged . . ." Or: The Clerkenwell Prison explosion of 1867'. Tuesday, 11 August 2011. http://thevictorianist.blogspot.com/2011/08/four-killed-and-forty-wounded-was-tally.html.

Vote, 1910. 'Miss Lena Connell'. Saturday, 7 May 1910, 16–17.

Vote, 1912. 'The pledge of Labour'. Saturday, 24 February 1912, 6.

Vote, 1914. 'The Women's Freedom League and the national crisis'. Friday, 14 August 1914, 278.

Vote, 1919. 'Equal franchise for women. Government defeat in committee'. Friday, 23 May 1919, 193.

Vote, 1923. 'Women in the assembly of the League of Nations'. Friday, 31 August 1923, 273.

Vote, 1925. 'Congratulations to Dame Millicent! An historic garden party'. Friday, 31 July 1925, 241.

Vote, 1927. 'In Trafalgar Square, July 16th'. Friday, 22 July 1927, 1–2.

Vote, 1928a. 'The Victory Breakfast. Hotel Cecil celebration'. Friday, 13 July 1928, 221–2.

Vote, 1928b. 'Presentation to Dame Millicent Fawcett'. Friday, 21 December 1928, 410.

Vote, 1929a. 'Faithful till the curtain drops. Dame Millicent Fawcett, G.B.E., J. P., L.L.D. A very gallant lady'. Friday, 9 August 1929, 249.

Vote, 1929b. 'Dame Millicent Fawcett'. Friday, 23 August 1929, 271.

Vote, 1930a. 'The unveiling of Mrs Pankhurst's statue'. Friday, 14 March 1930, 81.

Vote, 1930b. 'Dame Millicent for the nation'. Friday, 23 May 1930, 162.

Vote, 1932. 'Dame Millicent Garrett Fawcett unveiling in Westminster Abbey'. Friday, 11 March 1932, 86.

Votes for Women, 1908. 'Winston Churchill on votes for women'. Thursday, 30 April 1908, 131.

Votes for Women, 1910. 'Progress abroad'. Friday, 1 July 1910, 2.

Votes for Women, 1912. 'What will the cabinet do?'. Friday, 2 February 1912, 278.

Votes for Women, 1913. 'Miss Davison's funeral. "Give me liberty or give me death"'. Friday, 20 June 1913, 553–4.

Votes for Women, 1914a. 'Mass meeting in the Albert Hall. Constitutional suffragists demand government measure'. Friday, 20 February 1914, 311.
Votes for Women, 1914b. 'The outlook: Women must never return to subordination'. Friday, 7 August 1914, 678.
Votes for Women, 1914c. 'Women's Social and Political Union'. Friday, 21 August 1914, 703.
Votes for Women, 1915. 'Mr Asquith's first suffrage speech'. Friday, 14 May 1915, 4.
Votes for Women, 1917. 'Is it victory at last?'. Friday, 2 February 1917, 4.
Walsall Advertiser, 1906. 'Famine in Valenciennes lace'. Saturday, 21 July 1906, 3.
Ward, Mary A., 1908a. 'Is woman suffrage inevitable?'. *Times*. Tuesday, 30 June 1908, 9.
Ward, Mary A., 1908b. 'Some suffragist arguments'. *Times*. Tuesday, 1 September 1908, 11.
Ward, Mary A., 1908c. 'Woman suffrage in America'. *Times*. Saturday, 10 October 1908, 15.
Ward, Mary A., 1908d. 'Why I do not believe in woman suffrage'. *Ladies Home Journal*. Vol. 25, No. 15. In *Selected Articles on Woman Suffrage*, by Edith M. Phelps, 1910. Minneapolis: The H. W. Wilson Company, 251–6.
Ward, Mary Humphry, 1908. 'The women's anti-suffrage movement'. *The Nineteenth Century and After*. Vol. 64 (July–December 1908), 343–52.
Ward Howe, Julia, 1908. 'Woman suffrage in America'. *Times*. Thursday, 1 October 1908, 4.
Wearing, Gillian, 2017. 'The Artist's Statement. Gillian Wearing – Courage Calls, Millicent Fawcett statue, Parliament Square'. Donald Insall Associates, 2017. 'Design and Access Statement. Women's Suffrage Memorial', 4. In: Planning – Planning Application Documents, '17/05490/FULL | Erection of a Women's Suffrage memorial in the form of a bronze statue of non-militant Suffragist Millicent Fawcett, by Gillian Wearing. | Open Space Parliament Square London SW1A 0AA'. Available from https://idoxpa.westminster.gov.uk/online-applications/applicationDetails.do?activeTab=documents&keyVal=ORW9FURPHCE00. See 'Design and Access Statement DESIGN AND ACCESS STATEMENT', 21 June 2017.
Weigley, Frank Russell, 2004. *A Great Civil War: A military and political history, 1861–1865*. Bloomington, Indiana: Indiana University Press.
Western Chronicle, 1908. 'Women and the vote. Great march through London'. Friday, 19 June 1908, 2.
Western Daily Press, 1884. 'Great Liberal demonstration in Birmingham. Speeches of Mr Bright and Mr Chamberlain'. Tuesday, 5 August 1884, 8.
Western Daily Press, 1914. 'Cardinal Archbishop of Paris on Belgium and the war'. Wednesday, 16 December 1914, 3.
Western Daily Press, 1916. 'Progress of women workers'. Saturday, 8 January 1916, 9.
Western Daily Press, 1928. 'Suffragists' triumph'. Tuesday, 3 July 1928, 9.
Western Mail, 1914. 'The suffragettes. Unconditional release announced'. Tuesday, 11 August 1914, 2.
Western Mail, 1929. 'Social and personal'. Friday, 2 August 1929, 9.
Western Morning News, 1874. 'Mrs Fawcett on female characters of fiction'. Friday, 11 December 1874, 3.
Western Morning News and Mercury, 1928a. 'Who discovered Lionel Ellis?'. 8 March 1928, 6.
Western Morning News and Mercury, 1928b. 'Duveen exhibition of modern British art'. 13 April 1928, 4.
Western Morning News and Mercury, 1929. 'Dame Fawcett. Suggestion that ashes be buried in the Abbey'. Friday, 9 August 1929, 7.
Western Times, 1871. 'Women's claims to the suffrage. Mrs Fawcett at Exeter last night'. Thursday, 16 March 1871, 2.
Western Times, 1908a. 'Electoral reform'. Thursday, 21 May 1908, 2.
Western Times, 1908b. 'The prime minister and women's suffrage'. Friday, 29 May 1908, 9.
Western Times, 1909. 'Women's anti-suffrage campaign'. 6 January 1909, 4.
Westlake, John, 1906. 'The Trade Disputes Bill, To the editor of the Times'. Monday, 19 November 1906, 5.
Westminster Abbey, 1932. 'Unveiling of the memorial to Dame Millicent Garrett Fawcett'. https://www.westminster-abbey.org/media/6195/fawcett-dame-millicent-unveiling.pdf.
Westminster Abbey, 2021. 'Henry and Millicent Fawcett'. https://www.westminster-abbey.org/abbey-commemorations/commemorations/henry-and-millicent-fawcett.
Westminster Gazette, 1893. 'Chicago Exhibition and women teachers'. 17 February 1893, 10.
Westminster Gazette, 1906. 'The Welsh miners' strike'. Thursday, 6 September 1906, 6.
Westminster Gazette, 1917a. 'Electoral reform'. Wednesday, 17 January 1917, 5.

Westminster Gazette, 1917b. 'Woman suffrage. The speaker's committee in favour of the principle'. Monday, 22 January 1917.

Whitehead, Alfred North, 1906. *Liberty and the Enfranchisement of Women. Extract from the speech of A. N. Whitehead, Esq., Sc.D., at the Annual Meeting of the Cambridge Women's Suffrage Association, Nov. 5, 1906*. Cambridge Women's Suffrage Association. Available from http://www.religion-online.org/article/liberty-and-the-enfranchisement-of-women/.

Wilkinson, Ellen, 1925. 'Women police'. *Woman's Leader and Common Cause*. Friday, 11 December 1925, 364.

Williams, Llewellyn W., 1911. 'Henria Helen Leech Williams. A Memoir. To my sister's comrades in the army of freewomen'. *Votes for Women*. Friday, 20 January 1911, 256.

Wills, Stella, 1951. 'The Anglo-Jewish contribution to the education movement for women in the nineteenth century'. *Transactions (Jewish Historical Society of England)*. Vol. 17, 269–81.

Willson, Perry. 2009. *Women in Twentieth-Century Italy*. London: Macmillan International Higher Education.

Wollstonecraft, Mary, 1792. *A Vindication of the Rights of Woman, with Strictures on Political and Moral Subjects*. London: J. Johnson.

Wollstonecraft, Mary, 1879. *Letters to Imlay, With Prefatory Memoir By C. Kegan Paul*. London: C. Kegan Paul and Co.

Wollstonecraft, Mary, 1891. *A Vindication of the Rights of Woman, with Strictures on Political and Moral Subjects*. New edition, with an introduction by Mrs Henry Fawcett. London: T. Fisher Unwin. Available at https://archive.org/details/vindicationofrig00woll/.

Woman's Leader, 1920a. 'News from headquarters and from our societies. Parliament'. Friday, 7 May 1920.

Woman's Leader, 1920b. 'Maintenance orders'. Friday, 13 August 1920, 615.

Woman's Leader, 1921. 'The Married Woman (Maintenance) Act'. Friday, 21 January 1921, 1075.

Woman's Leader, 1922a. 'The Stansfeld lectures 1921–22'. Friday, 27 January 1922, 598.

Woman's Leader, 1922b. 'Equal Franchise Bill'. Friday, 10 March 1922, 41.

Woman's Leader, 1922c. 'Separation and Maintenance Orders Bill'. Friday, 14 July 1922, 190.

Woman's Leader, 1922d. 'News from Westminster'. Friday, 18 August 1922, 227.

Woman's Leader, 1923a. 'Equality of the sexes in marriage'. Friday, 23 February 1923, 26.

Woman's Leader, 1923b. 'Consultative committee of women's organizations'. Friday, 2 March 1923, 39.

Woman's Leader, 1923c. 'Equal Franchise.' Friday 27 April 1923, 97.

Woman's Leader, 1924. 'Representation of the People Act (1918) Amendment Bill'. Friday, 28 March 1924, 66.

Woman's Leader, 1925a. 'Three noble dames'. Friday, 9 January 1925, 398.

Woman's Leader, 1925b. 'A triumph for Lady Astor'. Friday, 17 July 1925, 194.

Woman's Leader, 1925c. 'In Aubrey House Garden'. Friday, 31 July 1925, 213.

Woman's Leader, 1925d. 'At last!'. Friday, 14 August 1925, 227.

Woman's Leader, 1926a. 'The illegitimate child'. Friday, 15 October 1926, 331.

Woman's Leader, 1926b. 'London Society for Women's Service'. Friday, 5 November 1926, 355.

Woman's Leader, 1927a. 'Parliament (Qualification of Peeresses Bill)'. Friday, 15 April 1927, 77.

Woman's Leader, 1927b. 'Notes and news. The prime minister's announcement'. Friday, 22 April 1927, 85.

Woman's Leader, 1927c. 'Cardiff'. Friday, 14 October 1927, 287.

Woman's Leader, 1928a. 'Portrait of Dame Millicent Fawcett'. Friday, 8 June 1928, 146.

Woman's Leader, 1928b. 'A happy ending'. Friday, 6 July 1928, 175.

Woman's Leader, 1928c. 'Members of the National Union of Societies for Equal Citizenship and Women's Freedom League attended the House of Lords to hear the assent of the Equal Franchise Bill'. Friday, 13 July 1928, 184.

Woman's Leader, 1928d. 'Equal franchise – A memento'. Friday, 7 September 1928, 239.

Woman's Leader, 1928e. 'Presentation to Dame Millicent Fawcett'. Friday, 21 December 21 1928, 359.

Woman's Leader, 1929a. 'The new headquarters of the London and National Society for Women's Service'. Friday, 19 April 1929, 82.

Woman's Leader, 1929b. 'Dame Millicent's last contribution to the "The Woman's Leader"'. Friday, 16 August 1929, 218.

Woman's Leader, 1929c. 'Dame Millicent Fawcett'. Friday, 16 August 1929, 219.

Woman's Leader, 1929d. 'A new recruit for the National Portrait Gallery'. Friday, 30 August 1929, 226.
Woman's Leader, 1929e. 'What we remember: Mr Lionel Ellis'. Friday, 15 November 1929, 316.
Woman's Leader, 1930. 'Another portrait of Dame Millicent'. Vol. 22, No. 14 (Friday, 9 May 1930), 102.
Woman's Leader, 1932. 'The Millicent Garrett Fawcett memorial'. Friday, 1 April 1932, 47.
Women's Franchise, 1908a. 'Notes'. Thursday, 5 March 1908, 1.
Women's Franchise, 1908b. 'Notes'. Thursday, 9 April 1908, 1.
Women's Freedom League (WFL), 1928. 'Victory Breakfast, Hotel Cecil'. London. Thursday, 5 July 1928.
Women's Group Executive, 1915. 'The war, women and unemployment'. *Fabian Tract*. No. 178 (March 1915). London: Fabian Society.
Women's Penny Paper, 1888. 'Interview. Mrs Garrett Fawcett'. Saturday, 3 November 1888, 4–5.
Wordsworth, William, 1882. *The Poetical Works of William Wordsworth*, edited by William Knight, Vol. 2. Edinburgh: William Paterson.
Wylie, William Howie, 1881. *Thomas Carlyle; The man and his books. Illustrated by personal reminiscences, table-talk, and anecdotes of himself and his friends.* London: Marshall Japp and Co.
Yorkshire Post and Leeds Intelligencer, 1925. 'New dames honoured. Presentation of gilt laurel wreaths'. Wednesday, 11 February 1925, 10.
Yorkshire Telegraph and Star, 1918. 'General election results'. Saturday, 28 December 1918, 4.
Young, Sue, 2009. 'Mary Lady Jeune 1849–1931'. https://www.sueyounghistories.com/2009-03-18-susan-marie-elizabeth-stewart-mackenzie-1849-1931/.
Zadra, Dan, 1999. *I Believe in You. To your heart, your dream, and the difference you make.* Washington: Compendium Incorporated.
Zimmeck, Meta, 1984. 'Strategies and stratagems for the employment of women in the British Civil Service, 1919–1939'. *Historical Journal*. Vol. 27, No. 4 (December 1984), 901–24.

Appendix:
Additions to Fawcett's bibliography

Publications by Millicent Garrett Fawcett found in the course of this research that were not previously listed in Rubinstein (1991, 291–9) include the following. There will no doubt be others still to find. Those marked * are featured in their entirety in this volume, those marked † are quoted in part and those marked ‡ are only known via advertisements.

1. *Fawcett, Millicent Garrett, 1871. 'Electoral disabilities of women'. A lecture delivered at the New Hall, Tavistock, March 11th 1871. Printed for the Bristol & West of England Society for Women's Suffrage. Tavistock: Tavistock Printing Company.
2. †Fawcett, Millicent Garrett, 1873. 'His influence as a practical politician'. In *John Stuart Mill: His life and works. Twelve sketches by Herbert Spencer, Henry Fawcett, Frederic Harrison and other distinguished authors.* Boston: James R. Osgood and Company, 81–7.
3. Fawcett, Millicent Garrett, 1873. 'The basis of the parliamentary suffrage, and the present exclusion of women'. *Cambridge Reform Club Papers, 1872–3*. 4 February 1873, No. 4. Cambridge: Macmillan and Co., 22–6.
4. *Fawcett, Millicent Garrett, 1874. 'Lecture on women of modern fiction', Glasgow. *Pictorial World*. 2 January 1875, 358.
5. *Fawcett, Millicent Garrett, 1874. 'Lecture on women of modern fiction', Kirkcaldy. *Fife Free Press*. 5 December 1874, 3.
6. *Fawcett, Millicent Garrett, 1887. 'Employment for girls. The civil service (the Post Office)'. *Atalanta*. Vol. 1, No. 3, 174–6.
7. Fawcett, Millicent Garrett, 1885. 'Paper read at the Bristol meeting of the Central Conference of Women Workers among Women and Children, November 1892, by Mrs Henry Fawcett, on the amendments required in the Criminal Law Amendment Act, 1885'. London: Women's Printing Society, 1892, 1–12.

8. †Fawcett, Millicent Garrett, 1892. 'Fawcett's Speech to National Society members, Galleries of the Royal Institute of Painters in Water Colours, Piccadilly, Tuesday 26 April 1892'. In National Society for Women's Suffrage 1892. 'Conversazione'. In *Occasional Paper*, May 1892. London: Vacher & Sons, Westminster, 72–5.
9. Fawcett, Millicent Garrett, 1898. 'Women's suffrage in Parliament'. *Outlook*. Saturday, 12 March 1898, 169–70.
10. Fawcett, Millicent Garrett, 1904. 'The women's congress in Berlin'. *Broad Views, A monthly review*, London. August 1904, 93–101.
11. Fawcett, Millicent Garrett, 1908. 'Women's suffrage to-day'. *Queen*. Saturday, 1 August 1908, 196.
12. †Fawcett, Millicent Garrett, 1912. 'How British women are organized in politics'. In *The Woman's Athenæum: The woman of affairs, business, professions, public life*, Vol. 9. New York: The Woman's Athenaeum, 333–6. Reprinted from 'Women and representative government' in the *Methodist Times*.
13. ‡Fawcett, Millicent Garrett, 1912. 'Woman's suffrage'. *Daily News and Leader Year Book*, 1912.
14. ‡Fawcett, Millicent Garrett, 1913. 'Preface'. *The Woman's Diary and Handbook for 1914*.
15. †Fawcett, Millicent Garrett, 1916. 'Foreword'. *Purchase of Women: The great economic blunder*, by Elizabeth Blackwell, 3rd edition. London: Bell, ix–xi.
16. Fawcett, Millicent Garrett, 1917. 'The problem of venereal diseases'. *Review of Reviews*. Vol. 55 (February 1917), 155–8.
17. Fawcett, Millicent Garrett, 1921. 'Foreword'. In *Advancing Woman*, by Holford Knight. London: Daniel O'Connor, 7.
18. Fawcett, Millicent Garrett, 1925. 'Foreword'. In *Women Under English Law*, by Maud Isabel Crofts. London: Published at the Office of the National Council of Women of Great Britain, with the assistance of the Stansfeld Trust, iii–iv.
19. Fawcett, Millicent Garrett, 1925. 'Foreword'. In *Report of a Conference on the Citizen Rights of Women Within the British Empire, Held by the British Commonwealth League*. London: British Commonwealth League, 3.
20. †Fawcett, Millicent Garrett, 1927. 'Women's rights', New edition. *Chambers's Encyclopedia*. Philadelphia: J. B. Lippincott Company, 693–8. (Authorship confirmed in *Nation and Athenaeum* 1929.)
21. †Fawcett, Millicent Garrett, 1927. 'The new feminism. What has the women's vote accomplished for the country?' *Good Housekeeping*. May 1927, 23 and 112.

22. †Fawcett, Millicent Garrett, 1928. 'Foreword'. In *Towards Citizenship: A handbook of women's emancipation*, by Phyllis Crawhall Challoner and Vera Laughton Mathews. London: P.S. King & Son, 7.
23. Strachey, Ray, 1928. 'The centenary of Josephine Butler: An interview with Dame Millicent Garrett Fawcett'. *Social Service Review*, Vol. 2, No. 1 (March 1928), 1–9.
24. *Fawcett, Millicent, 1928. Transcript of radio broadcast after the Royal Assent to the Equal Franchise Act. 2LO, British Broadcasting Corporation, 2 July 1928. In *Woman's Leader*, 1928c. 'Members of the National Union of Societies for Equal Citizenship and Women's Freedom League attended the House of Lords to hear the Assent of the Equal Franchise Bill'. Friday, 13 July 1928, 184.

Index

Acland-Hood, Sir Alexander 235
Adam, James 277
Adoption of Children Act (1926) 386
agricultural labourers 199, 202
Aldis, William and Mary Steadman 167
Aldrich-Blake, Louisa 373
Alençon, Duchess of 183–4
Anderson, Adelaide 339–40
Anderson, Elizabeth Garrett 3, 23, 157, 159, 255, 375
Anderson, Louisa Garrett 15
Anderson, Mary 123
Anne, Queen 393
Anonyma's diamonds 75
anti-suffragists 148, 266–74, 294, 297, 307–8, 348, 351
Armstrong, Eliza, case of 101–2
Arnold, Mathew 96, 141
Arnold, Thomas 28
Ascham, Roger 393
Asquith, Herbert 235, 239, 241, 251, 268, 293–4, 306, 318–19, 334, 342, 347–8, 361–2
Astell, Mary 393
Astor, Lord Waldorf 388
Astor, Lady Nancy 409
Atalanta (girls' magazine) 109
Atholl, Duchess of 380
Aubrey House *374*, 375
Australia 183, 188, 205, 273, 292
authority, abuse of 73
Avebury, Lord 275

Baker, Valentine 104
Baldwin, Stanley 386–7, 396
Balfour, A.J. 166, 189
Balfour, Lady Frances 251
Balfour, Gerald 203
Bath constituency 181
Beaconsfield, Lord *see* Disraeli, Benjamin
Beale, Dorothea 157–8, 236
Bear, Annette 122
Becker, Lydia 57
Bedford College, London 158, 195–6
Begg, Samuel 264, 266
Belgium 97
Bentham, Jeremy 337
Bigelow, Hosea 233–4
bi-metallism 185
Birrell, Augustine 234, 308
'Black Friday' (1910) 306
'blue-stockings' 29
Bostock, Elizabeth Anne 160
Boswell, James 142
Brackenbury, Georgina 305
Bradley, W. 64

Bright, Jacob 57
Bright, John 40–1, 51, 63, 94–5
Bristol 238–9
British Association 340
Brown, Ford Madox 58–9
Browning, Elizabeth Barrett 220–1, 277
Browning, Louisa 3
Bryant, Sophie 251–2
Bulgaria 103, 105
Buss, Frances Mary 158
Butler, Josephine 9, 163, 165

Cambridge University 5, 28–31, 34, 160, 165–9
Campbell, Janet 19
Campbell, R.J. 242
Campbell-Bannerman, Henry 232, 234
Carlyle, Thomas 130
Carpenter, Mary 394
Catherine the Great 64
Catholicism 97
Cavendish, Lord and Lady Frederick 112, 399
Conciliation Bills (1910–12) 307–8
Cecil, Lord 414
Chamberlain, Austen 356
Chamberlain, Joseph 93, 96, 274
Chantrey Bequest 305
Chapman Catt, Carrie 14, 270
chastity and unchastity 143–4
Chatauqua movement 164
Cheltenham Ladies' College 156–7, 160, 236
Chesterfield, Lord 136, 204
Chicago World's Fair (1893) 156
child labour 2, 212
    in theatres 118–26
China 51–2, 200
Christ's Hospital 29
Christianity 65, 85, 106, 186, 277, 289
Churchill, Sir Winston 2, 291–2
citizenship 40, 97, 277
    of women 361
civil disobedience 232, 238
Civil Service 380–1
Clark, Andrew 220
Clerkenwell Prison 242
Clough, Anne J. 162–6
Cobden, Richard 40
Cockburn, J. 205
Code Napoleon 415
competitive examination 111–14
concentration camps 2, 5 13, 15, 224–30
Connell, Lena 328–9
Conservative Party 63, 178–80, 183–5, 188–9
Coote, William Alexander 215
copyright restrictions 10
Corbett, Cameron 289, 291

'courage calls to courage everywhere' 1, 9, 365–9
Courtney, Kathleen d'Olier 317
Courtney, L. 125
Cowie, William Garden 205
Crewe, Lord 290
Criado Perez, Caroline 1, 367
Crimean War 158–9
criminal courts 74
Criminal Law Amendment Acts (1885 and 1922)) 102, 104, 382
Crowdy, Rachel 380
Crystal Palace 126
Curzon, Lord 165, 361

Daly, Mary 367
Dante Alighieri 337
Darwin, Charles 53
Davison, Emily 365–9
Davies, Emily 3, 24, 160–8, 251
Davies, Llewelyn 103, 105
Deakin, Alfred 373
deceased wives' sisters, marriage to 63
Defoe, Daniel 157–8
degrees for women 95, 167–70, 314, 392
  honorary 5, 197, 304
democracy 131
Denmark 317
Derby, Lord 342
despotism 132, 200
De Stael, Madame 185
Dicey, Albert Venn 235
Dickens, Charles 14, 34, 78, 64, 78, 81–4, 114
Dickinson, W.H. 349–50
Dilke, Sir Charles and Lady Emilia 59–60
Disraeli, Benjamin 41, 189, 399
dissimulation 134–5
divorce 63
domestic duties 132
Douglas, Robert 82
Downey, William and Daniel 128–9
Dring, William D. 16
drunkenness 152
Drury Lane theatre 125–6
Duveen, Sir Joseph 409

Edesleigh, Lord 174
Edgeworth, Maria 14, 139
Edis, Mary 255
Edis, Olive and Katherine 255
education of women 2, 5, 8, 24–7, 30–3, 97, 132, 135–8, 141–5, 153, 156–71, 170, 203, 217, 304, 391–5, 414
Elder, Isabella 169
electoral disabilities of women 37–9
Eliot, George 14, 34, 78, 81, 140, 158, 185
Elizabeth I, Queen of England 45, 64
Elliott & Fry (photographic studio) 19, 286, 287
Ellis, Lionel 16, 409–10
Elmy, Benjamin 102
employment of women 8, 34, 107, 115, 336–8, 341–4, 360–1
Endowed Schools Commission 160
enfranchisement 150–3, 233, 245, 265–7, 278; *see also* franchise reform

*Englishwoma*n (magazine) 11, 14, 266
Epsom Derby (1913) 365–70
equal franchise 386–7
equality between men and women 13, 16, 27–8, 31–2, 63, 69, 94, 97, 70–6, 106, 115–16, 131, 143, 150, 159–62, 165–80, 221, 238, 245, 278, 296, 307, 331, 349–50, 369–70, 396
Erasmus, Desiderius 131, 137

Factory Acts 118–22
fainting 154
family life 138–9
Fawcett, Henry 3–7, 22–5, 58–9, 69, 80, 82, 101, 109–14, 325, 412
Fawcett, Millicent Garrett
  autobiographical work 3–6, 9
  birth and family background 3, 15
  circle of contacts 14
  concern with public morality 212–13
  Damehood 5, 373–5
  death of and memorials to 1, 6–7, 13, 16, 329, 367–8, 411–12
  editorial approach 10–12
  love and knowledge of literature 8, 12, 14
  marriage of 22
  personal acquaintances of 128
  pictures of 16, 22–3, 78–9, 128–9, 250–1, 254–5, 264, 284–7, 302–5, 312–13, 328–9, 374, 403, 406–9
  political affiliation 179, 188
  political education 23
  public speaking by 4, 8, 12, 38, 61–2, 80–2, 149, 264–5
  signature 31
  voice recordings of 12
  writings by 3–12, 23–5, 37, 23–5,70, 85, 128–9, 195, 224, 232, 238, 412

Fawcett, Philippa 4–6, 23, 58–62, 194–6, 225, 329, 372–4, 391–2, 403, 411
Fawcett Commission 225
Fawcett Library 6
Fawcett Society 6, 367
feminism 2, 7–8, 13, 85, 130, 148, 213, 225–6, 367, 414–15
Fielding, Henry 14, 34
Finkelstein, Lord Daniel 367
Firbank, J.T. 180
First World War 5, 8, 10, 15, 324–5, 331–2, 336, 341–2, 345, 347, 352, 356, 359–62, 375, 414
Ford, I.O. 375
Fordyce, James 134, 136
Fowler, Henry 180–1, 202
France 217–18, 243, 295, 362, 414–15
franchise reform 3, 5, 37, 180, 189, 198–204; *see also* suffrage reform
Francis, John E. 257
free trade policy 199
Froude, James Anthony 168
Fry, Elizabeth 141, 394

Galloway, Janet Anne 169
Garrett, Agnes 3–5, 255, 304, 391–2, 403,

458   MILLICENT GARRETT FAWCETT

405, 411
Garrett, Edmund 15
Garrett, Louisa 3
Garrett, Newson 159
Garrett, Rhoda 3, 57, 304, 391–2
Garrison, Lindley Miller 333
Germany 297, 334, 362
Gey, Lord 399
Girton College 162, 165–7
Gladstone, William Ewart 41, 51, 94, 184–5, 189, 278, 399
Glasgow and West of Scotland Association for Women's Suffrage (GWSAWS) 288
Godolphin, Lady 393
Gohier, Urbain 217–18
Goldsmid, Lady Louisa 160
Gordon, Charles George 183
Great Pilgrimage (1913) 366, 368
Great Western Railway 341
Greece and Greek philosophy 98, 277
Green, J.R. 277
Gregory, John 133–6
Greville, Charles 239
Grey, Sir George 205
Grote, George 98, 159
Grotius, Hugo 337
Guardianship of Children Act 296

Hanover Square Rooms 57
Harcourt, Sir William 189
Hardie, Keir 232
Harris, Augustus 125–6
Harris, William T. 156
Hayti (Haiti) 276
Hills, John Waller 380
Hobhouse, Emily 15, 224–8
Hollins, Mary Letitia 195
Holloway Prison 25, 238, 241, 288
House of Commons, women elected to 359
House of Lords 355–7
householders 180–1, 188–9
    women as 202, 207
Hughes, E.P. 156–7
hunger strikes 288
Huxley, Thomas Henry 53, 129
Hyde Park rally (1913) 322–3, 366

Ibsen, Henrik 14, 144
Iddesleigh, Lord 170
idleness, enforced 34
imperialism 314
imprisonment 216, 221, 238–42
India 65, 289, 292–3, 309–10
Infanticide Act (1922) 381
Infants Bill 106–7
International Alliance of Women 285
International Woman Suffrage Alliance (IWSA) 284–5, 366, 413
Intoxicating Liquor Act (1923) 383
investigative journalism 101–2
Ireland 2, 8–9, 14, 170, 179, 307, 314–15, 319
Isle of Man 187–8
Italy 64, 103, 216, 295, 369

James, Lord 278
Janet Doncaster (novel) 80, 85–91

Jeune, Mary 118–26
Johnson, Samuel 142
Junior Constitutional Club 178–9

Kant, Immanuel 337
Karnie, Jim 78–9
Kennedy, Benjamin Hall 28
Kensington Society 24
Kingston, Charles Cameron 188
Kipling, Rudyard 274
Kitchener, Lord 338–9

Labouchère, Henry Du Pré 178–9, 188–9
Labour Party 315–19, 344
Ladies' Educational Council 163
Lamb, Mary 110
Law, Andrew Bonar 356
Law of Property Acts (1922 and 1925) 383–4
League of Nations 380, 414
Lees, Sarah Anne 362
Legat, Robert 255
legislation 202–3, 276
    affecting women 93–4
    bearing on the home and domestic life 150–2
    individual statutes 377–85
    protectionist 199
Legitimacy Bill (1925) 385–6
Leigh Smith, Barbara 158
liberal feminism 148
Liberal Party 61–2, 179, 188–9, 201, 348
liberty of the citizen 213
Lincoln, Abraham 23, 398
'Little Go' examinations 166
Liverpool Ladies' Educational Society 163
Lloyd George, David 343, 399
London, Brighton and South Coast Railway 341
London University 159, 167
Londonderry 239
Louch, Mary 156
Lowe, Robert 159
Lowell, Russell 150, 158, 171
Lubbock, John 75
Luther, Martin 131
Lyttleton, Dame Elizabeth 380
Lytton, Lord 306

MacArthur, Mary 342
McKay, Mrs Clarence 269
Macmillan, Alexander 25
Maine, Sir Henry 186
Maintenance Orders (Facilities for Enforcement) Act (1920) 381
Manchester 251, 291–2
Manchester (Victoria) University 164, 197
Maria Theresa, Holy Roman Empress 45, 64
Markby, Thomas 161
marriage 140, 296
married women 40, 132–3, 296
    legislation on 95–7, 381–2
Martineau, Harriet 110, 239, 394
Mason, Hugh 95
Mason, Mather 169
Massey, W.T. 342
mathematics 26

Matrimonial Causes Act (1923) 383
Maurice, Frederick Denison 3, 53, 143, 158
medical education 159, 167
medical profession 220
Medical Relief Bill (1885) 107
medical women, memorial to 272–3
Members of Parliament 199, 294, 298
    women as 180, 188
mental training and development 27–34
Meredith, George 239, 316
militancy 2–5, 8–10, 267–8, 287–9, 306, 368–9, 407
military operations 217–19
Mill, John Stuart 2–6, 25, 41, 69, 72, 103
Miller, Emma 103
Millett, Maude 129
Millicent Fawcett Court 6
Milner, Alfred 226, 274
Milton, John 139
Minto, Lord and Lady 292, 309
Montague. Jocelyn 124
Montmorency, Nina 124
moral standards 105, 107, 203, 216–17, 220–1
More, Sir Thomas 131, 337, 393
Morison, Rosa 392
Morley, Lord 137, 201–3, 309–10
motherhood 4, 149–50
Murray, Flora 15
Murray, Margaret 392

Napoleon 185, 337
National League for Opposing Women's Suffrage 267
National Portrait Gallery 60, 302, 305
National Union of Societies for Equal Citizenship (NUSEC) 365, 376–7, 400, 405
National Union of Women's Suffrage Societies (NUWSS) 1, 5–9, 13–14, 61, 149, 179, 197, 256–8, 288, 316–17, 325, 331–2, 336, 341–2, 347–51, 354, 365–6, 412
    new constitution (1907) 287
National Vigilance Association (NVA) 118, 212–13
needlework 28–9, 112
New Zealand 187–8, 205–6, 273, 292, 294, 297
Newnham College 5, 25, 92, 162–7, 410
Nicolay, C.G. 158
Nightingale, Florence 114, 159
Nonconformism 170–1
Northcote, Sir Stafford 189
Nottingham Castle 239
novels and novelists 2, 8, 16, 80–3

Oldham Council 362
'one man one vote' 203
O'Rell, Max 206
outdoor exercise 139
Oxford Union 264–5
Oxford University 28, 160, 168–9

pacifism 5, 8, 15, 285, 331–4, 361
Paget, Sir James 220
Pall Mall Gazette 101–6, 109
Pankhurst, Christabel 232
Pankhurst, Emmeline 232, 255–7, 305, 324

pantomime children 124–5
parental duties 120
parliamentary business 71, 92
parliamentary qualification of women 377–8, 388
Passmore Edwards Settlement 266–7
Paterson, Emma 149
patriotism 183, 336, 342–3
Pattison, Mrs Mark 57–60
Paul, St 103, 106
Paul, Kegan 139, 145
peace, promotion of 413–14
Penrose, Emily 196
physical strength and force 37, 139, 285
picketing 235
Plato 131, 337
Playfair, Lyon 57
policing 274–5
political education 23, 199–200, 272–3
Poor Law 186
Pope, Alexander 136
Post Office 109–11
    nomination system 110–12
Price, Thomas 297
Primrose League 183
Prince of Wales 129
professional occupations, women in 240
prostitution 102, 142, 212, 215
Prussia 362
Public Health (Smoke Abatement) Act (1926) 386–7
public opinion 102–6, 150, 158
Public Place Bill 388
Punch 297
purity movement 8, 213

Quakers 398
Queen's College, London 158

Rathbone, Eleanor 375, 391
Reed, Mark 168
Registration of Midwives Amending Act (1918) 378–9
Reid, Elizabeth Jesser 158
religion 134, 136, 200, 227–8, 277, 289, 295
    advantages of 93–4
Representation of the People Acts 354–7, 377, 386, 396, 404
representative government 97, 198, 201–2, 309
responsibility, national sense of 373
rights 24, 34–5, 38, 202, 204, 331, 377
    for women 13, 130–2, 139–45, 225
Roberts, Dorothea 195–6
Roosevelt, Theodore 205
Rose, Ernestine 57
Rosebery, Lord 189, 392–3
Rousseau, Jean-Jacques 135–8, 337
    wife of (Theresa) 137–8
Rowntree, Joshua 230
Royal Academy 304–5
Royal Holloway College 169, 196
Royal University, Ireland 170
Royden, Maude 414
Rubinstein, David 2–3, 7, 11–15
Russia 93, 200, 215, 276

Sabatier, Paul 276
St Andrews University 5, 304
Salisbury, Lord 41, 178, 189
Sanderson, Mrs Cobden 239, 241–2
Sargent, John Singer 305
school boards 186–7, 234
Scottish universities 28, 169
Seddon, Richard John 188
Seneca Falls convention (1848) 24
separation orders 384
settlement movement 149
Sex Disqualification (Removal) Act (1919) 380
Shakespeare, William 11, 13, 221
Shaw, Anna 268
Shorter Catechism, Scottish 138
Sidgwick, Henry 25, 163–8
Simon, Sir John 352
slavery and the slave trade 215, 398
Slocock, Emily 339
Smith, Adam 145
Smith, Goldwin 206
Smith, John Caswell 313
Smith, Lizzie Caswell 312–13
Smith, Mary Campbell 338
Smith, Samuel 184, 189
Smith, Sydney 158, 393–4
Snowden, Ethel 251
Snowden, Philip 290, 315, 318–19
Somerville, Mary 394
South Africa 5, 8, 13, 15, 205, 215, 224–30, 268, 273–4, 289, 293–4, 297
sovereigns, female 64
Speaker's Conference on Electoral Reform 348–51, 354–5
The Spectator 105, 268
Spencer, Herbert 43–6, 54
Squire, Rose 339
Stanley, Lady (Henrietta Maria) 158
statesmanship 291–3, 309–10
statues 1, 7, 13, 32, 367–8
Statutes of Labourers 199
Stead, William Thomas 101, 109, 129
Stephen, Sir James Fitzjames 69, 72–6
Stevenson, Louisa 169
Strachey, Ray (Mrs Oliver) 11, 38, 85, 285, 331–2, 336, 362, 366, 403, 405, 409, 412
Stuart, James 163
Sturge, Eliza Mary 61
suffrage reform 3–9, 13–14, 62, 92, 148–51, 179–80, 187–8, 198, 201–2, 205, 212, 232, 238–41, 245, 268–70, 277, 287–96, 315–16, 325–6, 348, 351
 agenda for 290
 benefitting both women and men 296–7
 see also franchise reform
suffragettes 5, 10, 178, 232–3, 267, 307, 323, 366–8, 373
suffragists 25, 232, 239, 268, 270, 285, 307–9, 334, 350, 357–61, 367–8, 398
Summary Jurisdiction Act (1925) 384
Swanwick, Helena 380
Sweden 317
Swynnerton, Annie Louisa 16, 302–5

Taine, M. 81

Tanner, Ethel M. 9
Tate Gallery 305
Taylor, Helen 166
teacher training 160–1
teachers' earnings 114
teaching as a career 33
Temple, Frederick 28
Tennant, Winifred Coombe 380
Tennyson, Lord Alfred 14, 152, 188
Terry Ellen 373
Terry, George 215
Thackeray, William Makepeace 34, 78, 81, 220
theatre children 118–26
The Times (newspaper) 14, 40–1, 66, 74–5, 105, 269, 295, 306
Times Literary Supplement (newspaper) 226
Tod, Isabella 170
Tolstoy, Leo 276
Torpey trial 70–1
Toynbee Hall 149
trade unions 94, 107, 271, 336, 344, 235
Trades Union Congress 197
trafficking 212–16, 278
training 342–3
transportation, sentences of 271
Trench, Richard Chevenix 158
Trinity College, Dublin 170, 314
Tripos examinations 160–2, 166–7
Turkey 103, 362
Twain, Mark 14, 205, 243, 268, 398
Tylor, Everard Burnett 64

Unionism, Irish 314
United States 103, 164, 187, 205, 268–9, 332–3, 362, 398, 413
unity of women's movement 238
University College, London 16, 392–5
university education 30–1
 for women 156, 159–64
university electors 349
University Extension 164
university tests 61

Vanderbilt, W.K. 269
venereal disease 102
vice 213, 216
Victoria, Queen 104, 129, 153-4, 184, 169
Victory Breakfast (1928) 407
vigilance committees 105
violence
 condemnation of 309
 use of 239

Ward, Mrs Humphry (Mary Augusta) 14–15, 266–8, 296, 373–8, 334
Ward Howe, Julia 268
warfare 273–4
Wearing, Gillian 1, 7, 16, 329, 367–8, 412
Westfield College 169
Westlake, John 235
Westminster Abbey 6–7, 16, 412
White, Sir George 219
White Slave Trade 212
Whitehead, Alfred North 275
Whitlock, Henry Joseph 22–3
Widows, Orphans and Old Age Contributory

Pensions Act (1925) 385
Wilhelm, Kaiser 361, 369
Willes, J. 66
Wirgman, May 195
Wirgman, Theodore Blake 194–5
Wollstonecraft, Mary 110, 130–45, 149, 158
Wolseley, Lord 219
Wolstenholme, Elizabeth 102
Woman's Leader (newspaper) 304–5, 376
womanliness 151, 154
women
    achievements of 233
    as women 270
    at home 273
    changes for 62, 65, 277
    characteristics of 64, 151–2, 244, 267
    duties of 15, 138, 144–5
    economic independence of 142, 144
    expertise of 294–5
    interests of 204
    maltreatment of 74–5
    offences committed by 296
    protection of 73–4, 134
    representation in fiction 80
    status of 92, 150, 201, 233, 236, 309
    subjection of 73–4, 107, 138–40
    trustworthiness of 140
Women Police acts (1918 to 1925) 381
Women's Franchise (newspaper) 257
Women's Freedom League (WFL) 256–7, 324
women's issues 14
women's movement 3, 130–2, 141, 150, 157, 162, 165, 221, 243, 305
    Victorian 148
Women's National Anti-Suffrage League (WNASL) 267
Women's Printing Society 149
Women's Social and Political Union (WSPU) 232, 238, 256–7, 288, 306–7, 324, 365–6
Wood, Mary 305
Wordsworth, William 14, 337
workhouses 186
working classes 63, 199, 271, 290
Wyllie, Sir Curzon 293, 309

Zenobia, Septima 45

Lightning Source UK Ltd.
Milton Keynes UK
UKHW051704170822
407438UK00021B/385